Lecture Notes in Computer Science   14416

Founding Editors

Gerhard Goos
Juris Hartmanis

The series Lecture Notes in Computer Science (LNCS), including its subseries Lecture Notes in Artificial Intelligence (LNAI) and Lecture Notes in Bioinformatics (LNBI), has established itself as a medium for the publication of new developments in computer science and information technology research, teaching, and education.

LNCS enjoys close cooperation with the computer science R & D community, the series counts many renowned academics among its volume editors and paper authors, and collaborates with prestigious societies. Its mission is to serve this international community by providing an invaluable service, mainly focused on the publication of conference and workshop proceedings and postproceedings. LNCS commenced publication in 1973.

Pari Delir Haghighi · Eric Pardede ·
Gillian Dobbie · Vithya Yogarajan ·
Ngurah Agus Sanjaya ER · Gabriele Kotsis ·
Ismail Khalil
Editors

Information Integration and Web Intelligence

25th International Conference, iiWAS 2023
Denpasar, Bali, Indonesia, December 4–6, 2023
Proceedings

 Springer

Editors
Pari Delir Haghighi
Monash University
Melbourne, VIC, Australia

Gillian Dobbie 🅾
University of Auckland
Auckland, New Zealand

Ngurah Agus Sanjaya ER
Udayana University
Denpasar, Indonesia

Ismail Khalil
Johannes Kepler University Linz
Linz, Austria

Eric Pardede
La Trobe University
Melbourne, VIC, Australia

Vithya Yogarajan
University of Auckland
Auckland, New Zealand

Gabriele Kotsis
Johannes Kepler University Linz
Linz, Austria

ISSN 0302-9743 ISSN 1611-3349 (electronic)
Lecture Notes in Computer Science
ISBN 978-3-031-48315-8 ISBN 978-3-031-48316-5 (eBook)
https://doi.org/10.1007/978-3-031-48316-5

This Springer imprint is published by the registered company Springer Nature Switzerland AG
The registered company address is: Gewerbestrasse 11, 6330 Cham, Switzerland

Paper in this product is recyclable.

Preface

Welcome to the 25th edition of the International Conference on Information Integration and Web Intelligence (iiWAS 2023) which was held from 4–6 December 2023 in Bali, Indonesia in conjunction with the 21st International Conference on Advances in Mobile Computing & Multimedia Intelligence (MoMM 2023).

This conference brought together researchers and practitioners from around the world to share their latest work on two of the most important trends in the field of information technology: information integration and web intelligence.

Information integration is the process of combining data from multiple sources into a single, unified view. This is a complex and challenging task, as the data may be in different formats, stored on different platforms, and have different semantics. However, information integration is essential for many modern applications, such as business intelligence, customer relationship management, and scientific research.

Web intelligence is the field of study that deals with the extraction of knowledge from the web. The web is a vast and ever-changing source of information, and web intelligence techniques can be used to extract this information in a structured and machine-readable format. Web intelligence has a wide range of applications, including search engines, social media analysis, and recommendation systems.

The field of information integration and web intelligence is rapidly evolving, and this conference was an important forum for sharing new ideas and advances. We were particularly excited to see the growing interest in the use of artificial intelligence and machine learning techniques for information integration and web intelligence tasks.

This year we received 96 papers from 28 different countries about a wide range of research topics including Data integration architectures and methodologies, Data quality and data cleaning, Data exchange and query languages, Web data extraction and mining, Ontology engineering and semantic web technologies, Social media analysis, and Recommendation systems.

The papers were thoroughly reviewed by at least three reviewers in terms of originality, contribution, and relevance. 24 papers were accepted as full papers and 24 papers were accepted as short papers, making the acceptance rate of full papers 25%.

The accepted papers are published by Springer in their Lecture Notes in Computer Science (LNCS). This distinguished conference proceedings series is submitted for indexing in the Conference Proceedings Citation Index (CPCI), part of Clarivate Analytics' Web of Science; Scopus; EI Engineering Index; Google Scholar; DBLP; etc.

This year, we were thrilled to have two distinguished keynote speakers, René Mayrhofer from Johannes Kepler University Linz, Austria and Maureen Tanner from University of Cape Town, South Africa. We also had our World ABC (AI-Big Data Convergence) Forum, which consisted this year of a tutorial on Demystifying Large Language Models and Generative Pretrained Transformer hosted by Won Kim from Gachon University, South Korea, and a panel on the future of LLMs which featured experts from a variety of fields, including academia, industry, and government, who shared their insights and perspectives on the future of LLMs and discussed the challenges and opportunities that lie ahead.

We would like to thank the authors of the papers in this volume for their contributions. We would also like to thank the members of the program committee and the organizing committee for their hard work in putting together this conference. Special thanks go to Udayana University for their generosity, unwavering commitment, and hard work in making iiWAS 2023 a big success.

We believe that this conference made a significant contribution to the advancement of the field, and we are grateful to all of the participants for their contributions.

We hope that you will find the papers in this volume to be informative and inspiring and that our participants enjoyed the conference and the discussions!

December 2023

Pari Delir Haghighi
Eric Pardede
Gillian Dobbie
Vithya Yogarajan
Ngurah Agus Sanjaya ER
Gabriele Kotsis
Ismail Khalil

Organization

Program Committee Chairs

Gillian Dobbie	University of Auckland, New Zealand
Vithya Yogarajan	University of Auckland, New Zealand

Steering Committee

Gabriele Kotsis	Johannes Kepler University Linz, Austria
Ismail Khalil	Johannes Kepler University Linz, Austria
Pari Delir Haghighi	Monash University, Australia
Eric Pardede	La Trobe University, Australia
Dirk Draheim	Tallinn University of Technology, Estonia
Syopiansyah Jaya Putra	Universitas Islam Negeri, Indonesia

Organising Committee

Ngurah Agus Sanjaya ER	Udayana University, Indonesia
I Putu Agung Bayupati	Udayana University, Indonesia

Program Committee Members

Akiyo Nadamoto	Konan University, Japan
Anne Kayem	Hasso Plattner Institute, Germany
Bala Srinivasan	Monash University, Australia
Barbara Catania	University of Genoa, Italy
Bartholomäus Wloka	University of Vienna, Austria
Bernardo Breve	University of Salerno, Italy
Brahim Ouhbi	ENSAM-Meknès, Morocco
Christine Strauss	University of Vienna, Austria
Dan Johansson	Umeå University, Sweden
Deborah Dahl	Conversational Technologies, USA
Devis Bianchini	University of Brescia, Italy
Dion Goh	Nanyang Technological University, Singapore
Donato Tiano	University of Modena and Reggio Emilia, Italy

Edgar Weippl	SBA Research, Austria
Elio Masciari	Federico II University, Italy
Emanuele Storti	Università Politecnica delle Marche, Italy
Enrico Gallinucci	University of Bologna, Italy
Erich Schikuta	University of Vienna, Austria
Francesc D. Muñoz-Escoí	Universitat Politècnica de València, Spain
Gaetano Cimino	University of Salerno, Italy
Giovanna Guerrini	University of Genova, Italy
Harald Wahl	University of Applied Sciences Technikum Wien, Austria
Hind Lamharhar	INSEA & Hightech, Morocco
Idir Amine Amarouche	University of Science and Technology Houari Boumediene, Algeria
Jeff Tan	IBM Research - Australia, Australia
Johannes Sametinger	Johannes Kepler University Linz, Austria
Jorge Lloret	University of Zaragoza, Spain
Kenji Hatano	Doshisha University, Japan
Kiki Maulana	Telkom University, Indonesia
Lars Moench	University of Hagen, Germany
Luca Gagliardelli	University of Modena and Reggio Emilia, Italy
Luca Zecchini	University of Modena and Reggio Emilia, Italy
Luca Mazzola	Lucerne University of Applied Sciences, Switzerland
Manolis Gergatsoulis	Ionian University, Greece
Marcin Zimniak	Leipzig University, Germany
Marco Mesiti	University of Milan, Italy
Marco Antonio Casanova	PUC - Rio, Brazil
Marinette Savonnet	University of Burgundy, France
Masayoshi Aritsugi	Kumamoto University, Japan
Massimo Ruffolo	ICAR-CNR, Italy
Matteo Francia	University of Bologna, Italy
Mauricio Soto Gomez	Università degli Studi di Milano, Italy
Michal Kratky	VSB-Technical University of Ostrava, Czech Republic
Michele Melchiori	University of Brescia, Italy
Muhammad Younas	Oxford Brookes University, UK
Naoko Kosugi	Takasaki University of Health and Welfare, Japan
Nuno Datia, ISEL	Instituto Superior de Engenharia de Lisboa, Portugal
Ngurah Agus Sanjaya ER	Udayana University, Indonesia
Peiquan Jin	University of Science and Technology of China, China

Petr Kremen	Czech Technical University in Prague, Czech Republic
Qiang Zhu	University of Michigan - Dearborn, USA
Qiang Ma	Kyoto University, Japan
Ronaldo Mello	Federal University of São Carlos, Brazil
Sami Habib	Kuwait University, Kuwait
Sergio Ilarri	University of Zaragoza, Spain
Soon Chun	City University of New York, USA
Sucha Smanchat	King Mongkut's University of Technology North Bangkok, Thailand
Sven Groppe	University of Lübeck, Germany
Takako Hashimoto	Chiba University of Commerce, Japan
Toshiyuki Amagasa	University of Tsukuba, Japan
Vincent Wang	City University of Hong Kong, China
Vincenzo Deufemia	University of Salerno, Italy
Werner Winiwarter	University of Vienna, Austria
Xuesong Lu	East China Normal University, China
Yousuke Watanabe	Nagoya University, Japan

External Reviewers

Alberto Cabri	University of Milano, Italy
Eleftherios Kelogeros	Ionian University, Greece
Emanuele Cavalleri	University of Milano, Italy
Hudson Silva	Instituto Federal do Pará, Brazil
Tomoya Kambara	Doshisha University, Japan

Organizers

ABC (AI-Big Data Convergence) Forum

Demystifying Large Language Models and Generative Pretrained Transformer (Tutorial)

Won Kim

Gachon University, South Korea

The release of ChatGPT from OpenAI has generated huge excitement and interest in Large Language Models (LLMs). Many companies have been busy developing their own LLMs and applications of LLMs.

An LLM is a computer algorithm that processes natural language inputs and predicts the next word based on what it has already seen. LLMs use the transformer, which is a type of neural network architecture. GPT (Generative Pre-trained Transformer) is the name OpenAI has given to its LLM, and it has become perhaps the best-known LLM.

In this tutorial, I will explore what LLM is and how it works, with emphasis on GPT. In particular, I will examine how input text is transformed into vectors and matrices of numbers, and how they flow through key layers of the transformer architecture. I will also discuss the opportunities and issues of LLMs.

The tutorial is organized as follows:

- Introduction to LLMs
- LLM training and inference
- GPT performance
- Input text tokenization
- Input token embedding and position encoding
- Attention concept
- Transformer architecture
- How Attention works
- Evolution of GPT models
- Opportunities and issues of LLMs

The Future of LLMs (Panel)

Ismail Khalil

Johannes Kepler University Linz, Austria

Large language models (LLMs) are a type of artificial intelligence that is trained on massive datasets of text and code. They can generate text, translate languages, write different kinds of creative content, and answer your questions in an informative way. LLMs are still under development, but they have already had a significant impact on a wide range of industries and applications.

This panel will discuss the future of LLMs, including the following topics:

- New and emerging applications of LLMs. How will LLMs be used in the future? What new possibilities will they open up?
- The challenges of developing and deploying LLMs. LLMs are complex and computationally expensive to train and deploy. What are the challenges that need to be overcome in order to make LLMs more accessible and affordable?
- The ethical and social implications of LLMs. LLMs have the potential to be used for good or for bad. What are the ethical and social implications of this technology? How can we ensure that LLMs are used responsibly?

The panel will feature experts from academia, industry, and government. They will share their insights and perspectives on the future of LLMs and discuss the challenges and opportunities that lie ahead.

This panel will provide a valuable opportunity to learn about the future of LLMs and the challenges and opportunities that lie ahead. It will also be a forum for discussion and debate about the ethical and social implications of this technology.

Contents

Generative AI

Image Data and Knowledge Graph

Business Data and Applications

How Domain Engineering Can Help to Raise Adoption Rates of Artificial Intelligence in Healthcare

Markus Bertl[1]([✉]) [ID], Toomas Klementi[1] [ID], Gunnar Piho[2] [ID], Peeter Ross[1,3] [ID], and Dirk Draheim[4] [ID]

[1] Department of Health Technologies, Tallinn University of Technology, Ehitajate tee 5, 12616 Tallinn, Estonia
mbertl@taltech.ee
[2] Department of Software Science, Tallinn University of Technology, Ehitajate tee 5, 12616 Tallinn, Estonia
[3] East Tallinn Central Hospital, Ravi 18, 10138 Tallinn, Estonia
[4] Information Systems Group, Tallinn University of Technology, Akadeemia tee 15a, 12169 Tallinn, Estonia

Abstract. Regardless of the often-claimed success of artificial intelligence (AI) and machine learning (ML), AI-based Digital Decision Support Systems (DDSSs) still suffer from low adoption rates. Much algorithmic research is done, but examples of AI bringing tangible benefits to the healthcare industry are rare. We argue that one of the reasons for low adoption rates is missing domain understanding and/or the heterogeneity of domain understanding among the DDSS developers and domain experts. To overcome this, we are working towards a methodology to utilize the Domain Engineering approach to create a shared common understanding of key concepts and relationships within the healthcare domain in a structured, formalized way. In the realm of complex interdisciplinary DDSS development within healthcare, the Domain Engineering approach can serve as a valuable instrument for bridging the gap between IT professionals and domain experts. It facilitates establishing a shared comprehension of the domain and hopefully contributes significantly to increasing the value and adoption rates of DDSSs in the clinical process. In this paper, we are proposing our work-in-progress ideas and preliminary results.

Keywords: Digital Decision Support System (DDSS) · DDSSs Adoption Rates · User Acceptance · Artificial Intelligence (AI) · Domain Engineering · Digital Health

1 Introduction

Artificial Intelligence (AI) is currently reporting unforeseen successes [15,17]. One example is large language models like ChatGPT. Retail companies like Amazon build their whole business model based on AI. Regardless of the reported successes in other domains, AI in healthcare, especially so-called Digital Decision Support Systems (DDSSs), suffer from low adoption rates [8,33,39]. One of the

P. Delir Haghighi et al. (Eds.): iiWAS 2023, LNCS 14416, pp. 3–12, 2023.
https://doi.org/10.1007/978-3-031-48316-5_1

key factors for creating successful DDSSs is the quality and depth of the domain knowledge incorporated into the decision algorithms. Domain knowledge refers to the understanding and expertise in a specific area, in this case, medicine and healthcare. DDSSs risk making incorrect, incomplete, or unuseful recommendations without a thorough understanding of the domain, which can have severe consequences for patients.

The importance of domain understanding and why a purely algorithmic approach for DDSS development is not enough to bring value to the clinical process can be observed in radiology, for example. Much AI research about detecting pathologies in radiological images has been published. Because of the high accuracy of machine learning and computer vision algorithms, some claim that AI will take over the field [36], and it, therefore, does not make sense to train radiologists anymore [14]. Proposing a DDSS to replace radiologists based on an algorithm that detects abnormalities in medical images is a prime example of insufficient domain knowledge. Only highlighting image abnormalities is not enough; radiologists perform this task reasonably quickly. However, the time-consuming part is interpreting the abnormalities, comparing them with previous images, setting them in context to the patient history, and providing meaningful recommendations. Additionally, considerations about digital data availability and quality [5], as well as security aspects [3], need to be considered.

This example illustrates that to ensure that DDSSs bring value to clinicians, knowledge from various domains must be incorporated into the design and development process. Usually, this is overcome through collaboration between domain experts like healthcare professionals and computer scientists, who can work together to identify relevant information. The knowledge within a domain like healthcare can be vast, complex, and constantly evolving. Domain engineering helps to systematically organize, model, and **formally represent** this knowledge ([11], pages 193-198) so that it can be understood and utilized by DDSSs. Professionals from different disciplines may have varied perspectives and terminologies, creating communication challenges like different viewpoints [13] about the domain facets. Domain engineering helps bridge these gaps by providing stakeholders with a common language and unified conceptual framework for the domain facets ([11], pages 251-318). Identifying the most critical and relevant information for a DDSS is challenging, as the system requirements may vary depending on the context and end-users. Domain engineering-based requirements analysis ([11], pages 479-492) enables a more methodological analysis of requirements by providing tools and methodologies to elicit, analyze, and prioritize them. Requirements acquisition (a part of domain-engineering-based requirements analysis) from the already engineered, common and unified domain models or theories leads hopefully to more interoperable DDSSs. Domain engineering also focuses on creating reusable and scalable domain knowledge formalized as domain models or formal domain theories [12].

Recent studies show that while adoption rates of DDSSs for production use cases are low, reported evaluation metrics like the accuracy of the decision technology (meaning the AI model) are promising [4,6,7]. So, the question arises as to why DDSSs still fail to bring value to real-world medical processes regardless of the well-performing algorithms. We propose that domain engineering is a valuable approach that complements collaboration between healthcare professionals, domain experts, and computer scientists. By demonstrating an understanding of the complexities of the healthcare domain, DDSSs can gain the support and acceptance of healthcare professionals and patients, which is essential for their widespread adoption and success.

2 Domain Engineering

Domain engineering is a software engineering discipline to analyse the discourse of the universe as it is. Examples of the domains (the area of expertise, the universe of discourse) are banking, transportation, trade, education, healthcare, etc. In addition to the ontologies that specify reusable, shared, agreed, and detailed sets of concepts (data structures) of a particular problem domain [25], a domain model, in addition, specifies the standard algorithms related to these concepts. Therefore, domain engineering is analyzing, defining, modelling and formalizing a particular domain's universally specific knowledge - concepts and algorithms. The goal of domain engineering is to create a shared understanding of the key concepts and relationships within a domain and to provide a structure and framework for representing and using this knowledge.

The theory behind this can be formalized [12] as $\mathcal{D}, \mathcal{S} \models \mathcal{R}$ - from domain model ($\mathcal{D}$) via requirements ($\mathcal{R}$) to useful and dependable software ($\mathcal{S}$). In practice, it is realized by software product lines [16] and software factory [20] initiatives. However, the biggest challenge of domain engineering is the semantic heterogeneity [21] and reusability of models, which also affects the semantic interoperability of data and systems [2]. Semantic heterogeneity means that models and data schemes describing the same or similar universe of discourse but developed by different independent parties are different. For example, despite the existence of various standards-based semantic interoperability initiatives in healthcare, such as HL7 CDA[1], LOINC[2], ICD-10[3] and SNOMED-CT[4], we still lack a unified approach and instead often use a divide-and-conquer strategy [19].

The OMG/MDA four-level modelling framework [9] can be a helpful strategy to follow in domain engineering and ontologies. According to this framework, four modelling layers are in use: namely, concrete level (M0), model level (M1), meta-model level (M2), and meta-meta-model level (M3). In [31], we proposed an interpretation for the OMG modelling framework from the software development viewpoint. We interpreted the M0 as data in some software system (e.g., a hospital or a laboratory information system) and M1 as a model (a domain model) that describes these data and that is used to interpret these data. These

---

[1] http://www.hl7.org/.
[2] https://loinc.org/.
[3] https://icd.who.int/browse10/.
[4] https://www.snomed.org/.

domain models include SNOMED, LOINC, ICD, HL7 RIM (Reference Information Model), openEHR RM (Reference Model), etc. In our understanding, and according to our experiences, these domain models are all local and, therefore, heterogeneous, even when claimed they use or follow some particular standard. The reason for that is, again, models and data schemes describing the same or similar universe of discourse but developed by different independent parties are different.

In our interpretation, the meta-meta-model (M3) is a pure abstraction of object orientation utilizing classes, objects, properties, methods, etc. What is left is M2, a meta-model that uses M3 (object orientation) as a language and that provides a (semi-)formal language for specifying M1 (domain) models. By analyzing different domain and data modelling approaches and patterns [1,10,18,22,37] we formulated an archetypes-based development methodology [26] on top of the Zachman framework [28] and developed a system of archetypes as a meta-model [31] for specifying requirements for enterprise applications and developing the software. This meta-model (similar to [1]) contains sub-models for parties and their roles, products and services, inventory, business processes, business orders, quantity, money, and rules. Our archetypes-based domain engineering approach is more precisely explained in [26,28–31], evaluated in real-life applications [27] and analysed based on HL7 RIM (reference information model) and openEHR RM (reference model) [32] as well as the interoperability issues that have been assessed in accordance with the LOINC [34], HL7 FHIR [35] and ContSys (ISO13940 [23]) [24,38] standards.

3 Applying Domain Engineering to Decision Support System Development

By applying domain engineering to healthcare, the knowledge and concepts specific to this domain can be formalized and structured, making it easier to develop DDSSs tailored to healthcare professionals' needs and providing accurate and relevant recommendations that improve the clinical process. We argue that this will result in a positive impact on the adoption rates of such systems. In developing DDSSs in healthcare, domain engineering can be applied in various ways to create effective and efficient solutions.

For example, in the field of radiology, domain engineering can be used to model the knowledge and concepts that are specific to the interpretation of medical images, including the effects of different imaging techniques, findings of previous images, patient conditions, and other factors that can impact the accuracy of the image interpretation and the diagnosis. The following is a possible step-by-step procedure for utilizing the domain engineering approach in the development of DDSSs in healthcare:

1. **Identify key domain concepts:** Identify the main entities or concepts within the healthcare domain, such as patients, diseases, treatments, healthcare providers, and medical devices. Include relevant attributes for each

entity, such as patient demographics, disease symptoms, treatment costs, and provider specialities. This can be applied to the above-mentioned example of radiology as follows. Instead of focusing only on algorithms, one should focus on the whole clinical process, from the initial referral letter of the patient to the final radiology report.

2. **Define relationships between concepts:** Determine how the identified concepts are related, such as the relationships between patients, diseases, and treatments. Specify the cardinality of the relationships, such as one-to-one, one-to-many, or many-to-many. If we have analyzed the complete clinical process, then we can model the domain. For the stated example, this means that the DDSS should be embedded into the reporting and imaging software (e.g., the hospital information system) so that the DDSS can support the specific clinical process. For this, the relationship between each process item must be considered.

3. **Establish rules and constraints:** Identify the domain's rules and constraints, such as medical guidelines, legal regulations, or clinical best practices. Specify the conditions under which these rules and constraints apply and any exceptions or special cases that may exist. An example of constraints and rules that might not be transparent to developers or data scientists is that the radiological image on the screen should never be the only input for the radiologist's conclusion. The physician does not only focus on one image but also on previous images and other data from the patient's health records. Therefore, providing a DDSS that only detects an abnormality in a medical image would break this constraint.

4. **Model workflows and processes:** Understand the typical workflows and processes within the healthcare domain, such as patient admission, diagnosis, treatment planning, and follow-up care. These workflows are sequences of steps, decision points, and interactions between domain concepts and actors. For a DDSS in radiology, this would mean defining how the referral report workflow is technically implemented. E.g., the standard in which a referral letter is saved is HL7, diagnoses are coded in ICD-10, and the standard for medical imaging is DICOM.

5. **Create a visual representation:** Use a suitable modelling language or notation, such as Unified Modeling Language (UML), to represent the domain model visually. Include diagrams to represent the various aspects of the domain, such as class diagrams for entities and relationships, sequence diagrams for workflows, and activity diagrams for processes. This means that the results from point 4 need to be represented in a standardized way.

6. **Validate the domain model:** Review the domain model with domain experts, such as physicians, nurses, and administrators, to ensure it accurately captures the relevant knowledge and requirements. Make any necessary revisions based on feedback from the domain experts. In the radiology example, the AI models are often evaluated based on the image (e.g., accuracy rates in detecting abnormalities) and not the whole clinical process. Therefore, the crucial part that brings benefit is often not evaluated.

7. **Iterate and refine the model:** As the DDSS development progresses, update and refine the domain model as needed to accommodate new requirements, address any identified issues, or incorporate changes in the healthcare domain. By following this procedure, you can create a comprehensive domain model that serves as a foundation for developing a decision support system tailored to the needs and requirements of a specific healthcare domain. Algorithms are trained initially on one modality (e.g., one kind of radiological image). However, the radiologist's daily work involves different modalities and anatomic regions. Therefore, new algorithms should be integrated into the DDSS if the full spectrum of the daily workload is not covered.

In addition to improving the accuracy and relevance of DDSSs, domain engineering can also help to improve the quality and consistency of healthcare applications and systems. By formalizing and representing domain knowledge in a structured and consistent manner, domain engineering enables software developers to create more effective and efficient solutions for the healthcare domain. It helps to improve the quality and consistency of software applications and systems. In previous research, we suggested using a framework for implementing and analyzing DDSSs to ensure a systematic and interdisciplinary approach that considers the technical and medical domain [8]. Domain engineering, as described in Sect. 2, can be used as a tool to describe those dimensions formally.

4   Conclusion

In summary, domain engineering provides a structured approach for developing DDSSs in healthcare that can lead to more effective, efficient, and tailored solutions, improved communication and collaboration among stakeholders, and increased adaptability and maintainability over time. Domain engineering offers several benefits in developing DDSSs in healthcare. Some of the key advantages include:

1. **A better understanding of the domain**: Domain engineering involves a systematic analysis of the healthcare domain, which helps developers and stakeholders understand the specific problems, requirements, and constraints in that domain.
2. **Reusability and modularity**: Domain engineering promotes identifying and implementing reusable components, such as libraries, APIs, or services, that can be shared across different DDSS applications.
3. **Tailored solutions**: Domain engineering enables the development of tailored solutions that address the unique challenges and requirements specific to health care.
4. **Enhanced communication and collaboration**: Using domain-specific languages and visual models facilitates communication and collaboration among developers, domain experts, and other stakeholders.

5. **Improved maintainability and adaptability**: Domain engineering supports continuous improvement and iterative development, making updating and maintaining the DDSS easier as new requirements emerge or healthcare practices change.
6. **Reduced development time and costs**: By leveraging domain knowledge, reusable components, and a well-defined development process, domain engineering can help reduce the time and costs of developing a DDSS in healthcare. These savings can be especially significant for large-scale or complex projects, where a structured approach can help avoid costly mistakes and rework.
7. **Increased interoperability**: Domain engineering encourages the integration of the DDSS with existing healthcare IT systems, such as electronic health records (EHRs) or health information exchanges (HIEs), by promoting standard data models and interfaces, and, therefore, can facilitate data sharing, streamline workflows, and ultimately enhance the overall quality of care.

By applying domain engineering in developing decision support systems in healthcare, organizations can create tailored solutions that address their domain's unique challenges and requirements, ultimately improving patient outcomes, reducing costs, and enhancing the overall quality of care. One major challenge for adopting AI-based DDSS in healthcare is that the system is right, meaning it delivers the desired results in terms of algorithmic correctness, but it is not the right system. So, it operates on assumptions that are not given in the real world, like unavailable data or output, which does not benefit the clinical process. To bridge that gap, a solid domain understanding is needed. Domain Engineering can be a useful tool to accomplish that.

Acknowledgements. This work in the project 'ICT programme' was supported by the European Union through the European Social Fund.

References

1. Arlow, J., Neustadt, I.: Enterprise Patterns and MDA: Building Better Software with Archetype Patterns and UML. Object Technology Series, Boston, Addison-Wesley (2003)
2. Beale, T.: Archetypes: constraint-based domain models for future-proof information systems. In: OOPSLA 2002 Workshop on Behavioural Semantics, November 4–8, Washington State Convention and Trade Center, vol. 105, pp. 1–69. Citeseer, Seattle, Washington, USA (2002)
3. Bertl, M.: News analysis for the detection of cyber security issues in digital healthcare: a text mining approach to uncover actors, attack methods and technologies for cyber defense. Young Inf. Sci. 4, 1–15 (2019)
4. Bertl, M., Bignoumba, N., Ross, P., Yahia, S.B., Draheim, D.: Evaluation of deep learning-based depression detection using medical claims data. SSRN (2023). https://doi.org/10.2139/ssrn.4478987

5. Bertl, M., Kankainen, K.J.I., Piho, G., Draheim, D., Ross, P.: Evaluation of data quality in the Estonia national health information system for digital decision support. In: Proceedings of the 3rd International Health Data Workshop (2023)
6. Bertl, M., Metsallik, J., Ross, P.: A systematic literature review of AI-based digital decision support systems for post-traumatic stress disorder. Front. Psychiatry **13** (2022). https://doi.org/10.3389/fpsyt.2022.923613. https://www.frontiersin.org/articles/10.3389/fpsyt.2022.923613
7. Bertl, M., Ross, P., Draheim, D.: A survey on AI and decision support systems in psychiatry - uncovering a dilemma. Expert Syst. Appl. **202**, 117464 (2022). https://doi.org/10.1016/j.eswa.2022.117464. https://www.sciencedirect.com/science/article/pii/S0957417422007965
8. Bertl, M., Ross, P., Draheim, D.: Systematic AI support for decision making in the healthcare sector: obstacles and success factors. Health Policy Technol. (2023)
9. Bézivin, J., Gerbé, O.: Towards a precise definition of the OMG/MDA framework. In: Proceedings 16th Annual International Conference on Automated Software Engineering (ASE 2001), pp. 273–280. IEEE (2001)
10. Bjørner, D.: Software Engineering 1: Abstraction and Modelling. Springer Science & Business Media, Berlin Heidelberg (2006)
11. Bjørner, D.: Software Engineering 3: Domains, Requirements, and Software Design. Springer Science & Business Media, Berlin Heidelberg (2006)
12. Bjørner, D.: Domain theory: practice and theories a discussion of possible research topics. In: Jones, C.B., Liu, Z., Woodcock, J. (eds.) ICTAC 2007. LNCS, vol. 4711, pp. 1–17. Springer, Heidelberg (2007). https://doi.org/10.1007/978-3-540-75292-9_1
13. Blobel, B., Oemig, F., Ruotsalainen, P., Lopez, D.M.: Transformation of health and social care systems-an interdisciplinary approach toward a foundational architecture. Front. Med. **9**, 802487 (2022)
14. Chockley, K., Emanuel, E.: The end of radiology? Three threats to the future practice of radiology. J. Am. College Radiol. **13**(12, Part A), 1415–1420 (2016). https://doi.org/10.1016/j.jacr.2016.07.010
15. Chui, M., Hall, B., Mayhew, H., Singla, A., Sukharevsky, A.: The state of AI in 2022 - and a half decade in review (2022). https://www.mckinsey.com/capabilities/quantumblack/our-insights/the-state-of-ai-in-2022-and-a-half-decade-in-review. Accessed 04 Apr 2023
16. Clements, P., Northrop, L.: Software Product Lines. Addison-Wesley Boston (2002)
17. Fast, E., Horvitz, E.: Long-term trends in the public perception of artificial intelligence. In: Proceedings of the AAAI Conference on Artificial Intelligence, vol. 31, pp. 963–969 (2017)
18. Fowler, M.: Analysis Patterns: Reusable Object Models. Addison-Wesley Professional (1997)
19. Gansel, X., Mary, M., van Belkum, A.: Semantic data interoperability, digital medicine, and e-health in infectious disease management: a review. Europ. J. Clin. Microbiol. Infect. Dis. **38**(6), 1023–1034 (2019). https://doi.org/10.1007/s10096-019-03501-6
20. Greenfield, J., Short, K.: Software factories: assembling applications with patterns, models, frameworks and tools. In: Companion of the 18th Annual ACM SIGPLAN Conference on Object-Oriented Programming, Systems, Languages, and Applications, pp. 16–27 (2003)
21. Halevy, A.: Why your data won't mix: new tools and techniques can help ease the pain of reconciling schemas. Queue **3**(8), 50–58 (2005)

22. Hay, D.C.: Data Model Patterns: Conventions of Thought. Pearson Education (2013)
23. ISO: 13940:2015 Health informatics - system of concepts to support continuity of care. International Organization for Standardization, Geneva. Switzerland (2015)
24. Kankainen, K.: Usages of the ContSys standard: a position paper. In: Bellatreche, L., Chernishev, G., Corral, A., Ouchani, S., Vain, J. (eds.) MEDI 2021. CCIS, vol. 1481, pp. 314–324. Springer, Cham (2021). https://doi.org/10.1007/978-3-030-87657-9_24
25. Munir, K., Sheraz Anjum, M.: The use of ontologies for effective knowledge modelling and information retrieval. Appl. Comput. Inf. **14**(2), 116–126 (2018). https://doi.org/10.1016/j.aci.2017.07.003. https://www.sciencedirect.com/science/article/pii/S2210832717300649
26. Piho, G., Roost, M., Perkins, D., Tepandi, J.: Towards archetypes-based software development. In: Sobh, T., Elleithy, K. (eds.) Innovations in Computing Sciences and Software Engineering, pp. 561–566. Springer, Dordrecht (2010)
27. Piho, G., Tepandi, J., Parman, M., Perkins, D.: From archetypes-based domain model of clinical laboratory to LIMS software. In: The 33rd International Convention MIPRO, pp. 1179–1184. IEEE, New York (2010)
28. Piho, G., Tepandi, J., Roost, M.: Domain analysis with archetype patterns based Zachman framework for enterprise architecture. In: 2010 International Symposium on Information Technology, vol. 3, pp. 1351–1356. IEEE, New York (2010)
29. Piho, G., Tepandi, J., Roost, M.: Evaluation of the archetypes based development. In: Databases and Information Systems VI, pp. 283–295. IOS Press, Amsterdam (2011)
30. Piho, G., Tepandi, J., Roost, M.: Archetypes based techniques for modelling of business domains, requirements and software. In: Information Modelling and Knowledge Bases XXIII, pp. 219–238. IOS Press, Amsterdam (2012)
31. Piho, G., Tepandi, J., Thompson, D., Tammer, T., Parman, M., Puusep, V.: Archetypes based meta-modeling towards evolutionary, dependable and interoperable healthcare information systems. Procedia Comput. Sci. **37**, 457–464 (2014). https://doi.org/10.1016/j.procs.2014.08.069. https://www.sciencedirect.com/science/article/pii/S1877050914010345
32. Piho, G., Tepandi, J., Thompson, D., Woerner, A., Parman, M.: Business archetypes and archetype patterns from the HL7 RIM and openEHR RM perspectives: towards interoperability and evolution of healthcare models and software systems. Procedia Comput. Sci. **63**, 553–560 (2015)
33. Prakash, A.V., Das, S.: Medical practitioner's adoption of intelligent clinical diagnostic decision support systems: a mixed-methods study. Inf. Manage. **58**(7), 103524 (2021)
34. Raavel, K.M., Kankainen (supervisor), K., Piho (supervisor), G.: Introduction of LOINC terminology to archetype patterns based ABC4HEDA base model (2022). https://digikogu.taltech.ee/et/Item/9086088f-5e01-446e-9e84-176dab21bfbe, B.Sc. thesis, in Estonian
35. Randmaa, R., Bossenko, I., Klementi, T., Piho, G., Ross, P.: Evaluating business meta-models for semantic interoperability with FHIR resources. In: HEDA-2022: The International Health Data Workshop, June 19–24, 2022, Bergen, p. 14. CEUR-RAT, Norway (2022)
36. Schwartz, W.B.: Medicine and the computer: the promise and problems of change. In: Anderson, J.G., Jay, S.J. (eds.) Use and Impact of Computers in Clinical Medicine, pp. 321–335. Springer, New York (1987). https://doi.org/10.1007/978-1-4613-8674-2_20

37. Silverston, L.: The Data Model Resource Book, Volume 1: A Library of Universal Data Models for All Enterprises. John Wiley & Sons (2011)
38. Sõerd, T., Kankainen, K., Piho, G., Klementi, T., Ross, P.: Specification of medical processes in accordance with international standards and agreements. In: 11th International Conference on Model-Based Software and Systems Engineering (Modelsward'2023), Feb 2023, Lisbonne, Portugal, p. 14 (2022)
39. Sutton, R.T., Pincock, D., Baumgart, D.C., Sadowski, D.C., Fedorak, R.N., Kroeker, K.I.: An overview of clinical decision support systems: benefits, risks, and strategies for success. NPJ Digit. Med. 3(1), 17 (2020)

Enhancing AI Adoption in Healthcare: A Data Strategy for Improved Heart Disease Prediction Accuracy Through Deep Learning Techniques

Rohan Deshamudre[1], Seyed Sahand Mohammadi Ziabari[1]([⊠]) [iD],
and Marc van Houten[2]

[1] Faculty of Science, Mathematics and Computer Science, University of Amsterdam,
1098 XH Amsterdam, The Netherlands
rohan.deshamudre@student.uva.nl, s.s.mohammadiziabari@uva.nl
[2] Microsoft, Amsterdam, The Netherlands
Marc.van.Houten@microsoft.com

Abstract. This paper presents the development of an artificial neural network (ANN) for the prediction of heart disease, along with a comprehensive data strategy aimed at improving the adoption of artificial intelligence (AI) in healthcare. The neural network architecture is carefully designed according to the dimensions of the data, transfer learning methods are used to increase generalizability, and hyperparameters are optimized to achieve high predictive accuracy. To address the challenges related to AI adoption in healthcare, a robust data strategy is devised, focusing on data quality, privacy, security, and regulatory compliance. The strategy incorporates comprehensive data governance frameworks, secure data sharing protocols, and privacy-preserving techniques to facilitate the responsible and ethical utilization of sensitive medical information. Furthermore, strategies for ensuring interoperability and scalability of AI systems within existing healthcare infrastructure are explored.

Keywords: Artificial Neural Network · Healthcare · Deep Learning

1 Introduction

The healthcare sector plays a critical role in ensuring the well-being of individuals and communities worldwide. Access to healthcare is a fundamental human right and is essential for maintaining good health and well-being [1]. The responsibility of this industry comes with a variety of challenges which can be categorized into three main areas: increasing patient complexity, shortage of healthcare staff, and rising costs [2]. Increasing patient complexity refers to the rising level of complexity in the healthcare needs and conditions of patients that require comprehensive and coordinated care. Patients today often present with multiple chronic conditions, comorbidities, and complex health needs that require comprehensive and coordinated care. The data available to provide personalized care and effective treatment is imbalanced and of low quality due to slow adoption of information technology [3]. Furthermore, the increasing global population, demand

© The Author(s), under exclusive license to Springer Nature Switzerland AG 2023
P. Delir Haghighi et al. (Eds.): iiWAS 2023, LNCS 14416, pp. 13–19, 2023.
https://doi.org/10.1007/978-3-031-48316-5_2

for healthcare services, and uneven distribution has resulted in a world wide shortage of healthcare workers. Factors like increased need for specialization due to advancements in technology, burnouts due to being overworked and many workers reaching retirement age contribute to the predicted shortage number of 18 million by [4]. Finally, healthcare costs continue to rise, posing challenges for individuals, families, employers, and governments. Factors such as the cost of medical technology, pharmaceuticals, and labor contribute to the increasing costs of healthcare services. With the ability to process and analyze vast amounts of data quickly and accurately, AI can help with use cases such as predicting optimal treatment strategies, making risk predictions, optimizing care processes and more. The Food and Drug Administration of the US has a vision to use Software as a Medical Device (SaMD) to leverage the AI's ability to deliver safe and effective solutions [5].

2　Related Work

This section goes over some of the relevant literature regarding the two aspects of the report. The paper by Suresh Renukappa et al. [6] goes over smart healthcare strategies as a potential solution to the growing problems within the healthcare sector. Three main themes affecting the adoption of smart solutions within healthcare have been identified based on the Technology-Organization-Environment (TOE) strategy. The main technology issues identified are: privacy and security issues, data governance and ethical concerns, interoperability issues, lack of data terminology and standards, poor data quality, functional and non-functional system issues, and costs. The main organizational issues are: disrupted workflows and reduced productivity, change culture, organizational readiness, organizational size, organizational structure, lack of management support and poor leadership, lack of knowledge, poor communication and engagement, poor planning, and rigid policies and procedures. Finally, the environmental issues are: end user behaviour, resistance to change, poor computer skills, and lack of training and support. A step by step approach considering all stakeholders involved and all the issues from all perspective needs to be constructed in detail to enable the digital transformation within these organizations.

3　Methodology

This paper will consist of two main parts: the designing of a data strategy for hospitals and development of an artificial neural network for heart disease prediction. The aim of the data strategy is to provide a road map to enable healthcare organizations to become data driven and take steps towards utilizing AI models in day to day patient diagnosis and other clinical applications. The data strategy is a broad topic which has many interdisciplinary aspects that need to be considered before envisioning a setup for a centralized data platform. The different aspects of the data strategy need to be considered to accommodate for the high regulatory barriers, sensitive data, data imbalance, scalability, and security concerns. An infrastructure needs to be built to ingest data from the different sources, process it into a well-defined structure and easy to use format, store it in the correct environment to have easy access and scalability, analyze and visualize it to gain insights, build predictive models and enable cognitive and automated systems to give real time responses. This entire infrastructure needs to be secured with a custom governance structure that ensures the quality, consistency, security, accountability and ownership, maintenance, and responsible use. The aim of this is to help improve transparency and safety of AI research, help increase knowledge of these technologies for the healthcare staff, and improve clinical implementation and usability. Once the data strategy is implemented and a centralized data platform that contains all the important information is available, analytics, AI and cognitive services can be used to improve efficiency of clinical processes, reduce workload of healthcare staff, automate administrative tasks, and more. The process can be seen in Fig. 1.

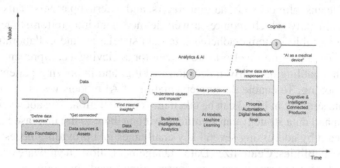

Fig. 1. The proposed data strategy.

In an ideal real-world scenario, the logical next step would be to implement the solutions required for various use cases. However, since hospitals are currently not well equipped to be able to use their own data to build the models they need, for the next steps, it is assumed that they have a well-structured data strategy in place which would allow for the development of the machine learning models. For the purpose of the research, external data sets that are publicly available are used. An artificial neural network will be the model that is going to be built and will be focusing on accurately predicting heart diseases based on patient data such as medical history, and symptoms.

The model building phase consists of several aspects such as data aggregation, exploratory data analysis, data processing, model training and evaluation, and hyper parameter fine tuning. The steps above are visualized in Fig. 2.

4   Results

This Section covers the data strategy that has been used, which in our case is the proposed cloud-based data strategy. It then proceeds to discuss data preprocessing and preparing it for deploying the ANN. In order to find out the typical data structure within today's healthcare facilities and the most important data sources, interviews with the IT team of two university medical centers were conducted. A hospital typically collects and maintains various types of data from different sources. In the current infrastructure, these systems are siloed and cannot be combined easily to extract valuable insights and run complex AI models that can be used for clinical diagnosis. All different forms of data such as Electronic Health Records, Laboratory Information Systems, Medical Imaging Systems, Administrative Systems, Research and Clinical Trials, Medical Devices, Pharmacy Systems, are stored in different systems, are in different formats, and have different data models with respect to structures and architectures. Based on interviews in the Netherlands, "EHR records are stored in vendor specific systems for most hospitals such as EPIC or ChipSoft whereas other admin related information is stored on Cloud ERP systems such as SAP. Clinical trial data is stored on systems such as Oracle Clinica, Open Clinica or Utopia". Therefore, combining data from multiple sources requires careful consideration of data governance policies, security measures, and privacy regulations. It requires collaboration and coordination among various stakeholders, including IT teams, clinical staff, administrators, and external partners. This introduces a level of complexity which requires a well-defined data integration strategy, investment in interoperable systems, adherence to data standards, and collaboration among stakeholders. Data integration efforts are crucial for achieving a comprehensive view of patient health, enabling data-driven decision-making, and improving patient outcomes in a hospital setting. To enable the implementation of AI models within healthcare, the following data strategy in Fig. 3 can be taken into consideration. The above cloud-based data platform and data strategy can significantly contribute to the increased adoption of AI in healthcare by addressing several key challenges and providing necessary infrastructure and capabilities. Centralized Data Management allows healthcare organizations to centralize their data from the various sources mentioned above this centralized data management enables easy access, integration, and sharing of data, ensuring that AI models have access to comprehensive and diverse datasets for training and validation. To start the pre-processing stage, a null check was conducted to see if there are any missing values and it was found that there were no missing values in the UCI dataset. However, the Framingham dataset consisted of multiple null values. Due to the small number of missing values for the columns BMI, chol, heartRate and cigsPerDay, these were imputed using the mean of the column. However, the glucose column had a larger number of missing values and hence was imputed using linear regression. Furthermore, in order to rectify the class imbalance within the Framingham dataset, the Synthetic Minority Over-sampling Technique (SMOTE) technique was used. This method identifies the minority class, randomly selects a minority class instance, finds k nearest neighbours of the sample point and creates a synthetic sample by interpolating between the reference point and the neighbour. This process is repeated for each instance of the minority class to result in a dataset with balanced class distribution. Once this is done, both datasets were merged to create one unified dataset. An artificial neural network is constructed to predict heart disease given a set of features from 2 different datasets - the UCI dataset and the Framingham dataset. The model is run individually on each of the datasets, as well as on the combined dataset to find prediction accuracies. The performance metrics achieved by each dataset are summarized in the Tables 1, 2, and 3. Table 3 contains the performance metrics for the merged dataset with the features from both UCI as well as the Framingham dataset. The accuracy, F1-score, precision and recall achieved by the ANN for this dataset is very high with all of them being above 0.98. As the next step, a genetic algorithm is applied to these datasets to find the most optimal subset of features to achieve best performance. Table 4 summarizes the optimal subset of features that result in the best accuracies for the different datasets.

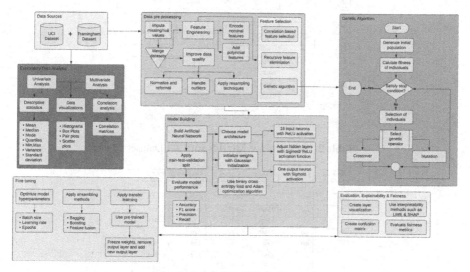

Fig. 2. Model Building diagram.

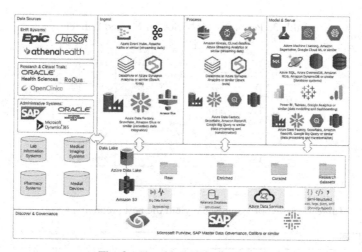

Fig. 3. Cloud based data strategy.

Table 1. Performance Metrics for UCI Dataset

Batch size	Epochs	Accuracy	F1 score	Precision	Recall
16	50	0.9805	0.9795	1.0	0.9597
16	100	0.9805	0.9795	1.0	0.9597
16	200	0.9903	0.9898	1.0	0.9797
32	50	0.9578	0.9562	0.9595	0.9530
32	100	0.9805	0.9795	1.0	0.9597
32	200	0.9805	0.9795	1.0	0.9597
64	50	0.9286	0.9247	0.9441	0.9060
64	100	0.9805	0.9795	1.0	0.9597
64	200	0.9805	0.9795	1.0	0.9597

Table 2. Performance Metrics for UCI Dataset

Batch size	Epochs	Accuracy	F1 score	Precision	Recall
16	50	0.7693	0.7669	0.7627	0.7712
16	100	0.7790	0.7834	0.7568	0.8121
16	200	0.7825	0.7759	0.7866	0.7655
32	50	0.7804	0.7740	0.7841	0.7641
32	100	0.7561	0.7516	0.7532	0.75
32	200	0.7901	0.7830	0.7968	0.7698
64	50	0.7582	0.7580	0.7466	0.7698
64	100	0.7887	0.7895	0.7746	0.8051
64	200	0.7783	0.7843	0.7523	0.8192

Table 3. Performance Metrics for Merged Dataset

Batch size	Epochs	Accuracy	F1 score	Precision	Recall
16	50	0.9958	0.9961	0.9964	0.9957
16	100	0.9988	0.9989	1.0	0.9977
16	200	0.9981	0.9982	0.9993	0.9972
32	50	0.9985	0.9986	0.9993	0.9977
32	100	0.9973	0.9975	0.9993	0.9957
32	200	0.9988	0.9989	0.9993	0.9986
64	50	0.9992	0.9993	0.9993	0.9993
64	100	0.9977	0.9979	0.9986	0.9972
64	200	0.9988	0.9989	0.9986	0.9993

Table 4. Subset of features that yield the best prediction accuracy

Dataset	Features
UCI Dataset	[age, sex, cp, trestbps, chol, thalach, exang, oldpeak, slope, ca]
Framingham Dataset	[sex, age, currentSmoker, cigsPerDay, prevelantHyp, chol, sysBP, diaBP, BMI, glucose]
Merged Dataset	[age, sysBP, chol, oldpeak, slope, ca, thal, cp, restecg, exang, cigsPerDay, diaBP, glucose]

5   Conclusion

This paper highlights the effectiveness of using an ANN with a genetic algorithm for feature selection to enhance the accuracy of heart disease prediction. By combining the UCI and Framingham datasets, which offer a larger number of samples and more diverse features, the ANN model achieved a predictive performance of over 98%. The integration of these datasets allowed the model to capture a comprehensive representation of factors influencing heart disease. The genetic algorithm further improved the model by identifying the most relevant features for prediction.

References

1. Knebel, E. Greiner, A.C.: 5 current issues in health care and what administrators can do: Regis, October 2022
2. Van Genderen, M.E., Smit, J.M., van de Sande, D.: Developing, implementing and governing artificial intelligence in medicine: a step-by-step approach to prevent an artificial intelligence winter. BMJ Health Care Inform. (2022)
3. Suleyman, M. , Corrado, G., King, D., Kelly, C.J., Karthikesalingam, A.: Key challenges for delivering clinical impact with artificial intelligence. BMC Med. (2019)
4. Boniol, M., Kunjumen, T., Nair, T.S., Siyam, A., Campbell, J., Diallo, K.: The global health workforce stock and distribution in 2020 and 2030: a threat to equity and 'universal' health coverage? (2022)
5. Software as a medical device (samd) (2021)
6. Renukappa, S., Mudiyi, P., Suresh, S., Abdalla, W., Subbarao, C.: Evaluation of challenges for adoption of smart healthcare strategies. Smart Health **26**, 100330 (2022)

WISHFUL - Website Extraction
of Institutional Sources
with Heterogeneous Factors
and User-Driven Linkage

Saijal Shahania[1,2]([✉]) [iD], Myra Spiliopoulou[2] [iD], and David Broneske[1,2] [iD]

[1] German Centre for Higher Education Research and Science Studies, Hannover,
Germany
broneske@dzhw.eu
[2] Faculty of Computer Science, University of Magdeburg, Magdeburg, Germany
shahania@dzhw.eu, myra@ovgu.de

Abstract. Extracting information from diverse websites is increasingly
important, especially for analyzing vast data sets to detect trends, gain
insights. By studying job ads, researchers can monitor employer demand
shifts, assisting policymakers in aiding affected workers and industries.
However, extraction faces challenges like varied website formats, dynamic
content, and duplicate data. This study introduces a method for extracting data from diverse private university websites involving keyword identification, website categorization, and extraction pipelines.

Keywords: Heterogeneous Information · Web Scraping · Job Ads

1 Introduction

Job advertisements from diverse sources offer valuable insights for researchers,
job seekers, and recruiters. Researchers leverage this data to track job market trends and ascertain the most sought-after skills, especially during economic downturns. Meanwhile, job seekers and recruiters can tailor their strategies, ensuring they align with current market needs [1,2]. The challenge lies
in data collection. A centralized repository for all job ads from private universities doesn't exist. This mandates extracting from varied sources, complicat-
ing the extraction process. Different university sites come with unique layouts
and designs, introducing data identification and extraction hurdles. Navigational
complexities can make locating the career portal on a university's homepage challenging. The diversity also extends to job ad formats - they can be PDFs, web

This work has been partially funded by the BMBF (FKZ: 16KOA008).

pages, or even Word documents. Special website features, such as infinite paginations or on-click data, further compound the issue. Manual data extraction, though possible, is tedious, error-prone, and resource-intensive.

Modern web scraping tools offer a potential solution. Tools like Scrapy (https://scrapy.org/), Selenium (https://www.selenium.dev/), and Beautiful Soup (https://www.crummy.com/software/BeautifulSoup/) cater to those with coding skills. In contrast, platforms like Import.io (https://www.import.io/), ParseHub (https://www.parsehub.com/), WebHarvy (https://www.webharvy.com/), and Octoparse(https://www.octoparse.com/) appeal to non-coders, simplifying the extraction process. However, their ease of use sometimes compromises flexibility, especially for intricate tasks. And these user-friendly tools often come at a financial cost. A significant gap in current tools is their primary focus on HTML or XML formats. Few can adeptly handle other formats like PDFs or Word documents.

Given these challenges, a comprehensive, adaptable solution is paramount. This would cater to the diverse formats and structures of university job ads while ensuring efficiency and accuracy in data extraction. To address these challenges, we will investigate the following research questions:

RQ 1: What are the different data representations and security features of a website that complicate data extraction?

RQ 2: What are the state-of-the-art techniques for extracting and integrating information from diverse sources, and how can they be integrated?

RQ 3: What is the impact of sourcing job openings from university websites directly versus third-party sources?

2   Concept and Implementation

This research presents a specialized web scraping framework for data extraction from varied sources, notably private university websites (c.f. Sect. 1). Built with adaptability in mind, the framework can adjust to changes in website structure and format [3]. Beyond mere data retrieval, it incorporates data pre-processing and cleaning features, ensuring the relevance and quality of job advertisement data. The methodology involves three core steps: 1) pinpointing the desired content, 2) organizing content based on recurring patterns, and 3) extracting content in its raw form, facilitating post-processing tailored to user needs. This approach enhances data collection efficiency and addresses diverse stakeholder needs (cf. Fig. 1).

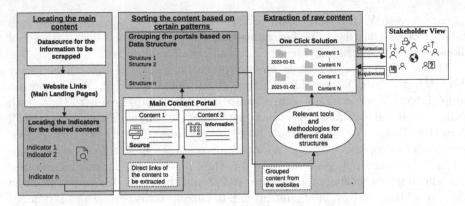

Fig. 1. The figure illustrates the main components of the proposed solution for customised scraping for heterogeneous websites.

2.1   Locating the Main Content

The first block identifies main content links, such as film reviews or job ads, using sources like IMDB for films or Google Finance for stocks. These URLs kickstart data extraction. The next step automates data access through website indicators, like keywords or filters [4]. Our focus was private university job ads. Directly sourcing from these sites ensures reliability, detailed job info, and cost benefits. University sites offer up-to-date listings and detailed application insights, often more affordably than third-party sources.

Using Hochschul Kompass (https://www.hochschulkompass.de/home.html), we sourced data on Germany's private universities, shortlisting 89. Keywords guided us to their job portals. Of these, 67 needed one keyword, yielding 44 unique terms. Another 11 required two steps, adding 11 unique keywords, and three sites took three steps, introducing 3 more terms. In total, we identified 58 distinct keywords. **Stellenangebote** was most frequent, followed by **Karriere** and **Stellenausschreibungen**. After excluding eight universities for missing job portals or required logins, we proceeded with 81 links.

While deeper navigation to a job portal might suggest ease, other elements can complicate extraction. Even single keyword sites can pose challenges with dynamic loading or infinite scrolls. The pipeline's goal is consistent data extraction via direct job portal links. With training on 58 terms, our system can handle any site, regardless of navigation depth to the main portal.

2.2   Sorting the Content Based on Certain Patterns

This phase delves into analyzing website structures to optimize extraction. Websites, though diverse in content-from movie reviews to job listings-can be classified based on their presentation styles, be it standard layouts or multimedia-rich designs. Identifying these styles is essential. Even if websites have standard sections, such as job openings, their navigation and functionalities can vary widely [5]. Most university sites prioritize user-friendly navigation and job search tools, but the extent of detail and features varies. For this project, the emphasis was on extracting universities' internal job listings sidestepping any pre-existing filters. We discerned three primary listing styles based on [6]:

- **Text-centric:** Direct textual job listings detailing roles, locations and salaries.
- **Interactive:** Dynamic job listings, such as grids or timelines. Grids use cards, while timelines spotlight recent openings.
- **Media-rich:** Visually engaging job listings, including formats like images, PDFs, or videos.

Of the 74 analyzed sites, 43 showcased interactive formats (with 34 employing cards), 14 were text-centric, and 8 utilized rich media. A few sites combined these styles, necessitating versatile extraction strategies. Within the rich media category, 5 employed PDFs, while 3 opted for images. Our extraction tool is designed to auto-detect these structures, ensuring adaptability. Websites with blended structures were particularly challenging, requiring a multi-faceted approach for effective data extraction.

2.3 Extraction of Raw Content

We tailored our extraction pipelines to address diverse website structures based on earlier classifications. We employed leading tools such as Selenium for website navigation and Beautiful Soup for precise data retrieval, with the latter also handling various character encodings. Processing non-textual formats like PDFs and images required special attention. Direct conversions risked data loss, and OCR methods sometimes misinterpreted content, as highlighted by Smith [7]. Though rich media websites were easy to interact with, extracting their actual content proved challenging. Interactive elements, once automated, facilitated data extraction due to their inherent structure. All raw extracted data was archived for versatile future usage. Researchers, watchdogs, and job seekers might focus on different facets of the data, emphasizing the need for such flexibility. Our automated module was calibrated to proficiently manage diverse data formats across the 74 university websites in our study.

3 Evaluation

Our study evaluated how well our data-gathering method worked and the quality of our data source. We judged our method based on its accuracy, speed, ability to work across multiple sites, adaptability, and ease of upkeep. The source's quality was assessed by its accuracy, fullness, and uniqueness, as mentioned by Lawson et al. [8]. A good data method should quickly fetch complete and correct data, work on many sites, and be easy to maintain.

Of the 89 websites from Hochschul Kompass, we collected data from 74. We skipped sites without job sections, no new jobs or that needed a special login. These university job listings are up-to-date and thorough. We checked the data's accuracy, collection speed, adaptability, strength, fullness, and range.

3.1 Effectiveness of the Proposed Web Extraction Approach

We conducted a qualitative analysis on random sites and job ads for quality assessment, ensuring accuracy and complete data extraction. This involved manual comparisons with the original sources. We performed stress tests over multiple scraping iterations to verify consistency, confirming identical data extraction across all sites and job listings.

We evaluated extraction speed based on two parameters: steps needed to access the primary job portal and the specific structural features of websites. To ensure server integrity, we integrated buffer sleep time between requests for each type of website, reducing the risk of IP bans. Our assessment looked at different categories, the number of websites in each category w_i, the total execution time t_t, individual buffer time t_b, total buffer time T_b, average time per website A_t, and the effective average time A_e. The effective time t_e is derived by subtracting T_b from t_t as shown in Eq. 1.

$$T_b = t_b \times w_i \quad \text{and} \quad t_t = t_e + T_b \quad \text{and} \quad A_t = \frac{t_t}{w_i} \quad \text{and} \quad A_e = \frac{t_e}{w_i} \quad (1)$$

For 60 sites, just one keyword was sufficient to navigate to the job portal, cumulatively taking 92 s. After accounting for a 67-second buffer, the effective time was 25 s. Extraction times varied across structures, influenced by factors like website interaction (as presented in Table 2). The interactive single format was prevalent in 34 websites (45.9%). However, the nine sites that featured interactive multiple or mixed media formats had longer extraction times. For example, mixed media sites took an average of 101.67 s, but the effective average was shorter at 88.67 s, indicating a notable buffer time. Text-only sites were the quickest, averaging 24.29 s, but their effective time was slightly longer due to their unstructured format.

In summary, structural features significantly influenced extraction durations. Websites with interactive multiple formats required the most time, while the extraction time for mixed media was shorter than expected. Factors such as third-party scripts, server locations, or the number of job listings on different sites also impacted extraction speeds.

Table 1. The table summarises the times to locate the main job portal depending on the steps taken to reach the same.

Steps required	w_i	t_t in s	t_b in s	T_b in s	t_e in s
1	67	92	1	67	25
2	11	32	2	22	10
3	3	13	3	9	4

Table 2. The table summarises times taken to extract the websites according to different structural features found.

Structural Feature	w_i	t_t seconds	t_b seconds	t_e seconds
Text Only	14	340	3	298
Interactive Single Format	34	732	4	596
Interactive Multiple Formats	9	957	7	894
Rich Media	8	772	10	692
Mixed Media	9	915	13	798

3.2   Usefulness of Chosen Source for Data Collection

In our second evaluation, we compared job ads from direct university websites (see Sect. 2.1) with those from third-party platforms to test our method's scalability and reliability. We focused on 74 universities with open job portals, using their listings as reference data. We compared them with reputable third-party platforms: Academics, Hochschul Job, and ZEIT Online Stellenmarkt, often used by universities to widen their job ad reach.

We assessed the coverage, completeness, and speed of data extraction. Direct university website extraction yielded 100% coverage and completeness. Third-party sources, however, had lesser coverage: Academia at 74%, ZEIT Online Stellenmarkt at 68%, and Hochschul Job at just 27%. Notably, Academia's potential affiliation with ZEIT group could influence these results (https://inserieren.academics.de/).

Direct extraction from university sites took longer due to their diverse structures, while third-party sites, having consistent formats, were faster. But, as mentioned in Sect. 3.1, speed isn't our main focus. Our method's adaptability ensures it works well across various sources; meeting stakeholder needs from quick job searches to in-depth research.

Table 3. The table contrasts data extraction from direct university websites and third-party sources. It evaluates based on coverage (universities represented), completeness (job listings per university), and extraction speed.

Source of job advertisements	Coverage (%)	Completeness (%)	t_t minutes	Total buffer time (minutes)	t_e minutes
University Websites	100	100	61,9	7,3	54,6
Academics	23	74	5,95	1,70	4,25
Hochschul Job	11	27	2,8	0,93	1,87
ZEIT Online Stellenmarkt	30	68	7,7	2,4	5,3

4   Summary and Conclusion

This paper presents a 3-step methodology for automated extraction of job listings from university websites. The steps involve navigating the main job portal, grouping websites based on navigation and search features, and selecting the appropriate extraction tool based on the format. The extracted content is stored efficiently for further processing. The approach is resilient to design variations and can be scaled to other data sources.

In the future, we improve the system by exploring data extraction beyond university job portals, including government and financial institutions. Moreover, we will use machine learning techniques to analyze extracted data for patterns and trends in the job and university sectors.

References

1. Baykal, E.: Digital era and new methods for employee recruitment. In: Handbook of Research on Strategic Fit and Design in Business Ecosystems. IGI Global (2020)
2. Kim, J., Angnakoon, P.: Research using job advertisements: a methodological assessment. Library Info. Sci. Res. **38**(4) (2016)
3. Torre-Bastida, A.I., Del Ser, J., Laña, I., Ilardia, M., Bilbao, M.N., Campos-Cordobés, S.: Big data for transportation and mobility: recent advances, trends and challenges. IET Intell. Transp. Syst. **12**(8) (2018)
4. Tarafdar, M., Zhang, J.: Determinants of reach and loyalty–a study of website performance and implications for website design. J. Comput. Inf. Syst. **48**(2) (2008)
5. Kalbach, J.: Designing Web Navigation: Optimizing the User Experience. O'Reilly Media Inc, Sebastopol (2007)
6. Sirisuriya, D.S., et al.: A comparative study on web scraping (2015)
7. Smith, R.: An overview of the tesseract OCR engine. In: International Conference on Document Analysis and Recognition (ICDAR 2007), vol. 2. IEEE (2007)
8. Lawson, R.: Web scraping with Python. Packt Publishing Ltd. (2015)

DISA - A Blockchain-Based Distributed Information Security Audit

Lukas König[✉][ID], Martin Pirker[ID], Herfried Geyer, Michael Feldmann,
Simon Tjoa[ID], and Peter Kieseberg[ID]

St. Pölten University of Applied Sciences, Campus-Platz 1, 3100 St. Pölten, Austria
{lukas.koenig,martin.pirker,herfried.geyer,michael.feldmann,
simon.tjoa,peter.kieseberg}@fhstp.ac.at
https://www.fhstp.ac.at/

Abstract. Information security audits are essential for the assessment
of enterprise cyber security maturity levels, both from a technical and
organizational perspective. A common way of conducting such an assessment is to carry out a security audit based on the international security
standard ISO 27001. However, modern organizations often have complex
or even global supply chains, which are hard to secure. Verification of
sufficient security levels across organizations is a non-trivial task and
requires trust between all entities. This paper explores the feasibility of
a blockchain-based distributed information security audit, highlights the
encountered challenges, and contributes to the discussion of distributed
security audits.

Keywords: Distributed Ledger · Blockchain · Information Security
Audit · Distributed Audit

1 Introduction

The National Institute of Standards and Technology (NIST) reported [2] on supply chain risks for organizations and their ICT systems. Security and resilience
are two of their main focus points to maintain quality and integrity of a supply chain. Adequately securing an organization that is a participant of a supply
chain is not only vital for that specific organization, but also for all the other
participants, e.g. due to domino effects or attack propagation.

One way to mitigate the overall cybersecurity risk of an organization is to
implement and regularly audit a so-called information security management system (ISMS). A commonly used and certifiable approach that follows the normative references stated in the ISO 27001 standard [4], and its subsequent supporting documents. An important pillar of security auditing is that such audits
provide an objective and independent overview of the organization [9], and how
security is managed to conform to existing security policies and reach security
objectives, especially with regards to the levels of confidentiality, integrity, and
availability.

P. Delir Haghighi et al. (Eds.): iiWAS 2023, LNCS 14416, pp. 27–34, 2023.
https://doi.org/10.1007/978-3-031-48316-5_4

The process of auditing IT [10] and information systems itself has gained increasing relevance and traction with the amounts of digital information that is processed and utilized within modern organizations.

Since a certified ISMS relies on information presented in an audit, as well as information of past audits to fulfill continuous improvement requirements, it is important that the correctness of all the available information can be validated. Such a validation includes that past audit results are kept as a reference to improve upon, which requires that stored audit results are resistant to tampering.

Due to the high level of sensitivity of information contained in the result of an information security audit, it is essential to ensure that these results are stored in a secure way. Additionally, it is important that the results are resistant to tampering. The use of a blockchain-based audit system [1] is a perfect fit for this task, due to the excellent record-keeping capabilities of blockchains. Such a system comes with the additional benefit that the audit information is replicated and therefore more resistant to data loss incidents.

This paper presents a new approach for the realization of a distributed information security audit system, using blockchains as the underlying technology. It uses the inherent security features of said technology to create an environment where proof of secure practices within an organization and compliance to international standardization become easily verifiable.

The remainder of this paper is structured as follows: Sect. 2 provides a brief technology overview and related work. Thereafter comes an overview of the approach and methods used in this work in Sect. 3, followed by a detailed description of the developed prototype in Sect. 4. The results are presented and discussed in Sect. 5, and finally, the paper concludes in Sect. 6.

2   Background and Related Work

2.1   Blockchain Technology

For the limited scope of this paper, a blockchain is one implementation variant of a distributed ledger system: Key attributes of a blockchain [7] are its immutability, increased security, and a consensus mechanism to settle block-appending transactions to the distributed system. One of the suitable use cases of a blockchain is record keeping, as a storage for records/transactions in the cryptographically linked data blocks/lists, which implicitly vouches for the authenticity of the stored data. Due to space constraints here, for additional discussion and future directions of blockchain technology see e.g. [5].

2.2   Related Work

Mounji et al. propose an approach for a distributed audit trail analysis [6] and highlight the importance of such a capability. Their analysis focuses on auditing network security via a rule-based language system, to then extract the desired information to a central host. However, it is not designed to be used for auditing information security management systems.

Another approach for a distributed audit is presented by Tsai and Gligor [8], which uses a combination of secure remote procedure calls and the network file system. Similar to the first approach, the purpose of their system is to collect information at a central point, where a security officer or administrator controls the entire system.

Guan et al. [3] present a different approach that uses a consortium blockchain and a distributed controller for software-defined networking. Their system aims to monitor information at the switching layer. The use of blockchain technology allows them to store information distributed across participating nodes.

However, there is no system that focuses on information security management system audit data regarding normative conformities of the ISO 27001 standard.

3 Approach

3.1 Concept and Purpose

We designed and developed a prototype (see Sect. 4) to demonstrate and trial distributed information security audit capabilities. This prototype serves as a platform for information security auditors and provides an audit catalogue, which is typically used by an auditor to facilitate the audit process. The basis for the audit catalogue are the security controls of the ISO 27001 standard.

Besides the base capability of distributed audits, important considerations of such a system are the trust in both the system and its participants, the confidentiality of audit information, and the possibility to verify audit results as an independent authority.

Distributed audits enable both auditors and affected organizations to quickly retrieve information about current and past audit results, and therefore details about the security levels of an organization. Aggregating the results in the audit history also reveals trends, e.g. about continuous improvement of the information security management system and the IT systems of an organization.

3.2 Data Structures and Operations

To map this to a practical example, an audit catalogue entry in the distributed audit system is comprised of three parts:

– A clear specification about which security control is the subject of each entry.
– The possibility for an auditor to store relevant information and the evaluation of the status of conformity/adherence to the standard.
– Evidence to prove the conformity to the respective security control.

The auditor inputs information for all three parts of a new audit entry into the system, where said information is then crafted into a new data block and added to the ledger. The distributed ledger design ensures traceability, immutability and non-repudiation of the audit results. Therefore, this enables future auditors to clearly trace back changes and improvements of the audited ISMS.

Each audit entry is unique due to the selected scope of the audit, the auditor's name, and a timestamp attached to it. The scope of the audit is typically negotiated between the auditor and the audited organization beforehand. The auditor selects the organizational units that have to be audited first, then the relevant audit catalogue dynamically provides more details/choices/tasks. The audit results must be signed by the auditor with a cryptographically secure signature, and a timestamp is set automatically by the software in order to guarantee the authenticity of the data.

The final result of an audit is a PDF report.

Since the file size of this document should not be limited by the constraints of the specific blockchain or distributed ledger, for this prototype we opted to store these outside of the blockchain, on the decentralized file system IPFS. Being a public data store, the data stored on IPFS needs to be secured, both by transport encryption and encryption of the data content itself.

4   Experimental Prototype

4.1   Substrate Prototype

Substrate nodes form the back-end of a distributed application and connect via a JSON-based remote procedure call (RPC) interface with the front-end. This is the interface with which the user interacts with the blockchain and visualizes data. Substrate uses a REST API for communication with nodes in the network, which makes it easy to connect and communicate via a web-based front-end.

Implementation: The functionality of a node is split up into different modules, which Substrate calls pallets. Pallets make it possible for a developer to re-use functionalities in other blockchain projects, and to integrate functionalities created by other developers. Multiple pallets assembled into one WebAssembly binary are then executed by the Substrate node.[1]

For our intended audit functionality, we created a new custom pallet which contains all the necessary logic for managing (e.g. queries) an audit storage. This audit pallet also contains a configuration data structure for customization of the pallet and import of code and data types from other pallets.

In our design, there is an `Event` type, for sending event notification when a new audit is created. The node passes these events to the user interface and enables the user interface to update in real-time.

```
#[pallet::event]
pub enum Event<T: Config> {
  AuditCreated(T::AccountId, T::Hash),
}
```

Further, importing the `TimeProvider` from the framework enables the pallet to receive time information from the already existing `time` pallet.

---

[1] See https://docs.substrate.io/build/build-process/.

Blockchain Data Storage: To store data on the Substrate network, a pallet has to have storage instances. These contain the values that are pushed onto the chain via the functions implemented at a later stage.[2] The audit use case requires storage of individual audits so that they can be retrieved at will based on their hashes, in order to obtain a list of all audits and a list of audits assigned to an organizational unit. For this purpose, we implemented a key-value storage map called `audits`, which uses the hash of an audit as key and the audit data as value. A second key-value map called `audits_location` then takes a value which represents the organizational unit as key and maps it to a list of audit hashes. The audit is stored once in the `audits` map and a second time in `audits_location` to retrieve the audit at a later stage. Hashes in the list are then queried in `audits` to get to the actual audit data.

For verification purposes there is an additional `audit_cnt` storage. This storage instance only contains a single integer value to track the total number of stored audits.

Audit Creation: In order to add a new audit entry to the blockchain, the storage instances described in previous paragraphs have to be updated via code. A method for the purpose of adding new audit entries is accessible through the front-end.

```
pub fn create_audit(
    origin: OriginFor<T>, answers: AuditAnswerVec<T>,
    ipfs: Vec<Vec<u8>>, comments: AuditCommentVec<T>, location: u32
) -> DispatchResult {
  let sender = ensure_signed(origin)?;
  let time = T::TimeProvider::now().as_secs();

  // this updates all storage instances
  let audit_id = Self::mint(&sender, &answers,
      &ipfs, &comments, location, time)?;

  Self::deposit_event(Event::AuditCreated(sender, audit_id));
  Ok(())
}
```

This method takes all information from an audit checklist form as input for an audit entry. On top of that, linked documents and the affected organizational unit represented by a numeric value are the second part, which is required to fill in when creating a new audit data instance. In addition to these parameters, the author of the audit is represented by a public key used to sign the method call to `create_audit`, also known as transaction. The current timestamp is created by retrieving the time from the time pallet, provided by the framework.

Since both the audit author and timestamp are automatically gathered through coded methods, those values can not be fabricated via the front-end. Therefore, one can trust that both the audit author and timestamp are always correct. The data gathered by the `create_audit` method is bundled into the Audit struct and stored in the audits storage. The hash of an audit is stored in

---

[2] See https://docs.substrate.io/build/runtime-storage/.

a list in `audits_location` based on the organizational unit. Additionally, the `audit_cnt` is incremented by one.

Supplemental Storage in IPFS: Substrate blockchain entries have a predetermined maximum size, which is determined automatically at compile time. To overcome this limitation for file storage, the audit PDF documents are stored on an alternative decentralized file system called IPFS. The IPFS upload and download functionality is implemented in the front-end and the Substrate node only stores the IPFS hash, which is used by the front-end to retrieve the document from IPFS at a later time again.

Prototype Testing: For testing, we set up two instances of a Substrate node on different virtual machines. The nodes are configured to run on a local network. This simulates the target environment of a private blockchain network. Since the nodes disallow external connections per default without a proxy, a ssh tunnel is used to connect front-end and back-end nodes on the virtual machines.

Core Audit Data Structure: The Audit structure describes the data stored on the blockchain:

- author is the account ID of the author that signed the transaction.
- answers is an array of bytes storing the checked yes/no question as a Boolean in each bit. So, every entry in this array stores 8 answers.
- ipfs stores the IPFS hashes as strings. On the blockchain strings are stored as byte arrays. Every control has one IPFS storage entry.
- comment stores the comments for each control directly on the blockchain; data is stored similar to the IPFS field.
- timestamp is a UNIX timestamp capturing the moment the audit was created.
- location is a number representing the organizational unit that was audited.

```
struct Audit {
  author: AccountOf, answers: AuditAnswerVec, ipfs: Vec<Vec<u8>>,
  comments: AuditCommentVec, timestamp: u64, location: u32
}
```

New Audit Instance: The audit pallet exposes a single function to create a new audit entry, with the following function signature. The 4 parameters are similar to the ones of the `Audit` structure.

```
fn create_audit( answers: AuditAnswerVec, ipfs: Vec<Vec<u8>>,
  comments: AuditCommentVec, location: u32 )
```

- answers is an array representing the results of the audit checklist as mentioned earlier in the Audit struct.
- ipfs is an array for the ipfs hashes for each control
- comments contains all additional comments for each control
- location is a number which represents the organizational unit that was audited

4.2   Results

With Substrate we were able to implement a comprehensive blockchain-based information security audit application prototype. Via a web-based application front-end, a user can connect to and communicate with the prototype. The back-end node takes care of the management of audit entries. Alternatively, by direct access via the Polkadot online wallet app, a user is also able to extract data from the blockchain, as well as to create new audit entries, independent of a web-application. This is convenient for debugging purposes.

5   Discussion

While it is possible to create a decentralized application with blockchain technology, this prototyping effort revealed important considerations during the development phase.

With Substrate, updating and the porting to new versions can be an issue, depending on the changes in the framework. In many cases it appeared easier to create a new project and copy most of the existing logic parts of an application over to the new project, as there is currently no assistance tool to support the update process of the framework.

In spite of these technical issues and limitations we were able to create a prototype for a distributed information security audit. However, while this prototype serves as a proof of concept for future work, it still heavily focuses on one blockchain implementation of a distributed audit system. A multi-layered blockchain support that connects a local blockchain within an organization to a global blockchain across an entire supply chain to enable interoperability between different distributed audits remains a task for future approaches.

Overall, we believe there still is high potential in the development of a distributed information security audit system that takes advantage of blockchain ideas and technology. As mentioned in the introduction of this work, secure supply chains are an increasingly important topic for many organizations, and proving security to partners becomes an easy task with verifiable information security certification.

6   Conclusion

In this paper we revisit the challenges of a distributed information security audit and present our prototype effort for a blockchain-based audit system. We use the security controls specified in the ISO 27001 standard as guide to provide an audit catalogue for the prototype. The technical basis for farthest implemented prototype is based on Substrate/Polkadot framework.

At the present state of work it does not seem feasible to invest more effort to continue development with the technologies currently used in the implementation of this prototype, as these technologies have proven to be not well-fitting to our initial design requirements for such a system.

A reflection of the lessons learned and the selection of a more suitable technology for the requirements of the distributed audit application scenario must form the basis for future work.

Acknowledgements. The work presented in this paper was done at the Josef Ressel Center for Blockchain Technologies and Security Management, St. Pölten University of Applied Sciences, Austria. The financial support by the Christian Doppler Research Association, the Austrian Federal Ministry for Digital, and Economic Affairs and the National Foundation for Research, Technology and Development is gratefully acknowledged. Furthermore, parts of this work were funded by the COIN-project "Secure Supply Chains for Critical Systems" (SSCCS, FFG-Nr. 883977) by the Austrian Research Promotion Agency (FFG).

References

1. Ahmad, A., Saad, M., Bassiouni, M., Mohaisen, A.: Towards blockchain-driven, secure and transparent audit logs. In: Proceedings of the 15th EAI International Conference on Mobile and Ubiquitous Systems: Computing, Networking and Services, pp. 443–448 (2018)
2. Boyens, J., Paulsen, C., Moorthy, R., Bartol, N., Shankles, S.A.: Supply chain risk management practices for federal information systems and organizations. NIST Spec. Publ. **800**(161), 32 (2015)
3. Guan, Z., Lyu, H., Zheng, H., Li, D., Liu, J.: Distributed audit system of SDN controller based on blockchain. In: Qiu, M. (ed.) SmartBlock 2019. LNCS, vol. 11911, pp. 21–31. Springer, Cham (2019). https://doi.org/10.1007/978-3-030-34083-4_3
4. ISO/IEC: Information technology - Security techniques - Information security management systems - Requirements. Standard, International Organization for Standardization, Geneva, CH, October 2013
5. Kolb, J., AbdelBaky, M., Katz, R.H., Culler, D.E.: Core concepts, challenges, and future directions in blockchain: A centralized tutorial. ACM Comput. Surv. **53**(1), February 2020. https://doi.org/10.1145/3366370
6. Mounji, A., Le Charlier, B., Zampunieris, D., Habra, N.: Distributed audit trail analysis. In: Proceedings of the Symposium on Network and Distributed System Security, pp. 102–112 (1995). https://doi.org/10.1109/NDSS.1995.390641
7. Panwar, A., Bhatnagar, V.: Distributed ledger technology (dlt): the beginning of a technological revolution for blockchain. In: 2nd International Conference on Data, Engineering and Applications (IDEA), pp. 1–5. IEEE (2020)
8. Tsai, C.R., Gligor, V.: Distributed audit with secure remote procedure calls. In: Proceedings. 25th Annual 1991 IEEE International Carnahan Conference on Security Technology, pp. 154–160 (1991). https://doi.org/10.1109/CCST.1991.202209
9. Vroom, C., von Solms, R.: Information security: auditing the behaviour of the employee. In: Gritzalis, D., De Capitani di Vimercati, S., Samarati, P., Katsikas, S. (eds.) SEC 2003. ITIFIP, vol. 122, pp. 401–404. Springer, Boston (2003). https://doi.org/10.1007/978-0-387-35691-4_35
10. Vroom, C., Von Solms, R.: Towards information security behavioural compliance. Comput. Secur. **23**(3), 191–198 (2004)

Analysing Online Review by Bank Employees: A Predictive Analytics Approach

Dominic Desmond Anil Abraham Emmanuel (ID), Swee Chuan Tan (ID), and Priyanka Gupta(✉) (ID)

Singapore University of Social Sciences, 463 Clement Road, Singapore 599494, Singapore
{dominic004,jamestansc,priyanka}@suss.edu.sg

Abstract. Publicly available data on the web is a rich and important resource for generating valuable insights about our world. In this paper, we present the analysis of bank employee online review data obtained from an online platform that collects anonymous employee reviews about the companies they work(ed) with. The feature of anonymity here is important, it helps (especially existing) employees to review their employers freely, without fear of repercussions. Employers can also capitalise on this platform to better understand their employees' opinions on the company's performance. However, there are several common issues associated with the data found on such platforms. These include: (i) relatively small number of reviews associated with each employer, (ii) multicollinearity among predictors, and (iii) missing values in the inputs. We propose a solution framework to address these issues. Firstly, we show that a transfer learning approach can help to augment the data size by combining data from different employers. Secondly, we address the missing value issues, which include the use of a rather uncommon method known as missing value replacements using a proxy variable. Finally, we apply a decision tree approach to build reasonably reliable model despite the presence of multicollinearity in the predictors. Our results show that all these solutions put together help to generate a more robust and comprehensible model. In addition, the results also show that augmentation of data is key to address some of the fundamental issues typically encountered in this type of online review data. Finally, we believe that the presented solution can be adapted or extended to other analytics projects that involve the analyses of online review data.

Keywords: Predictive analytics · Online Review · Employee satisfaction · Missing Values · Multicollinearity · Transfer Learning

1 Introduction

Publicly accessible data on the internet plays a crucial role in generating useful insights about the world we live in. In this paper, we focus on the analysis of online review data obtained from an online platform, where employees could anonymously share their reviews of the companies they have worked for or are currently working in. The feature of anonymity is crucial, it allows employees, both existing and former, to express their opinions about their employers freely, without the fear of facing repercussions. In

P. Delir Haghighi et al. (Eds.): iiWAS 2023, LNCS 14416, pp. 35–42, 2023.
https://doi.org/10.1007/978-3-031-48316-5_5

addition, an employer can leverage this platform to gain a deeper understanding of their employees' sentiment regarding the company's performance.

However, when collecting data from the online review platform, we encountered several data quality issues: (i) a small data size of 212 records only, (ii) a sizable proportion of missing entries found in the inputs, and (iii) the presence of multicollinearity found in the predictors. For the issue of small data size, it is primarily due to the small number of employees in the bank that we originally intended to study. To address this issue, we collected another 251 online review records of a second bank from the platform. Since both datasets are from the same online platform, they have a common set of variables and data format. This second bank was also carefully chosen based on bank type and location; and they are of similar size, scale, customer segments, and products-cum-services offerings. Furthermore, the review data was collected based on similar time periods. We then applied transfer learning [9] to confirm that these two sets of data are comparable and can be combined as a bigger set of bank review data.

We address the missing value issue by using decision trees, which can handle missing values naturally. We also explore the use of a less conventional method known as missing value replacements using a proxy variable. The missing value treatments were compared to understand the situations under which the methods are useful. Finally, we apply an ensemble learning approach to build a reliable model despite the presence of multicollinearity in the predictors. Our results show that all these solutions put together help to generate a more robust predictive model.

In short, our work suggests that the proposed solution framework can be adapted or extended to other analytics projects that involve the analyses of similar online review data. By addressing the inherent challenges with such data, our work contributes to a more systematic approach in the development of robust and useful model based on online review data. The rest of this paper is organized as follows. Section 2 reviews the related work. Section 3 presents the data and results. Finally, Sect. 4 provides some discussions and Sect. 5 concludes this paper.

2 Related Work

The issue of staff turnover has been of growing interest to many organizations worldwide. Unhappy employees not only result in reduced workplace productivity, but also high staff turnover rates, more hiring and training efforts, poor staff morale, and increased workloads. In recent years, much work on analyzing employee satisfaction has moved towards the use of machine learning algorithms, instead of classical statistical methods. For example, Atef et al. [2] used the k-nearest neighbors (KNN) and random forests (RF) machine learning algorithms for predicting the turnover intentions of workers during the recruitment process. Zhao et al. [12] evaluated the performance of ten supervised machine learning algorithms on human resource datasets. Ajit [1] conducted a comparative study to predict employee turnover, using several machine learning algorithms on the employee database of a global retailer.

Apart from the trend towards using machine learning algorithms, one common objective of these studies has been to identify important factors for employee satisfaction or turnover. For example, Jain & Nayyar [5] found that age, gender, marital status, years at the company, job satisfaction, and distance from home have the most significant effects on turnover among all attributes. Zhang et al. [11] attempted to find the most important factors of employee turnover using logistic regression. Other common modelling objectives include predicting who is likely to resign and why [2].

Web data or online review data is prone to noise, multi-collinearity issues, and missing information [1]. Koncar and Helic [7] deleted all records with missing values because the dataset was huge. Zhao et al. [12] replaced the numerical and categorical missing entries by the median and mode, respectively.

Although most of the research works mentioned above are problem-specific and difficult to generalize, they point to several useful directions for researchers. Firstly, they show that machine learning algorithms are promising methods for predictive modelling of employee satisfaction or turnover since inherent quality issues of online review data often render the use of classical statistical methods questionable. Secondly, common issues of online review data on the web, such as missing values and multicollinearity, deserve a more systematic study of the treatments required.

In our work, we will explore the use of transfer learning for data augmentation. This allows us to selectively combine two or more small but relevant datasets into a bigger dataset so that we could conduct more comprehensive sector-specific studies. Furthermore, the issues of missing values and multicollinearity are also present in the dataset, allowing us to study the effectiveness of possible treatments for online review data quality issues.

3 Dataset and Empirical Results

3.1 Dataset

The data used for this project came from the reviews of two similar banks extracted from an online review platform. The dataset was analyzed using the IBM SPSS Modeler [4], along with the use of Python scripts to perform repeated sampling of data for model constructions and evaluations. A total of 463 records were extracted. The employees were asked to rate seven job-related dimensions: *Work-Life Harmony*, *Organization Ethos*, *Equity & Belonging*, *Career Prospects*, *Renumeration and Benefits*, *Executive Leadership* and finally, *Overall (satisfaction) Rating*. The ratings were based on a Likert-scale of 1 to 5, where 1 is the most dissatisfied and 5 is the most satisfied.

We used all the reviews until the end of October 2022. Another attribute captured in the survey is the "willingness to recommend to a friend" as a dichotomous variable (named *Recommend*) with response options of either "Approve" or "Disapprove". In this dataset, 59% of the reviewers have expressed approval towards their employers. *Recommend* is highly correlated with the *Overall Rating* since happy employees are more likely to approve their employers.

There are high correlations between the *Overall Rating* and the six job-related ratings, ranging from 0.73 to 0.88. This suggests that the *Overall Rating* can be used as a proxy variable to replace missing values found in the six job-related dimensions. Moreover, the Overall Rating will not be used as an input because our interest is in understanding how the six job-related ratings affect the *Recommend* variable, which is the target of our models. The high correlations among the six inputs (correlations range from 0.64 to 0.848) also point to the issue of multicollinearity that needs to be addressed later.

Table 1 shows the frequencies of the missing values *in the inputs* across all the records. We can see that there are 301 complete records. On the other hand, 70 records with missing values across all six input variables do not serve any purpose and are discarded for good. "Equity & belonging" is a relatively new field introduced recently and it contains 154 missing values for the period prior to its introduction.

Since missing values may affect the validity of the models, we will evaluate four different methods of missing value treatments across different predictive models. They are namely: (i) Keep the null entries as they are and let the decision trees handle the missing values' (ii) Replace missing values with the means of individual attributes; (iii) Removing entries from the dataset entirely if they contain one or more missing values;)iv) Replace missing values with the Overall Rating as the proxy variable since Overall Rating is not an input but is highly correlated with the six input ratings.

Table 1. Missing values in the inputs across observations

Number of missing values	Number of observations	%
0	301	65.0
1	87	18.8
2	1	0.2
3	2	0.4
4	1	0.2
5	1	0.2
6	70	15.1
Total	463	100.0

3.2 Modelling and Performance Evaluation

The given dataset makes the decision tree approach particularly suitable for predictive modeling due to three reasons. Firstly, it is a non-parametric method that effectively addresses the multicollinearity issues mentioned earlier. Unlike parametric models, decision trees do not assume any relationship between predictors, and are robust in the presence of multicollinearity. Secondly, decision trees can handle missing values naturally, which is particularly useful in this case. This allows us to assess the effectiveness of decision trees in handing the missing values, versus other missing value treatment methods. Thirdly, decision trees are suitable for ensemble learning techniques, which can be used to create more accurate models. Finally, decision trees offer an intuitive visual representation of data partitioning, which is better than a black box algorithm such as Neural Networks.

The following decision tree algorithms were used for constructions and evaluations: (i) Classification and Regression Tree (CART) proposed by Breiman et al. [3], (ii) Chi-squared Automatic Interaction Detector (CHAID) developed by Kass [6], (iii) Quick Unbiased Efficient Statistical Tree (QUEST) introduced by Loh and Shih [8], and (iv) C5.0, which is a proprietary version of C4.5 [10]. The dataset was randomly split into 70% for training, and 30% for testing. This process is repeated 30 times, each with a unique random seed number from 1 to 30.

3.2.1 Model Performance

Table 2 shows the mean and standard deviation (which is enclosed in brackets) of the *test accuracy* for each model repeated over 30 runs. Of all the missing value treatment methods, it turns out that the best method is Method 3 (i.e., discarding all records with missing values). This is possible because we have already enlarged the dataset by combining two smaller datasets from two similar banks, and discarding the records with missing values in turn removes uncertainty in records and further improves model performance.

Under Method 3, it is interesting to note that the *CART with Bagging* is the best performing model, attaining the highest mean test accuracy of 87.7% and smallest standard deviation of 2.4%. Since it is hard to interpret this ensemble model, we can also use the second-best performing model, C5.0, which has a mean test accuracy of 87.5% and standard deviation of 3%.

At first sight, the rest of the methods work well too. For example, even Method 2, replacing missing values with the attribute's mean works quite well. A further check shows that most of the missing values are found in the *Equity & Belonging* attribute, which is one of the least important attributes according to the modelling results. Further, the presence of multicollinearity may have weakened its power as a predictor, making it less sensitive to the missing value treatments.

Table 2. Test performance of the predictive models: Mean and Standard Deviation (enclosed in brackets)

Missing Value Treatment Method	CART	CART + Bagging	CART + Boosting	QUEST	CHAID	C5.0
1) No change to input data	85.3% (3.1%)	86.8% (3.2%)	85.5% (2.5%)	85.6% (2.9%)	86.2% (2.7%)	86.1% (3.0%)
2) Replace missing entries with attributes' means	85.6% (3.2%)	86.6% (3.1%)	84.4% (3.5%)	85.0% (5.1%)	86.3% (2.8%)	85.8% (3.0%)
3) Discard records with missing entries	86.5% (2.9%)	**87.7% (2.4%)**	86.5% (3.7%)	86.4% (5.5%)	86.9% (3.3%)	**87.5% (3.0%)**
4) Replace missing entries with proxy values	85.2% (3.0%)	86.5% (3.1%)	86.1% (2.8%)	85.7% (2.9%)	85.7% (3.0%)	85.9% (3.0%)

3.2.2 Using Transfer Learning to Combine Online Review Data

So far, it appears that there is not much difference in model performance across various learning methods as well as different missing value treatments in Sect. 3.2.1. This was not true when we first started this research. Initially, we obtained the dataset from one local bank, which has 212 records only. With this small dataset, we found Method 4 to be the most effective method since every record count and should not be discarded. In fact, Method 3 did not work very well because we could not afford to discard the limited number of records available. Another issue of the small data size was overfitting, due to insufficient records for the algorithm to learn a generalized model.

To address these issues, we collected another 251 records of another similar bank from the same online platform. To ensure that the records can be merged, we applied transfer learning. We used the first bank's review data to train a CART model (M1) and tested it using the second bank's review data. Thereafter, we trained another CART model (M2) based on the second bank's review data and tested it using the first bank's review data. The overall test accuracy rates of models M1 and M2 are 88.84% and 87.25% respectively. This shows that the two datasets are highly similar and can be merged to build a more comprehensive predictive model. Additionally, we found that the testing accuracy of CART with Bagging improves from 82% to 87% as it is being trained with increasingly more records of the augmented dataset. This shows that the combination of datasets from similar employers is a useful and effective approach to improve model performance.

4 Discussion

In hindsight, we realise that most online review data share very similar structures and issues to the ones we study in this paper. Firstly, such data consists of a set of review ratings on different aspects of a product, service, or in our case, employment. These ratings are normally used as inputs to a predictive model to understand factors related to recommendation outcomes.

In addition, the data quality issues that one would encounter in such data are also highly similar. For example, these input ratings contain missing values, and are usually correlated. This makes it challenging to apply classical statistical methods on these data, but we found non-parametric machine learning methods work well here.

Most online review data contain an Overall Rating attribute that is also highly correlated with the inputs. Although this Overall Rating attribute is not meaningful as a predictor itself, it can serve as a valuable proxy variable for missing value treatment. This is especially relevant when working with limited data size and deletion of records with missing entries should be avoided.

Putting these ideas together, we present an applied framework for analytics practitioners to consider. This framework is shown in Fig. 1. It begins with the merger of similar datasets that can be verified using transfer learning. Thereafter, the inputs are extracted, and the missing values are treated. Finally, non-parametric machine learning methods are used to produce the predictions and factors needed for further analyses.

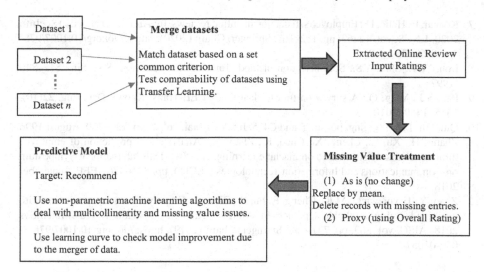

Fig. 1. A process framework recommended for analysing online review data.

5   Concluding Remarks

One key lesson learnt from this study is that the small size of online review data may be augmented by combining online review data from different but similar entities. We have demonstrated how this can be done by considering factors for assessing comparability, using transfer learning of predictive models to confirm that the records can be merged, and using a learning curve to verify the performance gain due to the augmented data.

Because of the possibility to merge review data using our approach, our study suggests that analysis of data can become more generalizable and impactful, since we are no longer limited to examining a small and isolated entity. Last but not least, our study also shows that the bigger dataset attained allows for more flexibility in missing value treatments, such as deleting records with missing entries rather than replacing them.

References

1. Ajit, P.: Prediction of employee turnover in organizations using machine learning algorithms. Algorithms **4**(5), C5 (2016)
2. Atef, M., Elzanfaly, D.S., Ouf, S.: Early prediction of employee turnover using machine learning algorithms. Int. J. Electr. Comput. Eng. Syst. **13**(2), 135–144 (2022)
3. Breiman, L., Friedman, J., Olshen, R., Stone, C.: CART. Classification and regression trees (1984)
4. IBM Corp: IBM SPSS Modeler (Version 18.2.2). IBM Corp., Armonk (2018)
5. Jain, R., Nayyar, A.: Predicting employee attrition using XGBoost machine learning approach. In: 2018 International Conference on System Modeling & Advancement in Research Trends (Smart), pp. 113–120. IEEE, November 2018
6. Kass, G.V.: An exploratory technique for investigating large quantities of categorical data. J. Roy. Stat. Soc. Ser. C (Appl. Stat.) **29**(2), 119–127 (1980)

7. Koncar, P., Helic, D.: Employee satisfaction in online reviews. In: Aref, S., et al. (eds.) SocInfo 2020. LNCS, vol. 12467, pp. 152–167. Springer, Cham (2020). https://doi.org/10.1007/978-3-030-60975-7_12

8. Loh, W.Y., Shih, Y.S.: Split selection methods for classification trees. Stat. Sin., 815–840 (1997)

9. Pan, S.J., Yang, Q.: A survey on transfer learning. IEEE Trans. Knowl. Data Eng. **22**(10), 1345–1359 (2010)

10. Quinlan, J.R.: Bagging, boosting, and C4. 5. In: Aaai/Iaai, vol. 1, pp. 725–730, August 1996

11. Zhang, H., Xu, L., Cheng, X., Chao, K., Zhao, X.: Analysis and prediction of employee turnover characteristics based on machine learning. In: 2018 18th International Symposium on Communications and Information Technologies (ISCIT), pp. 371–376. IEEE, September 2018

12. Zhao, Y., Hryniewicki, M.K., Cheng, F., Fu, B., Zhu, X.: Employee turnover prediction with machine learning: a reliable approach. In: Arai, K., Kapoor, S., Bhatia, R. (eds.) IntelliSys 2018. AISC, vol. 869, pp. 737–758. Springer, Cham (2019). https://doi.org/10.1007/978-3-030-01057-7_56

Optimizing Visit Booking at CERN: A Drools-Based Approach

Alberto Cortina Eduarte[✉], Jácome Costales Ballesteros,
José Antonio García Fuentes, Marcin Mazurek, and Cristian Schuszter

CERN, Esplanade des Particules 1, 1211 Meyrin, Switzerland
{alberto.cortina.eduarte,jacome.costales.ballesteros,
jose.antonio.garcia.fuentes,marcin.mazurek,cristian.schuszter}@cern.ch

Abstract. This paper describes the new rule-based booking system for external visitors, developed internally at CERN (the European Organization for Nuclear Research). The aim is to describe the architecture and the definition of complex business rules to reduce the rejection rate (thereby reducing manual work) and ensure equal opportunities for visitors to attend CERN. This paper presents the implementation and the structuring of the rules, while also providing metrics on the performance. Performance was an important factor in the implementation of the rule system, as visitors should be provided with an optimal booking experience that involves as little waiting time as possible. This paper discusses key factors contributing to high user satisfaction, confirming that the new system has successfully addressed previous shortcomings.

Keywords: Drools · booking · CERN · rule-based system

1 Introduction

One of the points in CERN's mission is to "engage all citizens in research and the values of science" [1], and one way of doing this is by offering free visits [2] to various CERN facilities.

The previous booking system faced several issues: visitors selected dates without being aware of availability, leading to numerous manual request rejections. Additionally, it appeared to favour certain visitors over others. As a result, CERN needed a more equitable solution.

These issues required the development of a new booking system addressing availability constraints and promoting equitable visit opportunities for a diverse range of visitors.

Supported by The European Organization for Nuclear Research (CERN).

2   State of the Art

Booking systems often grapple with efficient resource management and scheduling as their primary pain points. These aspects are crucial components in ensuring proper resource allocation, avoiding conflicts and maintaining accurate data availability.

When discussing various solutions for booking applications or similar systems, it becomes evident that there is a lack of in-depth discussion and a considerable shortage of publications addressing this topic with the attention it deserves. General problems like these are often overlooked or underestimated, as they may seem trivial at first glance. However, as the complexity increases, they can pose significant challenges during the design phases. Despite this, some researchers have documented different approaches to this problem and provided valuable insights.

An exhaustive study on booking systems, recently published, addresses the allocation of scarce goods and services through booking systems without pricing mechanisms or with limited price adjustments [3]. While not directly related to this paper, it is worth mentioning its relevance, particularly concerning the time cost of queues. The study addresses the significant time expenditure individuals face while waiting in queues, leading to potential productivity losses. It also offers valuable insights for market designers, providing a delicate balance between fairness and efficiency in choosing allocation rules. The aim is to optimise booking systems, ensuring equitable distribution and improved efficiency, benefiting both service providers and users.

Having said that, among various interesting proposals for analysis, there is an example of using basic `IF-THEN` rules in an expert hotel booking system. This system provides users access to a selection of the most suitable hotel services while offering choices for nearby activities and events [4].

Another noteworthy integration involves rule engines and agent-based systems. For instance, the integration between previous versions of Drools (formerly JBoss Rules), which implemented the ReteOO algorithm and JADE (Java Agent Development Framework), facilitates the development of object-oriented rule engines [5].

3   Implementation

3.1   Drools Rules

Drools [6] is the rule engine used to evaluate the quota system's rules. These rules, defined in a domain-specific language, can interact with the Java code within the program.

The rules in the system are triggered when specific conditions in the **when** block are met. Listing 1 shows an example of a rule that sets a daily maximum of 200 visitors per country to ensure an even distribution. Exceeding this limit makes the date unavailable.

```
rule "Country: Any [0-200] visitors / day"
  when
    $q : QuotaOutput()
    $v : DroolsVisitRequestInput()
    CountryRuleInput (
      country == $v.country,
      date == $q.date,
      numberOfVisitorsDay >= 0,
      numberOfVisitorsDay <= 200
    )
  then
    modify($q) {
      setCountryRulesPassed(true)
    }
end
```

Listing 1: Example of a definition of a rule restricting the maximum number of visitors per country on a date.

The results from each rule execution are aggregated to determine the outcome for a specific date. If any of the executed rules were to fail (indicated by the **passed** flag being false), the date would be considered unavailable. The implementation details are presented in Listing 2.

```
rule "Result: GREEN" no-loop
  when
    $q : QuotaOutput(visitTypeRulesPassed == true,
    languageRulesPassed == true,
    countryRulesPassed == true,
    busRulesPassed == true,
    dayRulesPassed == true,
    czeAndSvkRulesPassed == true)
  then
    modify($q) {
      setGuidedTourAvailable(true)
    }
end
```

Listing 2: Aggregation of results from executed rules.

3.2 Rules Engine Input and Output

Input. The rules engine uses user input and existing database information to generate availability forecasts for activities up to 9 months in advance.

Initially, the following data is passed from the user interface to the rules engine:

(a) country - the country ISO code [7] of the country from where the group originates.

(b) number of visitors - the number of people that will be part of the group.
(c) language - the language of the requested visit.
(d) own bus - whether the group will come with their bus or not (as bus availability on-demand from CERN is very limited).
(e) average age - the average age of the group in a specified categorical interval.
(f) visit type - the type of visit (whether it is a school group or a non-school group).
(g) a list of activity types - these can be any combination of a guided tour, a lab workshop or an exhibition.

Output. In the example from the previous section, a total of 9171 rule input objects are passed to the quota system for 274 dates (approximately 9 months) in the future. The output operates at the level of time slots, dividing each day into MORNING and AFTERNOON. Therefore, the system returns double the number of dates as outputs, resulting in 548 outputs for 274 dates.

Once all the rules are executed by the engine, the outputs are further aggregated, obtaining all the possible combinations. In Listing 3, an example of the final result for a date is shown.

```
{
    "2024-04-27": [
        [
            {
                "activityType": "GUIDED_TOUR",
                "timeSlot": "MORNING",
                "date": "2024-04-27"
            },
            {
                "activityType": "LAB",
                "timeSlot": "AFTERNOON",
                "date": "2024-04-27"
            }
        ],
    ],
}
```

Listing 3: Final result example. It shows that on the 27th of April 2024, the visitor will be able to do a guided tour in the morning and a lab workshop in the afternoon.

Finally, the results are presented to the user in an intuitive and simple interface allowing the selection of available dates according to his preferences.

4   Results

The system has been operational since June 23, 2021. However, due to the COVID-19 pandemic [8], all visits to CERN were suspended during this period, which affected the system's results. To analyse the outcome of the new approach, data from the year 2023 serves as the baseline for a typical scenario. The data presented in the following graphics is current as of the last document update on the 1st of October 2023.

With the implementation of the new booking system, a general increase in the approval rate is observed, as illustrated in Fig. 1, though it didn't quite meet the initial expectations. Notably, the unusual rise in rejections in April can be attributed to the planned opening of the Science Gateway [9] in September, which required all visit requests for that month to be declined.

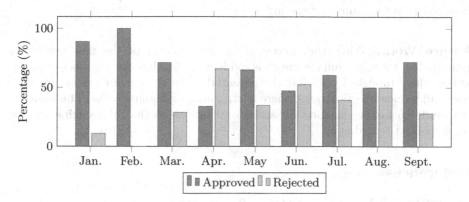

Fig. 1. Percentage of approved and rejected requests during 2023.

To evaluate the system's performance under varying load conditions, a load test was conducted using Gatling [10]. Figure 2 illustrates the response time distribution in three different categories during the load test. Out of the 1500 executed requests, nearly 1000 (64%) received responses from the system in less than 800 ms, indicating a very good percentage. On the other hand, approximately 300 requests (24%) took more than 1200 ms.

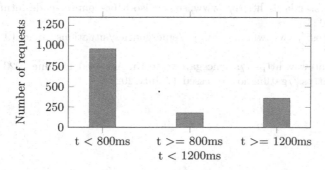

Fig. 2. Response time distribution for requests to the new system.

5 Conclusion

In conclusion, this paper has presented an innovative approach to handling the visit booking system at CERN by modelling the business requirements as rules.

The objectives were achieved with the implementation of this new system. A more equitable distribution of visitors with good performance that doesn't impact the user experience for visitors was observed.

In summary, adopting a Drools-based approach for visit booking has showcased the potential of rule-based modelling. The commitment to continually improving the system, making adjustments and aligning it optimally with business objectives remains unwavering.

Future Work. While the successful implementation of the new system is remarkable, room for improvement is evident. Adjusting the parameter values within the established rules has the potential to create a fairer system for visitors and reduce rejection rates, thereby streamlining manual tasks. This concept will undergo further exploration and modifications to the rules engine will be implemented accordingly.

References

1. CERN's mission statement. https://home.cern/about/who-we-are/our-mission. Accessed 15 June 2023
2. CERN's visit options. https://visit.cern/. Accessed 15 June 2023
3. Huang, L., Liu, T.X., Zhang, J.: Born to wait? A study on allocation rules in booking systems, pp. 1–5, 19–20, 32–33 (2023)
4. Walek, B., Hosek, O.: Proposal of Expert System for Hotel Booking System, pp. 1, 4 (2016)
5. Poggi, A., Tomaiuolo, M.: Rule Engines and Agent-Based Systems, pp. 1–4, 7 (2008)
6. Browne, P., Johnson, P.: JBoss Drools Business Rules, vol. 1847196063. Packt Publishing, Birmingham (2009)
7. ISO 3166 standard. https://www.iso.org/iso-3166-country-codes.html. Accessed 30 June 2023
8. WHO. https://www.who.int/europe/emergencies/situations/covid-19. Accessed 8 June 2023
9. Science Gateway. https://sciencegateway.cern. Accessed 11 June 2023
10. Gatling. https://gatling.io. Accessed 17 July 2023

A Label Aggregation Method Using Worker Quality in Crowdsourcing

Nana Ota[✉] and Yu Suzuki

Graduate School of Natural Science and Technology, Gifu University, 1–1 Yanagido, Gifu 5011193, Japan
ota.nana.f4@s.gifu-u.ac.jp, suzuki.yu.r4@f.gifu-u.ac.jp

Abstract. In this study, we propose a method to improve the quality of labels by considering the quality of workers. Our method constructs models that imitate workers' work to increase the pseudo-data. We calculate the worker's agreement rate using the pseudo-data obtained using the worker's imitation model and data worked by the worker. We calculate the weights of the worker's vote using the worker's agreement rate. The labels obtained by applying our method would be better quality than those obtained by a majority vote. Then, we experimented to verify the effectiveness of our method. The accuracy of the labels obtained by applying our method was 0.6685. We can reduce the influence of vandal workers and obtain high-quality labels.

Keywords: Crowdsourcing · Machine Learning · Text Classification · Natural Language Processing · BERT · Agreement Rate

1 Introduction

Good quality training data is necessary to create an accurate machine learning based classifier. Creating training data needs to label a large amount of data. However, labeling the huge amount of data is time consuming. For this reason, researchers use crowdsourcing to collect training data.

Crowdsourcing [4] is an outsourcing system to an unspecified number of people recruited over the Internet. There is a problem that there are a certain number of vandal workers who have a negative impact on the label aggregation. In addition, different workers feel different emotions from the same text data in the emotion classification task. Therefore, there are several labels that assigned by each worker for a single task. As a result, the work requesters cannot obtain the desired labels. More worker input would help us to obtain labels closer to those desired by the work requesters. However, recruiting a large number of workers is expensive and time-consuming. Therefore, if we construct a model that imitates a worker's work, we could increase the number of pseudo-workers. Increasing the number of pseudo-workers allows for aggregating the working data of many workers at a reduced cost and is time-consuming. A working data is the data that contains information of text data, about who assigned the labels, and labels assigned by the worker. We calculate worker quality from the pseudo-work

P. Delir Haghighi et al. (Eds.): iiWAS 2023, LNCS 14416, pp. 49–55, 2023.
https://doi.org/10.1007/978-3-031-48316-5_7

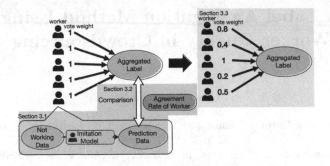

Fig. 1. Overview

data and the actual work data performed by the worker. We could reduce the influence of vandal workers by aggregating the labels considering the quality of workers calculated. Our goal is to obtain the labels desired by the work requester by aggregating the labels considering the quality of workers.

2   Related Work

There have been several studies on improving the quality of labels through crowdsourcing. Nishi et al.'s [5] research aims to improve worker quality through social networks. The worker can delegate work to one other person. If a worker correctly completes a task, they pay the worker who received the request and the worker who correctly completes the task. By paying rewards for correct answers to tasks, less capable workers delegate tasks to more capable workers. They can then obtain high-quality data from worker. Ashikawa et al.'s [1,2] research filters workers to see if they are qualified for the task. They aim to improve the quality of labels through crowdsourcing by filtering workers. They filter workers before, during, and after they finish a task. They select workers by filtering workers. They aim to improve the quality of crowdsourcing labels by selecting workers.

In our study, we construct an imitation model of a worker. We use the imitation model to increase the number of pseudo-data. By increasing the working data, we aim to improve the quality of labels. The above researches and our study are similar in that they aim to improve the quality of labels. However, the approach to improving quality is different.

3   Proposed Method

In this section, we describe how to identify the aggregated labels using workers' votes. Figure 1 shows the overview of our method.

3.1   Model Construction

In our study, we construct a model that imitated the worker. We use the BERT model to construct an imitation model of the worker. BERT [3] is a neural network model based on the Transformer [6] model for natural language processing. We use two different methods of fine-tuning for the BERT model. We describe each method in the following sections.

Model 1. The first method is to construct the model using only the data of each individual. First, we extract data for any given worker from the total data constructed by crowdsourcing. We construct the imitation model of the worker using the extracted their data. The amount of data used to construct the model depends on the number of tasks performed by the workers. Therefore, some workers have the disadvantage of having a small number of data. However, it is possible to construct a model that captures the characteristics of each worker.

Model 2. The second method is to construct a model with the total data and then fine-tune it with the data of each individual. We use data with multiple labels assigned to a single text data to create the total data. First, we assign a single label to each text data by a majority vote. The data with the labels assigned by the majority vote is the total data. We construct a model using this data. Then, we construct an imitation model by fine-tuning the model constructed using the total data with the data of each individual. As mentioned earlier, the Model 1 has the disadvantage of having a small number of data. The Model 2, however, can compensate for the drawback of a small number of data. Therefore, we could construct a model with good performance.

3.2   Calculation of Agreement Rates

In this section, we explain how to calculate the worker's agreement rate. We compute the worker's agreement rate by comparing the correct labels with the labels assigned by the worker. Here, the label assigned by the worker is the sum of the label actually worked by the worker and the label predicted by the worker's imitation model. Let $i(i = 1, 2, \cdots n)$ denote each worker, and let D_i denote the dataset on which worker i actually worked. In this case, let n be the number of workers. Then, let D_{all} denote the dataset to which the label is assigned by a majority vote. Let N denote the total number of text data to which label is assigned. Then, let each data denote d_j, $j = 1, 2, \cdots, N$. From the dataset D_{all} to which the label is assigned by a majority vote, we extract the data d_j that worker i is not working on. Then, we create the dataset $D_i' = \{d_j | d_j \in D_{all}, d_j \notin D_i\}$. We input to the imitation model the data d_j contained in the dataset D_i'. Then, we assign the output values as the label for data d_j. Let $l_i(d_j)$ be the label assigned to the data d_j contained in the datasets D_i and D_i'. We calculate the agreement rate A_i using the label $l_i(d_j)$ and the label $l_{all}(d_j)$ assigned by a majority vote. The formula for calculating the agreement rate A_i is as follows.

$$A_i = \frac{\sum_{j=1}^{N} M(l_i(d_j), l_{all}(d_j))}{N} \qquad (1)$$

$$M(l_i(d_j), l_{all}(d_j)) = \begin{cases} 1 & (l_i(d_j) = l_{all}(d_j)) \\ 0 & (l_i(d_j) \neq l_{all}(d_j)) \end{cases} \qquad (2)$$

Eq. 2 is a function that outputs 1 if the labels $l_i(d_j)$ and $l_{all}(d_j)$ are the same and 0 if they are different. In our study, we propose an label aggregation method using the agreement rate A_i calculated using Eq. 1.

3.3   Calculation the Weights of Workers' Votes

In this section, we explain the label aggregation method that weights each worker's votes based on the worker's agreement rate. We calculate the weights of the votes a worker has based on their agreement rate. We aggregate the labels by weighting the votes of the worker had. We can limit the influence of the tasks of vandal workers on the labels by using worker quality as a weight. Step A describes the process of calculating the agreement rate A_i for worker i. And then, Step B describes the process of taking a majority vote that weights each worker's vote based on the agreement rate.

Step A-1 Constructing an imitation model of worker i used the data selected from dataset D_i randomly as training data.
   A-2 Predicting the labels of text data d_j in dataset D_i' using the worker i's imitation model.
   A-3 Calculating the agreement rate A_i between the predictions of the worker i's imitation model and the labels assigned by a majority vote.
Step B-1 Weighting of worker i's vote based on the agreement rate A_i.
   B-2 Aggregating the label by taking a majority vote again.

We explain detail below weighting each worker's vote described in B-1. We decided to use the value obtained by normalizing the agreement rate as the weight of each worker's vote. If we normalize only by the worker's agreement rate, at least one person would not obtain a vote. It is possible that a task performed by a vandal worker may include useful working data. Therefore, we would like to give all workers the right to vote. Therefore, when calculating the weights, we normalize by including the chance rate C of k-class classifications.

We calculate the weight w_i of worker i's vote using the following formula.

$$w_i = \frac{A_i - x_{min}}{x_{max} - x_{min}} \qquad (3)$$

$$Q = \{x | x = C, A_i (i = 1, 2, \cdots, n)\}, \quad C = \frac{1}{k} \qquad (4)$$

Q, denoted by Equation (4), is the set containing the worker's agreement rate A_i and the chance rate C of k-class classification. The weight w_i calculated using the Equation (3) is the weight of the vote worker i has. We aggregate labels with the weight of the vote weighted by worker i as w_i.

4 Experiments

4.1 Experimental Setup

This experiment is to verify the usefulness of the method described in Sect. 3.3. The dataset we use is for tweets that contain the word "笑(laugh out loud; lol)" in the body of tweets. In constructing this dataset, 605 workers performed the work. There are 250,354 working data in this dataset. To evaluate the method, the authors assigned correct labels to the data d_j in the dataset D_{eva} in advance. Let D_{true} denote a dataset to which the correct answer label is assigned. We calculate accuracy score by comparing the correct labels with the labels assigned by the aggregation work or by applying the method. We then evaluate the method based on the calculated accuracy score.

In this experiment, we create an imitation model of worker i using the dataset D_i described in Sect. 4.1. We create two imitation models. The first imitation model is a model that categorizes positives or negatives. The second imitation model is a more detailed classification of negatives. The pre-trained model[1] for BERT used to create the imitation model is a BERT-base model from Tohoku University. We use this imitation model to predict label $l_i(d_j)$ for worker i's data d_j. Next, we calculate accuracy score using equation (1) and (2) in Sect. 3.2. Then, we calculate the weights w_i based on the agreement rate A_i of worker i using equation (3) in Sect. 3.3. At this time, we normalize the weights by including 0.125, the chance rate for the 8-class classification. Finally, we apply the method to the dataset D_{eva} using the weights w_i and take a majority vote. Then, we calculate accuracy score by comparing the labels assigned by applying the method with the correct labels. We evaluate the method by measuring accuracy.

4.2 Results and Discussion

The experimental results show that accuracy score is 0.6685 when this method is applied using Model 1, and accuracy score is 0.6625 when this method is applied using Model 2. The method of label aggregation by majority vote was defined as baseline. The accuracy was 0.6625. Comparing the baseline and the results of method application, accuracy is highest when the method is applied using Model 1.

Model 2 is a model created by fine-tuning a model created using the data used to calculate the baseline with the working data of each individual. The data used to calculate the baseline here is the correct data used to calculate the agreement rate of worker. Therefore, the less working data we have on workers, the smaller the amount of change in parameters due to fine-tuning, and the less we can capture the characteristics of each worker. This leads us to believe that Model 2 would predict almost the same labels as the baseline results. Therefore, the agreement rate is high regardless of the quality of the worker. In addition, the weights of each worker do not differ because the weights are normalized by

---

[1] https://github.com/cl-tohoku/bert-japanese.

including the chance rate when calculating the weights. Therefore, even if each worker's vote is weighted, the result is that it is easily assigned an label that is the same as the baseline. In fact, comparing the baseline with the results of applying the method using Model 2, only 9 out of 2,000 data show a change in the assigned labels.

On the other hand, Model1 can construct a model that directly reflects the characteristics of each worker. Therefore, it possible to calculate the worker i original agreement rate A_i. It is also possible to calculate weights w_i independent of the data used in the baseline. Therefore, the results of high-quality workers are more likely to be reflected in the results, and we can obtain better labels. In fact, comparing the baseline with the results of applying the method using Model 1, 85 out of 2,000 data show a change in the assigned labels.

5   Conclusion

This study aims to improve the quality of crowdsourcing by aggregating labels considering the quality of workers. We proposed an label aggregation method in which worker quality is the weight of the worker's vote. We conducted experiments to verify the effectiveness of the method. The experimental results show that accuracy score is 0.6685 when this method is applied using Model 1, and accuracy score is 0.6625 when this method is applied using Model 2. Model 1 allow the construction of a model that captures the characteristics of the worker. The imitation model can capture the characteristics of the worker, and thus the original quality of the worker can be determined. We can reduce the influence of vandal workers and obtain the labels close to the labels desired by the work requester. Therefore, accuracy score is highest when this method was applied using Model1.

We applied the method to dataset for which a work request completed. We can only identify vandal workers after we have completed a work request. As a future perspective, we consider extending this method to be applicable during a work request.

Acknowledgements. This paper is partly supported by JSPS KAKENHI 19H04218, 23H03694.

References

1. Ashikawa, M., Kawamura, T., Ohsuga, A.: Construction and management of high-quality private crowdsourcing platform. In: Proceedings of the National Conference on Artificial Intelligence 28th (2014), pp. 1J5OS18b4-1J5OS18b4. The Japanese Society for Artificial Intelligence (2014). (in Japanese)
2. Ashikawa, M., Kawamura, T., Ohsuga, A.: Development and evaluation of quality control methods in a microtask crowdsourcing platform. Trans. Japan. Soc. Artif. Intell. **29**(6), 503–515 (2014). (in Japanese)

3. Devlin, J., Chang, M.W., Lee, K., Toutanova, K.: BERT: pre-training of deep bidirectional transformers for language understanding. In: Proceedings of the 2019 Conference of the North American Chapter of the Association for Computational Linguistics: Human Language Technologies, Volume 1 (Long and Short Papers), pp. 4171–4186. Association for Computational Linguistics, Minneapolis, Minnesota (2019). https://doi.org/10.18653/v1/N19-1423, https://aclanthology.org/N19-1423
4. Howe, J., et al.: The rise of crowdsourcing. Wired Mag. **14**(6), 1–4 (2006)
5. Nishi, T., Koide, S., Ohno, H., Nagaya, T.: Improving data quality of crowdsourcing with social networks. In: Proceedings of the National Conference on Artificial Intelligence 27th (2013), pp. 3M3OS07d4-3M3OS07d4. The Japanese Society for Artificial Intelligence (2013). (in Japanese)
6. Vaswani, A., et al.: Attention is all you need. Adv. Neural. Inf. Process. Syst. **30**, 5998–6008 (2017)

ImputAnom: Anomaly Detection Framework Using Imputation Methods for Univariate Time Series

Tirana Noor Fatyanosa[1,2], Mahendra Data[2], Neni Alya Firdausanti[1],
Putu Hangga Nan Prayoga[3], Israel Mendonça[1(✉)], and Masayoshi Aritsugi[1]

[1] Kumamoto University, Kumamoto, Japan
{fatyanosa,nenialya}@dbms.cs.kumamoto-u.ac.jp,
{israel,aritsugi}@cs.kumamoto-u.ac.jp
[2] Brawijaya University, Malang, Indonesia
{fatyanosa,mahendra.data}@ub.ac.id
[3] MTI Co., Ltd., Tokyo, Japan
putu.hangga@monohakobi.com

Abstract. Anomaly detection plays a crucial role in various domains such as cybersecurity, fraud detection, and industrial asset condition monitoring. In these fields, identifying abnormal patterns or outliers is paramount for the business they support. This paper presents a new framework that utilizes imputation methods to effectively identify anomalies. To evaluate the performance of the proposed framework, experiments were conducted on different datasets that contain anomalies from different domains. Experimental results demonstrate the effectiveness of the framework in helping to detect anomalies. It provides improvements between 8.17% and 165.21% for all datasets. Experimental results also confirm the effectiveness of the proposed framework and its potential to be applied in real-world scenarios.

Keywords: Anomaly detection · Imputation

1 Introduction

Anomaly detection is a fundamental task in data analysis that focuses on finding patterns in data that do not follow an expected behavior. Such patterns are often referred to as anomalies, outliers, exceptions, and so forth. The applicability of anomaly detection techniques is quite broad and extends to many domains, including fraud detection, network intrusion detection, and health monitoring. The reason such techniques can be used in so many domains is due to the fact that anomalies usually translate to significant, and often critical, actionable information [2]. Traditional approaches often rely on statistical techniques or unsupervised learning algorithms. However, they usually struggle when the data is too complex and high-dimensional, which causes the anomalies to exhibit either a subtle or an over-complex pattern [8].

P. Delir Haghighi et al. (Eds.): iiWAS 2023, LNCS 14416, pp. 56–61, 2023.
https://doi.org/10.1007/978-3-031-48316-5_8

Imputation is a process used to handle missing data points within a dataset, and data imputation methods focus on automatically producing missing values with plausible substitutes, ensuring that the dataset remains complete and usable for subsequent analyses [4]. Due to the imputation methods' promising ability to learn the patterns of data, it gained increasing attention as a companion for anomaly detection methods.

In this paper, we propose a novel framework that utilizes imputation methods to support anomaly detection algorithms in the task of detecting anomalies in univariate time series. Existing anomaly detection methods often incorporate an imputation step before performing the detection process [3,9]. In contrast, our framework aims to enhance the anomaly detection process by accurately determining whether a specific row is truly an anomaly or not. By incorporating the imputation method directly into the anomaly detection framework, we aim to enhance the overall detection performance and efficiency. This integration allows us to leverage the strengths of both imputation and anomaly detection techniques, leading to more accurate and reliable anomaly detection results.

2   Methodology

In this section, we introduce our imputation framework, which comprises two main components: an imputation component and an anomaly detection component. The imputation method is applied to fill in missing values, and then an anomaly detection algorithm is applied to identify and flag anomalous rows. These steps are illustrated in Algorithm 1.

Algorithm 1. ImputAnom Framework

Input:
  X: Dataset
  y: A set of true labels
  P: Percentage of missing rows
  I: Imputation method
  A: Anomaly detection method

Output:
  $F1$: F1-Score
  y_{pred}: A set of predicted labels

1: $X_{nan} \leftarrow$ randomly removed P% of values in X
2: $X_{imp} \leftarrow$ impute X_{nan} using I
3: $y_{pred} \leftarrow$ detect anomaly from X_{imp} using A
4: $F1 \leftarrow$ calculate F1-Score from y and y_{pred}
5: **return** $F1$, y_{pred}

As we can see, imputation methods play a crucial role in effectively managing missing data within our framework. We integrate a range of well-established classical imputation techniques, including interpolation, mean, mode, and median, which serve as fundamental approaches to handling missing values. Additionally, we leverage advanced machine-learning-based imputation methods to enhance the accuracy and efficiency of data imputation. These include K-Nearest Neighbors (KNN) imputation, which involves inferring missing values based on the attributes of the nearest neighbors [7]. Moreover, we also employ Miceforest, a versatile imputation technique that utilizes a random forest approach to estimate missing data [10]. Lastly, our framework incorporates Generative Adversarial Imputation Nets (GAIN), a state-of-the-art imputation method that employs generative adversarial networks to predict and fill in missing values with high accuracy and efficiency [13].

For anomaly detection, we utilize two main types of methods: The first, statistical approaches, rely on diverse techniques like statistical measures, hypothesis testing, and data distribution analysis. Notable methods include Hotelling's T2, ChangeFinder, and the Variance-Based Method, each serving to detect deviations from expected patterns. For instance, Hotelling's T2 calculates distances from the center of a multivariate distribution, assessing abnormality based on mean and covariance structures [5]. ChangeFinder focuses on detecting shifts in statistical properties over time, identifying anomalies through significant deviations from expected patterns [11]. The Variance-Based Method identifies anomalies by assessing variances within features. The second approach employs machine learning techniques, involving models trained on labeled or unlabeled data to discern normal patterns and deviations. Notable methods here include One-Class Support Vector Machine (OSVM), Isolation Forest (IF), and Local Outlier Factor (LOF). OSVM constructs a model of normal data and identifies anomalies as significant deviations from this model [12]. Isolation Forest isolates outliers using random binary trees, leveraging the speed of isolation to distinguish anomalies [6]. LOF gauges the local deviation of an instance from its neighbors, determining anomaly scores based on instance density compared to its neighbors [1].

3 Experiments and Discussion

To evaluate our framework, we utilized publicly available datasets from the Numenta Anomaly Benchmark (NAB), specifically designed for evaluating anomaly detection algorithms in streaming and real-time applications. We worked with seven datasets, and further details can be found on the NAB online page[1]. For assessing anomaly detection effectiveness, we compared the F1-score, while for evaluating imputation performance, we utilized Mean Absolute Error (MAE), measuring the average absolute difference between actual and imputed values. Our imputation methods included mean, mode, median, interpolation, Miceforest, KNN, and GAIN. In terms of anomaly detection algorithms, we employed Hotelling's T2, ChangeFinder, Variance Based Method, One-Class Support Vector Machine (OSVM), Isolation Forest (IF), and Local Outlier Factor (LOF) for this study. Regarding the fraction, we conducted a comparative analysis across different fractions ranging from 0.1 to 0.9.

---

[1] https://github.com/numenta/NAB/tree/master/data/realKnownCause

Table 1 demonstrates ImputAnom's ability to boost F1-Scores across datasets, with enhancements ranging from 0.0275 to 0.1680 (8.17% to 165.21% improvement). This underscores the importance of integrating imputation and anomaly detection, significantly enhancing detection accuracy. Regarding Mean Absolute Error (MAE), the table shows that for all of the datasets, the method was able to achieve a lower MAE, consistently below 0.1. This indicates that the imputation methods are proficient at accurately filling in missing values, even when faced with a high fraction of missing data (greater than or equal to 0.5). The consistently low MAE values reinforce the robustness and effectiveness of our imputation methods, showcasing their ability to handle even high fractions of missing data and yield accurate imputations across different datasets.

Table 1. Overall comparison.

Data	F1-Score Original	F1-ImputAnom (Improvement%)	MAE
ambient_temperature_system_failure	0.3368	0.3644 (8.17%)	0.0362
cpu_utilization_asg_misconfiguration	0.1345	0.2621 (94.92%)	0.0541
ec2_request_latency_system_failure	0.1308	0.1586 (21.25%)	0.0583
machine_temperature_system_failure	0.2928	0.3216 (9.81%)	0.0234
nyc_taxi	0.0560	0.1268 (126.27%)	0.0842
rogue_agent_key_hold	0.1017	0.2697 (165.21%)	0.0255
rogue_agent_key_updown	0.0584	0.1112 (90.50%)	0.0035

Figure 1 provides a clear and insightful comparison between the original anomalous rows (Fig. 1a), and the results after employing our ImputAnom framework (Fig. 1c). We have only displayed the results of one data: *ambient_temperature_system_failure*, as the improvement pattern is clearly visible in the chart for this dataset. The blue point represents non-anomalous data, while the red point represents anomalous data. Upon closer inspection, it becomes evident that certain anomalies identified by the best anomaly detection algorithm are corrected by our ImputAnom framework. The corrected anomalies are more aligned with the ground truth and exhibit a better fit for the actual anomalous patterns in the data.

We can observe that the anomalous points exhibit a clustering pattern within specific periods of time, indicating a sequential nature rather than a spread-out distribution. Interestingly, the best anomaly detection algorithm primarily identifies anomalies in the peaks and valleys, as demonstrated in Fig. 1b. Our proposed algorithm, ImputAnom, demonstrates comparable performance to the best anomaly detection algorithm while also correcting some points, as evident in Fig. 1c. This correction is attributed to the random removal of a fraction of data, followed by imputation using an imputation method, which leads to the disappearance of some peaks and valleys. As a result, the anomaly detection

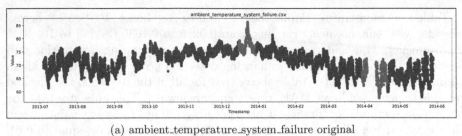

(a) ambient_temperature_system_failure original

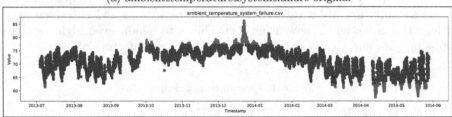

(b) ambient_temperature_system_failure using LOF

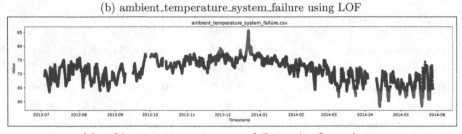

(c) ambient_temperature_system_failure using ImputAnom

Fig. 1. Before and After ImputAnom.

algorithm applied after the imputation step may not recognize these initially identified peak and valley points as anomalies. This observation confirms that our framework is capable of refining the results of the anomaly detection algorithm, making it more reliable and accurate in detecting anomalies.

4   Conclusion and Future Work

This paper introduced the ImputAnom framework, a novel approach that synergistically leverages imputation and anomaly detection methods to significantly enhance data analysis. The framework follows a two-step process: initially removing a fraction of data and employing imputation techniques to predict the missing values, followed by anomaly detection to identify potential anomalies. The experimental results vividly showcased the remarkable impact of this combined approach through ImputAnom, demonstrating improvements in F1-Score ranging from 8.17% to an impressive 165.21% across diverse datasets, thus highlighting its considerable effectiveness. In future work, we envisage extending the ImputAnom framework to handle multivariate data, enabling simultaneous analysis of multiple variables and providing exciting prospects for more comprehensive anomaly detection in complex datasets.

References

1. Alghushairy, O., Alsini, R., Soule, T., Ma, X.: A review of local outlier factor algorithms for outlier detection in big data streams. Big Data Cogn. Comput. **5**(1), 1 (2021). https://doi.org/10.3390/bdcc5010001, https://www.mdpi.com/2504-2289/5/1/1
2. Chandola, V., Banerjee, A., Kumar, V.: Anomaly detection: a survey. ACM Comput. Surv. **41**(3), 1–58 (2009). https://doi.org/10.1145/1541880.1541882
3. Duchi, J., Mackey, L., Wauthier, F.: Anomaly detection for asynchronous and incomplete data (2008). https://web.stanford.edu/lmackey/papers/anomaly-cs262a08.pdf, Advanced Topics in Computer Systems (UC Berkeley CS 262A, E. Brewer)
4. Fatyanosa, T.N., Firdausanti, N.A., Soto, L.F.J., Mendonça, I., Prayoga, P.H.N., Aritsugi, M.: Conducting vessel data imputation method selection based on dataset characteristics. IOP Conf. Ser.: Earth Environ. Sci. **1198**(1), 012017 (2023). https://doi.org/10.1088/1755-1315/1198/1/012017
5. Jensen, D.R., Ramirez, D.E.: Use of hotelling's T^2: outlier diagnostics in mixtures. Int. J. Stat. Probab. **6**(6), 24–34 (2017). https://doi.org/10.5539/ijsp.v6n6p24
6. Liu, F.T., Ting, K.M., Zhou, Z.H.: Isolation forest. In: 2008 Eighth IEEE International Conference on Data Mining, pp. 413–422 (2008). https://doi.org/10.1109/ICDM.2008.17
7. Murti, D.M.P., Pujianto, U., Wibawa, A.P., Akbar, M.I.: K-nearest neighbor (K-NN) based missing data imputation. In: 2019 5th International Conference on Science in Information Technology (ICSITech), pp. 83–88 (2019). https://doi.org/10.1109/ICSITech46713.2019.8987530
8. Thudumu, S., Branch, P., Jin, J., Singh, J.J.: A comprehensive survey of anomaly detection techniques for high dimensional big data. J. Big Data **7**(1), 1–30 (2020). https://doi.org/10.1186/s40537-020-00320-x
9. Vangipuram, R., Gunupudi, R.K., Puligadda, V.K., Vinjamuri, J.: A machine learning approach for imputation and anomaly detection in IoT environment. Expert Syst. **37**(5), e12556 (2020). https://doi.org/10.1111/exsy.12556, https://onlinelibrary.wiley.com/doi/abs/10.1111/exsy.12556
10. Wilson, S.V.: miceforest: fast, memory efficient imputation with LightGBM (2020). https://github.com/AnotherSamWilson/miceforest
11. Yamanishi, K., Takeuchi, J.: A unifying framework for detecting outliers and change points from non-stationary time series data. In: Proceedings of the Eighth ACM SIGKDD International Conference on Knowledge Discovery and Data Mining, pp. 676–681. KDD 2002, Association for Computing Machinery, New York, NY, USA (2002). https://doi.org/10.1145/775047.775148
12. Yang, K., Kpotufe, S., Feamster, N.: An efficient one-class SVM for anomaly detection in the internet of things. arXiv:2104.11146 (2021)
13. Yoon, J., Jordon, J., van der Schaar, M.: GAIN: missing data imputation using generative adversarial nets. In: Dy, J., Krause, A. (eds.) Proceedings of the 35th International Conference on Machine Learning, vol. 80, pp. 5689–5698. PMLR (2018). https://proceedings.mlr.press/v80/yoon18a.html

Smart Cities as Hubs: Navigating the Smart City Data Providers Landscape

Ioannis Nikolaou$^{(\boxtimes)}$ (iD) and Leonidas Anthopoulos (iD)

Department of Business Administration/Business School, University of Thessaly,
Larissa, Greece
{ionikolaou,lanthopo}@uth.gr

Abstract. Smart Cities produce a wealth of data from the network of
sensors and devices that are deployed at metropolitan scale. These data
are managed by Smart City platforms that may provide APIs for enabling
access them. The compatibility of these APIs however cannot be taken for
granted which creates challenges in the creation of value added products
and services towards the advancement of knowledge societies for smart
cities and communities. The Smart Cities as Hubs (SCHub) project has
been created with the goal to provide a layer that will simplify the access
to the Smart City data and enable their seamless flow thus enabling
the creation of innovative solutions for Smart Cities and communities.
Towards this end, several real life use cases of Smart City APIs have been
identified, documented and categorized in order to map the landscape of
the Smart City data providers.

Keywords: smart city platforms · software architecture · software
integration · APIs

1 Introduction

Smart cities are defined as a city model that uses state-of-the art ICT to a)
improve living, efficiency and competitiveness with respect to future generations,
[8] or to b) facilitate the planning, construction, management and smart services,
[7]; while the "smartness" of a city describes its ability to bring together all its
resources, to effectively and seamlessly achieve the goals and fulfill its purposes
which is to eventually improve the everyday life of its citizens. The way this
is achieved ranges from improved services, efficiency and safety to higher levels
of satisfaction through easier and more impactful citizen participation in the
Smart City's evolution. One of the key enablers of a Smart City is the sensors
and devices that comprise the Internet of Things (IoT) layer of a Smart City and
produce data of various types and origins ranging from energy and consumption
of resources like diesel and water, environmental and meteorological data to
health and activity data of the city's citizens. In order for the goal of the Smart
City to be achieved, the information should be able to flow in a unified, barrier
free environment that will allow the ease of data consumption, integration of data

P. Delir Haghighi et al. (Eds.): iiWAS 2023, LNCS 14416, pp. 62–67, 2023.
https://doi.org/10.1007/978-3-031-48316-5_9

from different sources and eventually the creation of added value products and services that will further advance the Smart City towards a knowledge society. In practice however, it has been observed that the Smart City landscape in general and the IoT layer in particular is fragmented and different solutions are deployed among Smart Cities or even within a single Smart City as discussed in [10,11].

In this context the SCHub project has been created to investigate the following questions:

- How the Smart City open innovation platform is being transformed to a hub (SCHub)?
- How can this SCHub become an "umbrella platform", able to integrate SC platforms and give back control to cities?
- What are the requirements and the architecture of the SCHub?

This article aims to present the first results of the ongoing SCHub project focusing on the Smart City data providers landscape. The paper is structured as follows: In Sect. 2 an overview of the SCHub concept and reference architecture is presented along with a set of functional and nonfunctional requirements that have been identified during the preliminary design phase. For the SCHub concept validation, a number of Smart City data providers have been contacted and access to their data has been requested. The data description and technical specifications are discussed in Sect. 3 along with their technical categorization. The paper concludes with a discussion of the current results, an overview of the challenges and opportunities of the SCHub project and future research directions.

2 The SCHub Concept

The concept of SCHub is presented in detail in [1]. In brief, the SCHub is using the analogy of the relationship between a traditional network hub and the various network resources in the context of the Smart Cities. In a typical computer network the various network nodes use a hub in an agnostic way to enable the communication among them in different protocols and for different purposes. In a similar fashion, the Smart City has many data sources, communication protocols and IoT platforms which are not able to easily communicate with each other, exchange data and enable the creation of value added services. The SCHub is envisioned to act as the layer that enables and facilitates these use cases.

2.1 SCHub Architecture

The SCHub architecture is inspired by the generic IoT architecture, whose main components have been extensively discussed in [3,4,9]. Their application in the SCHub concept however needs special attention to address the specific needs of the Smart City deployment environment and scale. More specifically, the SCHub reference architecture must meet the following requirements:

- **Generality**: the SCHub reference architecture must be technology agnostic and expandable in order to be able to support the integration of both existing and future data sources
- **Scalability/Elasticity**: the SCHub reference architecture must be able to support both small size pilots as well as full scale Smart City deployments. For this reason the architecture must be designed in a way that is both scalable (i.e. it can grow as needed) and elastic (i.e. it can adapt to the usage load).
- **Privacy**: the data and metadata available in Smart City applications can contain sensitive personal identifiable information which must be handled in accordance with the rules and regulations of each region. At the same time, the data are crucial for enabling the creation of value added services for the citizen. For this reason the SCHub must maintain a balance between these two requirements.

The key design principles of the SCHub reference architecture is presented in detail in [1] and are in brief the following:

- **API-first design** in order to ensure the data are easily accessible to third parties
- **Baked-in security** to be able comply with the strictest requirements for data consistency, integrity and availability
- **Privacy by default** to ensure any concerns regarding the handling of personal identifiable information are taken into consideration

2.2   Functional Requirements

The functional requirements for the SCHub platform that have been identified so far are as follows:

- The platform must support a modular architecture that will allow the implementation of connectors and gateways in an independent way according to the data sources and use cases identified.
- The platform must support role-based access for the consumption of the data in a fine-grained manner that will allow the users of the SCHub to access only the information required.
- The platform should be able to operate both on the cloud as well as in an on-premises environment in order to support a flexible deployment model according to each use cases' needs.

2.3   Non-functional Requirements

In addition to the functional requirements, the following non-functional requirements have been identified as key for the SCHub reference architecture:

- The SCHub will be able to scale horizontally in order to support the capacity required by the identified use cases
- The SCHub will support failover and geo-separated deployments in order to increase its availability and minimize the risk that any components can become a single point of failure.

3 Smart City Data Providers

In order to validate the SCHub concept, real data from Smart City data providers are needed to ensure that the introduction of the SCHub layer will have tangible benefits. A number of data providers of Smart City projects have been contacted and the process of collecting this data is ongoing. A first list of the data providers that have agreed to provide access in the context of the SCHub project are presented below. The identified data sources are categorized by various parameters in respect to their APIs in Table 1.

Table 1. Data sources API categorization.

Provider	Type	Data	Access	API	Format	Frequency	Doc
DEYAT	Public	Drinking water quality	Public	Pull	JSON	weekly	yes
IMBRIW	Public	Stream water quality	Auth	Pull	JSON	hourly	yes
WINGS	Private	Air quality	Public	Pull	JSON	minutes	no
AGENSO	Private	Meteorological Measurements	Public	Pull	CSV	daily	no

Water Quality Laboratory of the Municipality of Trikala, Greece (DEYAT). The Water Quality Laboratory of the municipality of Trikala (DEYAT) is performing weekly inspections at various points of the water supply network, including boreholes and network termination points. The Laboratory is accredited according to ISO 17025:2017 in the scope of the following tests: pH, Conductivity, Nitrates, Coliforms, E.coli, Enterococci. The weekly data are available in the laboratory's web page ([2]) and is also available in JSON format via a REST API.

Institute of Marine Biological Resources and Inland Waters, Greece (IMBRIW). Institute of Marine Biological Resources and Inland Waters (IMBRIW) is the leading public research institution in Greece, with a key role in the Mediterranean region and the EU, spearheading fisheries and inland water research. The main goals of IMBRIW are the production of knowledge related to structural and functional aspects of inland aquatic ecosystems and the high trophic level components (including fisheries) of marine ecosystems, and the application of this knowledge for integrated river basin and coastal zone management, ecosystem approach to fisheries and biodiversity conservation ([5]). The data collected are presented via the organization's web page as dashboards ([6]) and is also available in JSON format via a REST API.

Meteorological Data of Municipality of Trikala. The Municipality of Trikala is providing a portal for information regarding the air quality and meteorological data of the city ([12]). The data are retrieved from two external services providers that collect data for the air quality measurements ([13]) and meteorological measurements ([14]). The air quality measurements are available in JSON format via a REST API. The meteorological data latest measurements can be retrieved as a CSV file export upon request.

4 Discussion and Future Research Directions

From the data collected so far, it has been identified that the Smart City data providers can be both public and private sector companies. All of them allow public access to their data upon request however not all require authentication to access their API. The data are provided in a pull fashion and most of them use JSON as the preferred data format. The sampling interval varies and can range from minutes to weeks. In regards to the documentation of the API, it also varies from non-existent to extensive.

The initial mapping of the Smart City providers seems to confirm the hypothesis that the landscape is fragmented and that there is no common method for providing the data gathered in Smart Cities. The incompatibilities among the different technical aspects of the APIs make it challenging for external users to access, consume, combine and create additional value added services using this data. Inconsistencies in the data format, modeling and sampling frequency further increase the effort needed to re-use and increase the value of the collected data.

The introduction of the SCHub layer can contribute to the simplification of data discovery and consumption and allow third parties to focus their efforts in creating value added services rather than dealing with API incompatibilities and data manipulation. This can be a step towards the direction of implementing new use cases of collective intelligence and other innovative solutions for Smart Cities and communities

The SCHub project is ongoing. The identification and collection of additional real-life use cases of Smart City data providers for the southbound interfaces is of high priority in order to have an overview of the Smart City data providers landscape that is as wide as possible. Ongoing work is also focusing with equal priority on the standardization of the northbound APIs that will enable the seamless access to the identified data sources in a dynamic and consistent way.

Finally, a key research question in the context of the challenges of building knowledge societies for Smart Cities and communities is in regards to the centralization of the Smart City platforms and the impact this has on the privacy and self-soverance of the citizen's data. The data sources identified so far concern data that are at the metropolitan city scale without any kind of personal identifiable information. The wealth of sensors that are deployed in Smart Cities however allows the collection of data and metadata that can be linked to the citizens themselves. Examples of such data sources include the various types of smart meters like water, natural gas or electricity, occupancy sensors of parking spaces, health and biometric data provided by smart watches or other equipment. A layer like SCHub could provide the sanitization and anonymization for this kind of data in order to ensure that the citizen's privacy is not violated.

Acknowledgements. The SCHub research project is supported by the Hellenic Foundation for Research and Innovation (H.F.R.I.) under the "2nd Call for H.F.R.I. Research Projects to support Faculty Members & Researchers" (Project Number:2652).

References

1. Anthopoulos, L.G., Pourzolfaghar, Z., Lemmer, K., Siebenlist, T., Niehaves, B., Nikolaou, I.: Smart cities as hubs: connect, collect and control city flows. Cities **125**, 103660 (2022). https://doi.org/10.1016/j.cities.2022.103660
2. DEYAT: Water quality laboratory of the municipality of Trikala, Greece (deyat) (2018). https://www.deyat.gr/node/29
3. Fahmideh, M., Zowghi, D.: An exploration of IoT platform development. Inf. Syst. **87**, 101409 (2020). https://doi.org/10.1016/j.is.2019.06.005
4. Fremantle, P., Kopecký, J., Aziz, B.: Web API management meets the internet of things (2015). https://www.semanticscholar.org/paper/Web-API-Management-Meets-the-Internet-of-Things-Fremantle-Kopeck%C3%BD/13603dcb9e385c831e20703d4240c956ca9961cc
5. IMBRIW: Institute of marine biological resources and inland waters, Greece (IMBRIW) (2023). https://imbriw.hcmr.gr/mission/
6. IMBRIW: Institute of marine biological resources and inland waters, Greece (IMBRIW) - hydro stations (2023). https://hydro-stations.hcmr.gr
7. ISO: Smart cities (2015). https://www.iso.org/files/live/sites/isoorg/files/developing_standards/docs/en/smart_cities_report-jtc1.pdf
8. ITU-T: An overview of smart sustainable cities and the role of information and communication technologies (2014). https://www.itu.int/en/itu-t/focusgroups/ssc/documents/approved_deliverables/tr-overview-ssc.docx
9. Ray, P.P.: A survey of IoT cloud platforms. Future Comput. Inf. J. **1**, 35–46 (2016). https://doi.org/10.1016/j.fcij.2017.02.001, https://www.sciencedirect.com/science/article/pii/S2314728816300149
10. Sánchez-Corcuera, R., et al.: Smart cities survey: technologies, application domains and challenges for the cities of the future. Int. J. Distrib. Sens. Netw. **15**, 155014771985398 (2019). https://doi.org/10.1177/1550147719853984
11. Syed, A.S., Sierra-Sosa, D., Kumar, A., Elmaghraby, A.: Iot in smart cities: a survey of technologies, practices and challenges. Smart Cities **4**, 429–475 (2021). https://doi.org/10.3390/smartcities4020024
12. Trikala, M.: Municipality of trikala - dashboard (2022). https://trikalacity.gr/poiotita-zois-metriseis-2/
13. Trikala, M.: Municipality of trikala - air quality measurements (2023). https://trikalaws.mindrop.gr/
14. Trikala, M.: Municipality of trikala - meteorological measurements (2023). https://temperature.gr/details/%CE%9C%CF%8D%CE%BB%CE%BF%CF%82%20%CE%9C%CE%B1%CF%84%CF%83%CF%8C%CF%80%CE%BF%CF%85%CE%BB%CE%BF%CF%85%20%CE%A4%CF%81%CE%AF%CE%BA%CE%B1%CE%BB%CE%B1

Revolutionizing Real Estate: A Blockchain, NFT, and IPFS Multi-platform Approach

N. N. Hung[1]([✉]), Khoa T. Dang[1], M. N. Triet[1], K. Vo Hong[1], Bao Q. Tran[1],
H. G. Khiem[1], N. T. Phuc[1], M. D. Hieu[1], V. C. P. Loc[1], T. L. Quy[1],
N. T. Anh[1], Q. N. Hien[1], L. K. nd Bang[1], D. P. T. Nguyen[1], N. T. K. Ngan[2],
X. H. Son[3], and H. L. Huong[1]([✉])

[1] FPT University, Can Tho city, Vietnam
hungnnce171478@fpt.edu.vn, huonghoangluong@gmail.com
[2] FPT Polytecnic, Can Tho city, Vietnam
[3] RMIT University, Ho Chi Minh city, Vietnam

Abstract. Traditional real estate management faces challenges like lack of transparency, inefficiency, and fraud. Blockchain has been proposed as a solution, but its full potential remains untapped. Our paper introduces a sophisticated approach, combining Non-Fungible Tokens (NFTs), InterPlanetary File System (IPFS), and blockchain technology. Using Ethereum's ERC721 standard, we create unique NFTs for real estate assets, guaranteeing ownership and transferability. IPFS, integrated via Node.js, ensures permanent data storage for each NFT, preserving asset information integrity. What sets our model apart is its multi-platform deployment on Fantom, Polygon, Binance Smart Chain, and Celo networks, enhancing resilience and accessibility. This robust integration offers a transformative tool for real estate management, enabling transparent, secure, and efficient transactions, promoting market efficiency, and bolstering investor confidence.

Keywords: Real estate management · Blockchain · Smart contracts · NFT · IPFS · Ethereum · Fantom · Polygon · Celo · Binance Smart Chain

1 Introduction

The real estate sector is vital for economic stability and growth, accounting for a significant portion of the European Union's workforce and enterprises [1]. However, traditional real estate transactions suffer from issues like high fees, opacity, and fraud risks [4,7].

Blockchain, smart contracts, and NFTs offer promising solutions to these problems [2,5]. Blockchain's decentralization, immutability, and transparency can revolutionize asset transfers and recording [6,9]. Smart contracts enforce obligations, speeding up procedures and ensuring reliability.

P. Delir Haghighi et al. (Eds.): iiWAS 2023, LNCS 14416, pp. 68–73, 2023.
https://doi.org/10.1007/978-3-031-48316-5_10

Global initiatives like Sweden's Lantmäteriet and the Dutch government have explored blockchain in real estate [4,7]. Yet, they face legal and governance challenges.

This paper introduces a pioneering blockchain-based real estate system, addressing these challenges. It extends to multiple platforms like BNB Smart Chain, Fantom, Polygon, and Celo for flexibility. A detailed IPFS proof-of-concept ensures immutable data storage. These contributions advance the field significantly.

2 Related Work

Blockchain, Non-Fungible Tokens (NFTs), and the InterPlanetary File System (IPFS) hold transformative potential in real estate. This section reviews global initiatives, highlighting benefits and challenges.

The Netherlands has seen a surge in nationwide blockchain pilot projects, incorporating open data [4].

Bitfury partnered with Ukraine's State Agency of E-Government to explore blockchain for land cadastral [3].

In summary, these works demonstrate the transformative potential of blockchain, NFTs, and IPFS in real estate, warranting further research to address deployment challenges and harness their full potential.

3 Approach

3.1 Traditional Real Estate Management: An Overview

Traditional real estate management involves several essential components: assets (property or land), sellers (owners of assets), buyers (acquirers of assets), agencies (intermediaries like agents or brokers), and banks (providing loans or mortgages). Assets' characteristics determine their value, serving as the central element in real estate transactions. Sellers aim to transfer asset ownership for various reasons and must transparently disclose asset conditions. Buyers conduct due diligence to assess an asset's condition, legality, and value. Agencies facilitate transactions and provide market expertise but typically charge commissions. Banks play a role by offering loans, evaluating financial capacity, property value, and risk factors, using the property as collateral until the loan is repaid.

The traditional real estate transaction model, as depicted in Fig. 1, comprises four manual and paper-based steps, involving key roles played by the buyer, seller, agency, and bank. These steps encompass:

1. **Agreement to Transact:** It begins with a verbal agreement, followed by a formal written contract to document and validate transaction specifics.
2. **Asset Validation:** This step verifies property documents for legal ownership, but it's slow and error-prone due to manual processes.
3. **Financial Validation:** The bank assesses the buyer's financial capacity and property value, often involving paper-intensive, manual procedures.

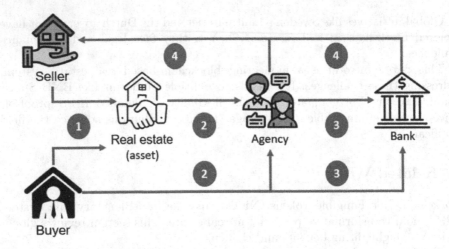

Fig. 1. The traditional real estate management model

4. **Information Transfer:** The final step transfers validated documents and contracts, often through physical means, risking sensitive information.

Traditional real estate transactions face problems like opacity, high costs, lengthy paperwork, fraud risks, and slow processes. Intermediaries lead to hefty fees and information imbalances. Physical paperwork and multiple stakeholders add delays and data inconsistencies. Blockchain, with its transparency and decentralization, can address these issues by cutting costs, automating processes, and reducing fraud. NFTs and IPFS further streamline operations. This paper examines how these technologies can transform real estate management, making it more efficient, transparent, and secure.

3.2 Proposed Architecture for Blockchain-Based Real Estate Transactions

Our architecture presents a blockchain-based system for real estate transactions, incorporating smart contracts, Non-Fungible Tokens (NFTs), and the InterPlanetary File System (IPFS). Figure 2 illustrates our model, consisting of key components: buyer, seller, agency, smart contract, distributed ledger, and IPFS, designed to enhance transparency, efficiency, and security in real estate transactions. The workflow comprises the following steps:

1. **Agreement to Transact:** The process starts with a buyer-seller agreement, defining transaction details and terms.
2. **Seller-Agency Interaction:** The seller engages the agency to validate and digitize real estate documents, preparing them for blockchain storage.
3. **Data Validation and Storage:** The agency validates and securely stores the seller's data, ensuring accuracy for the smart contract.

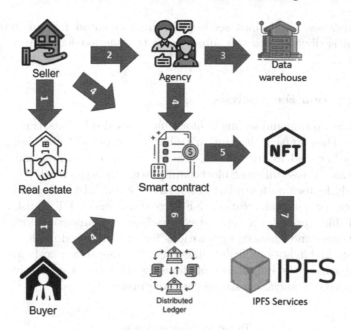

Fig. 2. Real estate management model based on blockchain technology, smart contract, and NFT

4. **Smart Contract Creation:** Validated data is transferred to a blockchain-based smart contract, created and deployed by the seller, encapsulating agreement terms and asset details.
5. **NFT Generation:** Upon successful smart contract deployment, an NFT representing the real estate asset is generated, initially containing all asset information and owner details.
6. **Blockchain Logging:** The smart contract, containing vital transaction data, is recorded in the blockchain, ensuring immutability and transparency.
7. **NFT Upload to IPFS:** The NFT is uploaded to IPFS, offering decentralized, tamper-resistant storage, bolstering security and resilience in our real estate transaction system.

4   Evaluation Scenarios

In this section, we practically deploy and assess our model across four Ethereum Virtual Machine (EVM) [8] compatible platforms: Binance Smart Chain (BNB)[1], Polygon (MATIC)[2], Celo (CELO)[3], and Fantom (FTM)[4]. These platforms were chosen due to their EVM compatibility, offering strong community support,

---

[1] https://github.com/bnb-chain/whitepaper/blob/master/WHITEPAPER.md.
[2] https://polygon.technology/lightpaper-polygon.pdf.
[3] https://celo.org/papers/whitepaper.
[4] https://whitepaper.io/document/438/fantom-whitepaper.

extensive libraries, and robust security features essential for our application. This section is divided into two subsections: transaction fee analysis, and gas limit analysis.

4.1 Transaction Fee Analysis

In the implementation and scaling of blockchain-based solutions, transaction fees are critical. They impact the system's viability, especially for high-frequency applications like real estate trading. Therefore, understanding and analyzing transaction fees across different blockchain platforms is essential.

Our study focuses on four platforms - BNB, FTM, MATIC, and CELO. We estimate fees for contract creation, NFT creation, and NFT transfer for each platform. Table 1 provides a detailed comparison of transaction fees, revealing cost-effectiveness and financial implications for our proposed model.

The table highlights significant differences in transaction costs among platforms, emphasizing the importance of choosing the most cost-effective platform based on specific financial constraints and requirements.

Table 1. Transaction fee

	Contract Creation	Create NFT	Transfer NFT
BNB Smart Chain	0.027311 BNB ($8.33)	0.00109162 BNB ($0.33)	0.00056991 BNB ($0.17)
Fantom	0.0095767 FTM ($0.003)	0.000405167 FTM ($0.000127)	0.0002380105 FTM ($0.000075)
Polygon	0.0068405000328344 MATIC($0.01)	0.000289405001273382 MATIC($0.00)	0.000170007500748033 MATIC($0.00)
Celo	0.00709722 CELO ($0.004)	0.0002840812 CELO ($0.000)	0.0001554878 CELO ($0.000)

4.2 Gas Limit Analysis

The gas limit is a critical consideration in Ethereum-based blockchains, denoting the computational effort required for operations like transactions and smart contracts. Each operation requires a specific amount of gas for successful execution, and the gas limit represents the maximum a user is willing to spend on an operation. Optimizing the gas limit is crucial for blockchain system efficiency and cost-effectiveness.

Table 2. Gas limit

	Contract Creation	Create NFT	Transfer NFT
BNB Smart Chain	2,731,100	109,162	71,991
Fantom	2,736,200	115,762	72,803
Polygon	2,736,476	115,762	72,803
Celo	3,548,610	142,040	85,673

This subsection analyzes the gas limit across four platforms: BNB, FTM, MATIC, and CELO, focusing on contract creation, NFT creation, and NFT transfer. The comprehensive comparison in Table 2 reveals varying computational resource requirements for each platform, impacting overall system performance and efficiency. This analysis helps make informed decisions on the optimal platform based on specific computational constraints and requirements.

The evaluation demonstrates the feasibility of deploying the proposed model on various platforms, offering insights into financial and computational implications. These findings guide future research and implementations in this rapidly evolving field.

5   Conclusion

This work explores blockchain, NFTs, and IPFS integration in real estate, proposing an NFT model. It analyzes EVM-compatible blockchain platforms, emphasizing platform selection's financial and computational impact. This research offers practical insights, contributing to advancing knowledge. Blockchain, NFTs, and IPFS hold the potential to enhance real estate's efficiency, transparency, and accessibility, paving the way for a tech-enhanced future in the sector.

References

1. EUROSTAT: Real estate activity statistics - nace rev. 2. [Online] (2015). https://ec.europa.eu/eurostat/statistics-explained/index.php?title=Real_estate_activity_statistics_-_NACE_Rev._2&oldid=572702
2. Ha, X.S., et al.: Dem-cod: novel access-control-based cash on delivery mechanism for decentralized marketplace. In: the International Conference on Trust, Security and Privacy in Computing and Communications (TrustCom), pp. 71–78 (2020)
3. Kalyuzhnova, N.: Transformation of the real estate market on the basis of use of the blockchain technologies: opportunities and problems. In: MATEC Web of Conferences 212 (2018)
4. Krupa, K.S.J., Akhil, M.S.: Reshaping the Real Estate Industry Using Blockchain, vol. 545, pp. 255–263 (2019)
5. Le, H.T., et al.: Introducing multi shippers mechanism for decentralized cash on delivery system. Int. J. Adv. Comput. Sci. Appl. 10(6) (2019)
6. Le, N.T.T., et al.: Assuring non-fraudulent transactions in cash on delivery by introducing double smart contracts. Int. J. Adv. Comput. Sci. Appl. 10(5), 677–684 (2019)
7. Nasarre-Aznar, S.: Collaborative housing and blockchain. Administration 66(2), 59–82 (2018)
8. Quoc, K.L., et al.: Sssb: an approach to insurance for cross-border exchange by using smart contracts. In: Mobile Web and Intelligent Information Systems: 18th International Conference, pp. 179–192. Springer, Cham (2022). https://doi.org/10.1007/978-3-031-14391-5_14
9. Veuger, J.: Trust in a viable real estate economy with disruption and blockchain. Facilities (2018)

Data Management

Towards a Unified Symbolic AI Framework for Mining High Utility Itemsets

Amel Hidouri[1]($\boxtimes$) (iD), Badran Raddaoui[2,3] (iD), and Said Jabbour[1] (iD)

[1] CRIL & CNRS, Université d'Artois, Lens, France
`hidouri@cril.fr`
[2] SAMOVAR, Télécom SudParis, Institut Polytechnique de Paris, Palaiseau, France
[3] Institute for Philosophy II, Ruhr University Bochum, Bochum, Germany

Abstract. This paper deals with the task of mining high utility itemsets. The proposed approach presents a unified framework for efficiently mining high utility patterns from transaction databases while handling effectively various condensed representations. In addition, this approach offers a way to integrate multiple constraints, including closedness, minimality, and maximality, while maintaining flexibility in the mining process. This allows to significantly enhance the efficiency and effectiveness of mining high utility patterns, making it a valuable tool for various data mining applications. Finally, we show through an extensive campaign of experiments on several popular real-life datasets the efficiency of our proposed approach.

Keywords: High Utility Itemsets · Symbolic Artificial Intelligence · Propositional Satisfiability · Constraints

1 Introduction

An essential task in the knowledge discovery process concerns *pattern extraction* w.r.t. various properties such as novelty, usefulness, and understandability. Pattern extraction is an active research topic in data mining. It involves automatically finding relevant patterns that represent the properties of the data according users' preferences. Typically, pattern mining methods can be roughly divided between *Frequent Itemset Mining* (FIM, for short) and *High Utility Itemset Mining* (HUIM, for short). FIM is based on the occurrence of items to measure its importance. However, HUIM is an extension of FIM and relies on the quantity and profit of items to determine the set of items that appear together and have a high utility in a transaction database. Such pattern is called High Utility Itemset (HUI, for short). The utility can be evaluated in profit, cost, or any other user preference measure. The task of HUIM was introduced in 2003 by Chan et al. [3] and it spans diverse fields, including retail marketing, customer behavior analysis, healthcare, and financial data analysis, among others (see [16]). For example, in a supermarket, retailers offer low-profit items or services at a reduced price or for free to customers who purchased more expensive products. The aim is to attract new customers and integrate new products into the market. Moreover, Microsoft's Xbox One video game console was sold at a low margin per unit, but Microsoft knew that there was potential to profit from the sale of video games with higher margins and subscriptions to the company's Xbox Live service [4].

Abundant literature has been dedicated to the task of high utility itemset mining (see [6,16] for a survey). Unfortunately, existing proposals for extracting high utility itemsets may be ineffective since they often generate an overwhelming number of patterns, a significant portion of which prove to be irrelevant or of little practical value. Moreover, the abundance of trivial or redundant patterns can lead to a time-consuming and resource-intensive post-processing phase to filter out irrelevant results. Consequently, the sheer volume of patterns generated makes it challenging for analysts and decision-makers to identify the most valuable and actionable insights. To tackle this issue, various condensed representations of high utility itemsets have been proposed and ranging from closed [9] and maximal [15] to generators [8] and minimal [7] itemsets.

Basically, existing approaches, commonly referred to as *specialized* or *imperative*, aim to find specific types of itemsets from transaction databases using some measures. More specifically, these algorithms can only extract the itemsets for which they were designed, and the user cannot easily incorporate new specifications into the application. In that sense, adding new constraints, i.e., user preference, cannot be easily integrated into the original approach. It often requires re-implementing the entire application, which might exceedingly challenging. However, adding new target patterns or combining existing properties of mined patterns may necessitate new complicated implementation modifications. Interestingly, constraint-based approaches have emerged as a promising framework for modeling diverse mining tasks due to their reliance on generic and declarative solvers. This approach allows users to incorporate specific constraints that define the characteristics of the patterns to be mined. As a result, this framework has garnered significant attention and has been applied in various data mining tasks, including frequent patterns, sequences, and association rules. The declarative nature of constraint-based languages facilitates adaptability, enabling the addition of new constraints or the combination of multiple constraints within a single framework by simply modifying the declarative specification. This flexibility empowers data miners to tailor the mining process to suit their specific needs while leveraging well-known and efficient solving techniques.

Our Contributions. The paper's topic falls under the data mining field in general and high utility itemsets extraction in particular. The first goal is to implement new effective reformulations to solve the problem of enumeration of high utility patterns using propositional logic resolution techniques. These reformulations should allow for more adaptable representations that can effortlessly incorporate new user constraints. In this paper, we review the approaches for mining high utility itemsets using propositional satisfiability. We show how the classical problem and some condensed forms can be easily translated into SAT or a problem around SAT.

This paper is organized as follows. Section 2 sketches some technical background and preliminary definitions. Then, we introduce some basic notions about Boolean Satisfiability problem and its variants. Afterwards, Sect. 3 presents the novel unified framework for high utility itemset mining. It explains how multiple constraints, such as closedness, minimality, and maximality, can be combined effectively within the constraint-based paradigm to extract valuable patterns. In Sect. 4, we present a decomposition strategy to improve the efficiency and effectiveness of the proposed framework. Finally, we discuss the experiments we carried out to assess the performance of our proposals in Sect. 5. Finally, we draw some conclusions in Sect. 6.

2   General Setting

In this section, we provide the essential preliminaries for understanding the high utility itemset enumeration task and the propositional satisfiability problem.

2.1   High Utility Intemset Mining Problem

In the high utility itemset mining problem, we consider a transactional database where each item $a \in \Omega$ is associated with two essential utility values: the *external utility* denoted by $w_{ext}(a)$ (e.g., unit profit) and the *internal utility* denoted by $w_{int}(a, T_i)$. More formally:

Definition 1 (Internal/External Utility). *Given a transaction database $T = \{T_1, \ldots, T_m\}$, for each transaction T_i such that $a \in T_i$, a positive number $w_{int}(a, T_i)$ is called the internal utility of the item a (e.g., purchase quantity). In addition, each item $a \in \Omega$ possesses a positive number $w_{ext}(a)$, called its external utility (e.g., unit profit).*

By considering both the external and internal utilities of items, one can easily compute the utility of an item in a transaction, as given in the following definition.

Definition 2 (Utility of an Item in a Transaction). *Given a transaction database $T = \{T_1, \ldots, T_m\}$, the utility of an item a in a transaction T_i, denoted by $u(a, T_i)$, is computed as: $u(a, T_i) = w_{int}(a, T_i) \times w_{ext}(a)$.*

Example 1. Consider an example of a transaction database depicted in Table 1 (we will use this table as a running example in this paper). Each item in each transaction is associated with a weight representing its internal utility (e.g., quantity). In addition, it has an external utility (e.g., unit profit), as shown in Table 2. Furthermore, the utility of the item a in the transaction T_2 is $u(a, T_2) = w_{int}(a, T_2) \times w_{ext}(a) = 2 \times 4 = 8$.

Table 1. Sample transaction database with utility.

TID	Items			
T_1	$(a,1)$	$(b,2)$	$(c,3)$	$(d,1)$
T_2	$(a,2)$	$(b,3)$	$(c,1)$	$(e,2)$
T_3	$(a,4)$	$(e,1)$		
T_4	$(a,1)$	$(d,2)$	$(e,2)$	
T_5	$(a,1)$	$(b,5)$		

Table 2. Profit table.

Item	Unit profit
a	4
b	2
c	1
d	2
e	3

Based on the utility of an item introduced in Definition 2, the utility of an itemset can be computed as follows:

Definition 3 (Utility of an Itemset in a Transaction). *The utility of an itemset X in a transaction T_i, denoted by $u(X, T_i)$, is the total utility of each item in that itemset in each transaction where it appears.*

$$u(X, T_i) = \sum_{a \in X \subseteq T_i} u(a, T_i)$$

Definition 4 (Utility of an Itemset in a Database). *Given a transaction database $T = \{T_1, \dots, T_m\}$, the utility of an itemset X in the entire database D, denoted by $u(X, D)$, is defined as the sum of its utility in each transaction $u(X, T_i)$ wherein it appears:*

$$u(X, D) = \sum_{(i,T) \in D \mid X \subseteq T_i} u(X, T_i)$$

In the following example, we give different expressions of Definition 4 and 3.

Example 2. Using Table 1 and Table 2, the utility of the itemset $\{a, b\}$ in the transaction T_1 is $u(\{a, b\}, T_1) = 1 \times 4 + 2 \times 2 = 8$. Hence, its utility in the database is the sum of its utilities in all transactions wherein it appears. More formally: $u(\{a, b\}, D) = u(\{a, b\}, T_1) + u(\{a, b\}, T_2) + u(\{a, b\}, T_5) = 8 + 14 + 14 = 36$.

The goal of high utility itemset mining problem is to find the set of all itemsets in a transaction database D whose utility value is no less than a given threshold θ. More formally,

$$HUI = \{X : u(X, D) \mid X \subseteq \Omega, u(X, D) \geq \theta\}$$

An itemset is called *high utility itemset* if it has a utility greater than the minimum utility threshold θ. Otherwise, it is called *low utility itemset*.

The next example shows all high utility itemsets in a database for a fixed minimum utility threshold.

Example 3. Let reconsider the database of Table 1 and a minimum utility threshold $\theta = 25$. Then, the set of all high utility itemsets is: $\{\{a\} : 36; \{a, b\} : 46; \{a, e\} : 43; \{a, b, c\} : 26\}$, where each number represents the utility of the itemset.

Now, we introduce the main concise representations of high utility itemsets commonly used in the HUIM literature.

Definition 5 (Concise Representations of HUIs). *Let D be a transaction database and X be an itemset.*

- *X is called a* **closed high utility itemset** *if there exists no itemset X' such that $X \subset X'$, and $\forall (i, T_i) \in D$, if $X \in T_i$ then $X' \in T_i$.*
- *X is called a* **maximal high utility itemset** *iff there exists no other high utility itemset Y such that $X \subset Y$, i.e., $\{X \subseteq \Omega \mid u(X) \geq \theta$ and $\nexists Y \supset X, Y \in HUI(D, \theta)\}$.*
- *X is called* **minimal high utility itemset** *iff there exists no other high utility itemset $Y \subset X$ in D, i.e., $\{X \subseteq \Omega \mid u(X) \geq \theta$ and $\nexists Y \subset X, Y \in HUI(D, \theta)\}$.*

In the sequel, we write CHUIs, MaxHUIs and MinHUIs for the set of all closed, maximal and minimal high utility itemsets in D, respectively.

Another task related to the HUIM problem consists in enumerating the set of HUIs while also considering the frequency measure in the target patterns. In this task, the objective is to find itemsets that not only have high utility but also occur frequently in the transactional database.

Definition 6. *Given a transaction database D, a support and utility minimum thresholds δ and θ respectively. An itemset X is a frequent high utility itemset (FHUI, for short). in D iff $\text{Supp}(X)$[1] $\geq \delta$ and $u(X) \geq \theta$.*

Clearly, the HUIM task is a particular case of Frequent High Utility Itemset Mining task (FHUIM, for short) where δ is set to 1.

A drawback of FHUIM setup is that when mining such patterns, the utility of itemsets is overestimated. This means that even if the utility of an itemset is relatively low, the transactions containing that itemset are still considered part of the cover of that itemset. In other words, the transactions are counted as supporting the itemset, regardless of the actual value of their utility. This can be accomplished by imposing additional constraints on the utility metric to assist filter out itemsets with low utility but high frequency, focusing on patterns that genuinely carry significant value. Simply put, the utility constraint is enforced on transaction level rather that the database level by restricting the cover of the itemset to only the transactions in which its utility is greater than a local minimum utility threshold. The following additional syntax is required to define such sets.

---

[1] $\text{Supp}(X, D) = |\{i \in [1..m] \mid (i, T) \in D \text{ and } X \subseteq T\}|..$

Definition 7 (Support-based cover). *Let D be a transaction database and X an itemset in D. Given a local minimum utility threshold θ', the utility-based cover of X in D:*

$$\text{Cover}_u(X, D) = \{(i, T) \in D \mid X \subseteq T_i, \text{ and } u(X, T_i) \geq \theta'\}$$

Then, the utility-based support of X is the cardinality of its utility-based cover, i.e., $\text{Supp}_u(X, D) = |\text{Cover}_u(X, D)|$. X is called a Frequent Local High Utility Itemset (FLHUI, for short) in a transaction database D iff. $\text{Supp}_u(X) \geq \delta$.[2]

2.2 The Satisfiability Problem in Propositional Logic

Consider a propositional language $\mathcal{L}$ built up from a countable set of propositional variables $\mathcal{P}$, the Boolean constants $\top$ (*True* or 1) and $\perp$ (*False* or 0) and the classical connectives $\{\neg, \wedge, \vee, \rightarrow, \leftrightarrow\}$ in the usual way. We use the letters $x, y, z, \ldots$ to range over the elements of $\mathcal{P}$. A **literal** is a propositional variable (x) of $\mathcal{P}$ or its negation $(\neg x)$. A **clause** is a (finite) disjunction of literals. Propositional formulas of $\mathcal{L}$ are denoted by Φ, Ψ, etc. For any formula Φ from $\mathcal{L}$, $\mathcal{P}(\Phi)$ denotes the symbols of $\mathcal{P}$ occurring in Φ. A formula in **conjunctive normal form** (or simply CNF) is a finite conjunction of clauses. A Boolean interpretation $\mathcal{I}$ of a CNF formula Φ is defined as a function from $\mathcal{P}(\Phi)$ to $\{0, 1\}$. A **model** of Φ is an interpretation $\mathcal{I}$ that satisfies Φ (denoted $\mathcal{I} \models \Phi$), that is, if there exists an interpretation $\mathcal{I} : \mathcal{P}(\Phi) \rightarrow \{0, 1\}$ that satisfies all clauses in Φ. The formula Φ is **satisfiable** if it has at least one model. We denote by $\mathcal{M}(\Phi)$ the set of all models of Φ.

The propositional satisfiability problem (SAT, for short) is a fundamental decision problem in propositional logic. It involves determining whether there exists a model for a given CNF formula. It has been extensively used in a wide range of real-world scenarios, thanks to its effectiveness in solving complex Boolean satisfiability problems, e.g., electronic design automation, software and hardware verification [14]. These applications enables the enumeration of all models of the underlying CNF formula. This task, called **model enumeration**, is a well-known problem in SAT community. It finds application in diagnosis where the user is interested in computing all explanations rather than just whether one exists. Model enumeration problems have been applied in various tasks, including network verification [17] as well as several data mining tasks, e.g., [2,10], and graph analysis [12,13]. A model M of Φ is called a *minimal model* or *prime implicant* if no proper subset $M' \subset M$ is a model of Φ. M_+ denotes the set of variables assigned to true in a model M.

Definition 8 (X-minimal model). *Let Φ be a propositional formula over a set of literals $\mathcal{L}$, $X \subseteq \mathcal{L}$ a set of variables, and M a model of Φ. Then, M is called an X-minimal model for Φ iff there exists no other model M' of Φ such that $M'_+ \cap X \subset M_+ \cap X$.*

---

[2] When there is no confusion, we note $\text{Cover}_u(X)$ instead of $\text{Cover}_u(X, D)$ and $\text{Supp}_u(X)$ instead of $\text{Supp}_u(X, D)$.

The problem of finding X-minimal models is about identifying all models of a given propositional formula Φ that minimize the set of literals X.

Next, we employ an unified constrained approach for enumerating HUIs. This framework is extended to leverage additional constraints in order guide the mining process and optimize the extraction of more concise patterns. These constraints serve as guidelines to restrict the search space and focus on patterns that satisfy specific conditions.

3   A Unified SAT-Based Framework for HUIM

In this section, we explore constraint-based HUIM algorithms to address lack of flexibility and support for multiple mining aims and provide more versatile solutions in that context. We provide SAT-based encoding of the HUIM task as a propositional satisfiability problem which will be expanded later to limit the search process to a specific type of patterns.

In the proposed encoding for the transaction database D, we associate each item a and transaction identifier i with a corresponding propositional variable. Specifically, for each item a in D, we introduce a propositional variable p_a. This variable represents whether the item a is included in a selected itemset or not. If p_a is assigned to *True*, it indicates that the item a occurs in the itemset. Conversely, if p_a is assigned *False*, it means that the item a is not included in the itemset. Similarly, for each transaction identifier i in the database, we introduce a propositional variable q_i. This variable represents whether a transaction T_i is considered in the mining process or not. If q_i is assigned a *True*, it indicates that the transaction T_i contains the itemset.

Given a Boolean interpretation Δ, the candidate high utility itemset and its cover are modelled as $\{a \in \Omega \mid \Delta(p_a) = 1\}$ and $\{i \in \mathbb{N} \mid \Delta(q_i) = 1\}$, respectively. Then, the encoding of HUIM problem into SAT is accomplished by imposing a set of constraints, as shown in Fig. 1. The propositional formula (1) expresses the itemset's cover, it indicates whether the itemset occurs in the transaction i, i.e., $q_i = 1$. More simply, the candidate motif does not supported by the transaction i i.e., q_i is *False*, if there exists an item a, such that $p_a = 1$ and a does not appear in the transaction ($a \in \Omega \backslash T_i$); when q_i is set to *False*. The constraint over the utility of an itemset X in D is expressed using the linear inequality (3) w.r.t. the user threshold θ. Finally, the propositional formula (2) aims to expand the framework for mining the set of closed HUIs. It ensures that if the candidate itemset is involved in all transactions containing the item a, then a must be added to the itemset. Clearly, the CNF formula (1) $\wedge$ (3) encodes the HUIM problem, while the formula (1) $\wedge$ (3) $\wedge$ (2) models the closed HUIM task.

Example 4. Let us consider the database of Table 1 as well as a minimum utility threshold of 10, respectively. The transaction database is encoded into the propositional formula Φ_{huim} is illustrated in Fig. 2.

$$\bigwedge_{i=1}^{m} (\neg q_i \leftrightarrow \bigvee_{a \in \Omega \setminus T_i} p_a) \qquad (1) \qquad\qquad \bigwedge_{a \in \Omega} (p_a \vee \bigvee_{a \notin T_i} q_i) \qquad (2)$$

$$\sum_{i=1}^{m} \sum_{a \in T_i} u(a, T_i) \times (p_a \wedge q_i) \geqslant \theta \qquad (3)$$

Fig. 1. SAT Encoding Scheme for (Closed) HUIM.

$$\Phi_{\text{huim}} = \left\{ \begin{array}{l} \neg q_1 \leftrightarrow (p_e) \\ \wedge \\ \neg q_2 \leftrightarrow (p_d) \\ \wedge \\ \neg q_3 \leftrightarrow (p_b \vee p_c \vee p_d) \\ \wedge \\ \neg q_4 \leftrightarrow (p_b \vee p_c) \\ \wedge \\ \neg q_5 \leftrightarrow (p_c \vee p_d \vee p_e) \\ \wedge \\ \begin{array}{l} 4 \times (p_a \wedge q_1) + 4 \times (p_b \wedge q_1) + 3 \times (p_c \wedge q_1) + 2 \times (p_d \wedge q_1) \\ + \\ 8 \times (p_a \wedge q_2) + 6 \times (p_b \wedge q_2) + (p_c \wedge q_2) + 6 \times (p_e \wedge q_2) \\ + \\ 16 \times (p_a \wedge q_3) + 3 \times (p_e \wedge q_3) \\ + \\ 4 \times (p_a \wedge q_4) + 4 \times (p_d \wedge q_4) + 6 \times (p_e \wedge q_4) \\ + \\ 4 \times (p_a \wedge q_5) + 10 \times (p_b \wedge q_5) \geq 10 \end{array} \end{array} \right.$$

Cover constraint

Utility constraint

To extend this encoding for mining CHUIs, simply add the closure to Φ^{huim} as follows:

$$\Phi_{\text{chuim}} = \left\{ \begin{array}{l} \Phi_{huim} \\ \wedge \\ p_a \\ \wedge \\ p_a \wedge p_b \vee q_3 \vee q_4 \\ \wedge \\ p_c \vee q_3 \vee q_4 \vee q_5 \\ \wedge \\ p_d \vee q_2 \vee q_3 \vee q_5 \\ \wedge \\ p_e \vee q_1 \vee q_5 \end{array} \right.$$

Closure constraint

Fig. 2. The encoding Φ_{huim} of the transaction database of Table 1.

It is important to note that the encoding of HUI involves Constraints (1) and (2) that can be easily translated into clausal form. The constraint (3) refers to a so-called *Pseudo-Boolean constraint* (PB, for short). Solving such kind of constraint has been a topic of significant interest in the SAT community. To solve problems with PB-constraints, one have to encode them as propositional formulas to leverage the powerful SAT solvers. However, this encoding can lead to formulas with an exponential number of constraints, which poses significant challenges in terms of computational efficiency and scalability [1] especially for long PB-constraints. As the length of the PB-constraints increases, the number of Boolean variables and coefficients in the linear combination also grows, which can result in an exponential increase in the number of clauses and literals in the corresponding propositional formula. One approach to handle this complexity is through the use of counters [11]. Counters are data structures that can efficiently manage and represent PB-constraints without explicitly encoding them as propositional formulas. Instead of expanding the PB-constraints into a large formula, counters provide a more compact and efficient representation. More precisely, $W = \sum_{i=1}^{m} \sum_{a \in T_i} u(a, T_i)$ is evaluated by subtracting $u(a, T_i)$ from W each time $q_i \wedge p_a$ becomes *False*.

To enumerate all models of the HUIM encoding, an extension of the Davis-Putnam-Logemann-Loveland (DPLL) procedure [5] is employed by adapting the algorithm to keep track of all solutions found instead of stopping after finding just one solution. This requires adding additional mechanisms to store and output the found models. The proposed algorithm (see Algorithm 1) enumerates the set of all models of a given CNF formula Φ. More precisely, the traditional DPLL procedure checks only the satisfiability of Φ without computing the models of Φ. However, Algorithm 1 checks first the satisfiability of Φ (line 11). If so, it returns the set of all models of Φ (line 16). In this procedure, a non assigned variable p of the formula Φ is selected, and the algorithm extends the current interpretation by assigning p to *True*. Next, unit propagation is performed (lines 1–2). If all literals are assigned without conflict, then Δ is selected as a model of the CNF formula (line 12).

Algorithm 1. DPLL_Enum: A backtracking search procedure for models enumeration

Input: Φ: a CNF formula, Δ: an interpretation
Output: The set of models of Φ

```
 1: if (Φ ⊨ p) then
 2:     return DPLL_Enum(Φ ∧ p, Δ ∪ {p}))                    ▷ unit clause rule
 3: end if
 4: if (Φ ⊨ ⊥) then
 5:     return ∅                                              ▷ conflict
 6: end if
 7: if (check_Utility_Constraint() == False) then
 8:     return ∅
 9: end if
10: p = select_variable(Var(Φ))
11: if (p == null) then                                      ▷ all variables are assigned
12:     return {Δ}                                           ▷ new found model
13: end if
14: S₁ ← DPLL_Enum(Φ ∧ p, Δ ∪ {p})                          ▷ recovering models with p
15: S₂ ← DPLL_Enum(Φ ∧ ¬p, Δ ∪ {¬p})                       ▷ recovering models with ¬p
16: return S₁ ∪ S₂
```

SAT-Based Approach to Mining Concise Representations of HUIs

Condensed forms have been proposed to reduce the output size i.e., the number of HUIs presented for the user. Similarly, prime implicants in propositional logic have been proposed to reduce the size of the output by taking into account those that encompass all models. Therefore, it is obvious that the two notions are related. Consider the traditional HUI encoding that was mentioned earlier. Now, the question is what the prime implicants of the formula (1) $\wedge$ (3) represents. Let's note that the variables for transactions q_i are expressed utilizing items' variables through the use of Boolean functions. As a result, each model of (1) $\wedge$ (3) assigns a value to transactions' variables. As defined, m is a prime implicant if m is a model and $\forall a \in m, m \backslash \{a\}$ is not a model. To satisfy the utility constraint, a subset of variables must be assigned to *True*. Thus, a prime implicant of (1) $\wedge$ (3) is equivalent to a minimal pattern in D. This mapping enables the generation of prime implicants using a symbolic method for finding minimal HUIs. As was previously said, the prime implicant in this case tends to minimize the set of item variables for minimal patterns. This also refers to the widely researched X-minimal model in the SAT community. Maximal HUIs and X-minimal models are related by the same logic. More formally the two following results hold:

1. There exists a one-to-one mapping between the MaxHUIs of D and the X-minimal models of Φ_{huim} where $X = \{\neg p_a \mid a \in \Omega\}$.
2. There exists a one-to-one mapping between the MinHUIs of D and the X-minimal models of Φ_{huim} where $X = \{p_a \mid a \in \Omega\}$.

Interestingly, item 1 shows the reduction of the task of computing maximal HUIs to the X-minimal models enumeration problem by finding the largest (w.r.t set inclusion) set of items. Similarly, item 2 shows the equivalence between the task of discovering the set of MinHUIs and the X-minimal models of the formula (1) $\wedge$ (3). Typically, traditional approaches for computing X-minimal models proceed in two phases: once a model is found, a minimization procedure is used to find the minimal ones. In our approach, we process in one phase in order to enumerate the X-minimal models of a given CNF formula. To compute all X-minimal models, an improved generic DPLL-based model enumeration of the previously described algorithm is used. It proceeds by assigning the variables of X first to False. Each time a model is found a blocking clause is added to prevent find models that are not minimal (see Algorithm 2).

Next, we deal with the task of FHUIM with into propositional logic. To do so, the encoding of classical HUIM problem is combined with the following *frequency* constraint:

$$\sum_{i=1}^{m} q_i \geq \delta \tag{4}$$

Then, our unified encoding allows us to combine both utility and frequency measures in order to derive the formula Φ_{fhuim} encoding the FHUIM problem.

$$\Phi_{fhuim} = (1) \wedge (3) \wedge (4)$$

Algorithm 2. Xmin-DPLL_Enum: A backtracking search procedure for X-minimal models enumeration

Input: Φ: a propositional formula ($X \subseteq Lit(\Phi)$)   ▷ $Lit(\Phi)$: literals of Φ
Output: S: the set of minimal models of Φ, Γ: the set of blocking clauses
1: $M = \emptyset$, $S = \emptyset$, $\Gamma = \emptyset$
2: **if** $(\Phi \models p)$ **then**
3:      **return** Xmin-DPLL_Enum($\Phi \wedge p, M \cup \{p\}$))   ▷ unit clause rule
4: **end if**
5: **if** $(\Phi \models \bot)$ **then**
6:      **return** $\emptyset$ ▷ conflict
7: **end if**
8: $p =$ select_variable($Var(\Phi)$)
9: **if** $(p == null)$ **then**   ▷ all variables are assigned
10:     $S \leftarrow S \cup \{M\}$ ▷ new found model
11:     $c_b \leftarrow (\bigvee_{x \in M \cap X} \neg x)$ ▷ blocking clause
12:     $\Phi \leftarrow \Phi \wedge c_b$
13:     $\Gamma \leftarrow \Gamma \wedge c_b$
14: **end if**
15: $S_1 \leftarrow$ Xmin $-$ DPLL_Enum($\Phi \wedge p, M \cup \{p\}$)   ▷ recovering models with p
16: $S_2 \leftarrow$ Xmin $-$ DPLL_Enum($\Phi \wedge \neg p, M \cup \{\neg p\}$)   ▷ recovering models with $\neg p$
17: **return** $S_1 \cup S_2$, Γ

More interestingly, $\Phi_{\texttt{fhuim}}$ can be extended to the closure constraint (2) to mine closed FHUIs (in short CFHUIs). We shall note the formula encoding the computation of CFHUIs as:

$$\Phi_{\texttt{cfhuim}} = \Phi_{\texttt{fhuim}} \wedge (2)$$

Proposition 1. *Let D be a transaction database, θ be a minimum high utility threshold, and δ be a minimum support threshold. Let $\Phi_{\texttt{cfhuim}} = \Phi_{\texttt{fhuim}} \wedge (2)$ be a propositional formula. Then, there exists a one-to-one mapping between the models of $\Phi_{\texttt{fhuim}}$ and the set of CFHUIs in D.*

To address the issue of overestimation in mining FHUIs, a specialized form of HUIM coined Frequent Local High Utility Itemset Mining (FLHUIM, for short) can be established. This specialized form aims to alleviate the overestimation by restricting the cover of the candidate itemset X to only those transactions T_i where the utility of X is greater than a local minimum utility threshold. Thus, the mining algorithm ensures that only those transactions containing X with utility values greater than the threshold will contribute to the support count of X. This representation can improve the quality of the mining results, obtain more meaningful frequent itemsets, and reduce the impact of overestimation on the utility values of the discovered itemsets.

In contrast to the previous SAT-based encoding of FHUIM, three subsets of propositional variables are introduced, namely $\{p_a \mid a \in \Omega\}$, $\{q_i \mid i \in [1..m]\}$, and $\{r_i \mid i \in [1..m]\}$. Each variable p_a is used to represent an item a and the variables $q_{1 \leq i \leq m}$ are used to represent each transaction T_i. In contrast, each variable $r_{1 \le i \le m}$ is used to indicate that the itemset appears in the ith transaction and has a utility value greater than a local minimum utility threshold. Afterward, the main idea is to restrict the frequency function to the transactions with the highest gain value. To do so, let us consider the next Constraint (5).

$$\bigwedge_{i=1}^{m} (r_i \leftrightarrow q_i \wedge (\sum_{a \in T_i} u(a, T_i)\, p_a \geq \theta')) \tag{5}$$

Intuitively, this constraint stipulates that a candidate itemset X is supported by a transaction T_i if it is contained in T_i and the utility of X in T_i meets the required local utility threshold. Notice that the cover and closedness constraints remain identical to the one of the FHUIM SAT-based encoding, i.e., Constraints (1) and (2). In other words, Constraint (5) can be rewritten as the following formula:

$$\bigwedge_{i=1}^{m} r_i \leftrightarrow \sum_{a \in T_i} u(a, T_i)(q_i \wedge p_a) \geq \theta'$$

Now, to enforce the candidate itemset to be frequent, i.e., to be covered by at least δ transactions, we add the cardinality constraint (i.e., Constraint (6)).

$$\sum_{i=1}^{m} r_i \geq \delta \tag{6}$$

Proposition 2. *Let D be a transaction database, θ' be a local minimum utility threshold, and δ be a minimum support threshold. Let the propositional formula $\Phi_{\texttt{flhuim}} = (1) \wedge (5) \wedge (6)$. Consequently, there is a one-to-one mapping between the models of $\Phi_{\texttt{flhuim}}$ and the set of FLHUIs in D. Similarly, $\Phi_{\texttt{cflhuim}} = \Phi_{\texttt{flhuim}} \wedge (2)$ is the formula used to encode the closed FLHUIM problem.*

4   Efficient Solving Strategy for HUIM Problem

The main idea of decomposition in data processing and problem-solving is to break down a large problem or dataset into smaller, more manageable sub-problems. Instead of encoding and dealing with the entire database as a single entity, decomposition allows us to solve many independent sub-problems of small size. Basically, given a classical formula Φ and a propositional variable x_1 in Φ (i.e., $x_1 \in \mathcal{P}(\Phi)$, where $\mathcal{P}(\Phi)$ denotes the set of variables occurring in Φ), the models (satisfying assignments) of Φ can be obtained by considering the models of two new formulas: $\Phi \wedge x_1$ and $\Phi \wedge \neg x_1$.

By generalizing the previous principle for a subset of variables $\{x_1, \ldots, x_n\}$, the models of Φ are those of $\Psi_1, \ldots, \Psi_n$ where $\Psi_i = \Phi \wedge x_i \wedge \bigwedge_{1 \le j < i} \neg x_j$. In our case, we have $\{x_1, \ldots, x_n\} = \{p_{a_1}, \ldots, p_{a_n}\}$ and Φ corresponds to $\Phi_{\texttt{huim}}$ (or $\Phi_{\texttt{chuim}}$ for closed patterns). Consequently, solving $\Psi_i = \Phi \wedge p_{a_i} \wedge \bigwedge_{1 \le j < i} \neg p_{a_j}$ can be obtained by considering only transactions containing the item a_i. In fact, since the variable p_{a_i} is *True*, the models of Φ_i is limited to those involving p_{a_i}, that is, the itemset including a_i. Clearly, partitioning the formula into many independent sub-formulas allows for the creation of smaller and more manageable problem instances that encode subsets of the original database. By managing subsets of transactions independently, the solution process becomes more feasible, and computational challenges are mitigated. By decomposing the original problem into independent sub-formulas, each sub-formula represents a smaller, self-contained problem with its own set of constraints. These sub-formulas retain the declarative nature, as they only describe the relationships between variables and do not prescribe the order or method of solving. The order in which we solve the generated sub-problems can significantly impact the effectiveness and efficiency of the overall approach. This order can influence how the search space is explored and how quickly a solution is found. Starting from the last sub-problem $\Phi \wedge \Psi_n$ can indeed be a strategic choice, often referred to as a "last-subproblem" strategy.

5   Empirical Evaluation

In this section, we present the experiments carried out to evaluate the performance of the proposed approach to discovering various high utility patterns embedded in transaction databases. Our empirical study was performed on a Linux machine 32GB of RAM running at 2.66 GHz. We test our approaches for mining classical HUIs (the algorithm coined SATHUIM), closed HUIs (SATCHUIM), minimal (SATminHUIM) and maximal HUIs (SATmaxHUIM), frequent HUIs (SATFHUIM) and frequent local HUIs (SATFLHUIM) while varying the minimum utility, i.e., θ and support, i.e., λ thresholds. The reported runtime is in seconds and the timeout is set to one hour for each test. For our empirical evaluation, experiments were carried out on various well-known datasets taken from the SPMF[3] repository. The different characteristics of these datasets are given in Table 3: the number of transactions ($|\mathcal{D}|$) and the number of items ($|\Omega|$). The runtime of the approaches described above against these datasets are also shown in Table 3 (in Fig. 3 for SATFLHUIM approach) under the fixed threshold (either the minimum utility or minimum support).

According to our experimental results, our approaches achieve across all datasets for all the considered minimum utility threshold values (also support threshold for SATFLHUIM). Moreover, the number of patterns clearly depends on the threshold values. More specifically, this number becomes huge even for small datasets with lowest threshold values. It is easy to observe how concise representation allows for large reductions in output size. For example, for $\theta = 400k$, the number of patterns decreases from more than 428 thousand HUIs to 154 minHUIs.

As illustrated in Table 3 and Fig. 3, it is clear that the performance of all algorithms depends on the overall dataset characteristics. Moreover, the minimum support and the minimum utility thresholds δ and θ (θ') have a significant

---

[3] https://www.philippe-fournier-viger.com/spmf/index.php?link=datasets.php.

Table 3. Comparative results using different minimum utility (and support) threshold values.

Dataset	θ	SATHUIM	#HUIs	CHUIM	#CHUIs	SATMinHUIM	#minHUIs	SATMaxHUIM	#maxHUIs	δ(%)	SATFHUIM	#FHUIs
Chess (3196, 75)	400k	39.88	428023	17.93	114660	6.02	154	3.88	211	30	51.29	427979
	500k	4.94	24979	2.79	10888	2.49	92	1.67	26		6.64	24979
	600k	1.35	583	1.17	394	1	26	1.15	6		1.29	583
Retail (16470, 1030)	10k	9.17	912	9.21	912	6.51	182	10.24	272	0.2	2,78	885
	25k	5.7	165	5.5	165	3.90	36	6.08	45		1,93	165
	30k	4.95	114	4.81	114	3.44	25	5.26	37		1,85	114
Kosarak (990002, 41270)	1M	121.01	125	128.65	125	88.47	8	98,19	8	4	7.2	34
	1.2M	108.76	87	116.45	87	86.15	6	97.61	6		6.97	31
	1.3M	94.28	78	110.95	78	81.65	6	92.86	6		6.52	31
Chainstore (1112949 46086)	1M	132.7	382	117.34	382	64.10	261	120.67	307	0.6	7,27	85
	1.4M	106.49	231	96.58	231	55.52	173	99.91	189		6,55	80
	1.8M	88.78	154	81.72	154	48	126	84.91	122		6,38	73

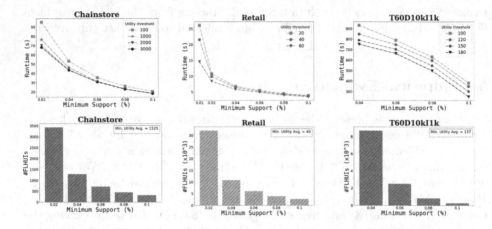

Fig. 3. Experimental results of SATFLHUIM on several datasets.

impact on the performance of the computing process of SATFHUIM and SATFLHUIM algorithms.

6 Conclusion

The suggested research developed methods for several related high utility mining problems using a SAT-based formulation. We proposed a unified framework for investigating a variety of constraints such as closedness, maximality, minimality, local utility, and frequency. Manipulation of the constraints can result in the desired patterns by adding or removing constraints according to particular requirements or preferences while offering flexibility and adaptability. Furthermore, the combination of decomposition and user-defined constraints keeps the SAT approach declarative while offering flexibility and customizability to successfully address specific real-world problems. For future consideration, more tests on other real-world datasets can be conducted to evaluate the proposed framework.

References

1. Biere, A., Heule, M., van Maaren, H.: Handbook of satisfiability. IOS press (2009)
2. Boudane, A., Jabbour, S., Sais, L., Salhi, Y.: Sat-based data mining. IJAIT, 1840002 (2018)
3. Chan, R., Yang, Q., Shen, Y.-D.: Mining high utility itemsets. In: ICDM, pp. 19–19 (2003)
4. Damon, P.: Like the PS4, Xbox One Being Built At a Loss (2013)
5. Davis, M., Logemann, G., Loveland, D.: A machine program for theorem-proving. Communications of the ACM, pp. 394–397 (1962)
6. Fournier-Viger, P., Chun-Wei Lin, J., Truong-Chi, T., Nkambou, R.: A survey of high utility itemset mining (2019)
7. Fournier-Viger, P., Chun-Wei Lin, J., Wu, C.-W., Tseng, V.S., Faghihi, U.: Mining minimal high-utility itemsets. In: DEXA (2016)
8. Fournier-Viger, P., Wu, C.-W., Tseng, V.S.: Novel concise representations of high utility itemsets using generator patterns. In: ADMA (2014)
9. Fournier-Viger, P., Zida, S., Chun-Wei Lin, J., Wu, C.-W., Tseng, V.S.: Efim-closed: fast and memory efficient discovery of closed high-utility itemsets. In: MLDM (2016)
10. Hidouri, A., Jabbour, S., Raddaoui, B.: On the enumeration of frequent high utility itemsets: a symbolic AI approach. In: CP, pp. 27:1–27:17 (2022)
11. Hölldobler, S., Manthey, N., Steinke, P.: A compact encoding of pseudo-boolean constraints into sat. In: Annual Conference on Artificial Intelligence, pp. 107–118 (2012)
12. Jabbour, S., Mhadhbi, N., Raddaoui, B., Sais, L.: Sat-based models for overlapping community detection in networks. Computing, pp. 1275–1299 (2020)
13. Jabbour, S., Mhadhbi, N., Raddaoui, B., Sais, L.: A declarative framework for maximal k-plex enumeration problems. In: AAMAS, pp. 660–668 (2022)
14. Morgado, A., Marques-Silva, J.: Algorithms for propositional model enumeration and counting (2005)
15. Wu, C.-W., Fournier-Viger, P., Gu, J.-Y., Tseng, V.S.: Mining compact high utility itemsets without candidate generation. In: High-Utility Pattern Mining: Theory, Algorithms and Applications (2019)
16. Zhang, C., Almpanidis, G., Wang, W., Liu, C.: An empirical evaluation of high utility itemset mining algorithms. Expert Systems with applications, pp. 91–115 (2018)
17. Zhang, S., Malik, S., McGeer, R.: Verification of computer switching networks: an overview. In: International Symposium on ATVA, pp. 1–16 (2012)

RDF Data Partitioning for Efficient SPARQL Query Processing with Spark SQL

Kosuke Yamasaki[1]([✉])[ID] and Toshiyuki Amagasa[1,2][ID]

[1] Graduate School of Science and Technology, University of Tsukuba,
Tsukuba, Japan
kosuke.y@kde.cs.tsukuba.ac.jp, amagasa@cs.tsukuba.ac.jp
[2] Center for Computational Sciences, University of Tsukuba, Tsukuba, Japan

Abstract. In the age of big data, the volume of RDF data has been exploding due to the growing demands for open data, including Linked Open Data (LOD), semantic data processing, and knowledge graphs. Large-scale RDF data may contain millions to hundreds of millions of triples, comprising subject, predicate, and object, making fast query processing on such datasets challenging. To address this issue, distributed parallel processing systems like Apache Spark has been successfully used. One of the key issues in such systems is to partition the data to maximize performance while balancing the load and minimizing communication between processing nodes by taking into account the dataset's characteristics and the workload. In this study, we propose a method of RDF data partitioning for efficient query processing by Spark SQL. We exploit the statistics of RDF data and the workload information representing typical user queries, allowing us to group strongly related RDF triples into the same partition. Moreover, we employ indexes whereby only the necessary partitions are loaded for answering a query, reducing the amount of data to be processed and improving query processing performance. Our evaluation experiments showed that the proposed scheme outperformed the comparative methods in table load time and query time for most benchmark queries in a single-node setting.

Keywords: RDF · data partitioning · workload · Spark SQL

1 Introduction

RDF (Resource Description Framework) [8] is a framework for expressing data in terms of triples consisting of subject, predicate, and object, and it has been extensively used in recent years due to the growing increasing demands for publishing data in a reusable way, such as LOD (Linked Open Data) or knowledge bases. To query RDF data, SPARQL [2] is one of the most popular query languages where one can specify the information needed in terms of a basic graph pattern (BGP). Generally, big RDF data contains millions to hundreds of millions of triples, and it is not easy to query such data at high speed. For this

P. Delir Haghighi et al. (Eds.): iiWAS 2023, LNCS 14416, pp. 92–106, 2023.
https://doi.org/10.1007/978-3-031-48316-5_12

reason, the demand for systems that can effectively and efficiently process large-scale RDF data has been growing. In particular, to process extremely large RDF data, a single-node computer is not sufficient, and there have been many works that try to exploit parallel-distributed processing frameworks, such as MapReduce [5] and Apache Spark [1], e.g., SPARQLGX [6], WORQ [9], S2RDF [12], and DIAERESIS [13].

One of the key challenges of these approaches is how to partition the dataset so that the performance is maximized – inappropriate data partitioning causes an unbalanced load distribution among processing nodes, resulting in performance degradation. Besides, minimizing the number of inter-node communications is desirable to attain better performance. In the case of processing a query, it would be better if necessary data for the query is stored in the local storage at the node to avoid inter-node communications.

Meanwhile, we can obtain typical workloads in terms of SPARQL queries as workload information in many systems. Such workload information allows us to extract strongly correlated data, which is useful for generating appropriate partitions for the workload.

There are several works for large-scale RDF processing. Some exploit workload information for generating RDF data partitioning for fast query processing. Adnan et al. [3] proposed a data partitioning method using workloads, where co-occurring predicates in a set of SPARQL queries are assigned to the same partition. Madkour et al. [9] also proposed a workload-based data partitioning method, aiming to minimize disk I/O and network shuffling overhead by focusing on join patterns in the query workload. Besides, Georgia [13] uses a two-stage data partitioning process exploiting the betweenness centrality for Apache Spark and Spark SQL.

Based on these research works, we propose in this study a method to achieve efficient query processing of RDF data using Spark SQL. Specifically, we propose partitioning and indexing methods that consider the co-occurrence of not only predicate but also subject and object in the workload, where we combine queried data into the same partition by introducing co-occurrence. Furthermore, using indexes, we try to reduce the amount of data to be processed. To evaluate the superiority of the proposed method, we compare it with DIAERESIS [13], the method using the betweenness centrality for schema graphs, in five aspects: data partitioning time, query execution time, data reading time, number of read triples, and the total time of query execution time and data reading time.

2 Preliminaries

2.1 RDF and SPARQL

RDF (Resource Description Framework) [8] is a framework for expressing relationships among resources. The basic construct is a triple structure of the form $(\langle s \rangle\ \langle p \rangle\ \langle o \rangle)$ using subject s, predicate p, and object o. The subject and object refer to the resources, and the predicate refers to their relationship. Any resource referenced by a triple is described by an IRI (international resource identifier), a unique identifier for a resource that allows us to identify any resource. Alternatively, a subject can be a blank node, and an object can be either a blank node or a literal.

To query RDF data, we use SPARQL (SPARQL Protocol and RDF Query Language for RDF) [2]. The basic syntax of SPARQL is similar to that of SQL. It consists of a SELECT and a WHERE clauses, where the SELECT clause describes the variables to be retrieved from the query result, and the WHERE clause describes the graph pattern to be retrieved from the RDF data, which is called BGP (basic graph pattern). Specifically, for all matches of a BGP, the values (?var) specified in the SELECT clause will be returned as a result.

2.2 Processing RDF Using Spark SQL

Apache Spark [1] is a distributed processing framework designed for large-scale data processing. It provides several APIs, including DataFrame, as a data access model for processing structural and semi-structured data, enabling flexible and high-speed parallel processing. We can use Spark SQL [4] to manipulate and query such data in a declarative way.

A straightforward way to process a SPARQL query using Spark SQL (or SQL) is as follows. First, store RDF triples with a table consisting of three attributes: subject, predicate, and object, called *triple store* [14]. Second, for a given SPARQL query, we extract the BGP. Then, we generate a join query in SQL according to the shared variables in the BGP. Besides, we convert the FILTER conditions to the conditions in the WHERE clause in the SQL query. Thus, we can convert a SPARQL query to an SQL query. Nevertheless, the size of the table storing the triples can be large, demanding an appropriate partitioning of the table to maximize the performance on Spark SQL.

3 Related Work

3.1 Workload-Based Methods

Adnan et al. [3] proposed a data partitioning method based on workloads. In their approach, they count co-occurring predicates from SPARQL queries. Given a query workload $Q = \{q_1, \ldots, q_{|Q|}\}$, where $|Q|$ represents the number of queries, the data is partitioned in such a way that predicate pairs frequently queried together are placed within the same cluster using a greedy clustering method. They store the partitioned data one by one on multiple SPARQL endpoints and process them using a federation engine, whereas this research targets a single Spark processor.

Madkour et al. [9] also proposed a workload-based data partitioning method. This approach aims to minimize disk I/O and network shuffling overhead by focusing on join patterns that are frequently repeated in multiple queries. They used a Bloom filter to reduce the number of elements in queries that require joins between multiple tables to achieve the aim. In addition, vertical partitioning of the obtained data based on subject or object is performed, and the results are cached to reduce the amount of data to be processed.

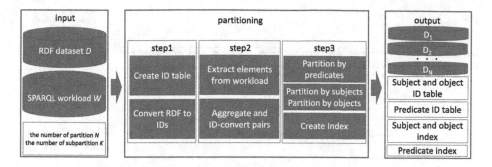

Fig. 1. An overview of the proposed scheme.

3.2 Methods Using Betweenness Centrality and Indexing

Georgia [13] uses a two-stage data partitioning process. In the first stage, betweenness centrality is computed for the schema graph of the data, and nodes with high centrality are identified as important nodes for generating the dependence used to group the non-schema nodes. In the second step, they apply a predicate-based vertical sub-partitioning so that each vertical partition contains a subject and an object for each predicate, reducing the data size of each partition. Besides, they generate indexes for these partitions so that the necessary sub-partition can be searched directly during query execution.

4   Proposed Method

In this work, we assume that the workload information (i.e., a set of SPARQL queries) is given, and the basic idea of the proposed method is to exploit the correlation among triples, thereby grouping highly correlated triples in the same partition to achieve efficient query processing in Spark SQL. Figure 1 shows an overview of the proposed scheme. It takes as input 1) RDF data D (where D is a set of RDF triples), 2) query workload $W = \{q_1, \ldots, q_{|W|}\}$ where q_i is a SPARQL query, 3) the number of partitions N, and K as the number of sub-partitions. The output consists of the RDF data partition $D_1, \ldots, D_N$ such that $D_1 \cap \cdots \cap D_N = \emptyset$, an ID table that records the relationship between data and IDs, and an index that records the path to the partition containing each piece of data.

The data partitioning process consists of three major steps. In Step 1, the data is assigned unique integer identifiers to reduce redundancy. Then, in Step 2, the subject, predicate, and object are each extracted from the workload, and the co-occurring elements are converted to IDs to create pairs. The number of occurrences of the pairs is then measured and sorted in order of frequency of occurrence. Finally, in Step 3, clustering is performed based on the number of co-occurrences of the predicates as the first segmentation. Then, for the result, in the second segmentation, two types of clustering are performed based on the

Fig. 2 queries:

```
SELECT * WHERE   SELECT * WHERE   SELECT * WHERE   SELECT * WHERE   SELECT * WHERE   SELECT * WHERE   SELECT * WHERE   SELECT * WHERE
{                {                {                {                {                {                {                {
?s p1 o1.        s1 p1 ?o.        ?s p1 o1.        ?s p1 o1.        ?s p1o1.         ?o p1 s1.        s1 p1 ?o.        ?s p1 ?o.
?s p2 o2         ?o p2 ?o2        ?s p3 o3         o1 p3 ?o3        ?s3 p3 o2        s1 p3 ?s3        s2 p2 ?o         ?s p2 ?o.
}                }                }                }                }                }                }                ?s p3 ?o.
                                                                                                                      ?s p4 ?o.
                                                                                                                      }
```

P1	P2	count
p1	p2	4
p1	p3	5
p1	p4	1
p2	p3	1
p2	p4	1
p3	p4	1

Fig. 2. Query example.   Fig. 3. Co-occurrence counts.

number of co-occurrences of the subject and the object, respectively, and the results of each type of clustering are produced as output. At the same time, indexes to the subject, predicate, and object partitions are also generated.

Notice that we use Apache Spark itself for RDF data partitioning for efficiency. For this reason, we use parallel constructs like MapReduce in the subsequent explanation.

4.1 Data Partitioning Process

Step 1: Assigning IDs. The IRIs and literals in RDF data are usually long strings that are costly to maintain and process as they are, while we mostly perform exact matches over IRIs when processing SPARQL queries. For this reason, we first convert IRIs and literals into unique IDs as integers.

Step 2: Workload Analysis. Next, we analyze the workload to extract the co-occurring pairs for the subject, predicate, and object, respectively. The input consists of the SPARQL workload W and the data-to-ID correspondence table generated in Step 1, while the output is a text summarizing each pair and its co-occurrence count.

Algorithm 1 presents the algorithm for this step. Initially, for a given workload $W = q_1, \ldots, q_{|W|}$, the WHERE clause is extracted, and the bound variables for the subject, predicate, and object are obtained from it. If there are elements containing multiple bound variables, they are converted to IDs and added to the respective co-occurrence lists $L_{sub}, L_{pre}, L_{obj}$ (Lines 2–14). The elements of these lists are tuples $p = \langle P_1, P_2 \rangle$, and the co-occurrence counts are aggregated (Lines 15–17).

For instance, when counting the co-occurrences of predicates for eight queries depicted in Fig. 2, $L_{pre} = (\langle p1, p2 \rangle, \ldots \langle p2, p4 \rangle, \langle p3, p4 \rangle)$ is obtained. Then, MapReduce aggregation is applied to it to count each pair efficiently, resulting in Fig. 3.

Step 3: Data Partitioning. Finally, we partition the dataset according to the information obtained in the previous steps. The input consists of the ID-encoded RDF dataset D_{ID}, co-occurrence counts for subjects, predicates, and

---

Algorithm 1. Workload Analysis.

Require: SPARQL workload W, Subject-object ID table ID_{so}, Predicate ID table ID_p
Ensure: Subject, predicate, and object co-occurrence counts denoted as $C_{sub}, C_{pre}, and C_{obj}$

1: Load ID_{so} and ID_p as HashMap
2: $L_{sub} := \emptyset; L_{pre} := \emptyset; L_{obj} := \emptyset$
3: **for all** $query \leftarrow W$ **do**
4:     $where = \text{extractInWhere}(query)$ ▷ Extract contents inside WHERE clause
5:     **for all** $(s, t) \leftarrow \text{extractBoundSubject}(where)$ **do**   ▷ Create subject pairs from WHERE clause
6:         $L_{sub} \leftarrow (\text{ID}_{so}(s), \text{ID}_{so}(t))$
7:     **end for**
8:     **for all** $(s, t) \leftarrow \text{extractBoundPredicate}(where)$ **do**   ▷ Create predicate pairs from WHERE clause
9:         $L_{pre} \leftarrow (\text{ID}_p(s), \text{ID}_p(t))$
10:     **end for**
11:     **for all** $(s, t) \leftarrow \text{extractBoundObject}(where)$ **do**   ▷ Create object pairs from WHERE clause
12:         $L_{obj} \leftarrow (\text{ID}_{so}(s), \text{ID}_{so}(t))$
13:     **end for**
14: **end for**
15: Convert all elements in L_{sub}, L_{pre}, and L_{obj} into ID using HashMap
16: $C_{sub} = \text{countAllPairsByMapReduce}(L_{sub})$
17: $C_{pre} = \text{countAllPairsByMapReduce}(L_{pre})$
18: $C_{obj} = \text{countAllPairsByMapReduce}(L_{obj})$
19: Output C_{sub}, C_{pre}, and C_{obj}

---

objects, denoted as C_{sub}, C_{pre}, and C_{obj}, respectively, along with the number of partitions N, and the number of subpartitions K. The output includes partitions $D_1, \ldots, D_N$ (where $D_{i_{sub1}} + \cdots + D_{i_{subK}} = D_i$, $D_{i_{obj1}} + \cdots + D_{i_{objK}} = D_i$, $D_{i_{sub1}} \cap \cdots \cap D_{i_{subK}} = \emptyset$, and $D_{i_{obj1}} \cap \cdots \cap D_{i_{objK}} = \emptyset$), subject and object indexes, and a predicate index. These indexes record in which partitions each element is contained. Figure 4 illustrates the data input/output structure in Step 3. In the proposed method, data is partitioned into two stages using the same clustering technique (Algorithm 2). So, we explain it first.

Clustering Algorithm. Initially, we make two HashMaps: a *cluster*, which records predicates belonging to each cluster, and an *Index*, which records clusters to which predicates belong. The size of a cluster, represented as t, indicates the maximum number of distinct predicates contained within a single cluster. It is computed by dividing the total number of distinct predicates by the number of partitions N (Lines 1–4). Next, the algorithm sorts each pair of predicates that co-occur in workload queries in descending order of frequency. This prioritization ensures that pairs with a stronger co-occurrence relationship, i.e., those appearing together more frequently, are considered first for clustering. This increases the likelihood that pairs with higher co-occurrence are grouped into the same cluster. The algorithm then tries to assign each pair to a cluster as follows: 1) if

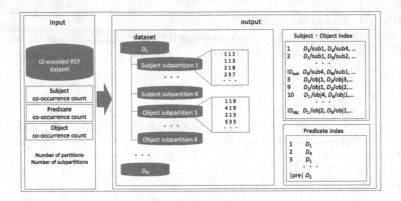

Fig. 4. Step 3 data layout.

both predicates are already assigned to either of the clusters, it does nothing; 2) if either of the predicates is assigned to one of the clusters, it assigns the other predicate to the cluster if the cluster's size is not greater than the limit t by the addition; or 3) if both predicates are not yet assigned to any cluster, it assigns the pair of predicates to the cluster with the least size. Finally, the algorithm adds predicates that could not be added in Lines 9–15 or that did not appear in the workload to the cluster with the smallest number of predicates in order. The same procedure is repeated not only for predicates but also for subjects and objects. In other words, based on the co-occurrence of predicates, each of the N partitions is further divided into K sub-partitions based on the co-occurrence of subjects and another K sub-partitions based on the co-occurrence of objects. As a result, we obtain a total of $N \times K \times 2$ partitions. Through this partitioning approach, we believe that the system can efficiently handle common query scenarios where predicates are bound, as well as cases where both the subject and the predicate, or the predicate and the object, are bound.

Step3 Details. The algorithm of Step 3 is shown in Algorithm 3. $Index_s$ and $Index_o$ are HashMaps whose keys are IDs and whose values are sets of partition numbers containing the IDs (Lines 1-2). In the first stage, the algorithm performs clustering based on predicate co-occurrence, using the entire ID-encoded RDF data, predicate co-occurrence counts, and the number of partitions as input for the clustering function (Line 3). In the second stage, the resulting clusters are used as input datasets, and the clustering is applied separately to the subject and object data. The resulting partitions are sequentially outputted in parquet format, and the Index is updated (Lines 4–15). Upon completion of all data partitions, the index is saved as well, and the process terminates.

4.2 Query Processing

When processing a user-given SPARQL query, we convert it so that Spark SQL can process it. More precisely, we assign IDs to bound variables during query

---

Algorithm 2. Clustering(D_{ID}, Co-occurrences$elem$, N)

Require: ID-encoded RDF dataset DID, Co-occurrence counts Co-occurrences$_{elem}$, ▷
elem is either subject, predicate, or object Number of partitions N
Ensure: Partitioned datasets $D_1, \ldots, D_N$, Index
1: cluster = $((0, \emptyset), \ldots, (N - 1, \emptyset))$: HashMap;   ▷ Record elements contained in each
    cluster
2: Index: HashMap;   ▷ Record the cluster to which an element belongs
3: t = $|\text{distinct}(elem)|/N$ ▷ The number of types of elem in one cluster
4: **for all** $(p_1, p_2) \leftarrow$ Co-occurrences **do**
5:     **if** p_1 in Index AND p_2 in Index **then**
6:         continue
7:     **end if**
8:     **if** One of them already belongs to a cluster **then**
9:         Let p_1 already belong to a cluster
10:        clusterNo = Index(p_1)
11:        **if** $|\text{cluster}(\text{clusterNo})| + 1 \leq$ t **then**   ▷ Compare the number of elem types
    after addition with t
12:            cluster(clusterNo) $\leftarrow p_2$
13:            Index(p_2) $\leftarrow$ clusterNo
14:        **end if**
15:    **end if**
16:    **if** Neither belongs to a cluster **then**
17:        clusterNo = cluster with the fewest number of elem
18:        cluster(clusterNo) $\leftarrow p_1, p_2$
19:        Index(p_1) $\leftarrow$ clusterNo
20:        Index(p_2) $\leftarrow$ clusterNo
21:    **end if**
22: **end for**
23: **for all** $p \leftarrow$ remaining elements **do**
24:    clusterNo = cluster with the fewest number of elem
25:    cluster(clusterNo) $\leftarrow p$
26:    Index$_p(p) \leftarrow$ clusterNo
27: **end for**
28: Output Index, cluster

---

conversion and, at the same time, identify partitions to be read in advance by using indexes created at the time of data partitioning, thereby reducing the amount of data to be read and enabling efficient query processing.

The system takes as input 1) the SPARQL query and 2) each index and ID table and outputs 1) a file containing the path to the file to be read, 2) the name of the table to be read, and 3) converted SQL. Note that the output is written in a single file.

The flow of the conversion process is as follows:

1. Extract triple patterns in WHERE clause from SPARQL query Q.
2. For each triple $(q_1, \ldots, q_{|Q|})$, apply the following process.
   (a) Extract the bound variables in triple q_i.

Algorithm 3. Data Partitioning Algorithm.

Require: ID-encoded RDF dataset D_{ID}, Subject co-occurrence counts Co-occurrences$_{sub}$, Predicate co-occurrence counts Co-occurrences$_{pre}$, Object co-occurrence counts Co-occurrences$_{obj}$, Number of partitions N, Number of sub-partitions K

Ensure: N partitions $D_1, \ldots, D_N$,
Subject index Index$_s$, Predicate index Index$_p$, Object index Index$_o$

1: Index$_s := ((\text{subject}_1, \emptyset), \ldots, (\text{subject}_{|subject|}, \emptyset))$: HashMap;
2: Index$_o := ((\text{object}_1, \emptyset), \ldots, (\text{object}_{|object|}, \emptyset))$: HashMap;
3: firstPartition, Index$_p$ = clustering(D_{ID}, Co-occurrences$_{pre}$, N)
4: **for all** partition ← firstPartition **do**
5:     secondPartition, Index = clustering(partition, Co-occurrences$_{sub}$, K)
6:     Output secondPartition
7:     **for all** (e, p) ← Index **do**
8:         Index$_s$(e) ← p
9:     **end for**
10:    secondPartition, Index = clustering(partition, Co-occurrences$_{obj}$, K)
11:    Output secondPartition
12:    **for all** (e, p) ← Index **do**
13:        Index$_o$(e) ← p
14:    **end for**
15: **end for**
16: Output Index$_s$, Index$_p$, Index$_o$

    (b) Determine the path to the file to be read based on the index and determine the table name.

    (c) Create a SQL subquery with the table name in the FROM clause, the bound variable in the WHERE clause, the unbound variable in the SELECT clause, and the result as table_i by the AS clause.

3. Specify the resulting $|Q|$ SQL subqueries in the FROM clause and specify the variables specified in the SELECT clause of the SPARQL query as variables in the SQL, creating the SQL WHERE clause based on the union of the unbound variables in the WHERE clause of the SPARQL query and output the resulting SQL, the path to the file to be read, and the table name together.

    The table name in Step 2(b) above is specified from the path to the file, and the table name is always the same if the paths are the same. The same paths and table names are consolidated. Therefore, if there are multiple SQL subqueries with the same path combination, only one table needs to be created for all of them, reducing the data loading time and the amount of data to be loaded. For queries with a WHERE clause composed of patterns like s1 ?p1 ?o1 and s2 ?p2 ?o2, the results for each subquery might be distributed across multiple files. If the results for one subquery pattern are found in file1, file2, and file4, and for another subquery pattern in file4, file5, and file6, the conversion process would group files 1, 2, and 4 into one table, and 4, 5, and 6 into another. This could lead to duplication of data from file4. Additionally, since indexes are created for all data in the set, if there's no index for a bound variable in a subquery, it indicates no matching data. In our speed evaluation, we queried such a subquery using a prepared empty table as the file to be read.

5   Performance Study

5.1   Setup

The experiments were conducted on a server equipped with an AMD EPYC 7502P 32-Core Processor and 128 GB RAM. This server was running Apache Spark (3.3.1) on Ubuntu 18.04.5 LTS. Please note that these experiments were carried out in a single-node setup. We intend to conduct experiments in a distributed environment as part of our future work. For our proposed method, we allocated 32 GB of both driver and executor memory, with an exception during the ID assignment phase where 50 GB was allocated. The number of partitions for the proposed method was set to 5 in the first stage and increased to 20 in the second stage. As a comparative baseline, we employed the DIAERESIS method [13], allocating 10 GB for both driver and executor memory.

5.2   Datasets

We employed the following two datasets:

LUBM. The Lehigh University Benchmark (LUBM) [7] is a synthetic data generator that takes the number of universities as a parameter and is widely used as a benchmark for RDF database systems. In our experiments, we created a dataset with a parameter value of 100, resulting in a data size of 2.37 GB and 13.8 million triples. We used 13 queries provided by the benchmark for the workload and performance evaluation.

SWDF. The Semantic Web Dog Food (SWDF) [10] is a real-world RDF dataset containing metadata from Semantic Web conferences about people, papers, and presentations. This dataset has a size of 50 MB and contains 304,583 triples. For workload and performance evaluation, we used 207 queries, which were taken from those used in the comparative method DIAERESIS. These queries were generated by the FEASIBLE benchmark generator [11] based on actual query logs.

5.3   Performance Measures

We use the following metrics for performance evaluation. Note that the time taken to convert SPARQL to SQL was not compared, as the comparison method did not measure it within the program. The reported times are the average of 5 executions.

- Preprocessing time: The time it takes to output the partitioned data.
- Query execution time: The time it takes from executing the SQL to obtaining the results.
- Table creation cost: The number of triples in the loaded data and the time it takes to create the table.
- Total time: The sum of the query execution and table creation time.

Table 1. Preprocessing time (ID conversion time and partitioning time in parentheses).

Method	Time	Data size
LUBM(13.4M triples)		
DIAERESIS	16.38 ± 0.30 min	762MB
Proposed method(with ID)	28.31 ±0.39 min (14.46 + 13.85)	199MB
Proposed method(without ID)	38.44 ±0.87 min	406 MB
SWDF(30.4K triples)		
DIAERESIS	1.80 ±0.02 min	14 MB
Proposed method(with ID)	1.27 ±0.03 min (0.20 + 1.07)	6.6 MB
Proposed method(without ID)	3.06 ±0.07 min	64 MB

Table 2. Average ratio of query execution times normalized to the comparison method.

Dataset	DIAERESIS	Proposed method (with ID)	Proposed method (without ID)
LUBM	1	0.80	0.95
SWDF	1	0.51	0.96

5.4   Results

Preprocessing Time. The preprocessing time is measured from when the original RDF dataset is input until the partitioned data is output. In addition to DIAERESIS, we compared the proposed method without ID conversion to evaluate its effectiveness. Table 1 summarizes the results.

When we see the time for the proposed method with and without IDs, the results show that the method with IDs is significantly better for all data sets. This confirms that converting data to IDs can significantly improve preprocessing efficiency. When comparing the processing times of the proposed method (with IDs) and DIAERESIS, the latter is faster for LUBM, while the proposed method is faster for SWDF. Additionally, when considering data size, the proposed method results in smaller sizes for both datasets and the difference is even more pronounced between using and not using IDs.

Query Execution Time. The query execution time measures only the SQL execution time. Table 2 shows the ratio of the average query execution times for all benchmark queries when DIAERESIS is set to 1.0. For LUBM, the proposed method (with ID) improves the performance by 20%, while, for SWDF, it improves the performance by 49%. On the other hand, the proposed method (without ID) also performs 5% faster on LUBM and 4% faster on SWDF than the comparison method.

Looking at the individual queries used in LUBM and their execution times in detail (Fig. 5), we can observe that the proposed method (with ID) is faster

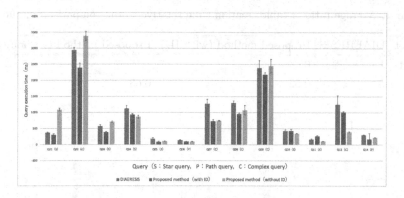

Fig. 5. Query execution time for LUBM.

Table 3. Average ratio of loaded triples relative to DIAERESIS.

Dataset	DIAERESIS	Proposed method (with ID)	Proposed method (without ID)
LUBM	1	2.01	2.59
SWDF	1	1.82	2.03

than DIAERESIS for 12 out of 13 queries. The difference is significant for Q2 and Q7, indicating that the proposed method (with ID) can efficiently handle complex queries.

A detailed breakdown of the comparison between the proposed method (with ID) and DIAERESIS for SWDF shows that the proposed method (with ID) outperforms DIAERESIS for 155 queries, successfully reducing processing time by an average of 73% and a maximum of 90%. On the other hand, the proposed method (with ID) was inferior to DIAERESIS in 52 queries, with an average of 23% and a maximum of 46%. These results demonstrate that the proposed method achieves significant performance improvement in many cases, although it is inferior to the comparison method for some queries.

Temporal Table Creation Cost. Both the proposed and DIAERESIS use indexes to identify the necessary data in advance, allowing us to access the minimum amount of data quickly. We investigate the cost of (temporal) table creation by examining the amount of data (number of triples) read during table creation and the time taken to create the table after reading the data.

Table 3 shows the average number of triples read by the proposed method when the number of triples read by DIAERESIS is set to 1.0 for each dataset. On average, the proposed method reads more triples for each dataset than the comparison method.

A detailed examination of the 13 queries for LUBM reveals that the proposed method tends to read a particularly large number of triples for complex queries. We also analyzed 207 queries for SWDF and found that the proposed method

Table 4. Average ratio of table creation time relative to the comparison method.

Dataset	DIAERESIS	Proposed method (with ID)	Proposed method (without ID)
LUBM	1	0.66	1.48
SWDF	1	0.52	0.68

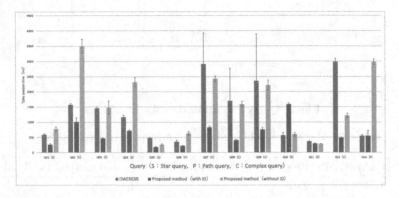

Fig. 6. Table creation time for LUBM.

read fewer triples than DIAERESIS for 113 queries, which is more than half of the 207 queries. These findings suggest that the proposed method reads many triples for queries containing specific patterns.

Table 4 presents a comparison of the average table creation times. The proposed method (with ID) completes the table creation more than 30% faster than the comparison method on all datasets.

Detailed data for LUBM (Fig. 6) shows that the proposed method (with ID) performs as well as the comparison method in Q14 and significantly worse in Q10, but significantly better in all other queries. Furthermore, the standard deviation shows that the table creation time tends to be more stable than that of the other methods. The proposed method (without ID) is faster than DIAERESIS for six queries. However, the difference is significant compared to the proposed method (with ID), suggesting the advantage of using ID. In SWDF, the proposed method (with ID) is faster than the comparison method in 205 out of 207 queries, and the difference in the remaining two queries is at most 19%, showing overall good performance.

Table 5. Average ratio of total time relative to the comparison method.

Dataset	DIAERESIS	Proposed method (with ID)	Proposed method (without ID)
LUBM	1	0.71	1.26
SWDF	1	0.47	0.84

Total Time. A comparison of the total query time, which includes both table creation and execution, is presented. Table 5 displays the average time ratio, with the comparison method's time set to 1.

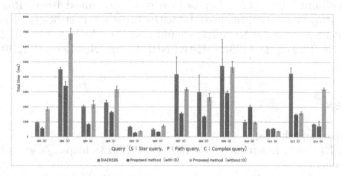

Fig. 7. Total time for LUBM.

The proposed method (with ID) shows consistent performance in both query execution time and table creation time and is the best in total time. In particular, the proposed method is more than 50% faster than the comparison method for SWDF, demonstrating its superior performance.

Figure 7 shows the breakdown for each query, revealing that Q11 performs at a similar level to the comparison method, while Q10 is about twice as slow. However, for all other queries, the proposed method significantly outperforms the comparison method, achieving a maximum speedup of approximately 75%. In SWDF, the proposed method (with ID) completed 198 queries faster than the comparison method, with a maximum difference of about 95%. Conversely, the total time for nine queries was inferior to that of the comparison method. Still, the difference was at most 15%, suggesting that the performance did not significantly drop compared to the comparison method.

6   Conclusions

This paper has presented a Spark-based method for efficiently partitioning and processing RDF data. By examining the co-occurrence of input workload queries, we placed related data in the same partition, enhancing the efficiency of data retrieval. An index was also introduced, which tracks each piece of data and its associated partition. Our experiments demonstrated that our approach surpassed existing techniques in a single-node context, primarily due to enhanced data access, the reduction of read triples leveraging co-occurrence, and the elimination of redundancy through IDs. Nevertheless, certain subquery structures resulted in reading duplicate data.

We try to adopt the algorithm to enhance DataFrame scalability. Our future endeavors will focus on testing in AWS-based distributed environments, incorporating larger datasets such as DBpedia, and refining the query order and handling of duplicate data reads based on statistical data. Moreover, we are committed to deepening our understanding of the ramifications of both the volume and the quality of the workload.

Acknowledgement. This paper is based on results obtained from "Research and Development Project of the Enhanced Infrastructures for Post-5G Information and Communication Systems" (JPNP20017) commissioned by NEDO, JST CREST Grant Number JPMJCR22M2, and JSPS KAKENHI Grant Numbers JP22H03694 and JP23H03399.

References

1. https://spark.apache.org
2. SPARQL 1.1 Query Language. Tech. rep., W3C (2013). https://www.w3.org/TR/sparql11-query
3. Akhter, A., Saleem, M., Bigerl, A., Ngomo, A.C.N.: Efficient RDF knowledge graph partitioning using querying workload. K-CAP 2021 (2021)
4. Apache: spark SQL guide. https://spark.apache.org/docs/latest/sql-distributed-sql-engine-spark-sql-cli.html
5. Dean, J., Ghemawat, S.: MapReduce: simplified data processing on large clusters (2004)
6. Graux, D., Jachiet, L., Genevès, P., Layaïda, N.: SPARQLGX: efficient distributed evaluation of SPARQL with apache spark. In: Groth, P., et al. (eds.) ISWC 2016. LNCS, vol. 9982, pp. 80–87. Springer, Cham (2016). https://doi.org/10.1007/978-3-319-46547-0_9
7. Guo, Y., Pan, Z., Heflin, J.: LUBM: a benchmark for owl knowledge base systems. J. Web Semant. **3**(2–3), 158–182 (2005). https://doi.org/10.1016/j.websem.2005.06.005
8. Klyne, G.: Resource description framework (rdf): concepts and abstract syntax. https://www.w3.org/TR/2004/REC-rdf-concepts-20040210/ (2004)
9. Madkour, A., Aly, A.M., Aref, W.G.: WORQ: workload-driven RDF query processing. In: Vrandečić, D., et al. (eds.) ISWC 2018. LNCS, vol. 11136, pp. 583–599. Springer, Cham (2018). https://doi.org/10.1007/978-3-030-00671-6_34
10. Möller, K., Heath, T., Handschuh, S., Domingue, J.: Recipes for semantic web dog food—the ESWC and ISWC Metadata projects. In: Aberer, K., et al. (eds.) ASWC/ISWC -2007. LNCS, vol. 4825, pp. 802–815. Springer, Heidelberg (2007). https://doi.org/10.1007/978-3-540-76298-0_58
11. Saleem, M., Mehmood, Q., Ngonga Ngomo, A.C.: FEASIBLE: a feature-based SPARQL benchmark generation framework. In: Arenas, M., et al. (eds.) ISWC 2015. LNCS, vol. 9366, pp. 52–69. Springer, Cham (2015). https://doi.org/10.1007/978-3-319-25007-6_4
12. Schätzle, A., Przyjaciel-Zablocki, M., Skilevic, S., Lausen, G.: S2RDF: RDF querying with SPARQL on spark. arXiv preprint arXiv:1512.07021 (2015)
13. Troullinou, G., Agathangelos, G., Kondylakis, H., Stefanidis, K., Plexousakis, D.: DIAERESIS: RDF data partitioning and query processing on spark, 07 October 2022. https://www.semantic-web-journal.net/content/diaeresis-rdf-data-partitioning-and-query-processing-spark
14. Wylot, M., Hauswirth, M., Cudré-Mauroux, P., Sakr, S.: RDF data storage and query processing schemes: a survey. ACM Comput. Surv. **51**(4), 1–36 (2018). https://doi.org/10.1145/3177850

A Comparative Evaluation of Additive Separability Tests for Physics-Informed Machine Learning

Zi-Yu Khoo[1]([✉]), Jonathan Sze Choong Low[2], and Stéphane Bressan[1,3]

[1] National University of Singapore, 21 Lower Kent Ridge Rd,
Singapore 119077, Singapore
khoozy@comp.nus.edu.sg, steph@nus.edu.sg
[2] Singapore Institute of Manufacturing Technology, Agency for Science,
Technology and Research (A*STAR), Singapore 138634, Singapore
sclow@simtech.a-star.edu.sg
[3] CNRS@CREATE LTD, 1 Create Way, Singapore 138602, Singapore

Abstract. Many functions characterizing physical systems are additively separable. This is the case, for instance, of mechanical Hamiltonian functions in physics, population growth equations in biology, and consumer preference and utility functions in economics. We consider the scenario in which a surrogate of a function is to be tested for additive separability. The detection that the surrogate is additively separable can be leveraged to improve further learning. Hence, it is beneficial to have the ability to test for such separability in surrogates. The mathematical approach is to test if the mixed partial derivative of the surrogate is zero; or empirically, lower than a threshold. We present and comparatively and empirically evaluate the eight methods to compute the mixed partial derivative of a surrogate function.

Keywords: Second-order bias · inductive bias · symbolic regression

1 Introduction

Many functions characterizing physical systems are *additively separable*, such as mechanical Hamiltonian functions in physics [16], population growth equations in biology [13], and consumer preference and utility functions in economics [26].

We consider the scenario in which a machine learning model is learning a surrogate of a function without the information that it is additively separable. Testing the surrogate for the property of additive separability is of interest. Physics-informed neural networks [10] combine the universal function approximation capability of neural networks [9] with the information of the symbolic properties, laws, and constraints of the underlying application domain [6,14,15,23,27]. With information regarding the additive separability of the function, physics-informed neural networks can leverage the additive separability property to improve further learning of the surrogate [11].

The mathematical approach to test for additive separability is to check if the mixed partial derivative of the surrogate is zero. Empirically, the mixed partial derivative of the surrogate should be lower than a small threshold close to zero.

© The Author(s), under exclusive license to Springer Nature Switzerland AG 2023
P. Delir Haghighi et al. (Eds.): iiWAS 2023, LNCS 14416, pp. 107–120, 2023.
https://doi.org/10.1007/978-3-031-48316-5_13

Information regarding the additive separability of a surrogate has seen several usages in physics-informed machine learning applications. In modelling Hamiltonian dynamics, for instance, Gruver et al., in [7] argue that almost all improvement of existing works [2] is due to a second-order bias. This second-order bias results from the additive separability of the modelled Hamiltonian into the system's potential and kinetic energy as functions of position and momentum, respectively. The additive separability allowed the physics-informed neural network to "*avoid[...] artificial complexity from its coordinate system*" (the input variables) and improve its performance [7]. In symbolic regression, Udrescu and Tegmark iteratively test an unknown function for additive separability to divide a symbolic regression problem into two simpler ones that can be tackled separately. This "*guarantee[s] that more accurate symbolic expressions [are] closer to the truth*", improving the performance of the symbolic regression algorithm [24]. Our work to test for additive separability creates the opportunity to leverage additive separability to improve the learning of surrogates as observed in the works of Gruver and Udrescu.

We introduce eight methods to compute the mixed partial derivative of a machine learning model, specifically a multilayer perceptron neural network learning a surrogate of a function. Our surrogate of choice is the multilayer perceptron neural network, although theoretically, any differentiable machine learning model will suffice. The first four of the eight methods compute the mixed partial derivative via finite difference of the multilayer perception neural network. Three methods arise from the different methods to automatically compute mixed partial derivatives using automatic differentiation of the multilayer perceptron neural network. The last method arises from the symbolic differentiation of a multilayer perceptron neural network. We present and comparatively and empirically evaluate the performance of eight methods in computing the mixed partial derivative of the surrogate functions.

The remainder of this paper is structured as follows. Section 2 presents the necessary background for additive separability and multilayer perception neural network surrogates. Section 3 presents the eight methods to compute the mixed partial derivative of a multilayer perception neural network. Section 4 presents and discusses the results of an empirical comparative evaluation of the eight methods. Section 5 concludes the paper.

2   Background and Related Work

2.1   Additive Separability

An additively separable real function $f(\vec{x}, \vec{y}) \in \mathbb{R}$ is of the form $f(\vec{x}, \vec{y}) = g(\vec{x}) + h(\vec{y})$, where $\vec{x} \in \mathbb{R}^n$, $\vec{y} \in \mathbb{R}^m$ are vectors representing disjoint subsets of $\mathbb{R}^{m+n}$ input variables and $g(\vec{x}), f(\vec{y}) \in \mathbb{R}$. x_n and y_m denote elements of $\vec{x}$ and $\vec{y}$.

The necessary and sufficient condition for a function to be additively separable is that the mixed partial derivative of the function equals zero. The mixed partial derivative is the second derivative of the function. The first derivative is taken with respect to an element in either $\vec{x}$ or $\vec{y}$, and the second derivative is taken with respect to an element in either $\vec{y}$ or $\vec{x}$. This condition is shown in Eq. 1, where the mixed partial derivative is found with respect to x_n, an element in $\vec{x}$ first, then y_m, an element in $\vec{y}$.

$$\frac{\partial^2 f(\vec{x}, \vec{y})}{\partial x_n \partial y_m} = \frac{\partial}{\partial y_m}\left(\frac{\partial(g(\vec{x}) + h(\vec{y}))}{\partial x_n}\right) = \frac{\partial}{\partial y_m}\left(\frac{\partial g(\vec{x})}{\partial x_n}\right) = 0 \qquad (1)$$

Finite difference methods refer to those that obtain a numerical solution for partial derivatives by replacing the derivatives with their appropriate numerical differentiation formulae. In general, a finite difference approximation of the value of some derivative of a scalar function $f(x)$ at a point in its domain relies on a suitable combination of sampled function values at its nearby points [17].

Starting with the first-order derivative, the simplest finite difference approximation for a multivariate function $f(\vec{x}, \vec{y})$ is the ordinary difference quotient shown in Eq. 2 where the function $f(\cdot)$ is sampled at $f(\vec{x}, \vec{y})|_{x_n=x_N+h}$ and $f(\vec{x}, \vec{y})|_{x_n=x_N}$ and all other elements are kept constant. x_N is a scalar sample of the element x_n in $\vec{x}$, and h is the scalar distance between the two samples of x_n. Indeed, if $f(\cdot)$ is differentiable at x_N then $\frac{\partial f(\vec{x}, \vec{y})}{\partial x}|_{x=x_N}$ is by definition, the limit, as $h \to 0$ of the finite difference quotients [17].

$$\frac{\partial f(\vec{x}, \vec{y})}{\partial \vec{x}}\Big|_{x_n=x_N} = \frac{f(\vec{x}, \vec{y})|_{x_n=x_N+h} - f(\vec{x}, \vec{y})|_{x_n=x_N}}{h} \qquad (2)$$

The finite difference for a multivariate function is analogous to partial derivatives in several variables. The finite difference analogue of Eq. 1 is shown in Eq. 3. The components of the numerator of Eq. 3 are defined in Eqs. 4 to 7. x_N and y_M are scalar samples of elements x_n and y_m respectively, and h and k are scalar. All other elements are kept constant.

$$\frac{\partial^2 f(\vec{x}, \vec{y})}{\partial x_n \partial y_m}\Big|_{\substack{x_n=x_N \\ y_m=y_M}}$$
$$= \frac{f(x_N + h, y_M + k) - f(x_N + h, y_M) - f(x_N, y_M + k) + f(x_N, y_M)}{h \times k} \qquad (3)$$

$$f(x_N + h, y_M + k) = f(\vec{x}, \vec{y})|_{x_n=x_N+h, y_m=y_M+k} \qquad (4)$$
$$f(x_N + h, y_M) = f(\vec{x}, \vec{y})|_{x_n=x_N+h, y_m=y_M} \qquad (5)$$
$$f(x_N, y_M + k) = f(\vec{x}, \vec{y})|_{x_n=x_N, y_m=y_M+k} \qquad (6)$$
$$f(x_N, y_M) = f(\vec{x}, \vec{y})|_{x_n=x_N, y_m=y_M} \qquad (7)$$

Seminal works that test for additive separability of a function make use of the finite difference of the function. Udrescu et al. [24] and Bellenot [1] state that for a function to be additively separable, for every pair of samples (x_a, y_a) and (x_b, y_b) where x is to be additively separable from y, the difference between the two pairwise sums of the values of the function at diagonally opposite corners of the rectangle $\langle(x_a, y_a), (x_b, y_a), (x_b, y_b), (x_a, y_b)\rangle$ equals zero [1,24]. This is shown for a bivariate function $f(x, y)$ in Eq. 8.

$$\forall x_a, x_b \in x \quad \forall y_a, y_b \in y$$
$$(f(x_a, y_a) + f(x_b, y_b)) - (f(x_a, y_b) + f(x_b, y_a)) = 0 \qquad (8)$$

Eq. 8 and Eq. 3 are equivalent in the case where Eq. 3 describes a bivariate function with the inputs x_N and y_M, after substituting $x_N = x_a$, $x_N + h = x_b$, $y_M = y_a$, $y_M + k = y_b$, and $h = k = 1$.

Equation 8 can be generalized to test multivariate functions for additive separability. A multivariate function $f(\vec{x}, \vec{y})$ is additive separable if Eq. 8 holds, and all elements of $\vec{x}$ and $\vec{y}$ except x_N and y_M are kept constant.

The set of additively separable functions is closed under operations including addition, multiplication by constants, partial derivatives, and integrals with respect to either of the disjoint subsets of input variables [1]. Therefore a test for additive separability only has to decompose a function into two components and can be applied repeatedly to a function that is multiply additively separable.

Several other tests for additive separability have been proposed in the literature, in particular in economics. These tests make assumptions that limit their applicability to specific families of functions. The seminal work of Leontief [12] proposed a test for additive separability for functions with three or more variables and non-zero first derivatives. Gorman [5], Varian [25], Diewert and Parkan [3] and Fleissig and Whitney [4] developed tests for additive separability that were specific to concave and monotonic functions. Polisson, Quah and Renou [21] and Polisson [20] developed tests for additive separability that assume non-satiation or a positive correlation between the input variables and output of a function.

2.2   Multilayer Perceptron Neural Network Surrogates

Multilayer perceptrons are regression tools [8] that are universal function approximators [9]. They can approximate any function to any degree of accuracy from one finite dimensional space to another.

We consider a multilayer perceptron neural network with one input layer, one hidden layer, and one output layer. The multilayer perception neural network regresses an output, shown in Eq. 9. In Eq. 9, the neural network has two inputs, x_1 and x_2, and one output, $f(x_1, x_2)$. σ_1 and σ_2 are the activation functions for the input and hidden layer respectively. F^{T} is the 3 by 2 weight matrix of the input layer, G^{T} is the 3 by 3 weight matrix of the hidden layer, and H^{T} is the 1 by 3 weight matrix of the output layer. B is the 1 by 3 bias matrix of the input layer, and C is the 1 by 3 bias matrix of the hidden layer. The elements of F^{T}, G^{T}, H^{T}, B and C are denoted by w, v, n, b and c respectively. Their subscripts indicate the row and column of the element in the matrix. The output of the input layer is denoted as W.

$$f(x_1, x_2) = n_1\sigma_2(v_{11}\sigma_1(W_1) + v_{12}\sigma_1(W_2) + v_{13}\sigma_1(W_3) + c_1)$$
$$+ n_2\sigma_2(v_{21}\sigma_1(W_1) + v_{22}\sigma_1(W_2) + v_{23}\sigma_1(W_3) + c_2)$$
$$+ n_3\sigma_2(v_{31}\sigma_1(W_1) + v_{32}\sigma_1(W_2) + v_{33}\sigma_1(W_3) + c_3) \tag{9}$$

where the outputs of the input layer are denoted as W and their subscripts enumerate the three outputs of the layer.

$$W_1 = w_{11}x_1 + w_{12}x_2 + b_1$$
$$W_2 = w_{21}x_1 + w_{22}x_2 + b_2$$
$$W_3 = w_{31}x_1 + w_{32}x_2 + b_3 \tag{10}$$

In the context of additively separable functions and their mixed partial derivatives, the derivatives of the output of the multilayer perceptron neural network should be considered. The first derivative of the output of the multilayer perceptron neural network, $f(x_1, x_2)$, with respect to its input, x_1, is computed in Eq. 11. σ'_{1,x_1} and σ'_{2,x_1} is the first derivative of the activation functions σ_1 and σ_2 with respect to x_1. The output of the hidden layer is denoted as V.

$$\frac{\partial f(x_1, x_2)}{\partial x_1}$$
$$= n_1\sigma'_{2,x_1}(V_1) \times (v_{11}w_{11}\sigma'_{1,x_1}(W_1) + v_{12}w_{21}\sigma'_{1,x_1}(W_2) + v_{13}w_{31}\sigma'_{1,x_1}(W_3))$$
$$+ n_2\sigma'_{2,x_1}(V_2) \times (v_{21}w_{11}\sigma'_{1,x_1}(W_1) + v_{22}w_{21}\sigma'_{1,x_1}(W_2) + v_{23}w_{31}\sigma'_{1,x_1}(W_3))$$
$$+ n_3\sigma'_{2,x_1}(V_3) \times (v_{31}w_{11}\sigma'_{1,x_1}(W_1) + v_{32}w_{21}\sigma'_{1,x_1}(W_2) + v_{33}w_{31}\sigma'_{1,x_1}(W_3))$$
$$\tag{11}$$

where

$$V_1 = v_{11}\sigma_1(W_1) + v_{12}\sigma_1(W_2) + v_{13}\sigma_1(W_3) + c_1$$
$$V_2 = v_{21}\sigma_1(W_1) + v_{22}\sigma_1(W_2) + v_{23}\sigma_1(W_3) + c_2$$
$$V_3 = v_{31}\sigma_1(W_1) + v_{32}\sigma_1(W_2) + v_{33}\sigma_1(W_3) + c_3$$

The mixed partial derivative of the multilayer perceptron neural network is shown in Eq. 12 where σ'_{1,x_1}, σ'_{1,x_2}, σ'_{2,x_1} and σ'_{2,x_2} are the first derivatives for the activation functions for the input and hidden layer with respect to x_1 and x_2 respectively, and σ''_1 and σ''_2 are the second derivatives for the activation functions for the input and hidden layer with respect to both x_1 and x_2 respectively.

$$\frac{\partial^2 f(x_1, x_2)}{\partial x_1 \partial x_2}$$
$$= n_1\sigma''_2(V_1) \times (VW_{1,x_1}) \times (VW_{1,x_2}) + n_1\sigma'_{2,x_1}(V_1) \times (VW''_1)$$
$$= n_2\sigma''_2(V_2) \times (VW_{2,x_1}) \times (VW_{2,x_2}) + n_2\sigma'_{2,x_1}(V_2) \times (VW''_2)$$
$$= n_3\sigma''_2(V_3) \times (VW_{3,x_1}) \times (VW_{3,x_2}) + n_3\sigma'_{2,x_1}(V_3) \times (VW''_3) \tag{12}$$

where VW'_{1,x_1}, VW'_{1,x_2}, VW'_{2,x_1}, VW'_{2,x_2}, VW'_{3,x_1}, VW'_{3,x_2}, VW''_1, VW''_2 and VW''_3 are computed using the chain rule.

$$VW'_{1,x_1} = v_{11} \times w_{11} \times \sigma'_{1,x_1}(W_1) + v_{12} \times w_{21} \times \sigma'_{1,x_1}(W_2) + v_{13} \times w_{31} \times \sigma'_{1,x_1}(W_3)$$

$$VW'_{1,x_2} = v_{11} \times w_{21} \times \sigma'_{1,x_2}(W_1) + v_{12} \times w_{22} \times \sigma'_{1,x_2}(W_2) + v_{13} \times w_{32} \times \sigma'_{1,x_2}(W_3)$$

$$VW''_1 = v_{11} \times w_{11} \times w_{12} \times \sigma''_1(W_1) + v_{12} \times w_{21} \times w_{22} \times \sigma''_1(W_2)$$
$$+ v_{13} \times w_{31} \times w_{32} \times \sigma''_1(W_3)$$

$$VW'_{2,x_1} = v_{21} \times w_{11} \times \sigma'_{1,x_1}(W_1) + v_{22} \times w_{21} \times \sigma'_{1,x_1}(W_2) + v_{23} \times w_{31} \times \sigma'_{1,x_1}(W_3)$$

$$VW'_{2,x_2} = v_{21} \times w_{21} \times \sigma'_{1,x_2}(W_1) + v_{22} \times w_{22} \times \sigma'_{1,x_2}(W_2) + v_{23} \times w_{32} \times \sigma'_{1,x_2}(W_3)$$

$$VW''_2 = v_{21} \times w_{11} \times w_{12} \times \sigma''_1(W_1) + v_{22} \times w_{21} \times w_{22} \times \sigma''_1(W_2)$$
$$+ v_{23} \times w_{31} \times w_{32} \times \sigma''_1(W_3)$$

$$VW'_{3,x_1} = v_{31} \times w_{11} \times \sigma'_{1,x_1}(W_1) + v_{32} \times w_{21} \times \sigma'_{1,x_1}(W_2) + v_{33} \times w_{31} \times \sigma'_{1,x_1}(W_3)$$

$$VW'_{3,x_2} = v_{31} \times w_{21} \times \sigma'_{1,x_2}(W_1) + v_{32} \times w_{22} \times \sigma'_{1,x_2}(W_2) + v_{33} \times w_{32} \times \sigma'_{1,x_2}(W_3)$$

$$VW''_3 = v_{31} \times w_{11} \times w_{12} \times \sigma''_1(W_1) + v_{32} \times w_{21} \times w_{22} \times \sigma''_1(W_2)$$
$$+ v_{33} \times w_{31} \times w_{32} \times \sigma''_1(W_3)$$

3   Methodology

We consider the scenario in which a machine learning model is a surrogate of a function without the information regarding additive separability of the function. The surrogate is a multilayer perceptron neural network that learns a multivariate function $f(\vec{x}, \vec{y})$. We design eight methods to compute the mixed partial derivative of the surrogate, to test the surrogate, and hence the unknown function, for additive separability. This section describes the design of the eight methods.

The first four methods compute the mixed partial derivative via finite difference. Three methods arise from the different methods to automatically compute mixed partial derivatives using automatic differentiation of the surrogate. The last method arises from the symbolic differentiation of the surrogate.

Method 1 computes the mixed partial derivative via Eq. 3 by evaluating the surrogate at (x_N, y_M), $(x_N + h, y_M)$, $(x_N, y_M + k)$ and $(x_N + h, y_M + k)$ in Eq. 3, and setting $h = k = 1$.

Method 2 computes the mixed partial derivative via Eq. 3 by evaluating the surrogate at (x_N, y_M), $(x_N + h, y_M)$, $(x_N, y_M + k)$ and $(x_N + h, y_M + k)$ in Eq. 3, and setting h and k to be the distances between x_N and $x_N + h$, y_M and $y_M + k$ respectively.

Method 3 computes the mixed partial derivative via Eq. 3 by evaluating the surrogate at (x_N, y_M), $(x_N + h, y_M)$, $(x_N, y_M + k)$ and $(x_N + h, y_M + k)$ in Eq. 3. However, it defines $x_N + h$ and $y_M + k$ to be the median of x_N and y_M respectively. It sets $h = k = 1$. We note that this is the methodology used by Udrescu et al. in their symbolic regression algorithm, AI Feynman [24].

Method 4 computes the mixed partial derivative via Eq. 3 by evaluating the surrogate at (x_N, y_M), $(x_N + h, y_M)$, $(x_N, y_M + k)$ and $(x_N + h, y_M + k)$ in Eq. 3. However, it defines $x_N + h$ and $y_M + k$ to be the median of x_N and y_M respectively. It sets h and k to be the distances between x_N and $x_N + h$, y_M and $y_M + k$ respectively.

We note that Methods 1 and 2 require a quadratic number of evaluations of the surrogate, while Methods 3 and 4 require a linear number of evaluations of the surrogate.

Method 5 computes the mixed partial derivative via Eq. 1. The mixed partial derivative of the surrogate is computed using automatic differentiation, by taking the first derivative of the surrogate with respect to an element in $\vec{x}$, then taking a second derivative of the surrogate with respect to an element in $\vec{y}$.

Method 6 computes the mixed partial derivative via Eq. 1. The mixed partial derivative of the surrogate is computed using automatic differentiation, by taking the first derivative of the surrogate with respect to an element in $\vec{y}$, then taking a second derivative of the surrogate with respect to an element in $\vec{x}$.

Method 7 computes the mixed partial derivative via Eq. 1. The mixed partial derivative of the surrogate is computed using automatic differentiation, by finding the Hessian of the surrogate with respect to an element in $\vec{x}$ and an element in $\vec{y}$.

Method 8 computes the mixed partial derivative of a surrogate multilayer perceptron neural network symbolically, following Eq. 12. Given a surrogate of a function, it creates a second surrogate multilayer perceptron neural network with the same weights and biases. This second surrogate multilayer perception neural network instead models the mixed partial derivative of the unknown function. The new surrogate multilayer perception neural network has layers and activations following Eq. 12. The inputs of the second surrogate are the same as the first. The mixed partial derivative of the unknown function is the output of the new surrogate multilayer perceptron neural network.

4   Performance Evaluation

Eight classifiers are created based on the eight methods listed in Sect. 3. Independently, functions that are either additively or non-additively separable are created, and one surrogate is trained on each function. Each classifier is then given a trained surrogate. The eight classifiers each return a test output. The test outputs are aggregated to compare the eight classifiers. This section presents and discusses the results of the comparison of the eight methods.

4.1 Experimental Setup

Setup of the Additively and Non-additively Separable Surrogates. We create unknown functions that are either additively or non-additively separable. We train one surrogate for each unknown function.

We create two- and three-variabled unknown functions comprising additive and multiplicative combinations of polynomial, trigonometric, exponential, radical and logarithmic uni-variate sub-functions, shown in Table 1. A total of 3744 additively and non-additively separable unknown functions were created.

Table 1. Twelve sub-functions with input n, a placeholder for variables x, y and z

Sub-functions			
$f(n) = n$	$f(n) = n^2$	$f(n) = (\frac{n}{3})^3$	$f(n) = \frac{1}{n+4}$
$f(n) = \sin(n)$	$f(n) = \cos(n)$	$f(n) = \sin(n)^2$	$f(n) = \cos(n)^2$
$f(n) = \exp(n)$	$f(n) = \log(n+4)$	$f(n) = \sqrt{|n|}$	$f(n) = n^{1/3}$

One multilayer perceptron neural network surrogate is trained per unknown function. We select 30 data points uniformly at random within the range of $[-3, 3]$ for each input variable of each unknown function[1]. The data is input to the analytical form of the created unknown functions to get function outputs, which we call output data. Tuples of the input and output data are used as training data for a surrogate multilayer perceptron. Each surrogate multilayer perception neural network has two hidden layers of width 26 with softplus activation, mean squared error loss, batch size of 128 and Adam optimizer with learning rate 0.01. 80% of the data is used for training and 20% for validation. All models are trained to convergence using a validation-based dynamic stopping criteria [22] with patience of 500 epochs. All models are trained and evaluated on two GeForce GTX1080 GPUs, with 64 GB of RAM and 12 processors.

Setup of the Eight Classifiers. The eight classifiers make use of the trained surrogate for each unknown function, $\hat{f}(\vec{x}, \vec{y})$ to evaluate additive separability. All eight classifiers compute the mixed partial derivative of the surrogate with respect to x_1 and y_1, which are the first elements in $\vec{x}$ and $\vec{y}$ respectively. The values of all other inputs to the surrogates are kept constant for each evaluation of each classifier. The eight classifiers compute the mixed partial derivatives on a test dataset, comprising 30 data points generated uniformly in a grid within the range of $[-3, 3]$ for each input variable of each unknown function.

Classifier 1 computes the mixed partial derivative via Eq. 3 by evaluating the surrogate at $\hat{f}(x_1, y_1)$, $\hat{f}(x_1 + h, y_1)$, $\hat{f}(x_1, y_1 + k)$ and $\hat{f}(x_1 + h, y_1 + k)$. The pair

---

[1] We note that if data is generated evenly in a grid, Eq. 1 (after computing the derivative between consecutive points) and Eq. 8 can be evaluated for each unknown function immediately without a surrogate.

of points (x_1, y_1) and $(x_1 + h, y_1 + k)$ correspond to all pairwise combinations of samples from the test dataset. h and k are set to 1. For a test dataset comprising n tuples of $(\vec{x}, \vec{y})$, this corresponds to $\frac{n(n-1)}{2}$ combinations of samples. The mixed partial derivative is averaged over all $\frac{n(n-1)}{2}$ combinations of samples for a comparative evaluation.

Classifier 2 computes the mixed partial derivative via Eq. 3 by evaluating the surrogate at $\hat{f}(x_1, y_1)$, $\hat{f}(x_1 + h, y_1)$, $\hat{f}(x_1, y_1 + k)$ and $\hat{f}(x_1 + h, y_1 + k)$. The pair of points (x_1, y_1) and $(x_1 + h, y_1 + k)$ correspond to all pairwise combinations of samples from the test dataset. h and k are set to be the distances between each pair of samples of (x_1, y_1) and $(x_1 + h, y_1 + k)$. For a test dataset comprising n tuples of $(\vec{x}, \vec{y})$, this corresponds to $\frac{n(n-1)}{2}$ combinations of samples. The mixed partial derivative is averaged over all $\frac{n(n-1)}{2}$ combinations of samples for a comparative evaluation.

Classifier 3 computes the mixed partial derivative via Eq. 3 by evaluating the surrogate at $\hat{f}(x_1, y_1)$, $\hat{f}(x_1 + h, y_1)$, $\hat{f}(x_1, y_1 + k)$ and $\hat{f}(x_1 + h, y_1 + k)$. $x_1 + h$ and $y_1 + k$ are the median from all samples of x_1 and y_1 from the test dataset respectively. h and k are set to 1. For a test dataset comprising n tuples of $(\vec{x}, \vec{y})$, the mixed partial derivative is averaged over all n samples for a comparative evaluation.

Classifier 4 computes the mixed partial derivative via Eq. 3 by evaluating the surrogate at $\hat{f}(x_1, y_1)$, $\hat{f}(x_1 + h, y_1)$, $\hat{f}(x_1, y_1 + k)$ and $\hat{f}(x_1 + h, y_1 + k)$. $x_1 + h$ and $y_1 + k$ are the median from all samples of x_1 and y_1 from the test dataset respectively. h and k are set to be the distances between each pair of samples of (x_1, y_1) and $(x_1 + h, y_1 + k)$. For a test dataset comprising n tuples of $(\vec{x}, \vec{y})$, the mixed partial derivative is averaged over all n samples for a comparative evaluation.

Classifier 5 computes the mixed partial derivative via Eq. 1. The mixed partial derivative of the surrogate, $\hat{f}(x_1, y_1)$, is computed using automatic differentiation via `autograd` in `pytorch` [18,19], at all samples (x_1, y_1) in the test dataset. This is done by taking the first derivative of the surrogate with respect to x_1, then finding the derivative of the surrogate again, but with respect to y_1. For a test dataset comprising n tuples of $(\vec{x}, \vec{y})$, the mixed partial derivative is averaged over all n samples for a comparative evaluation.

Classifier 6 computes the mixed partial derivative via Eq. 1. The mixed partial derivative of the surrogate, $\hat{f}(x_1, y_1)$, is computed using automatic differentiation via `autograd` in `pytorch` [18,19], at all samples (x_1, y_1) in the test dataset. This is done by taking the first derivative of the surrogate with respect to y_1, then finding the derivative of the surrogate again, but with respect to x_1. For a test dataset comprising n tuples of $(\vec{x}, \vec{y})$, the mixed partial derivative is averaged over all n samples for a comparative evaluation.

Classifier 7 computes the mixed partial derivative via Eq. 1. The mixed partial derivative of the surrogate, $\hat{f}(x_1, y_1)$, is computed using automatic differentiation via `torch.func` in `pytorch` [18,19], at all samples (x_1, y_1) in the test dataset. `torch.func` directly computes the Hessian of the surrogate. For a test dataset comprising n tuples of $(\vec{x}, \vec{y})$, the mixed partial derivative is averaged over all n samples for a comparative evaluation.

Classifier 8 computes the mixed partial derivative of a surrogate multilayer perceptron neural network symbolically, following Eq. 12. It models the mixed partial derivative of the unknown function by creating a second surrogate multilayer perceptron neural network with the same architecture. Instead of training the second surrogate multilayer perception neural network, the weights from the surrogate of the unknown function are transferred over. The mixed partial derivative of the surrogate, $\hat{f}(x_1, y_1)$, is computed using the second surrogate multilayer perception neural network at all samples (x_1, y_1) in the test dataset. For a test dataset comprising n tuples of $(\vec{x}, \vec{y})$, the mixed partial derivative is averaged over all n samples for a comparative evaluation.

The activation function of the surrogate multilayer perceptron neural network of the unknown function is the softplus activation function, of the form seen in Eq. 13. Therefore, the second surrogate multilayer perception neural network that computes the mixed partial derivative also uses the softplus activation function and its derivatives. The first and second derivatives of the softplus activation function are shown in Eqs. 14 and 15 respectively.

$$\sigma(x) = \log(\exp(x) + 1) \tag{13}$$

$$\sigma'_x = \frac{\partial \sigma(x)}{\partial x} = \frac{\exp(x)}{\exp(x) + 1} \tag{14}$$

$$\sigma'' = \frac{\partial^2 \sigma(x)}{\partial x^2} = \frac{\exp(x)}{(\exp(x) + 1)^2} \tag{15}$$

All code was implemented in `python`. The code to train the surrogates of the unknown functions, and to implement the eight classifiers, is available at https://github.com/zykhoo/AdditiveSeparabilityTest.git.

Evaluation Metrics. Each classifier computes an average mixed partial derivative for each of the 3744 unknown functions. A threshold value is set, and if the average mixed partial derivative of an unknown function falls below or is equal to the threshold, the classifier classifies that unknown function as additively separable. Otherwise, the classifier classifies the unknown function as non-additively separable. This is a binary classification problem.

The metric used to compare the eight methods is the accuracy of the classification, using the threshold that gives no false positives as the optimal threshold. The classification accuracy looks at fractions of correctly assigned positive and negative classifications. As half of the unknown functions are additively separable, and half are non-additively separable, the set of functions is balanced. Furthermore, it is equally important to identify both additively separable and non-additively separable unknown functions. Therefore the classification accuracy is used as a metric. The classification accuracy is computed as the count of true positives and negatives, divided by the count of all classifications. A higher accuracy is better.

4.2   Experimental Results

We report the accuracy for the eight classifiers and their respective thresholds in Table 2. Additionally, we report the time taken for each classifier to evaluate a surrogate in Table 3

Table 2. Accuracy and optimal threshold for the eight classifiers.

Classifier	1	2	3	4	5	6	7	8
Accuracy	0.8654	0.7647	0.7260	0.6571	0.6343	0.6343	0.6343	0.6343
Threshold	0.0109	0.0030	0.0053	0.0018	0.0050	0.0050	0.0050	0.0050

From Table 2 we observe that generally, all models have high classification accuracy and can be used to classify additively and non-additively separable functions. Classifier 1 performs the best, with an accuracy of 0.8654 at a threshold of 0.0109. Classifiers 2, 3 and 4 also perform well, with accuracies ranging between 0.7647 to 0.6571. Lastly. Classifiers 5, 6, 7 and 8 have an accuracy of 0.6343. It can also be observed from Table 2 that Classifiers 5, 6, 7 and 8 have the same accuracy and thresholds, as they all compute the mixed partial derivative of the neural network through automatic or symbolic differentiation. These mixed partial derivatives are instantaneous or at the limit, and computed at the same samples in the test dataset and, therefore have the same accuracy.

Classifiers 1 through 4 outperform Classifiers 5 through 8. Equation 1 implies that for an additively separable function $f(\vec{x}, \vec{y}) = g(\vec{x}) + h(\vec{y})$, Eqs. 16 and 17 hold, as the functions $g(\vec{x})$ and $h(\vec{y})$ are independent of $\vec{y}$ and $\vec{x}$ respectively. Therefore, Eqs. 16 and 17 should also hold even when the change in y_n or x_m is large, or when h and k is large. Classifiers 1 through 4, when computing the mixed partial derivative of a surrogate via finite difference, check that Eqs. 16 and 17 hold even for large changes in y_n and x_m, therefore outperform Classifiers 5 through 8 that only check to ensure that Eqs. 16 and 17 hold at the limit.

$$\frac{\partial g(\vec{x})}{\partial y_n} = 0 \tag{16}$$

$$\frac{\partial h(\vec{y})}{\partial x_m} = 0 \tag{17}$$

We make two notes about the observation above. Firstly, Classifiers 5 through 8 compute an instantaneous derivative whose magnitude may depend on the analytical form of the function. A non-additively separable function may have a small instantaneous derivative, and therefore be mistaken as additively separable when using Classifiers 5 through 8. For example, $f(\vec{x}, \vec{y}) = xy$ can have a small instantaneous derivative with respect to x of y and may potentially be classified as additively separable. Classifiers 1 to 4, by computing the partial derivative via finite difference instead of instantaneous derivative, compute the change in

$f(\vec{x}, \vec{y})$ and can check if $f(\vec{x}, \vec{y})$ changes greatly when y increases to identify that it is non-additively separable. Secondly, Classifiers 1 and 2 outperform Classifiers 3 and 4 because they compute the finite difference over larger changes in x_n and y_m. The former takes the distance between any two samples in the test data, while the latter takes the distance between any sample and the median of the test data.

It is for this same reason that Classifiers 1 and 3 outperform Classifiers 2 and 4. The latter normalize Classifiers 1 and 3 by the magnitude of x_n and y_m. The normalization obscures the effect of computing the finite differences.

Lastly, from Table 3, we observe that generally, Classifiers 5, 6 and 8 are the most time efficient. Classifiers 1 and 2 are time-consuming because they compute n^2 computations. Classifier 7 is also time-consuming because it computes the Hessian of the neural network at each sample in the test dataset. This involves not just computing the mixed partial derivative of the multilayer perceptron neural network, but all other second-order derivatives as well.

Table 3. Time taken in seconds for the eight classifiers to evaluate a surrogate over a test dataset.

Classifier	1	2	3	4	5	6	7	8
Time	48.3195	52.1720	0.0034	0.0032	0.0025	0.0025	136.4385	0.0029

5   Conclusion

We presented and comparatively and empirically evaluated the performance of eight classifiers for additive separability, to be used to compute the mixed partial derivatives of surrogate functions. Classifier 1 is the most effective, followed by Classifier 2 and Classifier 3. Classifiers 5, 6 and 8 are the most efficient, followed by Classifiers 3 and 4. Classifier 3 is the test of choice given a time constraint.

The surrogate of a function can be tested for additive separability using the methods introduced in this paper. The detection that the surrogate is additively separable can be leveraged to improve further learning. We are now working on the embedding of information regarding additive separability into a multilayer perceptron neural network surrogate that has been detected to be additively separable.

Acknowledgments. This research is supported by Singapore Ministry of Education, grant MOE-T2EP50120-0019, and by the National Research Foundation, Prime Minister's Office, Singapore, under its Campus for Research Excellence and Technological Enterprise (CREATE) programme as part of the programme Descartes.

References

1. Bellenot, S.F.: Additively separable functions of the form f(x, y)=f(x)+g(y). https://www.math.fsu.edu/~bellenot/class/s05/cal3/proj/project.pdf
2. Chen, R.T.Q., Rubanova, Y., Bettencourt, J., Duvenaud, D.K.: Neural ordinary differential equations. In: Bengio, S., Wallach, H., Larochelle, H., Grauman, K., Cesa-Bianchi, N., Garnett, R. (eds.) Advances in Neural Information Processing Systems, vol. 31. Curran Associates, Inc. (2018)
3. Diewert, W., Parkan, C.: Tests for the consistency of consumer data. J. Econometrics **30**(1), 127–147 (1985)
4. Fleissig, A.R., Whitney, G.A.: Testing additive separability. Econ. Lett. **96**(2), 215–220 (2007)
5. Gorman, W.M.: Conditions for additive separability. Econometrica **36**(3/4), 605–609 (1968). https://www.jstor.org/stable/1909527
6. Greydanus, S., Dzamba, M., Yosinski, J.: Hamiltonian neural networks. In: Wallach, H., Larochelle, H., Beygelzimer, A., d'Alché-Buc, F., Fox, E., Garnett, R. (eds.) Advances in Neural Information Processing Systems, vol. 32. Curran Associates, Inc. (2019)
7. Gruver, N., Finzi, M.A., Stanton, S.D., Wilson, A.G.: Deconstructing the inductive biases of Hamiltonian neural networks. In: International Conference on Learning Representations (2022)
8. Hastie, Trevor, Tibshirani, Robert, Friedman, Jerome: The Elements of Statistical Learning. SSS, Springer, New York (2009). https://doi.org/10.1007/978-0-387-84858-7
9. Hornik, K., Stinchcombe, M., White, H.: Multilayer feedforward networks are universal approximators. Neural Netw. **2**(5), 359–366 (1989)
10. Karniadakis, G.E., Kevrekidis, I.G., Lu, L., Perdikaris, P., Wang, S., Yang, L.: Physics-informed machine learning. Nature Reviews. Physics **3**(6), 422–440 (2021)
11. Khoo, Z.Y., Zhang, D., Bressan, S.: What's next? predicting Hamiltonian dynamics from discrete observations of a vector field. In: Strauss, C., Cuzzocrea, A., Kotsis, G., Tjoa, A.M., Khalil, I. (eds.) Database and Expert Systems Applications. DEXA 2022. Lecture Notes in Computer Science, vol. 13427, pp. 297–302. Springer, Cham (2022). https://doi.org/10.1007/978-3-031-12426-6_27
12. Leontief, W.: A note on the interrelation of subsets of independent variables of a continuous function with continuous first derivatives. Bull. Am. Math. Soc. **53**(4), 343–350 (1947)
13. Lotka, A.J.: Elements of physical biology. Nature **116**, 461–461 (1925)
14. Lu, Y., Lin, S., Chen, G., Pan, J.: ModLaNets: learning generalisable dynamics via modularity and physical inductive bias. In: Chaudhuri, K., Jegelka, S., Song, L., Szepesvari, C., Niu, G., Sabato, S. (eds.) Proceedings of the 39th International Conference on Machine Learning. Proceedings of Machine Learning Research, vol. 162, pp. 14384–14397. PMLR (2022)
15. McDonald, T., Álvarez, M.: Compositional modeling of nonlinear dynamical systems with ode-based random features. In: Ranzato, M., Beygelzimer, A., Dauphin, Y., Liang, P., Vaughan, J.W. (eds.) Advances in Neural Information Processing Systems, vol. 34, pp. 13809–13819. Curran Associates, Inc. (2021)
16. Meyer, K.R., Hall, G.R.: Hamiltonian Differential Equations and the N-Body Problem. In: Introduction to Hamiltonian Dynamical Systems and the N-Body Problem. Applied Mathematical Sciences, vol. 90, pp. 1–32. Springer, New York, NY (1992). https://doi.org/10.1007/978-1-4757-4073-8_1

17. Olver, P.: Introduction to Partial Differential Equations. Undergraduate Texts in Mathematics, Springer International Publishing (2013). https://doi.org/10.1007/978-3-319-48936-0, https://books.google.com.sg/books?id=aQ8JAgAAQBAJ

18. Paszke, A., et al.: Automatic differentiation in pytorch. In: 31st Conference on Neural Information Processing Systems (NIPS 2017), Long Beach, CA, USA (2017)

19. Paszke, A., et al.: Pytorch: an imperative style, high-performance deep learning library. In: Advances in Neural Information Processing Systems, vol. 32, pp. 8024–8035. Curran Associates, Inc. (2019). https://papers.neurips.cc/paper/9015-pytorch-an-imperative-style-high-performance-deep-learning-library.pdf

20. Polisson, M.: A lattice test for additive separability. IFS Working Papers W18/08, Institute for Fiscal Studies (2018)

21. Polisson, M., Quah, J.K.H., Renou, L.: Revealed preferences over risk and uncertainty. Am. Econ. Rev. **110**(6), 1782–1820 (2020)

22. Prechelt, L.: Early stopping - but when? In: Orr, G.B., Müller, K.R. (eds.) Neural Networks: Tricks of the Trade. Springer, Berlin Heidelberg, Berlin, Heidelberg (1998). https://doi.org/10.1007/978-3-642-35289-8

23. Shi, R., Mo, Z., Di, X.: Physics-informed deep learning for traffic state estimation: a hybrid paradigm informed by second-order traffic models. Proc. AAAI Conf. Artif. Intell. **35**(1), 540–547 (2021)

24. Udrescu, S.M., Tegmark, M.: AI Feynman: a physics-inspired method for symbolic regression. Sci. Adv. **6**(16), eaay2631 (2020)

25. Varian, H.R.: Non-parametric tests of consumer behaviour. Rev. Econ. Stud. **50**(1), 99–110 (1983). https://www.jstor.org/stable/2296957

26. Varian, H.R.: Microeconomic Analysis. Norton, New York, third edn (1992)

27. Zhang, G., Yu, Z., Jin, D., Li, Y.: Physics-infused machine learning for crowd simulation. In: Proceedings of the 28th ACM SIGKDD Conference on Knowledge Discovery and Data Mining, pp. 2439–2449. KDD 2022, Association for Computing Machinery, New York, NY, USA (2022)

Data Integration in a Multi-model Environment

Jaroslav Pokorný[1,2]([✉]) [iD]

[1] Faculty of Mathematics and Physics, Charles University, Prague, Czech Republic
jaroslav.pokorny@matfyz.cuni.cz, pokorny@savs.cz
[2] Škoda Auto University, Mladá Boleslav, Czech Republic

Abstract. A multi-model approach to heterogeneous database (DB) integration requires a more user-friendly solution, i.e., a possibility to see various conceptual or data schemas in a unified way. We use a functional approach based on so-called attributes named by short natural language expressions with associated expressions describing their type. Attributes are functions that can be manipulated by a version of typed lambda calculus, which with arithmetic and aggregation functions enables to build a powerful query language. We consider the relational, E-R, JSON, and graph data/conceptual models. A query over such integrated DB can be expressed by a term of the typed lambda calculus. A more user-friendly version of such language can serve as a powerful query tool in practice.

Keywords: functional approach · typed lambda calculus · multi-model approach

1 Introduction

Historically, data integration is associated with distributed databases (DB) developed mainly in 80ties. These DBs used mostly the relational DB model, a global schema and local schemas for DBs were placed in multiple DB nodes in a network. Then, two approaches based on DB schemas management occurred:

- top-down – starting with a global schema to design schemas for particular data stores in network sites,
- bottom-up – i.e., to use a schema mapping for schemas of data stores in sites with a middleware (e.g., JDBC). The process consists of integrating local DBs with their (local) schemas into a global DB with its global schema.

We remind that the former concerns rather homogenous DB models used in integrated data stores, using usually relational DBs, while the latter supports various DB models and consequently heterogeneous database systems (DBS).

Now, systems that store and process Big Data have become a common component of data management architectures. Generally, Big Data can be a combination of (i) structured data in DBs and data warehouses based on SQL, (ii) semi-structured data, such as web server logs or streaming data from sensors, organized by the means of, e.g., RDF graphs or XML documents, or (iii) unstructured data, such as document (or text) collections. Here, we will consider categories (i) and (ii).

P. Delir Haghighi et al. (Eds.): iiWAS 2023, LNCS 14416, pp. 121–127, 2023.
https://doi.org/10.1007/978-3-031-48316-5_14

A traditional problem how to approach data in such environment is the way how data is integrated. The remainder of the paper is organized as follows. Section 2 presents a functional modelling of conceptual and DB structures including tools appropriate for their querying, i.e., typed functions and a typed lambda calculus. Section 3 explores some approaches to data integrations. Section 4 presents also functional querying integrated data. Finally, Sect. 5 provides conclusions and topics for future works.

2 Functional Data Modelling

We start from classic approaches to functional DBs, that use a version of functional typing and a typed lambda calculus in Sects. 2.1 and Sect. 2.2. (for more details, e.g., [6]). In Sect. 2.3, we present how functional conceptual structures *attributes* can be described by expressions of a natural language. Combining attributes and typed lambda calculus we obtain a powerful query language (QL) presented in Sect. 2.4.

2.1 Functional Data Types

We assume the existence of some *elementary types* $S_1, \ldots, S_k$ $(k \geq 1)$ constituting a *base* **B**. More complex types are constructed in the following way:

If $S, R_1, \ldots, R_n$ $(n \geq 1)$ are types, then

(i) $(S{:}R_1, \ldots, R_n)$ is a (*functional*) *type*,
(ii) $(R_1, \ldots, R_n)$ is a (*tuple*) *type*.

The set of *types* **T** *over* **B** is the least set containing all types from **B** and those given by (i)–(ii). When S_i in **B** are interpreted as non-empty sets, then $(S{:}R_1, \ldots, R_n)$ denotes the set of all (total or partial) functions from $R_1 \times \ldots \times R_n$ into S, $(R_1, \ldots, R_n)$ denotes the Cartesian product $R_1 \times \ldots \times R_n$. Elementary type $Bool = \{\text{TRUE}, \text{FALSE}\}$ is also in **B**. It allows to model sets (resp. relations) as unary (resp. n-ary) characteristic functions. An object o of the type T is called a *T-object*. We denote it o/T. Logical connectives, quantifiers, and predicates are typed functions, e.g., **and**/$(Bool{:}\,Bool, Bool)$ and **implies**/$(Bool{:}\,Bool, Bool)$. Arithmetic operations are $(Number{:}\,Number, Number)$-objects. The aggregation functions have also associated types, e.g., SUM/$(Real{:}(Bool{:}Real))$. We use the infix notation for functions and arithmetic operations. We write '$\forall x \ldots$' and '$\exists x \ldots$', for application of the universal and existential quantifier, respectively. Relations are $(Bool{:}S_1, \ldots, S_m)$-objects, where S_i are descriptive elementary types.

2.2 Typed Lambda Calculus

Let **F** be a collection of constants, each having a fixed type, and suppose to have a denumerable set of variables of each type at disposal. The *language of lambda terms* **LT** is defined as follows:

Let types $R, S, R_1, \ldots, R_n$ $(n \geq 1)$ be elements of **T**. Then

(1) Every variable of type R is a term of type R.   (*variable*)
(2) Every constant (a member of **F**) of type R is a term of type R.   (*constant*)

(3) If M is a term of type $(S:R_1, ..., R_n)$, and $N_1, ..., N_n$ are terms of types $R_1, ..., R_n$, respectively, then $M(N_1, ..., N_n)$ is a term of type S.   (*application*)

(4) If $x_1, ..., x_n$ are distinct variables of types $R_1, ..., R_n$, respectively, and M is a term of type S, then $\lambda x_1, ..., x_n(M)$ is a term of type $(S:R_1, ..., R_n)$.   (*λ-abstraction*)

(5) If $N_1, ..., N_n$ are terms with types $R_1, ..., R_n$, respectively, then $(N_1, ..., N_n)$ is a term of type $(R_1, ..., R_n)$.   (*tuple*)

(6) If M is a term of type $(R_1, ..., R_n)$, then $M[1], ..., M[n]$ are terms of respective types $R_1, ..., R_n$.   (*components*)

Terms can be interpreted by an interpretation assigning to each function from **F** an object of the same type, and a semantic mapping from **LT** into all functions and Cartesian products given by the type of system **T**. Briefly, an application is evaluated as the application of an associated function to its arguments, the λ-abstraction "constructs" a new function. A tuple is a member of the Cartesian product of sets of typed objects.

2.3 Conceptual Modelling with Attributes

In general, attributes are parametrized by *possible worlds* (elementary type w) and *time moments* (elementary type t). Mathematical/logical functions are not dependent on w and t. For simplicity, we will not assume either possible worlds or time moments in the paper. For example, ACTORS/(*Bool:Name, Title, Role*) and MOVIES/(*Bool:Title, Released, Director, Genre*) represent named attributes - relations.

A_JOURNAL_TO_WHICH_ THE_USER_CONTRIBUTES/(*Journal:User*),
MOVIES_RATED_BY_A_USER/((*Bool:Stars, Movie*): *User*),

are rather functional attributes. We will denote them JU and SMU, respectively.

Other conceptual constructions are *propositions* of type *Bool*. Attributes generate certain basic propositions, e.g., "Mr. Baker contributes to the journal Computer Reviews". It is generated by the JU attribute. A *conceptual schema* is a tuple of attribute specifications and, possibly, a set of integrity constraints, i.e., certain propositions giving explicitly some information about attributes. An *information* base is a set of TRUE-propositions induced by attributes in an actual world and in a given time moment. Obviously, all known conceptual constructs used in conceptual modelling are cases of attributes. In [4] and [7] we applied this approach to XML and JSON data, respectively.

2.4 Querying with Attributes

The **LT** language can be used as a theoretical tool for building a functional QL. The choice of functions determines the expressive power of QL. A query in such language is expressed by a **LT** term, e.g.,

$$\lambda \, u^{User}, \, n^{Number}(n = \text{COUNT}(\lambda \, m^{Movie}(\exists \, s^{Stars} \, \text{SMU}(u)(s, \, m))))$$

of type (*Bool:User, Number*). Indexes of variables denote their types. The query means "Find for each user the number of rated movies".

A more complex example of a term uses a universal quantifier and implication:

$$\lambda\, n^{Name}(\forall t^{Title}\,(\exists\, re^{Rolasede},\, g^{Genre}\, \text{MOVIES}(t^{Title},\, re^{Relaesed},\, {}^{\prime}\text{Spielberg}^{\prime\, Director},\, g^{Genre})$$
$$\textbf{implies}\,\exists\, ro^{Role}\,\text{ACTORS}(n^{Name},\, t^{Title},\, ro^{Role}))$$

expressing the query "Find the names of actors, who play in each Spielberg film."

We gain a tool for common manipulation of relations and other typed functions. Then, the query results can be relations, nested relations, typed functions, etc. For Boolean queries, YES/NO can be a query result. It is important that there is no sharp line between conceptual and DB modelling with the functional approach. An application of the typed lambda calculus with equality is used in the approach of Hillebrand [2].

3   Multi-model Approach to Data Integration

Today, polystores and multi-model DBs are considered for DBs with multiple data stores [3]. In a *polystore* multiple storage engines are distinct and accessed separately through their own query engines. A more user-friendly solution of heterogeneous DB integration, is referred to as *multi-model DBs*. Typically, the relational data model can be one of them [1]. The query is then executed on more data sources, but an additional layer is often used to enable data integration.

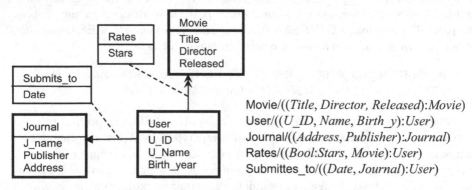

Movie/((*Title, Director, Released*):*Movie*)
User/((*U_ID, Name, Birth_y*):*User*)
Journal/((*Address, Publisher*):*Journal*)
Rates/((*Bool:Stars, Movie*):*User*)
Submittes_to/((*Date, Journal*):*User*)

Fig. 1. GDB conceptual schema Movies and its functional version

The notion of attribute applied in GDBs can be restricted to attributes of types (R:S), (Bool(R):S), or (Bool:R, S), where R and S are entity types. This strategy simply covers binary functional types, binary multivalued functional types, and binary relationships described as binary characteristic functions. The last option corresponds to M:N relationship types. For modelling directed graphs, the first two types are sufficient, because M:N relationship types can be expressed by two "inverse" binary multivalued functional types. For graphical expressing a graph conceptual schema, we use two types of arrows according to associated binary functional types (see Fig. 1).

Properties describing entity types can be of types $(S_1, \ldots, S_m:R)$, where S_i are descriptive elementary types and R is an entity type. They are of types $(S_1, \ldots, S_m, R_1:R_2)$ and $((Bool:S_1, \ldots, S_m, R_1):R_2)$ for binary functional and binary multivalued functional types, respectively. Functional querying in GDBs is described, e.g., in [5].

For relational DBs, we can assume the existence of an E-R schema describing the semantics of relations. Here we use attributes for conceptual schemas based on E-R models and sufficiently structured approach for expressing semantics of data in particular NoSQL DBs. The database schemas of these DBs are then described by sets of attributes, i.e. rather as *local conceptual schemas* (LCSs), a global schema is obtained by union of these LCSs. Such approach can be generalized to most NoSQL DBs [8].

In the case of NoSQL, even more than one data model is often included in one DB architecture. For example, the distributed DB Cassandra combines column-based and key-value data models, DynamoDB combines document-oriented and key-value data models. ArangoDB also represents a multi-model approach, meaning that it can address JSON documents, graphs, and key-values. OrientDB is a multi-model DB including geospatial, graph, fulltext, and key-valued data models. MarkLogic enables to store and search JSON and XML documents and RDF triples. In [10] the gap between SQL and NoSQL is solved via an abstraction level in which the NoSQL data are transformed to triples incorporated into SQL DB as virtual relations.

4 Querying Multi-model Data

In literature, we can find two basic general frameworks for unified modelling and management of multi-model data. The categorical approaches described [3, 9] use category theory for transformations between models and are usable also for conceptual querying. Querying multi-model data by a functional approach means to describe DB structures in particular DBs functionally by attributes. It means, in principle, that LCSs are specified. Since sets (relations) are modelled as their characteristic functions, we gain a tool for common manipulation of relations and functional data from NoSQL DBs. In consequence, the query results can be relations, nested relations or XML [4], JSON [7], graph data [5] as well, again expressed by **LT** terms.

Another approach uses a global schema similarly to the ANSI/SPARC approach. In such logical integration, the *global conceptual* (or *mediated*) *schema* (GCS) is entirely virtual and not materialized. The bottom-up design involves both the generation of the GCS and the mapping of individual LCSs to this GCS. In any case, there are difficulties in schema integration, because of different structures and semantics among local DBs. Details of integration of relational DBs and GDBs functionally are described in [6]. Data selection is performed in the source systems using SQL and Cypher. The results are mapped into data structures associated with the source query term.

Example 1: Suppose the relational attributes {ACTORS, MOVIES} from Sect. 2.3 and GDB described in Fig. 1, i.e., attributes {Movie, User, Journal, Rates, Submittes_to}. In the integrated DB, i.e., the multi-model system, the term in the simplified notation

$$\lambda u^{User} \lambda g^{Genre}, n^{Number}$$
$$(n^{Number} = \text{COUNT}_{Movie} (\lambda m^{Movie} (\text{Rates}(u^{User})(m^{Movie}) \textbf{ and}$$
$$\exists t^{Title} s^{Title} \text{Movie}(m^{Movie}).t^{Title} = s^{Title} \textbf{ and } \text{MOVIES}(s^{Title}, g^{Genre}))$$
$$))$$

expresses the query "Find for each user the genres and the number of reviews he/she made in them". The answer will be of type ((*Bool*: *Genre, Number*), *User*), i.e. a new multivalued attribute assigning to each user a binary relation with tuples containing a genre and the number of the rates created for this genre by a given user. The query term is decomposed and transformed into a query program that requires evaluation of the included attributes, e.g., by SQL and Cypher expressions, respectively. These partial results serve to the integration that generates the query result.

5 Conclusions

In the paper, we have focused on integration of relational and NoSQL DBs. Even a variant of the E-R model can be used in without problems. Formally, we used a functional typing system serving for specification of so-called attributes. The attributes can be named with expressions of a natural language, bringing database querying closer to conceptual querying. A typed lambda calculus can be used as a manipulation language.

The presented tools create a formal background covering querying an integrated multi-model DB. Such a language could be based on SQL-like syntax, in principle. Another interesting topic for research is the expressive power of the subsets of **LT** considered, the solution of their user variants, and the complexity of formulating queries in such apparatus. In general, the expressive power of a user QL depends on a choice of constant functions included into the QL. These are themes for future work.

References

1. Candel, C.J.F., Sevilla Ruiz, D., García-Molina, J.J.: A unified metamodel for NoSQL and relational databases. Inf. Syst. **104**, 101898 (2022)
2. Hillebrand, G., Kanellakis, P.C., Mairson, H.G.: Database query languages embedded in the typed lambda calculus. Inf. Comput. **127**(2), 117–144 (1996)
3. Lu, J., Holubová, I., Cautis, B.: Multi-model databases and tightly integrated polystores: current practices, comparisons, and open challenges. In: Proceedings of the CIKM 2018, 27th ACM International Conference on Information and Knowledge Management, pp. 2301–2302 (2018)
4. Pokorný, J.: XML functionally. In: Desai, B.C., Kioki, Y., Toyama, M. (eds.) Proceedings of the IDEAS2000, pp. 266–274. IEEE Computer Society (2000)
5. Pokorný, J.: Functional querying in graph databases. In: Nguyen, N., Tojo, S., Nguyen, L., Trawiński, B. (eds.) ACIIDS 2017, Part I. LNCS, vol. 10191, pp. 291–301. Springer, Cham (2017). https://doi.org/10.1007/978-3-319-54472-4_28
6. Pokorný, J.: Integration of relational and NoSQL databases. Vietnam J. Comput. Sci. **6**(4), 389–405 (2019)
7. Pokorný, J.: JSON functionally. In: Proceedings of ADBIS 2020, Lyon, France, August 25–27, pp. 139–153 (2020)
8. Pokorný, J., Richta, K.: Towards conceptual and logical modelling of NoSQL databases. In: Insfran, E., et al. (eds.) Advances in Information Systems Development. LNISO, vol. 55, pp. 255–272. Springer, Cham (2022). https://doi.org/10.1007/978-3-030-95354-6_15

9. Svoboda, M., Čontoš, P., Holubová, I.: Categorical modelling of multi-model data: one model to rule them all. In Proceedings of the 10th International Conference on MEDI 2021, Tallin, pp. 190–198 (2021)
10. Thant, P.T., Naing, T.T.: Hybrid query processing system (HQPS) for heterogeneous databases (relational and NoSQL). In: Proceedings of the International Conference on Computer Networks and Information Technology, pp. 53–58 (2014)

Character Entity Recognition Using Hybrid Binary-Particle Swarm Optimization and Conditional Random Field on Balinese Folklore Text

I Made Satria Bimantara[1] , Ngurah Agus Sanjaya ER[2(✉)] ,
and Diana Purwitasari[1]

[1] Institut Teknologi Sepuluh Nopember, Surabaya 60111, Indonesia
satriabimantara.imd@gmail.com, diana@if.its.ac.id
[2] Universitas Udayana, Badung 80361, Indonesia
agus_sanjaya@unud.ac.id

Abstract. Identifying the character entities correctly in a story becomes extremely challenging since an entity can refer to a proper noun, a phrase, or a particular definition. This study proposes BPSO-CRF, a hybrid NER method to extract character entities in Balinese stories. In addition, we develop a training dataset for balinese character named entities recognition task. We compare the proposed method against three baseline methods. Overall, BPSO-CRF obtains a relatively better recognition rate compared to the baseline method. Furthermore, only a few numbers of contextual features are relevant to improve the performance of the baseline CRF model.

Keywords: Charater Named Entity Recognition · Hybrid Binary Particle Swarm Optimization – Conditional Random Field (BPSO-CRF) · Balinese Folklore NER dataset

1 Introduction

Characters in a story are defined as entities who receive or perform actions in a plot in the story [1]. Identifying the characters becomes important when further understanding of the story is necessary [2]. However, character identification becomes challenging because entities in the story can refer to proper nouns, pronouns and noun phrases, or specific definitions. The challenge becomes even more significant in fiction genre texts [1], where the naming of characters may follow different rules than in the real world. Furthermore, the development of tools for NLP research and information retrieval generally focuses on high-resource language texts or literature, such as English. It is contradictory to the fact that large volumes of texts, documents, or literature are available in non-Western languages or low-resource languages.

Computation-based character identification in Balinese folklore is currently a challenging task. The rule and information-based named entity recognition (NER) approach with POS Tagger can be used to extract candidate characters from a text by extracting entities with the label "person" from nouns as characters [3]. However, characters in a story are not limited to a human [4]. They can also be inanimate objects or other living creatures (an elephant, a tiger, and a tree) [1], with human personification. In addition, characters in Balinese folklore are often displayed using some specific phrases and not proper nouns only. Therefore, a rule-based NER approach by extracting entities labeled "person" is insufficient [1].

The CRF model has been utilized in supervised learning-based NER to recognize various entities in text [5] as a single model or it has been added as an additional layer to deep learning and transformers-based architectures. However, no one has researched the optimal features used in learning on CRF. We utilize the advantages of BPSO which has been used in several previous studies to solve optimization problems [6]. Our research proposes a BPSO-based feature selection optimization process to train CRFs with optimal features.

This study aimed at proposing BPSO-CRF hybrid NER named SatuaNER for identifying character named entities from Balinese folklore text. We extract several feature sets in the CRF learning process to identify character entities and optimize using BPSO. In addition, this study introduces a new dataset to recognize character entities in Balinese folklore.

2 Character Named Entity on Balinese Folklore Dataset

Satua Bali (Balinese folklore) is one of the oral literature works from the island of Bali, which contains a collection of texts from folk tales [7]. Generally, a character named entity (CHAR NE) is a word or phrase consisting of five specific characteristics based on an analysis of the *Satua Bali* text. Each characteristic is given a particular label to mark CHAR NE. First, CHAR NE consists of noun phrases that show human characteristics that are usually used to name someone (ADJ), such as "*I Jemet*" (the diligent person). Second, CHAR NE consists of proper noun to name someone in Bali taken from the Sanskrit dictionary (PNAME), such as "*I Bima*". Third, CHAR NE consists of proper noun that show and/or have divine characteristics (GODS), such as "*Bhatara Shiva, Bhatara Wisnu*" (Gods in Hinduism). Fourth, CHAR NE consists of noun phrases or common noun of other living things that have human-like personifications (ANM), such as "*I Lutung*" (the monkey). Fifth, CHAR NE is a noun or pronoun phrase that refers to a human or things without mentioning specific names (OBJ), such as "*memene*" (his or her mother).

The dataset used in this study is 45 *Satua Bali* texts obtained by web-scraping. Documents obtained are then preprocessed, such as changing the special character é, normalizing words, removing punctuation, removing exclamations, breaking paragraphs into sentences, removing whitespace, and case folding. Two annotators fluent in Balinese label each token in the text using the Spreadsheet Tools. Each token consists of two labels: the part-of-speech (POS) label and the CHAR NE label. The annotator only gives CHAR NE labels, while POS labels are done automatically using the balinese-library package[1].

---

[1] HMM-based POS Tagging for balinese text was retrieved from https://pypi.org/project/balinese-library/

Table 1. Example sentence in *satua* Bali with corresponding CHAR NE label.

Sentence with CHAR NE tag (Balinese)	Sentence in English
I/**B-ANM** *Angsa*/**I-ANM** *lan*/**O** *I*/**B-ANM** *Kerkuak*/**I-ANM** *kema*/**O** *ka*/**O** *Tukad*/**O** *Dangin*/**O** *Desane*/**O** *ngalih*/**O** *amah*/**O** *amahan*/**O**./**O**	The Goose and The Crackling Bird went to the river east of the village to look for food

Table 2. CHAR NE statistics in training and test dataset.

Groups	ADJ	PNAME	GODS	ANM	OBJ	Percentage O label
Training	382	3,073	725	1,030	615	81.53%
Testing	74	864	189	258	153	81.34%

BIO encoding format [5] is used for labeling each CHAR NE. Label O marks every word that is not CHAR NE. Table 1 shows how to label each token in a sentence. Before labeling, a sample of 1,830 tokens was randomly selected to measure the reliability between annotators using Cohen's Kappa Coefficient at the start. The agreement score between the two annotators shows a value of 0.905 and is above 0.8 (perfect agreement). The final dataset consists of 2,860 sentences with 39,781 tokens from 45 Balinese texts (statistics in Table 2). The dataset is divided randomly into training and test data (80:20) using the group shuffle split.

3 Hybrid Binary Particle Swarm Optimization and Conditional Random Field for Character Named Entity Recognition

The architecture of the proposed hybrid model is shown in Fig. 1. BPSO stages from previous studies [6] were adopted in this study. We use binary vector format to represent particle solution with dimension of total number of features. A value of 1 indicates the feature is used and vice versa. BPSO is used to optimize feature selection in CRF learning in recognizing CHAR NE. The objective function at the optimization stage is to maximize the average F1-score value from 5-fold cross-validation of the CRF model. The best feature set combination from BPSO process is obtained from the last iteration or the solution from eight successive iterations does not change.

We extracted three types of local features, namely word features, part-of-speech (POS) features, and orthographic features with a total of 19 features. The i-th word (w_i) and contextual word around w_i of a sentence are extracted for word features with the addition of word prefix and suffix and contextual word prefix and suffix. Prefix and suffix features are extracted to overcome out-of-vocabulary. For contextual type of features, we use window width of one. POS tag label from w_i as p_i contextual POS tag label from word around w_i are then extracted for POS features. We extract some orthographical information from w_i and contextual w_i for ortographic features such as wheter w_i or contextual w_i is upper case, title case, lower case, number, at the beginning of sentence, at the end of sentence, greater than word length threshold or less than word length threshold.

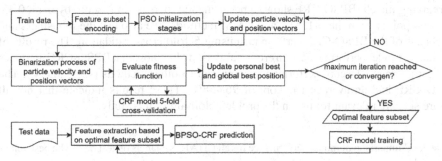

Fig. 1. Hybrid BPSO-CRF architecture for Character Named Entity Recognition on balinese folklore text.

4 Result and Discussion

We utilize AV-based HMM method[2], CRF model[3] trained with standard observation features (w_i and p_i) as M1, and CRF model trained with all feature sets as M2 for baseline methods. We use default parameters for CRF model from package settings. A, B, and π components for HMM are calculated directly based on our training data. We use 20 number of particles, maximum iterations of 40, inertia weight of 0.75, individual and social learning rate of 0.9 and 1.4 respectively for BPSO parameters. The same data composition for train and test data is used for all models to make comparisons fairs. The programming language Python v3.10 was used to develop the BPSO-CRF model. Precision, recall, and F1-score values [6] are used as performance metrics and are calculated from previous research. We also apply relax match calculations by removing B and I prefixes on CHAR NE label.

BPSO succeeded in optimizing the best features from initially producing an average F1-score of 96.38% to 96.60% in just 24 iterations. Based on the optimization results, the best feature subset was obtained by BPSO at the 24th iteration. The results suggest us to remove some insufficient features such as contextual features of word, word prefix, word suffix, and POS tag, and orthographic information such as *isEndWord* and *isDigit*. The best feature subset obtained by BPSO is then used to build and train the proposed CRF model, namely BPSO-CRF.

Based on Table 3, BPSO-CRF can give the best results compared to the other three baseline methods. Based on the calculation of model performance metrics without relax match, the BPSO-CRF yields an F1-score of 96.78%, while the baseline CRF without BPSO (M1 and M2) yields 96.35% and 96.48%, respectively. In addition, BPSO-CRF can provide a performance increase of 1.76 points from the HMM method. The CRF

---

[2] https://hmmlearn.readthedocs.io/en/latest/auto_examples/plot_multinomial_hmm.html
[3] https://sklearn-crfsuite.readthedocs.io/en/latest/

method that was trained with all feature sets (M2) gave better results when compared to the CRF that was trained with only two standard features (M1). BPSO-CRF also provided the best performance even though the calculation of model performance metrics is done by relaxing match. BPSO-CRF shows a performance increase in F-score by 0.44, 0.33, and 1.64 points from the M1, M2, and HMM methods. We also test the robustness and toughness of the BPSO-CRF performance using 5-fold cross-validation. The results of measuring model performance with cross-validation also show that BPSO-CRF produces the best average F1-score performance compared to other methods (see Table 4.). The BPSO-CRF had an average F1-score of 96.458%. These results indicate that not all feature sets are relevant for use in the problem domain of this study.

Table 3. Comparison of model performance for all CHAR NE labels on test data. The best values are in bold.

Without relax match				With relax match			
Metrics	HMM	M1	M2	Proposed	HMM	M1	M2	Proposed
Recall	94.70	96.48	96.57	**96.87**	96.57	96.64	96.71	**97.04**
Precision	95.55	96.34	96.43	**96.73**	96.43	96.50	96.59	**96.93**
F1-score	95.02	96.35	96.48	**96.78**	96.48	96.53	96.64	**96.97**

Table 4. F1-score performance comparison using 5-fold cross-validation from each model.

	Fold-1	Fold-2	Fold-3	Fold-4	Fold-5	Average
HMM	95.506	95.261	94.671	93.917	94.333	94.737
M1	96.331	95.782	96.215	95.796	95.379	95.901
M2	96.703	96.244	96.266	95.228	96.195	96.127
Proposed	**96.731**	**96.688**	**96.649**	**96.027**	**96.197**	**96.458**

Not all contextual features can help to recognize CHAR NE better. Using the current word feature, word prefix feature, word suffix feature, and current word POS Tag feature without the addition of contextual features can improve the M2 performance with all features. Based on the observations, several reasons related to the irrelevance of using the *isEndWord* and *isDigit* in this study were put forward. The tokens of each sentence in the dataset used to develop the model are always separated by a period as a marker for the end of the token. Thus, the CHAR NE label is never found at the end of the sentence. Therefore, the *isEndWord* feature does not help improve model performance. Almost the entire content of the CHAR NE labels in the dataset do not consist of numeric digits and are all composed of strings. Therefore, the *isDigit* feature is not recommended to use. However, the feature of whether the contextual w_i is digit or not is still used because the information around w_i can be a digit that can help better recognition of w_i labels, such as date and year which usually appear in legend texts.

5 Conclusion

This study proposes a BPSO-CRF hybrid NER method named SatuaNER, which identifies character entities in Balinese text. BPSO-CRF produces relatively better performance when compared to the baseline method. The performance of the baseline CRF model can increase if it is trained with the current word feature, word prefix feature, word suffix feature, and current word POS Tag feature without adding contextual features. Improvements in data labeling and the development of a larger dataset corpus are still needed in the future to improve the proposed model's performance.

Acknowledgments. This research was supported by the Udayana University's Institute for Research and Community Service (LPPM Unud), under Udayana's Invention Research (Penelitian Invensi Udayana) scheme and grant number B/1.3/UN14.4.A/PT.01.03/2023, May 2nd, 2023.

References

1. Barros, C., Vicente, M., Lloret, E.: Tackling the challenge of computational identification of characters in fictional narratives. In: Proceedings - 2019 IEEE International Conference on Cognitive Computing, ICCC 2019 - Part of the 2019 IEEE World Congress on Services, pp. 122–129. Institute of Electrical and Electronics Engineers Inc. (2019). https://doi.org/10.1109/ICCC.2019.00031
2. Carik, B., Yeniterzi, R.: A Twitter corpus for named entity recognition in Turkish. In: Proceedings of the 13th Conference on Language Resources and Evaluation (LREC 2022), pp. 4546–4551 (2022)
3. Bajracharya, A., Shrestha, S., Upadhyaya, S., Bk, S., Shakya, S.: Automated characters recognition and family relationship extraction from stories. In: 2018 8th International Conference on Cloud Computing, Data Science & Engineering (Confluence), Noida, pp. 314–319. IEEE (2018)
4. Jahan, L., Finlayson, M.A.: Character identification refined: a proposal. In: Proceedings of the First Workshop on Narrative Understanding, Minneapolis, pp. 12–18. Association for Computational Linguistics (2019)
5. Akmal, M., Romadhony, A.: Corpus development for indonesian product named entity recognition using semi-supervised approach. In: 2020 International Conference on Data Science and Its Applications (ICoDSA) (2020)
6. Ben Ali, B.A., Mihi, S., El Bazi, I., Laachfoubi, N.: Towards an approach based on particle swarm optimization for Arabic named entity recognition on social media. Indones. J. Electr. Eng. Comput. Sci. **27**, 1589–1600 (2022). https://doi.org/10.11591/ijeecs.v27.i3.pp1589-1600
7. ER, N.A.S.: Implementasi Latent Dirichlet Allocation (LDA) Untuk Klasterisasi Cerita Berbahasa Bali. Jurnal Teknologi Informasi dan Ilmu Komputer (JTIIK) **8**, 127–134 (2021). https://doi.org/10.25126/jtiik.202183556

On Observing Patterns of Correlations During Drill-Down

Sijo Arakkal Peious[1], Rahul Sharma[1,2][✉], Minakshi Kaushik[1][✉],
Mahtab Shahin[1][✉], and Dirk Draheim[1][✉]

[1] Information Systems Group, Tallinn University of Technology, Tallinn, Estonia
{sijo.arakkal,rahul.sharma,minakshi.kaushik,
mahtab.shahin,dirk.draheim}@taltech.ee
[2] Department of Information Technology, Ajay Kumar Garg Engineering College,
Ghaziabad, India

Abstract. Drill-down is a natural and extensive data analysis method that is widely used to analyse aggregate values of data at different levels of granularity. As such, drill-down has proven as an essential tool for informed decision-making in various scenarios. In this paper, we argue that drill-down can be equally utilised to analyse the behaviour of data patterns at various levels. To evaluate the usefulness of such an approach, we investigate the behaviour of Pearson correlation at different drill-down levels in the well-known meteorological data set CMDC. We test the hypothesis that the Pearson correlation between various attributes is preserved during drill-down and provide a systematic discussion of the outcome of these tests.

Keywords: Pearson correlation · drill-down

1 Introduction

Decision-makers need to do frequent data analysis to generate proper decisions. Going through a small amount of data is acceptable. However, there is a drastic change in the volume of the data produced every day [8]. It is undoubtedly good for decision-makers to understand all the available data before making any decision [14]. Due to the inability to go through each layer, decision-makers analyse the outermost margin or drill-down until they feel comfortable making the decision. They assume that the rest of the data follows the same pattern, which might result in the wrong conclusion.

Accessing the deeper layers of an organised dataset or a file structure is known as drill-down. Drill-down allows the decision-makers to analyse the granular layers of the dataset by combining more constraints. Drill-down can provide insights into each layer of data to decision-makers other than a marginal [10,16]. For example, a drill-down report which shows the salary distribution of each state in a country will also provide the capability to view and compare the salary distribution of each province or profession in the state. The drill-down method allows decision-makers to go deeper into each level for in-depth knowledge of each layer and compare it with each other. In the drill-down salary distribution report, decision-makers can compare the salaries in different provinces to identify which is the high-paying profession and high-paying province for the same profession. Seeing data from a different point of view will give a different perspective about the data; drill-down allows decision-makers to analyse the same data from a different point of view and compare it with different layers of results to make a better understating of data.

The rest of the paper is structured in the following manner: Sect. 2 delves into the issue or challenge being addressed in this paper. Then, Sect. 3 explains the data preprocessing method which is used in this study. In Sect. 4, we answer the question we raised in Sect. 2. Finally, Sect. 5 offers a concise overview of the findings from this study before proceeding to conclude the paper.

2   Problem Statement

In this paper, we calculate the bivariate Pearson correlation in each level and compare it with the outer marginal level. In bivariate analysis, the relationship of two variables is studied simultaneously [6,12]. Pearson correlation specifies the existence of a correlation between two variables and discovers the magnitude of the correlation between them. This method is commonly used for numerical variables [11]. A correlation shows the influence of one variable on another, but the actual causality might be in a different direction than we assume, so the correlation would not indicate causation. The correlation values vary from 1 (strong positive correlation) to -1 (strong negative correlation). The correlation value of uncorrelated variables will be 0 [2]. This correlation value shows, how a variable will behave when an increase or decrease happens to the other variable [15]. According to David(1938), the recommended sample size for calculating Pearson correlation is greater than or equal to 25 ($n \geq 25$) [3]. So, we can consider this number(25) as our minimum threshold for this study. The equation for the Person correlation of two variables is the sum of the covariance of variables divided by the sum of the square root of covariance [1].

$$\frac{\sum_{i=1}^{n}(x_i - \overline{x})(y_i - \overline{y})}{\sqrt{\sum_{i=1}^{n}(x_i - \overline{x})^2}\sqrt{\sum_{i=1}^{n}(y_i - \overline{y})^2}} \tag{1}$$

In recent times, individuals, particularly politicians and the media, often make inaccurate assertions regarding the causality of misleading or inappropriate correlations. These claims have a significant impact on decision-making. As we explained in the previous paragraph, correlation is not always the answer to causality. It does not mean that the correlated variable has a causal impact on each other. A vast volume of data is created on a daily basis, necessitating decision-makers to thoroughly review the data for informed decision-making. To alleviate this workload, they may opt to review the data at a superficial level or discretize the values. Selecting pertinent information and suitable features from the dataset has historically posed a challenge for decision-makers [14]. The system's performance has a vital role in finding these features and information [7]. Choosing unsuitable features will mislead the decision-makers, resulting in incorrect conclusions or confusion regarding the variables' impact.

Utilizing a drill-down approach enhances decision-makers' understanding of the data. In this study, we integrate drill-down capabilities with Pearson correlation to gain a deeper understanding of the data. This combined approach aids decision-makers in reaching more informed conclusions. To help the decision-makers, we have created a tool(Grandreport [5][1]) with multiple data mining techniques [13] and ACIF generator function [17]. The Grandreport will produce numerous rows of report. This is due to the absence of constraints on support and confidence, enabling generalized association rule mining. Analysts utilize this approach to integrate every line of the report into their decision-making process [5]. In Grandreport, we have integrated association rule mining, Pearson correlation and regression to improve the decision-making process. In association rule mining, the target columns are discretized for numeric values to facilitate the mining process [4]. In the Grandreport, we utilize values in their original form to achieve improved results. This stands as a primary advantage of our system. The main disadvantage of this tool is that it reports all possible combinations of influencing factors and generates a lengthy report. To tackle this problem, we decided to report only the exciting and valuable factors by analysing the output with the measures provided by integrated data mining techniques before showing it to the user. From this process, we noticed that some of the variables with high correlation in the marginal level are not showing correlation during the drill-down, and most decision-makers are not considering this pattern.

In this paper, we are trying to answer,

- Does the correlation shown in the marginal for a variable follow the same pattern during drill-down, or will it behave differently?

Our hypothesis is that the correlation observed at the marginal level for a variable will maintain a consistent pattern during drill-down.

3   Experimental Study

Within this research, we examine the patterns present at the marginal layer in comparison to each subsequent drill-down layer within a real-world dataset. Subsequently, we discuss our findings regarding the patterns observed in each dataset.

3.1   CMDC Dataset

For this study, Meteorological Data in China [9] (CMDC[2] is used. The establishment of this portal aimed to facilitate the sharing of daily meteorological data,

---

[1] http://grandreport.me/.

[2] http://data.cma.cn/en).

ultimately advancing science and technology. The CMDC dataset encompasses various meteorological attributes, including precipitation amount, sea level pressure, snow depth, temperature, visibility, wind speed, and more. Each attribute comprises one year's worth of data from 31 provinces.

3.2 Preprocessing

Pearson correlation involves a bivariate analysis and is most effective with numerical values. To enhance performance and reduce computation time, we refined the dataset by generating distinct tables for various attributes. Each column represents the mean value of a specific attribute for each day within a particular province(Table 1). The comparison between the provinces will generate an overview of climate differences in each province (Table 2).

Table 1. CMDC dataset separated by province.

Date	Beijing	Tianjin	Hebei	Shanxi	Neimenggu	Liaoning	Jilin	Heilongjiang
01-Jan	3.300	2.114	2.386	3.160	3.103	3.272	3.001	8.108
02-Jan	4.000	2.914	2.844	3.004	3.442	3.028	4.059	6.415
03-Jan	3.100	2.084	2.986	3.214	3.569	3.069	3.251	5.038
04-Jan	3.600	3.330	3.362	3.661	4.332	2.673	3.095	4.738
05-Jan	2.700	3.951	3.663	3.144	3.926	2.988	2.730	4.100
06-Jan	5.900	4.711	3.747	3.158	4.867	3.943	2.959	3.723
07-Jan	10.800	8.600	5.164	3.800	4.293	8.369	3.475	3.923
08-Jan	4.300	5.597	3.536	3.504	3.912	4.142	3.458	5.008
09-Jan	3.500	2.654	2.767	3.405	2.884	2.501	3.112	4.038
10-Jan	10.900	6.989	4.223	3.780	4.126	3.429	2.972	3.592

3.3 Setup

The objective of this study is to determine the correlation between variables and compare the Pearson correlation value of each drill-down layer against the marginal level. Using the above-described dataset (CMDC), we computed the Pearson correlation for each drill-down and compared it with the province's marginal layer. To ensure accuracy, we omitted correlation results with a count of less than 25 [3]. Put simply, if a month is absent or the number of values for a specific month is below 25 in any province, those months are excluded from the comparison. We developed a Python command line application to calculate correlation. To ensure accuracy and efficiency, we utilized the 'corrcoef' function from the 'NumPy' library.

As an example of the output generated by the application, see Table 3, which shows the correlations of the provinces Tianjin and Hunan for various months.

4   Evaluation

As previously mentioned, utilizing the drill-down approach enhances our understanding of the data. The outcomes confirm that drill-down helps to generate a deeper understanding of the data. Our experimentation with the CMDC dataset to verify the hypothesis, revealing diverse patterns across the dataset. The results shown here are for different meteorological attributes of Tianjin province. In this section, we address the questions posed earlier in this study.

– Whether the correlation shown in the marginal for a variable will follow the same pattern during drill-down or will it behave differently?

To answer this, we can compare the Figs. 1, 2, 3, 4 and 5. Our investigation revealed that nearly all combinations exhibit a consistent pattern with marginal level, with a few exceptions. The result shown in the Figs. 1, 2, 3, 4 and 5 can be divided into three groups.

1. The correlation patterns of drill-down have the same pattern as the marginal.
2. The correlation patterns of the majority drill-down are not the same as the marginal.
3. The correlation patterns of the drill-down and marginal behave in opposite directions.

The 'X' and 'Y' axes represent the correlation and number of elements.

Figures 1 and 2 show the same pattern for the marginal and drill-down. In this, the marginal shows a weak correlation, and the drill-down also shows the same pattern for most variables. However, a handful of variables (less than 5%) show strong correlations. Around 65% of attributes in the CMDC dataset follow this pattern.

Figures 3 and 4 show different patterns for drill-down and marginal. Here, the marginal will have a strong positive or negative correlation, while drill-down, we are getting different correlations. A strong positive correlation is generated for the marginal in Figs. 3 and 4. However, drill-down shows a weak or moderate correlation for the same dataset. Some exceptional variables(less than 10%) also show strong positive correlations. 25% of the attributes in the CMDC dataset follow this pattern.

The drill-down and marginal correlation patterns behave in opposite directions in Fig. 5. A negative correlation is generated for the marginal, while drill-down, strong or moderate positive correlations are generated for most of the variables. More than 60% of the variables behave in opposite directions. Figure 5 exemplifies the importance of drill-down techniques in data analysis. Only 10% of CMDC dataset attributes exhibit this pattern.

This result shows that it is always recommended to delve deep into the dataset to find the actual pattern before making any conclusions. In some cases, the correlation between the marginal and drill-down behaves differently (like Fig. 5). Moreover, the existence of the statistical paradoxes and other data fallacies (like confounding effects) have a significant impact on the outcome.

Table 2. Outer marginal correlations between (a) the mean temperature of 'Tianjin' and the mean temperature of various other provinces, and (b) the weighted mean sea level pressure of 'Tianjin' and the weighted mean sea level pressure of other provinces.

Province	(a) mean temperature correlation with 'Tianjin'	(b) sea level pressure correlation with 'Tianjin '
Anhui	0.9311	−0.4885
Fujian	0.8471	0.0413
Hebei	0.9897	−0.4860
Heilongjiang	0.9672	−0.4951
Jiangsu	0.9191	0.1049
Jiangxi	0.8910	−0.6206
Liaoning	0.9768	−0.0667
Neimenggu	0.9729	0.0736
Shanghai	0.8863	−0.8132
Shandong	0.9696	−0.1986
Zhejiang	0.8858	−0.7389

Table 3. Drill-down correlations between (a) the mean temperature of 'Tianjin' and 'Hunan', and (b) the weighted mean sea level pressure of 'Tianjin' and 'Hunan'.

Layer	(a) mean temperature correlation between 'Tianjin' and 'Hunan'	(b) sea level pressure correlation between 'Tianjin' and 'Hunan'
Year (Marginal)	*0.9018*	*0.0086*
January	0.2872	0.2913
February	0.6760	0.5680
March	0.4209	0.8667
April	0.5133	0.5599
May	−0.0876	0.0572
June	0.1998	0.3018
July	0.3676	0.9029
August	0.4704	−0.9963
September	−0.7657	0.8607
October	0.0351	0.7164
November	0.8734	0.8754
December	0.2183	0.9346

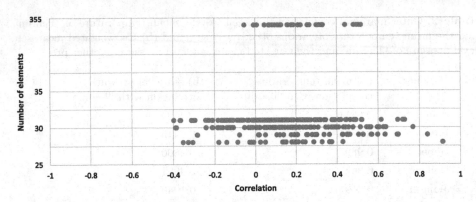

Fig. 1. Correlation plot for inverse-distance weighted maximum wind gust.

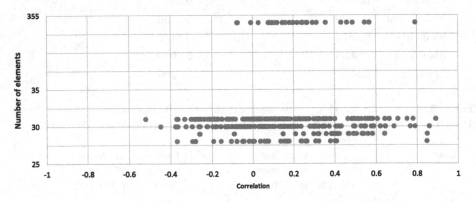

Fig. 2. Correlation plot for inverse-distance weighted maximum sustained wind speed.

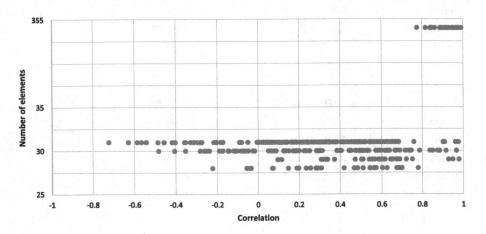

Fig. 3. Correlation plot for inverse-distance weighted mean temperature.

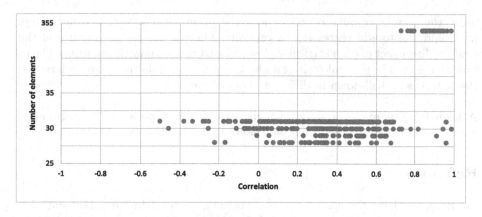

Fig. 4. Correlation plot for inverse-distance weighted mean dew point.

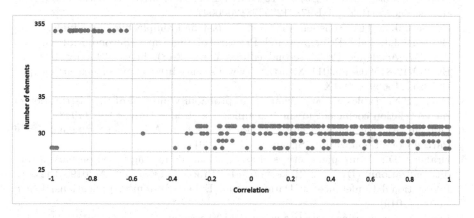

Fig. 5. Correlation plot for inverse-distance weighted mean sea level pressure.

5   Conclusion

The overall aim of this work is to identify the importance of the drill-down approach in data analysis. Given the importance of data analysis in decision-making, we wanted to understand the data more deeply and identify the patterns of each layer with the impact on the outcome. We calculated the correlation of each layer and compared it with the marginal correlation. This approach aims to identify the different patterns in drill-down and marginal. The results show three different patterns for CMDC data in this work.

The main confrontation faced in this work was to identify the proper statistical method to find the pattern to such scenarios. The experiment is carried out only on a small scale, with a limited number of meteorological attributes of CMDC data for one year. So, the presented results deliver only a general view of the importance of drill-down analysis. Further changes and more statistical analytical methods are required to enhance the results. For now, we are only using the correlation method to identify the patterns; however, as a next step, we would like to add regression to generate different perspectives and find the confounding effect of each attribute. Also, as part of future work, we would like to investigate on a larger scale(with hundreds of real-world datasets) to understand the patterns of drill-down in different types of datasets.

Acknowledgements. This work has been conducted in the project "ICT programme" which was supported by the European Union through the European Social Fund.

References

1. Berman, J.J.: Chapter 4 - understanding your data. In: Berman, J.J. (ed.) Data Simplification, pp. 135–187. Morgan Kaufmann, Boston (2016). https://doi.org/10.1016/B978-0-12-803781-2.00004-7, https://www.sciencedirect.com/science/article/pii/B9780128037812000047
2. Berman, J.J.: 11 - indispensable tips for fast and simple big data analysis. In: Berman, J.J. (ed.) Principles and Practice of Big Data (Second Edition), pp. 231–257. Academic Press, second edition edn. (2018). https://doi.org/10.1016/B978-0-12-815609-4.00011-X, https://www.sciencedirect.com/science/article/pii/B978012815609400011X
3. David, F.N.: Tables of the ordinates and probability integral of the distribution of the correlation coefficient in small samples. Cambridge Univ, Press (1938)
4. Draheim, D.: Generalized Jeffrey Conditionalization: A Frequentist Semantics of Partial Conditionalization. Springer, Cham (2017)
5. Draheim, D.: Future perspectives of association rule mining based on partial conditionalizationin (DEXA'2019 keynote). In: Proceedings of DEXA'2019 - the 30th International Conference on Database and Expert Systems Applications, LNCS 11706, (2019)
6. Field, A.: Discovering statistics using IBM SPSS statistics. sage (2013)
7. Gavel, S., Raghuvanshi, A.S., Tiwari, S.: Maximum correlation based mutual information scheme for intrusion detection in the data networks. Expert Syst. Appl. **189**, 116089 (2022). https://doi.org/10.1016/j.eswa.2021.116089, https://www.sciencedirect.com/science/article/pii/S095741742101424X
8. Han, J., Kamber, M.: Data Mining Concepts And Techniques, pp. 335–391. San Francisco, CA pp (2001)
9. Lab, C.D.: Meteorological Data (2020). https://doi.org/10.7910/DVN/TU0JDP, https://doi.org/10.7910/DVN/TU0JDP
10. Morar, N., et al.: Drilling into dashboards: responding to computer recommendation in fraud analysis. IEEE Trans. Human-Mach. Syst. **49**(6), 633–641 (2019). https://doi.org/10.1109/THMS.2019.2925619
11. Nettleton, D.: Chapter 6 - selection of variables and factor derivation. In: Nettleton, D. (ed.) Commercial Data Mining, pp. 79–104. Morgan Kaufmann, Boston (2014). https://doi.org/10.1016/B978-0-12-416602-8.00006-6, https://www.sciencedirect.com/science/article/pii/B9780124166028000066
12. Omilion-Hodges, L.: Sage Encyclopedia of Communication Research Methods, pp. 855–858. SAGE publications (2017). https://doi.org/10.4135/9781483381411.n293

13. Arakkal Peious, S., Sharma, R., Kaushik, M., Shah, S.A., Yahia, S.B.: Grand reports: a tool for generalizing association rule mining to numeric target values. In: Song, M., Song, I.-Y., Kotsis, G., Tjoa, A.M., Khalil, I. (eds.) DaWaK 2020. LNCS, vol. 12393, pp. 28–37. Springer, Cham (2020). https://doi.org/10.1007/978-3-030-59065-9_3
14. Peious, S.A., Suran, S., Pattanaik, V., Draheim, D.: Enabling sensemaking and trust in communities: an organizational perspective, p. 95–103. Association for Computing Machinery, New York, NY, USA (2021). https://doi.org/10.1145/3487664.3487678
15. Reshef, D., et al.: Detecting novel associations in large data sets. Science (New York, N.Y.) **334**, 1518–24 (2011). https://doi.org/10.1126/science.1205438
16. Shabaninejad, S., Khosravi, H., Indulska, M., Bakharia, A., Isaias, P.: Automated insightful drill-down recommendations for learning analytics dashboards. In: Proceedings of the Tenth International Conference on Learning Analytics & Knowledge, pp. 41–46. LAK '20, Association for Computing Machinery, New York, NY, USA (2020). https://doi.org/10.1145/3375462.3375539, https://doi.org/10.1145/3375462.3375539
17. Sharma, R., et al.: A novel framework for unification of association rule mining, online analytical processing and statistical reasoning. IEEE Access **10**, 12792–12813 (2022). https://doi.org/10.1109/ACCESS.2022.3142537

Deep and Machine Learning

Unsupervised Clustering and Explainable AI for Unveiling Behavioral Variations Across Time in Home-Appliance Generated Data

Ramona Tolas[(✉)] [iD], Raluca Portase[iD], Camelia Lemnaru[iD],
Mihaela Dinsoreanu[iD], and Rodica Potolea[iD]

Technical University of Cluj-Napoca, Cluj-Napoca, Romania
tolas.ramona@gmail.com

Abstract. The widespread adoption of smart home technologies has resulted in the generation of vast amounts of data related to home appliance usage. This research aims to harness the power of data analytics and pattern identification techniques to extract valuable insights from this data. We present an exploration of temporal dependency analysis applied to home-appliance generated data represented as user interactions events. Our approach converts the event data into time-series and historical data is segmented. Spectral features are extracted from each segmented time-boxed usage, and unsupervised clustering algorithms group similar usage patterns. Explainable AI techniques are employed to unravel the rules governing the occurrence of each usage pattern. Through this methodology, we unveil behavioral variations across time, providing insights into user behaviors and usage dynamics. Our findings contribute to the field of user profiling and provide a valuable framework for extracting meaningful insights from home-appliance generated data.

Keywords: Knowledge inference · Home appliance usage · Data analytics · Pattern identification · Unsupervised clustering · Explainable AI

1 Introduction

In recent years, the extensive adoption of home appliances equipped with sensors has facilitated the generation of rich datasets capturing user interactions. These datasets, represented as events recording the user's engagement with the home appliance, offer a valuable opportunity to gain insights into user behavior and uncover temporal dependencies in usage patterns. Understanding how user behaviors evolve across different time periods is essential for optimizing appliance design to fit the user needs, energy management, and personalized user experiences.

This paper presents a comprehensive exploration of temporal dependency analysis applied to usage patterns derived from home-appliance generated data. Our approach employs a completely unsupervised solution, aiming to identify and analyze behavioral variations that occur across time. The key steps of our

P. Delir Haghighi et al. (Eds.): iiWAS 2023, LNCS 14416, pp. 147–161, 2023.
https://doi.org/10.1007/978-3-031-48316-5_17

methodology involve converting the event data into time-series representations and segmenting the historical data into time-boxed snippets. By breaking the historical data into time-boxed snippets, we capture the temporal context within which behaviors occur, allowing us to examine usage patterns within specific time intervals. To uncover meaningful usage insights, spectral features are extracted from each time series, providing a compact representation that characterizes the usage patterns. This spectral feature extraction enables the identification of underlying patterns and variations, facilitating subsequent analysis and interpretation. Next, unsupervised clustering algorithms are employed to group similar usage patterns together. Each cluster represents a set of time-boxed usages of the appliance that share common characteristics from the usage perspective. Furthermore, our approach incorporates explainable AI techniques to unravel the rules governing the occurrence of the identified usage patterns. By leveraging explainable AI, we aim to shed light on the factors and conditions that contribute to the temporal dynamics of usage patterns, providing interpretable insights for appliance design and user behavior analysis.

In the subsequent sections, we present the details of our methodology, describe the experimental setup, present the results of our analysis, and discuss the implications of our findings.

2   Theoretical Background and Related Work

This study employs various machine learning techniques to unravel temporal dependency in usage patterns. The techniques utilized for the analysis combine time-series analysis with clustering and explainable AI. This section is focused on detailing all the theoretical aspects needed for understanding the proposed knowledge-mining solution.

2.1   Harnessing Temporal Insights: Machine Learning Algorithms for Time-Series Analysis

Time-series analysis enables the exploration of sequential patterns and trends within the temporal data, facilitating the detection of usage patterns over time. The main characteristic of this data format is that the property of interest is measured at successive equally spaced points in time [18]. Representing data in the syntactical form of time series is extremely common in the context of smart devices.

The data format popularity is also proven by a large number of available solutions in the research community. The need for processing and analyzing time series determined the development of libraries focused on data representation [8,9], data processing [24] and data visualization [5]. The already developed software solutions and their large community and stability determined the study of different transformations from other forms of representing the data into time series. In [31], the authors study different ways of transforming event-based signals (data format commonly used in storing user interaction with different devices) to time series. A taxonomy of this transformation is defined by the authors.

Feature extraction needs to be applied to time series in order to be compatible with machine learning techniques, such as classification or clustering. The extracted features can be from the spectral domain, from time domain or statistical [11]. Extracting features that retain information about the shape of the signal is widely used in the literature [19,37]. Frecvency domain has proven to be an effective way of characterizing time series and its usage is present in the medical field [10,22,34], automotive [33] or industrial engineering [30]. Discrete Fourier Transform algorithm [3] can be used for extracting shape-related characteristics of the data [31].

Pattern mining methods aim to extract valuable patterns from extensive datasets to enhance domain understanding and support decision-making processes. This objective can be achieved by employing clustering algorithms [14,25,38] to identify patterns of similarity and dissimilarity among objects. When the task is to retrieve information without apriori knowledge, the number of clusters is unknown. Density-based algorithms [12] such as DBSCAN [15] can be a good option in this case.

2.2   XAI - Explainable AI

In recent times, machine learning and especially deep learning has gained considerable attention and popularity due to its impressive performance in various domains. However, despite its notable successes, deep learning possesses a significant limitation: the explainability feature of the decision being taken by the AI solution. This deficiency necessitates the emergence of a distinct and critical area of research known as explainable AI. Addressing the limitations of deep learning, explainable AI serves as a standalone field, dedicated to developing methodologies and techniques that facilitate the interpretability and comprehensibility of AI systems, enabling stakeholders to gain insights into the factors driving their decisions.

As emphasized by the authors of [17], having explanations for the decision process can be an essential tool for users to understand, improve and detect reasoning biases. Because some critical domains need the conditions that lead to AI decisions, XAI topic is tackled by both academic and industrial communities. In [35], a review of the available XAI solutions is presented. Sensitivity analysis [28] and layer-wise relevance propagation [29] are methods presented in the review as techniques for making deep neural network decisions transparent. Explanatory graphs [36] are also analyzed as a method of extracting knowledge hierarchy hidden inside neural networks.

Even if the research in the XAI topic is focused on developing complex solutions for increasing the explainability of different kinds of neural networks, other machine learning techniques have the explainability built in [1]. One example of such an algorithm is Decision Tree [2]. The goal of the algorithm is to create a model that predicts the value of a target variable by learning simple decision rules inferred from the data features. Having also the advantage of being easy to understand, the algorithm is used in the literature as a XAI system [20, 21].

2.3   Analysing Data Produced by Smart Home Appliances

In recent times, there has been an increasing interest in academic research focused on home appliances, driven by the growing popularity of smart devices and the improved affordability of technology. The authors of [27] offer a methodology for analyzing data with multiple complexities, such as the data originating from home appliances. In [32] the transmission topic is tackled and transmission models are identified. The authors show how the periodicity in the transmission of a signal can be used to detect missing data and data duplication in the context of data generated by home appliances. Modern approaches for pre-processing the data applied on session-based data (running cycle for a washing machine can be an example) are presented in [23]. In [13], the authors present a pipeline of processing sensor-generated data with applications in data generated by home appliances. Knowledge inference techniques are present in the work [16] while the authors of [26] present an end-to-end pipeline for usage prediction. To the best of our knowledge, identifying patterns of usage is poorly tackled in this area, of home appliances. The authors of [31] present preliminary results for identifying one pattern usage in the historical data. The next section is detailing the work done while stating the limitations of the solution.

2.4   Mining Time-Boxed Usage Patterns

The authors of [31] are tackling the topic of profiling the user in the context of home-appliance usage. They introduce a formalized representation of generic home appliance-generated data. The input data for the presented pipeline is represented by the user interaction with the smart devices (the device is capable of capturing and transmitting the interaction and the moment of the interaction). The acronym UIES (user interaction events series) is used by the authors for referring to this syntactic form of the data. This acronym and the rest of the acronyms used by the authors in order to formulate the problem statement are used with the same meaning in this paper. Time-boxed usage, as defined in the mentioned work is symbolized by $TBES^T$ (T represents the time window), and the same time-boxed usage, represented by user interaction events in a certain time window but in the syntactical form of time-series, is symbolized by $TS.TBES$. A behavioral pattern is defined in these conditions as a sequence of probabilities. Each probability from the sequence represents the probability of the user interacting with the appliance.

The proposed pipeline is taking the input data (UIES) and as a first step is transforming it into $TS.TBES$, as a syntactical pre-processing step. From each $TS.TBES$, features are extracted using Discrete Fast Fourier Transform. A set of first N (input for pipeline) coefficients are used and with the time-boxed usage being now represented by a set of numbers, a clustering algorithm is applied to the data. If a majority cluster is found, it is concluded that a general usage pattern is found in the data and the usage pattern is inferred by applying the inverse Fast Fourier Transform on the centroid of the majority cluster.

The presented approach has good results if the appliance utilization follows a single and consistent pattern across time. However, the solution has some limitations. One of them is the fact that a single pattern can be extracted from the data. If the user is interacting with the device in different ways depending on the placement in time when the interaction is done, the patterns can not be inferred with the proposed approach. For example, the proposed pipeline is capable of mining the usage pattern of using the device between 8 AM and 10 AM each morning and also using the device in the evening. If the user has this pattern only during the weekdays, and on the weekend the usage pattern is completely different, due to various factors, this information will be lost. Only the pattern which is more predominant will be inferred.

Another limitation is the lack of explainability for the situation when the pattern is depicted in the data. In the case where a majority cluster exists, the only information that can be provided is that it is very likely that the user will act accordingly to that pattern, but there is no information under what conditions. In the above example, when a pattern of using the device two times a day is inferred, there is no information about the fact that only during the weekdays this pattern is likely to occur.

The goal of this work is to address these limitations. A processing pipeline for inferring multiple usage pattern is proposed. The pipeline is addressing also the problem of offering the conditions under which a pattern is likely to occur.

3   Proposed Processing Pipeline for Inference of Time-Dependent Usage Pattern

The proposed pipeline represented in Fig. 1 is extracting usage patterns based on the user interaction with a smart home-appliance by analyzing historical data. The input of the pipeline is represented by the events captured by the smart home-appliance related to user interactions. These events can be triggered by opening the door of the smart refrigerator or by using a certain washing program in the case of a smart washing machine. These interactions are identified by UIES (user interaction events series).

The pipeline starts with a pre-processing phase where the goal is to transform the UIES into TS.TBES. This part of the pipeline will not be detailed as it does not contribute to the novelty brought by the claim of this paper. The pre-processing steps are detailed in [31].

Fast Fourier Transform is used for the feature extraction phase. TS.TBES represent the time-boxed usage in the syntactical form of time series. In order to be compatible with the accepted input of numerical algorithms such as clustering algorithms, features for the time series need to be extracted. For minimizing the data dimensionality, not all the coefficients of the Fast Fourier Transform are used. The number of used parameters is given as input to the pipeline and should be determined in an empirical manner.

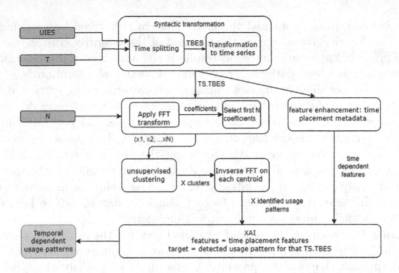

Fig. 1. Pipeline for mining time-boxed usage patterns which are time-dependent

Having the new feature space, an unsupervised clustering algorithm is applied on the time-boxed usages represented by time series. A number of X clusters are obtained. Each cluster is obtained by grouping similar usages. The centroid is a characterization of the general pattern from that cluster. In order to obtain the values from the same space as the input, the Inverse Fourier Transform is applied on the centroid. After this operation is performed, the centroid represents a usage pattern found in the dataset. Even if the information found until this moment is contributing to a profile of the user, there is still knowledge that can be further extracted to have a precise description of the user behavior.

XAI Component: A few examples of usage patterns that can be extracted with the previously mentioned steps are:

- **Usage Pattern 0**: the user is not interacting with the device
- **Usage Pattern 1**: the user is interacting with the device every evening, around 8 PM
- **Usage Pattern 2**: the user is interacting with the device between 8 AM and 2 PM

Just identifying these patterns in the data can not be enough for creating a profile of the user. The user might not use the home appliance in August because it is not home the entire month, every year. The user might follow the **Usage Pattern 1** during the weekdays, except Tuesday when he has the day off and is using the appliance with **Usage Pattern 2**. In weekends, having a different schedule is following **Usage Pattern 2**. The patterns, together with the conditions of occurrence from a temporal perspective offer a better and complete understanding of the appliance usage. These usage rules are represented in Fig. 2 in the form of a decision tree.

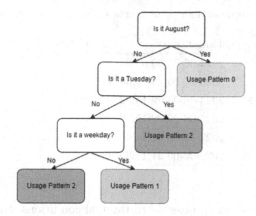

Fig. 2. Representation of the rules governing the usage model of a home appliance

The conditions under which a usage pattern occurs can be inferred by using an explainable AI solution applied to the time-dependent features extracted from the data.

Each TS.TBES (time-boxed usage), after the clusterization phase is done, is associated with a cluster. The goal of this phase is to discover what time features of the TS.TBES are influencing the cluster assignment (hence, the associated usage pattern).

In order to obtain this, the feature domain needs to be extracted from the TS.TBES. Month, year, day of the month, day of the week are valid features in this step. The entire feature space for this step is established based on the characteristics of the data. The target value is the associated cluster and an XAI solution applied to the generated data will construct an explanation of the temporal conditions when a pattern is occurring in the data.

4   Experiments and Results

The proposed usage profiling method is tested on data produced by the interaction of a user with a smart refrigerator. The interaction is stored in the form of events of opening and closing the door of the device. For evaluation purposes, complex patterns are planted in synthetically generated data. The time window used for splitting the analysed usage is one day. This implies that daily patterns and the conditions under which they occur in the data are mined.

4.1   Data Description

In Table 1, a snapshot from a synthetic data set representing the syntactic form of the data used is shown. The timestamp of the occurring event and encoding of the analyzed state is included in the data. The generated events are of type open/close the door, so numerical encoding of 1 is given for open door and numerical encoding 0 is given for closed door.

Table 1. Example of door open events from one smart refrigerator.

Timestamp	Door State
2023-06-05 09:04:35	1
2023-06-05 09:05:35	0
2023-06-05 09:15:02	1
2023-06-05 09:15:58	0
2023-06-05 21:11:00	1
2023-06-05 21:11:35	0

In order to be as close as possible to the real conditions, the characteristics of the real data are closely followed in the simulation process. The duration of keeping the door open, the frequency of openings and the noise were analyzed and replicated on the synthetic data.

4.2 Planted Patterns

A number of four devices are used in the experiments. For each device, a complex usage pattern was planted during the data simulation phase. The usage pattern is obtained by combining different day usage patterns. Examples of day usage patterns for the data described in the previous section are presented in Fig. 3. This section will associate an identifier for each appliance with the description of the planted usage patterns.

The planted behaviors are generated by varying the daily pattern based on temporal conditions in order to address the objective of this paper:

1. **1AP&2AP**: This device contains recordings of user interactions during one month. For the first part of the week (Monday, Tuesday, Wednesday) user is interacting with the device following 1AP model (one interaction during the day) and for the rest of the week interacts with the 2AP usage pattern model (interacts with the device two times a day)
2. **Alternative 1AP & 2AP**: The device contains user interactions spread across one month. The behavior is to alternate each day: one day is interacting in a 1AP model and in the other day in a 2AP model.
3. **Month dependent**: Containing four months of interactions, this behavior is following the 1AP model for two months and the 3AP for the rest of the months.
4. **Complex**: The device contains four months of interactions. If the day is a Monday, then 1AP model day pattern interaction is planted. If it is weekend and it is June, then the 2AP day usage pattern is planted and 3AP in the rest of the days.

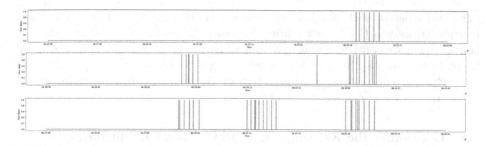

Fig. 3. Each figure represents a day usage. A day usage is represented by active periods (AP) - periods of time when the user is interacting with the device (in this case is opening the door of the fridge). The figure contains 1AP (one active period - the user is interacting with the device in one period of the day), 2AP (two active periods - the user is interacting with the device in three periods of the day) and 3AP. The X axis contains the time and the Y axis value 0 or 1 corresponds to the state of the door of the smart refrigerator.

4.3   Data Preparation and Feature Extraction

The data is pre-procesessed and from the event-based interaction, it is transformed into time series. Using the taxonomy defined in [31] for transforming the events into time series, a forward-filling method is used. This is practically implemented using specialized Python libraries [9].

To capture daily patterns in user interactions with the home appliance while reducing the data volume, a resampling technique is employed to transform the time granularity to one hour. This resampling process condenses the information about user interaction while maintaining all the interactions intact. The aggregation method used during the resampling phase involves summing the constituent aggregates. Consequently, the resulting signal represents the total duration, in seconds, that the door was open during each corresponding hour. Figure 4 illustrates a visual representation of the data snapshot after the completion of this resampling phase.

Fig. 4. Example of door open events from the smart refrigerator after the forward-filling and resampling to hours by aggregating the values is applied on the data

Discrete Fourier Transform [3] is used for constructing the feature space. Ten coefficients from the result of applying the Discrete Fourier Transform are further added to feature space because this number of coefficients provides good results in [31].

Following the aforementioned procedure, the events corresponding to a single day of user interaction with the appliance are represented by a set of 20 real numbers, wherein each number represents a coefficient derived from the Fast Fourier Transform (FFT), accounting for both the real and imaginary components. To ensure consistent scaling across all features, a normalization operation is conducted on the obtained feature set using a min-max scaler [7]. This scaling technique enables the transformation of the features to a common range, facilitating fair and comparable analysis.

4.4   Determining the Existing Usage Patterns with Clustering Algorithms

In the clustering phase, we employed the Python implementation of the DBSCAN algorithm [6]. The algorithm was configured with the Euclidean distance metric and the automatic selection of algorithmic optimizations. Specifically, we set the leaf size parameter to 30, while the values for the epsilon (EPS) parameter and the minimum samples parameter (minimum number of points required to form a dense region) were determined empirically.

All the time-boxed usages are associated with a cluster after this step. Each cluster represents the usage pattern (all the time-boxed usage patterns that are in that cluster are usages which are similar). For extracting the usage pattern from the cluster, the same procedure as defined in [31] is used: features of the centroid of each cluster are de-normalized and Inverse Fourier Transform [4] is then applied. In order to obtain a usage behavior as described in [31], the values are normalized to [0, 1] interval. This operation transforms one cluster into one usage pattern. In Fig. 5, a visualization of extracted daily patterns from the clusters is presented.

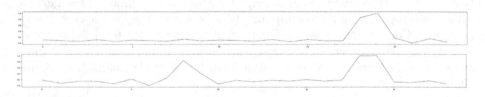

Fig. 5. Example of mined daily usage patterns from data produced by a smart refrigerator. The first pattern indicates that the user is interacting with the device by opening and closing the door only in a specific period of the day. The second pattern indicates that the user has two active periods of interaction with the device. The pattern is represented by the probability of the user interacting with the device at a certain hour of the day. The X-axis represents the time and the Y-axis represents the mentioned usage probability

In order to increase the results, various experiments were performed on the datasets. DBSCAN can be tuned by modifying the EPS (the maximum distance between two samples for one to be considered as in the neighborhood of the other). In Table 2, the results of the experiments are presented.

Table 2. Results of the experiments performed in the clustering phase with DBSCAN clustering algorithm. The experiments are made with the four data sets described in 4.1 *Data description* and 4.2 *Planted patterns* sections

Dataset	EPS	F1-score	Dataset	EPS	F1-score
1AP&2AP	0.45	0.821	Month dependent	0.45	0.522
	0.65	**0.966**		0.65	0.924
	0.75	0.966		0.75	**0.991**
	0.85	0.705		0.85	0.991
Alternative 1AP & 2AP	0.45	0.566	Complex	0.45	0.610
	0.65	**0.805**		0.65	**0.610**
	0.75	0.455		0.75	0.587
	0.85	0.448		0.85	0.551

4.5 Inferring Conditions of Occurrence for the Identified Usage Patterns

Previous steps of the pipeline revealed some usage patterns but there is no information about the conditions under which these usage patterns are occurring. The goal of this work is to find the temporal dependency of the identified patterns.

The explainable AI module from the pipeline was implemented with a Decision Tree algorithm. Before applying the Decision Tree algorithm in order to obtain a decision graph that will explain what rules are leading to a certain usage pattern, temporal descriptors need to be extracted from the usage pattern.

The temporal descriptors used in the experiments done as part of the current work are: **year, day of the year, day of the month, day of the week**. Each time-boxed usage (TS.TBES) is enhanced with these new features and with the label of the cluster where it was assigned by the clustering algorithm. With the feature space consisting of the above temporal features and target space being the cluster, Decision Tree algorithm is applied on the data set (experiments done on individual datasets - usage routine of one user is not impacted by the usage routine of other user). The result of this step is a decision graph as the one presented in Fig. 6 which shows the best result from the four data sets used when applying the XAI solution. In the same figure we can also see the real rules used for generating the data. As we can see, for 6 out of 7 possibilities, the XAI solution identified correctly the usage pattern.

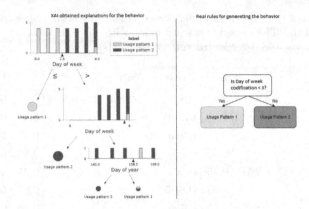

Fig. 6. Results after applying XAI solution based on Decision Tree on the dataset identified in the paper by 1AP&2AP. Left - the results obtained by the XAI solution for the rules under which the pattern occur. Right - real rules used in the generation of the data

5   Conclusions and Future Work

In this paper, we have explored the temporal dependency analysis of usage patterns derived from home-appliance generated data. By leveraging a completely unsupervised approach, we have successfully unveiled behavioral variations across time, offering valuable insights into user behaviors and usage dynamics.

Through the conversion of event data into time-series representations and the segmentation of historical data into time-boxed snippets, we have captured the temporal context within which usage patterns occur. This has allowed us to analyze usage patterns within specific time intervals and identify distinct clusters representing similar usage patterns. By extracting spectral features from each time series, we have effectively summarized the usage patterns, enabling the discovery of underlying patterns. Leveraging unsupervised clustering algorithms, we have successfully grouped similar usage patterns together. Furthermore, we have incorporated explainable AI techniques to unravel the rules governing the occurrence of usage patterns. This has provided insights into the factors and conditions that contribute to the temporal dynamics of usage patterns.

Future research directions could involve the exploration of additional clustering algorithms and the incorporation of domain-specific knowledge to further enhance the accuracy of the discovered usage patterns. Additionally, the integration of external contextual data, such as weather or user social data, could provide a more comprehensive understanding of the factors influencing temporal dependencies in usage patterns. By tuning and experimenting with other XAI solutions, the conditions under which a pattern in present in the overall usage could be mined in a precise manner.

In conclusion, this paper contributes to the field of knowledge inference from home-appliance generated data and user profiling by providing a robust framework for understanding usage patterns in home appliances. By uncovering behavioral variations across time, our approach offers valuable insights that can inform appliance design, energy management strategies, and personalized user experiences, ultimately improving overall user satisfaction and appliance efficiency.

References

1. DARPA. https://www.darpa.mil/program/explainable-artificial-intelligence. Accessed 21 May 2023
2. Decision Tree. https://en.wikipedia.org/wiki/Decision_tree. Accessed 29 Jun 2023
3. Discrete Fourier Transform. https://numpy.org/doc/stable/reference/routines.fft. Accessed 29 Jun 2023
4. Inverse Fourier Transform. https://numpy.org/doc/stable/reference/generated/numpy.fft.ifft.html. Accessed 29 Jun 2023
5. Matplotlib library. https://en.wikipedia.org/wiki/Matplotlib. Accessed 20 Feb 2023
6. Scikit-learn dbscan. https://scikit-learn.org/stable/modules/generated/sklearn.cluster.DBSCAN.html. Accessed 19 Jul 2022
7. Scikit-learn MinMaxScaler. https://scikit-learn.org/stable/modules/generated/sklearn.preprocessing.MinMaxScaler.html
8. Numpy. https://numpy.org/ (2022). Accessed 2 Jan 2022
9. Pandas. https://pandas.pydata.org/ (2022). Accessed 2 Jan 2022
10. Al-Fahoum, A.S., Al-Fraihat, A.A.: Methods of EEG signal features extraction using linear analysis in frequency and time-frequency domains. Int. Sch. Res. Not. **2014**, 730218 (2014)
11. Barandas, M., et al.: TSFEL: time series feature extraction library. SoftwareX **11**, 100456 (2020). https://doi.org/10.1016/j.softx.2020.100456, https://www.sciencedirect.com/science/article/pii/S2352711020300017
12. Campello, R.J.G.B., Kröger, P., Sander, J., Zimek, A.: Density-based clustering. WIREs Data Min. Knowl. Disc. **10**(2), e1343 (2020). https://doi.org/10.1002/widm.1343, https://wires.onlinelibrary.wiley.com/doi/abs/10.1002/widm.1343
13. Chira, C.M., Portase, R., Tolas, R., Lemnaru, C., Potolea, R.: A system for managing and processing industrial sensor data: SMS. In: 2020 IEEE 16th International Conference on Intelligent Computer Communication and Processing (ICCP), pp. 213–220 (2020). https://doi.org/10.1109/ICCP51029.2020.9266263
14. Djenouri, Y., Belhadi, A., Djenouri, D., Lin, J.C.W.: Cluster-based information retrieval using pattern mining. Appl. Intell. **51**, 1888–1903 (2021)
15. Ester, M., Kriegel, H.P., Sander, J., Xu, X.: A density-based algorithm for discovering clusters in large spatial databases with noise. In: Proceedings of the Second International Conference on Knowledge Discovery and Data Mining, pp. 226–231. KDD 1996, AAAI Press (1996)
16. Firte, C., et al.: Knowledge inference from home appliances data. In: 2022 IEEE International Conference on Intelligent Computer Communication and Processing (ICCP) (2022)
17. Gunning, D., Stefik, M., Choi, J., Miller, T., Stumpf, S., Yang, G.Z.: XAI—explainable artificial intelligence. Sci. Robot. **4**(37), eaay7120 (2019)
18. Hamilton, J.D.: Time Series Analysis. Princeton University Press (2020)
19. Lin, J., Williamson, S., Borne, K., DeBarr, D.: Pattern recognition in time series. Adv. Mach. Learn. Data Min. Astron. **1**(617–645), 3 (2012)

20. Lundberg, S.M., et al.: From local explanations to global understanding with explainable AI for trees. Nat. Mach. Intell. **2**(1), 56–67 (2020)
21. Mahbooba, B., Timilsina, M., Sahal, R., Serrano, M.: Explainable artificial intelligence (XAI) to enhance trust management in intrusion detection systems using decision tree model. Complexity **2021**, 1–11 (2021)
22. Nedelcu, E., Portase, R., Tolas, R., Muresan, R., Dinsoreanu, M., Potolea, R.: Artifact detection in EEG using machine learning. In: 2017 13th IEEE International Conference on Intelligent Computer Communication and Processing (ICCP), pp. 77–83 (2017). https://doi.org/10.1109/ICCP.2017.8116986
23. Olariu, E.M., Tolas, R., Portase, R., Dinsoreanu, M., Potolea, R.: Modern approaches to preprocessing industrial data. In: 2020 IEEE 16th International Conference on Intelligent Computer Communication and Processing (ICCP), pp. 221–226 (2020). https://doi.org/10.1109/ICCP51029.2020.9266215
24. Pedregosa, F., et al.: Scikit-learn: machine learning in Python. J. Mach. Learn. Res. **12**, 2825–2830 (2011)
25. Perera, D., Kay, J., Koprinska, I., Yacef, K., Zaïane, O.R.: Clustering and sequential pattern mining of online collaborative learning data. IEEE Trans. Knowl. Data Eng. **21**(6), 759–772 (2008)
26. Portase, R., Tolas, R., Lemnaru, C., Potolea, R.: Prediction pipeline on time series data applied for usage prediction on household devices. In: eKNOW 2023, The Fifteenth International Conference on Information, Process, and Knowledge Management (2023)
27. Portase, R., Tolas, R., Potolea, R.: MEDIS: analysis methodology for data with multiple complexities. In: Cucchiara, R., Fred, A.L.N., Filipe, J. (eds.) Proceedings of the 13th International Joint Conference on Knowledge Discovery, Knowledge Engineering and Knowledge Management, IC3K 2021, Volume 1: KDIR, Online Streaming, 25–27 October 2021, pp. 191–198. SCITEPRESS (2021). https://doi.org/10.5220/0010655100003064
28. Samek, W., Wiegand, T., Müller, K.R.: Explainable artificial intelligence: Understanding, visualizing and interpreting deep learning models. arXiv preprint arXiv:1708.08296 (2017)
29. Simonyan, K., Vedaldi, A., Zisserman, A.: Deep inside convolutional networks: Visualising image classification models and saliency maps. arXiv preprint arXiv:1312.6034 (2013)
30. Taylan, O., Sattari, M.A., Elhachfi Essoussi, I., Nazemi, E.: Frequency domain feature extraction investigation to increase the accuracy of an intelligent nondestructive system for volume fraction and regime determination of gas-water-oil three-phase flows. Mathematics **9**(17), 2091 (2021)
31. Tolas, R., Portase, R., Dinsoreanu, M., Potolea, R.: Mining user behavior: Inference of time-boxed usage patterns from household generated data. In: eKNOW 2023, The Fifteenth International Conference on Information, Process, and Knowledge Management (2023)
32. Tolas, R., Portase, R., Iosif, A., Potolea, R.: Periodicity detection algorithm and applications on IoT data. In: 2021 20th International Symposium on Parallel and Distributed Computing (ISPDC), pp. 81–88 (2021). https://doi.org/10.1109/ISPDC52870.2021.9521605
33. Wang, J., Li, S., Xin, Y., An, Z.: Gear fault intelligent diagnosis based on frequency-domain feature extraction. J. Vibr. Eng. Technol. **7**, 159–166 (2019)
34. Wen, T., Zhang, Z.: Effective and extensible feature extraction method using genetic algorithm-based frequency-domain feature search for epileptic EEG multi-classification. Medicine **96**(19), e6879 (2017)

35. Xu, F., Uszkoreit, H., Du, Y., Fan, W., Zhao, D., Zhu, J.: Explainable AI: a brief survey on history, research areas, approaches and challenges. In: Tang, J., Kan, M.-Y., Zhao, D., Li, S., Zan, H. (eds.) NLPCC 2019. LNCS (LNAI), vol. 11839, pp. 563–574. Springer, Cham (2019). https://doi.org/10.1007/978-3-030-32236-6_51
36. Zhang, Q., Cao, R., Shi, F., Wu, Y.N., Zhu, S.C.: Interpreting CNN knowledge via an explanatory graph. In: Proceedings of the AAAI Conference on Artificial Intelligence. vol. 32 (2018)
37. Zheng, Y., Si, Y.W., Wong, R.: Feature extraction for chart pattern classification in financial time series. Knowl. Inf. Syst. **63**(7), 1807–1848 (2021)
38. Zhou, K., Yang, S., Shao, Z.: Household monthly electricity consumption pattern mining: a fuzzy clustering-based model and a case study. J. Clean. Prod. **141**, 900–908 (2017)

A Deep Learning-Based Technique to Determine Various Stages of Alzheimer's Disease from 3D Brain MRI Images

Tahzib-E-Alindo, Pranto Kubi, Anika Islam, Md. Amir Hozaifa Bin Zaher, and Shamim H. Ripon$^{(\boxtimes)}$

Department of Computer Science and Engineering, East West University, Dhaka, Bangladesh
dshr@ewubd.edu

Abstract. Alzheimer's disease is a kind of dementia which leads in progressive loss of memory usually in elderly persons. Since there is not any cure for this condition it is vital to discover it as soon as possible. Machine learning algorithms are being used to detect various stages of Alzheimer's disease. ADNI, the most comprehensive dataset has been collected and used to conduct the experiments. The dataset comprises three classifications that include Alzheimer's Disease, Mild Cognitive Impairment and Cognitive Normal. The proposed approach illustrates multiple preprocessing methods to transform 3-D images into 2D images and employs various CNN models to achieve the best performing ones. Preprocessing approaches include brain segmentation, conversion to MNI space etc. VGG19 model has the overall best performance among all other models with an accuracy of 94.25% outperforming many other similar works.

Keywords: Alzheimer's Disease · MRI · ADNI · CNN · machine learning · multi classification

1 Introduction

Alzheimer's disease (AD) is a neurodegenerative illness that affects the central nervous system and complex genes [1]. AD affects many people worldwide, especially those over the age of 65. This is the most common cause of dementia worldwide. It is characterized by the gradual loss of cognitive function and memory, leading to a decline in the ability to perform activities of daily living. There were 46.8 million dementia sufferers in 2015, with the number expected to double in 20 years [2]. Currently, there is no cure for AD, and the available treatments only provide temporary relief of symptoms. For timely treatment and efficient therapy, early Alzheimer's disease detection is essential. A promising method for the identification of Alzheimer's disease is magnetic resonance imaging (MRI). The diversity and variability of brain regions make it difficult to accurately diagnose Alzheimer's disease from MRI imaging.

Machine learning algorithms have demonstrated significant progress in medical imaging analysis, especially in the identification and diagnosis of neurodegenerative

P. Delir Haghighi et al. (Eds.): iiWAS 2023, LNCS 14416, pp. 162–175, 2023.
https://doi.org/10.1007/978-3-031-48316-5_18

disorders. One promising approach for early diagnosis and prediction of AD is the use of magnetic resonance imaging (MRI) scans. MRI scans can provide detailed images of the brain, allowing for the detection of structural changes and abnormalities associated with AD. Several machine learning techniques have been presented in recent years for the accurate identification of Alzheimer's disease from MRI scans. Identifying the leading signals of Alzheimer's disease could reduce medical testing, expenses, and time, resulting in improved classification and prediction and providing a basis for clinical diagnosis [3]. These algorithms analyze MRI images and extract useful characteristics that can distinguish between healthy and diseased brain structures using a combination of machine learning algorithms and image processing techniques.

The application of machine learning for AD detection has shown considerable promise [4], but there are still obstacles to overcome. One of the issues is the necessity for huge datasets of MRI images from both healthy and Alzheimer's patients. Another problem is the creation of precise and robust machine learning algorithms capable of detecting tiny changes in brain structure and function. To overcome these issues, the purpose of this study is to develop a machine learning model for detecting Alzheimer's disease. The focus of this effort is to develop a highly accurate and efficient machine learning model for Alzheimer's disease detection and put the model into practice so that medical personnel may efficiently and quickly take required steps during and after recognizing the condition.

To mitigate the identified challenge, a key issue is to prepare the MRI image suitable for disease detection experiment. A series of rigorous preprocessing steps has been adapted to prepare the images collected from ADNI dataset. After that a set of deep learning models is utilized to successfully detect the disease. The proposed techniques successfully detect the disease with a comparable performance with the state of the art.

The rest of the paper is organized as follows. Section 2 gives a brief illustration of the related works in this area. After that a brief overview of the ADNI dataset is shown in Sect. 3. The proposed methodology of this paper is illustrated in Sect. 4 along with a schematic diagram. A crucial task of this paper is to perform preprocessing, which is demonstrated in Sect. 5. Result analysis and comparison with related works are shown in Sect. 6. Finally, Sect. 7 concludes the paper by summarizing the work and outlining our future plan.

2 Related Work

Our research tries to build a highly efficient machine learning model which can accurately predict stages of Alzheimer's disease from MRI images. We have surveyed a good number of research papers to find the effective methods for such a task. Almost all of the research papers used datasets from ADNI [5]. This section will give a brief description of our literature survey.

One of the objectives of our research is to find the best performing model. In our literature survey, CNN was the most used model. But the performance of CNN varied from paper to paper. Paper [6] and [7] used CNN and DCNN models respectively. In paper [6], three convolutional layers were used followed by pooling layers in CNN model. The features learned from CNN are then fed into an extreme learning Machine which is a feed forward neural network with a single layer of hidden nodes. Similarly, DCNN model of paper [7] used three convolutional layers but followed by max pooling layers and a flattening convolutional layer. Then it goes through two fully connected layers and a SoftMax classifier. Paper [6] achieved 79.9% accuracy whereas paper [7] had 87.72% accuracy.

In both paper [8] and [9], 3D and 2D CNN models have been used. Paper [8] took a two-stage approach where the first stage was about learning filters for convolutional operation using a sparse autoencoder. Then the second stage was building a 3D and 2D CNN model which uses filters learned with the auto encoder. Paper [9] used 2D-CNN which had 3 convolution layers, 3 max pooling layers, 1 flattening layer and 2 dense layers. The 3D-CNN had the same architecture but used 3D convolutional layers. Paper [8] had 85.53% and 89.47% accuracy for 2D and 3D CNN respectively in 3-way classification. Paper [9] achieved max accuracy of 98.4% and 97.1% for 3D and 2D CNN respectively in binary classification.

Transfer learning models like VGG-16, VGG-19, Resnet50, ResNet-18, AlexNet are some commonly used models in our literature survey. Paper [9] used VGG-19 which had a high accuracy of 97% in 4-way classification. In paper [10] authors used modified InceptionV3 named AlzheimerNet, ResNet50, AlexNet, MobileNetV2 and VGG16. Among the pertained model InceptionV3 had highest accuracy of 92.32% which then modified to AlzheimerNet that had an accuracy of 98.68% in 6-way classification. Paper [11] also used pretrained model like VGG-16 and ResNet-50 and had maximum accuracy of 78.57 and 75.1% respectively. Paper [12] used modified AlexNet with 8 layers of deep learnable parameters where 5 of them are convolutional layers and remaining three layers fully connected neural network. The dataset of the paper was from Kaggle. It had 91.7% accuracy in 4-way classification. Paper [13] also accommodates transfer learning models like GoogLeNet, ResNet-18, ResNet-152. In 4-way classification GoogLeNet, ResNet-18 and ResNet-152 output 98.88%, 98.1% and 98.14% accuracy respectively. Paper [14] proposes a deep sequence modeling using transfer-learning model ResNet-18. In the sequence modeling, temporal convolutional networks (TCN) and different types of recurrent neural networks (RNN) have been employed. Also, several deep sequence-based models and configurations were implemented and compared for AD detection. TCNs performed better than slice-based methods (using 2D CNNs), voxel-based methods (using 3D CNNs) and RNN-based methods. In the experiment, TCN with four residual blocks achieved the best classification performance, with 91% accuracy. Paper [15] implements ten pre-trained models with 2D-CNN. These are 1) LeNet-5, 2) AlexNet, 3) VGGNet-16, 4) SqueezeNet, 5) ResNet-18, 6) VGGNet-19, 7) GoogLeNet, 8) Inceptionv3, 9) ResNet-50, 10) ResNet-101. 3D CNN was also implemented with 1) LeNet-5, 2) ResNet-18, 3) ResNet-50, 4) ResNet-101. ResNet-18 and SqueezeNet performed comparatively well with 2D CNN and ResNet-101 performed better with 3D CNN.

Machine learning algorithms like Support Vector Machine, Random Forest were also used in some papers in the literature survey. Paper [16] and [17] uses Support Vector Machine and Random Forest for Alzheimer's disease detection. In paper [16] the MRI data was divided into several features to train the machine learning algorithms. The accuracy of the models is inconsistent and varies with classes. SVM had the lowest accuracy of 65.51% for binary classification (CN-EMCI) and had the highest accuracy of 91.07%. The Decision Tree used in the paper had a minimum accuracy of 61% and maximum of 87.27%. In paper [17] MRI images were processed to get numeric data which in turn is processed using machine learning algorithms. Random Forest had a much better accuracy of 97.86% along with the Neural Network used in the paper.

The highest achieved accuracies in our literature survey are paper [18] and [19]. Paper [18] had 99.5% accuracy using DNN with 300 hidden layers for 3-way classification. Histogram of oriented gradients (HOG) was used as a feature extractor and for optimization a rectified Adam optimizer was used here. Paper [19] achieved 99.1% accuracy for binary classification and 98.9% accuracy for multiclass classification using 3D-CNN-SVM.

Generalizability was a core focus of paper [20]. For that, cross-cohort datasets were used (NA-ADNI and J-ADNI) to evaluate the generalizability of the model. The authors used NA-ADNI for training and J-ADNI data for testing their CNN model. The accuracy of the model was 78% accuracy for only MRI input and 88% accuracy for MRI with other information (Cognitive scores, APOE, age).

Finally, image preprocessing was an important and inseparable part of many papers in our literature review. Most common preprocessing techniques in our literature survey are standardization, skull stripping, cervical stripping, segmentation of gray matter and white matter used by paper [11, 13] and [19]. There were also some unique image preprocessing techniques. Paper [6] creates a 2.5D patch using local patches of three different planes of the MRI which was transformed into an RGB patch for better feature representation. Paper [21] proposes an image fusion method to fuse Magnetic Resonance Images (MRI) with Positron Emission Tomography (PET) images of the subjects. The 3D convolution fused images are used to extract richer feature information. A 3D sparse autoencoder was trained to develop convolutional layers for the 3D CNN model. This method outputs a maximum accuracy of 93.21% for binary classification and 87.67% accuracy for 3-way classification. In paper [4] the authors use hippocampus segmentation from MRI images to predict Alzheimer's disease. The image segmentation was done on the left and right hippocampus. A Dense CNN model with two streams for left and right hippocampus segments was built. The proposed Dense CNN had an accuracy of 92.52%.

3   Dataset Overview

The dataset was collected from Alzheimer's Disease Neuroimaging Initiative (ADNI) [5]. Alzheimer's Disease Neuroimaging Initiative researchers collect, validate and utilize data, which include MRI and PET images, genetics, cognitive tests, CSF and blood biomarkers as predictors of the disease. ADNI has one of the largest collections of organized and variety of AD related data. The dataset consists of MRI images of 818 subjects. Table 1 shows the statistics of the dataset.

Table 1. Dataset statistics.

Diagnosed Group	Sex Ratio (M/F)	Number of patients
CN (Cognitive Normal)	119:110	209
MCI (Mild Cognitive impairment)	258:143	401
AD (Alzheimer's Disease)	99:89	188

In Fig. 1 the pie chart on the left shows that MCI, CN, AD respectively cover 49%, 28% and 23% of the dataset. This shows that a sizable population are in the MCI stage. The right chart of Fig. 1 shows the distribution of patients according to their sex. We can that see 58% (476) patients are male and 42% (342) are female.

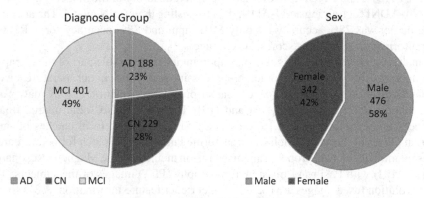

Fig. 1. Pie chart for diagnosed group (right), pie chart based on sex (left).

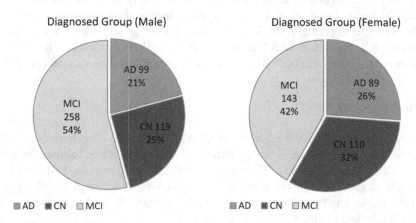

Fig. 2. Pie chart for diagnosed group based on male (right) and female (left).

Figure 2 shows the distribution of patients with different cognitive status categorized by their sex. It is seen that among the total 476 male patients the majority of patients (54%) are in MCI stage. This is followed by CN (25%) and AD (21%). Similarly, we see among the total 342 female patients MCI, CN and AD respectively covers 42%, 32% and 26%.

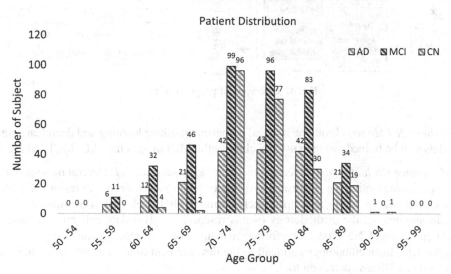

Fig. 3. Number of subject vs Age group multiple bar chart

Figure 3 represents the number of subject vs age group as multiple bar chart with their cognitive status. It is seen that as age increases the number of MCI and CN patients has increased. The number of AD patients is comparatively lower than MCI and CN patients. The majority of the patients are clustered within the age range of 70–89 years.

4 Proposed Method

The methodology for Alzheimer's disease detection using machine learning from MRI images consists of a sequence of steps shown in Fig. 4.

Data Collection and Creating Dataset Magnetic Resonance Imaging (MRI) data will be collected from a huge number of patients with Alzheimer's Disease, Mild Cognitive Impairment and Normal Control. The data will be provided by Alzheimer's Disease Neuroimaging Initiative (ADNI).

Data Preprocessing The MRI images will be preprocessed to standardize the images, remove skull and cervical spine, segment gray matter, white matter and hippocampus region, transform to MNI space and convert 3D MRI to 2D RGB image.

Dataset Split After preprocessing, the dataset will be split into two parts: the train set, and the validation set. The train set will be 67% of the original dataset and will be used to train the CNN models. The validation set will be 33% of the original dataset and will be used to evaluate the performance of those models.

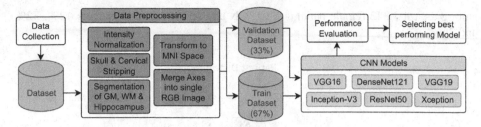

Fig. 4. Overview of preprocessing

Training CNN Models From the images, numerous machine learning and deep learning models will be trained and then used to classify the MRI images into AD, MCI and NC.

Performance Evaluation and Selecting the Best Performing Model Several metrics will be used for evaluating the performance of the trained models. From the results of each model, the best predicting and most efficient model will be selected as the final model.

To summarize, the methodology of this research involves data collection, preprocessing, training CNN models, performance evaluation and selecting the best performing model. This methodology can lead to the development of an accurate and efficient Alzheimer's Disease detection tool.

5   Image Preprocessing

The main objective of the project is to detect the stages of Alzheimer's Disease from 3D MRI files. To work with the MRI files, pre-processing with several steps needs to be performed. The preprocessing result provides us with 2D processed images which can be passed into 2D CNN to train and test the models (Figs. 5, 6 and 7).

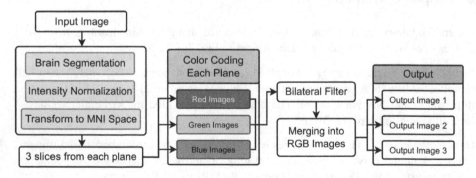

Fig. 5. Overview of preprocessing

Brain Segmentation & Intensity Normalization
First step of pre-processing is to segment the brain from the raw MRI scan. MRI consists of the brain, the skull and the cervical spine. Since we will only work with the brain,

segmentation needs to be performed. Intensity of each MRI can be different; hence intensity normalization also needs to be performed.

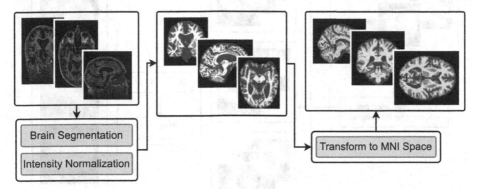

Fig. 6. Brain segmentation, intensity normalization & MNI space transformation

Transformation to MNI Space

MRI scans of all the patients are not aligned. The MNI (Montreal Neurological Institute) space refers to a standardized three-dimensional coordinate system which is used in neuroscience and brain imaging research. The MNI space serves as a template that researchers can use to transform individual brain images into a common space. This process, known as spatial normalization or registration, facilitates group analysis by aligning brain structures across participants. All of these steps were done using MATLAB SPM (Statistical Parametric Mapping) library and CAT12 (Computational Anatomy Toolbox).

2D RGB Image Generation

From a single transformed 3D image, we created 9 2D images each from different planes. 3 red images from the sagittal plane, 3 blue images from the coronal plane and 3 green images from the axial plane are created.

Bilateral Filter

Bilateral filter is a smoothing filter. It is used to preserve edges and reduce noise of an image. It is also a non-linear filter. Bilateral filter is defined by:

$$BF[I]_p = \frac{1}{W_p} \sum_{q \in S} G_{\sigma_s}(\|p - q\|) G_{\sigma_r}(|I_p - I_q|) I_q \#(1)$$

where normalization factor W_p is defined by:

$$W_p = \sum_{q \in S} G_{\sigma_s}(\|p - q\|) G_{\sigma_r}(|I_p - I_q|) \#(2)$$

where,
$|\cdot|$ denotes the absolute value.
$\| \cdot \|$ denotes the L2 norm.

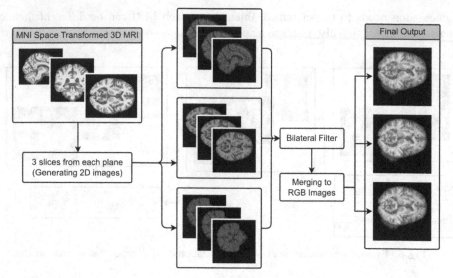

Fig. 7. RGB Images generation, bilateral filtering and merging (Color figure online)

$BF[I]_\mathbf{p}$ denotes the bilateral filter result at position $\mathbf{p}$.
I is the input image.
S denotes all image positions.
$G_\sigma(\cdot)$ denotes the 2D Gaussian kernel.
σ_s, σ_r denotes the amount of filtering.
The bilateral filter was applied on all of the 2D images.

Merging into RGB Images
Each red, green, and blue image were merged into a single RGB image, thus a total of three 2D RGB images were created from a single 3D MRI file. All the images were expanded to square images, since most CNN models take square images as inputs. RGB images were created so that CNN can pick features from all the planes. 3 images were generated to enlarge the dataset size.

6 Result Analysis

6.1 Results of Proposed Model

To train the CNN models, the dataset was split with 67% data on the train set and 33% data on the test set. We used 6 different CNN models to achieve the best results. These models were trained for 60 epochs. Among the 6 models, VGG-19 gave us the best validation accuracy and the lowest amount of validation loss. Whereas VGG-16 gave us the most training accuracy, and the least amount of training loss. Table 2 shows the results of our proposed model.

VGG-19, our best performing model gives us a validation accuracy of 94.25% and validation loss of 0.1762. It gives us a training accuracy of 98.35% and training loss of 0.0579. VGG-16 is the second-best performing model from the table. The training accuracy and training loss of that is better than VGG-19 but it underperformed just a bit in terms of validation. The VGG-16 model gives us training accuracy of 98.41% with 0.0339 training loss and 90.94% validation accuracy with 0.2584 validation loss. The rest of the four models underperformed compared to VGG-16 and VGG-19.

Table 2. Results of proposed model.

Model	Training Accuracy	Validation Accuracy	Training Loss	Validation Loss
VGG16	98.41%	90.94%	0.0339	0.2584
VGG19	**98.35%**	**94.25%**	**0.0579**	**0.1762**
DenseNet121	60.71%	64.14%	0.8328	0.8000
ResNet50	49.88%	52.14%	0.9825	0.9493
Xception	52.82%	54.35%	0.9556	0.9411

Figure 8 and Fig. 9 showcase the result metrics of our model. The x-axis represents the number of epochs, and the y-axis represents accuracy for Fig. 8 and loss for Fig. 9. VGG16 and VGG19 metrics are shown because of their comparatively better results on the dataset.

Here, the accuracy curve shows a consistent rising trend with the epoch number. The steady increase of model's accuracy from a very low point shows that the models are learning from training data. The training and validation accuracy indicate the models are more generalized and not overfitting to the training data.

The loss curve has a steady decreasing trend. This means that the model is effectively reducing the difference between its anticipated and real labels. As the loss gets lower, the model becomes more confident in predicting the data correctly.

The graph shows promising performance of our model. The accuracy and loss curves show consistency during the whole training period, whereas the validation accuracy indicated high generalization capability. Tuning the batch size or increasing the epoch might solve this issue which can be explored in future works. These results make us more positive about the model's dependability and capacity to generate correct predictions on previously unknown data.

6.2 Comparison

In our literature review, there were 2 works that used VGG-16 and only one used VGG-19. In [9], the authors used VGG-19 for multiclass classification (NC/EMCI/LMCI/AD) from 2D MRI. The preprocessing step includes data normalization which is done by changing pixel or voxel intensity. After that, resampling was done to the images followed by image augmentation. The paper claimed that it had around 97% accuracy in 4-way multiclass classification using this technique with the VGG-19 model. VGG-16 was one of the tested models in [10]. The image preprocessing had two steps. First one is applying CLAHE to enhance complicated structures and boosting local contrast. Other

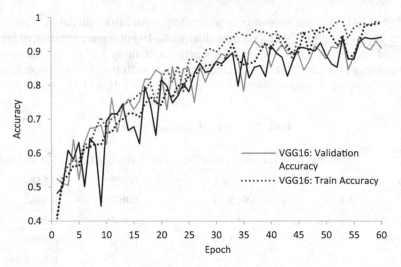

Fig. 8. Accuracy vs Epoch graph

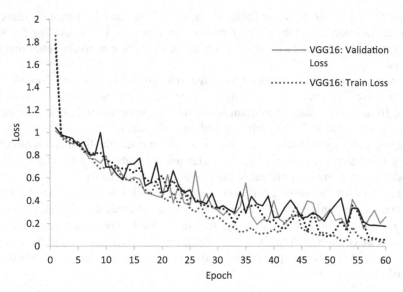

Fig. 9. Loss vs Epoch graph

one is selecting filters by applying different filters to MRI scans. Augmentation was done before model training. This method gave 78.85% accuracy for VGG-16 in 6-way multiclass classification. In [11] the VGG-16 model along with 2 other models are used as well. Its preprocessing had 6 steps. These were skull stripping, non-uniform intensity correction, segmentation, extraction of 2D images from 3D MRI volume, pixel value normalization and data augmentation. The accuracy of VGG-16 for the following method was 78.57%.

Table 3 below shows comparison among accuracies of different studies and our proposed model.

Table 3. Comparisons against other studies.

Study	Method		Accuracy	
			VGG16	VGG19
B. Y. Lim et al. (2017) [11]	VGG16		78.57%	
F. M. J. M. Shamrat et al. (2023) [10]	VGG16		78.85%	
Proposed model	**VGG16**	**VGG19**	**90.94%**	**94.25%**
H. A Helaly et al. (2021) [9]		VGG19		97%

From Table 3, we can see that our VGG-16 model outperforms the VGG-16 models in paper [10] and [11]. Here, our VGG-19 model was less accurate which is 94.25% compared to the VGG-19 model in paper [9] which had 97% accuracy.

7 Conclusion

Since Alzheimer's Disease can have a major impact on one's life, it is critically important to diagnose it as early as possible. Machine learning techniques such as CNN are highly useful for confirming the presence of Alzheimer's Disease. In this study we have exhibited our technique for Alzheimer's Disease identification utilizing several CNN models such as VGG16, VGG19 etc. The VGG16 model provides us 90.94% accuracy while the VGG19 model gives us 94.25% accuracy. These models categorize distinct phases of AD using 3D MRI images. Since we turned 3D MRI pictures into 2D images, there was a loss of information. Future research can be done using 3D images to improve accuracy and clinical applicability. Experimenting with a larger dataset can result in better training of the models consequently improved accuracy. The findings from this work might be valuable for people who work in the medical research sector, especially those dealing with Alzheimer's disease patients. They can gain essential knowledge on how to preprocess 3D images and apply deep learning algorithms on an Alzheimer's Disease related dataset.

Acknowledgement. The dataset was obtained from Alzheimer's Disease Neuroimaging Initiative also known as ADNI. Access to the ADNI database was granted upon request. We would like to thank ADNI for providing us with the necessary data for this research.

References

1. Massa, F., Meli, R., Morbelli, S., et al.: Serum neurofilament light chain rate of change in Alzheimer's disease: potential applications and notes of caution. Ann Transl Med **7**, S133 (2019)

2. Polson, N.G., Scott, J.G., Willard, B.T.: Proximal algorithms in statistics and machine learning. Stat. Sci. **30**, 559–581 (2015)
3. Goetz, J.N., Brenning, A., Petschko, H., et al.: Evaluating machine learning and statistical prediction techniques for landslide susceptibility modeling. Comput. Geosci. **81**, 1–11 (2015)
4. Katabathula, S., Wang, Q., Xu, R.: Predict Alzheimer's disease using hippocampus MRI data: a lightweight 3D deep convolutional network model with visual and global shape representations, Alzheimers Res Ther, vol. **13**, no. 1, Dec (2021), doi: https://doi.org/10.1186/s13195-021-00837-0
5. Petersen, R.C., et al.: Alzheimer's disease neuroimaging initiative (ADNI) clinical characterization, [Online]. Available: www.neurology.org (2010)
6. Lin, W., et al.: Convolutional neural networks-based MRI image analysis for the Alzheimer's disease prediction from mild cognitive impairment," Front Neurosci, vol. **12**, no. NOV, Nov., doi: https://doi.org/10.3389/fnins.2018.00777 (2018)
7. Kundaram, S.S., Pathak, K.C.: Deep learning-based Alzheimer disease detection. Lect. Notes in Electr. Eng. **673**, 587–597 (2021). https://doi.org/10.1007/978-981-15-5546-6_50
8. Payan, A., Montana. G.: Predicting Alzheimer's disease: a neuroimaging study with 3D convolutional neural networks, Feb., [Online]. Available: http://arxiv.org/abs/1502.02506 (2015)
9. Helaly, H.A., Badawy, M., Haikal, A.Y.: Deep learning approach for early detection of Alzheimer's disease. Cognit. Comput. **14**(5), 1711–1727 (2022). https://doi.org/10.1007/s12559-021-09946-2
10. Shamrat, F.M.J.M., et al.: An effective deep learning based proposition for Alzheimer's disease stages classification from functional brain changes in magnetic resonance images. IEEE Access **11**, 16376–16395 (2023). https://doi.org/10.1109/ACCESS.2023.3244952
11. B. Y. Lim et al., "Deep Learning Model for Prediction of Progressive Mild Cognitive Impairment to Alzheimer's Disease Using Structural MRI," Front Aging Neurosci, vol. 14, Jun., doi: https://doi.org/10.3389/fnagi.2022.876202 (2022)
12. Ghazal, T.M., et al.: Alzheimer disease detection empowered with transfer learning. Comput. Mater. Continua **70**(3), 5005–5019 (2022). https://doi.org/10.32604/cmc.2022.020866
13. Institute of Electrical and Electronics Engineers and IEEE Instrumentation and Measurement Society, "a deep CNN based multi-class classification of alzheimer's disease using MRI," (2017)
14. Ebrahimi, A., Luo, S., Chiong, R.: Deep sequence modelling for Alzheimer's disease detection using MRI," Comput Biol Med, vol. 134, Jul. 2021, doi: https://doi.org/10.1016/j.compbiomed.2021.104537
15. Ebrahimi, A. Luo, S.: A. Disease neuroimaging initiative, convolutional neural networks for Alzheimer's disease detection on MRI images,: Journal of Medical Imaging, vol. **8**, no. 02, Apr., doi: https://doi.org/10.1117/1.jmi.8.2.024503 (2021)
16. Tang, X., Liu, J.: Comparing different algorithms for the course of alzheimer's disease using machine learning. Ann Palliat Med **10**(9), 9715–9724 (2021). https://doi.org/10.21037/apm-21-2013
17. Lodha, P., Talele, A., Degaonkar, K.: diagnosis of alzheimer's disease using machine learning. In: Fourth International conference on Computer Communication Control and Automation (ICCUBEA) , (2018)
18. Suresha, H. S. Parthasarathy, S.S.: Alzheimer disease detection based on deep neural network with rectified adam optimization technique using MRI analysis, In: Proceedings of 2020 3rd International Conference on Advances in Electronics, Computers and Communications, ICAECC (2020), Dec. doi: https://doi.org/10.1109/ICAECC50550.2020.9339504
19. Feng, W., et al.: Automated MRI-based deep learning model for detection of alzheimer's disease process, Int J Neural Syst, vol. 30, no. 6, Jun. (2020), doi: https://doi.org/10.1142/S012906572050032X

20. Wang, C., et al.: A high-generalizability machine learning framework for predicting the progression of Alzheimer's disease using limited data, NPJ Digit Med, vol. 5, no. 1, Dec. (2022), doi: https://doi.org/10.1038/s41746-022-00577-x

21. Ismail, W.N., Fathimathul Rajeena, P.P., Ali, M.A.S.: : Multimodal MRI neuroimaging for Alzheimer's disease detection based on a 3d convolution model. Electronics 11(23), 3893 (2022). https://doi.org/10.3390/electronics11233893

22. Katabathula, S., Wang, Q. Xu, R.: Predict Alzheimer's disease using hippocampus MRI data: a lightweight 3D deep convolutional network model with visual and global shape representations," Alzheimers Res Ther, vol. 13, no. 1, Dec. (2021), doi: https://doi.org/10.1186/s13 195-021-00837-0.

23. Srivastava, S., Ahmad, R., Khare, S.K.: Alzheimer's disease and its treatment by different approaches: A review. Eur. J. Med. Chem. 216, 113320 (2021). https://doi.org/10.1016/j.ejm ech.2021.113320

Churn Prediction in Enterprises with High Customer Turnover

William Jones Beckhauser[✉] and Renato Fileto

Department of Informatics and Statistics Federal University of Santa Catarina,
Florianópolis, SC, Brazil
{william.beckhauser,r.fileto}@ufsc.br

Abstract. Most research about Machine Learning (ML) models for churn prediction has focused on sectors like telecommunications, while this problem can be particularly challenging in industries with High Customer Turnover (HCT) like food delivery, e-commerce, and gaming. This article addresses this gap by investigating the effectiveness of four alternative ML models that have been effective for churn prediction in particular HCT enterprises - Multilayer Perceptron, SVM, Decision Trees, and Random Forests. We trained and evaluated the models on three representative datasets from distinct sectors, aiming to identify the models and data features that provide the best results. We propose and employ a framework to help achieve this goal. It allowed high-performance churn prediction in our experiments, exploiting mainly the purchase data features of the distinct HCT enterprises. The Random Forest model achieved the best accuracy (around 90%) on the three datasets, and the best precision and F1-score on two of them.

Keywords: Churn Prediction · Machine Learning · Classification Model Comparison · High Customer Turnover · High Churn Rate

1 Introduction

Companies in competitive markets mainly depend on the profits that come from retained customers [24]. Many of these companies are resorting to Machine Learning (ML) techniques for churn analysis and prediction [30]. Churn prediction is a critical aspect of Customer Relationship Management (CRM), as it helps companies identify customers with a likelihood of churning (leaving) and take preventive measures. Effective churn prediction also enable identifying potentially lasting customers [25], to strengthen relationships with them. Retaining these customers can be easier and reduce the need to attract new ones (replacement), consequently decreasing the cost of offensive marketing [31].

Four key characteristics of enterprises make churn prediction particularly challenging and relevant: highly competitive sectors, non-contractual transactions, business-to-consumer operations, and high churn rates. Together, they exacerbate the difficulty of these companies to retain customers. High churn

P. Delir Haghighi et al. (Eds.): iiWAS 2023, LNCS 14416, pp. 176–191, 2023.
https://doi.org/10.1007/978-3-031-48316-5_19

rates usually results from the first three characteristics. Thus, in this article we refer to their combined occurrence as High Customer Turnover (HCT).

Accurate prediction of churn is particularly important for sectors with HCT, such as online games, as their costumers have no contractual obligations binding them. Studies have shown that 70% to 90% of players stop playing 10 d after the first match [10]. This high churn rate shows that it is crucial for companies to identify customers at risk of churn and take proactive measures to retain them. However, despite the growing interest in churn prediction for enterprises with HCT, there is a shortage of research in this area. Until 2020, the telecommunications and the finance sectors, which do not usually have HCT, accounted for 44% and 18% of the research in churn prediction, respectively, while the gaming sector accounted for just 2% [22].

This paper contributes to filling this research gap by introducing the CP-HCT framework (Churn Prediction in enterprises with HCT). It aims to streamline the identification of the most effective data features and models for predicting churn in sectors with HCT, by supporting a tailored extension of the CRISP-DM [3] process. We applied CP-HCT to train and evaluate Multilayer Perceptrons (MLP), Support Vector Machines (SVM), Decision Trees (DTs), and Random Forests (RF). Three transaction datasets were used for model training and evaluation: the first containing data of approximately 7249 customers from the food delivery sector; the second with data of 23902 customers from an e-commerce platform; and lastly a dataset of 1801 players from a gambling platform.

We first trained and tested the models using the standard configuration of the scikit-learn hyperparameters [18]. SVM performed the best for the Gambling dataset. For the other two datasets (Food Delivery and E-commerce) a Random Forest was the most successful model. The Multilayer Perceptron produced the second-best results for these datasets. A Random Forest was the second best model for the Gambling dataset. Then, we filter out the models with the lowest performance using the Mean Absolute Deviation (MAD) approach, taking only the best-performing models for the last and more computational intensive phases of hyperparameter setting, modeling and evaluation.

The major contributions of this paper are: (i) the systematic training and evaluation of ML models for churn prediction in industries with HCT; (ii) experimental results showing the superiority of the RF and the SVM models in the HCT contexts considered; and (iii) a framework to efficiently train a variety of ML models with distinct datasets and select the ones that provide best performance, which can be useful for the community. To the best of our knowledge, this is the first work to systematically compare the ML models that presented the best results in the literature on datasets from prominent HCT industries.

This article is structured in 5 sections. Section 2 lays the groundwork for understanding churn, HCT, and related work. Section 3 describes the framework developed for the experiments. Section 4 reports the experiments that we have realized and their results. Finally, Sect. 5 presents the conclusions derived from the research and suggestions for future research directions.

2   Foundations

Churn occurs when a customer discontinue using a product or service, becoming inactive. The term "chur" is commonly used to refer to any type of customer attrition, voluntary or involuntary [2]. Dissatisfaction with the quality of service, high costs, unattractive plans, lack of understanding of the service plan, poor support, and other factors may contribute to customer churn. Additionally, customers may terminate their contract without the intention of switching to a competitor due to changes in their situation, such as financial difficulties that prevent them from continuing to use the service or relocation to an area where the company does not operate or the service is not available [16].

Customer churn is measured by the churn rate (Z) during a specific period of time, such as a month or a year; whichever is relevant to the business. It can be calculated by the following formula, where Y refers to the number of customers who were inactive during the period; B the number of active customers in the period; and K the number of new customers during the period.

$$Z = Y/(B + K)$$

2.1   High Customer Turnover

High Customer Turnover (HCT) is a term proposed in this paper to refer to the following characteristics of enterprises in which churn is more common and its prediction usually more challenging and crucial than in most business.

High Churn Rate, for this research, is a churn rate above the average of industries that we are aware of in churn publications, i.e. an annual turnover rate between 20% and 40% [6]. Very differently, the gaming industry, for example, can have an astounding churn rate of up to 70% [10]. Companies with high churn rates usually have the other following characteristics that contribute to this.

Non-contractual Negotiations means that HCT organizations rely on informal and flexible negotiations that do not result in a legally binding relationship between the institution and the client, as in telecom companies. While non-contractual negotiations can be more collaborative and involve discussion, it also creates challenges in differentiating customers who have ended their relationship with the organization from those who are simply on a temporary pause between transactions [15]. Additionally, there are no constraints on discontinuing the usage of services or products since there is no formal link with the entity.

Business to Customer (B2C) interactions, i.e. between a company and an individual customer, is another characteristic of HCT. These interactions are often facilitated through retail channels such as brick-and-mortar stores, e-commerce websites, and mobile apps [7]. Companies that rely on B2C transactions need to be concerned with campaigns, targeting, behavioral research and retention. As a result, management differs from organizations in business to business or business to government systems.

Highly Competitive Sectors is a defining feature of HCT. In intensely competitive markets, there are many companies offering similar goods or services, creating fierce rivalry. This type of market structure creates pressure on HCT companies to increase efficiency and reduce costs to remain profitable, making it challenging for new companies to break through and exercise market creativity [14]. Thus, they have a greater need of accurate churn prediction.

2.2   Literature Review

We have done a bibliographical review for identifying advancements in machine learning models for predicting customer churn on datasets from HCT enterprises. Related work often used the keywords 'machine learning', 'customer churn', and 'non-contractual'. In addition, we consider that churn prediction is more relevant in B2C environments. Thus, we employed the search expression ('customer churn' OR 'churn prediction') AND ('machine learning') AND ('non-contractual') AND NOT ('B2B'). Then, we manually filtered by title, abstract, and keywords, considering only works published between January 2002 and February 2023.

The search was conducted across multiple databases, including IEEE Xplore, Google Scholar, and Periódicos Capes. The search process resulted in the identification of 146 articles. Then, we applied the following predetermined inclusion and exclusion criteria:

Inclusion criteria
- From 2002 to 2023
- HCT

Exclusion criteria
- Articles without English or Portuguese versions
- Book

These articles were classified in surveys or experimental. The 31 surveys found were cataloged separately. Of these, only 6 surveys had data from companies with non-contractual negotiation, such as [5], and only 1 survey made a distinction between companies with contractual and non-contractual data [1]. Upon excluding the surveys, 115 articles remained. However, only 7 of them met the criteria of non-contractual sales, high churn rate, and belonging to a highly competitive sector. However, out of the remaining 7, 1 article was focused on B2B and was excluded.

Table 1 allows comparing the selected works and our proposal according with the sector of the data used to train and evaluate de ML models, the models that provided the best accuracy in the respective works and their accuracy measures. Our bibliographical review and the survey of Sobreiro, Martinho, Alonso and Berrocal 2022 [22] revealed that 3 of the models chosen for our research are among the most used in published articles about churn prediction in general, namely: Random Forests in 30 articles, SVM in 29 articles, and Decision Trees in 52 articles. On the other hand, the Multilayer Perceptron was used in just 4 articles published until 2020, according to [22].

Four of the six articles listed in Table 1 do not publish the datasets used in their experiments [11,19,20,29], while one required prior request [28]. We were able to get just the "Gambling" dataset [4], which achieved an accuracy of 78% using the Random Forest algorithm. In our experiments the Random Forest achieved an accuracy of 92.52% on this dataset. It is important to notice

Table 1. Comparison of selected articles.

Work	Year	Sector	Best ML Model	Accuracy
Wu, Xing [28]	2021	Web Browser	Multilayer Perceptron	94%
Perianez, África [19]	2016	Gaming	SVM	96%
Perišić, Ana [20]	2021	Gaming	Random Forest	71%
Coussement, Kristof [4]	2013	Gambling	Random Forest	78%
Xiahou, Xiancheng [29]	2022	E-Commerce	SVM	91%
Kim, Sulim [11]	2022	E-Commerce	Decision Trees	90%
This Article	*2023*	*Food Delivery, E-Commerce and Gambling*	*Multilayer Perceptron, SVM, Decision Trees and Random Forest*	*88.41% - 92.52%*

that we used different filtering methods and apply the RF model segmentation technique. Our research also employs other datasets which were not used in previous studies, such as the "Food Delivery" and the "E-commerce" datasets. To the best of our knowledge, our work is the first to employ the former in churn prediction.

3   The CP-HCT Framework

We developed a framework called CP-HCT (Churn Prediction in enterprises with High Customer Turnover)[1] to help face the challenge of predicting churn effectively in HCT enterprises. It helps preliminary training and testing of a number of ML models with a variety of parameter configurations, and subsequently filtering and adjusting the best models. The goal is achieving the best results while reducing the computational costs for training of alternative models, with distinct hyperparemeter configurations for choosing the best ones.

Figure 1 illustrates the process supported by CP-HCT for training, testing, filtering, adjusting and evaluating ML models for churn prediction in HCT enterprises. It is an extension of the well-known CRISP-DM process [3], which has six phases in its traditional methodology. The main innovations of the CP-HCT framework are the modules to support the steps Quick Test, Filter and Hyperparameter Configuration. The other phases (Data Understanding Data, Peparation, Modeling and Evaluation) are those of CRISP-DM, but with a focus on churn in HCT enterprises. In the following subsections we explain each phase

---

[1] Available at https://github.com/WilliamBeckhauser/Churn-Prediction-in-enterprises-with-High-Customer-Turnover.

of the CP-HCT process that we have applied and the modules that we have developed to support some of them.

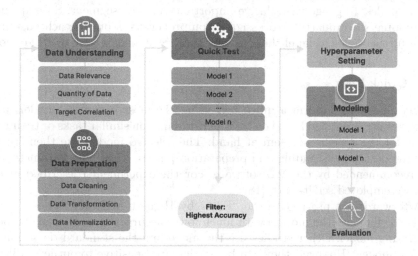

Fig. 1. The CP-HCT process for building and selecting churn prediction models

3.1   Data Understanding

During this phase, we evaluate relevance and volume of data available for training, testing and evaluating the ML models. We also examine the correlation between the target variable (churn) and the relevant data features. In addition, we make changes such as renaming and describing columns to facilitate analysis and identify issues such as data imbalance. It is important to ensure the balance between customers who churned out and those that did not, for properly train the ML models.

3.2   Data Preparation

In this phase, we harness the insights obtained from data understanding to effectively structure, balance, and cleanse the data. We define appropriate treatments for null values, either by excluding them entirely or substituting them with "0" where applicable. Furthermore, we perform data type conversions, such as transforming integers into floats, to ensure consistency. We employ the technique of one-hot encoding to handle categorical data like gender and country. This method allows us to represent categorical variables as binary vectors, enabling easier analysis and processing.

The datasets used in this article contain mainly transactional data about customer purchases. Though they are limited in terms of profile data availability, they still enable dataset segmentation strategies such as RFM (Recency,

Frequency, and Monetary value of customer transactions) [26]. This segmentation takes advantage of features present in all datasets (e.g. date of purchase, amount paid) to effectively categorize customers by feature values segmented into quartiles, to gauge the relative importance of each segment. Subsequently, we combine these quartiles to assign a comprehensive score to each customer, which further helps us label them as Not Fans, Switchers, Loyal, or Champions.

3.3 Quick Test

In this phase, we perform a quick test using the most promising models from search results, identified based on their performance on similar tasks or their suitability for the specific problem at hand. The selected models are then trained after the data understanding and preparation phases, with hyperparameter settings recommended by the ML software. For the experiments described in this work we employed scikit-learn [18].

Afterwards, we proceed to the "Filter by Highest Accuracy" phase, whose aim is to eliminate the models with much lower accuracy than that of the best-performing model. Other studies use the mean and the standard deviation for filtering models. However, they can be particularly sensitive to outliers [13]. We prefer to use the dispersion measure known as Mean Absolute Deviation (MAD) approach [9], which measures forecast accuracy by taking the average of the absolute error of each prediction. The MAD approach is more robust and less affected by outliers. MAD is calculated using the following formula:

$$MAD = \frac{\sum |x_i - \overline{x}|}{n} \tag{1}$$

where x_i stands for each value in a set of size n and $\overline{x}$ is the mean of the values. Therefore, the MAD quantifies the average distance between each value in the set and their mean. We employ a MAD limit of 2.5 for compatibility with [13].

3.4 Hyperparameter Setting

After the Quick Test, we conducted an extensive search for the best configuration of hyperparameters of the selected models, i.e., the configuration that yields optimal performance. In our experimentes, the filtering phase selected 4 models: Multilayer Perceptron, SVM, Decision Trees and Random Forest. The list of hyperparameters for each of these models with the respective values that we tried for the respective parameter (second column) are listed in Table 2. The hyperparameter tuning tried all the combinations of parameter configurations to identify the optimal settings for each model.

By fine-tuning the hyperparameters of each model, we aimed to extract the most valuable characteristics of each model to achieve the best possible performance. The resulting hyperparameter configuratios are used in subsequent phases to evaluate and compare the performance of each model.

3.5 Modeling

In this phase, we train the selected models with the best parameter configurations and make them available for the next evaluation and reporting. In our experiments, the models were trained on Google Colab PRO, which provided access to a GPU and 12GB of system RAM, in addition to 225GB of disk space.

3.6 Evaluation

During the Evaluation phase, we measure the performance of our models using various evaluation metrics such as accuracy, recall, F1 score, precision, specificity, true positive rate, false positive rate, ROC-AUC, and cross-validation ROC-AUC. In this article, we focus on three key evaluation metrics: accuracy, F1 score, and precision. These metrics provide insights into the overall performance of the model and its ability to correctly predict positive instances (precision) and false positives (precision).

Table 2. Hyperparameters of each model and their possible values

Multilayer Perceptron (MLP)	
Number of hidden layers	3, 5, 10, 16, 32, 64
Alphas (regularization strength)	0.001, 0.01, 0.1, 1
Solvers (optimization algorithm)	'sgd', 'adam'
Activations (hidden layers)	'relu', 'tanh'
Support Vector Machine (SVM)	
Kernels (used for transformation)	'linear', 'rbf', 'poly'
Cs (regularization)	0.1, 1, 10
Gammas (kernel coefficient)	'auto', 'scale'
Random Forest (RF)	
N estimators (number of trees)	10, 50, 100
Criterion (split quality measure)	'gini', 'entropy'
Max depth (trees depth maximum)	None, 10, 20
Random state	None, 42
Decision Tree (DT)	
Criterion (split quality measure)	'gini', 'entropy'
Max depth (trees depth maximum)	None, 10, 20
Min samples split	2, 5, 10
Min samples leaf	1, 2, 4

4   Experiments

4.1   Datasets

The quality and the quantity of data used for machine learning models are crucial factors that significantly impact their efficiency [23]. To ensure the best performance of these models, it is essential to use relevant and useful data. One way to achieve this is by using previously tested and validated data, Thus, in this work we use the well-known gambling [4] and e-commerce datasets [21]. Other valuable sources are companies that provide consistent and relevant data, such as the food delivery dataset especially obtained for our experiments. We standardized feature identifiers of these three datasets, made them available together for convenience[2] and describe them in the following.

[Food Delivery] data obtained from a prominent European food group whose identity is kept confidential at their request. It has data about 76446 deliveries to 7249 customers, mainly for lunch and dinner on weekdays (Monday to Friday), during the 12-month period between April 20, 2022, and April 21, 2023. It includes the number of purchases, location, type of orders (lunch or dinner), quantities of desserts, drinks, dishes, and other items, discounts offered, expenditure amounts, average spending, discounts availed, marketing communication, participation in the loyalty plan, types of discounts, gender, and customer reviews. Table 3 groups these features, including the ones derived by RFM, by their data types. For this dataset, we consider 30 d without purchasing as churn, because it is the period of time commonly waited in loyalty programs to intensify promotions [27], and we did not find references about churn in food delivery.

Table 3. Food Delivery dataset summary.

# of Variables	Data Type	Description
13	Numeric	Number of Purchases (absolute and by category); Average Spending; Amounts of Discounts; Review Score Average; Days since Last Order
3	String	Delivery; Language; Gender; RFM
8	Boolean	Dinner or Lunch Purchase; Marketing Comunication; First Order; Churn

---

[2] Available   at   https://github.com/WilliamBeckhauser/Churn-Prediction-in-enterprises-with-High-Customer-Turnover.

[Gambling] data generously provided by bwin Interactive Entertainment AG. This dataset is freely accessible from Cambridge Health Alliance, a teaching hospital affiliated with the Harvard Medical School. It consists of data from 2445 users spanning from February 2005 to February 2007, covering more than 99 variables, and the target "churn", grouped by data type in Table 4. It variables include customer profile details such as birthday, age, gender, language, and country. Additionally, transaction data metrics like average and frequency of purchases and purchases by type are also included. We use 120 d to consider customer churn in this dataset as in [4].

Table 4. Gambling dataset summary.

# of Variables	Data Type	Description
95	Numeric	Frequency; Amounts Spent; Lost Values; Sum of Errors and Gains; Year of Registration; Age *(Descriptions for each game on the platform)*
3	String	Country of Residence; Language; Gender; RFM
1	Boolean	Churn

[E-commerce] data sourced from Kaggle's public data repository. It is called "Brazilian E-Commerce Public Dataset" by Olist [8], and encompasses 24886 purchases of 23903 customers made between the years 2016 and 2018. The dataset provides extensive information regarding customer transactions, including the number of purchases, Amounts Spent, customer ratings, purchase integrity, purchase status, payment method, product weight, purchase category, as well as the geographical locations of both the seller and the buyer (refer to Table 5 for a summary). A period of 90 d is employed to ascertain customer churn in the e-commerce dataset as in [17].

Table 5. E-commerce dataset summary.

# of Variables	Data Type	Description
8	Numeric	Number of Purchases; Amounts Spent; Customer Ratings
10	String	Payment Method; Category; Product Discription; Seller State; Seller City; Customer State; Customer City; RFM
1	Boolean	Churn

Table 6 shows the distribution of churn and non-churn customers in the Food Delivery, Gambling, and E-commerce datasets. Notice that in the Food Delivery and E-commerce datasets, churners account for around 50% of the total customers, while in the gambling dataset, this percentage is slightly lower at 45%. Therefore, the data samples are quite balanced.

Table 6. Churn and non-churn distribution.

	Food Delivery		Gambling		E-commerce	
	Customers	Percentage	Customers	Percentage	Customers	Percentage
Churners	3620	49,94%	811	45,03%	12360	51,71%
Non-churners	3629	50,06%	990	54,97%	11542	48,29%
Total	7249	100,00%	1801	100,00%	23902	100,00%
Churn Time	30 d		120 d		90 d	

4.2 Results

The datasets were analyzed and prepared as described in Sect. 3 to train the four models: Multilayer Perceptron, SVM, Decision Trees and Random Forests. The default scikit-learn hyperparameters [18] were used to train the models for the quick test. Table 7 presents the preliminary results of this test. The Random Forest achieved the best accuracies on the Food Delivery and E-commerce datasets, namely 89.59% and 89.42%. However, SVM achieved the best accuracy of 92.52% on the Gambling dataset. Diff AVG refers to the difference between the accuracy of each model and the average accuracy (AVG) of the four models for the respective dataset. The models with DiFF AVG equal to −2.5% or below (highlighted in red in Table 7) were filtered out. Thus, SVM was excluded for the Food Delivery dataset, and Decision Tree for the E-commerce dataset.

Table 7. Preliminary results by default parameters

	Food Delivery		Gambling		E-commerce	
	Accuracy	Diff.AVG	Accuracy	Diff.AVG	Accuracy	Diff.AVG
Multilayer Perceptron	89.03%	1.72%	91.24%	−0.33%	87.70%	0.15%
Support Vector Machine	84.07%	−3.24%	**92.52%**	0.94%	88.37%	0.82%
Decision Trees	86.55%	−0.76%	91.14%	−0.44%	84.71%	−2.84%
Random Forest	**89.59%**	2.28%	91.41%	−0.17%	**89.42%**	1.87%
AVG	87.31%		91.58%		87.55%	

During the Hyperparameter Setting phase, we searched for the best combination of hyperparameters for each model and datased, by combining the selected values presented in Table 2. The combinations were generated using code created in this research. The resulting best combinations are shown in Table 8. The Random Forest best parameter configuration for the Gambling and E-commerce dasets combines the 'entropy' criterion, 100 estimators, None for the maximum depth and random state. For the Food Delivery dataset, the best configuration is 10 for the maximum depth set and 50 for the number of estimators. The SVM model uses 'rbf' kernel, C=1, 'scale' gamma for Gambling and E-commerce. However, the SVM model was removed Food Delivery in the quick test by the accuracy filter. The DT model vest configuration uses 'entropy' criterion, 10 for maximum depth, 2 for minimum samples split, and 4 for minimum samples leaf for the Gambling. For Food Delivery 10 is better for minimum samples split. The hyperparameters are the same for MLP on the three datasets, with hidden layer sizes 5, alpha=0.001, solver='adam', and activation='relu'.

Table 8. Best combination of hyperparameters

	Gambling	Food Delivery	E-commerce
RF	criterion: 'entropy' max depth: None n estimators: 100 random state: None	criterion: 'entropy' max depth: 10 n estimators: 50 random state: None	criterion: 'entropy' max depth: None n estimators: 100 random state: None
SVM	kernel': 'rbf' C: 1 gamma: 'scale'	Removed by the accuracy filter (Sect. 3.3)	kernel: 'linear' C: 10 gamma: 'auto'
DT	criterion: 'entropy' max_depth: 10 min_samples_split: 2 min_samples_leaf: 4 splitter: 'best'	criterion: 'entropy' max_depth: 10 min_samples_split: 10 min_samples_leaf: 4 splitter: 'best	Removed by the accuracy filter (Sect. 3.3)
MLP	hidden layer sizes: 5 alpha: 0.001 solver: 'adam' activation': 'relu'	hidden layer sizes: 5 alpha: 0.001 solver: 'adam' activation: 'relu'	hidden layer sizes: 5 alpha: 0.001 solver: 'adam' activation': 'relu'

A test set size of 0.2 was employed throughout the training process, i.e. taking 20% of the data for testing purposes. This ensured that the models' performance was assessed on unseen data, offering a dependable estimation of their ability to generalize.

Table 9 presents the final results. The Random Forest model provided the highest accuracy (90.69%) for the Food Delivery dataset, followed by the Decision Tree model (90.21%), and the Multilayer Perceptron model (88.41%). The precision scores for all models were close, with the Random Forest model having the highest precision score (91.09%).

For the Gambling datase, the Support Vector Machine and Random Forest models presented the highest accuracy scores (both at 92.52%), followed by the

Table 9. Final results of the algorithms.

		Accuracy	F1-score	Precision
Food Delivery	Multilayer Perceptron	88.41%	88.38%	89.70%
	Decision Tree	90.21%	89.92%	90.21%
	Random Forest	**90.69%**	**90.89%**	**91.09%**
Gambling	Multilayer Perceptron	90.58%	90.24%	91.36%
	Support Vector Machine	**92.52%**	**92.37%**	**93.17%**
	Decision Tree	90.86%	90.70%	90.95%
	Random Forest	**92.52%**	91.30%	92.60%
E-commerce	Multilayer Perceptron	89.17%	89.15%	90.12%
	Support Vector Machine	89.06%	89.00%	90.91%
	Random Forest	**89.56%**	**89.27%**	**90.85%**

Decision Tree (90.86%). The precision scores for all models are relatively close, with the Support Vector Machine having the highest precision score (93.17%).

Finally, for the E-commerce dataset, the Random Forest model yielded the highest accuracy (89.56%), followed by the Support Vector Machine (89.06%), and the Multilayer Perceptron (89.17%). The precision scores for all models are close, with the Support Vector Machine algorithm having the highest precision score (90.91%).

Overall, the results show that the Random Forest algorithm performs the best across the three domains, with the Support Vector Machine algorithm also performing well. The Multilayer Perceptron algorithm has the lowest accuracy scores across the datasets of the three domains, although the difference in performance between then is quite small. Due to space limitations, we do not present here further details of the results, such as the confusion matrices of the classifiers. They can be reproduced using the code available in the GitHub address indicated at the beginning of Sect. 3.

5   Conclusions and Future Work

This article compared alternative ML models for churn prediction on datasets of distinct HCT enterprises, using the CP-HCT framework introduced in this work. This framework, described in detail in Sect. 3, is available for reuse by the ML community. It allows efficiently training and selecting ML models by supporting an extension of the CRISP-DM process. Its main extension is a quick test, between the Data Preparation and the Hyperparameter Setting phases of CRISP-DM, to select models trained with default parameter configurations, based on their performance. It allows the speed-up of the subsequent Hyperparameter Setting, Modeling and Evaluation phases, by concentrating efforts on the most promising models for the datasets at hand. The CP-HCT framework also drives the data preparation phase for leveraging RFM segmentation of transactional data to create categorical data for training.

The goal of our experiments was to identify models and data features that provide the best results for churn prediction in industries with HCT. In our experiments, the quick test enabled the selection of the most promising ones. After careful hyperparamenter setting and modeling, the Random Forest consistently presented the best accuracy in most datasets considered. Other models used in related work (Sect. 2.2), such as SVM and Multilayer Perceptron, also yielded good results. Purchase transaction data was the basis for model training and evaluation in all the HCT scenarios considered. The best results presented in this paper were obtained by using RFM. Without it the results had 15% lower accuracy in average.

Our envision for future work include: (i) surveing related research on churn prediction in HCT enterprises to better determine key characteristics and differences from other areas; (ii) expanding research about churn prediction to more companies of distinct sectors with HCT; (iii) updating research that aims to compare customer acquisition costs versus retention costs in contexts with and without HCT; (iv) building a common database and benchmarks to compare alternative approaches for churn prediction in HCT enterprises; (v) analyzing the performance of the CP-HCT framework in other domains; (vi) enhance the CP-HCT framework with new approaches for feature selection, and ensemble learning, aiming to improve classification results, as done in [12], for example.

References

1. Ahn, J., Hwang, J., Kim, D., Choi, H., Kang, S.: A survey on churn analysis in various business domains. IEEE Access **8**, 220816–220839 (2020). https://doi.org/10.1109/ACCESS.2020.3042657
2. Berry, M.J., Linoff, G.S.: Data mining techniques: for marketing, sales, and customer relationship management. John Wiley & Sons (2004)
3. Chapman, P., et al.: Crisp-dm 1.0 step-by-step data mining guide. Tech. rep., The CRISP-DM consortium (August 2000). https://maestria-datamining-2010.googlecode.com/svn-history/r282/trunk/dmct-teorica/tp1/CRISPWP-0800.pdf
4. Coussement, K., De Bock, K.: Customer churn prediction in the online gambling industry: The beneficial effect of ensemble learning. J. Bus. Res. **66**(9), 1629–1636 (2013). https://EconPapers.repec.org/RePEc:eee:jbrese:v:66:y:2013:i:9:p:1629-1636
5. Geiler, L., Affeldt, S., Nadif, M.: A survey on machine learning methods for churn prediction. International J. Data Sci. Analy. **14**(3), 217–242 (2022). https://doi.org/10.1007/s41060-022-00312-5
6. Hashmi, N., Butt, N.A., Iqbal, D.: Customer churn prediction in telecommunication a decade review and classification. IJCSI **10**, 271–282 (2013)
7. Iacobucci, D., Hibbard, J.D.: Toward an encompassing theory of business marketing relationships (BMRS) and interpersonal commercial relationships (ICRS): An empirical generalization. J. Interact. Mark. **13**(3), 13–33 (1999)

8. Kaggle: Brazilian E-Commerce Public Dataset by Olist kernel description (2018). https://www.kaggle.com/olistbr/brazilian-ecommerce
9. Khair, U., Fahmi, H., Hakim, S.A., Rahim, R.: Forecasting error calculation with mean absolute deviation and mean absolute percentage error. J. Phys: Conf. Ser. **930**(1), 12002 (2017)
10. Kim, S., Choi, D., Lee, E., Rhee, W.: Churn prediction of mobile and online casual games using play log data. PLoS ONE **12**(7), e0180735–e0180735 (2017)
11. Kim, S., Lee, H.: Customer churn prediction in influencer commerce: An application of decision trees. Proc. Comput. Sci. **199**, 1332–1339 (2022). https://doi.org/10.1016/j.procs.2022.01.169,https://www.sciencedirect.com/science/article/pii/S1877050922001703, the 8th International Conference on Information Technology and Quantitative Management (ITQM 2020 & 2021): Developing Global Digital Economy after COVID-19
12. Lalwani, P., Mishra, M., Chadha, J., Sethi, P.: Customer churn prediction system: a machine learning approach. Computing **104**, 1–24 (2022). https://doi.org/10.1007/s00607-021-00908-y
13. Leys, C., Ley, C., Klein, O., Bernard, P., Licata, L.: Detecting outliers: do not use standard deviation around the mean, use absolute deviation around the median. J. Experi. Soc. Psychol. **49**(4), 764–766 (2013). https://doi.org/10.1016/j.jesp.2013.03.013, https://www.sciencedirect.com/science/article/pii/S0022103113000668
14. Makowski, L., Ostroy, J.M.: Perfect competition and the creativity of the market. J. Econ. Literat. **39**(2), 479–535 (2001)
15. Martínez, A., Schmuck, C., Pereverzyev, S., Pirker, C., Haltmeier, M.: A machine learning framework for customer purchase prediction in the non-contractual setting. Eur. J. Oper. Res. **281**(3), 588–596 (2020)
16. Mustafa, N., Sook Ling, L., Abdul Razak, S.F.: Customer churn prediction for telecommunication industry: a Malaysian case study [version 1; peer review: 2 approved]. F1000 Res. **110**, 1274–1274 (2021)
17. Oliveira, V.L.M.: Analytical customer relationship management in retailing supported by data mining techniques. Ph.D. thesis, University of Porto (Portugal) (2012)
18. Pedregosa, F., et al.: Scikit-learn: machine learning in Python. J. Mach. Learn. Res. **12**, 2825–2830 (2011)
19. Periáñez, f., Saas, A., Guitart, A., Magne, C.: Churn prediction in mobile social games: Towards a complete assessment using survival ensembles. Cornell University Library, Ithaca. arXiv.org (2017)
20. Perišić, A., Pahor, M.: Rfm-lir feature framework for churn prediction in the mobile games market. IEEE Trans. Games **14**(2), 126–137 (2022). https://doi.org/10.1109/TG.2021.3067114
21. dos Santos, L.G.M.: Domain generalization, invariance and the time robust forest (2021)
22. Sobreiro, P., Martinho, D.D.S., Alonso, J.G., Berrocal, J.: A slr on customer dropout prediction. IEEE Access **10**, 14529–14547 (2022)
23. de Souza, A.R.R., et al.: Mortality risk evaluation: a proposal for intensive care units patients exploring machine learning methods. In: Intelligent Systems: 11th Brazilian Conference, BRACIS 2022, Campinas, Brazil, 28 November - 1 December 2022, Proceedings, Part I, pp. 1–14. Springer-Verlag, Berlin (2022). https://doi.org/10.1007/978-3-031-21686-2_1
24. Tsai, C.F., Lu, Y.H.: Customer churn prediction by hybrid neural networks. Expert Syst. Appli. **36**(10), 12547–12553 (2009). https://doi.org/10.1016/j.eswa.2009.05.032, https://www.sciencedirect.com/science/article/pii/S0957417409004758

25. Vafeiadis, T., Diamantaras, K., Sarigiannidis, G., Chatzisavvas, K.: A comparison of machine learning techniques for customer churn prediction. Simul. Model. Pract. Theory **55**, 1–9 (2015)
26. Wei, J.T., Lin, S.Y., Wu, H.H.: A review of the application of rfm model. Afr. J. Bus. Manage. **4**, 4199–4206 (2010)
27. Wenger, M.: Strategic business models in the online food delivery industry - detailed analysis of the -order and delivery- business model (2021). http://hdl.handle.net/10362/140006
28. Wu, X., Li, P., Zhao, M., Liu, Y., Crespo, R.G., Herrera-Viedma, E.: Customer churn prediction for web browsers. Expert Syst. Appli. **209**, 118177 (2022). https://doi.org/10.1016/j.eswa.2022.118177, https://www.sciencedirect.com/science/article/pii/S0957417422013434
29. Xiahou, X., Harada, Y.: B2C e-commerce customer churn prediction based on K-Means and SVM. J. Theor. Appli. Elect. Commerce Res. **17**(2), 458–475 (2022). https://doi.org/10.3390/jtaer17020024, https://www.mdpi.com/0718-1876/17/2/24
30. Xie, Y., Li, X., Ngai, E., Ying, W.: Customer churn prediction using improved balanced random forests. Expert Syst. Appli. **36**(3, Part 1), 5445–5449 (2009). https://doi.org/10.1016/j.eswa.2008.06.121, https://www.sciencedirect.com/science/article/pii/S0957417408004326
31. Zineldin, M.: The royalty of loyalty: CRM, quality and retention. J. Consumer Market. **23**(7), 430–437 (2006)

Data Fusion Performance Prophecy: A Random Forest Revelation

Zhongmin Zhang[1] and Shengli Wu[1,2(✉)]

[1] School of Computer Science, Jiangsu University, Zhenjiang, China
swu@ujs.edu.cn
[2] School of Computing, Ulster University, Belfast, UK

Abstract. Data fusion synthesizes results from diverse sources, but the performance impact remains mysterious. This research reveals the inner workings of fusion through machine prophecy. Constructing a random forest model using TREC dataset benchmarks, we accurately predicted the performance of two fusion algorithms. The model achieved near perfect R^2 scores above 0.9 by exploiting meaningful statistical features. Compared to linear regression, the tree-based ensemble provides superior insight. The importance of newly identified drivers, like P@1000 metrics, is quantified. With this prescient view, researchers can refine fusion techniques to offer better search. By uncovering the secrets of fusion success, machine learning guides the path to retrieval excellence.

Keywords: data fusion · performance prediction · random forest · information retrieval

1 Introduction

Data fusion is a useful technique for merging multiple result lists in information retrieval [1, 2]. Its goal is to achieve better retrieval results by merging multiple lists, which can be obtained through different query representations, ranking functions and corpus, etc. The principle behind it is that simple aggregation functions also have the potential to improve retrieval performance by the chorus effect.

To find how the favorable condition is for data fusion methods to be successful, researchers conducted many experiments to evaluate the performance of fusion algorithms, but the results varied. It has been found that data fusion has significant uncertainty, and it does not always make the retrieval results better. It is affected by numerous factors such as the data fusion methods used, the number of component retrieval systems involved, performance of those retrieval systems, diversity of all component systems, the document collection underneath, the retrieval task to be taken, the metric used for evaluation, among many others. Some early experiments by a number of researchers explored the impact of those factors on fusion performance [3–6].

Due to the nature of uncertainty, predicting fusion performance is an important issue. It is a part of more broad performance prediction of information retrieval results [7–9]. It can be used in a few different ways such as deciding which fusion method to use [2, 3],

P. Delir Haghighi et al. (Eds.): iiWAS 2023, LNCS 14416, pp. 192–200, 2023.
https://doi.org/10.1007/978-3-031-48316-5_20

weights assignment for certain data fusion methods such as linear combination [4, 5, 7, 8], selecting a subset from a large number of component retrieval systems for fusion [9, 10], or instead of fusion selecting a single list from a group of candidates as the final result list [11, 12].

A few papers addressed the performance estimation/prediction on data fusion results [13–16]. Among them, [13–15] try to rank a group of queries based on their estimated performance; while [16] uses multiple linear regression to analyze and predict the performance of two typical data fusion methods CombSum and CombMNZ.

In the same vein as [16], this work investigates the fusion performance prediction issue through supervised learning. Although it costs more for relevance judgment, the much more accurate prediction is a big pay-off. It may be worthwhile for some situations which allow this cost. The main contributions of this work are as follows:

1. We propose a random forest-based approach. Experiments with three data sets from TREC confirm that its prediction is very accurate and more accurate than multiple linear regression [16].
2. A rank-based dissimilarity metric is proposed, which is more effective than the set-based dissimilarity metric in [16].
3. Some new features are identified as useful for performance prediction. Only MAP is used for performance-related features in [16]. We find that recall-based metrics also provide useful information for performance prediction.

2 Random Forest-Based Fusion Performance Prediction

In this section, we shall describe the random forest-based fusion performance prediction method and the feature groups selected for training and testing.

As in [16], we also deal with two fusion methods CombSum and CombMNZ. Note that quite a few different data fusion methods such as CombSum [17], CombMNZ [3, 17], Borda count [18], Condorcet fusion [19], and linear combination with multiple methods of weights assignment [4, 5, 8], among many others [20, 21], have been proposed. It is likely that CombSum and CombMNZ are the most commonly used.

Assuming for a given query q, n different component systems are selected to participate in fusion. CombSum calculates the sum of the scores of document d. The formula is as follows:

$$g(q, d) = \sum_{i=1}^{t} score_i(d) \tag{1}$$

where $score_i(d)$ denotes the score of document d in the i-th result list.

CombMNZ is essentially a variant of CombSum. It regards the times of occurrence of any document in all n result lists as an indicator of the importance of the document. The formula is as follows:

$$g(q, d) = \alpha * \sum_{i=1}^{t} score_i(d) \tag{2}$$

where α represents the number of component results containing document d.

Selecting a group of useful features is vital for the success of the prediction task. In [16], linear regression analysis was carried out with a group of selected features:

the average performance of all component systems, the standard deviation of the performance of all component systems, the total number of result lists, and the overlap rate among all component results. Among these features, performance of a component system is evaluated by MAP (Mean Average Precision). Based on their work with some modifications/extensions, we used the following eight features:

(1) the total number of component systems
(2) the average of MAP of all component systems
(3) standard deviation of MAP of all component systems
(4) the optimum AP in all component systems
(5) the average P@1000 of all component systems
(6) standard deviation of P@1000 of all component systems
(7) the optimum P@1000 of all component systems
(8) the dissimilarity among all component results.

Features 1–4 are the same as in [16]. Features 2–4 are MAP related features. However, there are many different metrics for retrieval performance evaluation. MAP is one of them and only reflects some but not all aspects of the evaluated result list. Now we add three P@1000 related features (5–8). P@1000 is a feature that can tell certain aspects about the result list and the number of relevant documents in the collection implicitly. As we will see later, all of them are useful features for the prediction task.

In [16], dissimilarity is considered by a measure of overlapping documents in two result lists. Here we define a rank-based method to compare the ranking differences of the same document in two result lists [22]. This method is better than the one used in [16] because more information is used.

To investigate the utility of the features introduced in this paper, the experimentation is performed in two steps. The first step is to set up three groups of features. Group 1 includes the number of all component systems, the mean of MAP of all component systems, the standard deviation of MAP of all component systems, and the optimum MAP in all component systems. Group 2 includes the number of all component systems, the average P@1000 of all component systems, the standard deviation of P@1000 of all component systems, and the optimum P@1000 in all component systems. Group 3 is a combination of Group 1 and Group 2 with one duplicate removed (the number of all component systems). Prediction is carried out with these three groups separately. The second step is to use all eight features to do the analysis.

Random forest [23] is used for analysis and prediction. We also tried SVM (Support Vector Machine, but it is not as good as random forest. Therefore, only results of using random forest are reported. For performance evaluation, we use MAP, because it is a commonly used single-valued metric.

3 Experimental Settings and Results

For the data sets used in the experiment, we used three data sets from TREC[1]: the 2004 Robust Track, the 2017 Common Core Track, and the 2018 Common Core Track. The information of these three data sets is summarized in Table 1. The major reason for

---

[1] Https://trec.nist.gov/

choosing the TREC Robust Track in 2004 is that this track contains 250 queries, which is relatively large and helpful for the training and testing of the prediction model. TREC Common Core Track in 2017 and 2018 were based on the New York Times corpus and Washington Post corpus, respectively. In terms of query set, they contain 50 queries with official relevance judgment respectively. In addition, query 672 in the TREC 2004 data set does not include any relevant documents, this query was excluded in the experiment. The figure under the title "No. Runs" indicates the total number of submissions to each task.

Table 1. Information of the data sets used in experiments

Collection	TREC Task	No. Topics	No. Runs
Disks 4&5 minus CR	Robust 2004	249	110
New York Times Corpus	Common Core 2017	50	75
Washington Post Corpus	Common Core 2018	50	72

For the component results for the experiment, we selected the result lists submitted by different organizations to those tasks. Two conditions were satisfied:

(1) MAP of all the queries is not lower than the threshold value of 0.15.
(2) The number of documents returned for each query is no less than 1000.

The former condition avoids the participation of poor lists in fusion, while the latter guarantees the homogeneity of the experimental environment. After screening these two conditions, 103 submissions met the requirements in 2004, 64 submissions met the requirements in 2017 and 55 submissions met the requirements in 2018.

Then the selected component results were normalized by the linear zero-one method [3]. For a given number, all component results were randomly selected from all available ones. Specifically, for the TREC 2004 set, the number of queries is 249, the number of component systems selected for fusion is 3–13, the round of random selection is 20, the combination of features is 6, and the types of fusion algorithms are 2. The final size of the training set is $249 * 11 * 20 * 6 * 2 = 657360$. In the same vein, the size of the training set is $50 * 10 * 20 * 6 * 2 = 120000$ and $50 * 7 * 20 * 6 * 2 = 84000$, for TREC 2017 and 2018 data sets, respectively.

A machine learning library for Python, scikit-learn, was used for the experimentation. Especially, we used its Random Forest Regressor[2], an ensemble method, with the default setting, for the random forest-based prediction. Five-fold shuffle-split cross-validation was used to evaluate the generalization performance of the model by R^2, whose value is in the [0, 1] interval. $R^2 = 1$ corresponds to the perfect prediction, $R^2 = 0$ corresponds to a constant model. The larger the R^2 value is, the denser the sample points are near the regression curve, which indicates that the higher the degree of interpretation of the target value (dependent variable) by the features (independent variable).

---

[2] It is sklearn.ensemble.RandomForestRegressor.

Linear regression and random forest regression models are constructed according to the three different feature groups described in Sect. 3. The prediction results of the two fusion algorithms for three different tasks are shown in Tables 2, 3, 4, 5, 6 and 7, respectively. In these tables, G1 includes all the features in Group 1, and G1+ includes all the features of Group 1 plus Dissimilarity. G2, G2+, G3, and G3+ are defined in the same way.

Table 2. Prediction results for the TREC 2004 data (CombSum). LR denotes linear regression, RF denotes random forest. The highest R^2 are shown in boldface.

Method	G1	G1+	G2	G2+	G3	G3+
LR	0.938	0.940	0.841	0.842	0.940	0.943
RF	**0.949**	**0.956**	**0.934**	**0.938**	**0.965**	**0.970**

Table 3. Prediction results for the TREC 2004 data (CombMNZ). LR denotes linear regression, RF denotes random forest. The highest R^2 are shown in boldface.

Method	G1	G1+	G2	G2+	G3	G3+
LR	0.922	0.925	0.831	0.832	0.924	0.928
RF	**0.937**	**0.946**	**0.933**	**0.938**	**0.958**	**0.963**

Table 4. Prediction results for the TREC 2017 data (CombSum). LR denotes linear regression, RF denotes random forest. The highest R^2 are shown in boldface.

Method	G1	G1+	G2	G2+	G3	G3+
LR	0.808	0.817	0.712	0.726	0.829	0.841
RF	**0.903**	**0.910**	**0.923**	**0.929**	**0.935**	**0.939**

Table 5. Prediction results for the TREC 2017 data (CombMNZ). LR denotes linear regression, RF denotes random forest. The highest R^2 are shown in boldface.

Method	G1	G1+	G2	G2+	G3	G3+
LR	0.816	0.823	0.710	0.723	0.830	0.841
RF	**0.901**	**0.909**	**0.925**	**0.932**	**0.936**	**0.940**

Firstly, Tables 2, 3, 4, 5, 6 and 7 show the role of the dissimilarity among component results. By comparing the results before and after adding the feature of Dissimilarity, we can find that it improves the fitting effect, whether the linear regression or random forest is applied. Although the improvement is small, which is no more than 0.1, can be seen in

Table 6. Prediction results for the TREC 2018 data (CombSum). LR denotes linear regression, RF denotes random forest. The highest R^2 are shown in boldface.

Method	G1	G1+	G2	G2+	G3	G3+
LR	0.869	0.873	0.743	0.747	0.872	0.876
RF	**0.904**	**0.908**	**0.915**	**0.920**	**0.931**	**0.933**

Table 7. Prediction results for the TREC 2018 data (CombMNZ). LR denotes linear regression, RF denotes random forest. The highest R^2 are shown in boldface.

Method	G1	G1+	G2	G2+	G3	G3+
LR	0.827	0.829	0.721	0.723	0.833	0.835
RF	**0.872**	**0.878**	**0.902**	**0.907**	**0.914**	**0.915**

almost all the cases. It demonstrates that this feature has a small but significant impact on fusion performance. By comparing the corresponding results of the two regression models, we can observe that the improvement for the random forest model is more than that for the linear regression model. It indicates that the random forest can take more advantage from this feature than the linear model does.

Secondly, it can be observed that the prediction for CombSum is always more accurate than for CombMNZ, although the difference is small. Understandably, CombMNZ is a little more complicated than CombSum on the fusion function used.

Thirdly, different accuracies are observed for different feature groups. Among all those feature groups, Group 3+ Dissimilarity is the best one. In TREC 2004, the R^2 values of the random forest model for CombSum and CombMNZ are 0.970 and 0.963 respectively, while the corresponding R^2 values of the linear model are 0.943 and 0.928 respectively. For the other two years, Group 3+ Dissimilarity is also the best combination. This result is in line with expectations because it contains all eight features and has more information available than Group 1 and Group 2. As all the results are very similar across three data sets, the following analysis is focused on the results of TREC 2004 data.

For linear regression analysis, all variables are standardized (scaled between 0 and 1) before modeling. The independent variable coefficients are the mean of AP of all component systems (1.012), the standard deviation of AP of all component systems (0.165), the optimum value of AP of all component systems (−0.069), the mean of P@1000 of all component systems (0.068), the standard deviation of P@1000 of all component systems (−0.023), the optimum value of P@1000 of all component systems (−0.069), the Dissimilarity (0.060) and the number of systems (0.050). All the above features can be identified as having statistical significance through the observation of the p-value ($p <= 0.05$). For the random forest-based method, the importance of different features is assessed by examining the contribution of each feature to each decision tree and taking the average value. The criteria for measuring the importance of a feature are the Gini index and the error rate of out-of-bag (OOB). For the TREC 2004 data set, the ranking of all the features in the random forest model is as follows: the mean of AP of all component systems (0.937), the mean of P@1000 of all component systems (0.013), the dissimilarity (0.012), the standard deviation of P@1000 of all component systems (0.009), the standard deviation of AP of all component systems (0.008), the optimum value of AP of all component systems (0.008), the optimum value of P@1000 of all component systems (0.007) and the number of component systems (0.005). Thus, the contributions of these features to the two models are quite different.

According to Tables 8 and 9, we find that the other two feature combinations, Group 1 and Group 2, have different performance for different regression methods, which are complex and difficult to distinguish. Group 1 contains features mainly from experiments conducted by Wu and Mcclean [16]. The results of this paper confirm that their proposed the mean of AP of all component systems, the standard deviation of AP of all component systems, the optimum value of AP of all component systems are representative. Group 2 contains the new features proposed in this paper: the mean of P@1000 of all component systems, the standard deviation of P@1000 of all component systems, the optimum value of P@1000 of all component systems, and also has a strong predictive ability. Interestingly, when Group 2 is used as the training data of random forest, the accuracy is much better than that of linear model. Specifically, when the linear model adopts Group 2, the determinant coefficient decreases to a certain extent compared with Group 1. The random forest model is less volatile and even better than the results of Group 1. This shows that random forest model is more effective in mining these features, especially the features in Group 2.

Table 8. Average R^2 for two methods using Group 1 vs. Group 2 (CombSum)

Method	Features	2004	2017	2018
Linear Regression	Group 1	0.938	0.808	0.869
	Group 2	0.841	0.712	0.743
Random Forest	Group 1	0.949	0.903	0.904
	Group 2	0.934	0.923	0.915

Table 9. Average R^2 for two methods using Group 1 vs. Group 2 (CombMNZ)

Method	Features	2004	2017	2018
Linear Regression	Group 1	0.922	0.816	0.827
	Group 2	0.831	0.710	0.721
Random Forest	Group 1	0.937	0.901	0.872
	Group 2	0.933	0.925	0.902

In summary, comparing the two methods of linear regression and random forest regression, it is obvious that the accuracy based on random forest prediction is higher.

Specifically, in all cases of different task data and different feature combinations, its determinant coefficients are higher than linear regression models. In particular, by observing the results of the above tasks and calculating the standard deviation, we can also find that the performance of the random forest model is more stable, while the prediction accuracy of the linear model for the data of TREC Common Core Track is obviously lower than that of TREC Robust Track. This indicates that the random forest model can make better use of the proposed features and predict the final fusion performance more accurately.

4 Conclusions

In this paper, we have proposed a random forest-based method for performance prediction of data fusion methods including CombSum and CombMNZ. Eight features were selected from different perspectives based on the data of different tasks in different years of TREC, and these features were tested in groups. The results of regression experiments show that the model is very good on fusion performance prediction. Especially, MAP, P@1000, and the dissimilarity among component results, are three most useful features and make significant contribution to the prediction task. The proposed method is very accurate, and it is better than the linear regression method by a clear margin. As our future work, we aim to apply it to some related retrieval tasks such as selecting a subgroup of component retrieval systems for better efficiency and performance.

References

1. Huang, Y., Xu, Q., Liu, Y., Xu, C., Wu, S.: Data Fusion Methods with Graded Relevance Judgment. WISA, pp. 227–239 (2022)
2. Kurland, O., Culpepper, J.S.: Fusion in Information Retrieval: SIGIR 2018 Half-Day Tutorial. SIGIR, pp. 1383–1386 (2018)
3. Lee, J.-H.: Analyses of Multiple Evidence Combination. SIGIR, pp. 267–276 (1997)
4. Vogt, C.C., Cottrell, G.W.: Predicting the Performance of Linearly Combined IR Systems. SIGIR, pp. 190–196 (1998)
5. Wu, S., Crestani, F.: Data fusion with estimated weights. CIKM, pp. 648–651 (2002)
6. Beitzel, S.M., Jensen, E.C., Chowdhury, A., Grossman, D.A., Frieder, O., Goharian, N.: Fusion of effective retrieval strategies in the same information retrieval system. J. Assoc. Inf. Sci. Technol. 55(10), 859–868 (2004)
7. Lillis, D., Zhang, L., Toolan, F., Collier, R.W., Leonard, D., Dunnion, J.: Estimating probabilities for effective data fusion. SIGIR, pp. 347–354 (2010)
8. Wu, S.: Linear combination of component results in information retrieval. Data Knowl. Eng. 71(1), 114–126 (2012)
9. Juárez-González, A., Montes-y-Gómez, M., Villaseñor-Pineda, L., Pinto-Avendaño, D., Pérez-Coutiño, M.: Selecting the N-top retrieval result lists for an effective data fusion. In: Gelbukh, A. (ed.) Computational Linguistics and Intelligent Text Processing, pp. 580–589. Springer Berlin Heidelberg, Berlin, Heidelberg (2010). https://doi.org/10.1007/978-3-642-12116-6_49
10. Wei, Z., Gao, W., El-Ganainy, T., Magdy, W., Wong, K.-F.: Ranking model selection and fusion for effective microblog search. SoMeRA@SIGIR, pp. 21–26 (2014)

11. Balasubramanian, N., Allan, J.: Learning to select rankers. SIGIR, 855–856 (2010)
12. Peng, J., Macdonald, C., Ounis, I.: Learning to Select a Ranking Function. ECIR, pp. 114–126 (2010)
13. Markovits, G., Shtok, A., Kurland, O., Carmel, D.: Predicting query performance for fusion-based retrieval. CIKM, pp. 813–822 (2012)
14. Roitman, H.: Enhanced Performance Prediction of Fusion-based Retrieval. ICTIR, pp. 195–198 (2018)
15. Faggioli, G.: Enabling Performance Prediction in Information Retrieval Evaluation. SIGIR, p. 2701 (2021)
16. Wu, S., McClean, S.I.: Performance prediction of data fusion for information retrieval. Inf. Process. Manag. **42**(4), 899–915 (2006)
17. Shaw, J.A., Fox, E.A.: Combination of Multiple Searches. TREC, pp. 105–108 (1994)
18. Javed A. Aslam, Mark H. Montague. Models for Metasearch. SIGIR 2001: 275–284
19. Montague, M.H., Aslam, J.A.: Condorcet fusion for improved retrieval. CIKM, pp. 538–548 (2002)
20. Sivaram, M., Batri, K., Mohammed, A.S., Porkodi, V., Kousik, N.V.: Data fusion using Tabu crossover genetic algorithm in information retrieval. J. Intell. Fuzzy Syst. **39**(4), 5407–5416 (2020)
21. Valadez, J.H., Morales-González, E., Fernández-Reyes, F.C., Montes-y-Gómez, M., Fuentes-Pacheco, J., Rendón-Mancha, J.M.: Exploiting hierarchical dependence structures for unsupervised rank fusion in information retrieval. J. Intell. Inf. Syst. **60**(3), 853–876 (2023)
22. Wu, S., Huang, C., Li, L., Crestani, F.: Fusion-based methods for result diversification in web search. Inf. Fusion **45**, 16–26 (2019)
23. Breiman, L.: Random forests. Mach. Learn. **45**(1), 5–32 (2001)

Celestial Machine Learning

Discovering the Planarity, Heliocentricity, and Orbital Equation of Mars with AI Feynman

Zi-Yu Khoo[1](✉), Gokul Rajiv[1], Abel Yang[1], Jonathan Sze Choong Low[2],
and Stéphane Bressan[1,3]

[1] National University of Singapore, 21 Lower Kent Ridge Rd,
Singapore 119077, Singapore
khoozy@comp.nus.edu.sg, grajiv@u.nus.edu, {phyyja,steph}@nus.edu.sg
[2] Singapore Institute of Manufacturing Technology, Agency for Science,Technology
and Research(A*STAR), Singapore 138634, Singapore
sclow@simtech.a-star.edu.sg
[3] CNRS@Create Ltd., 1 Create Way, Singapore 138602, Singapore

Abstract. Can a machine or algorithm discover or learn the elliptical orbit of Mars from astronomical sightings alone? Johannes Kepler required two paradigm shifts to discover his First Law regarding the elliptical orbit of Mars. Firstly, a shift from the geocentric to the heliocentric frame of reference. Secondly, the reduction of the orbit of Mars from a three- to a two-dimensional space. We extend AI Feynman, a physics-inspired tool for symbolic regression, to discover the heliocentricity and planarity of Mars' orbit and emulate his discovery of Kepler's first law.

Keywords: Machine Learning · Symbolic Regression · Pareto Optimisation

1 Introduction

In 2020, Silviu-Marian Udrescu and Max Tegmark introduced *AI Feynman* [13], a symbolic regression algorithm that could rediscover equations from the *Feynman Lectures on Physics* [2]. AI Feynman can even emulate Johannes Kepler's rediscovery of the orbital equation of Mars from the Rudolphine tables [7] [8].

In this work, we also use AI Feynman to emulate Kepler's rediscovery of the elliptical orbital equation of Mars, but from astronomical observations instead. Kepler's rediscovery of the orbital equation of Mars required two paradigm shifts in early astronomy which he embedded within the Rudolphine tables. Firstly, a shift from the geocentric to heliocentric frame of reference. Secondly, the reduction of the orbit from a three- to a two-dimensional space. Without observations from the Rudolphine tables, AI Feynman is ignorant of these two paradigm shifts and unable to emulate Kepler's rediscovery of the orbital equation of Mars. We therefore present two algorithms that embed the ability to change reference

P. Delir Haghighi et al. (Eds.): iiWAS 2023, LNCS 14416, pp. 201–207, 2023.
https://doi.org/10.1007/978-3-031-48316-5_21

frames and reduce dimensions in AI Feynman respectively, via biases in the style of physics-informed machine learning. We devise, present, and evaluate the performance of the two algorithms. The remainder of this paper details this advancement in symbolic regression algorithms and evaluates its performance.

2   Background and Related Work

Kepler's First Law states that each planet's orbit about the Sun is an ellipse with the Sun's center located at one focus. The planet follows the ellipse in its orbit, and the planet to Sun distance constantly changes [1]. The orbital equation of Mars in polar coordinates is shown in Eq. 1. It describes the distance of Mars from the Sun, r, as a function of the *anomalia coaequata*, θ, an angle between Mars and the Sun with respect to a horizontal. a and ϵ are constants representing the semi-major axis and eccentricity of the ellipse. The variables $r(t)$ and $\theta(t)$ are functions of time, and comprise observations at different times.

$$r(t) = \frac{a}{1 + \epsilon \cos(\theta(t))} \tag{1}$$

The same equation in cartesian coordinates is shown in Eq. 2. x and y are the coordinates of Mars relative to the Sun, and b and h are the semi-minor axis and distance between the center and focus of the ellipse respectively.

$$r(t) = \sqrt{y(t)^2 + x(t)^2} = \sqrt{b^2 \times \left(1 - \frac{(x(t) - h)^2}{a^2}\right) + x(t)^2} \tag{2}$$

The discovery of the orbital equation of Mars from sightings of the planet and the Sun is a combinatorial challenge [13]. To circumvent this, one may use universal function approximators such as multilayer perceptron neural networks [5].

Alternatively, symbolic regressions search for a parsimonious and elegant form of the unknown equation. There are three main classes of symbolic regression methods [10]: regression-based, expression tree-based and physics- or mathematics-inspired. We use AI Feynman, a physics-inspired algorithm [13].

Regression-based symbolic regression methods [10], given solutions to the unknown equation, find the coefficients of a fixed basis that minimise the prediction error. As the basis grows, the fit improves, but the functional form of the unknown equation becomes less sparse or parsimonious. Furthermore, committing to a basis limits the applicability of regression-based methods.

Expression tree-based symbolic regression methods based on genetic programming [9,10] can instead discover the form and coefficients of the unknown equation. However, genetic programmes may greedily mimic nuances of the unknown equation [12], limiting generalisability. Pareto optimisation can be used to balance the objectives of fit and parsimony in symbolic regression [4]. However, if an expression tree-based method finds a reasonably accurate equation with the wrong functional form, it risks getting stuck at a local optimum [13].

Physics-inspired symbolic regression methods such as AI Feynman use a neural network to test for properties of the unknown equation and recursively break its search into that of simpler equations [13]. Each equation is then regressed with a basis-set of nonlinear functions. This guarantees that more accurate approximations of an equation are symbolically closer to the truth [13]. AI Feynman outputs a sequence of increasingly complex equations with progressively better accuracy along a Pareto frontier, to balance fit and parsimony. We use AI Feynman to rediscover the orbital equation of Mars from observational data.

Seminal work by Khoo et al. [8] combined AI Feynman and physics-informed machine learning to rediscover the orbital equation of Mars. They used inductive and observational biases within the AI Feynman algorithm to inform the algorithm of the periodicity of Mars' orbit and the trigonometric nature of the data from the Rudolphine tables [8]. Additionally, they used data from the Rudolphine tables which embed observational biases of the heliocentricity and planarity of Mars' orbit [8]. We use the same inductive and observational biases as Khoo et al. [8]. However, we rediscover the orbital equation of Mars from three-dimensional, geocentric observations, and inform AI Feynman of heliocentricity and planarity of Mars' orbit using inductive biases.

3   Methodology

This section introduces two algorithms that correspond to two biases to aid AI Feynman in rediscovering the orbital equation of Mars. We evaluate the two algorithms on their ability to rediscover either Eq. 1 or 2.

The first algorithm considers the relationship between Mars and the Sun from varying reference frames. Observations of Mars, the Sun and the Earth are made from the three heliocentric, geocentric and areocentric reference frames. AI Feynman is used to discover the relationship between Mars and the Sun from each set of observations. All relationships are placed on one Pareto frontier as an inductive bias to compare their fit and parsimony. The second algorithm considers the relationship between Mars and the Sun from varying dimensional spaces. Three-dimensional geocentric observations of Mars and the Sun are made. The dimensional space of geocentric observations of Mars and the Sun is then gradually reduced by projecting the original observations into progressively lower dimensional spaces. AI Feynman is used to rediscover the relationship between Mars and the Sun from each set of lower-dimensional projections. All relationships are placed on one Pareto frontier as an inductive bias to compare their fit and parsimony. We evaluate the algorithms on their ability to rediscover equations that describe Mars' orbit around the Sun, namely Eqs. 1 or 2, from observations from a polar or cartesian coordinate system.

4   Performance Evaluation

Three experiments are designed. The first two correspond to the two algorithms described in Sect. 3. The third uses the results from the first two to rediscover the orbital equation of Mars. Their experimental setup and results are shown in this section. All experiments are run twice, once each for the cartesian and polar coordinate systems respectively.

Data for all experiments was obtained from the National Aeronautics and Space Administration's Horizons system and downloaded from `astropy` [3]. The data includes geocentric, polar observations of the angular width, AW, right ascension, RA and declination, DC, of Mars M and the Sun S from 1 January 1601 to 31 December 1602. The geocentric cartesian coordinates of Mars is a tuple (X_M, Y_M, Z_M), converted from polar coordinates using `astropy`. All computations are in astronomical units. The AI Feynman algorithm designed by Udrescu et al. [13] with modifications to embed inductive and observational biases by Khoo et al. [8] is used. The code and data are available at https:// github.com/zykhoo/AI-Feynman.

AI Feynman returns equations along a Pareto frontier. The Pareto frontier is a set of solutions that represents the best trade-off between fit and parsimony. No other solution has a better fit and is more parsimonious than an equation along the Pareto frontier. The measure of fit places a logarithm-scaled penalty on the absolute loss. The measure of parsimony places a logarithm-scaled penalty on real numbers, variables and operators in an equation. AI Feynman simultaneously attempts to minimise both penalties using the Pareto frontier.

Experiment 1. Three sets of observations are created, corresponding to the three reference frames for each coordinate system. The first set comprises the coordinates of Mars and the Sun from the geocentric reference frame, the second set comprises the coordinates of the Earth and Mars from the heliocentric reference frame, and the third set comprises the coordinates of the Sun and the Earth from the areocentric reference frame. The heliocentric and areocentric reference frames of Mars, the Earth and the Sun are computed using vector addition of the coordinates in the geocentric reference frame.

For the cartesian coordinate system, coordinates of the two bodies in each of the three reference frames are input to AI Feynman to describe the distance between Mars and the Sun. For the polar coordinate system, the declination and right ascension are replaced with their sines and cosines as an observational bias regarding the periodicity of Mars' orbital equation. The sine and cosine of the declination and right ascension, and the angular width are input to AI Feynman to describe the distance between Mars and the Sun. Independent runs of AI Feynman are completed for each of the three reference frames. The fit and parsimony of all equations output by AI Feynman from the runs for the cartesian and polar coordinate systems are compared on two separate Pareto frontiers. The equations that form the new, combined Pareto frontiers are examined.

Nine equations appear along the combined Pareto frontier for the cartesian coordinate system, of which six are heliocentric, one is geocentric, and one is areocentric. Four equations appear along the Pareto frontier for the polar coordinate system, of which one is heliocentric and three are geocentric. Generally, the majority of equations are heliocentric. Such equations fit the data parsimoniously and Pareto-dominate other equations that use observations of the Earth, suggesting a direct relationship between Mars and the Sun.

Experiment 2. The three-dimensional geocentric observations of Mars and the Sun in both the polar and cartesian coordinate systems are reduced to lower dimensional spaces by principal component analysis [6].

For the cartesian coordinate system, the three-dimensional geocentric x, y and z coordinates of Mars and the Sun are projected to three-dimensional, two-dimensional and one-dimensional spaces. Three independent runs of AI Feynman are made, one for the projections in each dimensional space. For polar coordinates, the three-dimensional polar coordinates of Mars and the Sun comprise the declination, right ascension and angular width. As the declination and right ascension are angles and the angular width is a measure of length, they cannot be simultaneously projected onto a lower dimensional space. Therefore, the two angles have to be projected onto a lower-dimensional space, after which they are replaced with their sines and cosines as an observational bias regarding the periodicity of Mars' orbital equation [8]. Two independent runs of AI Feynman are made, one for the projection in each dimensional space. The fit and parsimony of all equations output by AI Feynman from the runs for the cartesian and polar coordinate systems are compared on two separate Pareto frontiers. The equations that form the new, combined Pareto frontiers are examined.

Fifteen equations appear along the combined Pareto frontier for the cartesian coordinate system, fourteen of which suggest a two-dimensional space. The results overwhelmingly suggest the orbit of Mars to be in two-dimensional space.

Experiment 3. Following Experiments 1 and 2, the three-dimensional heliocentric observations of Mars in both the polar and cartesian coordinate systems are reduced to lower dimensional spaces by principal component analysis [6].

AI Feynman is used to describe the distance between Mars and the Sun for the cartesian and polar coordinate systems. For the cartesian coordinate system, The inputs are the two heliocentric projections of Mars in two-dimensional space. For the polar coordinate system, the three-dimensional heliocentric polar coordinates of Mars comprise the declination, right ascension and angular width. The angles are projected onto a lower dimensional space. The inputs to the run are the sine and cosine of the projections of the angles in a one-dimensional space.

For the cartesian coordinate system, AI Feynman rediscovers the equation of an ellipse with a semi-minor axis of 1.5165, a semi-major axis of 1.5241, and an eccentricity of 0.09974. The reported semi-major axis of Mars is 1.5237, and the reported eccentricity of Mars' orbit is 0.09341 [11]. For the polar coordinate system, AI Feynman rediscovers Kepler's first law, seen in Eq. 1, with a semi-major axis of 1.5227, and an eccentricity of 0.08306.

5   Conclusion

In this work, we have expanded the frontier of symbolic regression capabilities by extending AI Feynman using inductive biases to smartly explore changes in reference frames and reductions in dimension spaces. We found heliocentric and two-dimensional, planar projections of the data could parsimoniously fit and describe the distance of Mars from the Sun. This enhancement paves the way for AI Feynman to make paradigm shifts that were previously only possible with human intuition and understanding. Directly embedding an observational bias regarding the discovered heliocentricity and planarity allowed AI Feynman to rediscover the orbital equation of Mars.

We are now working on the equations of the orbit of various celestial objects, such as Mercury and the Moon, from various reference frames and dimensional spaces. The discovery of laws of physics can be seen as an optimisation problem for the discovery of maximally accurate and parsimonious models, as recommended by *Occam's razor*.

Acknowledgements. This research is supported by Singapore Ministry of Education, grant MOE-T2EP50120-0019, and by the National Research Foundation, Prime Minister's Office, Singapore, under its Campus for Research Excellence and Technological Enterprise (CREATE) programme as part of the programme Descartes.

References

1. Davis, P., Carney, S.: Orbits and Kepler's Laws. https://solarsystem.nasa.gov/resources/310/orbits-and-keplers-laws/
2. Feynman, R.P.: The Feynman lectures on physics, pp. c1963–c1965. Addison-Wesley Pub. Co., Reading, Mass (1965 c1963)
3. Ginsburg, A., et al.: The Astroquery collaboration, a subset of the astropy collaboration: astroquery: an Astronomical Web-querying Package in Python. Astrophys. J. **157**, 98 (2019)
4. Goldberg, D.E.: Genetic Algorithms in Search, 1st edn. Optimization and Machine Learning. Addison-Wesley Longman Publishing Co., Inc, USA (1989)
5. Hornik, K., Stinchcombe, M., White, H.: Multilayer feedforward networks are universal approximators. Neural Netw. **2**(5), 359–366 (1989)
6. Jolliffe, I.T.: Principal Component Analysis and Factor Analysis, pp. 115–128. Springer, New York (1986). https://doi.org/10.1007/978-1-4757-1904-8_7
7. Kepler, J., Brahe, T., Eckebrecht, P.: Tabulæ Rudolphinæ, quibus astronomicæ scientiæ, temporum longinquitate collapsæ restauratio continetur (1627)
8. Khoo, Z.Y., Abel, Y.: Low Sze Choong, J., Bressan, S.: Celestial Machine Learning From Data to Mars and Beyond with AI Feynman. In: Accepted for publication in Database and Expert Systems Applications: 34th International Conference, DEXA 2023, Penang, Malaysia, 28–30 August 2023, pp. 297–302. Springer-Verlag, Berlin (2023)
9. Koza, J.R.: Genetic Programming: On the Programming of Computers by Means of Natural Selection. MIT Press, Cambridge (1992)
10. Makke, N., Chawla, S.: Interpretable Scientific Discovery with Symbolic Regression: A Review. ArXiv (2022)

11. National Aeronautics and Space Administration: Mars fact sheet. https://nssdc.
gsfc.nasa.gov/planetary/factsheet/marsfact.html (2022)
12. Smits, G.F., Kotanchek, M.: Pareto-Front Exploitation in Symbolic Regression,
pp. 283–299. Springer, US (2005). https://doi.org/10.1007/0-387-23254-0_17
13. Udrescu, S.M., Tegmark, M.: AI Feynman: a physics-inspired method for symbolic
regression. Sci. Adv. **6**(16) (2020)

Deep Learning Based Emotion Recognition Using EEG Signal

Shamim Ripon[(✉)][iD], Tashfia Choudhury, Shabrina Akter Shara,
Sharmin Sharkar Rima, and Shaolin Jahan Aume

Department of Computer Science and Engineering, East West University,
Dhaka, Bangladesh
dshr@ewubd.edu

Abstract. Human-machine interface technology has shown success in recognizing emotions based on physiological data such as EEG signals, rather than facial expressions as facial expressions may not always provide accurate results. The paper proposes a deep learning method for recognizing emotions like arousal, valence, dominance, and liking from EEG signals. The proposed method use FFT for feature extraction, PCA for feature reduction, and deep learning models, namely, LSTM, ANN and CNN are employed. After conducting several experiments a novel combination of channels, number of channels and bandwidths has been identified. By adopting these combinations, the experimental results outperform the majority of the compared works. All research and comparisons were conducted by utilizing the DEAP dataset.

Keywords: EEG signal · Emotion Recognition · Fast Fourier Transform(FFT) · Principle Component Analysis(PCA) · Deep Learning · CNN · LSTM · ANN

1 Introduction

Emotions are combinations of feelings that cause mental and physical states. Emotions such as happiness, sorrow, surprise and excitement are crucial in various fields such as psychology, medical treatment, marketing and machine learning. Many people nowadays experience mental health conditions like anxiety, stress, hypertension etc. Emotion detection significantly contributes to enhancing patient care where doctors can adjust interventions as necessary by detecting and evaluating patient's emotional state [2]. Deep learning has made significant progress in identifying emotions by learning complex features from input information like Electroencephalography (EEG) signals. EEG is a neuro-imaging procedure that monitors brain activity and can capture patterns linked to specific emotions, offering excellent temporal accuracy and allowing researchers to observe rapid shifts in brain activity linked with emotional processes.

Realizing the significance of deep learning, this paper aims at creating a predictive model for emotion recognition from EEG signals, focusing on channel selection for better and faster performance. The selection of appropriate channels and bandwidth is crucial for effective emotion recognition from EEG signals. To

P. Delir Haghighi et al. (Eds.): iiWAS 2023, LNCS 14416, pp. 208–213, 2023.
https://doi.org/10.1007/978-3-031-48316-5_22

conduct this experiment, the dataset we used is Database for Emotion Analysis Using Physiological Signals (DEAP) [7] . The combination of EEG and other indicators in the DEAP dataset provides a valuable resource to investigate the complicated connection between signals from the brain, subjective feelings and emotions. The experiments are conducted by applying 3 deep learning models: LSTM, ANN and CNN. A number of experiments has been carried out by varying channels, number of channels and bandwidth along with tuning hyperparameters of the selected deep learning models.

The rest of the paper provides a brief overview of related work in emotion recognition in Sect. 2, an overview of the DEAP dataset and methodology in Sect. 3, experiments conducted, and results demonstrated in Sect. 4, in Sect. 5 concluding with a summary and outlining future plans.

2 Related Work

Recent experiments have explored extracting informative features from EEG data to recognize emotions from the DEAP dataset. In [6], the performance of an ANN classifier using EEG signals was examined, with 5 time-domain features computed for 3 frequency bands, achieving 85.60% accuracy for valence and 87.36% for arousal. Then again in [4], Discrete Wavelet Transform (DWT) was used to extract 4 frequency bands and 10 channels, followed by PCA and SVM, KNN, and ANN for emotion classification. The cross-validated SVM with Radial Basis Function kernel achieved 82.1% accuracy for valence and 84.7% accuracy for arousal. The authors in [10] used FFT with Power Spectral Density for feature extraction and PCA for reducing dimension, achieving 87.14% and 86.31% accuracy for predicting valence and arousal states, respectively.

In [1], they applied CNN and LSTM-based emotion recognition, with the best results for 'Liking' at 88.6% and 87.72%, respectively. Authors in [13] used SAE to build and solve linear EEG mixing models and emotion timing models based on LSTM-RNN, achieved accuracy of 81.10%(valence) and 74.38%(arousal). Then here they classified features from EEG signals using LSTM in [3]and achieved accuracy rates of 85.65%, 85.45%, and 87.99% for low/high arousal, valence, and liking respectively. In [5] PCA and CNN was applied for recognition emotion, achieved accuracy of 84.3%(valence) and 81.2%(arousal). A 3D-CNN was also applied in [12], achieved 87.44% and 88.49% accuracy respectively for valance and arousal.

3 Dataset and Methodology

DEAP dataset was established by a group of researchers at Queen Mary University of London [15]. It contains EEG signals and peripheral physiological signals. 32 healthy subjects ranging in age from 19 to 37 had recorded their physiological signals at a sampling rate of 512 Hz using 32 Channels. Each participant saw a music video that lasted one minute and evaluates their level of arousal, valence, like/dislike, and dominance after each trial or film.

Emotion detection from EEG signal requires a series of steps that constitutes the proposed methodology of the work. A schematic diagram of the proposed methodology is illustrated in Fig. 1 and a brief description of each step is presented as follows.

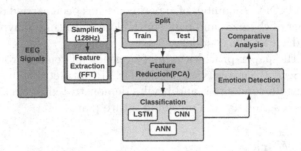

Fig. 1. Schematic diagram of the proposed methodology

1. **Signal PreProcessing:** To improve performance, preprocessing steps include downscaling each participant's EEG signal to 128 Hz using a band-pass filter, dividing the data into 60-second trials, eliminating the pre-trial baseline, and removing dead channels and artifacts. The data is then averaged to the standard reference for better performance.

2. **Feature Extraction:** Studies show that frequency domain feature extraction is more accurate for identifying emotional activities [14]. For frequency domain method FFT method is faster and better for this purpose [9]. This paper focuses on extracting a relevant and distinct channel list using 14 channels from 32 channels and five frequency bands: Delta (4–7 Hz), Theta (8–11 Hz), Alpha (12–15 Hz), Beta (16–24 Hz), and Gamma (25-45 Hz).

3. **Train-Test:** In our project we split training Dataset into 75:25. Also we determined to use a 5-fold cross validation procedure. In K-Fold, for each iteration we will get a test accuracy score and have to sum them all to find the average accuracy [11].

4. **Feature Reduction:** The study uses PCA for feature or dimensionality reduction, which reduces n-dimension features to k-dimension features [8]. Scale affects PCA, feature scalling is needed. The continuous initial variables range is standardized, ensuring equal contribution. The PCA function is applied, creating new features while retaining maximum variations of original features.

5. **Emotion Classification:** This paper uses three deep learning classifications: LSTM, ANN, and CNN, with hyperparameters like batch size(256), number of epochs(200), number of classes(10), input shape(50,1), number of folds for Kfold(5), loss function(Categorical Cross Entropy), and optimizer(Adam) are tuned carefully for optimal results.

(a) **LSTM:** The proposed LSTM model is consist with sequential layers combined with two convolution-1D with activation function 'relu', two LSTM, two maxpooling layers and two dense layers with 'tanh' and 'softmax' activation function for getting better performance. In the hidden layers, five dropout layers are added at a rate of 0.1.

(b) **ANN:** In this project ANN model consist with three dense layers: the first and second dense layers are hidden layers and the last one is the output layer. Dropout layers are introduced at a rate of 0.1, focusing on learning patterns rather than noise. The flatten function converts multi-dimensional input tensors to a single dimension, facilitating smooth data flow.

(c) **CNN:** In our CNN model, it is consists of layers like convolution, normalization, pooling, activation, and softmax. The convolution layer extracts features, and 1D CNN is commonly used for EEG signals. Input layers are connected to hidden layers, while hidden layers are connected to output layers. Different filters or kernels are applied to the input data, vectorizing the epoch at each convolutional layer. These layers analyze different EEG features.

4   Experiment and Result Analysis

The proposed technique involves various experiments by adjusting the channel list and selected band list before the final experiment, with the results displayed in this section.

1. **Experiment 1:** Similar to other works in the literature, the first used 14 channels and all 5 bands for feature extraction, applied PCA component 50 and a 5-fold train-test. The method achieved an accuracy of 88.72% and 88.13%for LSTM, 88.64% and 88.14%for ANN, and 88.58% and 87.75% for CNN for valence and arousal, respectively.

2. **Experiment 2:** The study used 10 randomly selected channels and 3 bands: Delta, Theta, and Alpha for feature extraction, applied PCA component 25 and a 5-fold train-test. The method achieved for LSTM 83.34% and 82.97% accuracy for valence and arousal, 67.03% and 68.91% for ANN, and 77.46% and 77.59% for CNN, it shows that LSTM performing best here.

3. **Experiment 3:** In contrast to earlier experiments, all 32 EEG channels selected here and 5 bands for feature extraction. After taking component 50 of PCA and training with 5-fold train-test, it achieves 87.79% and 87.59% accuracy for LSTM, 88.38% and 87.41% for ANN, and 87.65% and 86.50% for CNN for valence and arousal respectively.

Final Experiment: For this experiment we have chosen a unique combination of 14 channels and all 5 bands for feature extraction. We then applied component 50 of PCA and train-test applied with both 5-fold and 75–25 split set. This selection of the experimental parameters has shown a notable improvement in the

Table 1. Comparison With [1,3,13] applying LSTM and Comparison with [1,5,12] while applying CNN and Comparison with [4,6,10] while applying ANN.

Comparison With [1,3,13] applying LSTM					
Emotions	[1]		[13]	[3]	Proposed Work
	80-20	75-25			kfold	75-25
Arousal	85.07%	81.91%	74.38%	85.65%	**89.08%**	**90.38%**
Valance	83.83%	84.39%	81.10%	85.45%	**88.38%**	**89.74%**
Dominance	85.74%	88.60%	_	87.99%	**88.27%**	**89.00%**
Liking	81.43%	69.69%	_	_	**90.27%**	**92.06%**
Comparison with [1,5,12] while applying CNN					
Emotions	[1]		[12]	[5]	Proposed Work
	80-20	75-25			kfold	75-25
Arousal	84.77%	85.48%	88.49%	81.2%	**88.87%**	**91.00%**
Valence	85.01%	82.59%	87.44%	84%	**87.85%**	**90.27%**
Dominance	85.50%	83.61%	_	_	**88.05%**	**90.66%**
Liking	87.45%	87.72%	_	_	**89.74%**	**91.80%**
Comparison with [4,6,10] while applying ANN					
Emotions	[4]		[6]	[10]	Proposed Work
					kfold	75-25
Arousal	82.1%		87.36%	86.31%	**88.89%**	**90.12%**
Valence	84.7%		85.60%	87.14%	**88.17%**	**89.16%**
Dominance	_		_	_	**88.39%**	**89.48%**
Liking	_		_	_	**89.76%**	**90.88%**

experimental results. Table 1 demonstrates the comparison of the performance of classifiers, LSTM, ANN, and CNN with other works.

Table 1 shows that while classifying all four emotions, the proposed method performed better than those of [1,3,13] while using LSTM as the classifier. Considering ANN and CNN, shows considerable improvement of classification accuracy in comparison to those of [4,6,10] and of [1,5,12] respectively. It can be observed that two emotions, Dominance and Liking, are not considered in [4–6,10,12,13], where the present paper considers all four emotions. Apart from considering all four emotions, the paper experimented with a varieties of choices of channels and bandwidths added with cross-validation. Experiment with such variations gives us the confidence that the proposed model can be considered in other similar application and even with larger contexts.

5   Concluding Remarks

This research proposes 14 distinct combination of choosing EEG channels for feature extraction and for improved performance before categorizing emotions. The study used 5-fold cross validation and 75-25 train test split to train classifiers. CNN performed better than other deep learning approaches, demonstrating its potential for emotion identification. In the future, we can alter the suggested experimental configuration for real-time applications and utilize it to obtain valuable data on the individuals' emotions. We may add more frequency domain characteristics and assess their performance to make further advancements.

References

1. Acharya, D., et al.: Multi-class emotion classification Using EEG signals. In: Garg, D., Wong, K., Sarangapani, J., Gupta, S.K. (eds.) IACC 2020. CCIS, vol. 1367, pp. 474–491. Springer, Singapore (2021). https://doi.org/10.1007/978-981-16-0401-0_38
2. Acharya, D., et al.: An enhanced fitness function to recognize unbalanced human emotions data. Expert Syst. Appl. **166**, 114011 (2021)
3. Alhagry, S., Fahmy, A.A., El-Khoribi, R.A.: Emotion recognition based on eeg using lstm recurrent neural network. Inter. J. Adv. Comput. Sci. Appli. **8**(10) (2017)
4. Bazgir, O., Mohammadi, Z., Habibi, S.A.H.: Emotion recognition with machine learning using eeg signals. In: 2018 25th National and 3rd International Iranian Conference on Biomedical Engineering (ICBME), pp. 1–5. IEEE (2018)
5. Cao, G., Ma, Y., Meng, X., Gao, Y., Meng, M.: Emotion recognition based on cnn. In: 2019 Chinese Control Conference (CCC), pp. 8627–8630. IEEE (2019)
6. Chaudhary, R., Jaswal, R.A.: A review of emotion recognition based on eeg using deap dataset (2021)
7. Koelstra, S.: Deap: a database for emotion analysis; using physiological signals. IEEE Trans. Affect. Comput. **3**(1), 18–31 (2011)
8. Liu, H., Zhang, Y., Li, Y., Kong, X.: Review on emotion recognition based on electroencephalography. Front. Comput. Neurosci. **84** (2021)
9. Lokannavar, S., Lahane, P., Gangurde, A., Chidre, P.: Emotion recognition using eeg signals. Emotion **4**(5), 54–56 (2015)
10. Kanuboyina, S.N.V., Penmetsa, R.R.V.: Electroencephalograph based human emotion recognition using artificial neural network and principal component analysis. IETE J. Res., 1–10 (2021)
11. Pandian, S.: K-fold cross validation technique and its essentials. https://www.analyticsvidhya.com/blog/2022/02/k-fold-cross-validation-technique-and-its-essentials/ (Accessed 17 Feb 2022)
12. Salama, E.S., El-Khoribi, R.A., Shoman, M.E., Shalaby, M.A.W.: Eeg-based emotion recognition using 3d convolutional neural networks. Inter. J. Adv. Comput. Sci. Appli. **9**(8) (2018)
13. Saxena, S.: Introduction to long short term memory (lstm). https://www.analyticsvidhya.com/blog/2021/03/introduction-to-long-short-term-memory-lstm/ (Accessed 1 Mar 2021)
14. Vapnik, V.N.: Direct methods in statistical learning theory. In: The nature of statistical learning theory, pp. 225–265. Springer (2000). https://doi.org/10.1007/978-1-4757-3264-1_8
15. Zhang, Y.: An investigation of deep learning models for eeg-based emotion recognition. Front. Neurosc. **14**, 622759 (2020)

Generative AI

Generating Fine-Grained Aspect Names from Movie Review Sentences Using Generative Language Model

Tomohiro Ishii[1], Yoshiyuki Shoji[1,2]($\boxtimes$) (ID), Takehiro Yamamoto[3] (ID),
Hiroaki Ohshima[3] (ID), Sumio Fujita[4] (ID), and Martin J. Dürst[1] (ID)

[1] Aoyama Gakuin University, Sagamihara, Kanagawa 252–5258, Japan
{ishii,duerst}@sw.it.aoyama.ac.jp
[2] Shizuoka University, Hamamatsu, Shizuoka 432–8011, Japan
shojiy@inf.shizuoka.ac.jp
[3] University of Hyogo, Kobe, Hyogo 651–2197, Japan
t.yamamoto@sis.u-hyogo.ac.jp, ohshima@ai.u-hyogo.ac.jp
[4] Yahoo Japan Corporation, Chiyoda, Tokyo 102–8282, Japan
sufujita@yahoo-corp.jp

Abstract. This paper proposes a method for identifying an aspect highlighted in a sentence from a movie review, utilizing a generative language model. For example, the aspect "SFX Techniques" is identified for the sentence "The explosions in cosmic space were realistic." Classically, aspects are commonly estimated in the field of opinion mining within product reviews with classification or extraction approaches. However, because the aspects of movie reviews are diverse and innumerable, they cannot be listed in advance. Thus, we propose a generation-based approach using a generative language model to identify the aspect of a review sentence. We adopt T5 (Text-to-Text Transfer Transformer), a modern generative language model, providing additional pre-training and fine-tuning to reduce the training data. To verify the effectiveness of the learning techniques thus adopted, we conducted an experiment incorporating reviews of Yahoo! movies. Manual labeling of the correctness and diversity of the aspect names generated shows that our method can generates a variety of fine-grained aspect names using little training data.

Keywords: Opinion Mining · Aspect Detection · Generative
Language Model

1 Introduction

Even when they are watching the same movie, different people will pay attention to different parts of it. Some will focus on the script and others on the actors' performances. A person who has a specific interest may focus on a specific aspect. For example, a railroad enthusiast may focus on whether the trains shown in a movie are correct in relation to the temporal and spatial setting of the movie.

© The Author(s), under exclusive license to Springer Nature Switzerland AG 2023
P. Delir Haghighi et al. (Eds.): iiWAS 2023, LNCS 14416, pp. 217–232, 2023.
https://doi.org/10.1007/978-3-031-48316-5_23

Thanks to the rapid growth of information and communication technologies, the way that people watch movies and find reviews has changed in recent years. Subscription-based distribution services have brought more encounters with movies. People can decide what to watch from a vast pool of candidates. Movie review services, such as IMDb, have become widespread. Reading review posts to decide what movie to watch has become a part of everyday life.

However, the immense number of posted reviews makes it impossible to read them all. Additionally, as a large and diverse group of users contribute reviews, the aspects highlighted by different reviewers can vary. For instance, one user may want to read reviews that discuss the accuracy of the historical details in a movie, but most reviews concentrate on the actors' performances. Our hypothetical user will not be interested in this review. However, they cannot determine whether a review suits their purpose without reading the reviews.

To address this issue, numerous studies have focused on estimating the aspects of the text of reviews. However, conventional aspect classification and extraction approaches require each description to be categorized into predetermined aspects or extracting aspect names from the sentences. For instance, in common product domains, such as televisions or cameras, the sentence "I can see fine details" would typically be linked to the aspect of "resolution." At the same time, "I can bring it anywhere" would be associated with aspects such as "weight" or "size". For this categorization, a list of aspects must be provided in advance.

Reviews of entertainment content, such as movies and books, are necessarily more specific than reviews of traditional products. Different items may have different aspects; for example, even within the set of movies, the names of the aspects appearing in science fiction and romance movie reviews will be different. The number of such aspects is innumerable, so they cannot be listed in advance. New aspect names may become necessary when a new movie is released.

Therefore, this paper proposes a generative language model method that can generate aspect names from a given review sentence. Generative language models are capable of generating abstract aspect names that traditional classification and extraction approaches cannot address. For instance, take the case of creating an aspect name for the sentence "The explosions in cosmic space were realistic." Here, the review text has not included the phrase "scientific accuracy," and pre-enumerating specific aspect names for this case would be too fine-grained and laborious. This paper leverages state-of-the-art generative language models to comprehensively handle names of such fine-grained and specific aspects.

We adopt T5 (Text-to-Text Transfer Transformer), among the best-regarded text-to-text large language models, for this purpose. An overview of our training method is shown in Fig. 1. First, using crowdsourcing, we created a dataset consisting of sentences from reviews and the relevant aspect names. We then trained T5 using the review sentences and aspect names. In general, training a language model with an additional intermediate task improves the accuracy of its generation [10]. We interspersed two additional learning tasks that differ from the generation of aspect names: a task to binary classify whether a review

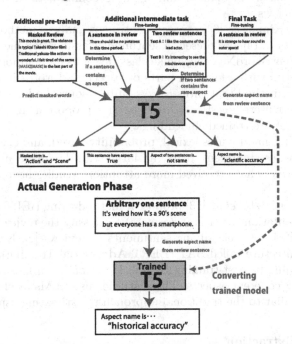

Fig. 1. Overview of our training steps of T5. The model was trained with an additional pre-training and two intermediate tasks before the main task.

contains a statement about an aspect and another to binary classify whether two given sentences refer to the same aspect. This model with additional training was fine-tuned with the task of generating aspect names.

The performance of this generative model was evaluated using real data. Aspect names were generated for review sentences that were collected from real online movie review sites. The experimental participants labeled each aspect name, assessing its correctness and fine grain. Thus, we confirmed the presence of fine-tuning and changes in accuracy depending on the additional tasks.

2   Related Work

This study was undertaken aims to identify the aspects mentioned in online reviews. To provide context and positioning, this section describes related studies on language models in online reviews, aspect extraction, and summarization, using language models.

2.1   Language Model in Online Review

Traditionally, review data are used as a general source of information for research. In addition, applications used to retrieve reviews have been widely studied. In particular, in opinion mining, it is common to analyze sentiment from product reviews.

For instance, Kim *et al.* [6] propose a sentiment analysis method using online reviews. Singh *et al.* [14] also present a sentiment classification method for movie reviews. Using SentiWordNet, they make classifications for emotional expressions and their polarities with a focus on parts of speech and words in proximity. Xu *et al.* [16] show a method that turns reviews into a source of knowledge that can be used to answer users' questions. Xu *et al.* [15] propose a simple CNN model using two types of pre-trained embeddings.

This research generally uses lexical, probability-based, and classical machine learning approaches. In recent years, as large-scale language models (LLMs) such as Transformers have received more attention, studies have come to focus on them.

For instance, Rietzler *et al.* [13] propose a method using BERT (Bidirectional Encoder Representations from Transformers) to classify the review aspect. Hasib *et al.* also use BERT for classifying sentiments of reviews [2]. Karimi *et al.* [5] propose an architecture called BAT (BERT Adversarial Training). BAT applies adversarial learning to post-training BERT. He *et al.* [3] propose a neural approach for finding coherent aspects. These studies use LLMs as classifiers. They are therefore similar to the traditional approach to estimating aspects.

2.2 Aspect Extraction

Aspect extraction has long been a topic of interest in opinion mining. In review posts, users can freely write their opinions about a product. To use reviews in product search, visualization, and analysis, it is important for shoppers to identify what aspects a specific description refers to [12].

Jo *et al.* [4] propose a method for automatically discovering different viewpoints and combinations of feelings on viewpoints from submission reviews. Peng *et al.* [9] propose a framework for dealing with the aspect of sentiment triplet extraction. Aspect sentiment triplet extraction refers to the task of extracting triples that can indicate what an aspect is, its sentiment polarity, and why it has this polarity. Angelidis *et al.* [1] present a neural network framework for summarizing opinions drawing on online product reviews. In their network, they combine two weak supervised components: an aspect extractor and a sentiment predictor.

Studies related to aspects of reviews are commonly used in both the categorical approach, where the aspect is applied to pre-prepared candidates, and in extracting aspects that are written directly in the review. This study seeks to address this problem with a generative language model.

2.3 Text Summarization Using Language Model

This study uses a language model to generate names of aspect from review sentences. This approach is similar to summarizing in that it extracts the subject matter from a text, abstracts it, and expresses it in a few words. Summaries of texts can be roughly divided into extractive and abstractive summarization; however, our study relates to abstractive summarization. In recent years, it has been common to use LLMs for abstractive summarization. Significant research has been conducted on summarization using a language model.

Among LLMs used in this area, Liu et al. [8] propose BERTSUM, an extractive summarization method using BERT. Pegasus, proposed by Zhang et al. [17], is another prominent example of a traditional language model based on the summarization method. Pegasus is also an extension of BERT, characterized the use of Gap Sentence Generation for pre-training. Lewis et al. [7] present Bidirectional and Auto Regressive Transformers, a denoising autoencoder for use in pre-training sequence-to-sequence models.

Some methods based on BERT specialize in discrimination by embedding. Generative language models such as GPT (Generative Pre-trained Transformer) and T5 are good at abstractive tasks in particular. Our method adopted T5, a generative LLM.

3   Aspect Name Generation with T5

This section describes a method for generating the names of aspects mentioned in a given movie review text. Our method consists of three steps:

- additional pre-training,
- fine-tuning via an additional intermediate task, and
- fine-tuning via the final task.

The additional pre-training is performed to ensure that the model understands the particular vocabulary and knowledge related to movies. This additional intermediate fine-tuning is intended to focus the model on aspects in particular. The final task is the task of actual generation task. It generates the names of the aspects of any input review text. We collected actual review data and had it labeled it using crowdsourcing to enable this training.

3.1   Creating Training Data Using Crowdsourcing

Initially, we created a dataset for use in machine learning. Actual movie reviews were collected from real online movie review sites. These reviews were divided into individual sentences through splitting at the periods. Crowd workers then identified the aspects that were mentioned in each sentence. In total, the aspect names for twenty sentences were input by each of the 100 crowd workers.

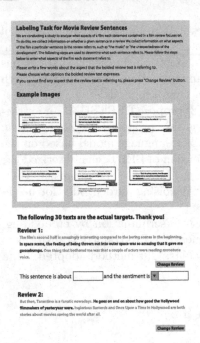

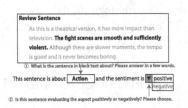

Fig. 2. Screenshot of the system used for labeling. Instructions are given at the gray section at the top. Below are six example images. Below these, the 20 review sentences are listed. (Color figure online)

Fig. 3. Example image is presented to the crowd workers. It includes a screenshot of the actual form, instructions in red text, and an inputted example answer. (Translated from Japanese) (Color figure online)

When the crowd workers accessed the system, they were first presented with an instruction. This included the following background statement "This is an experiment for analyzing reviews conducted at a university" and instructions stating, "Please input names of aspects and sentiments (*i.e.*, negative or positive) for the 20 review sentences displayed below." Additional detailed precautions are also provided. Below the instructions, six example images of correct labeling are presented. By clicking on an image, the workers could see examples of aspect names that could be assigned to specific review sentences.

Then, workers read and labeled 20 sentences from actual reviews. Each sentence was displayed together with the surrounding text (*i.e.*, the sentence before it and the one after it). The sentence to be labeled was marked in black, and the surrounding sentences were gray. Workers input the aspect names as free keywords into text boxes. Simultaneously, they also input the sentiment related to each aspect name. For example, a sentence like "The lead actress's strange pronunciation was rather refreshing" is a "positive" expression concerning "performance." It should be noted that not every sentence displayed in black mentioned any aspect. In this case, the workers could label a different sentence by pressing the button for "Change Review." This skipped statement is recorded and labeled as "no aspect."

3.2 Additional Pre-training: Predicting Masked Term in Movie Review Data

Additional pre-training is performed to prompt the language model to better learn vocabulary on movies and general knowledge about them. Many proper nouns and peculiar expressions appear in movie review data; This includes names of directors, actors, series, *etc.*

The T5 model, which is publicly available, has been pre-trained on public documents (*e.g.*, Wikipedia, OSCAR, and CC-100). Because these documents do not contain sufficient descriptions related to movies, we train the model with movie review data. This model is pre-trained with masked language modeling, in the same way as was done by Raffel *et al.* [11] For additional pre-training, the model should be trained on the same task as that when the original model was created, only using different data.

3.3 1st Intermediate Fine-Tuning: Binary Classification of Whether a Sentence Includes an Aspect

Next, we attempt to improve the quality of the model by fine-tuning it by means of intermediate tasks. In general, the accuracy of the final task can be improved by passing it through a task that is different from the original objective. Specifically, when training data for the final task are not large enough for training, it is adequate to fine tune it with different domains and tasks, so that it solves the same task with data from other domains or solves different related tasks using data from the same domain. Thus, here, the model solved tasks related to the goal of making the model understand what an aspect is.

To help the model understand aspects, it solves the most straightforward binary classification problem. In this task, the model receives one sentence and then learns to return 1 if the received sentence mentions an aspect and 0 otherwise. For this training, the sentences that the crowdworkers skipped as having "no aspect," and the sentences that were labeled with an aspect name were used as the answer data.

T5 can be trained using a prefix, which makes the different tasks explicit. Therefore, when fine-tuning this task, the prefix "contains-aspect:" was added.

3.4 2nd Intermediate Fine-Tuning: Binary Classification of Whether Two Reviews Have the Same Aspect

Next, we allow the model to solve a slightly more advanced intermediate task. It receives two sentences and determines whether both mention the same aspect. This task is intended to enable the model to learn the differences between aspects.

The review sentences containing aspect names that were collected through crowdsourcing are used for the training. We randomly selected two arbitrary sentences from the dataset and then combined the two sentences with a separator token.

The input is a text with a prefix like "same aspect: typical Takeshi Kitano's violence scene [SEP] it has surprising end part." In this example, the former refers to the director and the latter to the story. Thus, the model was trained to return 0 because the two sentences mention different aspects.

We used this training because we wanted to tune the model more efficiently using fewer training data. It is expensive to have people read sentences and label them with aspect names is expensive. This method, however, can use many combinations of two sentences in a given dataset, creating extensive training data.

3.5   Final Fine-Tuning: Aspect Name Generation

The model ultimately solved the same tasks as in the performance task. It input an arbitrary single sentence and outputs an aspect name. The prefix was also used for this training. For instance, the model was trained to generate aspect names, such as "direction," input such as the following is given: "aspect-generation: I was impressed with the way he expressed the main character's feelings by making it rain."

The same task was performed for the actual aspect name generation. A model trained in this way outputs aspect names even if they are input with review sentences that are not included in the training data. In such a case, the common linguistic sense obtained from training on public documents and knowledge of the movie studied in additional pre-training should be used. For example, the generated aspect name may be extracted from the review text, an abstraction of an expression in the review, or a completely new aspect name.

4   Evaluation

The evaluation tests were conducted to confirm the accuracy and effectiveness of the proposed aspect name generation and the effectiveness of the fine-tuning through the intermediate tasks. The experiment was conducted in two parts: first, a preliminary experiment was performed with automatic accuracy evaluation, followed by a main experiment that included subject evaluation. We created a dataset through the collection of reviews from real review sites and labeled them using crowdsourcing. Multiple comparative models were created for training using different fine-tuning methods. For each of these models, we evaluated the reproducibility (automatic evaluation) of the generated aspect names, their correctness, their fine granularity, and their novelty.

4.1   Dataset

We collected reviews from Yahoo! Movies, among the most extensive review sites in Japan. We extracted 176,970 of the reviews, avoiding those that were extremely short or too minor (this number was constrained by the graphic memory on the video card that was used for the training). All of these review data were first used for the additional pre-training of T5.

Next, sentences that were neither long nor short were extracted. We asked the crowdworkers to label the review sentences with the name of the aspect that they reviewed and to indicate whether they mentioned any aspect. Crowdsourcing continued until 1,500 sentences were labeled with the aspect name and collected.

The labeled review sentences thus obtained were used to create data for intermediate tasks. In the first intermediate task (the binary classification of whether an aspect was included), 3,759 reviews were prepared. For the second, (binary classification of whether two sentences refer to the same aspect), 1,000 pairs of review sentences were prepared.

During the creation of a dataset for the second intermediate task, we addressed the distortion of the notation of the aspect name, e.g., "story" and "scenario," were essentially the same aspect. For this purpose, the similarity of two aspect names was calculated using Sentence-BERT, and aspect names with a semantic similarity of 0.9 or higher were considered identical.

In addition to the training dataset, a dataset for the subject experiments was also generated. Review sentences not used for either training that have a standard length were extracted. We only used reviews that seemed to mention an aspect that was used for evaluation. We classified such reviews using a simple BERT classifier (accuracy 0.63).

4.2   Comparison Methods

We prepared different methods, and only some of the training was given to verify the effectiveness of each of the trainings described in Sect. 3. Specifically, one set was given no additional training at all, one set only had additional pre-training, and one set had only a part of the intermediates task. For the intermediate tasks, we also compared which task was solved most rapidly.

Table 1 shows the 10 methods compared in the evaluation. The methods of **Pre-training+Include>Same** and **Pre-training+Same>Include** are the proposed methods (that is, these are the models that successfully completed all training tasks).

4.3   Implementation

Hugging Face Transformers[1], a library of Transformer-based models was used to implement T5. We used the Japanese T5 pre-trained model[2]. Additional training

---

[1] Hugging Face Transformer: https://huggingface.co/docs/transformers/index.
[2] sonoisa/t5-base-japanese: https://huggingface.co/sonoisa/t5-base-japanese.

Table 1. Comparison of methods for evaluation and their accuracy during preliminary experiments. The precision assessment indicates whether the method generated the same aspect name as the test data during cross-validation (using BERT for distortion of the notation). The bottom two are the proposed methods (the ones that successfully completed all training).

Method	Additional Pre-training	Aarlier Task	Later Task	Final Task	# aspect name generated	# aspect names not in training data	Precision in Auto Evaluation	F1 Score in Auto Evaluation
FinalTask Only	None	None	None	Done	76	25	0.800	0.795
FinalTask+Include	None	Include	None	Done	74	28	0.795	0.791
FinalTask+Same	None	Same	None	Done	74	23	0.794	0.791
FinalTask+Include>Same	None	Include	Same	Done	69	27	0.798	0.795
FinalTask+Same>Include	None	Same	Include	Done	77	28	0.797	0.794
Pre-training Only	Done	None	None	Done	84	31	0.800	0.796
Pre-training+Include	Done	Include	None	Done	92	35	0.799	0.795
Pre-training+Same	Done	Same	None	Done	79	23	0.800	0.796
Pre-training+Include>Same	Done	Include	Same	Done	56	11	**0.802**	**0.797**
Pre-training+Same>Include	Done	Same	Include	Done	11	1	0.798	0.790

parameters were set as follows: Maximum sequence length, 512; batch size, 16; learning rate, 0.005; weight decay, 0.001; and warmup steps, 2,000.

The learning rate was 0.0003 (determined empirically). The other parameters were set to the default values for Hugging Face Transformers. SentenceTransformers[3] was used to evaluate whether the aspect name was correct. We used a pre-trained multilingual model[4] for it.

4.4   Preliminary Experiment: Automated Accuracy Evaluation

We first performed an automated cross-validation evaluation to roughly assess the generation accuracy. In this evaluation, we split the dataset, consisting of crowdsourced labeled review sentences and aspect names, into training and test sets.

The test set was then fed into the model trained on the training set. We determined whether the generated aspect names matched the original manually assigned aspect names. However, to deal with the notation distortion, we used BERT to determine the identity of the aspect name (as in Subsect. 4.1).

4.5   Experiment: Subject Evaluation of Generated Aspect Names

The participants manually assessed whether the aspect names generated for the unknown sentences were correct. They read one review sentence and the aspect names generated by each method and labeled them as correct or incorrect.

The three evaluation factors were as follows:

- **format**: Whether the aspect name generated is a likely aspect name (0 or 1),

---

[3] SentenceTransformers: https://www.sbert.net/.
[4] Hugging Face sentence-transformers https://huggingface.co/sentence-transformers/.

Table 2. Ratings for each method in the subject experiment (normalized to 0 – 1).

Method	Format	Correctness	Granularity
FinalTask Only	0.964	0.691	0.380
FinalTask+Include	0.969	0.677	0.399
FinalTask+Same	0.971	0.670	0.384
FinalTask+Include>Same	0.969	0.666	0.384
FinalTask+Same>Include	0.971	0.648	0.387
Pre-training Only	**0.973**	**0.700**	0.396
Pre-training+Include	0.962	0.677	**0.407**
Pre-training+Same	0.971	0.663	0.406
Pre-training+Include>Same	**0.973**	0.671	0.386
Pre-training+Same>Include	0.969	0.640	0.336

- **correctness**: How well the aspect name matches the content of the review sentence (scale of 1 to 5), and
- **granularity**: Whether the aspect name is sufficiently fine-grained (scale of 1 to 5).

Three participants read 100 review sentences. A maximum of 10 aspect names (with duplicates removed) were appended to each review text in random order. Participants labeled each aspect name.

4.6 Result

In this section, the results of the preliminary experiment and the subject experiment are described. Table 1 presents the results for the preliminary experiments. The model that had the highest accuracy had performed additional pre-training; it determined whether the aspect was included first and determined the same aspect name second. The models that had high accuracy had a lower probability of generating a new aspect name, often fitting an existing aspect names drawn from the training data.

Table 2 presents the results of the subject experiment. The method of **Pre-training Only** was evaluated as having the highest score. However, the differences were minor, and the models' performances were not significantly different from each other. The granularity of the generated aspect names was determined to be too rough in many cases.

5 Discussion

This section discusses the usefulness of the generative approach, the generation of aspect names by T5, and the effectiveness of every additional training according to the experimental results. Both the additional pre-training and the intermediate task showed increased accuracy. However, the additional pre-training was extremely effective, although the intermediate task had a limited effect.

Table 3. Example of a review text and the aspect name generated from it. The judgment is the evaluation of the appropriateness of the aspect name.

Review Sentences	Aspect Name	Type	Judge	Method
I must miss it if it kept its original title	Original Title	Extraction	1	Many methods
It is from an era I am unfamiliar with, but I recognized most of the songs	Song	Extraction	1	Many methods
I would have felt satisfied if they ended in the final scene :)	Last Scene	Classification	1	FinalTask Only
Regardless, it is undeniably a high-quality work that keeps you engaged till the end	Story	Classification	0	Many methods
All the other actors fit their comic roles perfectly and delivered high-quality performances	Casting	Classification	1	Pre-training Only, Pre-training+Include
I think that it is a black comedy that cleverly satirizes current social issues	Category	Classification	1	Pre-training Only
I think that it is a black comedy that cleverly satirizes current social issues	Story	Classification	0	Many methods
It is good for amateurs, but the previous anime version was better	Difference from Original	Generation	1	FinalTask+Include
The strangeness of this movie must came out from a director's taste	Director's Personality	Generation	1	Pre-training+Include
The dancing has improved and the singing is moving	Singing ability	Generation	1	Pre-training+Include
All the other actors fit their comic roles perfectly and delivered high-quality performances.	Difference from Original	Generation	1	FinalTask+Same, Pre-training+Same

Table 4. The ten aspect names most frequently generated by each method (translated from Japanese).

Pre-training Only	Pre-training +Same	Pre-training +Include	Pre-training +Same>Include	Pre-training +Include>Same	FinalTask Only	FinalTask +Same	FinalTask +Include	FinalTask +Same > Include	FinalTask +Include > Same
Cinema	Scale	Nature	Acting, Acting,	Dubbing	Tools	Translation	Drama	Entertainment	Tools
Culture	Love	Scale		Fans' Expectations	Landscape	Love	Love	Expression	Spoiler
Tears	Attraction	C		The Idea	Fatigue	Lighting	Spoilers	Love	Disappointment
Drama	Last Scene	Love		Passion	Love	Brainwashing	Sound Effects	Schedule	Original
Screenplay Award	Difference from Drama	Description		Commentary	Evaluation Criteria	Doraemon's tools	Love	Spoilers	Inclusion
Kissing Scene	Compilation	Lacrimal Gland		Generation	Spoiler	Crying Scene	Cooking	Talk of Cast	Dubbing
Disappointment	Dubbing	Language Difference		Scale	Last scene	Overseas travel	Scenery	Cooking	Travel Expenses
Special Makeup	Homage	Story		Cosmology	Brainwashing	Snow	Trailer	Disappointment	Animation
Target	Original Title	Brainwashing		Snow	Atmosphere of the Original	Travel Expenses	Dubbing	For Kids	Feeling of Support
Dubbing	Reproduction	Target		Travel Expenses	Overloaded	Original Title	Doraemon's Tools	Snow	Meet Expectations

First, we discuss the results of the automatic evaluation. To clarify the accuracy, we focus on the F_1 scores. As shown in Table 1, the model trained with all of the intermediate tasks achieved the highest accuracy. This model, developed with additional pre-training, first estimated the presence or absence of each aspect and then determined whether the aspect of the two sentences was identical. This suggested that the accuracy of the model could be improved through training it by solving aspect-related tasks.

In particular, fine-tuning with the intermediate task reduced accuracy in some cases. The model named **Pre-Training+Same>Include**, which trained on all tasks, was the least accurate. However, fine-tuning in general tended to lead to higher accuracy. In all cases except **Same>Include** models, the pre-trained models were more accurate than those models trained using the same task. For instance, F_1 value increased by 0.005 relative to **FinalTask+Same** to **Pre-training+Same**. From these results, it appears that increasing the amount of data and focusing on additional pre-training may be a more efficient approach than performing fine-tuning through increasing the number of intermediate tasks.

Next, we discuss the novelty, granularity, and quality of the aspects generated and not their accuracy. Each model differed in terms of the number of unknown aspect names that were generated. Some models did not generate novel aspect names but forcibly classified review sentences with aspect names that were contained in the training data labels.

For example, the model **Pre-training+Same>Include** generated only one new aspect name. It also tied all review sentences to a total of only 11 different aspect names. The novelty and the diversity of the aspect names that were generated tend to weaken with the amount of training. Models that were trained on both additional pre-training and two intermediate tasks output fewer aspect names.

This may be due to an overfitting to the training data. It is possible that the model was over-trained to consider the definition of the aspect names should refer only to the labels defined in the given dataset. There is room to investigate this effect in the future by increasing or decreasing the data for training and changing the ratio of fine-tuning.

Table 3 represents an example of the aspect names generated by the models[5]. Throughout this, reasonable aspect names are generated. These names included those derived from extraction, classification, and generation. The aspect names designated by extraction are those in which the model outputs words in the review text as they are. That is, the model extracts words based on the inference that these words are likely to be used as the aspect name. The aspect names according to classification are those that are not directly included in the input text but are included in the training data labels. Here, the model abstracts the review text to choose a word; however, these aspect names simply entail a classification as the pre-prepared aspect names. The aspect names according to generation are the output terms that are not included in the review text or in the training data labels. In these cases, the aspect names generated are completely abstracted from the meaning of the review sentences, and the model infers them from nothing.

Here, our discussion focuses only on the aspect names generated. Table 4 shows the top ten most frequent aspect names included in the output of the models. Many models generate valid aspect names that are fine-grained and are not included in the data set, excluding **Pre-train+Same>Include**. The only new aspect name generated by the **Pre-train+Same>Include** model was an incorrect name, simply repeating the word "acting" several times. At other times, this model either extracted a term in the review or applied a sentence to the label name in the training data.

One example of an incorrect aspect name was extraction using an incorrect word tokenization. The model **Pre-training+Include** output the aspect name "C." This indicates a failure to tokenize when reading the review text. The review text included statements on visual expressions, such as, "This visual effect is the kind of expression I see in TV$\underline{C}$M (Television Commercial Message)." Because the social review includes data with many colloquial expressions, it may be necessary to proofread the text using conventional methods before performing the language model.

In summary, T5 showed good performance, even without any fine-tuning or additional training. We had thought that generating aspect names in a generative language model would be more difficult. However, performing the same fine-tuning on plain T5 as in the production task achieved an F_1 value of 0.79. In addition, many of the aspect names generated were correct and were not found in the training data. A larger dataset that includes more fine-grained aspect names and that uses T5 in a straightforward manner could produce a more accurate and practical language model.

---

[5] For the sake of translation and anonymization, the reviews are fictitious, as the experiment was in Japanese and uses real review sentences prepared by an individual.

6   Conclusion

This paper proposed a method for generating aspect names for arbitrary sentences from reviews by training the generative language model T5. Evaluation experiments showed that the generative approach can also generate aspect names with high accuracy. We found that fine-tuning using intermediate tasks was less effective, but additional pre-training was highly effective.

The contributions of this paper are as follows:

- we revealed that a generative approach could be used for aspect name inferences, which is conventionally done using classification and extraction, and
- we revealed that additional pre-training is effective for training generative language models for the aspect name generation task.

In future work, we plan to enhance data cleansing and applied evaluation. Specifically, we plan to construct a system for searching for review sentences using generated aspect names. Recently, methods involving more extensive and more innovative language models have emerged (*e.g.*, GPT-4 and Bard). It may be possible to generate aspect names by prompts rather than using methods based on fine-tuning. Significant room remains for improvement in aspect name generation by generative AI.

Acknowledgements. This work was supported by JSPS KAKENHI Grants Number 21H03775, 21H03774, and 22H03905.

References

1. Angelidis, S., Lapata, M.: Summarizing opinions: aspect extraction meets sentiment prediction and they are both weakly supervised. In: Proceedings of the Conference on Empirical Methods in Natural Language Processing, pp. 3675–3686 (2018). https://doi.org/10.18653/v1/D18-1403
2. Hasib, K.M., Towhid, N.A., Alam, M.G.R.: Online review based sentiment classification on bangladesh airline service using supervised learning. In: 5th International Conference on Electrical Engineering and Information Communication Technology (ICEEICT), pp. 1–6. IEEE (2021)
3. He, R., Lee, W.S., Ng, H.T., Dahlmeier, D.: An unsupervised neural attention model for aspect extraction. In: Proc. of the 55th Annual Meeting of the Association for Computational Linguistics (Volume 1: Long Papers) (2017)
4. Jo, Y., Oh, A.H.: Aspect and sentiment unification model for online review analysis. In: Proc. of the Fourth ACM International Conference on Web Search and Data Mining, pp. 815–824 (2011). https://doi.org/10.1145/1935826.1935932
5. Karimi, A., Rossi, L., Prati, A.: Adversarial training for aspect-based sentiment analysis with bert. In: 2020 25th International Conference on Pattern Recognition (ICPR), pp. 8797–8803 (2021). https://doi.org/10.1109/ICPR48806.2021.9412167
6. Kim, R.Y.: Using online reviews for customer sentiment analysis. IEEE Eng. Manage. Rev. **49**(4), 162–168 (2021)

7. Lewis, M., et al.: BART: denoising sequence-to-sequence pre-training for natural language generation, translation, and comprehension. In: Proceedings of the 58th Annual Meeting of the Association for Computational Linguistics (2020). https://doi.org/10.18653/v1/2020.acl-main.703

8. Liu, Y.: Fine-tune bert for extractive summarization. arXiv preprint arXiv:1903.10318 (2019)

9. Peng, H., Xu, L., Bing, L., Huang, F., Lu, W., Si, L.: Knowing what, how and why: a near complete solution for aspect-based sentiment analysis. In: Proceedings of the AAAI Conference on Artificial Intelligence, vol. 34(05), pp. 8600–8607 (2020). https://doi.org/10.1609/aaai.v34i05.6383

10. Pruksachatkun, Y., et al.: Intermediate-task transfer learning with pretrained models for natural language understanding: When and why does it work? In: Proceedings of the 58th Annual Meeting of the Association for Computational Linguistics, pp. 5231–5247 (2020)

11. Raffel, C., et al.: Exploring the limits of transfer learning with a unified text-to-text transformer. J. Mach. Learn. Res. **21**(140), 1–67 (2020)

12. Ravi, K., Ravi, V.: A survey on opinion mining and sentiment analysis: tasks, approaches and applications. Knowl.-Based Syst. **89**, 14–46 (2015). https://doi.org/10.1016/j.knosys.2015.06.015

13. Rietzler, A., Stabinger, S., Opitz, P., Engl, S.: Adapt or get left behind: domain adaptation through BERT language model finetuning for aspect-target sentiment classification. In: Proceedings of the Twelfth Language Resources and Evaluation Conference, pp. 4933–4941 (2020)

14. Singh, V.K., Piryani, R., Uddin, A., Waila, P.: Sentiment analysis of movie reviews: a new feature-based heuristic for aspect-level sentiment classification. In: 2013 International Mutli-Conference on Automation, Computing, Communication, Control and Compressed Sensing (iMac4s), pp. 712–717 (2013). https://doi.org/10.1109/iMac4s.2013.6526500

15. Xu, H., Liu, B., Shu, L., Yu, P.S.: Double embeddings and cnn-based sequence labeling for aspect extraction. In: Proceedings of the 56th Annual Meeting of the Association for Computational Linguistics (2018)

16. Xu, H., Liu, B., Shu, L., Yu, P.S.: Bert post-training for review reading comprehension and aspect-based sentiment analysis. In: Proceedings of the Conference of the North American Chapter of the Association for Computational Linguistics (2019)

17. Zhang, J., Zhao, Y., Saleh, M., Liu, P.: PEGASUS: pre-training with extracted gap-sentences for abstractive summarization. In: International Conference on Machine Learning, pp. 11328–11339 (2020)

Reducing Human Effort in Keyphrase-Based Human-in-the-Loop Topic Models: A Method for Keyphrase Recommendations

Muhammad Haseeb UR Rehman Khan(ⓘ) and Kei Wakabayashi(✉)(ⓘ)

University of Tsukuba, Tsukuba, Ibaraki 305-8577, Japan
s2036048@s.tsukuba.ac.jp, kwakaba@slis.tsukuba.ac.jp
https://www.tsukuba.ac.jp

Abstract. Human-in-the-loop topic modeling (HLTM) empowers users to modify topic models and enhance their quality, by enabling them to directly refine the model. Prior studies have made significant strides in this area, specifically keyphrase-based refinements. However, the challenge is selecting suitable keyphrases from a large pool of them. To address this issue, we present a novel method for keyphrase recommendation that capitalizes on the connections between document-topic and document-keyphrases associations. The objective is to assist users of keyphrase-based HLTM by offering effective refinement recommendations. To evaluate the effectiveness in reducing human effort, we compared it with baseline and all-keyphrase approaches, while also evaluating F1 scores across multiple levels of human effort. Our method achieves comparable performance with minimal human effort, akin to ideal situations where human effort is maximized. Furthermore, our method surpasses the baseline and the approach of utilizing all keyphrases at the same level of human effort, demonstrating superior performance.

Keywords: Topic models · Latent Dirichlet Allocation ·
Human-in-the-loop topic modeling · Keyphrase generation model

1 Introduction

Topic modeling [3] is one of the most potent techniques in text mining [22], latent data discovery [10,39], and finding relationships among data and text documents [13,37]. Researchers use the topic models for many goals including but not limited to recommendation systems [7,40], social media analysis [1,18], time series analysis [11,16], and emotion classification [30,31]. This approach has been proven successful in cases where users aim to categorize documents but lack the knowledge or predefined categories to do so accurately. Let us consider a researcher processing the research articles related to the latest discoveries in the field of "neural networks". The researcher may have domain knowledge but it

P. Delir Haghighi et al. (Eds.): iiWAS 2023, LNCS 14416, pp. 233–248, 2023.
https://doi.org/10.1007/978-3-031-48316-5_24

is highly unlikely to come up with exact category themes beforehand. While this technique is remarkable for addressing such problems, it is important to note that typical topic models operate in an unsupervised manner, lacking human control. Consequently, this can lead to the extraction of unnecessary information during the process [18]. Additionally, topic models frequently produce incoherent, noisy, or loosely connected topics [5,6]. To address these challenges stemming from the unsupervised approach, researchers have proposed supervised and semi-supervised topic models [24,26]. However, these models necessitate labeled data for training, which poses a challenge as users may not possess prior knowledge of the topics to be presumed in advance.

Human-in-the-loop topic modeling (HLTM) tackles the issue of human control by involving human expertise in the modeling procedure. Basic HLTM systems present topic models to users in the form of topic words and documents, and users provide feedback through diverse refinement operations [33,35]. In the past, HLTM systems have primarily incorporated topic model refinements on the basis of assumptions made by algorithm developers regarding user considerations related to the ease of implementation [8,14,15]. However, Lee et al. [21] took a different approach by adopting a user-centered methodology to identify a specific set of topic refinement operations that users would anticipate in an HLTM system. With the help of previous studies, Kumar et al. [19] concluded the basic refinement operation and developed a UI-based HLTM system with seven refinement functions: add word, remove word, remove document, merge topics, split topic, change word order, and create topic. Subsequently, Khan et al. [17] introduced refinement functions centered around keyphrases, aiming to enhance document-topic associations. They argued that existing word- and document-based refinement functions fell short in effectively improving the document-topic associations across the entire document collection. To evaluate the efficacy of these refinement functions, experiments were conducted using the 20newsgroup dataset, simulating user behavior. The results demonstrated a substantial superiority of keyphrase-based refinements over the word- and document-based approaches, as evidenced by the remarkable improvement in F1 scores.

While keyphrase-based HLTM introduced effective refinement operations, the challenge lies in selecting appropriate keyphrases for refinement. The task of recommending keyphrases for keyphrase-based HLTM remains unexplored, with no existing research addressing this particular aspect to the best of our knowledge. The significance of this task cannot be overstated, as every keyphrase in an HLTM system holds the potential to serve as a refinement candidate. However, the process of examining each keyphrase for every topic and determining the most suitable candidates for refinement necessitates extensive human involvement. In an ideal HLTM system, it is imperative to minimize human effort while maximizing system effectiveness. Consequently, there is a pressing need for methods that can alleviate human effort and offer recommendations, enabling the HLTM system to operate optimally. This paper addresses the challenge of keyphrase recommendations for keyphrase-based HLTM with the intention to aid humans. Such recommendations aim to offer a reduced number of high-quality keyphrases that effectively enhance document-topic distribution. While Khan et al. [17] achieved a high F1 score improvement by examining all possible keyphrases and selecting the best on the basis of F1 score improvement, we aim to identify the optimal keyphrase for refinement operations with a limited set of keyphrases, while still maximizing F1 score improvement.

In this study, we introduce a novel approach that utilizes the relationships between documents, topics, and keyphrases to select recommendations. We evaluate the effectiveness of our recommended method through simulated user experiments. We compare the F1 score improvement of the proposed method with the baseline approach, which involves examining the top 10 most frequent keyphrases for each topic, and the all-keyphrase method, which considers all keyphrases for each topic at various human effort levels l. For this experiment, we used the 20Newsgroups dataset. As for the keyphrase generation (KPG) method, we used ChatGPT due to its superior performance when compared with other methods. The experimental results strongly support our claim, demonstrating the effectiveness and benefits of the proposed keyphrase recommendation method. The method significantly reduces human efforts while maintaining the quality of refinements, leading to a substantial improvement in efficiency.

2   Human-in-the-loop Topic Modeling

HLTM permits users to actively contribute their knowledge by enabling them to refine the topic models. But before going in-depth into HLTM, we briefly describe the underlying topic models. HLTM uses Latent Dirichlet Allocation as the underlying topic model.

Latent Dirichlet Allocation [4] is a probabilistic model that posits a fixed number of topics for each document. The topics are represented as multinomial distributions ϕ_z, over V. To generate a word token w_i within a d, LDA follows a two-step process. First, a topic assignment z_i is sampled from the document's topic distribution θ_d. Subsequently, the selected topic's distribution $\phi_{z,i}$ is sampled to generate w_i. The Dirichlet distributions are used to draw the multinomial distributions θ_d and ϕ_z. These Dirichlet distributions not only encode sparsity but also enable the inclusion of expert knowledge from users. In this context, sparsity refers to the expected occurrence of words within a topic or the number of topics within a document. In the following explanation, we will outline the process of incorporating user feedback into LDA by modifying the Dirichlet hyperparameters α and β. Specifically, adjusting α and β corresponds to integrating information about documents and topics, respectively. To compute the posterior distribution, we used collapsed Gibbs sampling [12] as an inference method. This iterative procedure involves sampling a topic assignment, denoted as $z_{d,i} = t$, given an observed token $x_{d,i} = v$ within document d, as well as other topic assignments $\tilde{\mathbf{Z}}_{\backslash d,i}$, from the subsequent distribution:

$$p(z_{d,i} = t \mid x_{d,i} = v, \mathbf{X}, \tilde{\mathbf{Z}}_{\backslash d,i}) = \frac{n_{d,t} + \alpha_{d,t}}{\sum_{t'} (n_{d,t'} + \alpha_{d,t'})} \frac{n_{t,v} + \beta_{t,v}}{\sum_{v'} (n_{t,v'} + \beta_{t,v'})} \quad (1)$$

Here $n_{d,t}$ represents the count of t within d, and $n_{t,v}$ is the count of t assigned to words of V. The calculation of the posterior for θ and ϕ is performed as follows:

$$\hat{\theta}_{d,t} = \frac{n_{d,t} + \alpha_{d,t}}{\sum_{t'} (n_{d,t'} + \alpha_{d,t'})} \quad (2)$$

$$\hat{\phi}_{t,v} = \frac{n_{t,v} + \beta_{t,v}}{\sum_{v'} (n_{t,v'} + \beta_{t,v'})} \quad (3)$$

We manipulate the hyperparameters α and β of the distributions mentioned previously to incorporate human knowledge and make modifications to the topic models.

Incorporating Feedback is the main objective of HLTM. There are numerous approaches available to accomplish this objective, such as "must-link" & "cannot-link" constraints [2,15] and extended variants of constraints [9,32], fragment quotation graph [14], document labels [38], matrix factorization [8,23], and informed priors [17,29]. The informed priors method is widely used for transferring knowledge into LDA. This approach is particularly popular due to its ease of comprehension for novice users, offering them greater control [19]. In this technique, the initial step involves discarding previous $\phi_{t,v}$ and $\theta_{d,t}$ assignments. The next step is to introduce new information by adjusting the hyperparameters (α or β). The specific modifications to the hyperparameters depend on the type of refinement. As a result, these injected changes gradually alter the posterior distributions over a few iterations of Gibbs sampling. This direct control over the distributions can be observed in Eqs. (2 & 3). Initially, among the various proposed refinement operations, the most popular ones were word-based and document-based refinements [19]. However, later research by Khan et al. [17] demonstrated that keyphrase-based refinements are more effective in improving document-topic associations. Keyphrase-based refinements leverage KPG methods and introduce an additional layer of information to topic models. This extra layer enables the grouping of documents and facilitates a distinct and effective approach to modifying the topic models. The proposed refinement functions work as follows:

Remove keyphrase refinement function enables users to specify a keyphrase kp that should be excluded as it is considered unsuitable for describing the topic t. Given the keyphrase kp, this function initially identifies all the associated documents with topic t using the following equation D_t.

$$D_t = \{d \in D \mid \arg\max_{t'} \hat{\theta}_{d,t'} = t\} \quad (4)$$

Subsequently, from D_t, a new document set D_{rem} is formed by including all documents related to kp as well as similar keyphrases to kp. This can be expressed as follows.

$$D_{rem} = \left\{ d \in D_t \mid \exists kp' \in f_{sim}^{(D_t)}(kp)\,(kp' \in KP_d) \right\} \tag{5}$$

Here $f_{sim}^{(D_t)}(kp)$ is constructed by applying density-based clustering on the embedding vectors. This process helps identify keyphrases that exhibit strong semantic similarity to kp, such as "neural network" and "neural net". These embedding vectors are generated for each keyphrase using Phrase-BERT [36]. Then "remove document" refinement is applied to each document in D_{rem}.

Add keyphrase refinement function offers a means for users to specify an appropriate keyphrase kp that effectively describes topic t. To add a keyphrase kp to topic t, the initial step is to obtain the set of documents that are *not* currently associated with topic t, as shown in the following.

$$D_{\setminus t} = \{ d \in D \mid \arg \max_{t'} \hat{\theta}_{d,t'} \neq t \} \tag{6}$$

Next, we compile a list of all keyphrases present in $D_{\setminus t}$. Following that, we proceed by either utilizing the same keyphrase kp if it is present in the previously mentioned list of keyphrases, or identifying the most closely related keyphrase. This is achieved by using cosine similarity on the embeddings generated by the Phrase-BERT model. This enables us to determine the documents to be included in the subsequent process. Then, we identify all the documents to which the "add document" refinement needs to be applied, using the following equation:

$$D_{add} = \left\{ d \in D_{\setminus t} \mid \exists kp' \in f_{sim}^{(D_{\setminus t})}(kp_{add})\,(kp' \in KP_d) \right\} \tag{7}$$

The final step of the refinement process involves re-training the LDA with fewer iterations of Gibbs sampling. This iterative process helps to update the topic assignments and optimize the model on the basis of the refined information.

Keyphrase Generation Model Vs ChatGPT: KPG is a critical component of this research as it plays a pivotal role in recommending keyphrases for a keyphrase-based HLTM. A keyphrase is a concise text snippet that encapsulates the primary semantic meaning of a longer text. Typically, a document consists of multiple important phrases, such as the keyword section found in scientific publications. These sections often contain more than one word and provide the core information of a paper. The KPG model is specifically designed to tackle the task of extracting keyphrases from the documents. It leverages advanced techniques and algorithms to effectively generate relevant and informative keyphrases. Traditional KPG algorithms have a long list of approaches, but the latest transformer-based KPG models have shown superior performance compared with older models [28]. These transformer-based models leverage the power of transformers and attention mechanisms to capture more nuanced and contextual information, leading to improved KPG capabilities. Khan et al. [17] used a Seq2Seq gated recurrent unit (GRU)-based model with a copy mechanism and coverage mechanism for KPG. They utilized the OpenNMT implementation[1] to generate keyphrases for the document dataset.

In this research, we utilized the aforementioned model with the same dataset and parameters as used by Khan et al. [17]. Additionally, as a sub-experiment, we compared the keyphrases generated by the model with the keyphrases generated by ChatGPT. In a subset of 500 documents from the 20Newsgroups dataset, the KPG model produced approximately 5,000 keyphrases, of which only 495 keyphrases appeared in two or more documents. On the other hand, ChatGPT generated approximately 9,000 keyphrases, of which around 1,500 keyphrases appeared twice or more in the subset. The keyphrase list generated by the KPG model contained numerous general, meaningless, and junk keyphrases. In contrast, the keyphrase list generated by ChatGPT did not include any such keyphrases. Given the significance of keyphrase occurrence in our experiment, we focused solely on keyphrases that appeared two or more times. Under these conditions, when using the KPG model, we found that 79 out of the 500 documents were keyphraseless, meaning they did not have any keyphrases that appeared twice or more. In contrast, when considering the keyphrase list generated by ChatGPT, not a single document was found to be keyphraseless. On the basis of these small-scale comparisons, we can conclude that ChatGPT outperforms the state-of-the-art transformer-based Seq2Seq model, trained on a large single dataset, in the task of KPG. This conclusion aligns with previous studies [25,34] that have also shown the superior performance of ChatGPT in various KPG tasks. Considering the aforementioned factors and the superior performance of ChatGPT in KPG, we decided to utilize ChatGPT as the KPG model for this experiment. Its effectiveness, along with its ability to produce meaningful and relevant keyphrases, made it the preferred choice for our research.

3   Keyphrase Recommendations

This work introduces a keyphrase recommendation method specifically designed for keyphrase-based refinements in HLTM. The primary goal is to minimize human efforts while enhancing document-topic association through the provision of keyphrase candidates. The proposed method builds upon keyphrase-based HLTM, utilizing similar primary steps as described in previous work [17]. Here, we present a concise overview of the one-time pre-processing steps, as follows:

- We utilize ChatGPT to generate keyphrases $KP^{(D)}$. These keyphrases are then transformed into embedding vectors using the Phrase-BERT model, which captures their semantic representations in a high dimensional vector space. Furthermore, we compute a similarity matrix by measuring the cosine similarity between all pairs of keyphrases. This matrix provides insights into the similarity and relationships between different keyphrases in our dataset.

---

[1] https://github.com/memray/OpenNMT-kpg-release.

– We train an initial topic model LDA with Gibbs sampling as an inference method on document dataset.

Next, we rank the top keyphrases to represent the topics, considering the frequency of each keyphrase in D_t defined in Eq. (4). This ranking enables us to emphasize the keyphrases that are most representative of each topic. Topic representation of initial LDA in the form of top keyphrases is shown in Fig. 1.

Topic	Top keyphrases(coma separated)
1	team, game, player, goal, league, nhl, season, playoff, point, standing
2	god, bible, christian, religion, jesus, faith, atheist, atheism, science, morality
3	window, mac, software, hardware, system, memory, do, apple, ibm, driver
4	space, armenian, turkey, muslim, serdar argic, jew, government, azerbaijan, crime, christian
5	space, nasa, shuttle, satellite, astronomy, moon, payload, launch, earth, jupiter

Fig. 1. Top 10 keyphrases based on the frequency of occurrence in the top documents of each topic. These keyphrases serve as representations of the respective topics.

To provide keyphrase recommendations, we calculate the proportion of each keyphrase within the current topic, which we refer to as the kp-doc ratio $\rho_{(kp,t)}$. This ratio represents the relative frequency or importance of kp in relation to the t under consideration. It is calculated using the following formula:

$$\rho_{(kp,t)} = \frac{N_{(kp,t)}}{N_{kp}} \tag{8}$$

where $N_{(kp,t)} = |\{d \in D_t \mid kp \in KP_d\}|$ is the number of documents associated with keyphrase kp in the current topic t, and $N_{kp} = |\{d \in D \mid kp \in KP_d\}|$ is the total number of documents associated with keyphrase kp.

For Remove Keyphrase refinement function, recommendations for topic t are generated by the procedure presented as follows:

– Initially, we compile a list of all the keyphrases $KP^{(D_t)}$ associated with the topic t that have been extracted from the documents D_t of Eq. (4).
– Next, we determine the dominant topic of each kp of $KP^{(D_t)}$ by examining the corresponding $\rho_{(kp,t)}$ value for each topic. This enables us to identify which topic exhibits the highest proportion or relevance for kp.
– If the dominant topic of a kp differs from the current t, then kp is considered a potential candidate for a recommendation. This means that if the keyphrase is more strongly associated with a different topic than the current topic, it is deemed relevant for removal in the context of the current topic.
– Since the remove keyphrase refinement is built upon the remove document refinement, the next step is to determine the number of documents to which the refinement will be applied. This value is referred to as the effective document number $N_{eff(kp,t)}$. It represents the count of documents affected by the removal of the identified keyphrase kp, which is similar to $N_{(kp,t)}$. For every potential candidate from the previous step, we calculate this value.

- Finally, we rank the keyphrases by effective document number $N_{eff(kp,t)}$. This ranking enables us to prioritize the candidate keyphrases. The keyphrases with a higher effective document number are given higher priority in the recommendation process.

For Add Keyphrase refinement function, recommendations for topic t are generated by the procedure presented as follows:

- First, we create a list of all the keyphrases $KP^{(D_t)}$ of the topic t, which have been extracted from the documents D_t of Eq. (4).
- Next, we determine the keyphrase kp from $KP^{(D_t)}$ that possesses the highest $\rho_{(kp,t)}$ value for topic t. This enables us to determine all the keyphrases that exhibit the strongest association with t compared with other topics.
- Since the add keyphrase refinement is built upon the add document refinement, we need to determine the number of documents to which the refinement will be applied. In this context, we refer to this as the effective document number $N_{eff(kp,t)}$, which can be calculated using the following formula:

$$N_{eff(kp,t)} = |\{d \in D_{\backslash t} \mid kp \in KP_d\}| \qquad (9)$$

- The final step involves ranking the keyphrases on the basis of their effective document number $N_{eff(kp,t)}$. This ranking helps prioritize the keyphrases in accordance with the number of documents that will be affected by their addition to the current topic t. Keyphrases with a higher effective document number are given a higher rank, indicating their significance in the refinement process.

4   Evaluation Experiments

To evaluate the performance of our keyphrase recommendation method, we conducted experiments focusing on two key aspects: the reduction of human effort and the quality of the recommended keyphrases. To achieve this objective, we used a simulated user-based experiment, leveraging a concept previously introduced in the literature [19]. In our study, we utilized a pre-classified dataset and applied an initial topic model. Then, we used our recommendation method, along with other approaches, to refine the topic distribution and align it more closely with the dataset's classification. The evaluation in this study revolves around measuring the similarity between the document-topic associations generated by the topic model and the document classifications specified in the dataset. This similarity is quantified using the F1 score as a metric. Initially, the simulated user generates a fixed number of recommended keyphrases, directly influencing the level of human effort (l) involved. These recommendations are derived from one of the three methods: our proposed method, a baseline method, or all keyphrases. Then, the simulated user systematically applies refinement operations for each recommended keyphrase and records the resulting document-topic distributions.

The F1 score is then computed, comparing the post-refinement document-topic distribution with our original document-class knowledge. In the next step, the simulated user selects the keyphrase and refinement operation that yields the highest F1 score. An illustrative example is presented in Fig. 2, showcasing this process.

Top keyphrases: team, game, player, goal, league, nhl, season, playoff, point, standing

Recommended keyphrases for refinement operations		Post-refinement F1 score (previous F1=0.75)		
For remove keyphrase	For add keyphrase	Refinement	Keyphrase	F1
season, point, standing	hockey, baseball, product	remove_kp	season	0.75
		remove_kp	point	0.73
		remove_kp	standing	0.73
"hockey" for add_kp is selected for next refinement loop		add_kp	hockey	0.77
		add_kp	baseball	0.76
		add_kp	product	0.74

Fig. 2. Example involving a single topic and three keyphrase recommendations for both refinement operations: remove keyphrase and add keyphrase. The refinement loop iteration involves selecting the keyphrase that yields the highest F1 score, thereby determining the most suitable refinement operation.

4.1   Experimental Setup

The text corpus used in this research is the *20Newsgroups*[2] dataset [20]. It comprises approximately 20,000 English text articles from 20 distinct categories. The length of the documents within the corpus varies significantly, ranging from a few words to several hundred words. In their study, Khan et al. [17] specifically selected the 2,000 longest documents from the available corpus. This decision was motivated by the observation that topic models tend to achieve optimal performance when working with longer documents, as longer texts provide a more comprehensive context for effective modeling. The researchers considered all the categories present in the dataset and treated each category as a distinct topic. However, it should be noted that certain newsgroups demonstrated a close relationship, such as the case of "ms-windows/windows-x". Through experimentation, we discovered that it is possible to use a smaller subset of documents to expedite the experimentation process. We specifically opted for entirely distinct categories, as topic models rely on word correlations, and distinct categories tend to exhibit stronger correlations among similar words. This approach enabled us

---

[2] http://qwone.com/~jason/20Newsgroups/.

to leverage the improved word correlations and accelerate the learning process within the topic model. Therefore, we created five categories by grouping similar newsgroups, as illustrated in Table 1.

We applied various pre-processing techniques, including removing stopwords, special characters, content consisting only of digits, and words with fewer than three characters. Additionally, we utilized word lemmatization as part of the pre-processing pipeline.

Table 1. The formed categories, accompanied by their respective newsgroup titles.

Category	Newsgroups
Religion	alt.atheism, soc.religion.christian, talk.religion.misc
Politics	talk.politics.guns, talk.politics.mideast, talk.politics.misc
Sports	rec.sport.baseball, rec.sport.hockey
Computer	comp.os.ms-windows.misc, comp.sys.ibm.pc.hardware, comp.sys.mac.hardware, comp.windows.x
Space	sci.space

We utilized the identical configuration of the keyphrase-based HLTM as used in the previous study [17]. The researchers used the Julia programming language and conducted LDA training with 1,000 iterations of Gibbs sampling. The prior β for words and the prior α for documents were set to a value of 0.01. The only variation in the hyperparameters lies in the number of topics. In their study, which examined 20 categories, the hyperparameter k was 20. However, since our analysis focuses on 5 categories, we set hyperparameter k to 5. Consequently, the LDA topic model was trained to extract 5 topics from the dataset.

Following the training, we applied the Gale-Shapley algorithm [27] to associate each topic with its corresponding dominant category. This association was established for evaluation. For instance, following the initial LDA training and the computation of topic distribution $\hat{\theta}$, we discovered that among the 500 documents, 76 had topic 1 as their dominant topic. Furthermore, out of those 76 documents, 72 were categorized as "sports". By applying the Gale-Shapley algorithm, we determined that the most suitable association for topic 1 is with the category "sports". The topic-category associations established in this manner are instrumental in our evaluation process, enabling us to quantify the variation in F1 scores before and after applying refinement operations.

4.2 Empirical Findings and Interpretation

In each experiment configuration, we begin by defining a human effort level l for each topic. The human effort level l refers to the number of keyphrases that the user needs to analyze for each topic. Since our experiments are simulated user-based, the parameter l corresponds to the number of recommended keyphrases in this context. Next, we identify the optimal refinement operation, keyphrase, and corresponding F1 score on the basis of the simulated user's behavior, as depicted in Fig. 2. The total number of iterations is 10, meaning that each configuration is tasked with finding 10 successive refinement operations to enhance the F1 score. For the proposed method, we use $l = 10$. Traditionally, LDA topics are represented with the top 10 words, but in our experiment, we use keyphrases, presenting the top 10 keyphrases for each of the 5 topics. This yields a total of 50 keyphrases. All of these keyphrases are included in our baseline method. The baseline method involves three values of l: $l = 10$ with 10 randomly recommended keyphrases for refinement, $l = 30$ with half of the keyphrases randomly chosen for recommendations, and $l = 60$ with all 50 keyphrases for "add keyphrase" and 10 keyphrases for "remove keyphrase" recommended. Similarly, for the "all keyphrases" configuration, where we use all keyphrases extracted from each document in the dataset, we examine three distinct values of l. First, we set $l = 10$, where 10 random keyphrases are selected as recommendations. Second, we set $l = 600$, where 500 keyphrases are randomly selected for the "add keyphrase" refinement and 100 keyphrases are randomly chosen for the "remove keyphrase" refinement for each topic. Third, for $l = 1500$, we utilize all the keyphrases as recommendations for the "add keyphrase" refinement, and all the keyphrases for each topic are recommended for the "remove keyphrase" refinement.

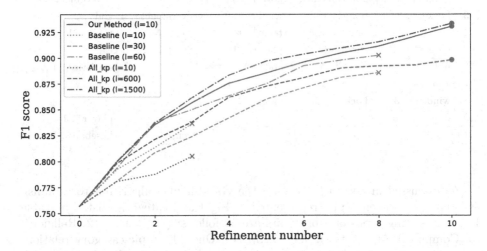

Fig. 3. Best F1 scores attained at each iteration of the refinement. The cyan lines depict the scores achieved by the baseline method, while the blue lines represent the scores of the all-keyphrase method. The value of l corresponds to the human effort level. (Color figure online)

Figure 3 illustrates the incremental improvement of the F1 score for each configuration throughout each iteration. The x symbol displayed on the graph indicates that there were no recommended keyphrases in the next iteration that could improve the F1 score. From the graph, it is evident that the baseline method, for all levels of human effort, was unable to complete the process of identifying 10 keyphrases that simultaneously improve the F1 score. In contrast, our proposed method consistently identified efficient keyphrases that led to continuous improvements in the F1 scores, even at lower levels of human effort ($l = 10$). Despite using a high human effort level ($l = 600$) for the all-keyphrase method, we were unable to achieve better F1 scores compared with the results of our method. When using all keyphrases with the highest human effort level ($l = 1500$), where each keyphrase is analyzed for each topic and refinement is applied, we achieved comparable results to those obtained with our method.

4.3 Discussion

Table 2. Comparison of the selected refinement and corresponding topic at each iteration loop across various approaches used in this study. kp^+ shows the added keyphrase, kp^- shows the remove keyphrase refinement.

N	Our Method	Baseline (l=30)	Baseline (l=60)	All (l=600)	All (l=1500)
1	space$^+$, 5	nasa$^+$, 5	space$^+$, 5	space$^+$, 5	space$^+$, 5
2	government$^+$, 4	government$^+$, 4	government$^+$, 4	uniform$^-$, 5	government$^+$, 4
3	hockey$^+$, 1	team$^+$, 1	window$^+$, 3	government$^+$, 4	god$^+$, 2
4	christian$^-$, 4	satellite$^+$, 5	team$^+$, 1	build$^-$, 5	team$^+$, 1
5	baseball$^+$, 1	christian$^+$, 2	player$^+$, 1	statistic$^-$, 2	lsd$^-$, 2
6	nhl$^+$, 1	moon$^+$, 5	god$^+$, 2	moon$^-$, 4	statistic$^+$, 4
7	gun$^+$, 4	game$^+$, 1	system$^+$, 3	devil$^-$, 4	window$^+$, 3
8	window$^+$, 3	hockey$^+$, 1	game$^+$, 1	search$^-$, 3	entry$^-$, 5
9	program$^-$, 5			hope$^-$, 4	player$^+$, 1
10	child$^-$, 2			license$^+$, 5	baseball$^+$, 1

As discussed in Sect. 4.1, we used the Gale-Shapley algorithm to establish associations between topics represented in Fig. 1 and categories listed in Table 1. The resulting topic-category pairs are as follows: (1, Sports), (2, Religion), (3, Computer), (4, Politics), and (5, Space). Once the topic-category relationships were established, refinements were applied by the simulated user, which are detailed in Table 2. Notably, there are highly evident keyphrases such as ($space^+$, 5) and ($government^+$, 4) that were unanimously recommended by all recommendation methods. These particular recommendations emerged as the most effective refinements operations for the initial iteration loops. As evident from Table 2, the simulated user did not select any "remove keyphrase" refinements in the baseline method. This is understandable since the recommended keyphrases primarily come from the top frequent keyphrases, which are often strongly associated with the topics. In contrast, the proposed method successfully identified a few "remove keyphrase" refinements that proved to be the most effective in terms of improving the F1 score. On the other hand, when compared with the all (l=1500) scenario, the keyphrases selected by our method exhibit several differences, although they result in almost the same F1 score improvement. For instance, there are common refinements such as $(baseball^+, 1)$ and $(window^+, 3)$, while the proposed method exclusively chooses refinements like $(hockey^+, 1)$ and $(gun^+, 4)$, which are also meaningful. This demonstrates that there are multiple effective ways to improve the topic-document association to the same degree, and the proposed method can uncover a number of them, even if they differ from the "best" one. From Table 2, it becomes evident that while the selected keyphrase may appear similar, there is a notable variation in terms of F1 score improvement. This indicates that discovering effective keyphrases for refinements can be a challenging task in the absence of a recommendation method. This highlights a significant advantage of our method in supporting human users in keyphrase-based HLTM.

5   Conclusion

To reduce human efforts, this study represents a pioneering investigation of a keyphrase recommendation method specifically designed for keyphrase-based HLTM. Our proposed method leverages the interplay between document-topic and document-keyphrases associations. The prospective recommendations for each topic and refinement are selected on the basis of the ratio of the kp proportion in t to the overall proportion of keyphrases in the dataset. These keyphrases are then ranked in accordance with the effective document number, representing the count of documents where refinements will be applied. To evaluate the efficacy of our method, we conducted experiments using a simulated user approach aimed at aligning document-topic associations with predetermined document-category ones. The results demonstrate that our keyphrase recommendation method achieves identical performance with minimal human effort, comparable with the ideal scenario where the human effort level is maximized. Moreover, our method outperforms the baseline and the approach of using all keyphrases at the same human effort level. Although our results highlight the substantial potential of our proposed keyphrase recommendation method, it is crucial to conduct real-user experiments to thoroughly evaluate its practical effectiveness because these experiments solely rely on the simulations.

Acknowledgements. This work was supported by JST SPRING grant number JPMJSP2124, JST CREST grant number JPMJCR22M2, and JSPS KAKENHI grant number 22K12039.

References

1. Abadah, M.S.K., Keikhosrokiani, P., Zhao, X.: Analytics of public reactions to the Covid-19 vaccine on twitter using sentiment analysis and topic modelling. In: Handbook of Research on Applied Artificial Intelligence and Robotics for Government Processes, pp. 156–188. IGI Global (2023)

2. Andrzejewski, D., Zhu, X., Craven, M.: Incorporating domain knowledge into topic modeling via dirichlet forest priors. In: Proceedings of the 26th Annual International Conference on Machine Learning, pp. 25–32 (2009)

3. Blei, D.M., Jordan, M.I.: Modeling annotated data. In: Proceedings of the 26th Annual International ACM SIGIR Conference on Research and Development in Information Retrieval, pp. 127–134 (2003)

4. Blei, D.M., Ng, A.Y., Jordan, M.I.: Latent dirichlet allocation. J. Mach. Learn. Res. **3**, 993–1022 (2003)

5. Boyd-Graber, J., Mimno, D., Newman, D.: Care and feeding of topic models: Problems, diagnostics, and improvements. Handbook Mixed Membership Models Appl. 225255 (2014)

6. Chang, J., Gerrish, S., Wang, C., Boyd-Graber, J., Blei, D.: Reading tea leaves: how humans interpret topic models. In: Advances in Neural Information Processing Systems 22 (2009)

7. Cheng, Z., Shen, J.: On effective location-aware music recommendation. ACM Trans. Inform. Syst. (TOIS) **34**(2), 1–32 (2016)

8. Choo, J., Lee, C., Reddy, C.K., Park, H.: Utopian: user-driven topic modeling based on interactive nonnegative matrix factorization. IEEE Trans. Visual Comput. Graphics **19**(12), 1992–2001 (2013)

9. Chuang, J., t al.: Document exploration with topic modeling: designing interactive visualizations to support effective analysis workflows. In: NIPS Workshop on Topic Models: Computation, Application, and Evaluation (2013)

10. Fang, D., Yang, H., Gao, B., Li, X.: Discovering research topics from library electronic references using latent dirichlet allocation. Library Hi Tech (2018)

11. Fukuyama, S., Wakabayashi, K.: Extracting time series variation of topic popularity in microblogs. In: Proceedings of the 20th International Conference on Information Integration and Web-based Applications and Services, pp. 365–369 (2018)

12. Griffiths, T.L., Steyvers, M.: Finding scientific topics. Proc. National Acad. Sci. **101**(suppl_1), 5228–5235 (2004)

13. Hagg, L.J., et al.: Examining analytic practices in latent dirichlet allocation within psychological science: scoping review. J. Med. Internet Res. **24**(11), e33166 (2022)

14. Hoque, E., Carenini, G.: Convisit: interactive topic modeling for exploring asynchronous online conversations. In: Proceedings of the 20th International Conference on Intelligent User Interfaces, pp. 169–180 (2015)

15. Hu, Y., Boyd-Graber, J., Satinoff, B., Smith, A.: Interactive topic modeling. Mach. Learn. **95**, 423–469 (2014)

16. Khan, M.H.U.R., Wakabayashi, K.: Drifting and popularity: a study of time series analysis of topics. In: The Seventh International Conference on Big Data, Small Data, Linked Data and Open Data, pp. 16–22 (2021)

17. Khan, M.H.U.R., Wakabayashi, K.: Keyphrase-based refinement functions for efficient improvement on document-topic association in human-in-the-loop topic models. J. Inform. Process. **31**, 353–364 (2023)

18. Khan, M.H.U.R., Wakabayashi, K., Fukuyama, S.: Events insights extraction from twitter using lda and day-hashtag pooling. In: Proceedings of the 21st International Conference on Information Integration and Web-based Applications and Services, pp. 240–244 (2019)

19. Kumar, V., Smith-Renner, A., Findlater, L., Seppi, K., Boyd-Graber, J.: Why didn't you listen to me? comparing user control of human-in-the-loop topic models. arXiv preprint arXiv:1905.09864 (2019)

20. Lang, K.: Newsweeder: learning to filter netnews. In: Machine Learning Proceedings 1995, pp. 331–339. Elsevier (1995)
21. Lee, T.Y., Smith, A., Seppi, K., Elmqvist, N., Boyd-Graber, J., Findlater, L.: The human touch: how non-expert users perceive, interpret, and fix topic models. Int. J. Hum Comput Stud. **105**, 28–42 (2017)
22. Liu, Z.: High performance latent dirichlet allocation for text mining. Ph.D. thesis, Brunel University School of Engineering and Design PhD Theses (2013)
23. Lund, J., Cook, C., Seppi, K., Boyd-Graber, J.: Tandem anchoring: a multiword anchor approach for interactive topic modeling. In: Proceedings of the 55th Annual Meeting of the Association for Computational Linguistics, pp. 896–905 (2017)
24. Mao, X.L., Ming, Z., Chua, T.S., Li, S., Yan, H., Li, X.: Sshlda: a semi-supervised hierarchical topic model. In: Proceedings of the 2012 Joint Conference on Empirical Methods in Natural Language Processing and Computational Natural Language Learning, pp. 800–809 (2012)
25. Martínez-Cruz, R., López-López, A.J., Portela, J.: Chatgpt vs state-of-the-art models: a benchmarking study in keyphrase generation task. arXiv preprint arXiv:2304.14177 (2023)
26. Mcauliffe, J., Blei, D.: Supervised topic models. In: Advances in Neural Information Processing Systems 20 (2007)
27. McVitie, D.G., Wilson, L.B.: The stable marriage problem. Commun. ACM **14**(7), 486–490 (1971)
28. Meng, R., Zhao, S., Han, S., He, D., Brusilovsky, P., Chi, Y.: Deep keyphrase generation. In: Proceedings of the 55th Annual Meeting of the Association for Computational Linguistics (Volume 1: Long Papers), pp. 582–592 (2017)
29. Musialek, C., Resnik, P., Stavisky, S.A.: Using text analytic techniques to create efficiencies in analyzing qualitative data: A comparison between traditional content analysis and a topic modeling approach. American Association for Public Opinion Research (2016)
30. Rao, Y.: Contextual sentiment topic model for adaptive social emotion classification. IEEE Intell. Syst. **31**(1), 41–47 (2015)
31. Rao, Y., Lei, J., Wenyin, L., Li, Q., Chen, M.: Building emotional dictionary for sentiment analysis of online news. World Wide Web **17**, 723–742 (2014)
32. Saeidi, A.M., Hage, J., Khadka, R., Jansen, S.: Itmviz: interactive topic modeling for source code analysis. In: 2015 IEEE 23rd International Conference on Program Comprehension, pp. 295–298. IEEE (2015)
33. Smith, A., Kumar, V., Boyd-Graber, J., Seppi, K., Findlater, L.: Closing the loop: user-centered design and evaluation of a human-in-the-loop topic modeling system. In: 23rd International Conference on Intelligent User Interfaces, pp. 293–304 (2018)
34. Song, M., et al.: Is chatgpt a good keyphrase generator? a preliminary study. arXiv preprint arXiv:2303.13001 (2023)
35. Wang, J., Zhao, C., Xiang, J., Uchino, K.: Interactive topic model with enhanced interpretability. In: IUI Workshops (2019)
36. Wang, S., Thompson, L., Iyyer, M.: Phrase-BERT: Improved phrase embeddings from bert with an application to corpus exploration. In: Proceedings of the 2021 Conference on Empirical Methods in Natural Language Processing, pp. 10837–10851 (2021)
37. Wang, Z., Ma, L., Zhang, Y.: A hybrid document feature extraction method using latent dirichlet allocation and word2vec. In: 2016 IEEE First International Conference on Data Science in Cyberspace (DSC), pp. 98–103. IEEE (2016)

38. Yang, Y., Downey, D., Boyd-Graber, J.: Efficient methods for incorporating knowledge into topic models. In: Proceedings of the 2015 Conference on Empirical Methods in Natural Language Processing, pp. 308–317 (2015)
39. Ye, S., Wakabayashi, K., Ho, K.K., Khan, M.H.: The relationships between users' negative tweets, topic choices, and subjective well-being in japan. In: Handbook of Research on Foundations and Applications of Intelligent Business Analytics, pp. 288–300. IGI Global (2022)
40. Zoghbi, S., Vulić, I., Moens, M.F.: Latent dirichlet allocation for linking user-generated content and e-commerce data. Inf. Sci. **367**, 573–599 (2016)

Movie Keyword Search Using Large-Scale Language Model with User-Generated Rankings and Reviews

Tensho Miyashita[1], Yoshiyuki Shoji[1,2]($\boxtimes$) (iD), Sumio Fujita[3] (iD),
and Martin J. Dürst[1] (iD)

[1] Aoyama Gakuin University, Sagamihara, Kanagawa 252 -5258, Japan
`tensho@sw.it.aoyama.ac.jp, duerst@it.aoyama.ac.jp`
[2] Shizuoka University, Hamamatsu, Shizuoka 432–8011, Japan
`shojiy@inf.shizuoka.ac.jp`
[3] Yahoo Japan Corporation,Chiyoda, Tokyo 102–8282, Japan
`sufujita@yahoo-corp.jp`

Abstract. The paper proposes a novel method for conducting keyword-based movie searches using user-generated rankings and reviews, by utilizing the BERT language model for task-specific fine-tuning. The model was trained on paired titles and reviews, enabling it to predict the likelihood of a movie appearing in a ranking that includes a particular keyword. An experiment using data from a reputable Japanese movie review site demonstrated that the method outperformed existing similarity-based approaches. However, some aspects, such as pooling methods, could be improved for accuracy.

Keywords: Movie Search · Online Review · BERT · Learning to Rank

1 Introduction

The shift towards on-demand and subscription-based movie services has changed how people select and watch movies. Traditional methods like going to a movie theater or video rental store limit the choices. Still, online platforms offer many options, making it challenging to select a movie based on specific preferences. Meanwhile, the changing attitudes towards movie-watching, such as viewing movies on computers and smartphones, often while multitasking, increased the demand for more efficient and personalized search technologies. These technologies should ideally consider not just metadata but also subjective elements like "beautiful scenery" or "flashy action," which are not typically included in conventional search algorithms.

We present a method that utilizes Bidirectional Encoder Representations from Transformers (BERT) to rank movies based on free queries, harnessing user-generated rankings and reviews. This approach is particularly tailored for user-generated ranking platforms where users can compile lists of up to ten of

P. Delir Haghighi et al. (Eds.): iiWAS 2023, LNCS 14416, pp. 249–255, 2023.
https://doi.org/10.1007/978-3-031-48316-5_25

their favorite movies along with a descriptive title, as seen in features like the "Round-Up" function on Yahoo! Movies, Japan.

We hypothesize that these descriptive titles can function as search keywords and proceed to train a model that can correlate these titles with the movies listed, thereby enabling more nuanced, keyword-based movie searches. The method assesses the likelihood of a movie appearing in user-generated rankings that contain the specified keyword, offering a more personalized search experience.

Our algorithm first vectorizes ranking titles and all reviews using BERT, and then it trains the neural network model to calculate the relevance between the ranking title and reviews of a particular movie. Finally, the model calculates the probability that a given movie will appear in the rankings with a given keyword in the title.

We conducted a subject experiment to confirm the accuracy and effectiveness of this ranking. Participants were asked to evaluate how closely the movies in the rankings generated by the proposed method, and several comparison methods were related to the query.

2   Related Work

This research aimed to make movies searchable using word of mouth (eWOM). BERT and Learning to Rank were used as enabling technologies.

Our research used reviews posted on movie sites, a type of eWOM, to find movies that were close to what users were looking for. Several examples of this kind of item search focus on eWOM. Ramanand et al. [5] proposed a method for extracting "wishes" that indicated suggestions about products and services and purchase intentions from documents, such as reviews and buyer surveys. Similarly, this study used user review information to search for movies using free queries.

We used BERT to search movies by using their review. BERT is a Large Language Model (LLM) proposed by Devlin et al. [1] that enables context reading. There are examples of BERT applied to information retrieval. Yang et al. [8] proposed a method for adapting BERT to the ad hoc retrieval of documents. Yunqiu et al. [6] proposed a BERT model for legal case retrieval, BERT-PLI, that can retrieve from much longer queries than general queries. The task of retrieving Lithuanian text and audio documents using the query and search corpus provided by IARPA's MATERIAL program revealed that this method enables more accurate retrieval than other methods. Since this research was conducted on movies, which are visual images, it is difficult to deal with the contents of movies in text; therefore, we used user-posted reviews. In addition, it is difficult to compare the similarity of review sentences and short queries because of the different natures of the sentences. Therefore, we used Learning to Rank to match queries and review sentences.

Our method is a type of Learning to Rank, an information retrieval technique that uses machine learning. Three main approaches to Learning to Rank [4] are pointwise, pairwise, and listwise methods. In this study, we used the pointwise method. As an example of retrieving documents belonging to a specific topic, Amir *et al.* [7] proposed a method that used BERT and Learning to Rank to retrieve evidence to support a claim. Yu *et al.* [9] proposed a method using Learning to Rank to find documents containing answers to a given question. Since the current research is concerned with retrieving an item (*i.e.*, a movie), we also discuss some examples of applying Learning to Rank to item retrieval. Shubhra *et al.* [2] proposed a method that applied Learning to Rank for product retrieval on an e-commerce site. Prior to this study, Kurihara *et al.* [3] proposed a method using Learning to Rank for movie retrieval based on review information. The current work solves the same task with a more modern method (*i.e.*, LLM).

3   Movie Keyword Search Using Review and LLM

This section introduces an algorithm to rank movies based on any keyword query. The procedure, illustrated in Fig. 1, initiates by retrieving titles and movies from user-generated movie rankings.

3.1   Vectorizing Movies Using Reviews

Movie websites feature reviews by various users. This research posits that these reviews encapsulate the movie's attributes. Consequently, review sentences, as opposed to movie metadata or visuals, were used to vectorize a movie.

For vectorization, the text underwent preprocessing. Sentences were segmented using punctuation, and superfluous characters and symbols were discarded. The average pooling is used to create a fixed-length vector of 768 dimensions.

3.2   Formatting User-Generated Rankings as Training Data

To facilitate movie retrieval for specific queries, data linking queries to movies is essential. The trend of users sharing personalized movie rankings online is increasingly prevalent. Many movie review sites allow users to create and register lists of favorite movies (*e.g.*, IMDB's Watchlist, Yahoo! Movies' Round-Up). User-generated rankings often have titles like "The 10 best movies that make me cry". Our method focuses on the relationship between this ranking title and the movies that appeared in the ranking. As preprocessing, unnecessary words (*e.g.*, "my", "all-time", "movie") were removed from the ranking titles.

3.3   Learning the Relationship Between Movies and Words
in the Ranking Title

Relevance between a query and a movie is computable by considering the ranking title as a keyword query. Here, a simple neural network was used to calculate relevance. When each movie and query has been represented as a vector of distributed representations, the proposed method trains a neural network as a

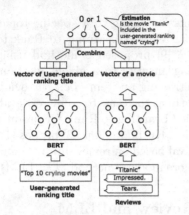

Fig. 1. Training that predicts whether a movie appears in user-generated rankings that include the query in the title.

Table 1. Queries used in the experiment and their features

Query	Features
Tearjerker Laughable Shocking	Emotion after watching the movie
Suitable for dating Suitable for children	Situation or scene when watching the movie
Suspense Animation	Category of the movie
Ghibli Surprise ending Takeshi Kitano	Content of the movie

binary classification task using these vectors, as shown in Fig. 1. The task is to combine vectors of movies and queries and then estimate whether the movie will likely appear in a ranking that includes the query in its title.

The input was a 1,536-dimensional vector: a combined pair of a 768-dimensional vector representing a movie and a 768-dimensional vector representing a ranking title. The output layer was binary since it performs a binary classification of whether a movie appears in the ranking whose title contains a given query. Note that, the output value is 0 or 1 during training, but it takes the probability during the inference phase. We used this probability as the final ranking score.

This trained model can rank movies in response to any given query. The keyword was vectorized using BERT, combined with a movie vector, and fed into the trained model. The model predicts the probability of a movie appearing in user-generated rankings with that keyword. By applying this to all movies, movies can be ranked based on this probability.

4   Evaluation

A subject experiment was conducted to verify whether the movie ranking generated by the proposed method was consistent with the user's perception. We compared three variant methods and the proposed methods as follows:

- **Proposed Method** uses deep learning to estimate the relevance of the query vector to the vectors generated from the movie reviews.
- **Movie Similarity** compares the vectors generated from the movie reviews and the query vectors using cosine similarity. It uses the cosine similarity between vectors of the query and the movie as the ranking score.

- **Review Sentence Similarity** calculates cosine similarity between input queries and review sentences, using the most similar review for movies with multiple reviews. This comparative method tests the risk of compressing movie reviews with average pooling.
- **Metadata Only** uses only metadata and no reviews. It finds movies containing query keywords in their metadata, and it sorts them by cosine similarities between the query and description.

Table 2. Precision at k and nDCG for each method

	p@1	p@5	p@10	nDCG
Proposed Method	0.50	0.56	0.58	0.64
Metadata Only	0.50	0.46	0.40	0.60
Movie Similarity	0.20	0.24	0.27	0.47
ReviewSentenceSimilarity	**0.80**	**0.74**	**0.72**	**0.75**

Table 3. Example output of the proposed method worked well (query: "Tearjerker")

Rank	Movie title	Participant Rating
1	What Dreams May Come	3.0
2	Gray Sunset	3.5
3	Glory Daze	3.0
4	The Boy Who Could Fly	4.0
5	Crayon Shin-chan: The Adult Empire	4.5
6	Pay It Forward	3.5
7	It's a Wonderful Life	4.0
8	Jack	3.5
9	Life is Beautiful	4.0
10	The Notebook	4.0

4.1 Experiment

We prepared the training dataset consisting of 15,000 movies, and 10,000 user-generated rankings taken from Yahoo! Movies Japan. We prepared ten queries in advance (see Table 1).

A subject experiment was conducted online in which participants were asked to label the relevance between the query and the movie. Ten participants labeled the 5-point scale relevance between a query and 40 movies; the top ten movies of four methods. Participants can search for the movie if they do not know about it.

For the actual experiment, we implemented an actual movie search system. The BERT Japanese pre-trained model[1] was used. A Japanese morphological analyzer "MeCab[2]" and it's dictionary called "mecab-ipadic-neologd[3]" was used for a tokenizer.

4.2 Experimental Results

The precision for each method is shown in Table 2. In nDCG and p@k, the proposed method performed better than simple cosine similarity to metadata

---

[1] Kurohashi Lab. Kyoto University: https://nlp.ist.i.kyoto-u.ac.jp/EN/.
[2] MeCab: Yet Another Part-of-Speech and Morphological Analyzer: https://taku910.github.io/mecab/.
[3] mecab-ipadic-NEologd: Neologism dictionary for MeCab https://github.com/neologd/mecab-ipadic-neologd.

and review. The method that worked best was the method using the most similar sentences rather than the entire review. Examples of outputs when the proposed method worked well are shown in Table 3. Many "tearjerker" movies can be retrieved correctly.

5   Discussion

Overall, the proposed method was more accurate for retrieval than the cosine similarity or metadata methods. However, a simple similarity calculation between a single sentence in a movie review and a keyword query was even more accurate.

The method's limitation lies in representing a movie with a single vector, which might retain major trends like "sad" or "funny" but dilute minor impressions from individual scenes. Despite this, the proposed method outperformed superficial cosine similarity, likely because using a neural network better captures the nuanced differences between short keyword queries and longer, multi-person reviews than just cosine similarity does.

The Review Sentence Similarity method offers superior accuracy due to the detailed variance representation derived from review sentences. The highest nDCG was observed in Review Sentence Similarity, underscoring the value of using reviews. The results suggest that in our test search task, the presence of elements relevant to the query was more crucial than the general trend of the movie.

6   Conclusion

This paper presents a method to determine the relevance between keywords and movies using user-generated rankings and reviews. Experimental results showed that our method outperformed traditional cosine similarity, but in some tasks, using metadata was more accurate.

We are planning a more detailed evaluation and refinement of our methodology. We also intend to use this method for the fine-tuning of the model itself.

Acknowledgments. This work was supported by JSPS KAKENHI Grants Numbers 21H03775, 21H03774, and 22H03905.

References

1. Devlin, J., Chang, M.W., Lee, K., Toutanova, K.: BERT: pre-training of deep bidirectional transformers for language understanding. In: Proceedings of NAACL 2019, pp. 4171–4186 (2019)
2. Karmaker Santu, S.K., Sondhi, P., Zhai, C.: On application of learning to rank for e-commerce search. In: Proceedings of SIGIR 2017, pp. 475–484 (2017)
3. Kurihara, K., Shoji, Y., Fujita, S., Dürst, M.J.: Learning to rank-based approach for movie search by keyword query and example query. In: Proceedings of iiWAS 2021, pp. 137–145 (2021)

4. Liu, T.Y.: Learning to rank for information retrieval. Found. Trends Inf. Retr. **3**, 225–331 (2009)
5. Ramanand, J., Bhavsar, K., Pedanekar, N.: Wishful thinking - finding suggestions and 'buy' wishes from product reviews. In: Proceedings of NAACL 2010, pp. 54–61 (2010)
6. Shao, Y., et al.: BERT-PLI: modeling paragraph-level interactions for legal case retrieval. In: IJCAI, pp. 3501–3507 (2020)
7. Soleimani, A., Monz, C., Worring, M.: Bert for evidence retrieval and claim verification. In: Proceedings of ECIR2020, pp. 359–366 (2020)
8. Yang, W., Zhang, H., Lin, J.: Simple applications of bert for ad hoc document retrieval. arXiv preprint arXiv:1903.10972 (2019)
9. Yu, L., Hermann, K., Blunsom, P., Pulman, S.: Deep learning for answer sentence selection. In: Proceedings of NIPS 2014 (2014)

Extraction News Components Methods for Fake News Correction

Masaya Sueyoshi[✉] and Akiyo Nadamoto

Konan University, Okamoto 8–9–1 Higashinada–ku, Kobe, Japan
m2324003@s.konan-u.ac.jp, nadamoto@konan-u.ac.jp

Abstract. There is a lot of fake news on the internet, and it is important to extract and correct the misinformation from the fake news. The purpose of this research is to extract and correct which parts of the news are misinformation based on 5 Ws including the main topic. In this paper as a first step of the research, we propose how to extract 5 Ws(without why) including the main topic using Masked-Language Modeling with BERT.

Keywords: Fake News · Correcting Misinformation · BERT

1 Introduction

There is a lot of fake news on the internet, and the number of them is increasing day by day. Many studies have been conducted to extract this fake news [1,3, 5]. Fake news is easily spread, and people unquestioningly believe it without knowing it is misinformation. Extracting and correcting the misinformation is important. However, to our knowledge, there is little research on correcting fake information. It is difficult for humans to manually extract and correct what parts of a large amount of news are different and what information is correct. In this study, we propose a method for automatically extracting and correcting the misinformation from the fake news. Specifically, we focus on the importance of the 5 Ws which are "who (what)," "where," "when," "what," and "why," in news articles, to determine whether the 5 Ws are correct or incorrect in news articles, and extract misinformation. Then, by comparing with similar articles on multiple news sites, we replace the incorrect 5 Ws with the correct 5 Ws. At this time, considering that "who (what)" is important in news, we consider "who (what)" as the main topic of the news, and determine whether "where," "when," "what," and "why," related to the main topic are incorrect or not, and correct them. In this study, "where," "when," "what," and "why," are collectively called "news components" for the main topic of the news article. In this paper, as a first step of the research, we propose the models that determine "when," "where," and "what" using each Masked-Language Modeling with BERT. Then, we conduct experiments to measure the benefits of our proposed methods.

P. Delir Haghighi et al. (Eds.): iiWAS 2023, LNCS 14416, pp. 256–261, 2023.
https://doi.org/10.1007/978-3-031-48316-5_26

2   Related Work

There are many studies about extracting fake news and analyzing fake news. Canhasi et al. [1] investigate the best combination of features for extracting fake news using lexical, syntactic, and psychological features. Wynne et al. [6] conduct fake news extraction using word n-grams and character n-grams. Zhou et al. [8] investigate news content at various levels. For example, lexicon-level, syntax-level, semantic-level, and discourse-level. These studies extract fake news based on news structures like vocabulary and grammar. However, we focus on 5 Ws and extract and correct fake news, and this is a different point from others. Imbwaga et al. [3] extract fake news with random forests, decision trees, gradient boosting, and logistic regression. Nagaraja et al. [5] classify news as correct news and fake news with Naive Bayes and Support Vector Machine. Helmstetter et al. [2] label tweets as reliable or unreliable to train classifiers and classify them. These studies extract fake news with machine learning. However, we create three models with Masked-Language Modeling with BERT and use them to correct fake news, and this is a different point from others.

3   Definition of Fake News

Fake news has been defined in various ways by various studies. For example, Lazer [4] et al. define fake news as "news that formally mimics the content of the news media but does not mimic their organizational ideas or intentions." Zhang [7] et al. define "fake news as any kind of information or story published and distributed mainly on the Internet to intentionally mislead, deceive, or lure readers for financial, political, or other gain." FIJ3[1] proposes and defines the 9 ratings which mean the evaluation and determination of the authenticity and accuracy of target statements in fact-checking articles. The 9 ratings are accurate, mostly accurate, misleading, inaccurate, unfounded, false, fake, suspend, and ineligible.

   In this study, we focus on "Mostly accurate," "False," and "Inaccurate." By definition of FIJ3, mostly accurate is that the main elements of the statement are factually accurate, but there are some minor or insignificant misinformation. False is that all or core elements of the claim are factually inaccurate. Inaccurate is that the claim lacks overall accuracy, but is a mixture of accurate and inaccurate elements. For example, "Shohei Ohtani returned to the Japan League to play in Japan this year" or "The fifth WBC tournament will be held in Qatar in 2023" are partially correct, partially incorrect, or fabricated news. We do not care about the political, financial, or other considerations behind the fake news. In this study, we also define fake news as all news, regardless of malicious intent, that is false or fake, such as lies or hoaxes, or news that contains mistakes, such as typos or omissions.

---

[1] https://en.fij.info/guidelines.

4   Extraction of Fake Passage

In this paper, we propose Masked-Language Modeling with BERT based model which is based on our proposed news component which is 5 Ws(without why).

4.1   News Component

In this study, we first focus on who is the main topic of the news and extract when, where, and what for this who. At this time, the reason we left out the "why" from the 5 Ws is that our study also targets unsubstantiated information in fake news. We believe that "why" indicates the basis of the news, so we left it out of our proposal in this paper. Since "Who" here is the main topic, it includes not only people but also objects and organizations. First, we extract the main topic MT for a target news article T. Then, for the MT, we extract the main topic MT. For MT, we extract DT_i (when) for the year and month, PT_i (where) for the place, and OT_i (what) for the purpose. Thus, the target news T is $TC = \{MT, DT_i, PT_j, OT_k\}$ and TC is called the target news component. where i,j,k denotes the number of each news component. This is because a news item has one main topic, but other elements may appear more than once. Next, let $CC_m = \{MT, DC_{mi}, PC_{mj}, OC_{mk}\}$ denote the news components CC_m of news from multiple news sites to be compared with the target news. The reason why the main topics of TC and CC_m are the same is that this study extracts and corrects fake news based on the assumption that the main topics are the same. where m is a number used to identify the news item of the news site to be compared.

4.2   Proposed Methods

Extracting the Main Topic
The main news topic is generally a person, an organization, or a thing. In addition, the title often contains the main topic of the news. Therefore, we first extract a noun as the subject from the title and make it a candidate for the main topic MT. If there is only one candidate MT in the title, it is assumed to be the MT. If there are multiple candidate MTs, the MT with the highest number of occurrences in the first paragraph of the news item is the MT.

Extracting News Component without Main Topic
When we extract elements of the news component, we use a BERT-based model and we propose a mode for each element. In our proposed system, we target Japanese news articles. Then, we use the same pre-trained BERT-model called bert-base-japanese-whole-word-masking[2]. We randomly select 10,000 news articles from the Mainichi Newspaper which is one of the famous Japanese newspaper companies from 2018 to 2021 for fine-tuning. We select 8,000 training

---

[2] https://huggingface.co/cl-tohoku/bert-base-japanese-whole-word-masking.

Table 1. The learning result of our proposed model

model	precision	recall	F1	Accuracy	AUC
When model	0.336	0.402	0.366	0.354	0.643
Where model	0.735	0.764	0.749	0.745	0.686
What model	0.684	0.616	0.648	0.657	0.694

data and 2,000 validation data from 10,000 news articles and train them by five-cross-validation. The when-model performs fine-tuning by masking out the parts manually determined to be DT_i. Similarly, the where-model performs fine-tuning by masking out the parts of the model that are manually determined to be PT_j. The what-model performs fine-tuning by masking out the parts of the model that are manually determined to be OT_k. The parameters of each BERT model are determined by grid search, the vector size is 768, the batch size is 32, the number of epochs is 5, the learning rate is 0.00002, and the optimizer is Adam.

5 Experiments

5.1 Evaluation of the Proposed Model

(1) Condition of Experiment

We evaluated the proposed BERT-based three models. We conducted five-cross-validation using 8,000 articles as training data which is masked by the target data in each model, and 2,000 articles as test data. For example, in the case of the when-model, we trained 8,000 articles by masking the dates, predicted the dates of the remaining 2,000 articles, and performed this five-cross-validation. Correct answers were determined manually. Table 1 shows the average of each result of our proposed model.

(2) Results and Discussion

The results of when-model are bad, we consider that this is because dates are often used after prepositions such as in and at, and the masked data are often mistaken for a location. This is an issue to be addressed in the future. The AUC results for all models are between 0.6 and 0.7. The results show that our model can learn, but should be improved to learn more. We consider that the training data is not enough. We have to train each model using more data.

5.2 Comparison of Proposed Methods with the Baseline

(1) Condition of Experiment

We conducted a comparison experiment with a rule-based baseline to demonstrate the usefulness of the proposed method.

Test Data

We measured the usefulness of the proposed model using fake news. Since it is difficult to collect a large amount of actual fake news, we considered the news

Table 2. the result of experiment

	Proposed model			Base line		
	Precision	Recall	F1	Precision	Recall	F1
When	0.243	0.421	0.308	0.722	0.683	0.702
Where	0.724	0.698	0.711	0.681	0.663	0.672
What	0.675	0.683	0.679	0.667	0.604	0.634

generated by ChatGPT as fake news. All queries in ChatGPT have the same main theme "Shohei Ohtani" and {date, place, purpose}. The date was randomly selected from year only, month only, year-month, month-day, and year-month-day. The place was selected randomly from {Japan, Tokyo, Osaka, Hokkaido, California, USA, Los Angeles, Anaheim}. The purpose was randomly selected from {Olympics, WBC, pitcher, batter, Koshien, game, home run derby, commercial, home run, major league}. All the elements are related to Shohei Ohtani. We created 1,000 queries combining {date, place, purpose}, and we generated 1,000 fake news by ChatGPT, which were used as test data. We used 1,000 fake news.

Baseline

When we compare the proposed methods with a baseline, we use the rule-based method as a baseline. We extract elements of news components that are related to the main topic. Then, we first remove the sentence whose subject is not the main topic from the target news articles.

- When (DT_i and DC_i)
  If the year, month, day, or hour appears in the target sentence, it is DT_i (or DC_i) in order of appearance.
- Where (PT_j and PC_j)
  If a proper noun indicating a region or at(in)+common noun occurs in order of appearance, then PT_j(or PC_j) in order of appearance.
- What (OT_k and OC_k)
  The object OT_k (or OC_k) is a verb and a noun occurring consecutively or with a verb + preposition + noun.

(2) Results and discussion

Table 2 shows the results of the comparison. When-model was lower for all results than the baseline. The baseline date decision had a higher F1 value than our proposed method. This indicates that using the rule base for when (DT_i) is better. On the other hand, the where-model and what-model are better than the baseline. Therefore, we use the rule-based for date extraction and the proposed model for Where and What extraction to extract news components.

6   Conclusion

The purpose of this research is to extract and correct what parts of the news are misinformation based on the main topic and 5 Ws. In this paper, as a first step of the research, we proposed how to extract 5 Ws(without why) including the main topic using Masked-Language Modeling with BERT. From our experiments, we find the extracting rule-based method of dates is better than the BERT model. However, our proposed where and what models are beneficial.

In future work, we will combine the two currently proposed models which are where and what into one and generate the model with more training data. Furthermore, we will propose a method that determines the correct information of the extracted fake passage of the fake news from the correct news and replace them.

Acknowledgements. This work was partially supported by Research Institute of Konan University.

References

1. Canhasi, E., Shijaku, R., Berisha, E.: Albanian fake news detection. ACM Trans. Asian Low-Resour. Lang. Inf. Process. **21**(5), 3487288 (2022). https://doi.org/10.1145/3487288
2. Helmstetter, S., Paulheim, H.: Weakly supervised learning for fake news detection on twitter. In: Proceedings of the 2018 IEEE/ACM International Conference on Advances in Social Networks Analysis and Mining, pp. 274–277. ASONAM 2018, IEEE Press (2020)
3. Imbwaga, J.L., Chittaragi, N., Koolagudi, S.: Fake news detection using machine learning algorithms. In: Proceedings of the 2022 Fourteenth International Conference on Contemporary Computing, pp. 271–275. IC3-2022, Association for Computing Machinery, New York, NY, USA (2022). https://doi.org/10.1145/3549206.3549256
4. Lazer, D.M.J., et al.: The science of fake news. Science. **359**, 1094–1096 (2018)
5. Nagaraja, A., Soumya, K.N., Sinha, A., Rajendra Kumar, J.V., Nayak, P.: Fake news detection using machine learning methods. In: International Conference on Data Science, E-Learning and Information Systems 2021, pp. 185–192. DATA 2021, Association for Computing Machinery, New York, NY, USA (2021). https://doi.org/10.1145/3460620.3460753
6. Wynne, H.E., Wint, Z.Z.: Content based fake news detection using n-gram models. In: Proceedings of the 21st International Conference on Information Integration and Web-Based Applications & Services, pp. 669–673. iiWAS2019, Association for Computing Machinery, New York, NY, USA (2020). https://doi.org/10.1145/3366030.3366116
7. Zhang, X., Ghorbani, A.A.: An overview of online fake news: characterization, detection, and discussion. Inf. Process. Manage. **57**, 102025 (2020)
8. Zhou, X., Jain, A., Phoha, V.V., Zafarani, R.: Fake news early detection: a theory-driven model. Digit. Threats **1**(2), 1–25 (2020). https://doi.org/10.1145/3377478

Image Data and Knowledge Graph

Buy Eye-Mask Instead of Alarm Clock!: Graph-Based Approach to Identify Functionally Equal Alternative Products

Tsukasa Hirano[1], Yoshiyuki Shoji[1,2]([✉])(iD), Takehiro Yamamoto[3](iD), and Martin J. Dürst[1](iD)

[1] Aoyama Gakuin University, Sagamihara, Kanagawa 252–5258, Japan
hirano@sw.it.aoyama.ac.jp, shojiy@inf.shizuoka.ac.jp,
duerst@it.aoyama.ac.jp
[2] Shizuoka University, Hamamatsu, Shizuoka 432–8011, Japan
[3] University of Hyogo, Kobe, Hyogo 651–2197, Japan
t.yamamoto@sis.u-hyogo.ac.jp

Abstract. This paper proposes a method to analyze product reviews to identify other products that can achieve the product's intended use. When people want to achieve the purpose of "getting up early in the morning," they generally tend to look only for an "alarm clock." In contrast, there are several products such as "smart curtains" that can directly achieve the purpose and "sleeping pills" that can indirectly achieve the purpose by replacing "getting up early in the morning" with "going to sleep early at night." The proposed method constructs a bipartite graph comprising product and uses purpose information from product review data. Then, the random walk with restart technique is employed to rank other products that can satisfy the use purpose of the input product. The proposed method was evaluated in subjective experiments, and the results suggest that the method is both accurate and useful in terms of identifying alternative products that satisfy similar use purposes.

Keywords: Information Retrieval · Review · Product Recommendation · Alternative Achievement

1 Introduction

Tunnel vision, which is also referred to as narrow-mindedness, is a significant obstacle in terms of product selection while shopping. Tunnel vision is a perceptual phenomenon whereby an individual experiences a significant reduction in peripheral vision. As a result, the individual focuses predominantly on their central vision, similar to looking through a tunnel. Most people have bought something they did not need on impulse due to tunnel vision at least once in their life. For example, after oversleeping and becoming upset, it is common for people to impulsively purchase an alarm clock in order to wake up at the necessary time. Conventional recommendation algorithms recommend various alarm clock devices when the user starts searching for an "alarm clock." In this case, the user can compare many "alarm clocks" to find the most suitable device for the given purpose, *i.e.*, waking up at the correct time.

However, solutions to avoid oversleeping are not limited to alarm clocks. For example, if you take sleeping pills the night before and go to bed early, you may reduce the risk of missing sleep the next day, and if you buy a pillow that allows you to sleep soundly, you may wake up more refreshed the next morning, even after a short sleep. As a result, when a person focuses singularly on alarm clock products, they are much more likely to purchase the product without considering any information about alternative products that are functionally equivalent." In many situations, consumers get tunnel vision and focus their attention on only a single purpose, thereby making it impossible to find an appropriate alternative product.

With the increasing ubiquity of the Internet and smartphones, various online shopping services and customer-to-customer marketplaces have become increasingly common in recent years. As a result, a wide variety of consumers can purchase desired products easily.

According to a survey conducted by the Japanese government, 73.4% of Japanese consumers have purchased items on an online shopping site. By age, 69.5% of those in their twenties and 78.0% of those aged 60 and older (regardless of gender or specific age) are using e-commerce sites[1].

A problem that can occur when casually shopping on the web in this manner is impulsive purchasing caused by tunnel vision. Online shopping services have made it considerably easier to purchase various products; however, it has also become increasingly difficult for users unfamiliar with the Internet to select the most suitable products. In fact, Zhang *et al.* [13] demonstrated that visual appeal and traditional recommendation methods create impulsive purchase intent in online shopping situations. To prevent this, it is necessary to present information that encourages logical thinking in consumers searching for a product to make them think about the purpose they need to address and the product they need once they have found it.

Generally, conventional product recommendation systems [5] have used collaborative filtering, which first recommends products of the same type, other products purchased by users who purchased that product, and products used in combination. Thus, if the user selects "alarm clock," another type of alarm clock or a related battery for such devices will be presented as a recommendation. Here, we consider the case where the user searches for an alarm clock to facilitate waking up early in the morning consistently and reliably. Many products can achieve this purpose, such as optical clocks, smart curtains, and smartwatches; however, conventional recommendation systems will limit the displayed recommendations

---

[1] The Ministry of Internal Affairs and Communications Japan: Usage of Internet shopping and auction flea markets (in Japanese) https://www.soumu.go.jp/johotsusintokei/whitepaper/ja/r03/pdf/n1100000.pdf.

to various types of alarm clocks. In other words, the user cannot find a way to achieve the given purpose other than purchasing an alarm clock. Thus, the user is likely to select an alarm clock even when other suitable options are available. In terms of recommendation systems, this problem can be solved by identifying the purpose of the purchase as a query, *e.g.*, "getting up early in the morning."

Thus, in this paper, we propose a product recommendation algorithm that outputs a ranking of different functionally equivalent products by defining the purpose in a query. For example, if the target product is an alarm clock, the proposed algorithm will show candidate purposes, *e.g.*, "wake up early in the morning," "avoid being late," and "make a loud sound." The user can select a single purpose, *e.g.*, "waking up early in the morning," which is then taken as the input to the proposed algorithm. Here, the proposed algorithm determines if each product in the dataset is suitable for the identified purpose. The algorithm then identifies, ranks, and displays specific alternative products that can achieve the given purpose, *e.g.*, "morning light," "pillows," and "supplements." To achieve this, we focused on product reviews to realize a product recommendation system that takes the purchase purpose as the query input. Note that most online shopping services allow users to post reviews of products, which may include information about how the purchaser used the product.

We consider using the purpose contained in product review information to identify products with the same purpose and present them as alternatives. Specifically, assume that an algorithm recommends products that directly include the words "awake early in the morning" in their reviews. Such an algorithm would not present alternative products, which is the goal of the proposed algorithm. The first problem is that review information frequently contains spelling errors and grouping the same purposes is impossible. The second problem is that a direct search may output common or similar products as effective alternatives. For example, if the query is "alarm clock," and the purpose is to "avoid being late," it is obvious that many other types of alarm clocks will be output, *e.g.*, "light clocks" or "wrist watches with alarms." However, these alternative products do not broaden the user's perspective or change the thinking that an alarm clock is a singularly best product to avoid being late. Thus, we created a bipartite graph with the product, segmented the purpose's word groups as nodes, and performed a random walk with restart (RWR) calculation. Using bipartite graphs and RWR allows us to discover a wide range of alternative products, which cannot be realized using conventional search systems. In the context of the "alarm clock" example, by performing an edge transition for the query "prevent being late," an indirect purpose, *e.g.*, "improve the quality of sleep" may be discovered, and various products will be output, *e.g.*, "pillow" and "eye-mask."

To demonstrate the effectiveness of the proposed method, we conducted evaluation experiments using accurate data. The proposed method outputs a ranking of alternative products for as input for the purpose. In the experiments, participants were asked to label how the output products could achieve their purposes, how useful they were for their purchase decisions, and the overall accuracy of the product rankings. The usefulness of the proposed method was revealed by evaluating each of the rankings and products.

The remainder of this paper is organized as follows. In Sect. 2, we summarize related studies and present the position of this study. Section 3 describes the proposed method, and Sect. 4 describes an experiment conducted to evaluate and compare the proposed method to a baseline method. The experimental results are then discussed in Sect. 5. Finally, the paper is concluded in Sect. 6.

2   Related Work

We propose a product recommendation algorithm to identify and display alternative products for a given purpose. Thus, this study is closely related to the study of product recommendation algorithms and studies related to achievement.

2.1   Recommendation and Search of Products by Purpose

In this study, we attempt to identify products based on the purpose of the product, which is related to the study of product recommendation systems. In a previous study that considered the relationships among products, Ruining *et al.* [2] proposed Monomer, a method that treats product relationships as multiple concepts and allows recommendations that are unrestricted by categories or symmetry. This study differs because the proposed method treats the relationship between products as a single concept that utilizes the relationship between product reviews.

We attempted to identify and collect the purchase purpose from product review information. In a study that used product reviews, Lei *et al.* [14] proposed a product recommendation algorithm that divides reviews into two types, *i.e.*, one for the user's actions, and one for the product, and uses a neural network that shares a layer trained on each review. In addition, the recommendation system proposed by Sopheaktra *et al.* [12] takes product features as input and extracts and uses purposes related to the features from reviews using LDA and Word2Vec. This study differs because the proposed method does not utilize product characteristics. Instead, the proposed method seeks products based on the relationship between the purposes and products. Previous studies have also investigated product recommendation algorithms that focus on the purpose of use. For example, McAuley *et al.* [6] proposed a recommendation system that divides the products they recommend for purchase into interchangeable substitutes and complementary products purchased in addition to the identified interchangeable replacements. The current study differs in that the product is a different type of product that can realize the given purpose.

2.2   Serendipity of Recommendation

The proposed method differs from conventional recommendation systems in that it attempts to recommend products that can have a different perspective. Thus, this study is related to the study of recommending unexpected products [3]. For example, Kotkov *et al.* defined serendipitous product recommendations as those with three specific elements, *i.e.*, relevance, novelty, and unexpectedness.

As an example of serendipitous product recommendation, Kensuke *et al.* [7] proposed a recommendation method that uses a bipartite graph of users and items, as well as a bridging score that represents the degree of association between the nodes and the degree of the anomaly of the nodes. In addition, Akiyama *et al.* [1] constructed a human preference model of serendipity using data from a questionnaire about serendipity, and they proposed a recommendation method ranked by the length of item distance.

2.3 Achievement Products for the Purpose

The proposed algorithm outputs an alternative product by finding possible alternative purposes for the product. To extract potential alternative purposes, Pothirattanachaikul *et al.* [8] proposed a method to extract alternatives that can achieve the purposes from community question answering (CQA) sites. For example, assume that we are focusing on the behavior of "taking sleeping pills" to achieve the purpose of "solving sleep problems." In that case, we present an alternative behavior of "taking a walk before bedtime." The relationship between actions and purposes is a bipartite graph that utilizes the question-and-answer information from the CQA site. In addition, the similarity is ranked to discover alternative measures.

In addition, Yamamoto *et al.* [10] and Yang *et al.* [11] proposed a method to identify alternatives based on the relationship between the primary purposes and sub-purposes. Here, they defined "exercise" and "diet pills" as sub-goals to achieve the primary goal of "losing weight," and they proposed a method to cluster the sub-goals using sponsored search data. Yang *et al.* defined sub-tasks as "selecting a hotel" and "recruiting volunteers," *etc.*, which are required to accomplish the main task of "organizing a meeting," and they proposed a method that connects queries with the functions described in wikiHow. Based on the definitions of these alternatives, the proposed method performs calculations to identify alternative achievement proposals.

3   Graph-Based Method to Identify Alternative Products

This section describes a method that inputs the purpose for why a user wants to buy a certain product, and then outputs a ranking of alternative products that can satisfy the purpose. To realize this algorithm, the proposed method extracts sentences from product review data corresponding to the use purpose. We hypothesize that products with the same purpose are similar and substitutable. Based on this hypothesis, we assume that a graph-based computation is appropriate, and we identify potential alternative products by constructing a graph that represents the relationship between products and purposes.

3.1 Extracting Purposes from Product Review Data

In the proposed method, product review information is used as data to obtain the purpose of using a given product. The proposed method extracts phrases from strings, primarily using syntactic patterns. Note that the dataset considered in this study is in Japanese; thus, we explain the extraction method using Japanese grammar and vocabulary. This process differs depending on the target language; however, for grammatical reasons, it is generally easier in English.

In the review text, only a few parts of the text are related to the purpose; thus, the proposed method utilizes syntactic patterns to isolate the purposes from the review text data. Here, a two-step process is employed to identify the purpose. The first step involves extracting the purpose based on language patterns, and the second step involves selecting sentences using morphological analysis.

Prior to extracting the purpose, the review data are cleaned in a preprocessing step. For example, sentences that mention shop, shipping, and price are removed. We also remove sentences that contain terms that are irrelevant to the purpose, *e.g.*, "postage" and "wrapping."

An overview of the proposed purpose extraction method is illustrated in Fig. 1. First, the purposes are extracted using regular expressions. Here, if the extraction utilizes typical syntactic patterns, the sentences may become redundant. Redundant sentences are those that contain many words besides the purpose word, which can result in an excessive number of nodes when using graph processing–based algorithms.

Thus, we must extract on the required words and construct subgraphs that are effective for the corresponding calculation. In Japanese, due to the grammatical order of words, it is necessary to specify the words before and after to be interposed when extracting the purpose phrase in a language pattern. The front patterns include "when" ("*-toki*" in Japanese), and the back patterns include "for this purpose" ("*-tame-ni*" in Japanese). For example, consider the sentence "... *neru toki, kuraku suru tame-ni* ..." ("When I sleep, I want to make the room dark." For this purpose, I bought an eye-mask."). Here, the phrase "*kuraku suru*" ("make the room dark") is extracted. We manually collected 15 eligible terms for the front and back patterns, and we used their combination. Sentences containing the purchase purpose are frequently followed by words like "utilize" ("*ri-you*" in Japanese); thus, the extraction process is performed when these words are found after the matching sentence. In addition, sentences exceeding a certain length are excluded because redundant sentences may be extracted even when a language pattern matching process is employed.

Next, morphological analysis is performed to filter out only those sentences extracted by syntactic patterns that contain the purpose. Note that some of these syntactic patterns are commonly used expressions. For example, if a phrase is extracted with the language pattern "For," it may express a purpose, as in "For sleeping well," or it may refer to an object, as in "For children." In such cases, it is necessary to classify the extracted sentences by focusing on the part of speech of the words. In other words, in this case, if it were a verbal noun phrase, it would be a purpose, and if it were a noun, it would not be a purpose.

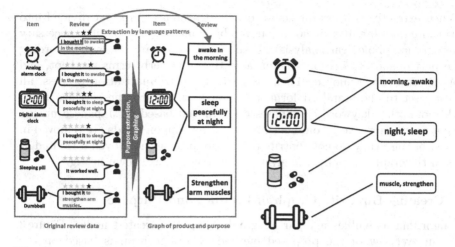

Fig. 1. Overview of generating product-purpose graphs using language pattern extraction.

Fig. 2. Example of nodes created by splitting purpose into words.

For each syntactic pattern, we created a list of the parts of speech from which the corresponding purpose could be extracted. Specific to the Japanese language, any noun can be converted into a verb using the suffix "-suru," and such verbs were treated as purposes by extracting the noun part.

Some other verbs related to "be" verbs and presence were listed and removed, e.g., "is," "are," "do," and "exist" (in Japanese: "aru," "iru," "suru," and "yaru").

In this study, we used the MeCab morphological analysis library[2]. In addition, as the word dictionary, Mecab-ipadic-NEologd[3], which includes new words and proper technical nouns, was used for the analysis.

3.2 Creating Nodes Comprising Multiple Purpose Terms

The proposed method constructs a bipartite graph using the extracted purposes; thus, the extracted purpose phrases are converted into a set of several terms to be used as nodes.

Note that these data can contain many different representations of the same purpose. For example, the simple purpose of "getting up early in the morning" can be expressed as "waking up before sunrise" or "early rising." However, the size of the graph would increase significantly if each of these unique expressions are used as nodes. Thus, we extract and lemmatize keywords from the purpose phrases. In the previous example, the words "wake," "early," and "morning" should be extracted. The extracted set of terms is then used as a node.

---

[2] MeCab: https://taku910.github.io/mecab/.
[3] Mecab-ipadic-Neologd : https://github.com/neologd/mecab-ipadic-neologd.

When extracting important keywords, short sentences are first divided into words (note that Japanese is not separated by white space; thus, it is necessary to perform morphological analysis). Then, some words are removed according to the part of speech, *i.e.*, only noun, adjective, and verb terms are kept, and all other terms are removed. Then, as part of the lemmatization process, all verbs are set to the standard form, and nouns are set to the singular form. In addition, other keyword candidates are removed based on Japanese unique frequent terms. Here, very common words and uncommon words are removed in this step because they do not contribute to score propagation (even if treated as nodes in the graph). Finally, the graph is constructed, as shown in Fig. 2.

3.3 Creating Bipartite Graph of Product and Purpose

Our algorithm assembles a bipartite graph using the created nodes. Figure 3 shows an overview of the proposed method. The algorithm is based on the hypothesis that if two products share many of the same achievable purposes, they may be substitutable for each other. Thus, the proposed method attempts to identify products that can achieve the same purpose by representing and calculating the relationship between similar products and purposes as a bipartite graph. Here, in the constructed graph, the reviewed products and word groups included in the purpose are nodes, which are connected by edges. The graphs are created as follows.

- Select a single product purpose and search for a product that has an edge to a word node contained in the purpose.
- For all obtained products, we search for products that have an edge to a word node in each purpose.
- The graph is constructed with the products obtained using the above process and the purpose word groups used in the search as nodes.

Rather than creating a graph using all product and purpose nodes, we select a particular product's purpose and create a subgraph using only the product and purpose nodes obtained from the two searches. This process is performed first because if all nodes are used, the size of the graph matrix will become too large to compute. Second, we attempt to prevent the edges from becoming less relevant as they are followed. If all nodes are used, there is a risk that they will be calculated as being related to a particular product, even if they are dozens of edges away. This is different from the substitutability defined in this study.

In addition, if a node is explored as it is, a recommendation of a purpose related to another purpose of the first product is made. For example, assume that a pillow has the purpose of "improving the quality of sleep at night" and "curing stiff shoulders," and that a search that selects the former finds the product. In this case, the following search finds the pillow again, thereby resulting in a search concerning the purpose of "curing stiff shoulders. " For this purpose, the edge to the first product is removed for the second and subsequent searches.

Here, let A be the adjacency matrix, let I be the set of commodity nodes, and let P be the set of destination nodes. In this case, matrix A comprises

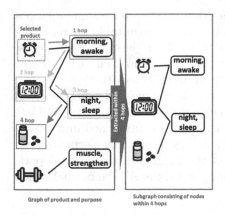

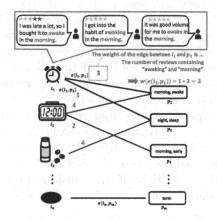

Fig. 3. Subgraph creation with graph search and extraction.

Fig. 4. Edge weighting using review texts containing purposes.

$(|I| + |P|) \times (|I| + |P|)$ dimensions, where the upper right and lower left of the matrix indicate the relationship from the product to the purpose and from the purpose to the product, respectively. Let $L_p(i_n)$ denote the set of P linked to i_n, and let $L_i(p_m)$ denote the set of I linked to p_n. In the upper right of the matrix, if I_n is contained in $L_i(p_m)$, the value of A_{nm} is 1; otherwise, the value is A_{nm} is 0.

3.4 Edge Weighting

The weight of each edge is set prior to performing the graph-based computation. Figure 4 shows an overview of the weighting technique used in the proposed method. Here, weighting is applied to focus on important words related to the product. Thus, weighting is performed using the occurrence frequency of words in the review text data. Some reviews were not extracted as purposes but contained the exact words as the extracted purposes. Thus, using the occurrence frequency of the purpose's words, it is possible to determine which words are essential. Here, if $|F_{nm}|$ is the frequency by which word p_m appears in the reviews of product i_n, the weight $w(e(i_n, p_m))$ of the edge $e(i_n, p_m)$ is expressed as follows:

$$w(e(i_n, p_m)) = |F_{nm}|. \qquad (1)$$

3.5 Random Walk with Restart

The method outputs a ranking of products that can achieve the desired purpose by calculating the degree of relevance between the nodes in the graph. Although many algorithms have been proposed to calculate the degree of association between nodes, the proposed method employs the RWR technique. Here, RWR is used in the proposed method based on the hypothesis that products have similar purposes and that the purposes of a given product have some relation-ship with each other. For example, "dish detergent" is unsuitable for removing stains from baths and cars; however, it can be used on glass. In other words, we can infer that another detergent used on glass can be used on dishes. These relationships can be obtained as values using the RWR calculation.

In the following, we describe the relevance calculation method using the RWR technique. First, the adjacency matrix A, which represents the graph of products and target word groups created up to the 3.4 clause, is transformed into a tran-sition probability matrix. This transformation is performed by normalization, where each column is divided by the sum of the weights of the edges depart-ing the node. Here, if the transition probability matrix is A', the normalization equation is defined as follows:

$$A'_{ij} = \frac{A_{ij}}{\sum_{k=1}^{|I|+|P|} A_{kj}}. \tag{2}$$

4 Evaluation

A subject experiment using real product data acquired from an e-commerce site (Rakuten Ichiba) was conducted to evaluate the usefulness of the proposed method. Two separate evaluations were considered in this experiment, one for the top-ranked alternatives and one for the rankings.

4.1 Dataset

In this experiment, we used product review data taken from Rakuten Ichiba, which is one of Japan's most popular e-commerce sites. The review data include review sentences, product names, and category data, and such data can be used to construct appropriate graphs. However, some of the review data were unsuit-able for our purpose; thus, the review data were filtered to eliminate inappro-priate data.

First, we excluded categorical data. There are 39 categories in the dataset, and each product is divided into large groups, e.g., "clothing," "home appli-ances," and "sports." The review data for products in the categories specified here were excluded. Examples of the excluded categories are only alternatives, e.g., "clothing" and "food," and those that cannot be substituted, e.g., "real estate" and "tickets."

Next, we excluded cases where the same review text was attached to multiple products. Products with the same review were excluded if they had the same review text at least once because this would affect the quality of the graph com-putation. After removing review data according to these processes, we obtained a dataset with a total of 44,834,987 reviews, and the number of products with review data was 180,910.

4.2   Implementation

The purposes were extracted from the acquired review data using regular expressions and MeCab, as described in Sect. 3.1. Finally, we obtained a total of 339,515 purposes.

Next, the words were segmented using MeCab to create word groups for the nodes. Here, only nouns, verbs, and adjectives were used, and the verbs were standardized. Finally, a total of 132,015 purpose nodes were obtained.

Then, the graph for the calculations was created. The preprepared query was divided into words, and the purpose node matching each word group was acquired. Then, we acquired the products related to the obtained word groups and searched for the products again using the word groups related to the products. A matrix representing the graphical relationships was created using the products and purposes obtained from these processes.

Finally, The RWR method was used to calculate the relevance of the product to the purpose. Here, the probability of a random jump to the query node was set to 0.8, and recursive calculations were performed until the results converged.

4.3   Compared Method

We prepared several variants to evaluate the usefulness of the proposed method.

1. **Proposed method.** This method calculates the relevance of the product-purpose graphs using the RWR technique.
2. **Unweighted graph.** Similar to the proposed method; however, edges are not weighted in this variant.
3. **Product description similarity.** This method calculates the similarity between the query and product descriptions using Doc2Vec.
4. **Keyword match.** This method finds products that contain all query terms in its review.
5. **Random**: This method selects products with reviews randomly.

4.4   Evaluation of Alternative Products

We prepared 25 queries and obtained product rankings in advance using the methods described in the previous section. Here, the participants labeled the top five items in all output rankings. The evaluation items included "Is it a direct solution?", "Is it an indirect solution?", "Did it help you in your purchasing decision?". In this evaluation, a four-point scale was used, with four being the most applicable, and one being the most minor practical.

4.5   Evaluation of Ranking

Three methods that enable ranking were considered in this study, *i.e.*, the proposed method, unweighted graph calculation, and the product description similarity calculation. These three methods were divided into two cases, *i.e.*, with and without category refinement, and a total of six methods were used to label the output rankings. The evaluation items included "Have you broadened your perspective?", "Is there diversity?", "Did you get motivated to buy products?", "Comprehensive evaluation." Here, a four-point scale is used, with four being the most applicable, and one being the most minor practical.

4.6 Experimental Results

In this study, the average of the responses of two participants was used as the evaluation value. In this case, Cohen's kappa values [4] for all items in each experiment was greater than 0.2, which indicates the reliability of the results.

Table 1 shows the mean values of the reasonable rates obtained in the evaluation experiments of the alternative products. The precision for each query is one if the average of the evaluated values is more significant than three on a five-point scale. The number of found is the average number of discoveries for all queries, the number of found for the proposed method, and the unweighted method is the number of nodes used in the calculation. We found that the unweighted graphing method was rated highly for all items. The proposed method exceeded the agreement of the purpose query in all reasonable rates, except for the "direct solution" item.

Table 2 shows the average values obtained in the ranking evaluation experiments. As can be seen, the proposed method narrowing was evaluated highly in terms of "perspective," and the unweighted graph calculation with narrowing for "diversity" received a high evaluation. The unweighted graph calculation without refinement was evaluated highly for the "motivated" to buy and "overall" rating items. The proposed method exceeds the baseline results (product description's similarity) in all terms.

Table 1. Precision of each method and each evaluation factor ($** : p < 0.01, * : p < 0.05$ to **Product Descriptions** method)

Methods	Direct solution	Indirect solution	Purchase decision	# Found
Proposed Method	**0.44	0.05	**0.50	759
Unweighted Graph	**0.46	0.06	**0.53	759
Product Description	0.34	0.04	0.14	-
Keyword Match	**0.43	0.04	**0.41	24
Random	**0.02	0.00	**0.03	-

Table 2. Average participant rating for each method when targeted to a specific product area (1 to 4, ** : $p < 0.01$, * : $p < 0.05$ to **Product Descriptions** method)

Methods	Categories	Perspective	Diversity	Motivating	Overall
Proposed method	Narrowed	**3.14	**3.44	**3.10	**3.14
Unweighted Graph	Narrowed	**3.12	**3.50	**3.24	**3.28
Product Descriptions	Narrowed	1.72	2.56	2.40	1.78
Proposed Method	All	**3.02	**3.30	**3.30	**3.12
Unweighted Graph	All	**3.04	**3.08	**3.60	**3.36
Product Descriptions	All	1.98	2.64	2.48	1.96

5 Discussion

First, an overall evaluation of the proposed method is discussed in terms of evaluating the alternative products. For all terms, we found that the proposed method exceeded the agreement on the baseline and the purpose keyword match. However, the results indicated that the unweighted graph calculation was the most effective method. Nonetheless, there were some cases where the proposed method was helpful for certain queries.

One such query was "Stretch out the wrinkles in your clothes." The higher precision can be attributed to many words related to the purpose, *e.g.*, "electric iron" and "sewing machine." For queries where the number of words is small and the types of products that can be explored are somewhat limited, words related reviews are more likely to appear.

A query for which the proposed method underperformed compared to the weighted computation was "Develop a sense of balance by training." One possible reason for the low precision for this query is that some words, *e.g.*, "house" and "home," that are unrelated to the original purpose, are assigned greater weight. Another reason may be that the weight is biased toward products with high review scores.

In addition, a query for which the results of both the proposed method and the weighted calculation were nearly the same was "Hang a picture on the wall." The reason why the precision results were similar for this query may be due to the small number of reviews for the selected products. To address this issue, the ratio of the number of reviews to the number of occurrences should be considered. The RWR algorithm enables the calculation of another indirect purpose or product that can achieve the same purpose.

The evaluation results of these experiments demonstrate that the proposed method can identify more products with higher accuracy than general search methods.

However, as a future issue, it will be necessary to reduce the number of oversight of words that express purpose. In the current search, there are cases where there is no combination of words in the query, and the search results must be examined. In addition, the extraction of purposes must be improved. In this study, the extraction process was based on language patterns; however, even if the expressions match, this does not necessarily mean that the identified product satisfies the given purpose. For example, when a product with a review that says it gets up early has a low rating, it is unlikely to solve the purpose. An effective weighting method must also be devised. The weighting technique implemented in the proposed method provides increased diversity; however, accuracy is reduced. Thus, more effective weighting methods should be investigated in future work.

6 Conclusion

In this paper, to prevent impulse buying, we have proposed a method to discover alternative products that can achieve the given purpose of using one product. For this purpose, the proposed method isolates the purpose of the product reviews according to language patterns and constructs a bipartite graph comprising products and purposes. Then, the weights of the edges are adjusted after the subgraphs are cut out for calculation. The RWR is then employed to calculate the graph, thereby making it possible to calculate another indirect purpose or product that can achieve the same purpose. [4]

Acknowledgments. This work was supported by JSPS KAKENHI Grants Number 21H03775, 21H03774, and 22H03905. We used "Rakuten Dataset [7]" provided by Rakuten Group, Inc. via IDR Dataset Service of National Institute of Informatics [9].

References

1. Akiyama, T., Obara, K., Tanizaki, M.: Proposal and evaluation of serendipitous recommendation method using general unexpectedness. In: PRSAT@ RecSys, pp. 3–10 (2010)
2. He, R., Packer, C., McAuley, J.J.: Monomer: non-metric mixtures-of-embeddings for learning visual compatibility across categories. arxiv abs/1603.09473 (2016). http://arxiv.org/abs/1603.09473
3. Kotkov, D., Wang, S., Veijalainen, J.: A survey of serendipity in recommender systems. Knowl.-Based Syst. **111**, 180–192 (2016). https://doi.org/10.1016/j.knosys.2016.08.014
4. Landis, J.R., Koch, G.G.: An application of hierarchical kappa-type statistics in the assessment of majority agreement among multiple observers. Biometrics, pp. 363–374 (1977)
5. Linden, G., Smith, B., York, J.: Amazon.com recommendations: item-to-item collaborative filtering. IEEE Internet Comput. **7**(1), 76–80 (2003). https://doi.org/10.1109/MIC.2003.1167344
6. McAuley, J., Pandey, R., Leskovec, J.: Inferring networks of substitutable and complementary products. In: Proceedings of the 21st ACM SIGKDD International Conference on Knowledge Discovery and Data Mining, p. 785–794 (2015). https://doi.org/10.1145/2783258.2783381

---

[4] Rakuten Dataset: https://rit.rakuten.com/data_release/.

7. Onuma, K., Tong, H., Faloutsos, C.: Tangent: A novel, 'surprise me', recommendation algorithm. In: Proceedings of the 15th ACM SIGKDD International Conference on Knowledge Discovery and Data Mining, p. 657–666 (2009). https://doi.org/10.1145/1557019.1557093

8. Pothirattanachaikul, S., Yamamoto, T., Fujita, S., Tajima, A., Tanaka, K.: Mining alternative actions from community q&a corpus for task-oriented web search. In: Proceedings of the International Conference on Web Intelligence, pp. 607–614 (2017). https://doi.org/10.1145/3106426.3106461

9. Rakuten Group, I.: Rakuten dataset (2020). https://doi.org/10.32130/idr.2.1, https://rit.rakuten.com/data_release/

10. Yamamoto, T., Sakai, T., Iwata, M., Yu, C., Wen, J.R., Tanaka, K.: The wisdom of advertisers: mining subgoals via query clustering. In: Proceedings of the 21st ACM International Conference on Information and Knowledge Management, CIKM 2012, pp. 505–514 (2012). https://doi.org/10.1145/2396761.2396827

11. Yang, Z., Nyberg, E.: Leveraging procedural knowledge for task-oriented search. In: Proceedings of the 38th International ACM SIGIR Conference on Research and Development in Information Retrieval, pp. 513–522 (2015). https://doi.org/10.1145/2766462.2767744

12. Yong, S., Asano, Y.: Purpose-feature relationship mining from online reviews towards purpose-oriented recommendation. IEICE Trans. Inf. Syst. **E101.D**(4), 1021–1029 (2018). https://doi.org/10.1587/transinf.2017DAP0013

13. Zhang, W., Leng, X., Liu, S.: Research on mobile impulse purchase intention in the perspective of system users during covid-19. In: Personal and Ubiquitous Computing, pp. 1–9 (2020)

14. Zheng, L., Noroozi, V., Yu, P.S.: Joint deep modeling of users and items using reviews for recommendation. In: Proceedings of the Tenth ACM International Conference on Web Search and Data Mining, pp. 425–434 (2017)

Deep Image Analysis for Microalgae Identification

Jeffrey Soar[1]([✉]) [iD], Oh Shu Lih[2] [iD], Loh Hui Wen[3] [iD], Aletha Ward[4] [iD],
Ekta Sharma[5] [iD], Ravinesh C. Deo[5] [iD], Prabal Datta Barua[1] [iD], Ru-San Tan[6] [iD],
Eliezer Rinen[7], and U Rajendra Acharya[5] [iD]

[1] School of Business, University of Southern Queensland, Springfield, Australia
soar@usq.edu.au
[2] Ngee Ann Polytechnic, Singapore, Singapore
[3] School of Science and Technology, Singapore University of Social Sciences, Singapore,
Singapore
[4] School of Nursing and Midwifery, University of Southern Queensland, Ipswich, Australia
[5] School of Mathematics, Physics and Computing, University of Southern Queensland,
Toowoomba, Australia
[6] Singapore National Heart Centre Singapore, and Duke-NUS Medical School, Singapore,
Singapore
[7] AlgaePharm, Goondiwindi 4390, Australia

Abstract. The current management of microalgae cultivation requires manual
microscopic examination in order to identify desired and competing species, as
well as predators. In this study, we trained and tested a transfer learning model
modified from EfficientNetV2 B3 model on 434 and 161 prospectively acquired
images of the preferred *Nanno-chloropsis* sp microalgae and competitor *Spirulina*,
respectively, and achieved >98% classification for both species on tenfold cross-
validation. The model was further enhanced with gradient-weighted class activation mapping, which allowed visualisation of regions of the input images that were
relevant to the classification, thereby improving its explainability. In this paper,
we demonstrate that a simple deep transfer learning model can help microalgae
farmers to identify and manage microalgae species. The application could enable
the widespread adoption of microalgae by more farmers as an enviroment-friendly,
drought-proof, and high-productive crop that can be grown on non-arable land and
use waste water.

Keywords: Microalgae · Artificial Intelligence · Deep Learning · Sustainability

1 Introduction

Burgeoning popularity and acceptance of plant-based protein consumption have brought
us a step closer to a more sustainable global food system. Among various sources of plant-
based products, wild edible seaweeds (or macroalgae) have traditionally been harvested
in many cultures [1, 2] but pressures on natural supplies [3] have instigated industrial-
scale marine macroalgae farming [4]; algae farming now supplies most of the market
demand. China is the largest producer of edible macroalgae farmed on suspended ropes
in the ocean; similar technology is used in Indonesia and other countries.

P. Delir Haghighi et al. (Eds.): iiWAS 2023, LNCS 14416, pp. 280–292, 2023.
https://doi.org/10.1007/978-3-031-48316-5_28

Macroalgae is an important source of hydrocolloids such as alginate, agar, and carrageenan which have been used as thickening and gelling agents in food, pharmaceuticals, and textile printing. Macroalgae have also long been used as a fertiliser, the high fibre content acts as a soil conditioner and the mineral content as a fertiliser. Increasing concerns about the environment as well as global warming and peak oil have driven interest in microalgae for biofuel. The potential for algae production particularly in developing countries has been recognised including by the Food and Agriculture Organisation of the United Nations [5].

Microalgae farming technology has enabled a shift in agricultural operations from the sea onto land over recent decades, offering better control, economies of scale, and greater ease of harvesting than macroalgae farming. Microalgae are a highly-productive and low-greenhouse-gas emission cash crop requiring only modest investment in equipment: a microalgae farm does not require arable land and can use waste water [6, 7]; microalgae grow fast, are continually harvestable [7], and can sequester carbon dioxide [8, 9]. Moreover, microalgae are highly nutritious with up to 60% protein content [8], rich in vitamins and minerals [10], and are associated with health benefits [10], which adds to their appeal and value. As a plant-based source of omega-3, microalgae are an alternative to unsustainable fish wild-catch which contain omega-3 only because of consumption of microalgae in the food-chain.

Microalgae farming has commonalities with other crops in that it needs water, nutrients as well as light to grow. As with any other crop grown in monoculture, microalgae crops can attract pests and diseases. Problems can include attack by predators, invasion by competitive species, toxic byproducts, bacteria, and viruses in the crop as well as in wastewater and harvested products. The harvested microalgae need to be dried as soon as possible before rot sets in. Management of the growing medium is one of the challenges of land-based microalgae farming. Water stagnation, toxic blooms, and slime proliferation are risks associated with poor quality control, which can cause concern among communities and jurisdictions located near microalgae production facilities. Local government approval of a microalgae farm in Goondiwindi, Queensland, Australia was contingent upon on the owners, AlgaePharm, properly managing water run-off, storm water, wastewater, security, landscaping, as well as fauna that might be attracted to the farm [11]. Meticulous monitoring of water and control of the media culture is critical to optimising the growth of the preferred microalgae species and for identifying and controlling competitor species and predators [12]. Manual media monitoring methods are laborious, require a high level of expertise and are prone to human error [13]. At the aforementioned AlgaePharm microalgae farm, which uses an open phototropic system to cultivate the *Nannochloropsis* oculate microalgae strain, manual microalgae crop monitoring at each pond currently requires one hour per day of skilled personnel trained in the microscopic analysis of microalgae species (AlgaePharm management, personal communication).

Considering the growth of digital automated technologies in applications of agriculture and the specific challenges faced by the microalgae farmers in managing their ponds, there is a need for efficient automated models for microalgae species identification. Deep learning-enabled image recognition, which has been widely applied to agricultural pest identification [14, 15], can be harnessed to automate the process of microalgae culture species classification, which is a key to building a sustainable healthy microalgae ecosystem and for detecting potential invaders and other threats. Wang et al., 2022 [16], reviewed IoT technologies that could be adopted for microalgae biorefinery and presented a model for microalgae environmental management that encompassed automation, sensors, lab-on-chip, machine learning, and the Internet of Things. Xu et al. 2022 [17], combined three-dimensional fluorescence with machine learning and deep learning to successfully distinguish microalgae that cause paralytic shellfish poisoning from those that do not. However, a fully automated microalgae species identification and pond management require more accurately trained models that are yet to be implemented

The purpose of this study was to develop a model for the systematic detection of microalgae species based on microscopic images, which is computationally lightweight and easy to implement for monitoring the growth media in microalgae farms using automatic detection models.

Specifically, this study: (i) acquired 595 images of the *Nannochloropsis sp* microalgae and competitor Spirulina and developed a transfer learning model, (ii) applied cross-validation to demonstrate excellent classification accuracy for both species on a tenfold cross-validation approach, and (iii) demonstrated the usefulness of the method in microalgae species identification and potential pond management applications for algae farming. Digital automation methods are essential to meet next-generation agriculture and food technologies needs [18]. Based on our studies, the proposed automation models can help streamline processes to reduce time and costs, increase accuracy, and allow for more data-driven decisions. The proposed automation approaches can also help increase efficiency of existing monitoring systems that are largely manual and reduce time spent, leading to a more sustainable future for agriculture and food production. The methods developed can give farmers a better approach for managing the algae ponds by automating monitoring and early detection of invader species and the other environmental perturbations that might require adjustments to environmental variables.

2 Materials and Methods

Our study is based on the premise that one of the challenges faced by researchers in this area is the limited availability of high-quality labelled image datasets to help identify the microalgae species, which constitute a barrier to research into and uptake of microalgae farming. For this study, we have prospectively acquired 434 images of healthy *Nannochloropsis sp.* microalgae, which was the preferred crop species, and 161 images of Spirulina from the Goondiwindi AlgaePharm growing ponds. The images were pre-processed by cropping with a 1:1 aspect ratio, resizing to 300×300, and then the step of converting the images to a red-green-blue (RGB) scale and normalising the pixels to -1 and 1.

Using an important technique of ten-fold cross-validation, the pre-processed images were fed to a pre-trained neural network called EfficientNetV2 B3 [19] which then classified them into *Nannochloropsis oculate* and Spirulina classes based on the pre-processed images. To visualise the most informative parts of the pre-processed input images, we also applied gradient-weighted class activation mapping (Grad-CAM) to the modified EfficientNetV2 B3 transfer learning model (Fig. 1). It should be noted that

EfficientNetV2 B3, like many deep learning models, is a "black box" model in which the inner workings of how the model predicts the results are indecipherable by design [20], which may prevent its acceptance by application developers. An explainable artificial intelligence technique, Grad-CAM is typically applied to the final layer of CNN models to generate a heatmap of the relative contributory importance of different regions within the input images to the prediction [21], which allows for some degree of interpretation of model predictions.

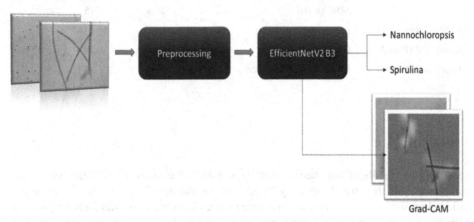

Fig. 1. Study workflow.

The present study employed a robust transfer learning model, EfficientNetV2 B3 [19], which is a type of convolutional neural network (CNN). While convolutional neural network models are widely used for image recognition tasks, EfficientNetV2 B3 takes it up to another level with training-aware neural architecture search, which accelerates the learning rate and improves parameter effectiveness. In our study, we have modified EfficientNetV2 B3 by freezing the base model except for the fully-connected layers, which were removed and replaced by batch normalisation, the dropout layer (0.2), and three other trainable fully-connected layers (Table 1). The model was trained with the Adam optimiser [22] with a 0.001 learning rate, batch size of 5, and run with 10 epochs. A weighted loss function was also incorporated into the model to mitigate dataset class imbalance during training.

Classification performance was evaluated using standard metrics: accuracy, sensitivity, specificity, and precision.

Table 1. The architecture of modified EfficientNetV2 B3 network used in this study.

Phase	Layer parameter	Stride	Filter No	No. of layers
1	Conv	2	24	1
2	Fused-MBConv1	1	24	2

(continued)

Table 1. (*continued*)

Phase	Layer parameter	Stride	Filter No	No. of layers
3	Fused-MBConv4	2	48	4
4	Fused-MBConv4	2	64	4
5	MBConv4	2	128	6
6	MBConv6	1	160	9
7	MBConv6	2	256	15
Modified 8 (Part 1)	Batch normalisation	–	–	1
Modified 8 (Part 2)	Dropout (0.2)	–	–	1
Modified 8 (Part 3)	Fully-connected layer	–	–	3

3 Results

Based on the results of the classification experiment, the modified EfficientNetV2 B3 model was able to correctly identify 98.32% of the dataset (Table 2). As shown in the table below, we have calculated performance metrics separately for Nannochloropsis and Spirulina samples. Our model is reliable since it can independently determine whether a sample is Nannochloropsis or Spirulina, it does not classify all samples in a binary fashion as one of the two. After training the model with multiple data augmentation techniques, we observed an increase in the accuracy of the model compared to the baseline model. This demonstrates that our model is able to identify the differences between Nannochloropsis and Spirulina samples more accurately. Furthermore, the model was able to correctly identify 98.32% of the dataset, which further confirms the robustness of our model.

Table 2. Performance metrics of modified EfficientNetV2 B3 model after 10-fold cross-validation.

	Nannochloropsis sp.	Spirulina
Accuracy	98.32%	98.32%
Sensitivity	98.85%	96.89%
Specificity	96.89%	98.85%
Precision	98.85%	96.89%

As can be seen from the confusion matrix, there is a very low rate of misclassification within each class, resulting in only five samples being classified incorrectly from each (Fig. 2). Based on the confusion matrix, the classification can either be binary or non-binary. For example, Nano 429/434 is correctly classified as Spirulina, while Spirulina

5/434 is incorrectly classified. As illustrated in Fig. 3, the performance graph generated during EfficientNetV2 B3 training also indicates that the model did not overfit, which corresponds to the number in brackets. The confusion matrix provides a visual representation of the model's performance. It shows the number of true positives, false positives, false negatives and true negatives, which can then be used to calculate the accuracy, precision, recall and other metrics that measure the model's performance. The performance graph also shows the model's performance over the course of training, which can be used to detect overfitting.

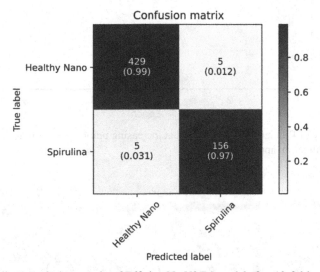

Fig. 2. Normalised confusion matrix of EfficientNetV2 B3 model after 10-fold cross-validation.

As illustrated in Fig. 4, heatmaps created by Grad-CAM were superimposed over preprocessed images of *Nannochloropsis sp.* and Spirulina samples as inputs. On the basis of a visual inspection, the regions that were flagged as highly relevant for model classification by Grad-CAM also overlap significantly with the microorganisms. It supports the contention that the EfficientNetV2 B3 model is capable of automatically focusing attention more specifically on relevant areas of an image to perform the classification process. This suggests that EfficientNetV2 B3 model has the potential to be a reliable classifier for microorganism identification in microscopic images.

Figure 4 shows Grad-CAM generated heatmaps for *Nannochloropsis sp.* (a) and Spirulina (b). The red regions denote regions that were highly relevant for classification; and the blue regions are irrelevant. These heatmaps enable us to quantitatively measure the relative importance of each region for the classification, with red regions indicating the most important features and blue regions indicating the least important features. By using the heatmaps, it became clear which regions of the images were most important for the classification and which were not, allowing us to gain a better understanding of the models used.

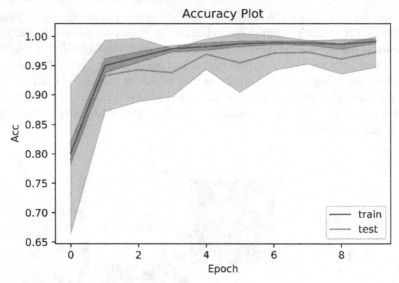

Fig. 3. Accuracy of EfficientNetV2 B3 model at increasing numbers of training epochs during a ten-fold cross-validation approach.

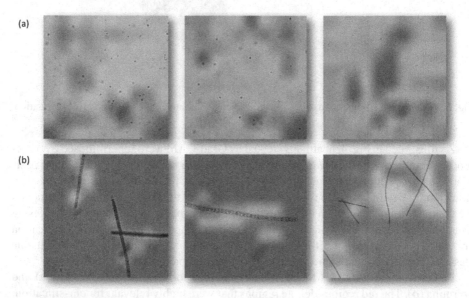

Fig. 4. Grad-CAM generated heatmaps for *Nannochloropsis sp.* (a) and Spirulina (b).

4   Discussion

We modified an existing deep transfer learning classifier, EfficientNetV2 B3, to per-form automated image-based classification of microalgae species. The application is novel and the proposed system is simpler, requires minimal pre-processing, is less computationally demanding and yields commensurate accuracy compared with previous works (Table 3). Luo et al. 2021 [23], proposed a support vector machine or deep learning model to distinguish one species of individual microalgae from another with high accuracy. They also demonstrated the feasibility of the use of a confocal hyper-spectral microscopic imager in the analysis of the concentration, species, and distribution differences of microalgae. Specifically, they used the model to identify the species of microalgae in a range of different concentrations, including those found in natural environments. The model was able to accurately classify the species with a high degree of accuracy, demonstrating the potential of the model for use in microalgae research.

Baladehi et al. 2021 [24], established an approach for rapidly identifying and metabolically profiling single cells, either cultured or uncultured, using pigment spectrum and whole spectrum, which could accelerate the mining of microalgae and their products. Mirasbekov et al. 2021 [25], employed machine learning to detect and quantify Microcystis colonial morphospecies using the FlowCAM-based imaging flow device. They demonstrated the proof-of-concept of how machine learning approaches could be applied to analyse microalgae. The authors used an imaging flow device to capture images of the microalgae and then used machine learning algorithms to analyse the images. They were able to accurately classify the different morphospecies of Microcystis, showing how machine learning can be used as a powerful tool for analysis.

Wang et al. 2020 [26], used a label-free method to identify living and dead algae cells based on digital holographic microscopy and machine learning. Memmolo et al 2020 [27], used convolutional neural network models to classify diatoms on dry slide images to avoid the time-consuming steps of water sampling and labelling by skilled marine biologists. The network model was then validated by using holographic recordings of live diatoms imaged in water samples. Xu et al. 2020 [28], performed hyperspectral imaging of three species of microalgae to verify their absorption characteristics. They demonstrated the feasibility of the technology for evaluating the growth state of microalgae through their transmission spectra.

Building on all these studies, we have developed a model that could automatically identify microalgae—both the preferred and invader species—with high accuracy, thereby realising the potential of transfer deep learning for real-world applications. With appropriate and larger training datasets, the work could be extended for the classification of other microalgae classes. For microalgae farming, species identification is but the first step. By linking the classification results to a real-time intelligent database, deep learning could provide timely decision-support: upon detecting populations it could advise the farmer of required interventions to produce the desired response in crop growth or time to harvest, e.g., water rotation, nutrient supply, water treatment, etc.

Our results are of practical value considering that in order to gain the most benefit from microalgae farming, farmers must have a thorough understanding of the species being grown, and the ability to implement the necessary adjustments to produce desired results. Deep learning technology can provide real-time decision-support, helping the farmer optimise crop growth and harvest times through interventions such as water rotation, nutrient supply, and water treatment.

Table 3. Comparison of our model with published literature on automated microalgae detection.

Study	Algae	Input	Model (DL/ML)	Accuracy
Luo et al. (2021)	Microalgae	Confocal hyperspectral microscopic imaging	DNN (DL)	98.34%
Baladehi et al. (2021)	Single-cell Raman	Pigment spectrum & whole spectrum	Ensemble learning (ML)	97%
Mirasbekov et al. (2021)	Microcystis colony	FlowCAM imaging	VisualSpreadsheet software (ML)	96–100%
Wang et al. (2020)	Living and dead microalgae cells	Digital holography amplitude & phase information	SVM (ML)	94.8%
Memmolo et al. (2020)	Diatoms	Holographic microscopy slides	Ensemble CNN (DL)	98%
Xu et al. (2020)	Microalgae	Transmission hyperspectral microscopic imaging	SVM (ML)	94.4%
This work	Microalgae	Microscopic imaging	EfficientNetV2 B3 (DL)	98.32%

The advantages of the proposed method in this study are as follows:

1. To the best of our knowledge, we are the first group to classify healthy *Nannochloropsis sp.* microalgae and Spirulina classes with an accuracy of >98%.
2. The developed model is robust as we have employed a ten-fold cross-validation strategy.
3. We have provided explainable AI to visualise the heatmaps in the *Nannochloropsis sp.* and Spirulina classes.

In spite of good performance of the proposed model for microalgae identification, one of the limitations of our work is that we have developed the model using a small dataset of 434 images of healthy *Nannochloropsis sp.* microalgae, which was the preferred crop species, and 161 images of Spirulina. In the future, we plan to validate our model using more images taken from other ponds. Also, we intend to consider more classes of algae images. This means that the model is unable to accurately identify microalgae of other species, as it has only been trained on images of Nannochloropsis and Spirulina. Additionally, since the dataset is relatively small, the model may not be able to generalise well to other ponds and environments, and more images from different ponds would be needed to improve accuracy. We used the balanced dataset but in the future we will explore the possibility of using problem of imbalanced label distribution problem and transfer-learning problem to mimic real-world scenarios.

In an era of increasing concern about the environment and global warnings as well as peak oil, there is potential for greater investment in microalgae for biofuel, for its high nutritional value and for its high productivity compared to other agricultural crops. Grown on non-arable land and utilising almost any source of water, microalgae farming has the potential internationally as an environmentally friendly source of biofuels, animal/human food, nutraceuticals, cosmetics, and plastics. A key threat to microalgae farming is pest attack, damaging a crop overnight (a 'crash'), and taking a long time to recover. Current pest or invader identification methods are largely manual, time-consuming, and prone to human error, impacting productivity. Our innovation will make microalgae farming accessible to more farmers around the world. Our innovation uses machine learning and image recognition technology to identify pests and invaders quickly and accurately. By automating the pest identification process, microalgae farmers will be able to act more quickly to protect their crops and reduce the risk of crop failure.

In the past the technology for algae farming was simple, such as harvesting from the sea or growing macroalgae on structures that can be pulled out to harvest it. Technology has opened up large-scale microalgae monoculture production in controlled environments primarily on land which provides economies of scale. It is a potential additional or main crop for many farmers; it could be an attractive option for Australia and many countries with abundant sunlight. Whilst building the required shallow ponds and installing equipment may not be challenging in terms of cost or expertise, few farmers are likely to have the expertise to identify and monitor the populations. An AI-based system could help farmers with monitoring their microalgae crop to identify the health of the preferred species and the presence of invaders and respond appropriately in adjusting variables. With an AI-based automation system, farmers will be able to monitor the health of the microalgae crop in real-time, while also being able to adjust variables in order to create an optimal environment for the desired species. Additionally, AI-based systems can also be used to detect any unwanted invaders before they become a problem, allowing farmers to take preventative measures to protect their crop.

The preliminary development of the modified EfficientNetV2 B3 model presented in this paper offers potential public benefit by making microalgae farming expertise more available to the farming community, improving drought resistance and farm productivity, reducing labour needs, and reducing pesticide use through early detection of unwanted species. Improving farm resilience benefits regions, the economy, and human health through the high nutritional value of microalgae and the environment to develop and improve productivity and environmental resilience.

5 Conclusions

In this study, we have demonstrated that a simple deep transfer learning model, denoted as modified EfficientNetV2 B3, developed for the classification of microalgae species can be feasible and accurate in order to classify microalgae. There is a practical need for robust automated monitoring of preferred and invader microalgae populations in industrial microalgae farms to ensure the sustainability of the farms. Therefore this detection model has been developed in order to satisfy that practical need. This model also has the potential to help improve the efficiency and sustainability of industrial microalgae farms, thereby helping to ensure their future success.

For effective management of the culture, it is necessary to identify the culture in a way that produces a consistent and predictable output. It is anticipated that if the model is successfully implemented, there is the potential to increase the productivity of microalgae farming, as well as to promote the use of microalgae as a viable alternative source of plant-based protein and other products once the model has been successfully implemented.

By creating a model that is based on the identification of the culture, managers can better understand the unique characteristics of the microalgae, allowing them to make informed decisions about how to best utilise the resources available to them. This in turn can lead to more efficient management of the microalgae farm, as well as improved outcomes for the products produced.

Acknowledgments. The authors acknowledge AlgaePharm, Goondiwindi, Australia for the supply of all images that were used in the research.

Author Contributions:. Conceptualisation, J.S., R.A., A.W.; methodology, R.A.; software, O.D.L, L.H.W.; validation, J.S., R.A., E.S, R.C.D.; formal analysis, R.A., E.S., R.C.D., O.S.L, L.H.W; investigation, J.S., R.A, O.S.L, E.S, R.C.D., A.W., L.H.W.; resources, E.R., L.H.W.; data curation, E.R., E.S, R.C.D.; writing—original draft preparation, J.S., R.A., E.S., R.C.D.; writing—review and editing, J.S., R.A., E.S, R.C.D., A.W.; visualisation, J.S., R.A.; supervision and project administration, J.S., R.A.; data acquisition, E.R. All authors have read and agreed to the published version of the manuscript.

Funding:. This research received no external funding.

Institutional Review Board Statement: Not applicable.

Data Availability Statement:. Data are available on request to the Corresponding Author.

Conflicts of Interest: The authors declare no conflict of interest.

Disclaimer/Publisher's Note: The statements, opinions and data contained in all publications are solely those of the individual author(s) and contributor(s) and not of MDPI and/or the editor(s). MDPI and/or the editor(s) disclaim responsibility for any injury to people or property resulting from any ideas, methods, instructions or products referred to in the content.

References

1. Buchholz, C.M., Krause, G., Buck, B.H.: Seaweed and man. In: Wiencke, C., Bischof, K. (eds.) Seaweed Biology: Novel Insights into Ecophysiology, Ecology and Utilization, pp. 471–493. Springer Berlin Heidelberg, Berlin, Heidelberg (2012). https://doi.org/10.1007/978-3-642-28451-9_22
2. Merz, C., Main, K.: Microalgae (diatom) production—the aquaculture and biofuel nexus. In: Oceans'14 MTS/IEEE Conference Proceedings – IEEE Xplore, St. John's, NL, Canada (2014). https://doi.org/10.1109/OCEANS.2014.7003242
3. Mac Monagail, M., Cornish, L., Morrison, L., Araújo, R., Critchley, A.T.: Sustainable harvesting of wild seaweed resources. Eur. J. Phycol. **52**, 371–390 (2017). https://doi.org/10.1080/09670262.2017.1365273

4. Marsham, S., Scott, G.W., Tobin, M.L.: Comparison of nutritive chemistry of a range of temperate seaweeds. Food Chem. **100**, 1331–1336 (2007). https://doi.org/10.1016/j.foodchem.2005.11.029

5. Cai, J., et al.: Seaweeds and microalgae: an overview for unlocking their potential in global aquaculture development. FAO Fisheries and Aquaculture Circular (1229) (2021). https://doi.org/10.4060/cb5670en

6. Griffiths, M.J., Harrison, S.T.L.: Lipid productivity as a key characteristic for choosing algal species for biodiesel production. J. Appl. Phycol. **21**, 493–507 (2009). https://doi.org/10.1007/s10811-008-9392-7

7. Andrade, D.S., et al.: Microalgae: cultivation, biotechnological, environmental, and agricultural applications. In: Maddela, N.R., García, L.C., Cruzatty, S.C. (eds.) Advances in the Domain of Environmental Biotechnology: Microbiological Developments in Industries, Wastewater Treatment and Agriculture, pp. 635–701. Springer Singapore, Singapore (2021). https://doi.org/10.1007/978-981-15-8999-7_23

8. Benedetti, M., Vecchi, V., Barera, S., Dall'Osto, L.: Biomass from microalgae: the potential of domestication towards sustainable biofactories. Microb. Cell Fact. **17** (2018). https://doi.org/10.1186/s12934-018-1019-3

9. McGinn, P.J., Dickinson, K.E., Bhatti, S., Frigon, J.-C., Guiot, S.R., O'Leary, S.J.B.: Integration of microalgae cultivation with industrial waste remediation for biofuel and bioenergy production: opportunities and limitations. Photosynth. Res. **109**, 231–247 (2011). https://doi.org/10.1007/s11120-011-9638-0

10. Caporgno, M.P., Mathys, A.: Trends in microalgae incorporation into innovative food products with potential health benefits. Front. Nutr. **5** (2018). https://doi.org/10.3389/fnut.2018.00058

11. Goondiwindi Regional Council. Communication of decision. mail@grc.qld.gov.au - Goondiwindi Regional Council. 27 November 2018 https://www.grc.qld.gov.au/downloads/file/1028/17-48g-decision-notice

12. Renuka, N., Guldhe, A., Prasanna, R., Singh, P., Bux, F.: Microalgae as multi-functional options in modern agriculture: current trends, prospects and challenges. Biotechnol. Adv. **36**, 1255–1273 (2018). https://doi.org/10.1016/j.biotechadv.2018.04.004

13. Deore, P., Beardall, J., Noronha, S.: A perspective on the current status of approaches for early detection of microalgal grazing. J. Appl. Phycol. **32**, 3723–3733 (2020). https://doi.org/10.1007/s10811-020-02241-x

14. He, Y., Zeng, H., Fan, Y., Ji, S., Wu, J.: Application of deep learning in integrated pest management: a real-time system for detection and diagnosis of oilseed rape pests. Mob. Inf. Syst. **2019**, 1–14 (2019). https://doi.org/10.1155/2019/4570808

15. Liu, L., et al.: PestNet: an end-to-end deep learning approach for large-scale multi-class pest detection and classification. IEEE Access **7**, 45301–45312 (2019). https://doi.org/10.1109/access.2019.2909522

16. Wang, K., et al.: How does the Internet of Things (IoT) help in microalgae biorefinery? Biotechnol. Adv. **54**, 107819 (2022). https://doi.org/10.1016/j.biotechadv.2021.107819

17. Xu, W., et al.: Identification of paralytic shellfish toxin-producing microalgae using machine learning and deep learning methods. J. Ocean. Limnol. **40**, 2202–2217 (2022). https://doi.org/10.1007/s00343-022-1312-1

18. Austrade, Australian Government. Australia: shaping the future of food and agriculture. https://www.austrade.gov.au/agriculture. Accessed 11 Feb 2022

19. Tan, M., Le, Q.: EfficientNetV2: smaller models and faster training. In Proceedings of the 38th International Conference on Machine Learning/Proceedings of Machine Learning Research. PMLR 139, 14 December 2021. https://proceedings.mlr.press/v139/tan21a.html

20. Selvaraju, R.R., Das, A., Vedantam, R., Cogswell, M., Parikh, D., Batra, D.: Grad-CAM: Why did you say that?. arXiv preprint arXiv:1611.07450. 2016 Nov 22

21. Selvaraju, R.R., Cogswell, M., Das, A., Vedantam, R., Parikh, D., Batra, D.: Grad-CAM: visual explanations from deep networks via gradient-based localization. Int. J. Comput. Vis. **128**, 336–359 (2020). https://doi.org/10.1007/s11263-019-01228-7
22. Zhang, Z.: Improved adam optimizer for deep neural networks. In: IEEE/ACM 26th International Symposium on Quality of Service (IWQoS) (2018). https://doi.org/10.1109/IWQoS.2018.8624183
23. Luo, J., et al.: Confocal hyperspectral microscopic imager for the detection and classification of individual microalgae. Opt. Express **29**, 37281 (2021). https://doi.org/10.1364/OE.438253
24. Heidari Baladehi, M., et al.: Culture-free identification and metabolic profiling of microalgal single cells via ensemble learning of ramanomes. Anal. Chem. **93**, 8872–8880 (2021). https://doi.org/10.1021/acs.analchem.1c01015
25. Mirasbekov, Y., et al.: Semi-automated classification of colonial Microcystis by FlowCAM imaging flow cytometry in mesocosm experiment reveals high heterogeneity during seasonal bloom. Sci. Rep. **11** (2021). https://doi.org/10.1038/s41598-021-88661-2
26. Wang, Y., Ju, P., Wang, S., Su, J., Zhai, W., Wu, C.: Identification of living and dead microalgae cells with digital holography and verified in the East China Sea. Mar. Pollut. Bull. **163**, 111927 (2021). https://doi.org/10.1016/j.marpolbul.2020.111927
27. Memmolo, P., et al.: Learning diatoms classification from a dry test slide by holographic microscopy. Sensors **20**, 6353 (2020). https://doi.org/10.3390/s20216353
28. Xu, Z., Jiang, Y., Ji, J., Forsberg, E., Li, Y., He, S.: Classification, identification, and growth stage estimation of microalgae based on transmission hyperspectral microscopic imaging and machine learning. Opt. Express **28**, 30686 (2020). https://doi.org/10.1364/OE.406036

Provenance-Aware Data Integration and Summarization Querying for Knowledge Graphs

Pei-Yu Hou[✉], Jing Ao, Kara Schatz, Alexey V. Gulyuk,
Yaroslava G. Yingling, and Rada Chirkova

North Carolina State University, Raleigh 27695, USA
{hpeiyu,jao,kmschat2,agulyuk,ygyingli,rychirko}@ncsu.edu

Abstract. Knowledge graphs are an increasingly popular choice for integrating heterogeneous data that have been collected independently from multiple sources. In many scenarios, including research and industry collaborations, the source data can be provided at different granularities, that is at more detailed and independently at more summarized levels, each with its own ontology. In such scenarios it is often important to find justifications at a more detailed data level for the data at a more summarized level, that is to find correct *provenance of the existing summarized data*. To address this previously unexplored challenge, in this paper we present a framework for enabling provenance-aware knowledge-graph integration and querying for such hierarchical data. We introduce the proposed domain-independent algorithms, outline their implementation, and report experimental results for two real-life application domains. The findings suggest that our proposed framework can be effective and efficient in enabling provenance-aware summarization querying across hierarchical knowledge-graph data.

Keywords: Knowledge graphs · Data integration · Data provenance

1 Introduction

Understanding the provenance of the data of interest may help disclose and explain potential root causes of phenomena or problems in many applications. For this reason, the topic of provenance has been extensively studied in data analytics, see, e.g., [1,7,16]. In this paper, we focus on provenance-derivation challenges that arise in real-life scenarios in which *pre-summarized* (lower-level) and *summarized* (higher-level) data are collected independently from disparate sources. This process causes the collected data to be *hierarchical,* with the pre-summarized data being more fine-grained and detailed, and the summarized data providing higher-level information. Such scenarios apply to a variety of domains, including materials science, pharmaceutics, and antimicrobial resistance.

In this scope, we formulate and address the novel problem of *provenance-aware summarization querying*. We use this term to refer to retrieval from the

P. Delir Haghighi et al. (Eds.): iiWAS 2023, LNCS 14416, pp. 293–308, 2023.
https://doi.org/10.1007/978-3-031-48316-5_29

data of the pre-summarized values that have contributed to the derivation of the summarized values of interest. In this paper, we consider this problem for cases where the data are stored using the popular *knowledge-graph (KG)* data model.

To enable provenance-aware summarization querying across hierarchical (that is, pre-summarized *and* summarized) data, the data need to be integrated first. Unfortunately, existing data-integration and provenance solutions, see, e.g., [14,19], do not focus on building meaningful connections between existing data values at different summarization levels that come from different sources. This shortcoming can pose significant challenges to data analysts in performing effective and efficient provenance-aware summarization querying in practice. The approaches introduced in this paper can be used to address the challenges.

Motivating Example. Figure 1 showcases a toy example involving biomedical data that are represented in the KG format, with pre-summarized data shown in Fig. 1(a) and summarized data shown in Fig. 1(b). We refer to these data as *standard-level* and *summary-level*, respectively. Figure 1(a) details biological interactions between the drug Losartan and the disease hypertension through two genes, AGTR1 and REN; among the two paths, only the path that involves AGTR1 is the biological justification for the drug treating the disease. Figure 1(b) shows summary-level drug-treats-disease relationships involving Losartan, another drug Captopril, and hypertension; the relationships indicate that both drugs treat the disease, but do not detail the nature of the interactions.

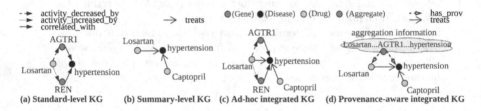

Fig. 1. The motivating example.

Suppose that, after observing the Losartan-treats-hypertension relationship in Fig. 1(b), a research team would like to pose a provenance-aware summarization query to understand the mechanism of the treatment, that is the biological interactions enabling the treats relationship. For this purpose, the team needs to first integrate the KGs of Fig. 1(a) and 1(b), and then pose the query on the existing summarized data of interest in the integrated graph. The team can easily integrate the graphs by merging (by node ID) their common entities and by listing all the relationships present in the input KGs, see Fig. 1(c). Unfortunately, the resulting integrated KG cannot single out the gene AGTR1 that biologically justifies the Losartan-treats-hypertension relationship, since the integration procedure has not specified how the treats relationship arises from the underlying biological evidence.

Alternatively, suppose that the provenance information of the `Losartan-treats-hypertension` relationship is introduced to the integration process as suggested in Fig. 1(d). Note how the integrated KG provides just the biologically meaningful provenance information for the relationship, as shown via the dotted line in Fig. 1(d), referring correctly to the gene `AGTR1` whose involvement explains the relationship. The research team can now obtain a correct answer to their provenance-aware summarization query on `Losartan-treats-hypertension`.

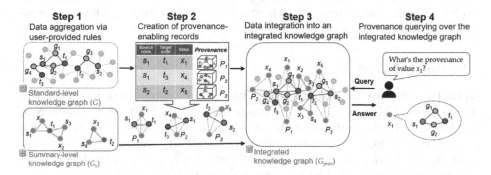

Fig. 2. The workflow for the proposed approach for setting up and retrieving provenance information for data in knowledge graphs across granularity levels.

The Proposed Approach. In this paper, we formulate and address the problem of automatically enabling provenance-aware data integration and summarization querying across hierarchical KG data. We focus on the scenario in which the summary-level (aggregate) data and the standard-level (provenance) data were collected independently in different KGs, rules for aggregating standard-level data into summary-level data are available from domain experts, and the users are interested in correct and efficient processing of provenance queries posed on the summary-level data. Our proposed approach is a data-integration and query-answering framework shown in Fig. 2 that (i) automatically integrates provenance and aggregate data from the input KGs, and (ii) enables answering of provenance-aware summarization queries over the integrated graph using the ontology of the summary-level graph in the queries. Our integration process uses novel algorithms to identify and retain correct provenance for the given aggregate (summarized) data. The algorithms also enable effective and efficient retrieval of the provenance data for the aggregate data of interest to users.

Our specific contributions are as follows.

- We formalize the problem of provenance-aware data integration and summarization querying of hierarchical data in the context of knowledge graphs;
- We address the problem by introducing an approach that enriches the aggregate data with provenance information during integration, and then uses the enriched integrated graph to correctly answer provenance queries on the existing summarized data; and

– We report experimental results for two real-life application domains with an implementation of the proposed approach. The results suggest that the proposed approach consistently enriches the given aggregated data with correct provenance information, and that the summarization-querying process is effective and efficient in retrieving the correct provenance information.

Paper Outline. We review related work in Sect. 1.1 and formalize the problem in Sect. 2. Section 3 introduces our proposed approach. Section 4 details the implementation and reports our experimental results with respect to two real-world application domains. We conclude in Sect. 5.

1.1   Related Work

Data Integration for Knowledge Graphs. In general, data integration in the context of KGs focuses on merging common entities [6,12,15], to enable connectivity and interoperability of the data coming from different sources. Some projects use machine-learning techniques and similarity metrics for entity alignment [6,12,15], while others use specific predicates (e.g., `owl:sameAs` in RDF) to construct mappings and assign canonical identifiers to entities [25].

In contrast, in this paper we focus on tracking the pre-summarized provenance information of summary-level data across different KGs during data integration, as well as on enabling correct and efficient provenance-query answering on the integrated KGs. Our contributions are complementary to those in the projects that focus on entity alignment, as we assume that the entity alignment between the KGs in question has already been performed. Thus, our work can be viewed as a downstream step following entity alignment in data integration.

Provenance-aware Data Querying. Existing projects that are related to provenance-aware data aggregation mostly focus on processing relational queries that perform data summarization (that is, aggregation) at runtime [2,17]. We, on the other hand, provide integration of knowledge-graph data at two different levels of detail (summarized and pre-summarized), while enabling provenance querying on the already existing summarized data. Some recent works have reported results on provenance-aware data querying over a single KG; however, the focus of their provenance analysis is in identifying the document source [21]. In contrast, our aim is to find all the data that contribute to a certain aggregate value. Some works use semi-rings [3,8], with *why* provenance explaining why an answer is part of a query result [5], and with *how* provenance providing information about the derivation of the answers [9]. While these works study the provenance issues for common insert, delete, and update operations, they do not directly address the provenance of aggregated values, which is our focus in this current paper. In addition, to the best of our knowledge, unlike our work none of these projects consider scenarios that involve multiple KGs with different ontologies.

2   Preliminaries and Problem Statement

In this section we formalize the novel problems of provenance-aware integration of hierarchical knowledge-graph data and of summarization querying on knowledge graphs. In the formal development, we view a *knowledge graph (KG) G* as a directed graph $G = (\mathcal{V}, \mathcal{E}, T_{\mathcal{V}}, T_{\mathcal{E}})$, in which each *node* $v \in \mathcal{V}$ and each *edge* $e \in \mathcal{E}$ has an associated type in $T_{\mathcal{V}}$ and $T_{\mathcal{E}}$, respectively. We define a KG *ontology* as a specification of a shared conceptualization [10]:

Definition 1. Ontology. *Let C be a conceptualization and $V = (N, E)$ be a vocabulary where N is a set of node-type labels, E is a set of edge-type labels, and L be a set of logical formulae defined on the vocabulary V [11]. An ontology O for C is defined as $O_c = \{V, L\}$ [14]. A KG $G = (\mathcal{V}, \mathcal{E}, T_{\mathcal{V}}, T_{\mathcal{E}})$ is compliant with an ontology $O_c = \{V, L\}$ iff (i) $T_{\mathcal{V}} \subseteq N$, (ii) $T_{\mathcal{E}} \subseteq E$, and (iii) there is no node $v \in \mathcal{V}$ and no edge $e \in \mathcal{E}$ that would violate L.*

Data aggregation transforms relationships between objects into relationships between higher-level objects [22]. In this paper we consider two common types of aggregation, logical and numerical aggregation; both are formalized below.

Definition 2. Data aggregation [4]. *Given an ontology O_{c_1} with set of edge types E_1, an ontology O_{c_2} with set of edge types E_2, and an operator $o \in \{count, sum, average, max, min, \varnothing\}$, a data aggregation $\mathcal{M}$ from O_{c_1} to O_{c_2} with operator o is a tuple $(\Sigma_1, \Sigma_2, o, \mathcal{T})$, where $\mathcal{T}$ is a rule of the form $\phi_{s_1}(\bar{x}) \rightarrow \varphi_{s_2}(\bar{y}) \wedge o(\bar{z})$, with $\bar{x}$ ($\bar{y}$ and $\bar{z}$, resp.) over $\Sigma_1 \subseteq E_1$ (over $\Sigma_2 \subseteq E_2$, resp.), and $\phi_{s_1}(\bar{x})$ and $\varphi_{s_2}(\bar{y})$ are conjunctions and/or disjunctions over $\bar{x}$ and $\bar{y}$, respectively. The left-hand (right-hand) side of $\mathcal{T}$ is the body (head) of $\mathcal{M}$.*

In this study, cases with $o = \varnothing$ are those of *logical aggregation*, and cases with $o \in \{count, sum, average, max, min\}$ are those of *numerical aggregation*.

Note that a data aggregation $\mathcal{M}$ from an ontology O_{c_1} to an ontology O_{c_2} is also a data aggregation from O_{c_1} to O_{c_3} if $O_{c_2} \subseteq O_{c_3}$. Given a set of values g that satisfies the body of $\mathcal{M}$, $\mathcal{M}(g)$ denotes the instantiation of the head of $\mathcal{M}$.

Let $\mathcal{G}$ and $\mathcal{G}^s$ be two KGs compliant with ontologies O_c and O_{c^s}, respectively. We call $\mathcal{G}$ a *standard-level KG* and $\mathcal{G}^s$ the respective *summary-level KG* iff there exists at least one data aggregation from O_c to O_{c^s}.

Definition 3. Provenance information for data aggregation. *Given a standard-level KG $\mathcal{G}$ compliant with ontology O_c, a summary-level KG $\mathcal{G}^s$ compliant with ontology O_{c^s}, and a data aggregation $\mathcal{M}$ from O_c to O_{c^s}, the provenance information in $\mathcal{G}$ with respect to $\mathcal{M}$ of a subgraph S of $\mathcal{G}^s$ is the maximal set g of node/edge labels of $\mathcal{G}$ that satisfies the body of $\mathcal{M}$ and such that $\mathcal{M}(g) \subseteq S$.*

Problem Statement.   Given a standard-level KG $\mathcal{G}$ compliant with ontology O_c, a summary-level KG $\mathcal{G}^s$ compliant with ontology O_{c^s}, and a set $\mathcal{M}_{\mathcal{T}}$ of data aggregations *(aggregation rules)* from O_c to O_{c^s} provided by domain experts, our goal is to integrate $\mathcal{G}$ and $\mathcal{G}^s$ into a KG $\mathcal{G}^s_{prov}$ compliant with ontology $O_{c^s_{prov}}$ such that

1. $\mathcal{G}^s \subseteq \mathcal{G}^s_{prov}$ and $O_{c^s} \subseteq O_{c^s_{prov}}$;
2. For each $g \subseteq \mathcal{G}$ that satisfies the body of $\mathcal{M} \in \mathcal{M}_T$, $\mathcal{M}(g) \subseteq \mathcal{G}^s_{prov}$; and
3. Provenance-aware summarization querying is enabled over $\mathcal{G}^s_{prov}$, such that evaluating a provenance query over a subgraph S of $\mathcal{G}^s_{prov}$ returns for S the correct provenance information in $\mathcal{G}$ with respect to all the rules $\mathcal{M}$ in $\mathcal{M}_T$.

3   The Proposed Approach

Our proposed provenance-aware data-integration approach is sketched in Fig. 2. Typically, the standard-level KG has some entities of interest (e.g., s_1 and t_1) connected via some intermediate nodes (e.g., g_1 and g_2). The summary-level KG might involve the same entities of interest (s_1 and t_1), either (1) without intermediate nodes, but with a new relationship connecting them (see, e.g., Fig. 1b), or (2) with intermediate summary-level nodes (e.g., node x_1 in Fig. 2) storing *average*, *count*, or *sum* aggregations associated with s_1 and t_1.

In the proposed approach, the integrated KG $\mathcal{G}^s_{prov}$ is generated by enriching the summary-level KG $\mathcal{G}^s$ with additional nodes and edges, and by reflecting the changes also at the ontology level. In Step 1 of Fig. 2, given a standard-level KG $\mathcal{G}$ and a summary-level KG $\mathcal{G}^s$, we first aggregate the information in $\mathcal{G}$ using the *data-aggregation rules* $\mathcal{M}_T$ provided by the user. Then, in Step 2 of Fig. 2, we generate in $\mathcal{G}^s$ *summary subgraphs* that (i) represent the result of aggregating (logically or numerically) the information from $\mathcal{G}$, and (ii) point back to the provenance of the aggregation in the KG $\mathcal{G}$.

Conceptually, the summary subgraphs can be organized using *reification* style constructs, which provide a mechanism for making statements about statements [13]. Using reification, we can anchor a pair (s, t) of nodes of interest in the summary-level KG $\mathcal{G}^s$, and connect that pair both to (a) the aggregation introduced to $\mathcal{G}^s$ via the rules, and to (b) the fragment of the standard-level KG $\mathcal{G}$ that provides the provenance of the aggregation. In the implementation of our approach reported in this paper, we have used a lightweight version of reification expressed through node and triple annotations that are available in Neo4j,[1] the graph database system used in our experiments. In graph database systems that do not make such annotations available (e.g., RDF stores), our approach can be implemented using the structural version [13] of reification.

In the proposed integration process (i.e., Step 3 of Fig. 2), the results of aggregating data for nodes of interest s and t can be incorporated into the summary-level graph $\mathcal{G}^s$ in two ways. Suppose first that the aggregation produces a construct that is already present in $\mathcal{G}^s$, either (1) a statement node x for a relationship from s to t (via logical aggregation), or (2) a numerical node x relating s to t (via numerical aggregation). In this case, the approach adds the provenance information to the special newly generated *aggregate-node* and *provenance-node* in $\mathcal{G}^s$, and connects them via *has_prov* edges to x in $\mathcal{G}^s$. (The *provenance information* is a listing of the fragment of $\mathcal{G}$ that the data aggregation has used to derive x in $\mathcal{G}^s$, see the shaded area in Fig. 1(d) for an illustration.) If,

---

[1]   https://neo4j.com.

on the other hand, the aggregation produces results that are not present in $\mathcal{G}^s$, then the corresponding new nodes are created in $\mathcal{G}^s$ along with the provenance information. Running the above process with all the rules in $\mathcal{M}_T$ produces the integrated KG $\mathcal{G}^s_{prov}$, the results of enriching $\mathcal{G}^s$ with provenance information and with potentially previously missing aggregation results. Finally, in Step 4 of Fig. 2, the user is able to find provenance for the summarized item of interest.

3.1 Provenance-Aware Data Integration

The proposed approach for provenance-aware data integration is outlined in Algorithm 1. The algorithm iteratively generates the integrated KG G^s_{prov}, by using one data-aggregation rule at a time to enrich the summary-level KG $\mathcal{G}^s$ with the provenance information coming from the standard-level KG $\mathcal{G}$. Once generated, $\mathcal{G}^s_{prov}$ can be used to answer provenance queries, which return standard-level provenance information for aggregate values in $\mathcal{G}^s$ of interest to the users.

Algorithm 1: Generation of the integrated KG $\mathcal{G}^s_{prov}$ by using aggregation rules $\mathcal{M}_T$ to add to $\mathcal{G}^s$ provenance information from $\mathcal{G}$.

Data: Standard-level KG $\mathcal{G}$; summary-level KG $\mathcal{G}^s$; set $\mathcal{M}_T$ of expert-provided data-aggregation rules from $\mathcal{G}$ to $\mathcal{G}^s$.

Result: Integrated KG $\mathcal{G}^s_{prov}$ that enables processing of provenance queries.

```
1  begin
2  |   G^s_prov ← G^s;
3  |   for each rule M ∈ M_T do
4  |   |   for each result M of applying M to G do
5  |   |   |   construct record r = (s,t,x,p); // nodes s and t of G^s,
   |   |   |   // aggregate result x, provenance subgraph p of G
6  |   |   |   q^s ← AddProvenance(r); // see Algorithm 2
7  |   |   |   G^s_prov ← G^s_prov ∪ q^s(G);
8  |   return G^s_prov;
```

Algorithm 1 takes as inputs a standard-level KG $\mathcal{G}$, a summary-level KG $\mathcal{G}^s$, and aggregation rules $\mathcal{M}_T$ from $\mathcal{G}$ to $\mathcal{G}^s$ provided by domain experts. It uses the rules to aggregate data in $\mathcal{G}$ while generating appropriate provenance information. The integration is done by locating the aggregate results that are already present in $\mathcal{G}^s$ and adding the missing ones, with the provenance information added appropriately. The algorithm outputs the integrated KG $\mathcal{G}^s_{prov}$.

In more detail, after initializing the integrated KG $\mathcal{G}^s_{prov}$ with $\mathcal{G}^s$ (line 2), the algorithm iterates over the rules in $\mathcal{M}_T$ (line 3). Consider the set of all the results of applying one such rule $\mathcal{M}$ on the KG $\mathcal{G}$. For each element M of this set (line 4), the algorithm creates (line 5) a record r that stores the nodes s and t of the KG $\mathcal{G}^s$ and the aggregate value x mentioned in the head of M, as well as the subgraph p of $\mathcal{G}$ that justifies the provenance of x in $\mathcal{G}^s$ and is expressed by the body of M. For each such record r, the subroutine *AddProvenance* (Algorithm 2) generates a query q^s (line 6) for transforming the elements of r into graph nodes and edges. Merging the results of applying each such query q^s to the KG $\mathcal{G}$ contributes to enriching the KG $\mathcal{G}^s_{prov}$ (line 7); the latter KG is output by the algorithm once all the rules and records have been processed.

Algorithm 2: Procedure AddProvenance.

Data: Record $r = (s, t, x, p)$, where s and t are nodes in $\mathcal{G}^s$, x is the aggregate value for (s, t), and p is the provenance subgraph of $\mathcal{G}$ that justifies x.

Result: Merge-query q^s that contributes to the integration of $\mathcal{G}$ and $\mathcal{G}^s$.

1 **begin**
2      $n_x \leftarrow$ create an aggregate-node with value x;
3      $n_p \leftarrow$ create a provenance-node with the provenance subgraph p of $\mathcal{G}$;
4      $q^s \leftarrow$ create a merge-query for nodes s, t, n_x, and n_p, with *has_prov* edges added between s and n_p, between t and n_p, and between n_x and n_p in $\mathcal{G}^s$;
5   **if** *a node $m \in \mathcal{G}^s$ has value x* **then**
6          $q^s \leftarrow q^s \cup$ query adding a connection statement for nodes n_x and m;
7   **return** q^s;

We now discuss the procedure *AddProvenance* given in Algorithm 2. For a rule M in $M_{\mathcal{T}}$, consider an aggregate record r whose components are nodes s and t in $\mathcal{G}^s$, node x with the aggregate result, and subgraph p of $\mathcal{G}$ that involves s and t and satisfies the body of M. The goal of the *AddProvenance* subroutine is to generate a query, q^s, that contributes to the integration of $\mathcal{G}$ and $\mathcal{G}^s$ by introducing the information in r into the integrated graph $\mathcal{G}^s_{prov}$ being constructed. The subroutine creates an aggregate-node n_x that stores in its properties the aggregate result x (line 2), as well as a provenance-node n_p that stores the information of the provenance subgraph p of $\mathcal{G}$ (line 3). Then the subroutine creates a query q^s introducing *has_prov* edges between the provenance-node n_p and the nodes s, t, and the aggregate-node n_x (line 4). If a node m with value x already exists in $\mathcal{G}^s$, q^s would be enhanced with a component that adds appropriate *has_prov* edges between m and n_x to connect these nodes (lines 5–6). The resulting query is returned to Algorithm 1.

We illustrate the work of the proposed approach with the following example. Consider an aggregation rule $M = (\Sigma_1, \Sigma_2, \mathcal{T})$ with $\Sigma_1 = \{activity\_decreased\_by, correlated\_with\}$, $\Sigma_2 = \{treats\}$, and $\mathcal{T} = activity\_decreased\_by(x, y) \wedge correlated\_with(y, z) \rightarrow treats(x, z)$. This rule expresses one of the known mechanisms of action between drugs and diseases provided by biomedical experts. Let `treats(Losartan, hypertension)` be the result of applying M to the KG of Fig. 1(a), with the provenance information p being the path in the KG between the nodes for `Losartan` and `hypertension` that goes through the node `AGTR1`. The *AddProvenance* subroutine of Algorithm 1 will incorporate this information into the KG of Fig. 1(b) as suggested in Fig. 1(d). The resulting KG integrates into the KG of Fig. 1(b) provenance information for its `Losartan-treats-hypertension` part, with the provenance arising from the KG of Fig. 1(a) based on a real-life domain rule provided by biomedical experts.

3.2 Provenance-Aware Summarization Querying

In this section we discuss how the integrated KG $\mathcal{G}^s_{prov}$ generated by Algorithm 1 of Sect. 3.1 can be used to look up the provenance information for aggregate values of interest in the KG $\mathcal{G}^s$. Our proposed approach, outlined in pseudocode in Algorithm 3, is as follows: For any given aggregate-node n in $\mathcal{G}^s_{prov}$, the approach returns all the subgraphs of the standard-level KG $\mathcal{G}$ that have contributed to the aggregate value in n.

Algorithm 3 takes as inputs the integrated KG $\mathcal{G}^s_{prov}$ and a user-specified aggregate-node n in $\mathcal{G}^s_{prov}$. The algorithm first checks whether the target aggregate-node n connects to a provenance-node, n_p, by a `has_prov` edge, which stores the provenance information in $\mathcal{G}$ for the aggregate result in n (line 3). If such a provenance-node n_p exists for n, the algorithm retrieves its provenance subgraph $\mathcal{R}^P$ stored in the `provPaths` property of n_p (line 4). The provenance subgraph $\mathcal{R}^P$ is returned by the algorithm.

Algorithm 3: Retrieving provenance information for aggregate results.

Data: Integrated summary-level KG with provenance $\mathcal{G}^s_{prov}$; aggregate-node n of interest to the user in $\mathcal{G}^s_{prov}$.

Result: Set $\mathcal{R}^P$ of provenance subgraphs of $\mathcal{G}$ that justify n in $\mathcal{G}^s_{prov}$.

1 **begin**
2      $\mathcal{R}^P \leftarrow \varnothing$; // initialization
3   **if** n *is connected to provenance-node* n_p **then**
4          $\mathcal{R}^P \leftarrow n_p.$`provPaths`; // provenance information from n_p
5   **return** $\mathcal{R}^P$;

In our implementation of the approach, the Cypher query-language version of the provenance-query in lines 3–4 of Algorithm 3 that can be used to find the provenance subgraph for the aggregate-node of the user's interest is as follows.

```
MATCH(x : Aggregate{value :x}) − [: has_prov]− > (p : Provenance)
RETURN p.provPaths
```

4 Implementation and Experimental Results

In this section we report on the results of the experiments that we performed to help us understand whether our proposed approach introduced in Sect. 3 can be used to address the problem of provenance-aware query answering on hierarchical knowledge-graph (KG) data, see Sect. 2. In summary, the approach presents a natural tradeoff, in which the time spent offline in integrating KGs with data at different granularity levels pays off in terms of the effectiveness and efficiency of processing provenance-aware queries on the integrated data.

4.1   The Data Sets

We performed the experiments on two real-world data sets from the biomedical and antimicrobial-resistance (AMR) domains. From each data set we built a standard-level and a summary-level KG; Table 1 provides details on the results.

Table 1. KG statistics for the ROBOKOP and AMR data sets.

Data set	Standard-level KG			Summary-level KG		
	Size	Nodes	Edges	Size	Nodes	Edges
ROBOKOP	97.8KB	436	832	3.12MB	228	215
AMR	2.03MB	1,017	8,946	7.22MB	97	225

The ROBOKOP Data set. This biomedical data set contains a subset of drug-to-disease paths extracted from the ROBOKOP KG [18][2] in August 2022. The standard-level KG has 436 nodes (145 drugs, 43 diseases, and 248 genes) and 832 edges (497 drug-to-gene relationships and 335 gene-to-disease relationships). There are ten different types of drug-to-gene relationships, e.g., *correlated_ with*, *increases_ secretion_ of*, and *decreases_ response_ to*, and three different types of gene-to-disease relationships, including *correlated_ with*, *genetic_ association*, and *gene_ associated_ with_ condition*. The summary-level KG has 228 nodes (91 drugs and 137 diseases) and 215 drug-to-disease *treats* edges.

The AMR Data set. This data set contains antimicrobial-resistance data collected from the College of Veterinary Medicine at NCSU in 2019. It includes experimental results on the degrees of resistance of serotype[3] samples to antimicrobial agents. The standard-level KG has 1,017 nodes (15 serotypes, 8 antimicrobial agents, and 994 samples) and 8,946 edges (994 serotype-to-sample *bacteria_ used* relationships and 7,952 agent-to-sample *tested_ on* relationships). The summary-level KG has 97 nodes (5 serotypes, 15 antimicrobial agents, 75 measures, and 2 reports) and 225 edges (75 serotype-to-measure *bacteria_ used* relationships, 75 agent-to-measure *tested_ on* relationships, and 75 measure-to-report *reported_ in* relationships).

4.2   The Implementation and Experimental Setup

We implemented the proposed approach as follows. For each data set, we used as inputs to the approach (i) the standard-level KG $\mathcal{G}$ and the summary-level KG

---

[2]   http://robokopkg.renci.org/browser/.
[3]   A *serotype* is a distinct variation within a species of bacteria.

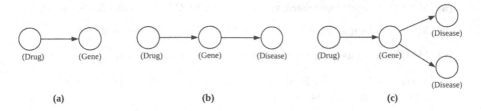

Fig. 3. Types of aggregation rules: one-hop aggregation denoted as T_1 (a), two-hop aggregation denoted as T_2 (b), and Y-shape aggregation denoted as T_3 (c).

$\mathcal{G}^s$, both represented as labeled property graphs and stored in Neo4j [23, 24], and (ii) user-provided data aggregations written in the Cypher query language. The graph values stored in Neo4j were processed with Java and Neo4j Java driver v.4.4.2. Our experiments were conducted on a computer with an Intel i7-1165G7 CPU processor running at 2.8 GHz with 16GB of RAM and Windows 11.

Our goal was to assess the effectiveness and efficiency of the proposed approach. We measured effectiveness by the degree of correctness of the answers to provenance-aware queries on the integrated KG $\mathcal{G}^s_{prov}$ generated by the approach, compared to the answers obtained via the baseline approach described below. We measured efficiency by the processing time of provenance-aware queries.

Baseline. The baseline approach poses provenance-aware queries on the result of merging the standard-level and summary-level KGs on the common-node IDs. Figure 1(c) shows the result of such integration of the KGs of Fig. 1(a)–(b).

To achieve generality in our results, we compared the effectiveness and efficiency of the proposed approach to the baseline with respect to three types of data aggregation: (i) one-hop aggregation, (ii) two-hop aggregation, and (iii) Y-shape aggregation. We refer to the three aggregation types as T_1, T_2, and T_3, respectively. Fig. 3 provides examples of T_1 through T_3 in the biomedical domain. We chose these types of data aggregation for the experiments due to their being representative of aggregation rules in multiple application domains. For instance, one-hop aggregations (T_1) can be used to aggregate the number of genes that are connected to a specified drug by a specified relationship; two-hop aggregations (T_2) can be used to aggregate the number of genes that are connected to the specified drug and disease with the matched semantics; and Y-shape aggregations (T_3) can be used to aggregate the number of genes that are connected to a specified drug and two specified diseases with the matched semantics. Similar examples can be provided for the AMR and other domains.

For each aggregation type from among T_1, T_2, and T_3, we tested in each domain three specific aggregation rules Q_1, Q_2, Q_3, varying the types of nodes or the types of edges involved in the aggregation. For example, given one-hop type queries T_1, an example of a Cypher query for T_1Q_1 is shown in Fig. 4(a); an example for T_1Q_2 is shown in Fig. 4(b); and an example for T_1Q_3 is shown in Fig. 4(c). That is, all the T_1Q_i are one-hop type queries with different specifications. Similarly, a two-hop query T_2Q_1 is shown in Fig. 4(d), and a Y-shape type

(a) MATCH (a:Drug)-[:correlated_with]->(g:Gene) RETURN a, count(distinct g) as x

(b) MATCH (a:Drug)-[:treats]->(d:Disease) RETURN a, count(distinct d) as x

(c) MATCH (a:Drug)-[]->(g:Gene) RETURN a, count(distinct g) as x

(d) MATCH (a:Drug)-[:correlated_with]-(g:Gene)-[:correlated_with]-(b:Disease)
    RETURN a, b, count(distinct g) as x

(e) MATCH (a:Drug)-[r1:correlated_with]-(g:Gene)-[r2:correlated_with] -(b:Disease)
    MATCH (g)-[r3:correlated_with]-(c:Disease)
    WHERE b <> c
    RETURN a, b, c, count(distinct g) AS x

Fig. 4. Example queries that could be used in the biomedical domain for each aggregation type T_1(a)-(c), T_2(d), and T_3(e).

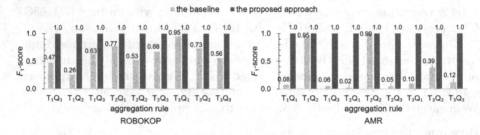

Fig. 5. Effectiveness results for our proposed approach versus the baseline, for the ROBOKOP (left) and AMR (right) data sets. The x-axis shows the aggregation rules, and the y-axis shows the average F_1-scores.

query T_3Q_1 is shown in Fig. 4(e). Then, with respect to each specific data aggregation, we evaluated three distinct provenance-aware queries. For example, for the query T_1Q_1, we evaluated it for three different drugs by replacing the node name. We then compared and reported the degrees of correctness of the query answers over the integrated KGs produced by our approach and by the baseline, measuring the results by the F_1-scores of the query answers, see [20].

4.3 The Experimental Results

We now report the experimental results. As already mentioned, the proposed approach presents a natural tradeoff, in which the time spent in integrating pre-summarized and summarized KGs pays off in terms of the effectiveness and efficiency of processing provenance-aware querying on the integrated data.

We first present the effectiveness results. Figure 5 shows the average F_1-scores of the query answers to the three provenance-aware queries for each specific data-aggregation type, over the integrated KGs produced by the proposed approach and by the baseline. We can see that the proposed approach returns correct query answers for both data sets, i.e., F_1-score = 1 in all cases. This is due to

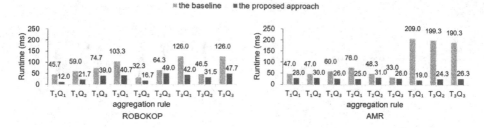

Fig. 6. Efficiency results for our proposed approach versus the baseline, for the ROBOKOP (left) and AMR (right) data sets. The x-axis shows the aggregation rules, and the y-axis shows the average runtimes in milliseconds.

the fact that our framework captures all paths in the subgraph that contribute to the aggregate result and stores them into a provenance node when the user executes the aggregation rule. That is, no information is lost during the query execution, regardless of the aggregation rule used. In contrast, given the same aggregation rule, the baseline cannot guarantee correctness of the results for all the queries, i.e., F_1-score < 1 in many cases. This is because the baseline does not record any information when the user executes the aggregation rule, causing the information to be lost when the user wants to query its provenance. Specifically, if the data aggregation involves more detailed information, such as specifying edge types or properties, the F_1-score for the answer returned by the baseline would be even lower.

For example, the data-aggregation rule that underlies Fig. 1(d) is

$$activity\_decreased\_by(drug, X) \wedge correlated\_with(X, disease) \rightarrow treats(drug, disease).$$

Since the baseline approach lacks information on which edge types in the standard-level graph contribute to which edge types in the summary-level graph during integration, the downstream data queries are unable to correctly determine which of the standard-level paths between Losartan and hypertension is the correct provenance information for the summary-level edge between them.

We conclude that the results support the claim that the proposed approach enables correct provenance-aware query answering over the integrated KG.

We report the efficiency results in Fig. 6, which compares the average runtime (measured in milliseconds) of the execution of the provenance-aware queries over the integrated KG $\mathcal{G}^s_{prov}$ using the proposed approach and the baseline approach. We see that the proposed approach consistently outperforms the baseline, with the runtimes of the proposed approach staying at or below 49 ms on both data sets. This is not surprising, as the focus of the proposed data-integration framework is on retaining with the integrated knowledge graph as much information as possible about the provenance of its summarized data.

We conclude that the results support the claim that the proposed approach enables efficient provenance-aware query answering over the integrated KG.

Finally, we discuss the aggregation-performance results reported in Fig. 7. We can see that, while the runtimes for the proposed approach are greater than

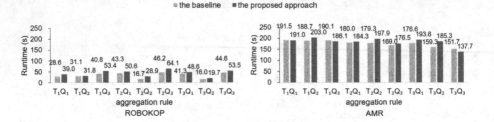

Fig. 7. Data-integration performance for our proposed approach and for the baseline, for the ROBOKOP (left) and AMR (right) data sets. The x-axis shows the aggregate rules, and the y-axis shows the average runtimes in seconds.

those for the baseline in almost all cases, the time differences are not significant. As data integration can be done offline and as the proposed approach is superior to the baseline in terms of the effectiveness and efficiency of provenance-aware query answering, we conclude that this is an acceptable tradeoff.

5   Conclusion

Provenance-aware summarization querying, in which the expected answers include the pre-summarized data that have contributed to the calculation of the existing summarized data of interest, is an important part of data analysis in many real-life scenarios in a range of application domains. As pre-summarized and summarized data are in many cases collected independently, in such scenarios they have to be integrated in ways that would enable correct processing of provenance-aware summarizaton queries. In this paper we formalized the problems of provenance-aware data integration and summarization querying in this context, and proposed a framework for addressing these problems on knowledge graphs (KGs) that represent data at different levels of granularity, that is at the *standard* (pre-summarized) and *summary* levels of detail.

The scenarios that we focused on in this paper are those of analysts and domain scientists looking to find in the standard-level KGs those data that contribute to the existing aggregate data of interest in the summary-level KGs. Our proposed domain-independent approach enables integration of such different-granularity knowledge graphs, while simultaneously enriching the integrated KGs with provenance information that enables effective and efficient processing of real-life provenance-aware summarization queries posed by users on the existing aggregate data of interest. Our experimental results for two real-life application domains provide supporting evidence for the effectiveness and efficiency of the proposed approach. Based on these results, we believe that the proposed approach can be used to help analysts and domain scientists accomplish their goals in research and industry collaborations in a range of application domains, by enabling effective and efficient retrieval from knowledge graphs of pre-summarized provenance information for the existing summarized data of interest. Future work includes developing user interfaces that would make it easier for domain scientists to query and explore the integrated data with provenance.

Acknowledgment. This work has been supported by the National Science Foundation under Grant No. CBET-2019435.

References

1. Ahlstrøm, K., Hose, K., Pedersen, T.B.: Towards answering provenance-enabled SPARQL queries over RDF data cubes. In: Li, Y.-F., et al. (eds.) JIST 2016. LNCS, vol. 10055, pp. 186–203. Springer, Cham (2016). https://doi.org/10.1007/978-3-319-50112-3_14
2. Amsterdamer, Y., Deutch, D., et al.: Provenance for aggregate queries. In: PODS, pp. 153–164 (2011)
3. Avgoustaki, A., Flouris, G., Fundulaki, I., Plexousakis, D.: Provenance management for evolving RDF datasets. In: Sack, H., Blomqvist, E., d'Aquin, M., Ghidini, C., Ponzetto, S.P., Lange, C. (eds.) ESWC 2016. LNCS, vol. 9678, pp. 575–592. Springer, Cham (2016). https://doi.org/10.1007/978-3-319-34129-3_35
4. Barceló, P., Pérez, J., et al.: Schema mappings and data exchange for graph databases. In: ICDT, pp. 189–200 (2013)
5. Buneman, P., Khanna, S., et al.: Why and where: a characterization of data provenance. In: ICDT, vol. 1973, pp. 316–330 (2001)
6. Collarana, D., Galkin, M., et al.: Semantic data integration for knowledge graph construction at query time. In: ICSC, pp. 109–116 (2017)
7. Galárraga, L., Ahlstrøm, K., Hose, K., Pedersen, T.B.: Answering provenance-aware queries on RDF data cubes under memory budgets. In: Vrandečić, D., et al. (eds.) ISWC 2018. LNCS, vol. 11136, pp. 547–565. Springer, Cham (2018). https://doi.org/10.1007/978-3-030-00671-6_32
8. Gaur, G., Bhattacharya, A., et al.: How and why is an answer (still) correct? Maintaining provenance in dynamic knowledge graphs. In: CIKM, pp. 405–414 (2020)
9. Green, T.J., Karvounarakis, G., et al.: Provenance semirings. In: PODS, pp. 31–40 (2007)
10. Gruber, T.R.: A translation approach to portable ontology specifications. Knowl. Acquis. **5**(2), 199–220 (1993)
11. Guarino, N., Oberle, D., Staab, S.: What is an ontology? Handbook on Ontologies, pp. 1–17 (2009)
12. Hao, X., Ji, Z., et al.: Construction and application of a knowledge graph. Rem. Sens. **13**(13), 2511 (2021)
13. Hayes, P.J., Patel-Schneider, P.F.: RDF 1.1 Semantics. W3C Recommendation (2014)
14. Kalfoglou, Y., Schorlemmer, M.: Ontology mapping: the state of the art. Knowl. Eng. Rev. **18**(1), 1–31 (2003)
15. Kieler, B.: Semantic data integration across different scales: automatic learning generalization rules. ISPRS Arch. **37**, 685–690 (2008)
16. Knap, T., Michelfeit, J., et al.: Linked open data aggregation: conflict resolution and aggregate quality. In: COMPSAC, pp. 106–111 (2012)

17. Mohammadi, S., Shiri, N.: ARDBS: efficient processing of provenance queries over annotated relations. In: DEXA, pp. 263–269 (2022)
18. Morton, K., Wang, P., et al.: ROBOKOP: an abstraction layer and user interface for knowledge graphs to support question answering. Bioinformatics **35**(24), 5382–5384 (2019)
19. Noy, N.F.: Semantic integration: a survey of ontology-based approaches. SIGMOD Rec. **33**(4), 65–70 (2004)
20. Sasaki, Y., et al.: The truth of the f-measure. Teach. Tutor Mater. **1**(5), 1–5 (2007)
21. Sikos, L.F., Philp, D.: Provenance-aware knowledge representation: a survey of data models and contextualized knowledge graphs. DSE **5**, 293–316 (2020)
22. Smith, J.M., Smith, D.C.: Database abstractions: aggregation. Commun. ACM **20**(6), 405–413 (1977)
23. Vukotic, A., Watt, N., et al.: Neo4j in action, vol. 22. Manning Shelter Island (2015)
24. Webber, J.: A programmatic introduction to Neo4j. In: SPLASH, pp. 217–218 (2012)
25. Xiao, G., Hovland, D., Bilidas, D., Rezk, M., Giese, M., Calvanese, D.: Efficient ontology-based data integration with canonical IRIs. In: Gangemi, A., et al. (eds.) ESWC 2018. LNCS, vol. 10843, pp. 697–713. Springer, Cham (2018). https://doi.org/10.1007/978-3-319-93417-4_45

Integration of Knowledge Bases and External Information Sources via Magic Properties and Query-Driven Entity Linking

Yuuki Ohmori[1,2]($\boxtimes$)(iD), Hiroyuki Kitagawa[1,2](iD), Toshiyuki Amagasa[1](iD),
and Akiyoshi Matono[2](iD)

[1] University of Tsukuba, Tsukuba, Japan
`omori.yuki.sm@alumni.tsukuba.ac.jp`, {`kitagawa,amagasa`}`@cs.tsukuba.ac.jp`
[2] Artificial Intelligence Research Center, National Institute of Advanced Industrial
Science and Technology, Tokyo, Japan
`a.matono@aist.go.jp`

Abstract. A knowledge base (KB) accumulates human knowledge in
resource description framework (RDF), which forms a knowledge graph
consisting of subject-predicate-object triples. Although RDF KBs are
essential information sources for various knowledge processing, many
non-RDF information sources exist. Therefore, integrating RDF KBs
and external sources will be beneficial in supporting various applications.
However, external sources have diverse access methods and input/output
formats. In addition, their integration with the KB involves identifying
correct entities which correspond to objects in the external sources, which
is challenging. In this paper, we present an architecture for an integrated
environment (named *Knowledge Mediator*) in which the user can query
the KB as if external sources were an integral part using the *Magic Properties* of SPARQL. We also propose novel query-driven on-demand entity
linking, to select correct entities in the KB for objects in the external
sources.

Keywords: Knowledge Graph · SPARQL · Data Integration · Entity
Linking · Query Processing

1 Introduction

As the amount of knowledge increases, it is imperative to devise techniques that
can process data from various sources. Recently, resource description framework
(RDF)-style knowledge bases (KBs) and a query language SPARQL have been
commonly used for knowledge management and processing. However, not all
knowledge is accumulated in RDF KBs. For example, information that requires
immediacy such as weather or traffic information is unsuitable for static accu-
mulation. Additionally, other sources provide specialized information for specific

The original version of this chapter was revised: A typo in the first author's family
name has been corrected. The correction to this chapter is available at
https://doi.org/10.1007//978-3-031-48316-5_49

domains. Thus, it is essential to use both RDF KBs and non-RDF external information sources in a coordinated manner to effectively utilize information.

Because external sources often use their own access methods and formats for queries and returned values, they need to be accessed according to their unique methods, and information must be interpreted according to their unique formats. Consequently, querying a KB integrating with external sources is an extremely time-consuming process. Query processing requires matching the results of both the KB and the external sources while dealing with diverse formats. However, the correspondence between entities in the KB and external sources is often unclear, making manual determination difficult. For example, when using a map application as an external source to search for churches near a particular train station and using information in a KB to narrow the search to churches of a specific denomination, the correspondence between objects on the map and entities in the KB must be examined one-by-one and aggregated.

This paper proposes an architecture for an integrated environment named *Knowledge Mediator*. It accesses external sources and treats them as an integral part of an RDF KB (Fig. 1). Knowledge Mediator has two significant features: (1) External sources are accessed using *Magic Properties* and incorporated into the query results. *Magic Properties* are user-defined predicates, which allow the application specific information processing to be implemented. (2) Query-driven on-demand entity linking selects the correct entities in the KB for objects obtained from the external sources in the query processing, using the intermediate query results as context.

A KB supported by Knowledge Mediator includes two types of predicates: *Knowledge Base Predicate (KBP)* and *External Source Predicate (ESP)*. KBPs are ordinary predicates in the original KB. ESPs are defined as Magic Properties and execute accesses to external sources by calling the user-defined functions.

For example, a query to find "the establishment date of San Francisco and its neighboring cities" using an external source (i.e., a map application) can be expressed in the following SPARQL query which includes ESP `udp:m:AdminDivNext`.

```
SELECT DISTINCT * WHERE {
?x rdfs:label "San Francisco"@en . ?x rdf:type dbo:City .
?x dbp:establishedDate ?date . ?x <udp:m:AdminDivNext> ?y .}
```

In this query, finding entity $?y$ adjacent to $?x$, namely entities that satisfy $\langle ?x, \text{udp:m:AdminDivNext}, ?y \rangle$, is performed by `udp:m:AdminDivNext`, which invokes access to the map application. The map application searches for and returns objects (e.g., "Richmond") whose locations are adjacent to the object corresponding to the entity $?x$. To compile the query result, we need to find entities (e.g., `dbr:Richmond,_California`) in the KB which correspond to the returned objects. This is achieved by our query-driven on-demand entity linking, and Knowledge Mediator finds the correct entities in the KB corresponding to $?y$.

This paper makes the following contributions:

(1) We propose Knowledge Mediator architecture. It provides an extended knowledge graph including ESPs via Magic Properties, which seamlessly integrate accesses to external sources into the original knowledge graph.

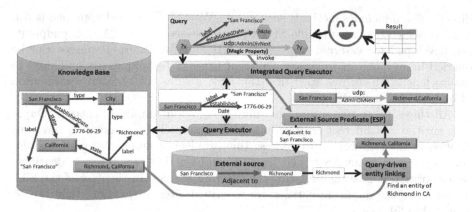

Fig. 1. Knowledge Mediator architecture for integrating KBs and non-RDF information sources.

(2) We propose novel query-driven on-demand entity linking to address the problem of finding correct entities in the KB for objects obtained from external sources, taking the query context into consideration.

(3) We implemented a prototype system of Knowledge Mediator and experimentally proved the advantages of the proposed query-driven on-demand entity-linking methods.

The rest of this paper is organized as follows. Section 2 describes related works. Section 3 provides the preliminary knowledge. Section 4 overviews the architecture of the proposed method. Section 5 details the query-driven on-demand entity linking, and Sect. 6 explains our experimental evaluation, and discusses the experimental results. Finally, Sect. 7 concludes this study. RDF KBs are simply referred to as KBs in the remaining part.

2   Related Work

Integration of external sources with KBs has been studied by many researches for a long time. They can be classified into three groups. The first approach transforms the entire external sources into RDF using mapping rules and stores the RDF datasets [20]. The derived RDF datasets can be accessed together with KBs via SPARQL, with possible support by the federation techniques shown below. Extract Transform Load (ETL) models are often used for the transformations, and they include CSV2RDF[1] (for CSV) and SPARQL Anything [2] (for various file formats). This approach first transforms external sources into RDF. Therefore, it is not easy to integrate dynamically changing external sources. The second approach is to develop a wrapper which provides an RDF view on top of each external source. The wrapper accesses the external source when queries are given and returns query results based on pre-registered mapping rules [7]. Ontology-Based Data Integration (OBDI) [5,7,11] is a wrapper/mediator approach in this

---

[1] https://github.com/AtomGraph/CSV2RDF.

direction, and includes methods such as Obi-Wan [6]. The third approach is *federation*, which queries multiple SPARQL endpoints. Once SPARQL endpoints are developed for external sources, the KB and the external sources can be queried in an integrated manner. Different types of techniques are employed to realize federation such as statistics [15], ASK queries [13,17], and combination of multiple methods [16].

All these integration approaches may bring about duplicate entities. Duplicate entities are different entities in RDF but actually correspond to the same entities in the real world. To address this problem, a number of methods also generate the owl:sameAS triples [8] and common IRIs [21] if some identification information is available inside the external sources. In the case of the ETL model, once the duplicate entities are identified after integration, they can be removed [9,20] using GNN [22].

Duplicate entity identification has also been studied in non-SPARQL query processing contexts. QuERy [1] discusses duplicate entities identification in the context of relational database query. Duplicate entity identification is usually an expensive operator. Therefore, they proposed to reduce the overall query processing cost including de-duplication. The work in [3] proposed de-duplication using hyper-edge structures over entities as well as attributes of entities.

Entity Linking (EL) has been studied in the context of natural language text analysis. It assigns entities in the KB corresponding to mentions (words) that refer to real world entities [19]. The EL process is divided into three stages: Mention Detection, Candidate Selection (CS), and Linking Decision (LD). Mention Detection identifies mentions that reference entities in sentences. CS chooses candidate entities that may correspond to the mentions. LD narrows down and decides the correct entities [18]. TAGME [12] uses the relevance of candidate entities for linking decisions. It calculates the relationship strength between entities using the destination overlap of anchor links in Wikipedia. Yamada et al. [23] proposed EL using BERT with simultaneous input of words and entities.

This study proposes to integrate external sources with KB by using Magic Properties. To the best of our knowledge, no other work has proposed to use Magic Properties for the integration purpose. In addition, we propose novel query-driven on-demand entity linking to find the correct entities corresponding to objects obtained from the external sources. It is inspired by the entity linking for text, but it features the use of the query context, which makes the proposal fit to the integration problem. Existing studies on integration of KBs and external sources have not directly addressed this problem.

3   Preliminaries

RDF: RDF describes information as a collection of triples consisting of subject, predicate, and object. It is also used to describe semantic information[2] [14]. The subject is an entity corresponding to a real object or concept and designated

---

[2] https://www.w3.org/TR/rdf11-concepts/.

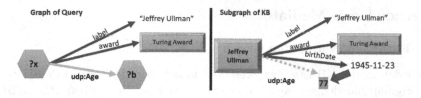

Fig. 2. Example of a Magic Property to obtain the age from the date of birth stored in the knowledge base.

by an IRI. The object can be an entity IRI or a literal such as a number or a string. Finally, predicates have IRIs to represent the relationship between the subject and the object. SPARQL is a query language commonly used to search KBs. Queries perform pattern matching against a knowledge graph of the KB and obtain desired information[3]. The query result of a SPARQL query is a set of tuples consisting of variable assignments, namely a table, where each variable and its assigned values are represented as a column. For example, let us consider the following query:

SELECT DISTINCT * WHERE {?x rdfs:label "Jeffrey Ullman"@en . }
The WHERE clause defines the matching pattern against a knowledge graph. The essential components of this pattern are the subject, object, and predicate. The subject can be an IRI or a variable. The object can be an IRI, a literal, or a variable. The predicate is an IRI or a variable. The subject-predicate-object pattern is called a *triple pattern*. The set of triple patterns forms a graph called a *Basic Graph Pattern (BGP)* and is the basic content of the WHERE clause. Executing the above query will yield a table which only contains the IRI for the entity of Jeffrey Ullman in the $?x$ variable column.

Magic Property: The SPARQL processor allows users to specify user-defined predicates[4,5]. This feature is called Magic Property. It is intended to incorporate application-specific computation procedures into SPARQL queries to meet the application demands[6]. To define a user-defined predicate, the user needs to give a function to calculate the object of the predicate from a subject or vice versa. For example, Fig. 2 shows an example of a user-defined predicate udp:Age to obtain the age from the date of birth value stored in the KB. In this example, the age information is not directly stored in the KB, but can be calculated on demand using the calculation function associated with udp:Age. When a SPARQL query includes the predicate udp:Age, the SPARQL processor calls the function with the argument dbr:Jeffrey_Ullman to calculate the age. It retrieves the triple ⟨dbr : Jeffrey_Ullman, dbo : birthDate,1945-11-23⟩, obtains the date of birth, and calculates the current age, say 77. In this study, Magic Property is employed to access external sources to integrate their information with the KB.

---

[3] https://www.w3.org/TR/2013/REC-sparql11-query-20130321/.

[4] https://www.w3.org/Submission/spin-modeling/#spin-magic.

[5] https://jena.apache.org/documentation/query/writing_propfuncs.html.

[6] https://www.w3.org/2009/sparql/wiki/Feature:JavaScriptFunctions.

4   Knowledge Mediator

4.1   Extended Knowledge Graph

Knowledge in the KB can be represented in a knowledge graph. Predicates in this original knowledge graph are called *Knowledge Base Predicates (KBPs)*. Knowledge Mediator extends the original knowledge graph with *External Source Predicates (ESPs)*. ESPs are defined as Magic Properties in SPARQL, and their associated functions are used to derive object entities from a subject entity or vice versa.

Figure 3 shows how ESP extends the knowledge graph. In the original KB, entities and literals such as dbr:San_Francisco and dbr:Richmond_California are represented as vertices and connected by edges representing KBPs. Although dbr:San_Francisco and dbr:Richmond_California are geographically adjacent with each other, this relationship is not expressed in the original knowledge graph. If we use some map application such as Openstreetmap (OSM), we can augment the original knowledge graph with geographical information from the map application. Actually, OSM contains information of geographical objects such as coordinates, polygons, and relationships between objects. Therefore, OSM provides information that San Francisco and Richmond (California) are adjacent. Knowledge Mediator allows users to define a new ESP udp:AdminDivNext to express this geographical adjacency relationship. The function associated with udp:AdminDivNext accesses OSM and finds geographically adjacent objects. Then, dbr:San_Francisco and dbr:Richmond_California are connected with each other by the ESP udp:AdminDivNext in the extended knowledge graph. The user of Knowledge Mediator can issue SPARQL queries for the extended knowledge graph, and query processing involving accesses to the underlying KB and external source, query results compilation, and EL is performed all inside Knowledge Mediator.

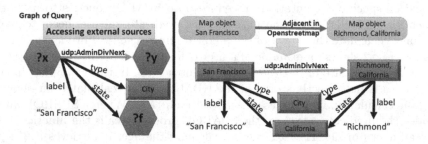

Fig. 3. Example of an extended BGP (Left) and the extended knowledge graph relevant to this BGP (Right).

4.2   Overall Architecture

Figure 1 overviews Knowledge Mediator architecture. As mentioned, it extends the original knowledge graph with ESPs, and the user can issue SPARQL queries for the extended knowledge graph. The SPARQL query example in Sect. 1 includes the ESP udp:m:AdminDivNext. The object entities of this ESP for the given subject entity are obtained by accessing OSM. In this example, the establishment date of San Francisco can be obtained from the KB using the KBP dbp:establishedDate. Neighboring municipalities are obtained using the ESP udp:AdminDivNext. The evaluation of the ESP generates a triple ⟨dbr : San_Francisco, udp : m : AdminDivNext, dbr : Richmond_California⟩.

The following subsections show more details of Knowledge Mediator design. Especially, we will elaborate the following three points:

Registration of ESPs: Although external sources to be integrated are diverse, registering ESPs should be done in a unified manner.

Execution of Extended SPARQL Queries: We need to develop a query processing algorithm for SPARQL queries against the extended KB including ESPs.

Mapping of External Source Objects to Entities: To compile the query results, objects obtained from external sources need to be mapped to corresponding entities in the KB. For example, if the external source returns the string "Richmond," many entities with the same name exist in the United States (e.g., Richmond, Virginia). From here, dbr:Richmond_California must be selected. This EL is done inside Knowledge Mediator by the query-driven on-demand entity linking.

For simplicity of our discussion in the following part, we assume that objects of ESPs are entities, and ESPs are evaluated in the direction from the subject to the object. (ESPs are used to derive object entities for a given subject entity.) However, these restrictions can be easily relaxed.

4.3   Registration of ESPs

To evaluate an ESP, the system must (1) generate a *key* from a given subject entity to access the external source, (2) access the external source using the key, and (3) find entities in the KB corresponding to objects obtained from

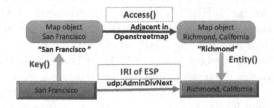

Fig. 4. How each ESP occurrence is processed.

the external source. Figure 4 schematically diagrams this process. To register an ESP, the user needs to specify functions for (1) and (2). Therefore, the following items need to be specified at the time of ESP registration:

a) IRI of ESP: The user should register IRI of ESP, for example, *udp:m:AdminDivNext*. If this IRI appears in the query, the query processor calls the external source access function shown in c) below.

b) Key generation function $Key()$**:** We model that an external source is accessible via some kind of key. To generate a key from a given subject entity x, the user needs to register a function (program code) that performs the process described in (1) above. The subject entity's name, coordinates, etc., are actually used as keys depending to the type of the subject entity and external source. In the above example, $Key(x) = $ "San Francisco" could be derived for the subject entity $x = $ dbr : San_Francisco since "San Francisco" is the object value for rdfs:label in the registered $Key()$ function.

c) External source access function $Access()$**:** The user should register a function (program code) which actually accesses the external source using $Key(x)$ defined in b) and obtains information about object entities. External objects $R = Access(Key(x))$ are obtained from the external source. In the above example, the $Access()$ function will query OSM using for $Key(x) = $ "San Francisco", and returns $R = \{$ "Richmond", "Oakland".... $\}$, which is a set of adjacent municipality names.

Once the above three items are registered, Knowledge Mediator allows ESPs to be used in queries.

4.4 Mapping External Objects to KB Entities

For each subject entity x, we get the set of external objects $R = Access(Key(x))$ in the evaluation of the ESP. We need to find a correct entity in the KB for each $r \in R$ and return it as an object entity $y = Entity(x, r)$. If an appropriate entity does not exist in the KB for r, $Entity(x, r)$ should return Null. The function $Entiy()$ is provided in Knowledge Mediator. Details of this part are described in Sect. 5.

4.5 Execution of Extended SPARQL Query

The extended SPARQL query adds ESPs to the traditional SPARQL query. A BGP representing the WHERE clause in the extended SPARQL query is a directed labeled graph, which consists of vertices representing variables, entities, and literals and edges representing KBPs and ESPs.

When we exclude ESP edges from the BGP, it is decomposed into a number of connected subgraphs. Each remaining connected subgraph is called a *segment*. Figure 5 shows how the BGP of an extended SPARQL query is partitioned into segments by excluding ESPs. A segment contains variables, entities, and literals as vertices and KBPs as edges. Segments are connected via ESPs. That is, each

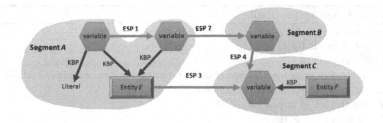

Fig. 5. Example of extended BGP and segments.

ESP has a segment (called *subject segment*) on the subject side and one (called *object segment*) on the object side.

Since the BGP inside a segment is equivalent to an ordinary SPARQL query (we call it a *local query*), it can directly query the KB. Then, we get a table representing the query results for each segment. It should contain columns corresponding to the entities directly appearing in the query as well as columns corresponding to variables.

Algorithm 1 describes the overall query processing procedure. Note that $R = Access(Key(x))$ represents the access result of the external source for ESP, $Entity(x, r)$ for $r \in R$ represents the object entity obtained by the EL, and $subjects(p)$ is the set of subject entities for ESP p. The followings are basic points considered in the design of Algorithm 1.

(1) When executing $Key()$ and $Access()$ for ESP, the subject entity x should be specified.

(2) Executing $Access()$ and $Entity()$ for ESP involves accesses to external source and EL process. Since they are generally expensive, the number of their invocations should be minimized.

(3) After executing $Key()$, $Access()$, and $Entity()$ for ESP, pairs of subject and object entities instantiating the ESP are obtained, and they can be treated as the ordinary query result table.

5   Entity Linking (EL)

Algorithm 2 shows a procedure $Entity()$ to execute the EL for an external object $r \in Access(Key(x))$. This study proposes novel query-driven on-demand entity linking for this purpose. "On-demand" means that the entity linking is performed triggered by processing queries including ESPs. "Query-driven" means that it utilizes information of entities included in the current intermediate query results, namely query context, to find out the correct entities which should be linked to objects obtained from external sources. Therefore, the entity linking here is designed to be best fit to this problem, and is quite different from existing entity linking methods. For simplicity, we assume that objects obtained from external sources are strings representing names of entities. Also, we assume DBpedia as target KB. Relaxing these restrictions is our future research issues.

Algorithm 1. Query processing

Input: extended BGP G
Output: query result for G
1: Find all segments in G
2: Evaluate local queries for all segments that contain triple patterns, and insert the result into a set of intermediate result tables I_{result}.
3: Let P_u be the set of unprocessed ESPs.
4: **while** $count(P_u) \neq \emptyset$ **do**
5:     $p_{min} = \arg\min_{p \in P_u} count(subjects(p))$ (If multiple ESPs give the same minimum, choose one of them at random.)
6:     $X = subjects(p_{min})$
7:     **for** $x \in X$ **do**
8:         $R = Access(Key(x))$: Access the external source.
9:         **for** $r \in R$ **do**
10:            $y = Entity(x, r)$: Assign an object entity (y can be Null).
11:         **end for**
12:     **end for**
13:     Update I_{result} by joining the evaluation result for ESP p_{min} with intermediate result tables for its subject and object segments.
14:     $P_u = P_u - \{p_{min}\}$
15: **end while**
16: Outputs the final result of the query from I_{result}.

5.1 Candidate Selection (CS)

Entity linking first requires the process Candidate Selection (CS), which selects the set of candidate entities for each target string. The most common way for CS is string similarity matching combined with aliases [17]. We employ the following two simple methods for CS.

LabelCS: Given a string r, word-by-word partial match to a word sequence in `rdfs:label` of an entity is performed, and entities with similar word sequences are extracted as candidates.

Algorithm 2. Entity linking: $y = Entity(x, r)$

Input: subject entity x, external object r
Output: object entity y
1: **Candidate Selection:** Select a set of candidate entities C for a given external object $r \in R$.
2: **if** I_{result} can be used to narrow down candidate entities in C. **then**
3:     Do this filtering.
4: **end if**
5: **Linking Decision:** Based on the relation between the subject entity x and a candidate entity $c \in C$, choose the most appropriate object entity $y = LD(C, x)$ for each external object (y can be Null).

Algorithm 3. Linking Decision: $y = LD(C, x)$

Input: subject entity x, candidate entities C
Output: object entity y
1: Obtain $QCtx(x)$, set of entities in the same rows as x in I_{result}
2: **for** $c \in C$ **do**
3:    Obtain $QCtx(c)$, set of entities in the same rows as c in I_{result}
4:    Calculating weighted averages: $Conf(x, c)$
5: **end for**
6: **if** $\max_{c \in C} Conf(x, c) \geq th$ **then**
7:    $y = \arg\max_{c \in C} Conf(c)$
8: **else**
9:    $y = Null$
10: **end if**

DictCS: A dictionary of candidate entities for entry words can be prepared in advance using article names and anchor link information collected from the English version of Wikipedia [4,10,19]. *Anchor links* are links that jump from words or phrases in a Wikipedia document to Wikipedia pages, providing the correspondence between the word or phrase and the Wikipedia page. Converting the string of the Wikipedia page to the DBpedia entity gives the IRI of DBpedia entity. When searching the dictionary, entry words are matched with the given string r and its suffixes.

Note that the candidates obtained by these methods are narrowed down if there is an intermediate result table for the object segment in Algorithm 2.

5.2 Linking Decision (LD)

Linking Decision (LD) follows the CS and chooses the most appropriate entity from the candidate entities. Algorithm 3 shows a procedure $LD()$ to execute the LD.

From a set of candidate entities C, it needs to select the most appropriate object entity $y = LD(C, x)$ for a given subject entity x. If there is no appropriate entity in C, $LD(C, x)$ returns Null. The appropriate entity $y \in C$ is supposed to have some semantic relationship with the subject entity x. Therefore, LD evaluates the relationship degree between the subject entity x and each candidate entity $c \in C$. Additionally, the proposed query-driven on-demand entity linking considers relationships among entities in the query context of x and c (entities appearing together with x or c in the intermediate query tables).

More concretely, the relationship degree between two entities a and b is measured by $rel(a, b) = \frac{\log(max(|W_a|, |W_b|)) - \log(|W_a \cap W_b|)}{\log(|W|) - \log(min(|W_a|, |W_b|))}$, where W_i stands for the set of pages reachable by following anchor links from the Wikipedia page w_i corresponding to entity i. This calculation is inspired by TAGME [12].

Then, we define the query context $QCtx(x)$ for the subject entity x. Let $I_x \in I_{result}$ be the intermediate result table for the subject segment. $QCtx(x)$ is defined as the set of entities which appear in the same rows as x in I_x. Also, we define the query context $QCtx(y)$ for the candidate entity c. If the intermediate result table $I_y \in I_{result}$ exits for the object segment, $QCtx(c)$ is defined as the set of entities which appear in the same rows as c in I_y. If there is not I_y, then $QCtx(c)$ is empty.

We calculate the confidence of each candidate entity by the following formula $Conf(x, c)$.

$$\frac{rel(x,c) + \alpha \left(\sum_{a \in QCtx(x)} rel(a,c) + \sum_{b \in QCtx(c)} rel(x,b) + \sum_{a \in QCtx(x)} \sum_{b \in QCtx(c)} rel(a,b) \right)}{1 + \alpha(|QCtx(x)| + |QCtx(c)| + |QCtx(x)||QCtx(c)|)}$$

Then, $LD(C, x)$ selects entity $y = \arg\max_c Conf(x, c)$. If the maximum sum is less than to the threshold (Θ) value, $LD(C, x)$ decides there is no appropriate object for x, and returns Null.

6   Experiment

6.1   Experimental Environment

Accuracy of extended SPARQL query results depend on the above mentioned entity-linking process. We implemented a prototype of Knowledge Mediator, registered ESPs, and verified how accurately the proposed algorithm executes queries. We used the June 2020 snapshot of the English version of DBpedia as a KB, and OSM as an external source.

The following three ESPs were implemented for this study. Their $Access()$ functions access OSM search services, Nominatim and Overpass, using English names of OSM nodes as keys and retrieve OSM node names. EL is performed for the returned OSM node names.

udp:m:AdminDivNext: Object entities are administrative districts adjacent to the given subject entity on the map.

udp:m:Dist1km, udp:m:Dist5km: Object entities are within 1 km and 5 km distance area from the given subject entity, respectively.

We used 25 extended SPARQL queries including these ESPs. The queries were designed to have variations in BGP. The set of correct answers for the 25 queries was provided by the authors. The ranges of parameters are $\Theta = \{0.1, 0.3, 0.5, 0.7, 0.9\}$ and $\alpha = \{0.1, 0.5, 1.0\}$. We evaluated the result returned by Knowledge Mediator and the correct answer set, and measured Recall, Precision, and F1 by counting tuples.

There is no directly comparable method that provides an equivalent functionality to the proposal. Hence, we employed the following two methods as a baseline methods for $Entity()$ for comparison.

WikipediaEL: Given a key (string), it returns entities corresponding to the search results of the English version of Wikipedia. We used the Python "wikipedia" package to implement this method.

ReturnCandidates: A method that returns all candidate entities as results.

Table 1. Performance evaluation of EL methods. Average and Standard Deviation of F1, Precision, and Recall for 25 queries. CS denotes Candidate Selection. Direction denotes OUT and IN. For each combination, only the best Θ and α is listed. If all entities are null, the value is 0.

Context	Direction	CS	F1	Precision	Recall	Θ	α
QCtx (Proposed)	**OUT** (Proposed)	LabelCS	**0.841**±0.198	0.853±0.211	0.840±0.203	0.5	0.1
		DictCS	0.797±0.129	0.745±0.183	0.886±0.135	0.5	1.0
	IN	LabelCS	0.703±0.279	0.856±0.246	0.652±0.300	0.1	0.1
		DictCS	0.702±0.191	0.688±0.211	0.797±0.228	0.1	0.5
NoCtx	OUT	LabelCS	0.831±0.221	0.838±0.247	0.840±0.203	0.5	
		DictCS	0.742±0.170	0.656±0.206	0.902±0.108	0.5	
	IN	LabelCS	0.650±0.289	0.857±0.283	0.567±0.300	0.5	
		DictCS	0.597±0.269	0.686±0.296	0.589±0.298	0.5	
NeighborCtx	OUT	LabelCS	0.000±0.000	0.000±0.000	0.000±0.000	all	all
		DictCS	0.000±0.000	0.000±0.000	0.000±0.000	all	all
	IN	LabelCS	0.775±0.310	**0.869**±0.271	0.760±0.357	0.1	all
		DictCS	0.571±0.271	0.629±0.326	0.610±0.316	0.1	0.1
ReturnCandidates		LabelCS	0.674±0.384	0.640±0.411	0.853±0.208		
ReturnCandidates		DictCS	0.504±0.281	0.392±0.293	**0.955**±0.060		
WikipediaEL			0.207±0.277	0.360±0.468	0.146±0.200		

To evaluate the efficacy of the proposed use of the query context, we also implemented the following two methods which differ in the use of context entities.
NoCtx: It uses no context entities.
NeighborCtx: It uses all the neighboring entities of the subject entity x and a candidate entity c in the KB as the context. In the definition of $rel(a, b)$, we use W_i the set of pages reachable from w_i. Some works use the set of pages which can reach w_i for W_i instead. In the experiment, we evaluate both cases. They are denoted as *OUT* and *IN*, respectively.

6.2 Experimental Results

Table 1 shows the experimental results measuring the average and standard deviation of F1, Precision, and Recall. The best F1 is achieved by the proposed method (QCtx, OUT, LabelCS).

The methods (QCtx, OUT) outperform WikipediaEL and ReturnCandidates in F1 and Precision. This proves that EL including LD is essential and simple keyword-based search does not work well for the purpose.

In addition, OUT is superior in QCtx. In general, Wikipedia pages of well known entities collect far more incoming links from other pages compared than pages of ordinary entities. Therefore, in the case of IN, well known entities tend to give much impact in the calculation of $Conf(x, c)$. In the case of OUT, this problem is alleviated. However, (NeighborCtx, OUT) fails because LD returns Null in all queries.

Comparing the proposed methods (QCtx, OUT) with the baselines (NoCtx, OUT), F1 is improved in LabelCS and DictCS, and the standard deviations also tend to be smaller. This is due to the improvement in Precision. One reason will be that (QCtx, OUT) is superior in its ability to return Null when there is no appropriate entity and more stable for various queries. Although F1 of (NoCtx, OUT, LabelCS) is 0.831, the one-sided Wilcoxon signed rank test statistically conforms advantages of (QCtx, OUT, LabelCS) over (NoCtx, OUT, LabelCS) with $p = 0.032$ ($p < 0.05$).

Comparing the proposed method (QCtx, OUT, LabelCS) with the baseline (NeighborCtx, IN, LabelCS), Precision is slightly lower, but a large increase in Recall leads to the improved F1. Furthermore, (QCtx, OUT, DictCS) exceeds (NeighborCtx, IN, DictCS). These results suggest that, restricting contexts to the same row of the intermediate result table works well.

From the above, it has been shown that the proposed query-driven entity linking method can obtain more accurate entities by considering the query context.

7   Conclusion

RDF knowledge bases (KB) statically accumulates semantic information and can be queried with SPARQL. In contrast, non-RDF external sources often have their own access methods and formats for queries and return objects. In this study, we proposed Knowledge Mediator to integrate KBs and non-RDF external sources. It utilizes the Magic Properties in SPARQL to access external sources and extend the predicates in the KB by incorporating information from external sources. We also proposed novel query-driven on-demand entity linking to address the problem of finding correct entities in the KB for objects obtained from external sources, considering query context. Through the experiments, we confirmed that extended SPARQL queries often return results at the reasonable level, and query-driven on-demand entity linking improves the quality of the query results.

Future works include relaxing the restrictions mentioned in Sect. 5 and development of more sophisticated entity linking schemes, which will allow user-defined entity linking schemes. Extending a knowledge graph by including new entities is also an interesting issue.

Acknowledgement. This work was supported in part by "Research and Development Project of the Enhanced Infrastructures for Post-5G Information and Communication Systems" (JPNP20017) commissioned by NEDO, JSPS Grants-in-Aid for Scientific Research (JP23H03399, JP22K19802, JP22H03694), JST CREST (JP-MJCR22M2), AMED (JP21zf0127005), and collaboration research with Sky Co., LTD.

References

1. Altwaijry, H., Mehrotra, S., Kalashnikov, D.V.: QuERy: a framework for integrating entity resolution with query processing. Proc. VLDB Endow. **9**(3), 120–131 (2015)

2. Asprino, L., Daga, E., Gangemi, A., Mulholland, P.: Knowledge graph construction with a Façade: a unified method to access heterogeneous data sources on the web. ACM Trans. Internet Technol. **23**(1), 1–31 (2023)
3. Bhattacharya, I., Getoor, L.: Query-time entity resolution. J. Artif. Int. Res. **30**(1), 621–657 (2007)
4. Bunescu, R., Paşca, M.: Using encyclopedic knowledge for named entity disambiguation. In: Proceedings 11th Conference of the European Chapter of the Association for Computational Linguistics, pp. 9–16 (2006)
5. Buron, M., et al.: Ontology-based RDF integration of heterogeneous data. In: Proceedings 23rd International Conference on Extending Database Technology, pp. 299–310 (2020)
6. Buron, M., Goasdoué, F., Manolescu, I., Mugnier, M.L.: Obi-Wan: ontology-based RDF integration of heterogeneous data. Proc. VLDB Endow. **13**(12), 2933–2936 (2020)
7. Calvanese, D., et al.: Ontop: answering SPARQL queries over relational databases. Semant. Web **8**(3), 471–487 (2017)
8. Calvanese, D., Giese, M., Hovland, D., Rezk, M.: Ontology-based integration of cross-linked datasets. In: Arenas, M., et al. (eds.) ISWC 2015. LNCS, vol. 9366, pp. 199–216. Springer, Cham (2015). https://doi.org/10.1007/978-3-319-25007-6_12
9. Christophides, V., Efthymiou, V., Palpanas, T., Papadakis, G., Stefanidis, K.: An overview of end-to-end entity resolution for big data. ACM Comput. Surv. **53**(6), 1–42 (2021). https://doi.org/10.1145/3418896
10. Cucerzan, S.: Large-scale named entity disambiguation based on Wikipedia data. In: Proceedings 2007 Joint Conference on Empirical Methods in Natural Language Processing and Computational Natural Language Learning, pp. 708–716 (2007)
11. Ekaputra, F., et al.: Ontology-based data integration in multi-disciplinary engineering environments: a review. Open J. Inf. Syst. **4**(1), 1–26 (2017)
12. Ferragina, P., Scaiella, U.: TAGME: on-the-fly annotation of short text fragments (by Wikipedia entities). In: Proceedings 19th ACM International Conference on Information and Knowledge Management, pp. 1625–1628 (2010)
13. Görlitz, O., Staab, S.: SPLENDID: SPARQL endpoint federation exploiting VOID descriptions. In: Proceedings 2nd International Conference on Consuming Linked Data, pp. 13–24 (2011)
14. Mahdisoltani, F., Biega, J.A., Suchanek, F.M.: YAGO3: a knowledge base from multilingual Wikipedias. In: Proceedings 7th Conference on Innovative Data Systems Research (2015)
15. Saleem, M., et al.: CostFed: cost-based query optimization for SPARQL endpoint federation. Procedia Comput. Sci. **137**, 163–174 (2018)
16. Saleem, M., Ngonga Ngomo, A.-C.: HiBISCuS: hypergraph-based source selection for SPARQL endpoint federation. In: Presutti, V., d'Amato, C., Gandon, F., d'Aquin, M., Staab, S., Tordai, A. (eds.) ESWC 2014. LNCS, vol. 8465, pp. 176–191. Springer, Cham (2014). https://doi.org/10.1007/978-3-319-07443-6_13
17. Schwarte, A., Haase, P., Hose, K., Schenkel, R., Schmidt, M.: FedX: optimization techniques for federated query processing on linked data. In: Aroyo, L., et al. (eds.) The Semantic Web – ISWC 2011, pp. 601–616. Springer, Heidelberg (2011). https://doi.org/10.1007/978-3-642-25073-6_38
18. Sevgili, Ö., et al.: Neural entity linking: a survey of models based on deep learning. Semant. Web **13**(3), 527–570 (2022)
19. Shen, W., et al.: Entity linking with a knowledge base: issues, techniques, and solutions. IEEE Trans. Knowl. Data Eng. **27**(2), 443–460 (2015)

20. Tamašauskaitė, G., Groth, P.: Defining a knowledge graph development process through a systematic review. ACM Trans. Softw. Eng. Methodol. **32**(1), 1–40 (2023). https://doi.org/10.1145/3522586

21. Xiao, G., Hovland, D., Bilidas, D., Rezk, M., Giese, M., Calvanese, D.: Efficient ontology-based data integration with canonical IRIs. In: Gangemi, A., et al. (eds.) ESWC 2018. LNCS, vol. 10843, pp. 697–713. Springer, Cham (2018). https://doi.org/10.1007/978-3-319-93417-4_45

22. Xin, K., et al.: Large-scale entity alignment via knowledge graph merging, partitioning and embedding. In: Proceedings of the 31st ACM International Conference on Information and Knowledge Management, pp. 2240–2249 (2022)

23. Yamada, I., et al.: Global entity disambiguation with BERT. In: Proceedings 2022 Conference of the North American Chapter of the Association for Computational Linguistics: Human Language Technologies, pp. 3264–3271 (2022)

Enhancing Taxi Placement in Urban Areas Using Dominating Set Algorithm with Node and Edge Weights

Sonia Khetarpaul[1]([✉]) [ID], Dolly Sharma[1] [ID], Somya Ranjan Padhi[2], and Saurabh Mishra[3] [ID]

[1] Shiv Nadar Institution of Eminence, Delhi NCR, India
{sonia.khetarpaul,dolly.sharma}@snu.edu.in
[2] Bhavans Vivekananda College, Hyderabad, India
[3] Manipal University Jaipur, Jaipur, India
saurabh.mishra@jaipur.manipal.edu

Abstract. This paper aims to improve the identification of taxi hotspots in spatio-temporal space. We propose an approach that combines ensemble-weighted degree and node entropy measures within a dominating set to enhance the identification of taxi hotspots. First, we construct a graph representation of the spatio-temporal space, where nodes represent potential taxi hotspots. The weighted degree of each node is computed by considering the weights of its adjacent edges, which correspond to the distances between the two adjacent nodes on the road network. This measure quantifies the importance and connectivity of a node. We calculate node entropy to capture the level of uncertainty and randomness associated with each node. The entropy measure provides insights into the diversity of each potential hotspot, helping to distinguish between highly active and less predictable areas. We then integrate the ensemble weighted degree and node entropy measures into a dominating set approach. By iteratively selecting the nodes with the highest combined scores, we construct an optimal set of taxi hotspots that effectively cover the spatio-temporal space while considering both connectivity and uncertainty. The proposed approach enables a more comprehensive identification of taxi hotspots, taking into account the connectivity and importance of potential locations and their level of uncertainty. To evaluate the effectiveness of the proposed approach, we conducted experiments using New York taxi trip data. The results demonstrate that the ensemble weighted degree and node entropy measures enhance the identification of taxi hot spots compared to traditional dominating set methods.

Keywords: Dominating Set · Entropy · Hotspots detection · taxi Demand · Location based service

1 Introduction

This research focuses on enhancing the taxi allocation strategy in a city by incorporating edge weights into the dominating set problem. The dominating set prob-

P. Delir Haghighi et al. (Eds.): iiWAS 2023, LNCS 14416, pp. 325–338, 2023.
https://doi.org/10.1007/978-3-031-48316-5_31

lem aims to 'identify a subset of nodes in a graph that "dominates" or covers all other nodes of that graph. By considering edge weights, which represent varying travel times between pick-up and drop-off locations, the allocation strategy can be optimized to reduce passenger waiting times, increase revenue for taxi companies, and mitigate traffic congestion and negative environmental impacts.

The research aims to address the limitations of traditional taxi allocation approaches by introducing the concept of edge weights into the dominating set problem. By incorporating actual travel times, the allocation algorithm can make more informed decisions about taxi deployment, ensuring that taxis are assigned optimally to minimize passenger wait times and maximize overall efficiency.

This work involves developing and implementing methods that integrate edge weights into the dominating set problem. Edge weights representing travel time are utilized to evaluate the effectiveness of the proposed approach. The research outcomes are measured based on waiting times and revenue generation metrics.

The findings of this research can have practical implications for taxi companies, transportation authorities, and urban planners, ultimately improving the quality of taxi services, optimizing resource utilization, and contributing to a more sustainable and efficient transportation system.

1.1   Motivation and Contributions

Identifying taxi hotspots is essential for optimizing taxi services and improving transportation systems. Traditional methods often focus on factors such as demand density or historical data, overlooking the dynamic nature and uncertainty associated with taxi hot spots. Therefore, there is a need for a more comprehensive approach that considers both the connectivity of potential hotspots and the level of uncertainty or randomness associated with them.

This research is an extension of our previous work [28], in which we predicted and recommended taxi hotspots using k-hop dominating set considering the number of taxi request in a road network graph. In this work, we incorporate edge weights, which represent travel distances, and provide a realistic representation of the conditions in a city's road network. By considering historical travel time data, our approach captures the dynamic nature of requests from each node pattern. It gives a more accurate estimation of the time required to travel between pick-up and drop-off nodes. We used dominating set problem and optimization techniques to minimize the taxis required for efficient allocation. By identifying the minimum dominating set in the graph, the approach aims to optimize resource utilization, ensuring that a minimal number of taxis can cover the entire network effectively. It leads to improved operational efficiency and increased revenue for taxi companies.

Further, we customized and adapted to specific city contexts and requirements. It allows incorporating additional factors or constraints, such as driver preferences, providing flexibility in designing allocation strategies that align with the city's unique characteristics and the taxi service.

Focusing on these issues, the key contributions of this paper are as follows:

1. The proposed method helps reduce the cruising time of the drivers and maximizes their revenues by determining the optimal number of taxis in a city.
2. And, maximizes the coverage of taxi services in a city with the optimum resource allocation.
3. We propose an ensemble weighted degree measure, which considers the weights of adjacent edges (trip distances) to quantify the importance and connectivity of potential taxi hotspots.
4. We evaluate node entropy to quantify the level of uncertainty and randomness associated with each potential hotspot.
5. The incorporation of uncertainty measures in our approach enhances the recommendations provided to taxi drivers regarding the pickup of the next customer at the earliest. By considering both connectivity and uncertainty.

2   Literature Review

Identifying taxi hotspots is a relatively recent and upcoming field of research [3–7]. Many researchers have been working on identifying taxi hotspots. Li et al. [1] have proposed a simple Dijkstra-based algorithm for an approachable kNN query on moving objects for the ride-hailing service, which considers the occupation of objects. They improved its efficiency by applying a grid-based Destination-Oriented index for occupied and non-occupied moving objects.

Chang et al. [2] mined historical data to predict the demand distributions concerning different contexts of time, weather, and taxi location for predicting the taxi demand hotspots. In many of the existing approaches, the researchers have applied various clustering algorithms, like K-means [5], DBSCAN algorithm [4,7–9], fuzzy clustering [11], or taxi-data mining algorithms, such as the density-based hierarchical clustering method [6], to identify taxi pick-up locations. Those clustering-based models mainly focused on spatial features of historical data to understand the taxi requirements. To understand the taxi demands more accurately, many researchers have explored the temporal properties [10,12]. Sumi et al. [13] proposed a personal mobile-based expert system for guidance system for exhibition tours.

Davis et al. [25] proposed a multi-level clustering technique for hotspot prediction. They used time series decomposition and correlation between adjacent geo hashes to reduce the Mean Absolute percentage error, improving the hotspot forecasting accuracy. Tang et al. [26] proposed the Entropy Maximization theory to model taxi trip distribution in a city using GPS trajectories. They partitioned traffic zones using K-means clustering and calibrated the procedure of Entropy-Maximizing. They compared Entropy-Maximizing with the Gravity model and proved its superiority. Bucella et al. [27] proposed an ontology-driven system (GeoMergeP) described for the semantic integration of geographic information sources.

The recent development of deep learning techniques has led some researchers to apply these techniques for traffic predictions, such as short-term traffic flow [14,15], real-time traffic speed [16], and passenger-demand for real-time ride service [17,18].

Dominating sets are one of the most discussed topics in graph analysis. It is used to find the most influential nodes in a graph for the communication networks, social networks, and road networks [19,20]. Wang et al. [21] used the dominating set problem to find the most influential nodes in a social network graph. He et al. [22] used the dominating set problem for quality improvement in the wireless sensor network. They proposed a neural network model to find the minimum weakly connected dominating sets (WCDS) in a wireless sensor network.

As discussed, most researchers have used different clustering and deep learning techniques for hotspot detection and analysis. In summary, the existing literature demonstrates the significance of taxi allocation strategies, the foundational concepts of dominating set problems, and the integration of edge weights into optimization problems. However, there is a research gap in exploring the specific application of incorporating edge weights into dominating set problems for taxi allocation in a city.

This research aims to bridge this gap and contribute to the field by proposing a novel methodology that optimizes taxi allocation by considering edge weights representing varying travel times between pick-up and drop-off locations. Most approaches do not consider edge weights, which represent varying travel times between pick-up and drop-off locations. Ignoring edge weights can result in suboptimal allocation decisions and longer travel times for passengers.

3   Preliminaries

Here, we define the necessary definitions and notations used.

1. **Road Network Graph:** A road network graph $G(V, E)$ is a planar graph in which each road segment corresponds to an edge (E) of the graph, and road intersections are represented as vertices (V) of the graph G. The road network graph represents the connectivity of the road network, where vertices represent intersections, and edges represent road segments.

2. **Dominating Set:** A dominating set in a road network graph $G(V, E)$ is a subset of vertices $D \subseteq V$ such that every vertex in V is either in D or adjacent to at least one vertex in D. In other words, every vertex in V is either part of the dominating set or has a neighbor in the dominating set.

3. **k-Hop-Dominating Set:** A k-hop dominating set [28] in a road network graph $G(V, E)$ is a subset of vertices $D \subseteq V$ such that every vertex in V is either in D or within a distance of at most k-hops from a vertex in D. In other words, for every vertex in V, there exists a path of at most k edges that leads to a vertex in D.

4. **Node Entropy:** Node entropy measures uncertainty or randomness associated with a node in a road network graph. It quantifies the diversity or variability of traffic flow, connectivity, or other relevant characteristics at a specific node. It can be used to calculate the uncertainty of a node based on its probability distribution.

5. **Weighted Degree:** The weighted degree of a vertex in a road network graph is a measure that incorporates the weights assigned to the edges connected to that vertex. Our weight represents the total travel distance. The weighted degree of a vertex considers the number of edges incident to the vertex and the associated weights of those edges.

6. **Ensembled Node Entropy and Weighted Degree with k-hop Dominating Set:** The ensembled node entropy and weighted degree with k-hop dominating set is a combined measure that incorporates both node entropy and weighted degree, considering the k-hop dominating set. It aims to optimize taxi placements or decision-making in the road network by balancing the uncertainty or randomness (node entropy) and the vertices' importance or influence (weighted degree) within the k-hop dominating set. The ensembled measure can be defined as the weighted sum of the node entropy and weighted degree, considering the vertices within the k-hop dominating set, with appropriate weights assigned to each measure.

4   Problem Definition

Given a road network graph $G = (V,E)$, and node features(historical taxi dataset and event dataset). The proposed method aims that predicts the hotspots for the given road network graph G using ensemble node entropy and weighted degree. The goal is to maximize overall revenue for the taxi drivers available in the region(G) by recommending them to move to the nearest hotspot in case of no pick-up request in the region they dropped a customer.

5   Proposed Approach

In this section, we define the proposed methods to address the problem of optimal placement of taxis in a city to improve the availability of taxis for customers and maximize revenue. Figure 1 shows the system diagram of the proposed model. The road network of a city is a planar graph. Using the available taxi data set and road network data sets, we can determine the demands for taxis arising at each node per unit of time in a city.

To convert the road network graph to a weighted graph, first, we map taxi pick-up requests to the nearest node of the road network graph. Further, we use the total number of taxi pick-up requests per time slot as the node's weights. Therefore, we use "weight/weights" for the total number of requests generated on each node in each time slot.

After creating the weighted graph, we calculated the node entropy of each taxi pick-up and dropoff location to calculate the uncertainty on it, and then with assigned trip distance as edge weight, we calculated the weighted degree of the graph to increase our accuracy in finding the best possible locations the greater the weighted degree, the higher the probability the taxi will go on that direction.

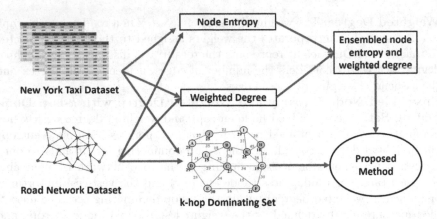

Fig. 1. Proposed Approach

This model uses historical data to predict the subsequent request-generating nodes or the most prominent point for drivers to wait. For identifying the prominent nodes, we have used k-hop domination set algorithm [28]. The dominating nodes, node entropies, and weighted degrees are combined together to identify the optimal taxi hotspots.

5.1 Dominating Set Example

Figure 2 represents a prototype of our proposed approach. We constructed a graph G that has twelve nodes from node A to node K. The request generated from different nodes is assigned as weights, and the trip distance between the different nodes is as edge weights. Then, we applied the k-hop dominating set algorithm [28]. The authors in [28] experimentally evaluated k value based upon different matrices like number of drivers, and distance covered to pick-up next customer.

The figure shows 12 node graph and it has resultant k-hop dominating set nodes displayed in **yellow** color nodes. In this example, we got five nodes as dominating set nodes. Now, we calculate the node entropy of all those dominating set nodes considering the node and edge weights.

5.2 Node Entropy

Next, we calculated the node entropy; Eq. 1 represents the formula used to compute the node entropy. It takes a list of probabilities as input and calculates the entropy for each non-zero probability node. Here the *prob* refers to the probability of finding the customer at a particular node.

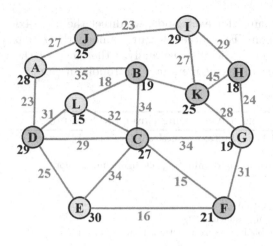

K-hop dominating set
according to Mishra et al.[28]
{A,E,I,G,L}

Node Entropy of Dominating set
node

Node A : 3.098098833270442

Node E : 3.224895714463846

Node I : 2.599390184600164

Node G : 2.584962500721156

Node L : 3.895540993544492

Fig. 2. Dominating set with node entropy measure execution representation

$$\ddot{N}ode\ entropy = -\sum(prob * log_2(prob)) \tag{1}$$

5.3 Weighted Degree

Next, we calculated the weighted degree for each node, Eq. 2 represents the weighted degree calculated for each node in the graph. It iterates over each node in the graph and computes the sum of the weights of its neighboring edges.

$$\ddot{w}eighted\ degree = \sum(weight)_{N_G} \ \forall\ neighbours\ of\ node\ N_G \tag{2}$$

5.4 Ensembled Node Entropy and Weighted Degree with k-Hop Dominating Set

Next, we calculated the normalized measure function using node entropy and weighted degree measures. The normalization is performed to bring the measures to the range [0, 1], where the minimum value is subtracted from each measure and then divided by the difference between the maximum and minimum values, as shown in Eq. 3. The normalized measures are combined into an ensembled measures by adding each node's normalized node entropy and weighted degree. The normalization done for ensembling node entropy and weighted degree is given as:

$$\ddot{n}ormalized\ measure = (measure - min\_val)/(max\_val - min\_val)) \tag{3}$$

Here the measure represents the original measure value, min_val is the minimum measure value across all nodes, and max_val is the maximum measure value across all nodes.

Once we get the "Ensemble Measure" for each node, we direct the idle taxi driver to the node with the maximum 'Ensemble Measure' among the k-hop nodes away from his present location. In Sect. 6, we analyze the effect of the proposed method on the performance of taxi drivers in a metropolitan city.

Algorithm 1: Task assignment to the drivers using Ensemble Measure

---

Input: : (a) Road Network Graph $G(V,E)$ (b) Taxi request data (c) List of Drivers
Output: Recommendation to the drivers
1: calculate the dominating set D using k-hop dominating set algorithm [28] for graph $G(V,E)$
2: **for** each node in D **do**
3:     calculate node entropy using equation (1)
4:     calculate the weighted degree using equation (2)
5:     calculated the normalized ensembled measure function using equation (3)
6:
7: **end for**
8: **if** if driver is idle **then**
9:     move driver to the node with maximum entropy
10:     update the driver information
11: **end if**
12: **return** updated driver information

5.5   Recommendation Phase

Recommendation to taxi drivers in a spatial region is one of the most important part in this research and assigning the right job(request) to the right person(driver) is a complex problem. As shown in algorithm 1, line 2–4, we first calculated the node entropy for each node of the road network graph using Eq. 1. Then we calculated the weighted degree for each node using edge weights as shown in Sect. 5.3, once we calculated the ensembled measure for each node, we recommend the driver to the node with the maximum "Ensemble Measure".

6   Experiments and Results

This section discusses the experimental setup and dataset used and analyzes the results for the k-hop dominating set approach.

6.1   Experimental Setup

In our experiments, we have used NY city road network graph [23] and NY taxi dataset [24]. The taxi data has 3.8 million taxi requests, and 99 percent of these requests are extended from $40.5N$ to $41.0N$ latitude and $-74.2E$ to $-73.5E$ longitude. We cleaned the road map data, and in the NY-city road map, we had 20,700 nodes and 33,000 edges. The NY-city taxi dataset has attributes:

date-time, pickup location, and drop-off location, and there are approximately five to six thousand requests per day. Table 1 show the details of our datasets and Table 2 shows an instance of cleaned NY taxi dataset.

We combine both datasets, which enables the exploration and analysis of the relationships between taxi allocations, travel times, and the efficiency of the dominating set problem. It provides a realistic representation of the taxi service dynamics and allows for evaluating and validating the proposed approaches for taxi allocation optimization.

Table 1. Datasets Used

	#Nodes	#Edges
NY road graph	20,700	33000
	#Taxi Requests	Latitudes & Longitudes
NY Taxi dataset	3.8M	(40.5N, 41.0N), (-74.2E, -73.5E)

Table 2. Sample Dataset

Pickup_datetime	Dropoff_datetime	Pickup_point	Dropoff_point	Trip_distance
2014-01-01 00:15:22	2014-01-01 00:17:57	188588	188592	0.03
2014-01-01 00:27:59	2014-01-01 00:28:44	197900	197899	0.01

We conducted a series of experiments to evaluate the effectiveness of our approach for incorporating edge weights into the dominating set problem for taxi allocation. The experiments were performed on a machine with a 12th Gen Intel®Core™i9-12900K × 24 processors, 64GB of RAM, and Ubuntu 20.04.

Performance Metrics: To evaluate the effectiveness of our approach and ensure reliable and reproducible results, we used the following parameters and configurations:

- **Average waiting time for passengers:** The average time a passenger had to wait for a taxi.
- **Revenue generated:** The total revenue earned by taxi companies during the simulation.
- **Traffic congestion reduction:** The decrease in overall traffic congestion in the city, measured in terms of average travel times.

We conducted a series of experiments to evaluate the effectiveness of our approach for incorporating edge weights into the dominating set problem for taxi allocation. The experiments were performed on a dataset of 50 taxi trips in New York City.

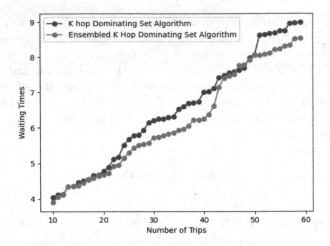

Fig. 3. Comparison of waiting time Between k-hop dominating set algorithm and ensembled k-hop dominating set algorithm

We first analyzed the comparison between the waiting times for a customer to get a taxi after they request the k-hop dominating set algorithm [28] and the ensembled k-hop dominating set algorithm, and we can see the graphical representation of the results that we got in Fig. 3. Furthermore, in the results obtained, we observed that our approach has approximately a five percent reduction in waiting time as compared to k-hop dominating set algorithm.

After this, we then analyzed the comparison between the revenue generated by trips we got from the k-hop dominating set algorithm and the ensembled k-hop dominating set algorithm, and we can see the graphical representation of the results that we got in Fig. 4. Furthermore, in the output results, our proposed method shows an increase of approximately 13 percent in revenue generation as compared to the k-hop dominating set algorithm.

Then we analyzed the comparison between the number of drivers who got more customers between the k-hop dominating set algorithm [28] and the ensembled k-hop dominating set algorithm, and we can see the graphical representation of the results we got in Fig. 5. Furthermore, in the output results, we observed that our proposed method shows a decrease of approximately two percent in number of drivers as compared to the k-hop dominating set algorithm.

Finally, we compared the average travel time to reach the k-hop dominating set algorithm and the ensembled k-hop dominating set algorithm. We can see the graphical representation of our results in Fig. 6. The output result shows that the proposed method displays approximately a 10 percent reduction in the average travel time as compared to the k-hop dominating set algorithm.

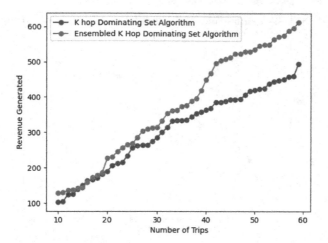

Fig. 4. Comparison of revenue generated between k-hop dominating set algorithm and ensembled k-hop dominating set algorithm

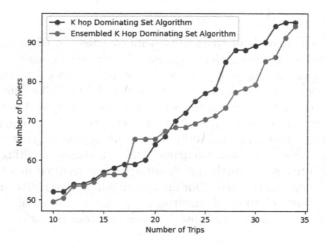

Fig. 5. Comparison of the number of drivers who got trips using k-hop dominating set algorithm and ensembled k-hop dominating set algorithm

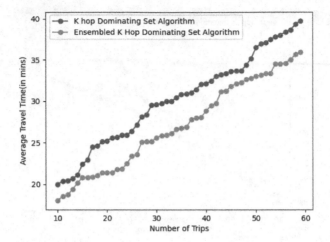

Fig. 6. Comparison of average travel time for trips using k-hop dominating set algorithm and ensembled k-hop dominating set algorithm

6.2   Result Analysis

In summary, our analysis of the results demonstrates the effectiveness of our approach in reducing waiting times, increasing revenue, decreasing the number of drivers, and decreasing average travel times. By incorporating edge weights and node entropy into the dominating set problem for taxi allocation, we significantly decreased average waiting times by ten percent compared to the baseline approach. This improvement enhances customer satisfaction and improves the overall quality of taxi services. Additionally, our approach generates thirteen percent higher revenue for taxi companies through reduced waiting times and improved taxi utilization. Furthermore, our approach resulted in a five percent reduction in average travel times. Our findings highlight the significance of incorporating edge weights into the dominating set problem, showcasing its potential for more efficient, profitable, and sustainable urban transportation.

7   Conclusion and Future Scope

Our research on incorporating edge weights into the dominating set problem for taxi allocation has yielded several significant outcomes. Our approach outperforms existing methods by optimizing taxi routes based on accurate travel time estimates. The practical implications of our research include improved passenger experience and enhanced revenue generation. These outcomes are relevant and significant for addressing the research problem of optimizing taxi allocation in urban areas and offering practical solutions to improve efficiency, customer satisfaction, and overall transportation systems.

We modified the dominating set problem formulation to minimize the maximum weighted distance between any location and its nearest vertex in the dominating set. Collect data on travel times between locations in the city. Investigated the impact of edge weights on the size and structure of the dominating set and determined how this affects the overall taxi allocation strategy. It enhances the dominating set algorithm by incorporating ensembling the weighted degree and node entropy. We developed an ensemble method to efficiently solve the modified dominating set problem, with the minimum dominating set considering the added complexity of the edge weights.

This work considers the entropy-based hotspot prediction. The work can be further extended, and the entropy of each node can be improved by considering additional attributes like weather conditions, events happening in a spatial region, etc. This will increase the certainty of finding a customer in a particular spatial region.

References

1. Li, M., He, D., Zhou, X.: Efficient kNN search with occupation in large-scale on-demand ride-hailing. In: Borovica-Gajic, R., Qi, J., Wang, W. (eds.) ADC 2020. LNCS, vol. 12008, pp. 29–41. Springer, Cham (2020). https://doi.org/10.1007/978-3-030-39469-1_3

2. Chang, H.W., Tai, Y.C., Hsu, J.Y.J.: Context-aware taxi demand hotspots prediction. Int. J. Bus. Intell. Data Mining 5(1), 3–18 (2010)

3. Dwork, C., Kumar, R., Naor, M., Sivakumar, D.: Rank aggregation methods for the web. In: WWW, pp. 613–622 (2001)

4. Ailon, N., Charikar, M., Newman, A.: Aggregating inconsistent information: ranking and clustering. JACM 55(5), 23 (2008)

5. Shekhar, S., Feiner, S.K., Aref, W.G.: Spatial computing. Commun. ACM 59(1), 72–81 (2016)

6. Mouratidis, K., Bakiras, S., Papadias, D.: Continuous monitoring of top-k queries over sliding windows. In: SIGMOD, pp. 635–646 (2006)

7. Bohm, C., Ooi, B.C., Plant, C., Yan, Y.: Efficiently processing continuous k-nn queries on data streams. In: ICDE, pp. 156–165 (2007)

8. Korn, F., Muthukrishnan, S., Srivastava, D.: Reverse nearest neighbor aggregates over data streams. In: PVLDB, pp. 814–825 (2002)

9. Li, C., Gu, Y., Qi, J., Yu, G., Zhang, R., Yi, W.: Processing moving knn queries using influential neighbor sets. PVLDB 8(2), 113–124 (2014)

10. Cheema, M., Zhang, W., Lin, X., Zhang, Y., Li, X.: Continuous reverse k nearest neighbors queries in Euclidean space and in spatial networks. VLDB J. 21(1), 69–95 (2012)

11. Khetarpaul, S., Gupta, S.K., Malhotra, S., Subramaniam, L.V.: Bus arrival time prediction using a modified amalgamation of fuzzy clustering and neural network on spatio-temporal data. In: Sharaf, M.A., Cheema, M.A., Qi, J. (eds.) ADC 2015. LNCS, vol. 9093, pp. 142–154. Springer, Cham (2015). https://doi.org/10.1007/978-3-319-19548-3_12

12. Xia, T., Zhang, D., Kanoulas, E., Du, Y.: On computing top-t most influential spatial sites. In: PVLDB, pp. 946–957 (2005)

13. Sumi, Y., Mase, K.: Toward a real-world knowledge medium: building a guidance system for exhibition tours. N. Gener. Comput. 17(4), 407–416 (1999)

14. Koh, J.-L., Lin, C.-Y., Chen, A.P.: Finding k most favorite products based on reverse top-t queries. PVLDB 23(4), 541–564 (2014)

15. Vlachou, A., Doulkeridis, C., Nørvåg, K., Kotidis, Y.: Identifying the most influential data objects with reverse top-k queries, PVLDB, vol. 3, no. 1–2, pp. 364–372 (2010)
16. Wong, R.C.-W., Özsu, M.T., Yu, P.S., Fu, A.W.-C., Liu, L.: Efficient method for maximizing bichromatic reverse nearest neighbor, PVLDB 2(1), 1126–1137 (2009)
17. Gkorgkas, O., Vlachou, A., Doulkeridis, C., Nørvåg, K.: Discovering influential data objects over time. In: SSTD, pp. 110–127 (2013)
18. Choudhury, F.M., Bao, Z., Culpepper, J.S., Sellis, T.: Monitoring the top-m aggregation in a sliding window of spatial queries (2016)
19. Sampathkumar, E., Walikar, H.B.: Connected domination number of a graph. J. Math. Phys. (1979)
20. Pang, C., Zhang, R., Zhang, Q., Wang, J.: Dominating sets in directed graphs. Inf. Sci. 180(19), 3647–365 (2010)
21. Wang, G., Wang, H., Tao, X., Zhang, J.: A self-stabilizing algorithm for finding a minimal positive influence dominating set in social networks. In: Proceedings of the 24th Australasian Database Conference (ADC 2013), pp. 93–100. Australian Computer Society Inc. (2013)
22. He, H., Zhu, Z., Makinen, E.: A neural network model to minimize the connected dominating set for self-configuration of wireless sensor networks. IEEE Trans. Neural Networks 20(6), 973–982 (2009)
23. https://users.diag.uniroma1.it/challenge9/download.shtml
24. https://www1.nyc.gov/site/tlc/about/tlc-trip-record-data.page
25. Davis, N., Raina, G., Jagannathan, K.: A multi-level clustering approach for forecasting taxi travel demand. In: 2016 IEEE 19th International Conference on Intelligent Transportation Systems (ITSC), pp. 223–228. IEEE, November 2016
26. Tang, J., Zhang, S., Chen, X., Liu, F., Zou, Y.: Taxi trips distribution modeling based on Entropy-Maximizing theory: a case study in Harbin city-China. Phys. A 493, 430–443 (2018)
27. Buccella, A., Cechich, A., Gendarmi, D., Lanubile, F., Semeraro, G., Colagrossi, A.: GeoMergeP: geographic information integration through enriched ontology matching. N. Gener. Comput. 28(1), 41–71 (2010)
28. Mishra, S., Khetarpaul, S.: Optimal placement of Taxis in a city using dominating set problem. In: Qiao, M., Vossen, G., Wang, S., Li, L. (eds.) ADC 2021. LNCS, vol. 12610, pp. 111–124. Springer, Cham (2021). https://doi.org/10.1007/978-3-030-69377-0_10

Fast Correlated DNA Subsequence Search via Graph-Based Representation

Ryuichi Yagi[1]([✉])(iD), Yuma Naoi[1](iD), and Hiroaki Shiokawa[2](iD)

[1] Department of Computer Science, University of Tsukuba, Tsukuba, Japan
{yagi,naoi}@kde.cs.tsukuba.ac.jp
[2] Center for Computational Sciences, University of Tsukuba, Tsukuba, Japan
shiokawa@cs.tsukuba.ac.jp

Abstract. Numerous fields employ correlation-based searches to provide insights about relationships in a database. Herein we propose a correlated DNA subsequence search for DNA databases to extract DNA subsequences that frequently co-occur with a query. Typical search methods must evaluate the entire database for potential candidates, which is computationally expensive. To overcome this, we propose a threshold-based algorithm to achieve efficient computation. The proposed algorithm extracts all DNA subsequences whose correlation is more significant than the threshold and excludes unlikely candidates. Experiments involving real-world DNA databases show that the proposed method achieves a faster search than baseline algorithms while maintaining a high accuracy.

Keywords: DNA database · Similarity search · Correlation

1 Introduction

Biologically closer lifeforms tend to have similar DNA sequences, which are long strings composed of four characters ("A", "C", "G", and "T"). DNA functionalities, which may be potential biomarkers for specific diseases, can be estimated by analyzing the relationships of DNA subsequences in a database. For this reason, a DNA similarity search is an essential building block for fundamental biological research, medical diagnosis, and bioinformatics [7–9].

To achieve efficient and effective DNA searches, various algorithms have been proposed [8,11]. String-based similarity search methods model a DNA database as a set of character strings. Although string-based similarity search methods are helpful for DNA analysis, they have two critical weaknesses. First, the edit distance is computationally expensive. Second, the edit distance is highly biased by the subsequence length. To overcome these limitations, we define a novel class of the DNA search problem called *correlated DNA subsequence (CDS) searches*. Unlike traditional similarity search methods, a CDS search evaluates the relevance of a DNA subsequence to a query based on the co-occurrence in a database. For a given query DNA sequence and a DNA database, a CDS search finds DNA

P. Delir Haghighi et al. (Eds.): iiWAS 2023, LNCS 14416, pp. 339–347, 2023.
https://doi.org/10.1007/978-3-031-48316-5_32

subsequences in the database that frequently co-occur with the query in the database. Since a CDS search explores subsequences based on the co-occurrences, similar or related DNA subsequences can be identified regardless of length.

This study proposes an efficient algorithm for a CDS search that returns all DNA subsequences with co-occurrences greater than a user-specified threshold. In the CDS search, computing co-occurrences incurs an expensive cost. However, our proposed algorithm excludes unpromising DNA subsequences to avoid expensive overhead. First, we convert DNA subsequences into the corresponding graph representations. Then, we employ graph-based bounds of the correlation, which can identify unpromising subsequences in the database. Finally, based on the lower bound and the user-specified threshold, subsequence pruning rules are designed. These rules are inspired by frequent subgraph mining methods [1,10].

2 Preliminary

Let s be a DNA sequence with a length of m_s, where m_s indicates the number of characters in s. For simplification, m is used instead of m_s if it is clear from the context. Given two DNA sequences, s_i and s_j, $s_i \subseteq s_j$ if an injective function $f : s_i \rightarrow s_j$ exists. If $s_i \subseteq s_j$, then s_i is a *subsequence* of s_j. Let $\mathcal{B}(s)$ be a set of all subsequences of s. Then it is defined as $\mathcal{B}(s) = \{s_i \mid s_i \subseteq s\}$. A DNA database that consists of N DNA sequences is denoted as $\mathcal{D} = \{s_1, s_2, \ldots, s_N\}$. Given $\mathcal{D}$, we denote $\mathcal{D}_s = \{s' \in \mathcal{D} \mid s \subseteq s'\}$ as a projected database of s.

Inspired by frequent subgraph mining [1,10], we define the correlation between subsequences to measure the co-occurrence of subsequences. Let $supp(s; \mathcal{D})$ be the support of s in $\mathcal{D}$ defined as $supp(s; \mathcal{D}) = \frac{|\mathcal{D}_s|}{|\mathcal{D}|}$. Unless otherwise stated, $supp(s)$ is used instead of $supp(s; \mathcal{D})$. Given two subsequences, s_i and s_j, their joint support in $\mathcal{D}$, which is denoted by $supp(s_i, s_j)$, is defined as $supp(s_i, s_j) = \frac{|\mathcal{D}_{s_i} \cap \mathcal{D}_{s_j}|}{|\mathcal{D}|}$. If $s_i \subseteq s_j$, then $supp(s_j) \leq supp(s_i)$ holds. Additionally, the joint support implies $supp(s_i, s_j) \leq supp(s_i)$ and $supp(s_i, s_j) \leq supp(s_j)$.

By using the support, we define the correlation between subsequences based on the Pearson coefficient [3] as follows:

Definition 1 (Correlation between subsequences). *Given two subsequences, s_i and s_j, their correlation is denoted by $\phi(s_i, s_j)$ and is defined as*

$$\phi(s_i, s_j) = \frac{supp(s_i, s_j) - supp(s_i)supp(s_j)}{\sqrt{supp(s_i)supp(s_j)(1 - supp(s_i))(1 - supp(s_j))}}. \tag{1}$$

Note that $\phi(s_i, s_j) = 0$ if $supp(s_i)supp(s_j)(1 - supp(s_i))(1 - supp(s_j)) = 0$.

Finally, using Definition 1, a CDS search is defined as follows:

Problem 1 (CDS search). *Given a DNA database $\mathcal{D} = \{s_1, s_2, \ldots, s_N\}$, a query DNA sequence q, and a threshold $\theta \in [-1, 1]$, a CDS search finds a set of correlated subsequences $\mathcal{T}_\theta(q)$, which is defined as*

$$\mathcal{T}_\theta(q) = \left\{ s \in \bigcup_{s' \in \mathcal{D}} \mathcal{B}(s') \,\middle|\, \phi(q, s) \geq \theta \right\}. \tag{2}$$

Problem 1 indicates that a CDS search finds all subsequences induced from $\mathcal{D}$ such that the subsequences yield a larger correlation than θ. Since each DNA sequence includes $\mathcal{O}(\frac{m(m+1)}{2}) = \mathcal{O}(m^2)$ subsequences, a CDS search incurs $\mathcal{O}(Nm^2)$ times in a naïve way. Because practical DNA sequences have large m, it is important to develop an efficient algorithm for a CDS search.

3 Proposed Method: Pruning-Based Algorithm

Our proposed algorithm finds the correlated subsequences from $\mathcal{D}$ within a short computation time. For Problem 1, a naïve algorithm measures the correlation for all subsequences induced from $\mathcal{D}$, entailing $\mathcal{O}(Nm^2)$ time. In contrast, our proposed algorithm excludes unpromising subsequences that yield a correlation smaller than θ without computing the correlation. Our algorithm improves the efficiency of the CDS search by reducing the number of computed subsequences.

3.1 A DNA Graph

We begin by theoretically discussing the equivalence between a DNA sequence and a graph. Let $g = (V, E, L)$ be a labeled graph, where V, E, and L are the sets of nodes, edges, and node-labels, respectively. We define a DNA graph as follows:

Definition 2 (DNA graph). *Let $s = S^1, S^2, \ldots, S^m$ be a DNA sequence of length m, where S^i is the i-th character of s. A DNA graph of s, denoted by g_s, is defined as $g_s = (V, E, L)$, where $V = \{1, 2, \ldots, m\}$, $E = \{(v_i, v_j) \in V^2 \mid i + 1 = j\}$, and $L = \{S^1, S^2, \ldots, S^m\}$.*

Definition 2 indicates that a DNA sequence s is transformed into a path graph g_s whose edges represent adjacency of characters in s. That is, a DNA database $\mathcal{D} = \{s_1, s_2, \ldots, s_N\}$ can be regarded as a graph database $\mathcal{G} = \{g_{s_1}, g_{s_2}, \ldots, g_{s_N}\}$. From Definition 1, the correlation between two DNA graphs is derived as follows:

Definition 3 (Correlation between DNA graphs). *Let $\mathcal{G}_{g_i}$ be a set of supergraphs of g_i in $\mathcal{G}$. Given two DNA graphs, g_i and g_j, their correlation is defined as $\phi(g_i, g_j)$.*

From Definitions 1, 2, and 3, we can derive the following lemma:

Lemma 1. *Given two DNA subsequences, s_i, s_j and their corresponding DNA graphs, g_i, g_j, $\phi(s_i, s_j) = \phi(g_i, g_j)$ always holds.*

Proof. For DNA sequence s_k and its corresponding DNA graph g_{s_k}, if $s_k \subseteq s_i$, then g_{s_k} is a subgraph of g_{s_i}. As shown in Definition 2, a bijection mapping exists between s_k and g_{s_k}. Thus, we always have $|\mathcal{D}_{s_i}| = |\mathcal{G}_{g_{s_i}}|$ for any pair of a DNA sequence and its corresponding DNA graph. Hence, from Definitions 1, 2, and 3, $\phi(s_i, s_j) = \phi(g_i, g_j)$ always holds. □

Lemma 1 indicates that if a DNA graph yields a smaller correlation with the query, then its corresponding subsequence is not correlated to the query.

3.2   Graph-Based Pruning Rules

A DNA subsequence and its corresponding DNA graph are equivalent in a correlation-based search. Based on this property, graph-based pruning rules [1] can be applied to a CDS search. Specifically, several graph-based pruning approaches [1] are applicable to a CDS search by converting DNA subsequences into DNA graphs.

Rule 1. *Given a query graph g_q and a threshold θ, a necessary condition that satisfies $\phi(g_q, g) \geq \theta$ for $g \in \mathcal{G}$ is*

$$supp(g; \mathcal{G}_q) \geq \frac{1}{\theta^{-2}(1 - supp(q)) + supp(q)}. \tag{3}$$

Rule 1 indicates that only DNA subsequences corresponding to g need to be computed.

Additionally, the following heuristic pruning rules [1] are applicable to a CDS search.

Rule 2. *Given a query graph g_q, a graph $g \in \mathcal{G}$, and a threshold θ, if g_q is a subgraph of g, then $\phi(g_q, g) \geq \theta$.*

Rule 3. *For a given query graph g_q, suppose a graph g and its subgraph g' satisfy $supp(g_q, g) = supp(g_q, g')$. In this case, if $\phi(g_q, g) < \theta$, then $\phi(g_q, g') < \theta$ holds.*

Rule 4. *For a given query graph g_q, suppose a graph g and its subgraph g' satisfy $supp(g_q, g') < f(g_q, g)$. In this case, if $\phi(g_q, g) < \theta$, then $\phi(g_q, g') < \theta$ holds. Note that $f(g_q, g)$ is defined as*

$$f(g_q, g) = \theta \sqrt{supp(g_q) supp(g)(1 - supp(g_q))(1 - supp(g))} + supp(g_q) supp(g). \tag{4}$$

The proposed algorithm uses the above rules over DNA graphs converted by Definition 2 to exclude unpromising DNA subsequences included in $\mathcal{D}$.

Algorithm 1. Threshold-based method

Input: $\mathcal{D}$, q, and θ
Output: $\mathcal{T}_\theta(q)$
 1: Convert $\mathcal{D}$ to $\mathcal{G}$ by Definition 2;
 2: Obtain $\mathcal{G}_q$, $\mathcal{T}_\theta(q) = \emptyset$;
 3: Obtain $\mathcal{C}$ from $\mathcal{G}_q$ by on Rule 1;
 4: **for each** $g \in \mathcal{C}$ **do**
 5:     **if** g contains g_q **then**
 6:         Obtain a DNA subsequence s corresponding to g;
 7:         Add s to $\mathcal{T}_\theta(q)$ by Rule 2;
 8:     **else**
 9:         Compute $\phi(g_q, g)$;
10:         **if** $\phi(g_q, g) \geq \theta$ **then**
11:             Obtain a DNA subsequence s corresponding to g;
12:             Add s to $\mathcal{T}_\theta(q)$;
13:         **else**
14:             Remove $g' \in \mathcal{C}$ by Rule 3;
15:             Remove $g' \in \mathcal{C}$ by Rule 4;
     return $\mathcal{T}_\theta(q)$;

3.3 Algorithm

Algorithm 1 shows the pseudocode of our proposed method. Given a query q and a DNA database $\mathcal{D}$, the proposed method converts them into DNA graphs by Definition 2. Then our algorithm applies the graph-based pruning rules to explore correlated subsequences by dynamically excluding unpromising subsequences. First, the projected database $\mathcal{G}_q$ (line 2) is obtained. By applying Rule 1 to $\mathcal{G}_q$, a set of DNA subgraphs $\mathcal{C}$ are generated (line 3). Second, a frequent subgraph mining method [2] is employed to efficiently compute $\mathcal{C}$. For each DNA subgraph $g \in \mathcal{C}$, graph-based pruning rules Rules 2, 3, and 4 are performed (lines 4–15). In lines 5–7, Rule 2 is applied to g. If g satisfies the condition shown in Rule 2, its corresponding DNA subsequence s is added to $\mathcal{T}_\theta(q)$. Otherwise, $\phi(g_q, g)$ is computed, and if its value is greater than or equal to θ, s corresponding to g is added to $\mathcal{T}_\theta(q)$ (lines 9–12). Finally, Rules 3 and 4 are applied to prune unpromising DNA subgraphs from $\mathcal{C}$ (lines 14–15).

4 Experiments

4.1 Experimental Setup

To validate the proposed method, we experimentally compared Algorithm 1 with the baseline methods. The baseline methods consist of the following steps:

1. A set of subsequences, denoted by $\mathcal{O}$, whose occurrence in $\mathcal{D}_q$ is greater than $\hat{\mu}$ is extracted.

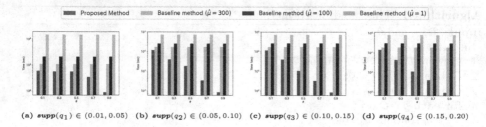

Fig. 1. Query Processing Time of GEN20kS

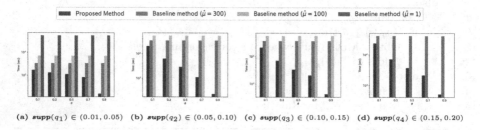

Fig. 2. Query Processing Time of GEN20kM

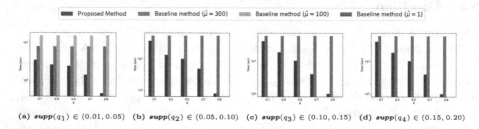

Fig. 3. Query Processing Time of GEN20kL

2. The correlation $\phi(q, s)$ is computed for each $s \in \mathcal{O}$.
3. s is added into $\mathcal{T}_\theta(q)$ if $\phi(q, s) \geq \theta$.

In our experimental analysis, $\hat{\mu}$ was varied as 300, 200, and 1. If $\hat{\mu} = 1$, the Baseline method needs to compute all subsequences included in $\mathcal{D}$, which entails $\mathcal{O}(Nm^2)$ time as described in Sect. 2. In contrast, as $\hat{\mu}$ increases, not all subsequences need to be computed.

All algorithms were implemented by C++ and compiled with the -O3 option. All experiments were conducted on a Linux server with an Intel Xeon 2.7 GHz CPU and 768 GiB RAM. We used three real-world DNA databases provided by [11]. All databases included 20,000 DNA sequences with different average lengths (Table 1).

4.2   Efficiency

Four types of queries, q_1, q_2, q_3 and q_4 were set by varying their support values. The supports were set as $supp(q_1) \in (0.01, 0.05)$, $supp(q_2) \in (0.05, 0.10)$, $supp(q_3) \in (0.10, 0.15)$, and $supp(q_4) \in (0.15, 0.20)$.

Figures 1, 2, and 3 show the query processing time for each dataset. If the method did not finish with 24 h, the results were omitted. Our proposed algorithm outperformed the other methods examined in this experiment. Of interest, our proposed method was up to two orders of magnitude faster than the fastest baseline method (*i.e.*, Baseline method ($\hat{\mu} = 300$)). In contrast, the baseline methods often failed to finish the CDS search if the average DNA sequence was large. In each figure, our proposed achieved a better running time as θ increased because the pruning rules excluded many candidates for large θ values. For small θ settings, our algorithm still required a long running time. However, setting θ to a small value for the CDS search is unreasonable because the obtained results are almost independent of the query. Therefore, our algorithm can drastically reduce the running time in many use cases.

Table 1. Details of the datasets

Datasets	N	Avg. length	Min. length	Max. length
GEN20kS	20,000	5,000	4,829	5,109
GEN20kM	20,000	10,000	9,843	10,154
GEN20kL	20,000	20,000	19,821	20,109

Table 2. Recall on GEN20kS

Method	q_1	q_2	q_3	q_4
Our proposed method	1.0	1.0	1.0	1.0
Baseline method ($\hat{\mu} = 300$)	0.81	0.77	0.77	0.78
Baseline method ($\hat{\mu} = 100$)	1.0	1.0	1.0	1.0

4.3   Accuracy

Next, we assessed the search accuracy of our proposed method. Since the baseline method returned all correlated subsequences from $\mathcal{D}$ if $\hat{\mu} = 1$, these results were regarded as the ground truth.

Table 2 shows the Recall values of each method on GEN20kS. Our proposed method reproduced the ground truth, while the other methods failed to find the exact search results. To find exact subsequences, the baseline method needs to tune $\hat{\mu}$, although this is computationally expensive as discussed in Sect. 4.2. In contrast, as discussed in Sect. 3.1, we theoretically bridged the CDS search into a graph-based representation, leading to effective pruning rules inspired by graph-based correlation analysis. In addition, as discussed in [1], the pruning rules theoretically guarantee the exact search results. Hence, our algorithm achieves the exact search results in all settings.

5   Conclusion

This study proposes a method to overcome the limitations of existing string-based approaches for a class of the DNA search problem called the CDS search. A CDS search is a problem in finding correlated subsequences to a user-specified query sequence. Since a CDS search incurs $\mathcal{O}(Nm^2)$ time in the worst case, in this paper, we propose an efficient algorithm for a CDS search based on graph-based pruning. Our method converts DNA databases into corresponding graph databases and efficiently explores the correlated subsequences by excluding unpromising ones. Our experimental analysis using real-world DNA databases demonstrates that our proposed method is up to two orders of magnitude faster than the others while keeping exact search results. As for future work, we plan to adopt our algorithm to actual DNA screening tasks in collaboration with medical science researchers. To this end, we will further experimentally discuss the effectiveness of the CDS search in comparison with traditional string-based searches based on the edit distance. In addition, the computational efficiency of our proposed algorithm still looks limited if a threshold θ is small. Hence, we plan to extend the pruning approaches further to enhance computational efficiency by using data aggregation approaches [4–6].

Acknowledgements. This work is partly supported by JST PRESTO JPMJPR2033 and JSPS KAKENHI JP22K17894.

References

1. Ke, Y., Cheng, J., Ng, W.: Correlation search in graph databases. In: Proceedings of the 13th ACM SIGKDD International Conference on Knowledge Discovery and Data Mining, KDD 2007, pp. 390–399 (2007)
2. Ke, Y., Cheng, J., Yu, J.X.: Top-k Correlative Graph Mining. In: Proceedings of the SIAM International Conference on Data Mining, SDM 2009, pp. 1038–1049 (2009)
3. Reynolds, H.T.: The Analysis of Cross-Classifications. The Free Press, New York (1977)
4. Shiokawa, H.: Scalable affinity propagation for massive datasets. In: Proceedings of the AAAI Conference on Artificial Intelligence 35(11), pp. 9639–9646 (2021)
5. Shiokawa, H., Amagasa, T., Kitagawa, H.: Scaling fine-grained modularity clustering for massive graphs. In: Proceedings of the 28th International Joint Conference on Artificial Intelligence, IJCAI 2019, pp. 4597–4604 (2019)
6. Shiokawa, H., Fujiwara, Y., Onizuka, M.: Fast algorithm for modularity-based graph clustering. In: Proceedings of the 27th AAAI Conference on Artificial Intelligence (AAAI 2013) (2013)

7. Suzuki, Y., Sato, M., Shiokawa, H., Yanagisawa, M., Kitagawa, H.: MASC: automatic sleep stage classification based on brain and myoelectric signals. In: 2017 IEEE 33rd International Conference on Data Engineering (ICDE), pp. 1489–1496 (2017). https://doi.org/10.1109/ICDE.2017.218
8. Yagi, R., Shiokawa, H.: Fast Top-k similar sequence search on DNA databases. In: Proceedings of the 24th International Conference on Information Integration and Web Intelligence (iiWAS 2022), pp. 145–150 (2022)
9. Yamabe, M., Horie, K., Shiokawa, H., Funato, H., Yanagisawa, M., Kitagawa, H.: MC-SleepNet: large-scale sleep stage scoring in mice by deep neural networks. Sci. Rep. 9(15793), October 2019
10. Yan, X., Han, J.: gSpan: graph-based substructure pattern mining. In: 2002 IEEE International Conference on Data Mining, 2002. Proceedings, pp. 721–724 (2002)
11. Zhang, H., Zhang, Q.: EmbedJoin: efficient edit similarity joins via embeddings. In: Proceedings of the 23rd ACM SIGKDD International Conference on Knowledge Discovery and Data Mining, KDD 2017, pp. 585–594 (2017)

Efficient Maximum k-plex Search
via Selective Branch-and-Bound

Shohei Matsugu[1(✉)] and Hiroaki Shiokawa[2]

[1] Graduate School of Science and Technology, University of Tsukuba,
Tsukuba, Japan
matsugu@kde.cs.tsukuba.ac.jp
[2] Center for Computational Sciences, University of Tsukuba, Tsukuba, Japan
shiokawa@cs.tsukuba.ac.jp

Abstract. Maximum k-plex search (MPS) finds the largest dense subgraph in a graph. Although it is a fundamental task in many AI and DB applications, MPS is computationally expensive. It searches a maximum k-plex, which is a generalization model of a clique, by removing nodes not included in the k-plex. However, handling massive graphs with numerous nodes and edges is challenging because existing MPS algorithms repeatedly compute the entire graph to remove non-k-plex nodes. Herein we propose a fast algorithm, *SBnB*, which outputs an exact maximum k-plex in a shorter computation time as it dynamically finds non-k-plex nodes without exploring the entire graph. Additionally, we experimentally demonstrate that SBnB outperforms state-of-the-art MPS algorithms in terms of running time by up to two orders of magnitude.

Keywords: Dense subgraph search · Graph database · k-plex

1 Introduction

Finding the largest dense subgraph is a fundamental task to discover an insightful community in many AI and DB applications [3,6,16]. The *maximum k-plex search* (MPS) algorithm can identify such subgraphs. A k-plex is a subgraph containing n nodes, where each node is adjacent to at least $n - k$ nodes [1]. Since k-plex can effectively model complex communities observed in real-world phenomena, MPS is suitable to find the largest dense subgraph for complex real-world networks.

Although MPS is useful in many applications, it is NP-hard [2] because it must repeatedly search for all nodes. If V is a set of nodes, the MPS algorithm requires $O(2^{|V|}|V|)$ time. As dataset resources increase both in size and ubiquity, applications repeatedly handle massive graphs with at least 10^5 nodes [11]. Consequently, current MPS algorithms require a large running time on massive graphs.

1.1 Existing Approaches and Challenges

Many studies have strived to overcome the expensive cost [5,20]. Traditional MPS algorithms explore the maximum k-plex among $O(2^{|V|})$ search spaces.

© The Author(s), under exclusive license to Springer Nature Switzerland AG 2023
P. Delir Haghighi et al. (Eds.): iiWAS 2023, LNCS 14416, pp. 348–357, 2023.
https://doi.org/10.1007/978-3-031-48316-5_33

However, searching only essential nodes, which may be included in k-plexes, is more reasonable. Gao *et al.* recently proposed *branch-and-bound* (BnB) [8]. They found that a lower bound size of a k-plex can be estimated from the nodes included in a specific search space, derived graph reduction techniques to estimate the boundary, and eventually designed an MPS algorithm that can return the maximum k-plex with a reasonable running time even if the graph size exceeds 10^4 nodes.

Although BnB improves efficiency, it still requires high computational costs to handle massive graphs [19]. In BnB, three graph reduction techniques explore all nodes repeatedly, incurring $O(|V|(|V| + |E|))$ time [8], where $|V|$ and $|E|$ are the number of nodes and edges in a graph, respectively. To find the maximum k-plex, BnB incurs $O(|V|)$ search trials. If each trial involves graph reduction $O(\tau)$ time, then the total time complexity of BnB is $O(\tau|V|^2(|V| + |E|))$ time. Hence, it is a challenging task to develop an efficient MPS algorithm to handle massive graphs.

1.2   Our Approaches and Contributions

Our goal is to efficiently compute MPS on massive graphs. Here, we present a fast algorithm called *selective BnB* (SBnB). SBnB removes redundant search subspaces computed in the graph reduction algorithms. To identify which subspaces to exclude, SBnB focuses on the bounding properties of graph reduction. We theoretically clarify that finding structurally similar nodes can tightly bound most search subspaces explored by the algorithms (Lemmas 1–4). Thus, exhaustively searching all nodes is unnecessary.

Based on these properties, we employ two approaches to enhance efficiency. First, we theoretically derive *removable nodes*, which provide SBnB with the bounding properties for graph reduction (Sect. 3.2). Second, we introduce *selective graph reduction* to efficiently skip redundant search spaces for removable nodes (Sect. 3.3). Consequently, SBnB has the following attractive characteristics:

- **Efficiency:** SBnB achieves faster computations than state-of-the-art MPS algorithms (Theorem 1 and Sect. 4.1).
- **Exactness:** SBnB always outputs the maximum k-plex in a graph, even though it significantly reduces search spaces (Theorem 2).
- **Easy to deploy:** Unlike BnB, SBnB does not require additional parameters.

SBnB is the first solution that simultaneously achieves efficient MPS on massive graphs and the exactness of the search results. It outperforms state-of-the-art algorithms by up to two orders of magnitude in terms of running time. Moreover, SBnB should contribute to various applications due to its scalability. By providing scalable approaches, SBnB should contribute to various applications.

2   Preliminaries

Here, we define the basic notations and briefly review BnB [8]. Let $G = (V, E)$ be an undirected graph, where V and E are a set of nodes and edges, respectively.

Let d_G represent the degree of a node u in G, and $N(u)$ indicate a set of neighbor nodes of node u (including u). Given $S \subseteq V$, $G[S]$ represents an induced subgraph. For convenience, $N(S)$ represents a set of neighbor nodes of a subgraph S and $N^2(u) = N(N(u))$.

2.1 Maximum k-plex Search (MPS) Problem

MPS is a task to find the largest k-plex in a graph G, where k-plex is a dense subgraph model proposed by [1]. Since k-plex relaxes the topological constraints of a clique, several edges in a subgraph can be omitted. Formally, k-plex is defined as:

Definition 1 (k-plex). *Given a graph $G = (V, E)$, and a positive integer k, k-plex is an induced subgraph $G[S]$ such that $S \subseteq V$ and $d_{G[S]}(v) \geq |S| - k$ for all $v \in S$.*

That is, k-plex is subgraph S in which the degree of each node is at least $|S| - k$. Based on Definition 1, the MPS problem is formally defined as:

Problem 1 (MPS Problem). *Given a graph G, and a positive integer k, the MPS problem is a task to find $G[S]$ that maximizes $|S|$ in G.*

If $k = 1$, Problem 1 is equivalent to the maximum clique problem [4]. Hence, the MPS problem is NP-hard [1,12,17].

2.2 Branch-and-Bound (BnB)

To efficiently compute MPS, Gao *et al.* recently proposed BnB [8]. First, BnB selects a starting node u, and k-plex is initialized as $S = \{u\}$. Second, it selects a node $v \in V \backslash \{u\}$ and applies binary branching rule. The rule states that either (1) node v is merged into k-plex S (*i.e.*, $S = S \cup \{v\}$) or (2) it is discarded. Thus, the search space is split into two subspaces: $S = \{u, v\}$ or $S = \{u\}$. Third, BnB invokes the bounding rule to estimate the lower k-plex bound size, which can be extracted in each subspace. Then the process is repeated by selecting another node from $V \setminus S$. Hence, BnB explores all subspaces until $|S|$ is maximized. To speed up this process, BnB employs the graph reduction algorithms shown in Definitions 2, 3, and 4 to prune unpromising nodes for each subspace. Unpromising nodes are excluded because they are unlikely to be in any k-plexes in the subspace. Specifically, these algorithms are defined as:

Definition 2 (k-reduction). *Given G and k-plex nodes $S_u = S \cup \{u\}$, let $\overline{S}_u(w) = S_u \backslash N(w)$. k-reduction removes $f_k(V, S_u) = f_k^1(V, S_u) \cup f_k^2(V, S_u)$ from G, where $f_k^1(V, S_u)$ and $f_k^2(V, S_u)$ are given as $f_k^1(V, S_u) = \{w \in V \backslash S_u \mid |\overline{S}_u(w)| > k-1\}$ and $f_k^2(V, S_u) = \bigcup_{w \in \{w' \in S_u \mid |\overline{S}_u(w')| = k-1\}} V \backslash (N(w) \cup S_u)$.*

Definition 3 (vertex-reduction). *Given G and integer l, vertex-reduction removes the following nodes from G: $f_x(V, l) = \{u \in V \mid d_G(u) + k \leq l\}$.*

Definition 4 (v-reduction). *Given G, k-plex nodes $S_u = S \cup \{u\}$, and an integer l, v-reduction removes $f_v(S, u, l) = \{v \in N(u)\backslash S \mid c_{G,S}(u,v) + |S| - 1 \le l\}$ from G. Note that $c_{G,S}$ is defined as $c_{G,S}(u,v) = \min\{d_{G'}(u) + r_{G,S}(u) + 1, |N(v)\backslash S|\} + r_{G,S}(v)$, where $G' = G[N(v)\backslash S]$, and $r_{G,S}(u) = k - |S\backslash N(u)|$.*

BnB removes nodes that cannot be included in any k-plexes larger than l using a combination of the above definitions for each subspace. As the k-plex search progresses, the subspace size is gradually reduced. As described in Sect. 1.2, BnB requires $O(\tau |V|^2(|V| + |E|))$ time. Hence, MPS via BnB fails on massive graphs due to the long running time of BnB for large graphs.

3 Selective Branch-and-Bound (SBnB)

Our proposal, SBnB, can efficiently compute MPS. Here, we describe the concept of SBnB and then provide details. Proofs of lemmas are omitted due to space limitations.

3.1 Ideas

Our goal is to efficiently find the maximum k-plex. SBnB explores only essential nodes in each subspace using the following approaches. First, we derive removable nodes. These nodes determine which nodes to prune in multiple search subspaces. Second, we employ selective graph reduction to minimize redundant searches based on removable nodes while maintaining the same results as BnB.

SBnB finds the maximum k-plex within a shorter running time. Our approach successfully handles the power-law degree distribution [7]. Because SBnB can effectively bound search spaces for selective graph reduction if most nodes have a small degree, it can efficiently find the maximum k-plex.

3.2 Removable Nodes

We define *removable nodes*, which derive tightly bounded search spaces for graph reduction algorithms as follows:

Definition 5 (Removable nodes). *Given k-plex $G[S]$ and node $u \in V\backslash S$, a set of removable nodes $\mathcal{R}(S, u)$ is defined as $\mathcal{R}(S, u) = \{v \in V\backslash S \mid N(u) \cap S = N(v) \cap S\}$.*

Definition 5 indicates that $\mathcal{R}(S, u)$ includes all non k-plex nodes that share the same neighbor nodes in k-plex $G[S]$ with node u. Definition 5 leads to the following bounding properties, which are crucial for selective graph reduction (Sect. 4.2):

Lemma 1. *Given k-plex $G[S]$, $v \in \mathcal{R}(S, u)$, $S_v = S \cup \{v\}$, $S_u = S \cup \{u\}$ and $V' = V\backslash f_k^1(V, S_u)$, $f_k^1(V', S_v) \subseteq N(u)$ always holds.*

After k-reduction gives V', Lemma 1 indicates that the nodes removed by $f_k^1(V', S_v)$ are always bounded. A similar bounding property for k-reduction can be derived, as shown in Definition 2.

Lemma 2. *Given k-plex $G[S]$, node $v \in R(S, u)$, and $V' = V \backslash f_k^2(V, S_u)$, $f_k^2(V', S_v) \subseteq N(u)$ always holds.*

From Definition 2 and Lemmas 1 and 2, we can theoretically derive that $f_k(V', S_v)$ is bounded by $N(u)$ for all $v \in \mathcal{R}(S, u)$ once V' is obtained. Consequently, the entire graph does not need to be explored to identify which nodes can be removed by k-reduction.

Analogously, we introduce similar properties for vertex-reduction and v-reduction.

Lemma 3. *Given k-plex $G[S]$, $v \in \mathcal{R}(S, u)$, and $V' = V \backslash (f_k(V, S_u) \cup f_x(V, l))$, $f_x(V'', l) \subseteq N^2(v)$ always holds, where $V'' = V' \backslash f_k(V', S_v)$.*

If $v \in \mathcal{R}(S, u)$, Lemma 3 indicates that the search spaces explored by vertex-reduction are bounded by $N^2(u)$.

Lemma 4. *Given k-plex $G[S]$, and $u \in V \backslash S$, $f_v(S, u, l) \subseteq N(u)$ always holds.*

From Lemma 4, v-reduction removes only nodes in $N(u)$ regardless if u is the removable node or not.

Finally, we theoretically assess the time complexity to obtain the removable nodes.

Lemma 5. *Given k-plex $G[S]$ and $u \in V \backslash S$, $\mathcal{R}(S, u)$ is obtained in $O(\overline{d}^2)$ time, where $\overline{d}$ is the average degree in G.*

3.3   Selective Graph Reduction

We introduce *selective graph reduction* to remove unnecessary graph reduction processes in BnB. If nodes are included in the removable nodes of node u, the search spaces explored by the three graph reduction algorithms are tightly bounded by $N(u)$ or $N^2(u)$, as proved in Lemmas 1–4. Thus, nodes removed by the graph reductions can be identified without exploring all nodes.

To leverage the above properties, SBnB replaces three graph reductions with selective graph reduction, which is given as follows:

Definition 6 (Selective graph reduction). *Given k-plex $G[S]$ and $u, v \in V \backslash S$, selective graph reduction removes nodes in $\hat{f}(S_v, l)$ for a node v, which is defined as*

$$\hat{f}(S_v, l) = \begin{cases} f_\Delta(S_v, l) \cup f_v(S, v, l) & (v \in \mathcal{R}(S, u)) \\ f_k(V, S_v) \cup f_x(V, l) \cup f_v(S, v, l) & (Otherwise) \end{cases},$$

where $f_\Delta(S_v, l) = f_k(N(u), S_u) \cup f_x(N^2(u), l)$.

In Definition 6, SBnB explores which nodes to remove by graph reduction from $V \backslash S$ by following Definitions 2–4 only if a node v is not included in the removable nodes. Otherwise, it bounds the search spaces explored in the graph reduction algorithms by $N(u)$, $N^2(u)$, and $N(v)$.

To discuss the theoretical aspects of Definition 6, we derive the following property:

Lemma 6. *Given k-plex $G[S]$, $u, v \in V \backslash S$, and $V' = V \backslash (f_k(V, S_u) \cup f_x(V, l))$, $\hat{f}(S_v, l) = f_k(V', S_v) \cup f_x(V', l) \cup f_v(S, v, l)$ always holds.*

Although SBnB and BnB differ, Lemma 6 indicates that SBnB can remove the same nodes from search spaces as the three graph reduction methods in BnB. This is because $N(v)$, $N^2(v)$, and $N(u)$ bound both search spaces.

3.4   Algorithm, Optimization, and Analysis

We overview an algorithm of SBnB. It iteratively performs MPS by varying the starting node. Once node u is selected as a starting node, the MPS function is invoked to explore the maximum k-plex from u. In the MPS function, SBnB initially selects node v from $V \backslash S$. Then the search space is split based on whether k-plex S includes v. If v is a k-plex node, SBnB invokes selective graph reduction based on Definition 6. If $v \in \mathcal{R}(S, u)$, $\hat{f}(S_v, l)$ is computed in $O(\overline{d}^2)$ time by Lemma 6. Otherwise, it requires $O(|V_G|)$ time, where V_G represents the nodes in G. These processes are recursively performed until SBnB finds the largest k-plex S starting from u. Finally, the maximum k-plex is returned from all starting nodes.

Theoretical analysis: Finally, we theoretically assess the efficiency and exactness. Here, let $\overline{d}$, c, and τ be the average degree, the pairwise clustering coefficient [9], and the average number of graph reductions invoked by $\text{MPS}_k(G, S, l, u)$, respectively.

Theorem 1 (Efficiency). *Given a graph G and an integer k, SBnB incurs $O(\tau |V|(c\overline{d}^2 + (1 - c)|V|))$ time.*

Proof. SBnB repeats the MPS_k search in $O(|V|)$ time. In each search, SBnB invokes Definition 6 in $O(\tau)$ time. Each search incurs $O(\overline{d}^2 + \overline{d}^2) = O(\overline{d}^2)$ time for removable nodes by Lemma 5, whereas the remaining nodes require $O(|V|)$. From [14], pairwise nodes share $O((c\overline{d}/2)/\overline{d}) = O(c)$ fraction of neighbors on average. Since SBnB incurs $O(c\overline{d}^2 + (1 - c)|V|)$ time on average, SBnB requires $O(\tau |V|(c\overline{d}^2 + (1 - c)|V|))$ time.   □

As shown in Sect. 2, BnB requires $O(\tau |V|^2(|V| + |E|))$ time. Consequently, Theorem 1 indicates that SBnB is dramatically faster than BnB. In practice, $\overline{d}$ should be a small constant since real-world graphs follow a power-law degree distribution [7]. Thus, $\overline{d}^2$ is negligible, and SBnB has $O(\tau |V|(c\overline{d}^2 + (1-c)|V|)) \approx O(\tau(1-c)|V|^2)$ time on real-world graphs.

Theorem 2 (Exactness). *SBnB always outputs the exact maximum k-plex.*

Proof. As proved in Lemma 6, our selective graph reduction prunes the same nodes as BnB even if the entire V isnot computed by Definition 6. Therefore, SBnB always outputs the exact maximum k-plex same as the BnB.   □

Table 1. Running time in seconds.

Graphs	$|V|$	$|E|$	$\overline{d}$	Type	$k = 5$		$k = 10$		$k = 15$	
					SBnB	BnB	SBnB	BnB	SBnB	BnB
soc-livejournal	4,033,137	27,933,062	6.93	Social	18.06	**17.64**	**31.02**	33.79	**16.55**	17.66
rt-retweet-crawl	1,112,702	2,278,852	2.05	Social	1.92	**1.82**	**1.53**	1.58	**1.44**	**1.44**
inf-roadNet-PA	1,087,562	1,541,514	1.42	Road	–	–	**0.80**	–	**0.81**	–
ca-hollywood-2009	1,069,126	56,306,653	52.67	Collaboration	**31.99**	32.40	31.93	**31.79**	32.09	**32.02**
soc-delicious	536,108	1,365,961	2.55	Social	**0.33**	0.79	1.29	**0.96**	**1.06**	1.15
ca-MathSciNet	332,689	820,644	2.47	Collaboration	0.61	**0.45**	–	–	**3.90**	–
ca-dblp-2012	317,080	1,049,866	3.31	Collaboration	**0.44**	0.46	**0.47**	0.54	–	–
ca-citeseer	227,320	814,134	3.58	Collaboration	0.33	**0.30**	**0.31**	0.35	**0.33**	0.37
ca-dblp-2010	226,413	716,460	3.16	Collaboration	**0.25**	**0.25**	**0.26**	0.34	–	–
tech-RL-caida	190,914	607,610	3.18	Technological	**0.68**	**0.68**	**0.54**	0.60	**0.42**	0.48
sc-shipsec5	179,104	2,200,076	12.28	Scientific	**2.12**	–	**4.58**	–	–	–
web-arabic-2005	163,598	1,747,269	10.68	Web	**0.61**	0.62	**0.64**	0.68	**0.63**	0.69
soc-douban	154,908	327,162	2.11	Social	**0.20**	**0.20**	**0.30**	–	**6.36**	–
sc-shipsec1	140,385	1,707,759	12.16	Scientific	**2.27**	–	**3.28**	–	–	–

4   Experimental Evaluation

We experimentally evaluated the effectiveness of SBnB by comparing it with the following algorithms for MPS.

- **BS:** As the state-of-the-art GB algorithm for MPS [18], BS recursively partitions and searches subspaces until the maximum k-plex is obtained.
- **BnB:** As the standard BnB algorithm [8], it estimates a lower bound size of k-plex and prunes unpromising subspaces based on graph reduction.
- **Maplex:** As the state-of-the-art MPS algorithm to compute large-scale graphs [19], Maplex provides a tighter lower bound than BnB based on the graph coloring approach [15] and accelerates MPS using a tighter lower bound.

All experiments were conducted on a Linux server with Intel Xeon E5-2690 CPU 2.60 GHz and 128 GiB RAM. All algorithms were implemented in C/C++ using the "−O3" option as a single-threaded program. For BS, BnB, and Maplex, we used C/C++ source codes, which were downloaded from the authors' websites.

We used massive real-world graphs originally published by the Network Repository. Similar to [8], we selected the same 139 massive graphs shown in Table 1 from the repository. These graphs are the standard benchmarks for evaluating various graph mining algorithms on massive real-world graphs [10,13]. In the results below, "−" indicates that the algorithm did not finish MPS within 100 s.

4.1   Efficiency

We first discuss the running time efficiency of SBnB on massive real-world graphs. Figure 1 shows the fraction of solved instances among the 139 real-world graphs for $k = 5, 10$, and 15. Specifically, the number of MPS completed within 100 s is summed for each algorithm. SBnB completes MPS for more graphs than the other methods examined in the experiments. These results imply that SBnB is faster than the others on the massive real-world graphs.

We then assessed the impact of the k value. SBnB shows the best performances even if k is large, whereas, the running times of the other methods degrades significantly for large k settings in Fig. 1. The graph reductions prune unpromising nodes from each search subspace using k-plex S and the k value. However, if k is large, the removed nodes significantly decrease according to Definitions 2 and 3 despite their exhaustive search costs. Because each requires $O(|V|(|V| + |E|))$ time, the running time of BnB is not reduced for large k settings. In contrast, SBnB performs selective graph reduction in $O(\overline{d}^2)$ time regardless of the size of k. Consequently, SBnB can mitigate the search costs on massive graphs even if k is large.

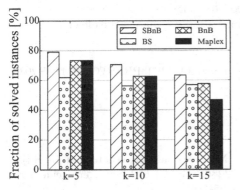

Fig. 1. Overall results.

Table 2. Number of computed nodes in SBnB.

Graphs	$k = 10$		$k = 15$	
	SBnB	3GR	SBnB	3GR
soc-delicious	1.15 M	**816 K**	970 K	1.06 M
tech-RL-caida	–	–	**220 K**	279 K
soc-slashdot	**38.9 M**	43.3 M	–	–
socfb-OR	**254 K**	328 K	**241 K**	331 K
socfb-Penn94	**490 K**	546 K	**485 K**	655 K
tech-internet-as	**195 K**	369 K	**53 K**	94 K
socfb-Texas84	**280 K**	8.12 M	**15.1 M**	15.1 M
socfb-UF	–	–	**17.3 K**	17.8 K
ia-enron-large	**1.12 M**	5.49 M	–	–
ia-email-EU	**2.16 M**	3.95 M	–	–
socfb-Indiana	**10.8 M**	13.3 M	–	–
soc-epinions	**153 K**	189 K	**11.3 M**	25.7 M
tech-as-caida2007	**155 M**	183 K	**65 K**	80 K
socfb-Wisconsin87	878 K	**785 K**	**218 K**	329 K
socfb-Berkeley13	38.8 M	**23.3 M**	–	–
socfb-UConn	**194 K**	266 K	**186 K**	240 K

4.2   Effectiveness of Selective Graph Reduction

Our key contribution is reducing search costs by using the selective graph reduction. Here, we experimentally compare the effectiveness of selective graph reduction to the original BnB. Specifically, we verified whether SBnB effectively reduces the number of computed nodes during MPS. Table 2 compares the number of computed nodes between SBnB and SBnB-3GR, which is a variant of

SBnB without selective graph reduction. In Table 2, we selected 16 middle-sized instances from Table 1 for a fair comparison since SBnB-3GR cannot return k-plexes from large graphs. As shown in Table 2, SBnB effectively reduces the number of computed nodes. For example, SBnB computes 3.25 times and 5.77 times fewer nodes than SBnB-3GR at $k = 10$ and 15, respectively.

Selective graph reduction enhances the efficiency even though it requires $O(\overline{d}^2)$ time (Theorem 1). Real-world graphs generally have small values of $\overline{d}$ due to the power-law degree distribution. Thus, the time complexity $O(\overline{d}^2)$ becomes small in real-world graphs. Furthermore, as proved in Theorem 1, SBnB does not exhaustively explore for graph reduction, which incurs $O(|V|)$ time if the clustering coefficient c is large. In general, real-world graphs have large values of c [14]. Consequently, the running time of SBnB can be effectively reduced.

5 Conclusion

SBnB is an efficient algorithm to find the exact maximum k-plex because it has a faster computation time compared to state-of-the-art methods. During a k-plex search, SBnB finds removable nodes to exclude unnecessary search spaces. In our experiments, SBnB offers improved efficiency on massive graphs. Consequently, employing SBnB for massive graphs should enhance the effectiveness of applications.

Acknowledgement. This paper is partly supported by JST PRESTO JPMJPR2033 and JSPS KAKENHI 22KJ0398.

References

1. Abello, J., Resende, M.G.C., Sudarsky, S.: Massive quasi-clique detection. In: Rajsbaum, S. (ed.) LATIN 2002. LNCS, vol. 2286, pp. 598–612. Springer, Heidelberg (2002). https://doi.org/10.1007/3-540-45995-2_51
2. Balasundaram, B., Butenko, S., Hicks, I.V.: Clique relaxations in social network analysis: the maximum k-plex problem. Oper. Res. **59**(1), 133–142 (2011)
3. Bodaghi, A., Oliveira, J.: The theater of fake news spreading, who plays which role? A study on real graphs of spreading on Twitter. Expert Syst. Appl. **189**, 116110 (2022)
4. Bomze, I.M., Budinich, M., Pardalos, P.M., Pelillo, M.: The maximum clique problem. In: Du, D.Z., Pardalos, P.M. (eds.) Handbook of Combinatorial Optimization, vol. 4, pp. 1–74. Springer, Boston (1999). https://doi.org/10.1007/978-1-4757-3023-4_1
5. Conte, A., De Matteis, T., De Sensi, D., Grossi, R., Marino, A., Versari, L.: D2K: scalable community detection in massive networks via small-diameter k-Plexes. In: KDD '18, Association for Computing Machinery, pp. 1272–1281, New York, NY, USA (2018)
6. Doerr, B., Fouz, M., Friedrich, T.: Why rumors spread so quickly in social networks. Commun. ACM **55**(6), 70–75 (2012)

7. Faloutsos, M., Faloutsos, P., Faloutsos, C.: On power-law relationships of the internet topology. SIGCOMM Comput. Commun. Rev. **29**(4), 251–262 (1999)
8. Gao, J., Chen, J., Yin, M., Chen, R., Wang, Y.: An exact algorithm for maximum k-plexes in massive graphs. In: Proceedings of the Twenty-Seventh International Joint Conference on Artificial Intelligence, IJCAI-18, pp. 1449–1455 (2018)
9. Latapy, M.: Main-memory triangle computations for very large (sparse (power-law)) graphs. Theoret. Comput. Sci. **407**(1), 458–473 (2008)
10. Lin, J., Cai, S., Luo, C., Su, K.: A reduction based method for coloring very large graphs. In: Proceedings of the 26th International Joint Conference on Artificial Intelligence, IJCAI'17, pp. 517–523 (2017)
11. Matsugu, S., Fujiwara, Y., Shiokawa, H.: Uncovering the largest community in social networks at scale. In: Proceedings of the Thirty-Second International Joint Conference on Artificial Intelligence, IJCAI-23, pp. 2251–2260 (2023)
12. McClosky, B., Hicks, I.V.: Combinatorial algorithms for the maximum k-plex problem. J. Comb. Optim. **23**(1), 29–49 (2012)
13. Rossi, R., Ahmed, N.: Coloring large complex networks. Soc. Netw. Anal. Min. **4**, 1–37 (2014)
14. Shiokawa, H., Fujiwara, Y., Onizuka, M.: Scan++: efficient algorithm for finding clusters, hubs and outliers on large-scale graphs. Proc. VLDB Endow. **8**(11), 1178–1189 (2015)
15. Tomita, E., Seki, T.: An efficient branch-and-bound algorithm for finding a maximum clique. In: Calude, C.S., Dinneen, M.J., Vajnovszki, V. (eds.) DMTCS 2003. LNCS, vol. 2731, pp. 278–289. Springer, Heidelberg (2003). https://doi.org/10.1007/3-540-45066-1_22
16. Wang, L., Dai, G.Z.: Global stability of virus spreading in complex heterogeneous networks. SIAM J. Appl. Math. **68**(5), 1495–1502 (2008)
17. Xiao, M., Kou, S.: Exact algorithms for the maximum dissociation set and minimum 3-path vertex cover problems. Theor. Comput. Sci. **657**(PA), 86–97 (2017)
18. Xiao, M., Lin, W., Dai, Y., Zeng, Y.: A fast algorithm to compute maximum k-plexes in social network analysis. In: Thirty-First AAAI Conference on Artificial Intelligence (2017)
19. Zhou, Y., Hu, S., Xiao, M., Fu, Z.H.: Improving maximum k-plex solver via second-order reduction and graph color bounding. In: Proceedings of the AAAI Conference on Artificial Intelligence, vol. 35, pp. 12453–12460 (2021)
20. Zhu, J., Chen, B., Zeng, Y.: Community Detection Based on Modularity and k-Plexes. Inf. Sci. **513**, 127–142 (2020)

Automatic Hypotheses Testing Over Heterogeneous Biological Databases Using Open Knowledge Networks

Hasan M. Jamil[1]($\boxtimes$), Stephen Krawetz[2], and Alexander Gow[2]

[1] Department of Computer Science, University of Idaho, Moscow, ID 83844, USA
jamil@uidaho.edu
[2] School of Medicine, Wayne State University, Detroit, MI 48201, USA
steve@compbio.med.wayne.edu, agow@med.wayne.edu

Abstract. An understanding of the molecular basis of musculoskeletal pain is necessary for the development of therapeutics, their management, and possible personalization. One-in-three Americans use OTC pain killers, and one tenth use prescription drugs to manage pain. The CDC also estimates that about 20% Americans suffer from chronic pain. As the experience of acute or chronic pain varies due to individual genetics and physiology, it is imperative that researchers continue to find novel therapeutics to treat or manage symptoms. In this paper, our goal is to develop a seed knowledgebased computational platform, called *BioNursery*, that will allow biologists to computationally hypothesize, define and test molecular mechanisms underlying pain. In our knowledge ecosystem, we accumulate curated information from users about the relationships among biological databases, analysis tools, and database contents to generate biological analyses modules, called π-graphs, or process graphs. We propose a mapping function from a natural language description of a hypothesized molecular model to a computational workflow for testing in BioNursery. We use a crowd computing feedback and curation system, called *Explorer*, to improve proposed computational models for molecular mechanism discovery, and growing the knowledge ecosystem.

Keywords: Molecular Mechanism · Knowledge Ecosystem · Computational Models · Crowdsourcing · Biological Databases · Data Integration

1 Introduction

Evidence driven biology is usually expensive as it demands laboratory experiments to validate testable hypotheses. Much of the evidence sought today is also available in the form of data [5] and knowledge [9] in databases toward hypothesis generation and refinement prior to laboratory testing. While computational tools and modeling [1] are being used by some researchers at great expense, there is a paucity of hypothesis testing tools that leverage the huge volume of complementary and redundant data, computational tools and models, and structured knowledge to aid researchers in generating novel theses.

For example, consider the fact that Americans are most likely the largest group of consumers of painkillers and opioids in the world. They spend more than $18 billion on pain medications, and pain contributes to about $635 billion in lost productivity [8]. While many medications generally manage pain, variations in genetics and physiology of individual patients often contribute to serious side effects such as acute liver failure, spinal cord damage, opioid addiction, and respiratory complications. Idiopathic pain is also difficult to treat and manage due to multiple or unknown etiologies. It is therefore imperative that new therapeutics are continuously developed to ease the incidence, prevalence and cost of treating and managing pain.

These needs notwithstanding, to investigate the prevailing state of addiction and pain, and develop novel interventions, an inquisitive biologist has no simple way of posing the following query to a computational system for a satisfactory scientific response,

> Define the expression profiles of spinal cord pain gate interneurons in superficial layers of the dorsal horn (SDH) that play major roles in processing touch/thermal/pain signals from skin nociceptors. The interneurons can be either excitatory or inhibitory. They receive sensory input from dorsal root ganglia neurons and deliver these signals to projection neurons that relay the mechanical/thermal pain signals to the brain.

which is sufficiently informative to allow one to formulate the hypothesis

> "Novel cell type specific ion channels or G protein coupled receptors expressed by SDH neurons may contribute to sensory information processing and can be modulated pharmacologically to mitigate transmission of pain signals to the sensory cortex in disease states."

for laboratory testing. However, one of the ways this evidence can be gathered would be to follow the steps outlined below by an informed biologist.

1. Harvest Data from the single cell database SeqSeek [10], and cluster expressed genes of different cell types. Medlock et al. [6] describes a number of interneuron cell types based on gene expression data. These genes may be sufficient to complete the clustering and cell type identification, but if not, then other gene marker sets need to be identified.
2. Ion channels and G coupled receptors are widely considered important pharmacological targets for mitigating pain. Many of these protein complexes are broadly expressed in most neurons; however, we are interested in those with restricted expression profiles. To find them, the data from SeqSeek can be correlated with spatial expression patterns of the genes in the Allen mouse spinal cord atlas. Spatial protein expression databases may also be used to identify the channels of interest.

3. Cells that express restricted channels need to be identified using cell-type specific gene marker groups published in the literature or other databases.
4. Where possible, the densities and electrophysiological properties of the channels should be determined so they can be modeled and inserted into computational pain gate models.

The question we address in this article is whether a generalized computational hypothesis testing tool can be developed that not only suggests the steps above, but also computes the model and responds affirmatively. We discuss the outline of a possible system that leverages available resources and a knowledge ecosystem for biological research, in particular, the pain research outlined above. We do so by presenting an interaction with a large language model (LLM), Chat-GPT, about pain models and identifying its potentials as a hypothesis generator, its limitations as a trusted platform and its current handicap as a computational tool for hypothesis validation. Based on these observations, we propose a new biological hypothesis generation and testing system architecture, called *BioNursery*, in which we aim to determine if a proposed computational strategy is a valid model, and can be successfully tested over available digital resources. If valid, the corresponding computational model will be added to the BioNursery ecosystem. If not, we will submit the hypothesized model to the crowd (the community) for curation and re-evaluation until it is sufficiently refined. BioNursery thus serves as a knowledge ecosystem in which biological hypotheses are constantly generated, tested and validated, refined and re-used in creating new knowledge to advance science and its understanding.

2   Proposed Architecture of BioNursery

The interaction with ChatGPT[1] sufficiently highlights two realities – LLMs such as ChatGPT, or BardAI, may be more appropriately the BioMedLM[2], have significant potentials in hypothesis generation and testing using a simple natural language prompt from a naive user, but also cannot be fully trusted[3] because it has the capacity to convincingly fake the truth. The question then becomes whether it is possible to leverage the power of LLMs and shorten the distance between hypotheses generation and testing by using LLMs to generate the models and then validate the generated models by inserting humans in the loop as curators in the knowledge gathering ecosystem. The BioNursery architecture aims to answer this question affirmatively.

Figure 1 shows the main components of the BioNursery system and their functional relationships. In this system, user queries are processed by the *user interface* module, which transmits the query either to the *BioSmart query translator* via the *digital assistant* (when a process description is not included in the

---

[1] https://chat.openai.com/share/b8250057-780d-4bf0-94d3-a95349d91fc2.

[2] https://crfm.stanford.edu/2022/12/15/biomedlm.html.

[3] https://crfm.stanford.edu/report.html.

query, as in the infertility Gene-Disease Association example [2]) for the generation of a process description, or directly to the *BioSmart query translator* (as in the pain example [3]), for onward processing.

The BioSmart system analyzes the natural language description of the suggested computational procedure and maps it into a set of so called possible π-graphs using the BioNursery knowledgebase. Recall that the BioNursery knowledgebase includes all curated process descriptions in the form of conceptual resource description (CRD), and node description of resources (NDR). If BioSmart fails to generate a π-graph, it initiates a crowd computing request by forwarding the missing process description specifications to the *community curator* database for help. Once a response is submitted by members of the community, it enters the system and is checked for completeness. Once a complete π-graph becomes available, it is then sent to the *graph generator* to generate a template for a Needle [2] query sequence as an implementation of the workflow, more specifically, a *testable graph*, or a testable hypothesis.

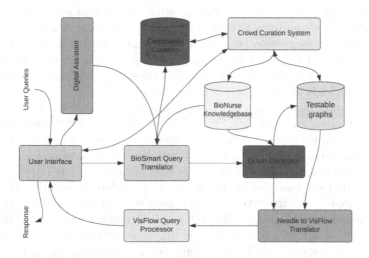

Fig. 1. BioNursery system architecture.

The testable graph is then converted to a VisFlow program [7], executed by the VisFlow system, and the responses forwarded to the user for consideration. If the generated response is accepted by the user as valid, it is forwarded to the curation system for community curation. Once the procedure, or the π-graph, surpasses a curation threshold, it is appended to the BioNursery knowledgebase as a valid process. The π-graph remains searchable and usable at all times, but starting with lower credibility until it reaches the credibility threshold and enters the curated knowledge pool. However, inclusion in the knowledge pool does not alter the attained credibility of the hypotheses.

3   Crowd Computing as an Open Knowledge Ecosystem

As discussed earlier in Sect. 2, BioNursery system relies mainly on three components – an LLM-based digital assistant, a process graph constructor and ranker, and an executable workflow query generator. The latter two components rely heavily on a fourth component, we call *Open Knowledge Ecosystem* (OKE), created and curated by the community of researchers and users using a crowd computing platform similar to CrowdCure [4], called the Crowd Curation System (CCS). CCS has access to three databases – a community of curators, a testable hypotheses repository (THR), and a biological resource description knowledgebase (RDK). Combined, they serve as the OKE of BioNursery.

Both THR and RDK are in constant flux and therefore are constantly evolving. If a biological resource such as a database or a computational tool is missing a description in OKE, a request for crowd help to describe it is received by CCS from the user interface of BioNursery. CCS then communicates this task as a broadcast to all relevant community users, who then respond to the request within a defined time frame, and the resource description enters the RDK as an accessible resource in the form of a textual declaration. A graph, more precisely a node, representation corresponding to the resource description is also registered in the THR. A testable hypothesis in general is an abstract graph of resource descriptions. The workflow generator uses these descriptions to generate executable workflow queries.

These resource descriptions and the hypothesis graphs are constantly curated to ensure relevance and accuracy. Since the resource descriptions are either contributed by community users, or are harvested by automated web-crawlers, they can be erroneous due to algorithmic deficiencies. Since meaningful hypothesis construction depends on the completeness and accuracy of the process descriptions, they in turn can also be flawed. It is therefore imperative that some form of revision and corrective opportunities are available. In BioNursery, the crowd computing model uses a well developed Information Source Tracking (IST) method [11] to assign credibility of the resource descriptions. We invite readers to [11] for a discussion on the IST method, and to [4] for a discussion on CrowdCure in which IST has been used to assign credibility to stored information.

4   Conclusion and Future Research

Though we have discussed BioNursery features using simple, intuitive and small examples throughout the article, our goal in this paper was to show that BioNursery holds promise for constructing and testing complex and arbitrary hypotheses of the form shown as the π-graph in Fig. 2 generated against the query Q below using BioNursery knowledgebase.

Q: Could you suggest a procedure to identify genes associated with male infertility using semen expression and pathway data?

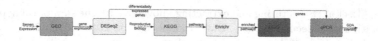

Fig. 2. Computational model of an infertility-related hypothesis discussed in [2].

Our reliance on a community curated knowledge ecosystem BioNursery indicates a good chance that we can develop an automated hypothesis testing system and an open knowledge ecosystem for molecular modeling of pain. We do not insist on a flawless generation of a computational procedure. Instead, we propose a mechanism that expects possible erroneous suggestions or mappings, but can eventually be cured successfully. The model proposed relies on expert and user participation in the knowledge ecosystem in their role as curators. The crowd computing model accommodates a reliability assignment mechanism [11] that tracks user curation efforts to identify reliable curators using a possible world trust model that changes over time and adjusts to new realities.

Acknowledgement. This research was partially supported by an Institutional Development Award (IDeA) from the National Institute of General Medical Sciences of the National Institutes of Health under Grant #P20GM103408.

References

1. Clark, C.A.C., Helikar, T., Dauer, J.: Simulating a computational biological model, rather than reading, elicits changes in brain activity during biological reasoning. CBE Life Sci. Educ. **19**(3), ar45 (2020)
2. Jamil, H., Naha, K.: Mapping strategies for declarative queries over online heterogeneous biological databases for intelligent responses. In: SAC 2023, Tallinn, 27–31 March 2023. ACM (2023)
3. Jamil, H.M.: Knowledge rich natural language queries over structured biological databases. In: BCB 2017, Boston, 20–23 August 2017, pp. 352–361 (2017)
4. Jamil, H.M., Sadri, F.: Crowd enabled curation and querying of large and noisy text mined protein interaction data. Distribut. Parall. Datab. **36**(1), 9–45 (2018)
5. Liu, G.,et al.: Aging atlas: a multi-omics database for aging biology. Nucl. Acids Res. **49**(Database-Issue), D825–D830 (2021)
6. Medlock, L., Sekiguchi, K., Hong, S., Dura-Bernal, S., Lytton, W.W., Prescott, S.A.: Multiscale computer model of the spinal dorsal horn reveals changes in network processing associated with chronic pain. J. Neurosci. **42**(15), 3133–3149 (2022)
7. Mou, X., Jamil, H.M.: Visual life sciences workflow design using distributed and heterogeneous resources. IEEE/ACM TCBB **17**(4), 1459–1473 (2020)
8. Rasu, R., et al.: Cost of pain medication to treat adult patients with nonmalignant chronic pain in the United States. J. Manag. Care Spec. Pharm. **20**(9), 921–928 (2014)

9. Roos, M., et al.: Structuring and extracting knowledge for the support of hypothesis generation in molecular biology. BMC Bioinformatcis **10**(S-10), 9 (2009)
10. Russ, D.E., et al.: A harmonized atlas of mouse spinal cord cell types and their spatial organization. Nat. Commun. **12**(1) (2021)
11. Sadri, F.: On the foundations of probabilistic information integration. In: CIKM, Maui, 29 October–02 November 2012, pp. 882–891 (2012)

Recommendation Systems

Using Derived Sequential Pattern Mining for E-Commerce Recommendations in Multiple Sources

Ritu Chaturvedi[1]([✉]), Christie I. Ezeife[2], and Md. Burhan Uddin[2]

[1] School of Computer Science, University of Guelph, Guelph, Canada
chaturvr@uoguelph.ca
[2] School of Computer Science, University of Windsor, 401 Sunset Avenue, Windsor, ON N9B3P4, Canada

Abstract. Existing multi-source E-Commerce recommendation algorithms, such as Multi-source Category Extension system (ECCF19), use item categories to improve the quality of the user-item rating matrix input to the collaborative filtering (CF) process for better recommendations. HPCRec18 model derives a consequential bond between clicks and purchases to predict preferences for users with no purchase history, whereas HSPRec19 uses sequential purchase patterns from historical data as well as consequential bond in mined patterns to improve the user-item matrix for CF. None of these systems use both the historical and item description data to address the CF limitations.

This paper proposes a Multi-source Category Extended Historical Sequential Pattern Recommendation System (MCE-HSPRec), an extension of the HSPRec19 system to increase recommendation coverage and alleviate new item problem by enriching item category information. MCE-HSPRec derives enriched category-based user profiles by analyzing item categories that are frequently purchased together. Results show that HSPRec achieves 36.64% more prediction coverage compared to HSPRec. MCE-HSPRec also obtains high precision and recall values (0.94716, 0.94781) in comparison to HSPRec19 (0.8985, 0.90002).

Keywords: Multi-Source · Sequential Pattern Mining · Category Co-occurrence · Recommendation System · Implicit feedback

1 Introduction

Modern daily life is now highly dependent on different internet-based services. As a result, we are surrounded by the various implementation of recommendation systems. Recommendation Systems are a collection of software tools and techniques that suggest items to users that vary from physical items to entertainment content to consume [7]. Some common examples of recommendation systems in different domains are Movies/Dramas (Netflix), Video (YouTube), Music (Spotify), E-commerce (Amazon), Friends (Facebook). Platforms implement recommendation systems based on their varying interests. When making a recommendation, among many common operational and technical goals are relevance, novelty, serendipity, and increasing recommendation diversity [1]. According to Schafer et al. [14], in addition to these common goals, a recommendation system has a few other important goals including the ones listed next: (i). Increase sales: one of the most important goals of a commercial RS is to increase sales by recommending products the customer will likely buy. Profit is a major driving factor for the development of commercial recommendation systems. (ii). Recommend diverse products: another important goal is to diversify recommended products. Instead of recommending only highly-rated, recommend more diverse and harder-to-find products. (iii). Increase user retention: by improving user experience, RS can also increase user loyalty to the website or application. This is achieved by recommending users tailored, relevant, and exciting items.

Traditional recommendation systems, such as the most widely used Collaborative filtering (CF) technique, uses user ratings on items to derive recommendations. In the explicit dataset, the collaborative filtering method works with highly sparse user explicit ratings as many items are not rated or purchased by the users [13]. The ratings themselves then become questionable as many vendors and E-commerce platforms were found bribing the users for fake positive ratings [4]. To resolve both the sparsity and honesty problem, implicit rating techniques [3] derive user preferences from user behaviors such as clicks and purchases. The Content-Based filtering (CBF) approach to recommendation [16] utilizes user profile information (i.e., age, gender, location) and product features (i.e., price, category, attributes) to derive recommendations. Hybrid recommendation approaches [6,10] combine techniques from both the collaborative and content-based approaches to achieve a better result. However, hybrid recommendation systems [3,18] that can alleviate new user problems cannot address new item issues with only one source of information. Therefore, a question arose: Can implicit multi-relational information be obtained and used for decision-making tasks? The necessity of mining multiple sources includes comparative analysis, finding product sequence patterns in the local and global scope, finding alternative information on product sequence patterns mined in one source, and many more [5].

The proposed MCE-HSPRec system as in an unpublished thesis [17], extends the HSPRec19 system using item category information and increases prediction coverage for the domain. It derives recommendations for new items (Cold start) and derives a rich user profile based on category preference, in addition to deriving category co-occurrence pattern in user clicks.

Section 2 discusses related work, Sect. 3 describes the proposed MCE-HSPRe system with an example application of the proposed technique, Sect. 4 compares the proposed system with HSPRec19 and analyses its performance. Section 5 presents the limitations of the proposed system and conclusions.

2   Related Work

The related work is divided into 4 different categories: (i) Historical Sequential Pattern Approach system, HSPRec19 [3] derives the relation between click and purchase as sequential rules through sequential pattern mining in historical e-commerce data. It then uses the derived rule to compute weights for items in sequence and predict recommendations to enrich the user-item frequency matrix. (ii) Matrix Factorization Approach, MuSIF19 [15] uses a multi-source approach to alleviate the CF method's data sparsity issue. It generates the user-item frequency matrix from historical user interaction information, such as view action, adding different weights for each action while computing the rating for each user-item pair. It then derives a binary preference score from the populated user-item matrix. (iii) Multi-source Category Extension system called ECCF19 [11] uses item category to extend the CF method of an explicit rating matrix and alleviate the new item problem. The ECCF19 system derives category co-relation from the user search history and generates a category co-occurrence graph. They then generate a user-category frequency matrix from the user-item rating matrix. Finally, it computes the user-category preference matrix incorporating the user-item matrix, user-category frequency matrix, and the category co-occurrence graph before applying the CF method. (iv) Ontology-based Matrix Factorization Approach [12] called HCR18, a hybrid approach for CF systems using semantic similarity and dimensionality reduction techniques. They first cluster the users based on their preference similarity and the items based on their semantic similarity. They used an ontological knowledge representation to store item semantic information. SVD is used on the user and item clusters to reduce their dimensionality. Prediction for missing rating is computed through approximation based on matrix factorization. Ontology Enhanced Collaborative Filtering Approach [2] utilizes ontological knowledge to derive item similarity to enrich the user-item matrix. They use the weighted path length formula applied in cross-domain knowledge to find semantic similarity. Using an adjusted cosine similarity and SVD method, the CD-SPM system predicts rating before applying the CF method.

Major drawbacks of these existing systems are (i) HSPRec19 [3] cannot derive recommendations for new items, and does not take into account, item attribute information while enriching user-item matrix (ii) MuSIF19 [15] has different user interaction adding noise to the matrix and contributing to inaccurate predictions. In addition, ARM used in it does not significantly increase the matrix density (iii) ECCF19 [11] is unable to capture user purchase behavior as it does not mine patterns in user purchase history, and therefore, it cannot generate a recommendation for new users (iv) HCR18 [12] depends on explicit user rating and density of the matrix. It does not capture purchase behavior as it does not use historical e-commerce information (v) CD-SPM [2] does not use sequential pattern mining to capture changes in user purchase behavior, and only one domain is benefited from the cross-domain knowledge transfer.

In order to mitigate these limitations, the proposed system MCE-HSPRe extends HSPRec19 [3] to (i) derive recommendations for new items (i.e., for a cold start): (ii). derive a rich user profile by extending the user-item matrix derived by HSPRec19 with user category preference information and (iii) deriving category co-occurrence pattern in user clicks.

3   The Proposed Multi-source Recommendation System MCE-HSPRec

The primary goal of the proposed MCE-HSPRec system is to mine both an item purchase sequence database and category sequence database to derive an enriched categorical preference user item rating matrix. The historical sequential pattern recommendation system (HSPRec19) mines user clicks and purchase behavior to derive recommendations for a new user with no purchase history. As it does not consider item attribute information such as category, the HSPRec19 system is unable to predict ratings for a new item in the domain. New items are recommended to increase sales in the interest of both seller and customer. The proposed MCE-HSPRec system uses the category information available in the item database to extend the HSPRec [3] system for new item coverage. In the e-commerce platform, many items share a category. The customer purchase history is converted into a user-category frequency matrix. Then category co-relation is derived as co-occurrences in historical user click sequence. The co-occurrence data is stored in a graph called co-occurrence graph (CCG). The HSPRec module helps to generate a rich user-item preference matrix through sequential pattern mining in the user click and purchase click sequence database. As the final step of MCE-HSPRec, user preference is computed to a category from the user-item matrix, user-category and CCG. User preference are being computed to individual categories. Therefore, this allows addressing new item recommendations if the item is from an existing category in the system.

Figure 1 shows the flow of steps proposed in MCE-HSPRec, whereas the main proposed MCE-HSPRec algorithms is given as Algorithm 1, which calls the sub algorithms 2 to 5. As the aim is to generate a rich user-item preference matrix, the first step of the proposed algorithm is to apply the HSPRec module to the historical click and purchase data that contains user clickstream and purchases event to generate a user-item preference matrix. Note that details of HSPRec19 algorithm ([3]) are beyond the scope of this paper due to space limitations. The rich user-item preference matrix is extended to a richer user-category (UC) preference matrix by executing UC, CCG, and the MCE-HSPRec module in sequence. The result of this MCE-HSPRec program is fed to collaborative filtering [1,8] program to generate recommendations (Top-N categories of items, highest rated categories of items). Section 3.1 demonstrates the flow of data shown in Fig. 1 using a working example. It runs the example input through each step of algorithms 1 to 5 to achieve the final output, which is an enriched normalized user-preference matrix.

The formula to generate an enriched preference matrix in step 1 of Algorithm 5 is adapted from ECCF19 [11]. This method uses a user-defined threshold value called PositiveRating to determine which rating will be considered as positive.

In step 2 of Algorithm 5, the enriched user-item frequency matrix is normalized according to the unit vector formula adapted from Bhatta et al. [3].

$$Normalization(r_{uc}) = r_{uc}/\sqrt{(r_{uc_1}^2 + r_{uc_2}^2 + ...r_{uc_n}^2)}, \tag{1}$$

where r_{uc} is the level of user interest in categories as a value between 0 and 1.

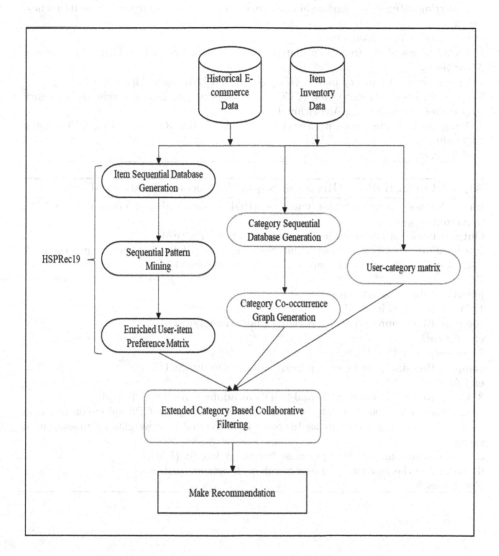

Fig. 1. Dataflow of the proposed MCE-HSPRec system

Algorithm 1 . MCE-HSPRec (Multi Source Category Extended Historical Sequential Recommendation)

Input: historical user purchase database (PDB), historical user clicks data (CDB), minimum support (s). user-item purchase frequency matrix (M), item attribute database (IDB) containing item category information, positive rating threshold (pr)
Output: Enriched user preference matrix (EPM) using sequential purchase patterns, co-occurring category preference in clickstream data, and category purchase frequency.
Begin
For each table in a database
1. Enriched user-item frequency matrix (EM) ← HSPRec (PDB, CDB, M, s) using Algorithm 2.
2. User category frequency matrix (UC) ← UCM(PDB) using Algorithm 3.
3. Category co-occurrence graph (CCG) ← CCG(CSD) to create a weighted category co-occurrence graph using Algorithm 4.
4. Enriched user preference matrix (EPM) ← MCE-HSPRec (EM, UC, CCG) using Algorithm 5.
End for each

Algorithm 2. HSPRec (Historical Sequential Recommendation) Module

Input: historical user purchase database (PDB), historical user clicks data (CDB), minimum support (s).
Output: Enriched user-item purchase frequency matrix (EM).
Intermediate: historical sequential purchase database (SDB), historical sequential click database (SCDB), enriched user-item frequency matrix (EM),
Begin
For each table in a database
1. for each user U in PDB,
compare timestamp and create periodic (daily, weekly) SDB
end for each
2. for each user U in CDB,
compare timestamp and create periodic (daily, weekly) SCDB
end for each
3. Compute CPS between SDB and SCDB as adapted from HSPRec [3]
4. Compute weighted frequent patterns for user u using the CPS value computed in step 4. Use the weighted sequence to compute individual item weights for missing item ratings
5. Generate an enriched user purchase frequency matrix (EM)
6. Normalize the new enriched user purchase frequency matrix.
End for each

Algorithm 3. UC (User Category Preference Matrix) Module

Input: Historical user purchase data, Item profile data.
Output: User category preference (UC) matrix.
Begin
For each table in a database
1. Map user purchase of item to the category id of the item
2. for each user-category purchase event, count frequency and update UC matrix
End for each

Algorithm 4. CCG (Category Co-occurrence Graph) Module

Input: Historical user clickstream data, Item profile data, CSD (Category Sequence Database).
Output: Weighted edge category graph (CCG).
Begin
For each sequence in a database
1. Map user-item click event to the category id of the item
2. Using the modified sequence database generator to create CSD
3. Create a weighted category co-occurrence graph (CCG).
4. for each category c in a sequence do: count co-occurrence of two categories (c1, c2) update CCG
End for each

Algorithm 5. MCE-HSPRec (Multi-source Category Extended HSPRec) Module

Input: Enriched user-item frequency matrix (EM), category co-occurrence graph (CCG), user-category frequency matrix (UC)
Output: Enriched user preference matrix (EPM).
Begin
For each table in a database
1. for each user for each category compute user preference using EM, UC and CCG update enrich preference matrix (EPM) end for each
2. Normalize the matrix using equation
3. Apply collaborative filtering (CF) to generate recommendations

---

3.1 Running Example of MCE-HSPRec (Algorithms 1–5)

Input: user clicks database (Table 1), user purchase database (Table 2), and item details database (Table 3)
Output: rich user-item frequency matrix (Table 4), rich user-category preference matrix (Table 5) and normalized user preference matrix (Table 8b).

Step 1: Create the rich user-item preference matrix by using Algorithm 2 that extends the user-item matrix generated by HSPRec module [3]. Table 4 shows the matrix generated for the given input. The detailed steps used to generate this user-item matrix from the given user-clicks, user-purchase and items database adapted from HSPRec19 algorithm ([3]) are beyond the scope of this paper due to space limitation.

Table 1. Input1: User clicks database

User_id	Items	Session_start	Session_end
U1	Galaxy_s21, Iphone_12, Galaxy_s21, Case_s21, Samsung_tv, Fast_charger	2021.04.12.11.30.21	2021.04.12.12.30.21
U1	Iphone_12, Airpod, Fast_charger	2021.06.23.11.43.21	2021.06.23.12.26.21
U2	Iphone_12, Airpod, Case_s21	2021.04.14.09.20.30	2021.04.14.10.00.10
U3	Airpod, Iphone_12, Fast_charger, Galaxy_s21	2021.05.11.10.02.40	2021.05.11.10.45.40
U3	Galaxy_s21, Samsung_tv, Fast_charger	2021.07.22.11.30.21	2021.07.22.12.40.11
U4	Iphone_12, Galaxy_s21	2021.09.23.11.43.21	2021.09.23.12.14.21

Table 2. Input2: User purchase database

User_id	Items	Timestamp
U1	Galaxy_s21,Case_s21, Samsung_tv, Fast_charger	2021.04.12.12.30.21
U1	Iphone_12, Fast_charger	2021.06.23.12.26.21
U2	Iphone_12, Airpod	2021.04.14.10.00.10
U3	Iphone_12, Airpod, Galaxy_s21	2021.05.11.10.45.40
U3	Fast_charger, Samsung_tv	2021.07.22.12.40.11
U4	?	2021.09.23.12.14.21

Table 3. Item details database

Item	CategoryId	Category
Iphone_12	C1	Phone
Galaxy_s21	C1	Phone
Samsung_tv	C2	Television
Airpod	C3	Phone_accessory
Fast_charger	C4	Phone_charger
Case_s22	C3	Phone_accessory
Case_12	C3	Phone_accessory

Table 4. Rich user-item purchase frequency matrix

Item-> User	Galaxy_s2	Samsung_tv	Iphone_1	Airpod	Fast-charger	Case_s2	Case_12
U1	0.354	0.354	0.354	?	0.707	0.354	?
U2	?	?	0.707	0.707	?	?	?
U3	0.354	0.354	0.354	0.707	0.354	?	?
U4	0.457	0.457	0.420	0.305	0.305	0.468	?

Step 2: Create the user-category preference matrix from historical purchase database base and the item details database using Algorithm 3. Mapping item category to purchase through item id we get following matrix (Table 5)

Table 5. User-category purchase frequency matrix

Category-> User	C1	C2	C3	C4
U1	2	1	1	2
U2	1	0	1	0
U3	2	1	2	1
U4	0	0	0	0

Table 6. Category click sequence

User_id	Click Category Sequence
U1	<(Phone, Phone, Phone, Phone_accessory, Television, Phone_charger), (Phone, Phone_accessory, Phone_charger)>
U2	<(Phone, Phone_accessory, Phone_accessory)>
U3	<(Phone_accessory, Phone, Phone_charger, Phone), (Phone, Television, Phone_charger)>
U4	<(Phone, Phone)>

Step 3: This step uses step 1 of Algorithm 4 to first create category click sequence database by mapping items to their categories through the primary key – foreign key relation. The result is as shown in Table 6.

As the target for the proposed algorithm is the correlation between the categories, for each sequence we keep first appearance of each category and prune the repetitive occurrences (step 2 of Algorithm 4). For example, the sequence <(Phone, Phone, Phone, Phone_accessory, Television, Phone_charger), (Phone, Phone_accessory, Phone_charger)> becomes <(Phone, Phone_accessory, Television, Phone_charger), (Phone, Phone_accessory, Phone_charger)> after pruning. We use category id for easier computation and representation. The pruned sequence database is shown in Table 7.

Table 7. Pruned category click sequences

S_id	Click Category Sequence
S1	<(C1, C3, C2, C4), (C1, C3, C4)>
S2	<(C1, C3)>
S3	<(C3, C1, C4), (C1, C2, C4)>
S4	<(C1)>

In step 3 of Algorithm 4, we first count co-occurrences frequency of each category pair with respect to their distance in each sequence and update the category co-occurrence graph (CCG). Co-occurrence for the sequence <(Phone, Phone_accessory, Television, Phone_charger), (Phone, Phone_accessory, Phone_charger)> is computed with respect to category "Phone".

$Phone(C1) - PhoneAccessory(C3) = w_{(x,y)} = \sum_S 1/d_{(x,y)} = 1/1 + 1/1 = 2$
$Phone(C1) - Television(C2) = 1/1 = 0.50$
$Phone(C1) - PhoneCharger(C4) = 1/3 + 1/2 = 0.83$

For this example, the CCG is as shown in Fig. 2, by counting for all sequence pair in order and for all sequences. For example, weight of the edge between categories C1 and C3 is calculated by adding co-occurrence frequency of the pair (C1, C3) with respect to their distance in each of the four sequences S1 to S4 shown in Table 7, i.e., by adding 2 from S1, 1 from S2 and 1 from S3, to get a total of 4 on the edge between C1 and C3.

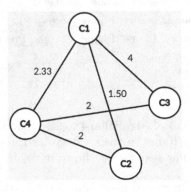

Fig. 2. Category Co-occurence Graph (CCG)

Step 4: In this step, we demonstrate Algorithm 5 by combining the rich user-item purchase frequency matrix (Table 4), user-category purchase frequency matrix (Table 5), the category co-occurrence matrix (Table 7) and the category co-occurrence Graph (CCG)) shown in Fig. 2 to compute rich user-category preference matrix. Assuming that the *PositiveRating* is set to 0.60 (the rating scale is 0–1), the resulting rich user-category preference matrix generated is shown in Table 8a. For example, frequency for user U1 and category C4 is enriched and updated from 2 to 3, since U1 has interest in fast_charger, which belongs to category C4 and has a frequency of 0.707, as shown in Table 4. Since this value is greater than the given *PositiveRating*, U1->C4 gets an updated value of 3, as shown in bold in Table 8a.

Final step: The final step of Algorithm 5 applies a unit normalization formula (Eq. 1) to capture user level of interest between 0 and 1 and generates a normalized user preference matrix as shown in Table 8b, which is the final output generated. For example, U1->C1 is computed as $2/sqrt(2^2 + 1^2 + 1^2 + 3^2) = 2/sqrt(15) = 0.516$.

Table 8. Enriched and normalized user preference matrix

(a) User-category purchase frequency

Category-> User	C1	C2	C3	C4
U1	2	1	1	**3**
U2	**2**	0	**2**	0
U3	2	1	3	1
U4	0	0	0	0

(b) Normalized user preference matrix

Category-> User	C1	C2	C3	C4
U1	0.516	0.258	0.258	**0.775**
U2	**0.707**	0	**0.707**	0
U3	0.516	0.258	**0.775**	0.258
U4	0	0	0	0

4   Results and Analysis

As a historical e-commerce dataset, the "eCommerce events history in electronics store" provided by Kechinov ([9]) was selected. This dataset was collected under the Open CDP (2019) project and contains events related to users and products of a large online electronics store over five months. The dataset contains 845041 events of which there are 793748 clicks and 37346 purchases. There is total 53453 products of 718 categories. This dataset was chosen since it provides both historical e-commerce data and item category information.

A performance analysis of the proposed MCE_HSPRec system using user-based collaborative filtering over the historical dataset is presented in this section. The proposed system performance is evaluated with respect to MAE (Mean absolute error), RMSE (Root Mean Square Error), Precision, Recall, F1-score, and Prediction coverage compared with U2UCF [1], ECCF [11] and HSPRec19 [3] systems.

For the comparative performance analysis, user-based collaborative filtering was first applied on the implicit rating matrix derived from the "eCommerce events history in electronics store" dataset. The baseline recommendation system used in the proposed research is U2U [1]. Then HSPRec19 [3] is implemented, which integrates user purchase and click behavior by deriving sequential rules mined from the historical e-commerce data. After mapping category to user purchase, collaborative filtering is applied over the user-category frequency matrix giving CCF [11]. Algorithm ECCF [11], which utilizes item categories, is used next to extend the user-based collaborative filtering method. Lastly, the proposed multi-source category extended historical sequential recommended system (MCE-HSPRec) is implemented that utilizes the rich user-item frequency matrix derived from HSPRec19 [3]. Thereafter, category correlations from the co-occurrences in user click sequence are captured into a category co-occurrence graph. Finally, the user-category frequency matrix is combined with category co-occurrence graph, and the rich user-item frequency matrix to derive a rich user-category preference matrix by applying collaborative filtering to it. Then, preference matrix is derived for three different PositiveRating (0.6, 0.8, 1.0) thresholds giving three matrix, namely mcehsprec0.6, mcehsprec0.8, mcehsprec1.0. A 10-fold evaluation is run for all the recommendation systems to validate performance. Figure 3 displays graphs showing the comparative performance of each recommendation system on 10-fold for k nearest neighbor (k@10). It can be seen

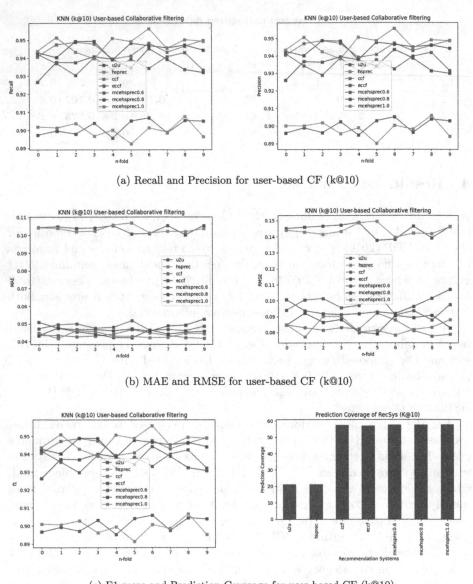

(a) Recall and Precision for user-based CF (k@10)

(b) MAE and RMSE for user-based CF (k@10)

(c) F1-score and Prediction Coverage for user-based CF (k@10)

Fig. 3. Performance evaluation measures using 10-fold cross validation on kNN for User-based Collaborative filtering

from the graphs that MCE-HSPRec consistently improves CF results over the HSPRec19 [3] system.

Table shown in Fig. 3a shows the average performance of different recommendation systems. As demonstrated, the proposed MCE-HSPRec system outperforms both user-item frequency-based (U2U, HSPRec19) recommendation

Model\Metrics	MAE	RMSE	Precision	Recall	F1	Prediction Coverage
U2U	0.10348	0.14427	0.89992	0.90147	0.90069	21.198
HSPREC	0.10339	0.14404	0.8985	0.90002	0.89926	21.238
CCF	**0.04356**	**0.08322**	0.94474	0.9452	0.94497	57.349
ECCF	0.04815	0.09591	0.93533	0.93651	0.93592	56.988
MCEHSPREC0.6	0.04819	0.09635	0.93574	0.93726	0.9365	57.567
MCEHSPREC0.8	0.04464	0.08642	0.94466	0.94518	0.94492	57.638
MCEHSPREC1.0	0.04377	0.08354	**0.94716**	**0.94781**	**0.94749**	**57.878**

(a) Comparative Performance Analysis

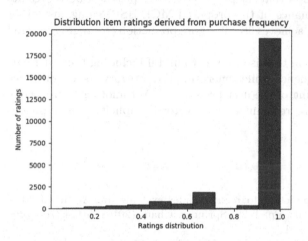

(b) Distribution of ratings in user-item frequency matrix

Fig. 4. Performance analysis @k10

systems. The proposed system only loses to the CCF model in MAE and RMSE metrics, although achieving very close results. The metric error results can be explained through the rating value distribution in our user-item frequency matrix. In Fig. 4b, it can be seen that the rating matrix is highly skewed, resulting in more errors in the collaborative filtering part. The CCF model only takes the category purchase frequency as input and does not consider the user preference of the category and purchase behavior present in the historical data. It also does not consider category co-relation, which the proposed model is able to capture in the category co-occurrence graph. The best accuracy achieved is when the PositiveRating threshold is set to be 1.0. The results also show that denser user-category preference matrix can increase the prediction coverage on the domain to more than double.

5   Conclusion and Future Work

To conclude, by deriving user interest from categories instead of specific items, this research is able to create a denser preference matrix and increase the prediction coverage of the domain. In comparison to other collaborative filtering systems that utilize historical e-commerce data (HSPRec19), our proposed MCE-HSPRec system has improved recommendation performance. The proposed method can generate a recommendation for new items if it shares the category with an existing item, helping sellers increase recognition and sales of a new item. The proposed MCE-HSPRec system can also incorporate user purchase behavior into a recommendation, whereas existing category-based CF systems (ECCF) do not. This helps us generate more relevant recommendations for that user. Experiments show that the proposed system produces better results after evaluating the performance of the proposed MCE-HSPRec against other systems. The MCE-HSPRec achieves 36.64% more prediction coverage compared to HSPRec.

A possible future extension to this study is to find if including the order category co-occurrence in a sequence while generating the category co-coocurrence graph improves understanding of the user preferences. Yet another future scope is a possible way to overcome recommendation error if implicit rating distribution is highly skewed.

References

1. Aggarwal, C.C.: An introduction to recommender systems. In: Aggarwal, C.C. (ed.) Recommender Systems, pp. 1–28. Springer, Cham (2016). https://doi.org/10.1007/978-3-319-29659-3_1
2. Anwar, T., Uma, V.: CD-SPM: cross-domain book recommendation using sequential pattern mining and rule mining. J. King Saud Univ.-Comput. Inf. Sci. **34**(3), 793–800 (2022)
3. Bhatta, R., Ezeife, C.I., Butt, M.N.: Mining sequential patterns of historical purchases for e-commerce recommendation. In: Ordonez, C., Song, I.-Y., Anderst-Kotsis, G., Tjoa, A.M., Khalil, I. (eds.) DaWaK 2019. LNCS, vol. 11708, pp. 57–72. Springer, Cham (2019). https://doi.org/10.1007/978-3-030-27520-4_5
4. Brown, S.: Amazon sellers beg and bribe customers to delete negative reviews (2021). https://www.cnet.com/tech/services-and-software/
5. Ezeife, C.I., Aravindan, V., Chaturvedi, R.: Mining integrated sequential patterns from multiple databases. Int. J. Data Warehous. Min. (IJDWM) **16**(1), 1–21 (2020)
6. Ghazanfar, M.A., Prugel-Bennett, A.: A scalable, accurate hybrid recommender system. In: 2010 Third International Conference on Knowledge Discovery and Data Mining, pp. 94–98. IEEE (2010)
7. Gupta, S., Dave, M.: An overview of recommendation system: methods and techniques. In: Sharma, H., Govindan, K., Poonia, R.C., Kumar, S., El-Medany, W.M. (eds.) Advances in Computing and Intelligent Systems. AIS, pp. 231–237. Springer, Singapore (2020). https://doi.org/10.1007/978-981-15-0222-4_20
8. Hug, N.: Surprise: a Python library for recommender systems. J. Open Source Softw. **5**(52), 2174 (2020)

9. Kechinov, M.: Ecommerce events history in electronics store (2019). https://www.kaggle.com/mkechinov/ecommerce-events-history-in-electronics-store
10. Kumar, N.P., Fan, Z.: Hybrid user-item based collaborative filtering. Procedia Comput. Sci. **60**, 1453–1461 (2015)
11. Mauro, N., Ardissono, L.: Extending a tag-based collaborative recommender with co-occurring information interests. In: Proceedings of the 27th ACM Conference on User Modeling, Adaptation and Personalization, pp. 181–190 (2019)
12. Nilashi, M., Ibrahim, O., Bagherifard, K.: A recommender system based on collaborative filtering using ontology and dimensionality reduction techniques. Expert Syst. Appl. **92**, 507–520 (2018)
13. Sarwar, B., Karypis, G., Konstan, J., Riedl, J.: Analysis of recommendation algorithms for e-commerce. In: Proceedings of the 2nd ACM Conference on Electronic Commerce, pp. 158–167 (2000)
14. Schafer, J.B., Frankowski, D., Herlocker, J., Sen, S.: Collaborative filtering recommender systems. In: Brusilovsky, P., Kobsa, A., Nejdl, W. (eds.) The Adaptive Web. LNCS, vol. 4321, pp. 291–324. Springer, Heidelberg (2007). https://doi.org/10.1007/978-3-540-72079-9_9
15. Schoinas, I., Tjortjis, C.: MuSIF: a product recommendation system based on multi-source implicit feedback. In: MacIntyre, J., Maglogiannis, I., Iliadis, L., Pimenidis, E. (eds.) Artificial Intelligence Applications and Innovations. IFIP Advances in Information and Communication Technology, vol. 559, pp. 660–672. Springer, Cham (2019). https://doi.org/10.1007/978-3-030-19823-7_55
16. Shu, J., Shen, X., Liu, H., Yi, B., Zhang, Z.: A content-based recommendation algorithm for learning resources. Multimedia Syst. **24**(2), 163–173 (2018)
17. Uddin, B.: Multi-data source recommendations with derived sequential pattern mining. Electronic Theses and Dissertations. 9046 (2023). https://scholar.uwindsor.ca/etd/9046
18. Xiao, Y., Ezeife, C.I.: E-commerce product recommendation using historical purchases and clickstream data. In: Ordonez, C., Bellatreche, L. (eds.) DaWaK 2018. LNCS, vol. 11031, pp. 70–82. Springer, Cham (2018). https://doi.org/10.1007/978-3-319-98539-8_6

Taste Representation Learning Toward Food Recommendation Balancing Curiosity and Comfort

Yuto Sakai[1]([✉]) [iD] and Qiang Ma[2] [iD]

[1] Kyoto University, Kyoto, Japan
sakai.yuto.47e@st.kyoto-u.ac.jp
[2] Kyoto Institute of Technology, Kyoto, Japan
qiang@kit.ac.jp

Abstract. One of the best aspects of traveling is getting to try new dishes or regional delicacies that one has never had before. It is an act of satisfying our curiosity, which is one of the most important motivations to travel. However, there may be concerns about whether such dishes can be eaten. Many studies on food recommendations are based on user preferences or dish popularity, and consideration for enjoying unknown local dishes with a feeling of comfort is often insufficient. To address the challenge of balancing curiosity and a sense of comfort, this study determines a sense of comfort toward food from the acceptability of taste and curiosity towards food from the adventurousness of ingredients. This study proposes a neural network model for learning and estimating representation vectors that represent the taste and ingredients of food to compare the taste and ingredients of the recommended food with those of the food the user has had in the past. We also verify the feasibility of recommending dishes that balance both a sense of comfort and curiosity using the estimated acceptability and adventurousness. Through a case study, we demonstrate that reducing the dimensionality of the ingredient representation vectors through principal component analysis results in a certain bias in the distribution on the plane. We also confirm that differences in taste can be estimated by measuring the distance between past distributions and current taste representation vectors.

Keywords: Food Recommendation · Travel · Acceptablity · Adventurousness

1 Introduction

Trying new dishes or local specialties that one has never eaten before is one of the most enjoyable aspects of traveling, satisfying our curiosity, which is one of the most important motivations to travel. It is desirable that the dishes that are eaten are made up of ingredients that one can eat and they taste good according to one's own taste. Especially when it comes to food during travel, there is often

P. Delir Haghighi et al. (Eds.): iiWAS 2023, LNCS 14416, pp. 382–397, 2023.
https://doi.org/10.1007/978-3-031-48316-5_36

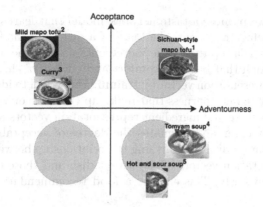

Fig. 1. Recommendation factor and the resulting food (https://lostplate.com/recipes/mapo-tofu-recipe; https://bit.ly/3XoC0sx; https://www.sbfoods.co.jp/recipe/detail/08678.html; https://www.food.com/recipe/tomyamsoup-thailand-479094; https://littlespoonfarm.com/hot-and-sour-soup-recipe)

no second chance to make a different choice if the food does not meet one's expectations. Therefore, one must be comfortable while accepting food.

In recent years, research on food recommendations has been actively conducted. Gao et al. [4] and Thongsri et al. [8] proposed food recommendation systems that satisfy users' food preferences. When it comes to meals during travel, if recommendations are made based on a user's food preferences, as in the conventional methods introduced here, the dishes obtained through recommendations may be closer to the user's preferred taste, providing a sense of comfort that they can be enjoyed. However, a sense of curiosity is absent because the tastes of the dishes that one prefers to eat frequently are similar.

Correia et al. [3] concluded that the uniqueness and tradition of food are important elements in recommending dishes to tourists. Users' curiosity can be satisfied by recommending dishes based on regional and popular cuisine. However, the recommended dishes may contain ingredients that the user cannot eat or that have strong tastes that do not suit the user's palate; therefore, a sense of comfort cannot be ensured.

To the best of our knowledge, currently, no method for recommending unfamiliar dishes at travel destinations combines both curiosity and a sense of comfort. Figure 1 illustrates an example of the correspondence between recommendation factors and the resulting recommended dishes. As of now, recommending dishes in the third and fourth quadrants of Fig. 1 is undesirable, as they contain dishes that may be difficult for users to accept. Additionally, dishes in the second quadrant of Fig. 1 are easily acceptable to users but lack adventurousness, and conventional recommendation methods based on taste preferences would recommend dishes in this area. Dishes that balance both curiosity and a sense of comfort are those included in the first quadrant of Fig. 1.

In this study, we propose a taste network model that learns the taste representation vector, which represents the taste of a dish, and the ingredient representation vector, which represents the ingredients used in the dish, to achieve a food recommendation that balances comfort and curiosity. The proposed model learns the taste representation vector by training the model to identify the degree of hotness, sweetness, and sourness that make up the taste of a dish. The model then calculates the taste and ingredient representation vectors for the dishes the user has previously eaten and estimates the degree of acceptability and adventurousness of the target dish by analyzing the relationship between the taste and ingredient representation vectors of the target dish and those of the dishes the user has eaten previously; This enables a food recommendation that balances comfort and curiosity.

The major contributions of this study are as follows:

- We proposed a neural network model that outputs two types of representation vectors that represent the two elements that constitute a dish: taste and ingredients, using image and recipe data (Sect. 3).
- We demonstrated the possibility of identifying the degree of hotness, sweetness, and sourness in dishes from image and recipe data using a taste network model (Sect. 3).
- We conducted cross-validation and user experiments to measure the discriminative performance of the proposed model in identifying the degree of taste. Additionally, we proposed a data sampling method from existing datasets (Sects. 3 and 4).
- We analyzed the degree of acceptability and adventurousness of the target dish using the user's food history data (Sect. 4).

2 Related Work

Conventional studies on food recommendation systems focus on recommending food based on users' food preferences. Gao et al. [4] proposed a recommendation system based on a neural network called hierarchical attention-based food recommendation to estimate the user's food preferences. Ueda et al. [9] proposed a recipe recommendation method based on food preferences. They estimated the user's food preferences, including their favorite and least liked ingredients, based on recipes they have viewed or cooked in the past. Thongsri et al. [8] proposed a personalized healthy food recommendation system based on collaborative filtering and Knapsack methods.

Yu et al. [10] argue that aesthetic elements are crucial in predicting users' preferences. They incorporate aesthetic features of items extracted from a deep aesthetic network into recommendation systems. Zhang et al. [11] proposed a personalized restaurant recommendation system by extracting visual features of images using deep convolutional neural networks and using them with collaborative filtering methods.

Ahmadian et al. [1] proposed a recommendation approach that takes into account temporal reliability and confidence measures. Similarly, Zhao el al. [12]

considered the temporal changes in users' rating preferences and proposed a tensor factorization model that includes time-varying user and item bias terms.

Travel and food are inseparable companions. Kauppinen et al. [6] conducted focus group interviews to investigate memorable and positive meal experiences and understand the nature of past experiences. They identified the typical characteristics of a meal or food experience as a tourist, including the willingness to try new types of food. Jiménez et al. [5] conducted a study that analyzed the relationship between gastronomy, culture, and tourism. As a result, it was revealed that tourists consider food to be an essential part of the cultural identity of a tourist destination. Correia et al. [3] investigated the impact of local food attributes on customer satisfaction using fuzzy set qualitative comparative analysis. They identified four factors that contributed to recommendations: the quality of the cuisine, its uniqueness, tradition, and the quality of service.

Marín et al. [7] proposed a neural network model called the joint neural embedding model (JNEM) to achieve cross-modal food search. JNEM outputs recipe representation vectors from text data representing ingredients and cooking procedures that constitute a dish and image representation vectors from image data representing dish images. The recipe and image representation vectors output from the same dish are trained to have a small cosine similarity so that representation vectors obtained from different types of data, such as text and images, can be handled in the same space.

3   Proposed Method

In this section, we explain the taste network model, which learns taste and ingredient representation vectors. Furthermore, we describe a method for estimating acceptability and adventurousness using this model. The taste network takes as input the ingredients data, cooking procedure data, and image data of a dish, and outputs representation vectors of the ingredients and taste of the dish by considering both visual semantic and textual semantic to obtain rich features. Figure 2 illustrates the structure of the taste network. In Sect. 3.1, we explain the model proposed by Marín et al. [7], JNEM, which is incorporated into the taste network model. Section 3.2 summarizes the processing within the components that constitute the model. In Sect. 3.3, we explain the method for estimating the ingredient and taste representation vectors. In Sect. 3.4, we describe the training task of the proposed model, and in Sect. 3.5, we explain the dataset used for training and testing the proposed model. Finally, in Sect. 3.6, we summarize the training method and evaluation results of the proposed model.

3.1   JNEM

The JNEM consists mainly of three encoder parts and a fully connected layer, as shown in Fig. 3. The inputs are recipe data consisting of a set of ingredients and cooking procedures included in the dish and the image data of the dish. The mechanisms of each encoder part are as follows.

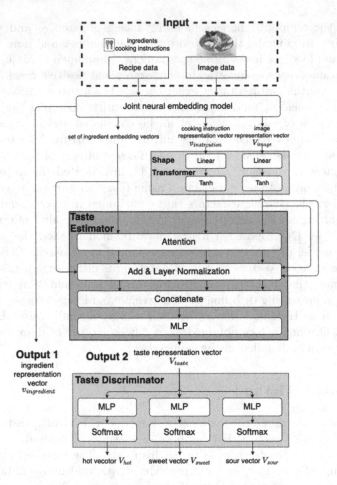

Fig. 2. Structure of Taste Network Model.

Ingredients-Encoder. Each ingredient in the recipe's ingredient set is first converted into a 300-dimensional semantic vector using word2vec. These are denoted as $\{v_{ingr}^1, v_{ingr}^2, \ldots, v_{ingr}^m\}$, where m is the number of ingredients in the recipe. Subsequently, considering that the ingredient set is a non-ordered relation, each ingredient vector $v_{ingr}^1, v_{ingr}^2, \ldots, v_{ingr}^m$ is input into a bidirectional Long Short Term Memory(LSTM), and a single 600-dimensional vector $v_{ingredient}$ is obtained as the output, which represents the ingredient vector.

Instructions-Encoder. Typically, the cooking instructions of a recipe comprise multiple sentences and steps. Therefore, we first encode each sentence that represents a step using a method based on Skip-thought. The Skip-thought model is modified by replacing the Gated Recurrent Unit(GRU) part with LSTM and adding instructions to represent the beginning and end of the cooking instructions.

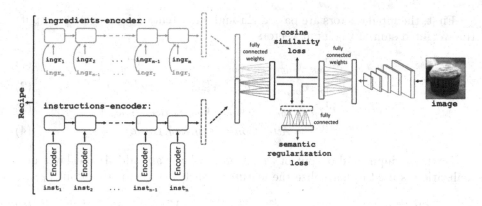

Fig. 3. Structure of JNEM. [7]

This model converts each sentence of the cooking instructions into a 1024-dimensional vector. Finally, we input the vectors obtained earlier into a regular LSTM to obtain a single 1024-dimensional vector, which represents the cooking instructions of the recipe. Here, let us denote the cooking instruction representation vector as $v_{instruction}$.

Image-Encoder. The food image is encoded into a 2048-dimensional vector v_{image} by a model that removes the classification layer from the pre-trained ResNet50 based on the ImageNet dataset.

3.2 Component Description

The taste network comprises three components: the shape transformer, taste estimator, and taste discriminator. We will discuss the processing that occurs within each component in this section.

Shape Transformer. In the shape transformer, $v_{instruction}$ and V_{image} are input, and they are transformed into 300-dimensional vectors $v'_{instruction}$ and V'_{image} by passing them through a linear layer and the *tanh* activation function.

Taste Estimator. The taste estimator takes $v^1_{ingr}, v^2_{ingr}, \ldots, v^{20}_{ingr}$, $v'_{instruction}, V'_{image}$ as input and outputs the taste representation vector V_{taste}.

First, the input vectors are passed through an attention layer, which outputs the weighted sum of the input vectors.

$$query = [v_{ingr}^1, v_{ingr}^2, \ldots, v_{ingr}^{20}, v_{instruction}', V_{image}'] \tag{1}$$

$$key = [v_{ingr}^1, v_{ingr}^2, \ldots, v_{ingr}^{20}, v_{instruction}', V_{image}'] \tag{2}$$

$$value = [v_{ingr}^1, v_{ingr}^2, \ldots, v_{ingr}^{20}, v_{instruction}', V_{image}'] \tag{3}$$

$$V^{attention} = Attention(query, key, value) \tag{4}$$

Next, the input and output of the attention layer are added, and layer normalization is used to normalize the feature of each row vector to obtain V_{LN}.

$$V^{add} = [v_{ingr}^1, v_{ingr}^2, \ldots, v_{ingr}^{20}, v_{instruction}', V_{image}'] + V^{attention} \tag{5}$$

$$V^{LN} = LayerNormalization(V^{add}) \tag{6}$$

The row vectors of V^{LN} are then concatenated to form a single vector $V^{\prime attention}$. Finally, $V^{\prime attention}$ is passed through a 3-layer multilayer perceptron(MLP) with a rectified linear unit activation function in the hidden layer. Dropout is applied with a dropout rate of 0.5 for the non-activated nodes in the hidden layer. The output of the MLP is a 6-dimensional taste representation vector V_{taste}, which is the output of the taste estimator.

Taste Discriminator. The taste discriminator takes the taste representation vector V_{taste} as input and outputs 3-dimensional vectors $V_{hot}, V_{sweet}, V_{sour}$ indicating the degree of hotness, sweetness, and sourness, respectively.

First, V_{taste} is input into a 3-layer MLP with rectified linear unit activation function in the hidden layers, and the output layer applies the softmax function to obtain V_{hot}. Here, V_{hot} is a hotness vector that represents *not hot, slightly hot*, and *very hot* in order from the first element. Similarly, V_{taste} is input to an MLP to obtain V_{sweet} and V_{sour}. V_{sweet} is a sweetness vector that represents *not sweet, slightly sweet*, and *very sweet* in order from the first element, and V_{sour} is a sourness vector that represents *not sour, slightly sour*, and *very sour* in order from the first element.

3.3 Estimation Method for Ingredient and Taste Representation Vectors

In this section, we describe the method for estimating ingredient and taste representation vectors output by the taste network.

Ingredient Representation Vector. The ingredient representation vector $v_{ingredient}$ is output from JNEM.

Taste Representation Vector. First, the recipe and image data of the food are input into the JNEM to obtain a set of ingredients processed by word2vec, denoted as $\{v_{ingr}^1, v_{ingr}^2, \ldots, v_{ingr}^m, v_{ingr}^{m+1}, \ldots, v_{ingr}^{20}\}$, an encoding of the cooking instructions denoted as $v_{instruction}$, and an encoding of the image denoted as V_{image}. Here, m is the number of ingredients, and $v_{ingr}^{m+1}, \ldots, v_{ingr}^{20}$ are dummy ingredient embeddings processed by word2vec for a dummy ingredient (ingredient ID: 0) prepared to align the sequence length of the ingredient set. Next, $v_{instruction}$ and V_{image} are input into the shape transformer to obtain 300-dimensional $v'_{instruction}$ and V'_{image}. Finally, $\{v_{ingr}^1, v_{ingr}^2, \ldots, v_{ingr}^m, v_{ingr}^{m+1}, \ldots, v_{ingr}^{20}\}$, $v'_{instruction}$, and V'_{image} are input into the taste estimator to obtain the taste representation vector V_{taste} from the output.

3.4 Training Task of Taste Network

Chandrashekar et al. [2] demonstrated that the tastes humans perceive through their tongues are generally classified into five categories: sweetness, saltiness, sourness, bitterness, and umami. However, hotness (spiciness) is an important factor in our choice of food. Consequently, we represents taste in a six-dimensional manner: sweetness, saltiness, sourness, bitterness, umami, and hotness.

Among these six elements, we considered that hotness, sweetness, and sourness strongly affect the acceptability of human taste. Currently, in the labeling task described in Sect. 3.5, we only considered the hotness, sweetness, and sourness because they are easily discernible elements from recipe data and image data. Therefore, in the training task of the taste network, we impose a training task to recognize how much hotness, sweetness, and sourness are present in the input food to learn how to output the taste representation vector V_{taste}.

Hotness, sweetness, and sourness are all classified into one of the following categories: 1, 2, or 3.

1. None (hot, sweet, or sour)
2. Slightly (hot, sweet, or sour)
3. Very (hot, sweet, or sour)

The hotness, sweetness, and sourness of the dishes used as training data are expressed as three-dimensional one-hot vectors, and the cross-entropy error between the outputs of the taste discriminator $V_{hot}, V_{sweet}, V_{sour}$ and the one-hot vectors is used as the loss for training.

3.5 Dataset

Recipe1M [7] comprises recipe and image data collected from 24 cooking websites, with approximately 1 million recipes and 800,000 images. Recipe1M contains the following data:

(*Recipe ID, Recipe name, Ingredients, Cooking instructions, Recipe image, Course label*)

Each recipe is uniquely identified by a recipe ID and contains data such as recipe name, ingredients, cooking instructions, and course labels such as appetizer or dessert. Additionally, multiple recipe images are associated with each recipe.

For this study, a portion of the recipes from Recipe1M were used as the training and test data for the model. Because Recipe1M does not contain data indicating the degree of hotness, sweetness, or sourness, we labeled them and used them as training and test data. Recipes with strong tastes in each category, corresponding to labels 2 and 3, were selected as positive training to efficiently train the model for hotness, sweetness, and sourness data. The specific method used for hotness is shown as an example.

1. Three representative dishes that prominently exhibit hotness are extracted from the dishes included in Recipe1M.
2. For each recipe data point in Recipe1M, V_{image} is calculated by passing v_{image} through a fully connected layer and activation function, and V_{recipe} is calculated by combining $v_{ingredient}$ and $v_{instruction}$ and passing the result through a fully connected layer and activation function. These will be referred to as V_{im}^{tar} and V_{rec}^{tar}, respectively. Similarly, V_{im}^i and V_{rec}^i are calculated for the three representative recipes extracted in step 1, where $i = 1, 2, 3$.
3. The cosine similarity between the vectors is calculated to obtain the image similarity sim_{image} and recipe similarity sim_{recipe} between the representative and other dishes.

$$sim_{image} = \frac{cos(V_{im}^{tar}, V_{im}^1) + cos(V_{im}^{tar}, V_{im}^2) + cos(V_{im}^{tar}, V_{im}^3)}{3} \qquad (7)$$

$$sim_{recipe} = \frac{cos(V_{rec}^{tar}, V_{rec}^1) + cos(V_{rec}^{tar}, V_{rec}^2) + cos(V_{rec}^{tar}, V_{rec}^3)}{3} \qquad (8)$$

Furthermore, the food similarity sim_{food} is calculated as a weighted average of sim_{image} and sim_{recipe} to measure the similarity between dishes.

$$sim_{food} = \frac{1}{10} sim_{image} + \frac{9}{10} sim_{recipe} \qquad (9)$$

4. The top 100 dishes are adopted in the descending order of sim_{food} obtained in step 3.

Furthermore, to sample both negative and positive examples, 100 dishes with low sim_{food} were also selected in order. Through these steps, a dataset consisting of 600 dishes was constructed and used.

3.6   Learning and Evaluation of the Taste Network

The dataset of 600 recipes described in Sect. 3.5 was randomly split into a training set of 540 recipes and a test set of 60 recipes to evaluate the performance of the model with a ratio of 9:1. The cross-entropy error was used as the loss function, Adam was used as the optimization method, and the learning rate was fixed at 0.001 for training.

The accuracy of the trained model was measured on a test set of 60 instances, resulting in 85% accuracy for the "hot" label, 85% for the "sweet" label, and 75% for the "sour" label. Table 1 lists the number and proportion of each label in the test data.

Table 1. Number and proportion of each label

taste	none(1)	slightly(2)	very(3)
hotness	51(85%)	7(11.7%)	2(3.3%)
sweetness	25(41.7%)	31(51.7%)	4(6.7%)
sourness	40(66.6%)	18(30.0%)	2(3.3%)

Table 2. Accuracy of cross-validations

fold	hot		sweet		sour	
	baseline	Our Method	baseline	Our Method	baseline	Our Method
1	73.3%	83.3%	40.3%	85.0%	61.7%	71.6%
2	73.0%	81.7%	35.5%	86.7%	55.2%	66.7%
3	75.0%	85.0%	42.2%	75.0%	56.7%	78.3%
4	74.0%	90.0%	41.5%	80.0%	52.3%	75.0%
5	74.0%	81.7%	40.2%	73.3%	49.3%	73.3%
6	78.8%	90.0%	42.0%	86.7%	60.5%	73.3%
7	74.0%	73.3%	42.0%	88.3%	58.8%	68.3%
8	71.2%	88.3%	42.3%	71.7%	60.3%	71.6%
9	74.7%	78.3%	41.2%	83.3%	52.7%	75.0%
10	71.5%	83.3%	42.7%	78.3%	55.5%	73.3%
Average	73.9%	83.5%	41.0%	80.8%	56.3%	72.7%

Furthermore, k-fold cross-validation was conducted with $k = 10$, and the accuracy shown in Table 2 was obtained. The average accuracies over the 10 folds were 83.5%, 80.8%, and 72.7% for the hotness, sweetness, and sourness labels, respectively. To the best of our knowledge, there have been no previous studies that focus on the task of discriminating the degree of taste. Furthermore, as the output of JNEM is a ingredient representation vector, it cannot be introduced as a comparative method. It is to say, there is no existing methods could be used for comparison. Therefore, we calculated the distribution of labels of training data per each cross-validation, and then set it predict the labels by sampling according to that distribution.

Based on the results of the test data and cross-validation, the taste discriminator with an accuracy of 70 − 80% was considered to have been achieved for each taste.

4   User Experiment and Case Study

4.1   User Experiment

In this section, we further evaluate how accurately the taste discrimination for hotness, sweetness, and sourness can be achieved through a user experiment.

We used the dataset "foodRecSys-V1"[1] published on Kaggle. This dataset contains approximately 3.8 million interactions between users and recipes.

We selected five users with a food history of 10 or more dishes, including a bias towards certain dishes from the perspective of taste or ingredients. We prepared the user experiment data by replacing their food history with the corresponding recipe from the Recipe1M dataset for the same dish or with the same name. The participants of the user experiment were an undergraduate and two postgraduate students (hereinafter referred to as participants A, B, and C).

We presented 59 dishes to the participants using a Google Form and asked them to report three levels of hotness, sweetness, and sourness. The discrimination accuracy of the proposed model for both the answers of subjects A, B and C and the most-voted label among their answers is shown in Fig. 4.

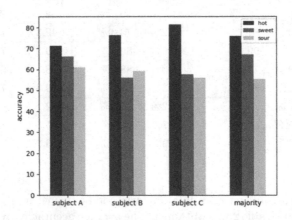

Fig. 4. Accuracy of each taste category (hot, sweet, sour).

The accuracy for the labels obtained by majority voting was 7.6% lower for hotness, 13.6% lower for sweetness, and 17.5% lower for sourness compared with the average accuracy obtained by cross-validation in Sect. 3.6. This is because taste has a subjective aspect that is difficult to measure quantitatively. We

---

[1] https://www.kaggle.com/datasets/elisaxxygao/foodrecsysv1.

assigned the hotness, sweetness, and sourness labels in the training data, and some differences existed between the model trained on the training data and the subjects' taste preferences.

4.2 Case Study

In this section, we report a case study to demonstrate the provision of food recommendations while balancing acceptability and adventurousness, using the food history data of five users used in the user experiment in Sect. 4.1. The procedure is as follows:

– For all dishes in the food history data, we calculate the taste representation vector V_{taste}, assume that they form one cluster, and calculate the centroid of the taste representation vectors V_{center} for all dishes. We then measure the Mahalanobis distance between each dish's V_{taste} and V_{center} and set the maximum value as d_{max}. Furthermore, we calculate the Mahalanobis distance d' between the target dish's V_{taste} and V_{center} and determine the dish as acceptable if $d' \leq d_{max}$. We use Mahalanobis distance to detect the outlier comparing with the distribution of previously eaten dishes.

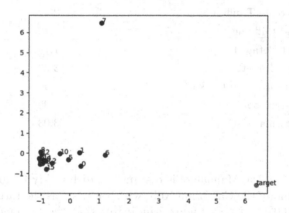

Fig. 5. User 1's scatter plot of ingredient representation vectors

– For all dishes in the food history data, we calculate the ingredient representation vector $v_{ingredient}$, compress the dimensionality to a 2D vector through PCA, and plot them on a scatter plot. Similarly, we compress the target dish's ingredient representation vector $v_{ingredient}$ through PCA and judge it as adventurous if it is located away from the position formed by the points created by the food history data on the same plane.

We summarize the analysis of two cases, one in which the proposal of a dish that balances acceptability and adventurousness was successful, and one in which it failed, out of five cases.

Case 1. User 1 in Case 1's history data includes many desserts such as cake, cookies, and pie. Figure 5 depicts the scatter plot of the ingredient representation vectors of the 16 dishes included in the food history data and the target dish, and Table 3 lists the dish names and Mahalanobis distances.

Table 3. User 1's food history

index	title	mahalanobis distance
0	Red Velvet cupcake	2.58
1	Turkish Delight	2.06
2	Dark Chocolate cake	2.53
3	Best Big, Fat, Chewy Chocolate Chip Cookie	2.73
4	Molasses Cookies	1.02
5	Tiramisu cheesecake	1.77
6	My Crab Cakes	3.31
7	Mie Goreng	2.86
8	Sweet Potato Casserole	2.18
9	Favorite Old Fashioned Gingerbread	1.93
10	Chocolate Truffle Pie	2.47
11	Bread Pudding	1.12
12	Sweet Potato Pie	1.76
13	Green Tomato Cake	3.23
14	Oatmeal Raisin Cookies	2.40
15	Easy blueberry pie	1.90
target	California Roll	3.03

d_{max} is equal to the Mahalanobis distance of dish 6: My Crab Cakes, which is 3.31. Furthermore, the California Roll, which was set as the target dish in this case, has $d' = 3.03 (\leq d_{max})$. Figure 5 indicates that the target dish is located far to the right, away from the previously eaten dishes whose ingredient vectors are biased towards the lower left of the plot. Therefore, the California Roll is likely to be a dish that incorporates adventure while maintaining acceptability for the user, making it a candidate for a dish that balances a sense of comfort and curiosity.

Case 2. User 2's history data in Case 2 contains meat dishes and spicy dishes such as salsa and chili con carne. The scatter plot of the ingredient representation vectors of 10 dishes included in the history data, and the target dish is shown in Fig. 6, and the dish names and Mahalanobis distances are listed in Table 4.

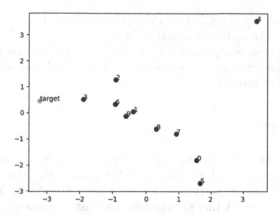

Fig. 6. User 2's scatter plot of ingredient representation vectors

Table 4. User 2's food history

index	title	mahalanobis distance
0	Pork Barbeque	1.95
1	Spicy Salsa	2.83
2	Italian Pork Tenderloin	2.87
3	Pumpkin, Sweet Potato, Leek and Coconut Milk Soup	1.53
4	Flank Steak a la Willyboy	2.88
5	Emily's Famous Sloppy Joes	1.90
6	Canadian Cod Au Gratin	2.24
7	The Ultimate Chili	1.47
8	Wheat Bran and Walnut Bagels	2.52
9	Easy blueberry pie	1.82
target	Taiwan Ramen	2.98

The d_{max} is equal to the Mahalanobis distance of dish 4, Flank Steak a la Willyboy, which is 2.88. The target dish, Taiwan Ramen, has $d' = 2.98 (> d_{max})$, indicating that it may not be very acceptable. Furthermore, Fig. 6 indicates that the ingredient representation vector for the target dish is outside the bias of the representation vector for the usual dishes consumed. Therefore, Taiwan Ramen may have some adventurousness, but it cannot be recommended as a dish that balances both comfort and curiosity.

Conclusion and Discussion. In conclusion, the results of the case study demonstrate that reducing the dimensionality of the ingredient representation vectors through principal component analysis results in a certain bias in the distribution on the plane and that differences in taste can be estimated by measuring the distance between past distributions and current taste representation vectors. However, there are cases where similar-tasting dishes, such as Dish 8: Sweet Potato

Casserole and Dish 12: Sweet Potato Pie in Case 1, have different distances from
the centroid of the taste history distribution.

Given that the taste representation vectors are six-dimensional, using data
with even more food history for each user would be ideal. Therefore, we plan to
collect such data in future.

5   Conclusion

This study addresses the challenge of discovering dishes that satisfy both the
user's sense of comfort and curiosity by obtaining both taste and ingredient
representation vectors for each dish. We propose a proprietary neural network
model called taste network that incorporates an existing research model to realize
the estimation of these vectors. The taste network is trained on the task of
discriminating the hotness, sweetness, and sourness of dishes. The performance
of the discriminator was evaluated using a test dataset prepared by the authors
and a user experiment, resulting in an average accuracy of 81.7% for the test
dataset and 68.5% for user responses.

This study retrieved the food histories of five users and applied the proposed
model to demonstrate the discovery of dishes that ensured both acceptability
and adventurousness in a case study using a dataset that preserved the mutual
relationship between users and the dishes on recipe websites.

The challenges and prospects for future research can be summarized as
follows:

- The amount of training data used in the training task, which is 540 in this
research, is insufficient for learning. Therefore, future research must aim to
increase the number of training data. In addition, personalization is planned
to discussed.
- A limitation is that the ability to obtain taste and ingredient representation
vectors is limited to the recipes contained in Recipe1M. Therefore, we plan
to expand it to enable the application of the taste network to any recipe.

Acknowledgements. This work was partly supported by JSPS KAKENHI
(23H03404).

References

1. Ahmadian, S., Joorabloo, N., Jalili, M., Ahmadian, M.: Alleviating data sparsity
problem in time-aware recommender systems using a reliable rating profile enrich-
ment approach. Exp. Syst. Appl. **187**, 115849 (2022)
2. Chandrashekar, J., Hoon, M., Ryba, N., Zuker, C.: The receptors and cells for
mammalian taste. Nature **444**, 288–294 (2006)
3. Correia, A., Kim, S.(Sam)., Kozak, M.: Gastronomy experiential traits and their
effects on intentions for recommendation: a fuzzy set approach. Int. J. Tour. Res.
22(3), 351–363 (2020)

4. Gao, X., et al.: Hierarchical attention network for visually-aware food recommendation. IEEE Trans. Multim. **22**(6), 1647–1659 (2020)
5. Jiménez-Beltrán, F., López-Guzmán, T., González Santa Cruz, F.: Analysis of the relationship between tourism and food culture. Sustainability **8**(5), 418 (2016)
6. Kauppinen-Räisänen, H., Gummerus, J., Lehtola, K.: Remembered eating experiences described by the self, place, food, context and time. Br. Food J. **115**, 666–685 (2013)
7. Marin, J., et al.: Recipe1m+: a dataset for learning cross-modal embeddings for cooking recipes and food images (2018)
8. Thongsri, N., Warintarawej, P., Chotkaew, S., Saetang, W.: Implementation of a personalized food recommendation system based on collaborative filtering and knapsack method. Int. J. Electric. Comput. Eng. **12**(1), 630 (2022)
9. Ueda, M., Asanuma, S., Miyawaki, Y., Nakajima, S.: Recipe recommendation method by considering the user's preference and ingredient quantity of target recipe. Lect. Notes Eng. Comput. Sci. **2209**, 519–523 (2014)
10. Yu, W., et al.: Visually aware recommendation with aesthetic features. VLDB J. **30**, 495–513 (2021)
11. Zhang, X., Luo, H., Chen, B., Guo, G.: Multi-view visual Bayesian personalized ranking for restaurant recommendation. Appl. Intell. **50**, 2901–2915 (2020)
12. Zhao, J., Yang, S., Huo, H., Sun, Q., Geng, X.: Tbtf: an effective time-varying bias tensor factorization algorithm for recommender system. Appl. Intell. **51**, 4933–4944 (2021)

Tag2Seq: Enhancing Session-Based Recommender Systems with Tag-Based LSTM

Yahya Bougteb[1]([✉])(iD), Elyazid Akachar[1], Brahim Ouhbi[1], and Bouchra Frikh[2]

[1] LM2I Lab, ENSAM, Moulay Ismaïl University, Marjane II, B.P.5290, Meknès, Morocco
y.bougteb@edu.umi.ac.ma, b.ouhbi@umi.ac.ma
[2] LIASSE Lab, Ecole Nationale Supérieure des Sciences Appliquées, B.P. 1796 Atlas, Fès, Morocco
bouchra.frikh@usmba.ac.ma

Abstract. A key problem of session-based recommendation (sequence pattern or neighborhood-based recommendation) is to predict items of interest based on anonymous user's current interaction session or unavailable profile user. While recurrent neural networks (RNNs) have been applied to the recommender systems with remarkable success, little attention has been paid to the semantic and contextual information about tags. In this work we argue that long-short-term memory recurrent neural network (LSTM-RNN) incorporating pre-trained global vectors embeddings can be applied to capture semantic and contextual information about tags in session-based recommendation systems with remarkable results. Therefore, this paper introduces Tag2Seq, a novel recommendation system based on a recurrent neural network architecture that utilizes LSTM to leverage user's tags. Our method is evaluated on the Movielens 20M dataset, Experimental results indicate that Tag2Seq outperforms state-of-the-art session-based recommendation methods on large real-world dataset.

Keywords: Session-based Recommender System · LSTM · RNN · Deep Learning · GloVe

1 Introduction

As the number of web resources continues to increase, users are presented with an overwhelming amount of information to sift through. This phenomenon, commonly known as information overload, can be addressed by implementing personalized recommender systems (RS). RS have become one of the most important information systems services in the last two decades [9], owing to their highly practical value, especially in social media, e-commerce, education, and other domains. Usually, it creates suggestions based on users' prior intentions. In fact, it analyzes a user's past behavior to identify their preferences to recommend resources that align with his/her interests. By doing so, personalized

P. Delir Haghighi et al. (Eds.): iiWAS 2023, LNCS 14416, pp. 398–407, 2023.
https://doi.org/10.1007/978-3-031-48316-5_37

RS assist users in obtaining and accessing resources that are relevant to their needs, thus alleviating the problem of information overload [4,13,18,19]. However, these methods usually overlook the changes in a user's preference over time, as they mainly focus on exploring all historical data. Therefore, the user's recent interactions with items are not given much attention.

Recently, there was a growing interest in the RS literature on session-based recommender systems (SBRS) aiming to provide personalized recommendations based on a given sequence of user actions, without considering the longer-term user histories [17]. This is particularly relevant for non-registered users, whose short-term interests are assumed based on their current session. The main goal of SBRS is to provide relevant item recommendations that match the user's short-term interests, without relying on longer-term user histories [24]. However, this approach had limitations in capturing more complex dependencies in the user's behavior. Over the past decade, SBRS have evolved from traditional factorization approach to advanced deep neural networks-based model [3]. A key problem of session-based recommendation (sequence pattern or neighborhood-based recommendation) is to predict items of interest based on anonymous user's current interaction session or unavailable profile user. Therefore, it is challenging to recommend relevant content instantly to users by simulating their long-term behavior pattern [10]. In other words, instead of assuming that each user has a fixed preference they tend to discover user preferences changes since a user's interests can change over time. Discovering such a change is crucial for producing personalized suggestions. Moreover, session-based recommendation is misleading by popularity bias and always favors short-head items with more popularity.

Deep neural network techniques have been widely adopted in the session-based recommendation systems. RNNs, CNNs, GNNs, and attention mechanisms are the most used approaches for deep learning-based sequential recommendation. RNN-based architectures have been extensively used in sequential recommendation. Hence, the LSTM network was introduced to enable the learning of long-term dependencies [11]. An LSTM has the advantage of having a long-term memory module that can better handle long-term dependencies. As a result, LSTMs have been widely used in various fields, such as natural language processing, speech recognition, and others that involve sequential data [20]. Despite the improvements brought by RNN-based methods, they still suffer from limited short-term memory and have difficulty in memorizing long sequences of actions [20]. Therefore, in certain real-world scenarios, these methods still could not better simulate the real intention of users or consider the complex pattern transformation between interacted items [22]. In fact, the aforementioned memory network-based methods for session-based recommendations often ignore the potential of using metadata such as tags, which could provide valuable information to improve the accuracy of recommendations.

To address these limitations, we propose to Incorporating tags metadata in RS to capture more nuanced user preferences and enhance recommendation accuracy. This approach enables the recommender system to provide more personalized and precise recommendations that align with the user's actual preferences.

Furthermore, tag-based SBRS can prove especially useful in cases where there is a lack of user interaction history or limited data available. In this paper, we propose Tag2Seq: an LSTM-RNN session-based recommender system that utilizes pre-trained GloVe embeddings to represent both tags and items in a dense vector space [15]. This approach aims to enhance recommendation accuracy by leveraging the more nuanced user preferences captured through tag information. The LSTM-RNN architecture is chosen because it is able to capture long-term dependencies in user behavior, which is important for session-based recommendation scenarios. To further enhance the performance of the model, GloVe embeddings are used to represent the items and tags. GloVe embeddings are a popular method for generating word embeddings, which are numerical representations of words or phrases that capture semantic meaning. By representing the items and tags with GloVe embeddings, the model is able to capture the semantic relationships between them, which can lead to more accurate recommendations. To the best of our knowledge, there is no LSTM-RNN incorporating pre-trained global vectors embeddings to capture semantic and contextual information about tags in session-based recommendation systems. This paper is structured as follows: in Sect. 2, we provide a brief summary of the related work. The proposed approach is detailed in Sect. 3, and in Sect. 4, we present the results of our experiments. Finally, we conclude our paper in Sect. 5.

2   Related Work

Explicit data such as likes and ratings have been the primary source of information used in traditional recommendation systems, implicit data such as clickstream and browsing history can also be used. Thus, it is crucial to analyze a user's behavior and preferences. Hence, research is constantly being conducted on methods to improve the accuracy of recommendations by continuously refining insights based on a user's past history of selected item [21].

SBRS are a kind of recommender system that utilizes a user's previous interactions with a system to suggest new items. These systems can be employed for both registered users and anonymous visitors, making them popular in both academic research and industry. Early studies on SBRS were based mainly on Markov chains, which modeled the local sequential behavior between adjacent items [7]. However, this approach had limitations in capturing more complex dependencies in the user's behavior. Recently, deep learning models such as RNNs have been used to model sequences of user interactions in a session. In [10], an RNN-based approach is suggested for SBRS. The paper also takes into consideration practical aspects of the task and introduces several modifications to classic RNNs, such as a ranking loss function, to make the approach more feasible for short session-based data. The LSTM-RNN was designed to address the problem of long-term dependencies that traditional RNNs were not able to effectively handle. Since its introduction, many variants of LSTMs have been proposed, including the Gated Recurrent Unit (GRU) [5], as well as GRU-1, GRU-2, and GRU-3 [6]. A movie recommendation system, named GRU4RecBE, is proposed in [16]. The architecture of that model is an extension of the GRU4Rec [10].

Incorporating contextual information, as described in [23], is one way to model a user's ongoing session. This approach leverages various types of rich metadata, such as location, time, device information, etc., to enhance the accuracy of the recommender system. By incorporating this additional information, the system can provide more informative recommendations to the users. Furthermore, the widespread use of tags has spurred the development of a vast body of literature on tag recommendation methods [25]. These methods are designed to aid users in the tagging process and enhance the quality of tags that are generated. Meanwhile, there has been some studies that take advantage of available tags to recommend items. Authors in [1] propose a sparse deep autoencoder that constructs low-dimensional latent features based on both trust relationships between users and tag information. [26] introduce a music recommendation system based on Gaussian state-space models that incorporate tags associated with a particular song or artist to generate personalized recommendations.

So, exploration of utilizing tags in SBRS to discover semantic relationships between tags and items to enhance the accuracy of recommendations is still a challenging task. The key contributions of this paper are summarized as follows:

- We highlight that there has been limited exploration of utilizing tags in SBRS to discover semantic relationships between tags and items.
- We propose the Tag2Seq model which utilizes an embedding layer to represent both tags and items in a dense vector space using pre-trained GloVe embeddings.
- By incorporating tags in the user session, the recurrent neural network can better capture these relationships and enhance the accuracy of recommendations.
- Experiment results on a benchmark dataset demonstrate the strong performance of Tag2Seq model over state-of-the-art baselines.

3   Tag2Seq Recommendation Model

This section introduces the Tag2Seq model, which utilizes an LSTM-RNN for session-based recommendation. Our proposed method leverages pre-trained GloVe embeddings to represent items and tags in a dense vector space, allowing for the capture of semantic relations between them. By incorporating tags in user sessions, the model can capture a wider range of user interests and preferences, while the LSTM architecture is used to capture long-term dependencies in user behavior. The framework of Tag2Seq is illustrated in Fig. 1.

3.1   Embedding Layers

We consider a user session as an input sequence consisting of the items that the user has positively interacted within a session, such as watching a movie,

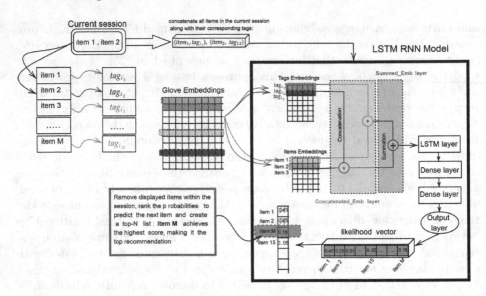

Fig. 1. Tag2Seq framework architecture

buying an item, clicking an item, or rating an item positively, along with their corresponding tags: $\tau = [(item1, tag_{item1}), (item2, tag_{item2}), ..., (iteml, tag_{iteml})]$ where l is the number of items in the current session. Tag2Seq is used to extract latent representations through two embedding layers. The first layer receives the item Id and generates its vector embedding $I_{emb} \in \mathbb{R}^d$, where d=100. We used d=100 for word embeddings because we utilized pre-trained GloVe embeddings that have 100 dimensions. The second layer receives the corresponding tag and extracts its vector embedding $Tag_{emb} \in \mathbb{R}^d$. The parameters of the embedding layers are initialized with pre-trained GloVe embeddings. By representing the items and tags with GloVe embeddings, the Tag2Seq is able to capture the semantic relationships between them, which can improve the relevance and diversity of recommended items.

Next, a **concatenated_Emb** layer is used for concatenation of both embedding vectors I_{emb} and Tag_{emb}. By concatenating two vectors of the same dimension, we are essentially creating a new vector that contains the information from both original vectors. This allows the model to consider both the item and tag information when making predictions. Then, a **summed_Emb** layer is used to compute the sum of the concatenated embeddings along the time axis (i.e., across the sequence of items and tags). This produces a single fixed-length vector representation of the session that captures the user's interests across all the items they interacted with. The use of concatenation followed by summation is a common technique in sequence modeling tasks, as it allows the model to capture both local and global dependencies within the sequence [14]. Specifically, concatenation allows the model to learn relationships between adjacent items and tags, while summation allows the model to aggregate information from across the entire sequence. The final embeddings $E_{sum} \in \mathbb{R}^d$ and the concatenated embeddings $E \in \mathbb{R}^{2d}$ can be defined as follows:

$$E = [I_{emb}; Tag_{emb}] \tag{1}$$

$$E_{sum} = \sum_{i=1}^{2d} E_i \tag{2}$$

where E_i denotes the i-th element of the concatenated embedding E.

3.2 LSTM

LSTMs utilize gated cells that selectively retain or discard information, making them highly effective at processing sequential data over long periods of time. The basic architecture of an LSTM consists of three gates: an input gate, an output gate, and a forget gate, which control the flow of information into and out of the LSTM [12]. Each gate is a separate neural network that acts as a filter, controlling the flow of information into and out of the LSTM. By selectively retaining and forgetting information, LSTMs are able to maintain a more accurate and useful memory of long sequences. LSTMs have been shown to outperform traditional RNNs on various tasks, such as language modeling, machine translation, and speech recognition [2]. The activations for the input gate, denoted by y^{in}, and the output gate, denoted by y^{out}, are calculated using the following equations [8]:

$$net_{out_j}(t) = \sum_m w_{out_j m} y^m(t-1); y^{out_j}(t) = f_{out_j}(net_{out_j}(t)) \tag{3}$$

$$net_{in_j}(t) = \sum_m w_{in_j m} y^m(t-1); y^{in_j}(t) = f_{in_j}(net_{in_j}(t)) \tag{4}$$

where the weight on the connection from unit m is denoted by w, and f represents the sigmoid function. the formula for the output layer k is calculated as follows:

$$net_{k_j}(t) = \sum_m w_{km} y^m(t-1); y^k(t) = f_k(net_{k_j}(t)) \tag{5}$$

The LSTM layer plays a crucial role in Tag2Seq by processing the sequential information from the input sequence of (item, tag) pairs. It takes in the concatenated and summed embeddings as input and generates a sequence of hidden states. Each hidden state at time t in the sequence represents the model's understanding of the sequence up to that point. The LSTM layer is designed to selectively retain and forget information from previous hidden states, allowing it to model long-term dependencies.

After processing the sequence of item-tag pairs with the LSTM layer, the final hidden state encapsulates the model's understanding of the entire sequence. This hidden state is then fed through two dense layers to obtain a probability vector

$I_{next} \in \mathbb{R}^M$, where M is the total number of items in the system. The vector I_{next} contains the probabilities of all items in the system being the next one in the sequence. To generate the recommendation list, the items are sorted in descending order based on their probabilities, and the top n items are selected. The item with the highest probability is the first recommendation, followed by the item with the second highest probability, and so on.

4   Experimental Evaluation

In this section, we conduct multiple experiments on the MovieLens 20M dataset to compare the effectiveness of our proposed model, Tag2Seq, with other methods.

4.1   Dataset Description

The MovieLens 20M dataset is a widely used and stable benchmark dataset in the field of movie recommendation. It contains 20 million movie ratings and 465,000 tag applications given by 138,000 users for 27,000 movies. Additionally, it includes tag genome data with 12 million relevance scores across 1,100 tags. The dataset was initially released in April 2015 and updated in October 2016.

To ensure accurate and effective recommendations, it is crucial to preprocess the dataset before feeding it into a neural network. In our case, we begin by cleaning the MovieLens 20M dataset by removing entries without tags or with tags composed solely of numerical or special characters. We also preprocess the tags by removing special characters. After cleaning the dataset, we split it into a training set (80%) and a test set (20%).

4.2   Results and Discussion

To evaluate the performance of our proposed approach, Tag2Seq, we compare it against state-of-the-art session-based methods using two common metrics: hit ratio (HR) and Normalized Discounted Cumulative Gain (NDCG). We compared our proposed Tag2Seq model with several baseline methods, including POP that recommends the most frequent items in the training set and the current session, as well as three other state-of-the-art session-based recommendation models: GRU4Rec, GRU4RecBE, and SR-GNN. While GRU4Rec uses RNNs to model user sequences, GRU4RecBE extracts features from item descriptions and SR-GNN models session sequences as graphs with Graph Neural Networks. Table 1 reports the final results.

Results show that our proposed method Tag2Seq achieved the highest performance compared to other methods in terms of hit@10 and NDCG@10, indicating its superiority in the session-based recommendation task. This is attributed to its ability to capture semantic information embedded in the tags associated with the movies. Additionally, GRU4Rec models performed better than SR-GNN and POP because they use RNNs to model the user's sequence of interactions with

Table 1. The performance of Tag2Seq with other baseline methods on the MovieLens 20m dataset

Metrics	hit@10	NDCG@10
GRU4Rec	0.5844	0.3637
GRU4RecBE	0.7908	0.5670
SR-GNN	0.4913	0.2931
POP	0.1378	0.0695
Tag2Seq	**0.8117**	**0.5741**

the system. RNNs are particularly good at capturing temporal dependencies in the data, which is important in session-based recommendation. Furthermore, The GRU4RecBE model performed even better than the original GRU4Rec model, as it takes into account the text descriptions of the items of interest, which provides additional contextual information for the model to learn from. On the other hand, SR-GNN models the session sequences as graph-structured data with Graph Neural Networks (GNNs). While GNNs have shown great success in modeling graph-structured data, they may not be as effective in capturing temporal dependencies in the data. Additionally, POP simply recommends the most popular items in the training set or in the current session, which does not take into account the user's individual preferences and history.

5   Conclusion

Session-based recommendations have achieved encouraging results. However, these methods often ignore the potential of using tags as metadata, which could provide valuable information to improve the accuracy of recommendations. In this paper, we proposed Tag2Seq, a SBRS that leverages tags to enhance recommendations. In future work, it would be interesting to apply Tag2Seq to other datasets and compare its performance with other state-of-the-art methods. Additionally, evaluating the impact of the number of tags associated with each item on the performance of the model can also be explored.

References

1. Ahmadian, S., Ahmadian, M., Jalili, M.: A deep learning based trust-and tag-aware recommender system. Neurocomputing **488**, 557–571 (2022)
2. Bhaskar, S., Thasleema, T.: LSTM model for visual speech recognition through facial expressions. Multimed. Tools Appl. **82**(4), 5455–5472 (2023)
3. Bougteb, Y., Ouhbi, B., Frikh, B., Zemmouri, E.M.: A deep autoencoder based multi-criteria recommender system. In: Hassanien, A.E., et al. (eds.) Proceedings of the International Conference on Artificial Intelligence and Computer Vision (AICV2021), pp. 56–65. Springer, Cham (2021). https://doi.org/10.1007/978-3-030-76346-6_6

4. Bougteb, Y., Ouhbi, B., Frikh, B., Zemmouri, E.: A deep autoencoder-based hybrid recommender system. Int. J. Mobile Comput. Multimed. Commun. (IJMCMC) **13**(1), 1–19 (2022)

5. Cho, K., et al.: Learning phrase representations using RNN encoder-decoder for statistical machine translation. arXiv preprint arXiv:1406.1078 (2014)

6. Dey, R., Salem, F.M.: Gate-variants of gated recurrent unit (GRU) neural networks. In: 2017 IEEE 60th International Midwest Symposium on Circuits and Systems (MWSCAS), pp. 1597–1600. IEEE (2017)

7. Eirinaki, M., Vazirgiannis, M., Kapogiannis, D.: Web path recommendations based on page ranking and markov models. In: Proceedings of the 7th Annual ACM International Workshop on Web Information And Data Management, pp. 2–9 (2005)

8. Gers, F.A., Schmidhuber, J., Cummins, F.: Learning to forget: continual prediction with LSTM. Neural Comput. **12**(10), 2451–2471 (2000)

9. Hdioud, F., Frikh, B., Ouhbi, B.: Multi-criteria recommender systems based on multi-attribute decision making. In: Proceedings of International Conference on Information Integration and Web-based Applications and Services, pp. 203–210 (2013)

10. Hidasi, B., Karatzoglou, A., Baltrunas, L., Tikk, D.: Session-based recommendations with recurrent neural networks. arXiv preprint arXiv:1511.06939 (2015)

11. Hochreiter, S., Schmidhuber, J.: Long short-term memory. Neural Comput. **9**(8), 1735–1780 (1997)

12. Krause, B., Lu, L., Murray, I., Renals, S.: Multiplicative LSTM for sequence modelling. arXiv preprint arXiv:1609.07959 (2016)

13. Liao, M., Sundar, S.S.: When e-commerce personalization systems show and tell: Investigating the relative persuasive appeal of content-based versus collaborative filtering. J. Advert. **51**(2), 256–267 (2022)

14. Ng, P.: dna2vec: Consistent vector representations of variable-length k-mers. arXiv preprint arXiv:1701.06279 (2017)

15. Pennington, J., Socher, R., Manning, C.D.: Glove: Global vectors for word representation. In: Proceedings of the 2014 Conference on Empirical Methods in Natural Language Processing (EMNLP), pp. 1532–1543 (2014)

16. Potter, M., Liu, H., Lala, Y., Loanzon, C., Sun, Y.: Gru4recbe: a hybrid session-based movie recommendation system (student abstract). In: Proceedings of the AAAI Conference on Artificial Intelligence. vol. 36, pp. 13029–13030 (2022)

17. Ranjbar Kermany, N., Yang, J., Wu, J., Pizzato, L.: Fair-SRS: a fair session-based recommendation system. In: Proceedings of the Fifteenth ACM International Conference on Web Search and Data Mining, pp. 1601–1604 (2022)

18. Ricci, F., Rokach, L., Shapira, B.: Recommender systems: introduction and challenges. Recommender systems handbook, pp. 1–34 (2015)

19. Shambour, Q., Hussein, A.H., Kharma, Q., Abu-Alhaj, M.M.: Effective hybrid content-based collaborative filtering approach for requirements engineering. Comput. Syst. Sci. Eng. **40**(1), 113–125 (2022)

20. Smagulova, K., James, A.P.: A survey on LSTM memristive neural network architectures and applications. Europ. Phys. J. Special Topics **228**(10), 2313–2324 (2019)

21. Wang, S., Cao, L., Wang, Y., Sheng, Q.Z., Orgun, M.A., Lian, D.: A survey on session-based recommender systems. ACM Comput. Surv. (CSUR) **54**(7), 1–38 (2021)

22. Wu, S., Tang, Y., Zhu, Y., Wang, L., Xie, X., Tan, T.: Session-based recommendation with graph neural networks. In: Proceedings of the AAAI Conference on Artificial Intelligence. vol. 33, pp. 346–353 (2019)

23. Wu, T., Sun, F., Dong, J., Wang, Z., Li, Y.: Context-aware session recommendation based on recurrent neural networks. Comput. Electr. Eng. **100**, 107916 (2022)
24. Zhang, Q., Wang, S., Lu, W., Feng, C., Peng, X., Wang, Q.: Rethinking adjacent dependency in session-based recommendations. In: Gama, J., Li, T., Yu, Y., Chen, E., Zheng, Yu., Teng, F. (eds.) Advances in Knowledge Discovery and Data Mining: 26th Pacific-Asia Conference, PAKDD 2022, Chengdu, China, May 16–19, 2022, Proceedings, Part III, pp. 301–313. Springer International Publishing, Cham (2022). https://doi.org/10.1007/978-3-031-05981-0_24
25. Zhao, W., et al.: Hyperbolic personalized tag recommendation. In: Bhattacharya, A., et al. (eds.) Database Systems for Advanced Applications: 27th International Conference, DASFAA 2022, Virtual Event, April 11–14, 2022, Proceedings, Part II, pp. 216–231. Springer, Cham (2022). https://doi.org/10.1007/978-3-031-00126-0_14
26. Zheng, E., Kondo, G.Y., Zilora, S., Yu, Q.: Tag-aware dynamic music recommendation. Expert Syst. Appl. **106**, 244–251 (2018)

ClinLearning: An Online Clinical Tutoring and Crowdsourced Treatment Recommendation System

Hasan M. Jamil[1]([⊠]), Tyler Bland[2], Evanthia Bernitsas[3], Nancy Carr[4], Derrick Phillips[2], Farjahan Shawon[5], Berhane Seyoum[3], and Alexander Gow[3]

[1] Department of Computer Science, University of Idaho, Moscow, ID 83844, USA
`jamil@uidaho.edu`
[2] WWAMI Medical Education, University of Idaho, Moscow, ID 83844, USA
`{tbland,dphillips}@uidaho.edu`
[3] School of Medicine, Wayne State University, Detroit, MI 48201, USA
`{ebernits,bseyoum,agow}@med.wayne.edu`
[4] Moore School of Education, Carolina University, Winston-Salem, NC 27101, USA
`carrn@carolinau.edu`
[5] College of Education, University of Idaho, Moscow, ID 83844, USA
`shaw0901@vandals.uidaho.edu`

Abstract. Tutoring and training clinical practitioners are the corner stones of quality healthcare systems. While formal education and training give medical students the basis of human physiology, anatomy, health, and medicine, internships and hospital mentorships offer more hands-on practice, real life experiences and clinical insights to become a successful young physician. A digital tutoring and assessment system can aid in the training and learning process immensely. While there are several clinical tutoring and e-learning systems around, most do not support community contributed learning challenges to introduce new learning experiences. In this paper, we introduce a new clinical e-learning and tutoring system, called *ClinLearning*, for online training and assessment of medical students. In this system, we allow inclusion of partitioned EHRs for focused training, and submission and inclusion of challenging real life case scenarios for the recommendation of interventions. We highlight ClinLearning's promises and discuss potential research opportunities.

Keywords: Clinical tutoring · crowdsourcing · EHR · machine learning

1 Introduction

One of the most essential skills medical students learn to diagnose and treat patients is clinical reasoning. The ability to link acquired knowledge and experience for the synthesis of an intervention depends almost entirely on the students' ability to reason and infer based on the facts of the case at hand. Traditional ways

P. Delir Haghighi et al. (Eds.): iiWAS 2023, LNCS 14416, pp. 408–413, 2023.
https://doi.org/10.1007/978-3-031-48316-5_38

of imparting this reasoning capabilities has been hospital rounds and internships. In its traditional form, this process amounts to problem-based learning (PBL) [1] and collaborative learning (CL) [4]. In this approach, students are presented with a case, mentored by an experienced physician, and are asked to hypothesize a treatment plan. Students in the group reason, discuss and suggest possible solutions, and learn by watching the mentor's solutions and self-correction.

Digital incarnation of PBL tries to simulate the mentoring experience at a larger and wider scale. While the instructional model and its implementation varies, the common substrate involves a mentor who designs a problem with a mental model of learning outcome, presents the problem to a student, and helps the student develop the solution hypothesis through reasoning and process of elimination offering only minimal help just enough to keep the student on the right track [2]. To help correct a mistake in the process, hints are generated by the system and a conversation ensues [3]. In this paper, our goal is to discuss a new machine learning based conversational clinical tutoring system, called *Clin-Learnig*, for novice medical students to aid in clinical reasoning based learning. We adopted a two stage approach to its development. In the first stage, we have implemented an experimental prototype called MedSchool$^+$ as a tutoring system for United States Medical Licensing Examination (USMLE) Step 3 Exam[1]. ClinLearning is planned as its natural second stage. We present a brief discussion on the early development of ClinLearning and introduce its characteristic features. We plan to present a complete discussion on this system elsewhere.

2   A Document Model for Cases

Figure 1 is an EHR document for the ER patient John Doe. He was attended and treated by Dr. Jane Doe on March 10, 2023, then on March 17, 2023 by Dr. John Smith, and finally on May 1, 2023 by Dr. Jane Doe. This the document contains three episodes temporally ordered as E_1, E_2 and E_3.

During episode 1, John broke his forearm, a physical exam and X-ray were performed, and then a splint was applied and a painkiller was prescribed following a diagnosis of a bone fracture. In episode 2, he returned a week later with a complaint of increased pain and temperature. Following a physical exam, blood test and MRI, an infection was diagnosed at the site of the fracture. Surgical drainage of the infection was performed, and an antibiotic was prescribed. Finally, in episode 3, he returned for a follow-up, and the case was closed after a X-ray of the fracture site revealed that bone had healed.

While John's EHR only lists the episodes and not the actual medical knowledge to guide the process underlying the treatments, a digital tutoring system is unable to offer any guidance or feedback to the students if they followed a different set of interventions, except to say it was different, and not much else. Inclusion of the guiding medical knowledge and established treatment protocols could enable a tutoring system to offer insights. Practice of medicine and treatment reflect a physician's best judgement, and, thus, it can vary from case to

---

[1] http://medplus.codeartisanlab.com/medplus_game/public/login.

```
Patient: John Doe
Age: 65
State: Idaho
Employer: University of Idaho
Insurance: Idaho Blue Cross

Blood group: O+
History: appendix removed, has PGM, elevated LDL, megaloblastic anemia

Episode List A:
    Episode 1:
        Date: March 10, 2023
        Physician: Dr. Jane Doe
        History: Admitted to ER, deformity in the right forearm from a fall,
            pain, swelling, bruising, and dizziness
        Tests: physical exam, X-ray
        Diagnosis: closed fracture
        Treatment: splint, analgesic

    Episode 2:
        Date: March 17, 2023
        Physician: Dr. Marry Doe
        History: Increased pain, warmth at injury site, high temperature,
            splint in place
        Tests: physical exam, blood test, MRI
        Diagnosis: infection
        Treatment: wound drainage, dressing, reapply splint, antibiotic

Episode List B:
    Episode 1:
        Date: July 5, 2023
        Physician: Dr. Jane Doe
        History: abdominal pain, diarrhea, blood in stool, fatigue
            and joint pain
        Tests: blood test, stool test, colon MRI, sigmoidoscopy
        Diagnosis: ulcerative colitis
        Treatment: corticosteroid, immunomodulator
```

Fig. 1. Example EHR of John Doe showing the two episode lists A and B.

case. In most countries, these judgements must follow protocols as well as insurance and laws, which may limit choices. Therefore, an intervention must attempt to maximize the three independent factors – medical knowledge, protocols, and the laws.

2.1   Medical Knowledge

The medical knowledge underlying the EHR in Fig. 1 can be represented in multiple different ways. The simplest one may have the following form.

Facts: Fresh Injury, Severe Pain, Swelling, Bruising
Required: Physical Exam
Suggested: Closed Fracture
Required: X-Ray
Confirmed: Closed Fracture

Diagnosed: Fracture
Required: Splint, Analgesic

The above knowledge could be represented as an IF-THEN type of graph as shown in Fig. 2(a). In this representation, we have used several predefined concepts. The ellipse represents facts – known/established, observed or suspected (green, yellow and white), diamonds represent tests/procedures that produce findings as facts – confirmed or unconfirmed (green, white), cross represents diagnosis (red), and finally a rectangle represents treatments – procedure and medication (light blue, and grey). An arrow represents requirement, and a line connecting/crossing two or more arrows means all the arrows are ANDed, and no line means ORed.

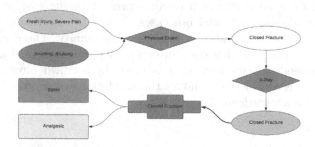

(a) Medical knowledge for episode 1.

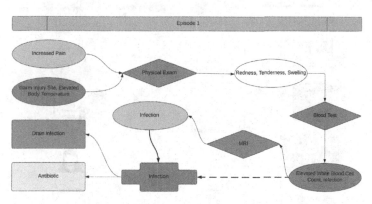

(b) Follow-up of episode 1.

Fig. 2. Knowledge representation, protocols and laws.

The medical knowledge contained in Fig. 2(a) is that to make a diagnosis of "Closed Fracture", a physician must make a positive determination of closed fracture. This is shown as a thicker arrow into the diagnosis block. Only by making this diagnosis, a procedure "Splint" and a prescription for medication of analgesic can be, or is, made. Similarly, in Fig. 2(b), a drainage procedure can be performed only if a diagnosis of infection is made, and antibiotics can be prescribed. Since episode takes place in the context of episode 1 (shown as a predefined process atop the knowledge graph), the wound site is unambiguous, as well as previous interventions are in full view.

3   Components of ClinLearning

Figure 3 shows a high level view of the main components of ClinLearning. In this figure, the EHR/Cases database stores patients' health records using the document model presented in Sect. 2. The ever evolving knowledge ecosystem of ClinLearning also includes a medical protocol database, a legal and insurance rule database, and a medical knowledge database. A crowd EHR database is also linked to the system to which doctors present challenging/novel cases as community knowledge or tutorial use cases. They also use this portal to seek medical treatment recommendation from the community. These use cases are incorporated into the EHR database after proper representational adjustments. Once a recommendation for treatment is made by a crowd physician and the recommendation is considered sound by the validation system, the knowledge is added in medical knowledgebase.

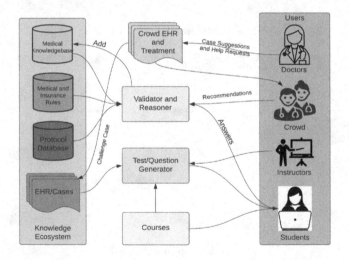

Fig. 3. Components of ClinLearning Tutoring System.

The central tutoring activities are piloted by an instructor via the design of a course in which students enroll. They interact with the system through a GUI inside their respective instructor's and student's dashboards. ClinLearning also has GUI for external physicians as members of the crowd to access ClinLearning for treatment recommendations, or to contribute challenging and novel use cases. The test or tutoring questions are generated by ClinLearning based on the question parameters chosen by the instructor – difficulty level, time allotted, extent of novelty of cases, level of mutation of real cases, etc. It is important to note here that novel cases still have a known treatment plan that will pass the validation test by the reasoner. But not all mutated cases in the question will pass the validation because some of the mutations could be so far off that no known protocol, legal/insurance rules or medical knowledge appear to exist, yet a human inspection may yield a feasible treatment plan. These questions invite manual grading, or crowd validation. Feasible treatment plans may suggest a new protocol to tentatively add to the protocol database.

The medical knowledge database is a collection of treatment rules derived within ClinLearning, or collected from databases such as Cleveland Clinic, Mayo Clinic, WebMD, etc. The database also have a set of derivation rules that the validation and reasoning system uses to test if a suggested protocol is valid, and the process is medically sound. It does so by reasoning about the episodic, and historical information of the case and establishing similarity with existing protocols, and prevailing legal and insurance rules.

4   Conclusion and Future Research

ClinLearning clinical tutoring and assessment system is at its early stage of development as a proof of concept. The novelty of ClinLearning is that it uses a semantic distance based least suggestive hint generation to guide medical students in the learning pursuit. It also considers applicable laws, institutional and insurance policies, and body of relevant medical knowledge for the reconstruction of episodes and possible interventions or treatments. The decoupling of the knowledge, health policies, and protocols make it possible to add new knowledge and information to change or improve the system without redesigning the reasoner or the system.

Acknowledgement. This research was partially supported by an Institutional Development Award (IDeA) from the National Institute of General Medical Sciences of the National Institutes of Health under Grant #P20GM103408.

References

1. Khoiriyah, U., Roberts, C., Jorm, C., Van der Vleuten, C.P.M.: Enhancing students' learning in problem based learning: validation of a self-assessment scale for active learning and critical thinking. BMC Med. Educ. **14**, 140 (2015)
2. Servant, V.F.C., Schmidt, H.G.: Revisiting foundations of problem-based learning: some explanatory notes. Med. Educ. **50**(7), 698–701 (2016)
3. Suebnukarn, S., Haddawy, P.: A bayesian approach to generating tutorial hints in a collaborative medical problem-based learning system. Artif. Intell. Med. **38**(1), 5–24, 2006
4. Suebnukarn, S., Haddawy, P.: Comet: a collaborative tutoring system for medical problem-based learning. Intelligent Systems, IEEE, **22**, 70–77 (2007)

Similarity Measure and Metric

Similarity Measures and Metrics

The Actualization of TikTok Affordances to Challenge Female Unrealistic Standards of Beauty

Saffiya Ebrahim and Maureen Tanner[(✉)] [iD]

University of Cape Town, Cape Town, South Africa
mc.tanner@uct.ac.za

Abstract. While social media platforms have often been used to perpetuate unrealistic standards of beauty, a new trend is emerging whereby social media users are purposefully creating content that challenges these standards set by society. This trend is particularly prominent on TikTok. However, insufficient research has been conducted into this phenomenon. The study thus explores how users actualize the affordances offered by TikTok to challenge and deconstruct the standards of beauty set by society. Through a single case study approach, data were collected through semi-structured interviews and observation. The research was guided by the Affordance Theory which assisted in understanding how female social media users actualize TikTok affordances to challenge beauty stereotypes and promote body positivity. Four propositions were formulated, centered around the actualization of association, editability, sharing, and browsing others' content affordances. The study also contributes to self-presentation and impression formation theories, by describing how beauty standards are deconstructed when supported by the actualization of TikTok affordances.

Keywords: TikTok · Affordances · Deconstructing Beauty Standards · Self-Presentation · Impression Formation

1 Introduction

Social media enables the sharing of digital content in various formats including text, images, and videos (Sweet et al. 2020). Since its inception, social media has been used as a platform to promote beauty standards, often unattainable ones, by social media influencers and celebrities alike. As a result, social media has influenced the standards of beauty of millions of individuals in diverse parts of the world (Siddiqui 2021). It is important to note that many women suffer adverse consequences when subjected to unattainable standards of beauty (Balcetis et al. 2013).

More recently, social media has been increasingly used to deconstruct the inaccessible and narrowly scoped body ideals set by society. The aim is to empower women by promoting a more inclusive and positive concept of beauty (Cohen et al. 2019). This had led to the emergence of the "body positive movement" which challenges the ideal body type promoted by media outlets and encourages the acceptance and admiration of a

P. Delir Haghighi et al. (Eds.): iiWAS 2023, LNCS 14416, pp. 417–430, 2023.
https://doi.org/10.1007/978-3-031-48316-5_39

variety of body types (Cohen et al. 2019). For example, Instagram users can benefit from the hashtag feature to find content that increases visibility as well as the normalization of a wide range of common body types which are often underrepresented by the media (Cohen et al. 2019). A simple search for a hashtag that promotes the normalization of bodies would be "#body positivity". This displays more than two million Instagram posts that promote a wide range of common body types (Cohen et al. 2019). TikTok is another popular social media platform that can be used to challenge unattainable beauty standards. TikTok is a social media platform that has been downloaded more than three billion times since its international launch in 2017 (Bhandari & Bimo 2020; Ceci 2022). TikTok currently has over 30 million active users on Android and more than 120 million active users on iOS devices (Ceci 2022).

Despite the rise in the body positivity movement, insufficient research has been conducted to understand how social media affordances can be used to successfully deconstruct societal standards of beauty and advocate the normalization of beauty standards to empower women. In addition, despite the rise in popularity of TikTok (Vijay & Gekker 2021), this platform has not yet been sufficiently researched (Bhandari & Bimo 2020).

Given the above-mentioned research gap, this study explores how female users of TikTok actualize the affordances of this social media platform to challenge the unattainable standards of beauty set by society. An affordance can be defined as the "multifaceted relational structure between an object/technology and the user that enables potential behavioral outcomes in a particular context" (Kim & Ellison 2021, p. 3). Actualization refers to the action that actors take when they use technology to take advantage of perceived affordances (Pozzi et al. 2014). Therefore, a social media platform like TikTok, has features that affords the user an opportunity to cause an action that will have an outcome. The paper addresses the following research question: How does the actualization of TikTok affordances challenge unrealistic standards of beauty for female users?

The study reveals how female users can creatively use social media platforms like TikTok to break the status quo around beauty standards. The study also reveals that through mechanisms related to self-presentation and impression formation on social media, women can actively challenge unrealistic standards of beauty.

The paper is structured as follows: First, a review of literature is presented on TikTok, the concepts of influencers and followers, standards of beauty, and how these are promoted online through impression formation and self-presentation. The chosen theoretical framework and the methodology are then discussed. This is followed by insights into the findings as well as a discussion of these findings. The paper is then concluded.

2   Literature Review

This section provides a summary of literature on TikTok as a social media application. The concepts of social media followers and influencers, as well as societal standards of beauty, are then discussed. This section also provides insights into theories of self-presentation and impression formation.

2.1 TikTok as a Social Media Application

TikTok is a social media application that is well known for the video content shared by its users daily (Bhandari & Bimo 2020). Features of the TikTok application include video uploading, social sharing, likes and comments, hashtags, live streams, notifications, duets, reactions, filters, and effects. TikTok is used to create and share content on various topics including beauty, technology, politics, fashion, and health amongst others (Audrezet et al. 2020). In addition, users can post on various social media platforms, share their opinions and beliefs, and their experience within a particular field (Audrezet et al. 2020).

TikTok relies on the use of an algorithm to provide the user with a personalized TikTok feed that is specifically directed at the user through a landing page known as "For You" (Bhandari & Bimo 2020). The "For You" feed recommends and curates specific content which is targeted at the user based on their preferences and various factors such as the user's interactions, video information, device, and account settings. The user's interactions include likes, shares, comments, and the accounts followed. Video information refers to video uploads or posts that contain captions, sounds, and hashtags. Device and account settings relate to the type of device, the preferred language, and the user's country (TikTok 2020a).

It is important to note that the For You feed will provide the TikTok user with content that was posted within the time frame of the last three months (TikTok 2020b). The TikTok user is thus exposed to a wide variety of content based on their preferences through the For You feed. Content that has been recently uploaded generally triggers higher degrees of engagement shortly after they have been posted on TikTok (TikTok 2020b). Even though a TikTok user with a large follower base might receive more views, this does not imply that the follower count or a high view count will influence the algorithm (TikTok 2020b). The algorithm thus targets videos to TikTok users who display similar interests (Vaterlaus & Winter 2021).

2.2 Social Media Followers and Influencers

A social media follower is an individual that follows a social media user - either another social media user or an influencer. The follower therefore automatically receives posts of the social media user within their feed, actively participates and engages with these social media posts as well as creates a virtual community with the social media user (Farivar et al. 2022).

A social media influencer is an individual that has a large and actively engaged follower base of more than 5000 followers on their social media platforms that the social media follower would not be aware of unless they have followed them (Haenlein et al. 2020; Ruiz-Gomez 2019). The social media influencer can connect to this community of followers and inspire them based on their social media posts (Haenlein et al. 2020).

An influencer can be subdivided into two main categories: a micro influencer and macro influencer. A micro influencer is one of the largest groups of content creators and has a follower base from 5 000 to 100 000 social media users (Ruiz-Gomez 2019). A macro influencer falls under a more professional group of content creators and tend to work fulltime with a follower base that ranges from 100 000 to 1 000 000 social media users (Ruiz-Gomez 2019).

2.3   Social Media and Societal Standards of Beauty

Beauty is a concept that has existed and constantly changed for thousands of years. For a while, the most prominent standard of beauty stemmed from colonialism by the West and enforced a Euro-centric standard of beauty on people of color (Montle 2020). This standard advocate for a thin ideal whereby women are expected to have a tiny waist, a flat stomach as well as a slender physique (McComb & Mills 2022). However, there has recently been a shift from a small and petite figure to a more curvaceous, voluptuous, and hourglass standard of beauty. In this new trend, a body type known as the hourglass or slim-thick body type has emerged. This body type advocates for a tiny waist, a flat stomach, wide hips, and thighs, as well as enhanced bottoms and breasts (McComb & Mills 2022). The evolving and often unattainable beauty standards are popularized on social media by influencers (often using filters to accentuate features (Siddiqui 2021)) and impact the physical and mental health of women (McComb & Mills, 2022).

Social media can thus contribute towards the formation of an unrealistic and difficult standard of beauty for women. This can lead to women's dissatisfaction with regards to their weight and physique (McComb & Mills 2022; Fioravanti et al. 2022) and lead to body dysmorphia (Lazuka et al. 2020).

Despite the use of social media to promote unattainable standards of beauty, there has also been an emergence of social media influencers who advocate for body inclusivity and the normalization of bodies. Recently, there has been a visible growth in the number of social media influencers who promote self-love and body positivity. Body positivity focuses on the promotion and acceptance of various body types, sizes and appearances in order to challenge the unrealistic standards of beauty portrayed in the media – i.e., the acceptance of various bodily features such as stomach rolls, skin imperfections such as acne and hyperpigmentation, and cellulite (Lazuka et al. 2020).

2.4   Self-Presentation on Social Media

Self-presentation is defined as "the goal-directed activity of controlling information to influence the impressions formed by an audience about the self" (Schlosser 2020, p. 1). The theory of self-presentation focuses on how the user selectively provides information about themselves online to influence others' impressions. The user profile is critical in self-presentation as it enables an individual to express themselves and create an opportunity for relationships to foster (Tong et al. 2020). Self-presentation includes an individual communicating textual information or images about themselves to create an attractive public image that could either be authentic or inauthentic (Schlosser, 2020). An authentic image could assist with challenging beauty standards.

2.5   Impression Formation on Social Media

"Impression formation is the process by which individuals perceive, organize, and ultimately integrate information to form unified and coherent situated impressions of others." (Moore 2015, p. 1). Online profiles, more specifically, words form an integral part of impression formation as they enable users to express valuable information (Tong et al.

2020). Social media offers users an opportunity to keep in touch with existing acquaintances as well as create new online relationships. These relationships are primarily based on the user viewing an individual's account and forming a judgment based on their online persona (Scott 2014).

3 Theoretical Framework

This section provides insights into the Affordance theoretical framework as well as the specific affordances of TikTok as a social media platform.

3.1 Affordance Theoretical Framework

This study employed the Affordance Theory to shed light on the phenomenon of interest. The existence of an affordance emerges because of an interaction between the user and the object and/or IT artifact (Thapa & Zheng 2019). In the context of the study, the IT artifact specifically refers to the social media application (i.e., TikTok), while the user refers to the TikTok user who has a valid account of more than 3 months. Affordance perception is formed due to the user's ability to perceive as well as recognize the affordance of this IT artifact to exploit its potential (Thapa & Zheng 2019). This recognition process is influenced by the features of the tool, the experience, capabilities, culture, and goals of the actor as well as external information (Pozzi et al. 2014). Affordance actualization relates to the actions undertaken by actors as they use and take advantage of one or more perceived affordances to fulfill specific goals (Pozzi et al. 2014; Thapa & Zheng 2019). In other words, users of TikTok would perceive the relevant affordances of the social media platform to exploit their potential. Lastly, as affordances are actualized, the process may result in an 'affordance effect' (Pozzi, et al. 2014) and the achievement of the users' goals (Alraddadi 2020; Strong et al. 2014).

3.2 Social Media Affordances

Social media applications like TikTok depict a distinct set of affordances (Karahanna et al. 2018) namely: visibility, persistence, editability, association (Kim & Ellison 2021), Multimediality (Ranzini & Lutz 2017), self-presentation, collaboration, sharing (Karahanna et al. 2018), and browsing others' content (Jiao et al. 2021).

- *Visibility* affords the social media user the ability to reveal their previously invisible behaviors, knowledge, preferences, and networks to other users (Kim & Ellison 2021).
- *Persistence* affords the social media user the ability to communicate as well as record and archive their communication. The recorded and archived communication is then accessible at any given time (Kim & Ellison 2021).
- *Editability* affords the social media user the opportunity to edit and perfect the content that they post before it is viewed by others. Editability also affords the user the opportunity to edit this message after it has been posted (Kim & Ellison 2021).
- *Association* affords users the ability to establish a connection with pieces of information as well as with other individual users (Kim & Ellison 2021).

- *Multimediality* affords the user the possibility to combine various methods of communication. For example, this could relate to the ability to text as well as share photos or videos on TikTok (Ranzini & Lutz 2017).
- *Self-presentation* is the ability to "create and demonstrate a personal image and identity" (Karahanna et al. 2018, p. 5) or the ability of social media users to present and portray information about themselves online (Karahanna et al. 2018).
- *Collaboration* affords the social media user the ability to work together as a team with various other social media users (Karahanna et al. 2018).
- *Sharing* affords the social media user the opportunity to exchange, distribute and receive content (Karahanna et al. 2018).
- *Browsing Others' Content* affords the social media user an opportunity to view another social media user's content as well as receive alerts so that they will be attentive to the other user's content (Jiao et al. 2021).

4 Methodology

This study employed an interpretive philosophy. The research purpose selected for the study was exploratory, to gain an in-depth understanding of how the social media platform, TikTok, can be used to challenge standards of beauty. A deductive approach to theory was chosen whereby the Affordance Theory, was drawn upon to explore the above-mentioned social phenomenon.

The research strategy was that of a single case study of TikTok. This was selected as it provided the researchers with an opportunity to observe as well as analyze a phenomenon rarely analyzed previously (Saunders et al. 2009). The researcher was thus able to observe and analyze how the affordances of TikTok were actualized by female users to challenge the standards of beauty set by society. A cross-sectional time frame was also chosen.

The target audience selected for the purpose of this study related to TikTok users who identify as female and are aged between 18–30 years old. Purposive sampling was used to choose respondents. The sampling criteria included gender as well as a TikTok account of more than 3 months.

To target respondents, the researchers created a poster that was promoted on the social media platforms Instagram, WhatsApp, and Facebook. A Tik Tok video about the study was also created and posted on the social media platform. The researchers made use of the following features: filter, music, text-to-speech, captions, and hashtags, and received over 100 views within the first day.

Data was collected using 15 semi-structured interviews. The demographics of the respondents are depicted in Table 1. The questionnaire was designed in line with the concepts derived from the theoretical framework. The questionnaire comprised 20 questions to gather information about the existing affordances of TikTok and how they are recognized, perceived, and actualized to challenge unrealistic standards of beauty.

The interviews lasted approximately 60 min and were conducted either in-person or on MS Teams depending on the respondent's location. All interviews were recorded and securely stored on a password-protected file. The respondents' TikTok profiles and videos were also analyzed to better understand how they presented themselves on the social media platform. This further allowed for data triangulation.

Table 1. Respondent Demographics

#	Respondent Code	User Type	Age	Follower Count	Following Count
1	TT1	Follower	22	43	23
2	TT2	Follower	22	0	6
3	TT3	Follower	21	2	933
4	TT4	Follower	22	0	89
5	TT5	Follower	22	117	300
6	TT6	Follower	20	4 623	516
7	TT7	Follower	18	1	20
8	TT8	Follower	23	30	48
9	TT9	Follower	22	50	1 200
10	MICROI1	Micro Influencer	24	71 000	44
11	MICROI2	Micro Influencer	18	66 189	1 556
12	MICROI3	Micro Influencer	23	5 831	502
13	MICROI4	Micro Influencer	30	8 583	4 117
14	MICROI5	Micro Influencer	24	11 700	63
15	MACROI1	Macro Influencer	24	1 500 000	196

The interview recordings were then transcribed and analyzed using thematic analysis in NVIVO (Braun & Clarke 2006). All transcripts were anonymized and respondents given acronyms as shown in Table 1. As part of the analysis, the transcripts were reviewed to familiarize oneself with the data. The dataset was then coded to reveal initial insights into how the affordances are actualized. Initial codes were then regrouped into themes. Each theme was reviewed to ensure that it aligned with the code extract. Themes were regrouped into categories (Braun & Clarke 2006).

In addition to ensuring anonymity, the respondents were allowed to withdraw from the study at any point in time. In order to ensure that the data was kept safe and secure, it was stored on OneDrive and only the researchers had access to it.

5 Findings

The findings of the study are now presented. This section describes how TikTok affordances (association, editability, sharing, browsing others' content), are actualized to challenge unrealistic standards of beauty for female users.

5.1 Association

The study found that users actualized the association affordance to fulfill their goal of challenging standards of beauty (see Table 2). The association information is integral to the creation of a community of TikTok users that can deconstruct beauty standards and empower women to feel better in their bodies, no matter their shape or size. Both followers and influencers could actualise the association affordance through the use of profile content creation and follow features. Followers could identify relevant influencers based on their profile (e.g. username) and follow them to access their content. In turn, influencers could curate their profile and content to broaden their user base and ensure that their content reaches a wide audience. Through the actualisation of the association affordance, influencers and followers worked together to ensure that content that challenge beauty standards were viewed and heard far and wide.

For example, TT6 (a follower) associated the username with the type of content she would view: *you just see the username and then it's a content creator who is well known for spreading body positivity and helping with one's mental health. I guess you would get curious and be like, oh okay, I know this content creator, and then you click on their profile and go through a bunch of videos.* In turn, MACROI1 (an influencer) curated her profile (e.g., username, bio, and profile picture) to align with the overall message that she is intent on spreading (i.e., deconstructing a certain type of beauty standards). She then associated her username with any content that she created: *I'll use my bio and my profile picture to give an idea of what the content is that I'm posting, and in this case, normalizing body hair on women. And then also the content that I'm creating will speak to that topic.* MICROI2 is an 18-year-old micro-influencer who also actualized the association affordance using her profile. Her username revealed a direct link to her birth name as well as the month she was born. In addition, MICROI2's profile picture is an illustration that promotes self-acceptance. This is further reiterated in her bio (text) which promotes "self -love/disrupting beauty standards" and provides an email address that contains the username and the term "self-love". The audience thus becomes aware of exactly what MICROI2 intends to accomplish with her account. Furthermore, she includes links to her other social media accounts to ensure that other users can view her content on more than one social media platform.

Table 2. Association Affordance Actualization

Perceived Affordance: Association		
Features of Tik Tok	**Affordance**	**Actualized Affordance**
Profile content creation	Association	• Creating profile content that aligns with the overall body positivity message that they would like to spread • Visually expressing their identity through a profile picture • The use of language in their bio reveals what their account focuses on • The quick links to other social media accounts to form a connection
Follow feature		Following TikTok users (e.g., influencers) who create and share relevant videos about body positivity

Outcome: To form a community of users with similar body types and features, create more awareness as well as promote self-acceptance and body positivity

The association affordance was further supported by the TikTok algorithm which ensures that users are presented with content based on whom they follow and the type of content they follow (For You page). For instance, TT2 stated that *when I follow creators that focus on these unrealistic standards of beauty, because I'm following them, it's really cool on the Tik Tok app, the algorithm will see then what kind of content I like, and similar content will show up on my For You Page. And then I'll be introduced to more content creators within this niche and I'll be able to follow them or engage with their content. So that's really cool.*

5.2 Editability

The study found that the actualization of the editability affordance was imperative in attracting a certain audience whilst challenging beauty standards (see Table 3). The editability affordance enables users to edit and perfect their content before and after posting. While the editability affordance can be detrimental to the body positivity message (e.g., using filters), users who seek to challenge existing beauty standards have found ways of actualizing this affordance to also meet their goals.

The filter feature is used to either overlay the content with a different shade or to overlay the user's physical features to enhance their content. The filter feature can thus be actualized to deconstruct societal standards of beauty when the user shows themselves with and without the filter in a video. MACRO1 actualized the editability affordance to create a video where half of the screen displayed a filtered video with make-up and smooth skin, while the other half was unfiltered and showed how she looked in real life: *"You start on the left side of the screen, where the filter is on you. And then you move to the right side of the screen, and as you do that, the filter goes away, and you're left with how your face looks in real life. Macro11 also added captions to explain how natural beauty and who we are as just ourselves is beautiful and amazing as is, we don't need to conform to what we're "supposed to look like".* The caption was created using the Speech to Text/Text to Speech feature.

The actualization of the editability affordance through The Speech to Text/Text to Speech feature also ensures that the content is more understandable to the audience, and further assists in fulfilling the goal of challenging beauty standards. As mentioned by TT1: *"Not many people can accurately hear, even if they can hear they can't hear if someone is talking too fast or too slow. So, to use that feature, then it's easy for them to just read. So, it's I think it's a very, very good feature to have".*

5.3 Sharing

The study found that users actualized the sharing affordance to fulfill their intention of deconstructing beauty standards (see Table 4). Sharing refers to a user's ability to exchange, distribute and receive content. The actualization of the sharing affordance is essential to the creation of a community of users centered around body positivity. Users actualize the sharing affordance to target an audience that might suffer from poor self-esteem to raise awareness. The sharing affordance was actualized through the following features: share, download, and repost.

Table 3. Editability Affordance Actualization

Perceived Affordance: Editability

Features of Tinder	Affordance	Actualized Affordance
Filters	Editability	The use of filters to explicitly demonstrate how certain features can be artificially enhanced
Speech to Text/Text to Speech		The use of the Speech to Text/Text to Speech feature to reinforce the message and ensure that it is accessible to all

Outcome:
- Demonstrating reality vs. filtered videos to challenge beauty standards
- Reinforcing the message and making it accessible to all

According to TT3, sharing content (using the sharing feature) increases awareness amongst individuals who may have self-esteem issues: *"I do share some of it and it has to do with the normalization of body features. It creates public awareness and even if it's just to my friends who feel insecure, it increases awareness, and they feel more secure"*. In turn, TT6 actualized the sharing affordance by downloading and sharing videos to her device. She then later shared these videos with her friends and family who struggle with body dysmorphia and need motivation: *"You download it, and then you can share it to your friend and be like, oh, this person is struggling as well. But they're trying to do better for themselves. And then they relate to it and feel comfortable, and it helps them cope"*.

TikTok recently launched a repost feature that users make use of, to actualize the sharing affordance. The repost feature enables a user to share content with their followers and share a message that they may resonate with to create more awareness on the topic. For example, MICROI2 stated: *"If I see a video, I like about beauty standards or whatever, I will repost it because I think it's something that people need to see. It helps get the message out"*.

Table 4. Sharing Affordance Actualization

Perceived Affordance: Sharing

Features of Tinder	Affordance	Actualized Affordance
Share (link)		Explicitly spreading awareness on deconstructed beauty standards
Download	Sharing	Reliance on creator enabling the download feature so that users can download the video
Repost		To share content with all their followers

Outcome: To create awareness of beauty standards, and to communicate with TiTok users on their perspectives of beauty. In addition, the algorithm uses the sharing and repost feature to further curate content that promotes body positivity

5.4 Browsing Others' Content

The study found that the actualization of the browsing other's content affordance was integral to exposing users to content that deconstructed beauty standards (see Table 5). Browsing other's content refers to a user's ability to view another user's profile and posts and receive alerts about changes to that content. The browsing others' content was actualized through the following features: search, hashtag, follow, report, and not interested.

The respondents actualized the browsing others' content affordance through the search feature. For instance, the search feature enabled users to browse beauty-related content based on their body type. Another instance was through the hashtag feature where the user clicked on a certain hashtag and was redirected to a page with videos containing that specific hashtag. TT5 was able to use the hashtag feature to narrow her search to body-positive content that would change her perspective on beauty: *"Using the hashtag feature to narrow so many videos into just one genre or category is easier. You say 'love all bodies hashtag' and you'll see different types of bodies and an array of that.... And it's just like, okay, maybe I do fit in!, It changes your perspective on yourself as well. So that's how I feel about it"*.

TT7 chose to follow Tik Tok users who portrayed a certain body type like hers so that her self-esteem would not suffer: *"Normally, because like I'm very slim, I follow people who are very slim. I follow someone who obviously has big boobs and maybe a big bum, then I will want to look like them and probably feel insecure about myself. So, I try to, follow and engage with people who look like me, so I don't feel insecure"*.

MicroI3 has used the not interested feature which actualizes the browse others' content affordance and ensures that she would not come across beauty content that would trigger her: *"So if I see anything that I don't like, or videos, the types of videos or messages that I don't like, then I will filter it out by using the not interested feature. Because I don't want to be triggered or anything"*.

Table 5. Browsing Others' Content Affordance Actualization

Perceived Affordance: Browsing Others' Content		
Features of Tinder	**Affordance**	**Actualized Affordance**
Search		Enables users to access specific content or users
Hashtag	Browsing	Enables users to access content within a specific category
Follow	Other's Content	Expands the content they come across based on preference
Not Interested		Ensures that certain types of content will not appear on their FYP

Outcome: To access relevant content based on their preferences and maintain a sense of community. Moreover, this fosters body positivity as users browse content they can relate to as opposed to content that will reduce self-esteem or promote body dysmorphia

6 Discussion

The study found that TikTok enables users to actualize the Association, Editability, Sharing, and Browsing Others' Content affordances to create awareness, deconstruct societal standards of beauty, and normalize body shapes. As users actualize these affordances, they engage in two key strategies: self-presentation and impression formation.

Self-presentation is a strategy predominantly used by individuals to control and shape how others perceive them (Tong et al. 2020). Self-presentation strategies are useful within the digital space whereby users can present themselves through text or imagery (Schlosser 2020). For instance, by crafting their content, users would authentically disclose their views on beauty standards to attract like-minded individuals. Self-presentation strategies predominantly emerged during the actualization of the editability affordance, to reveal users' true selves on TikTok. Beauty standards were further challenged given that users could create content that promoted diverse body types and features (Lazuka et al. 2020; Cohen et al. 2019).

Through impression formation strategies, users form an impression of an individual based on the information available online (Moore, 2015; Tong et al., 2020). Like self-presentation, this strategy is quite useful given that it enables a user to foster a relationship with another user and form an opinion based on the content of the post (Scott 2014). The impression formation strategies employed through the actualization of the association affordance, allowed other users to change their perceptions of beauty standards.

Given the empirical findings derived from this study, the following theoretical propositions have been formulated:

Proposition 1: Users actualize the association affordance by devising impression formation strategies, to form a community of users with similar body types and features, create more awareness as well as promote self-acceptance and body positivity.

Proposition 2: Users actualize the editability affordance by devising self-presentation strategies, to unravel the difference between real and filtered videos and reinforce their intended message, to challenge established beauty standards.

Proposition 3: Users actualize the sharing affordance by devising mechanisms to spread awareness with the aim of broadening the community, thus perpetually reinforcing their message on body positivity.

Proposition 4: Users actualize the browsing others' content affordance to curate the content that they access and are presented with, thus ensuring that their intended goal around body positivity is achieved.

7 Conclusion

The use of the social media application TikTok has swiftly spread internationally and influenced the lives of many. However, existing research has not explored how female users actualize these TikTok affordances to challenge unrealistic beauty standards. This paper contributed to theories of self-presentation, and impression formation, by describing how beauty standards are deconstructed when supported by the actualization of

TikTok affordances. The theoretical contributions are summarized in four propositions centered around the association, editability, sharing, and browsing of others' content affordances.

Given that the study was cross-sectional, a limitation of the case study would be time constraints. In addition, the researchers were not able to expand the geographical reach of the target population. In future, other similar studies would benefit from a longitudinal timeframe as this would enable researchers to identify how this phenomenon of deconstructing beauty standards would evolve over time, combined with a larger target population across more countries.

Nonetheless, the study presents some practical contributions which might benefit TikTok users. Firstly, individuals who wish to challenge the status quo of societal beauty standards would have access to research that has recently been conducted in that regard. They could broaden the strategies that they employ to challenge standards of beauty and ultimately create a broader community of users whose aim is to promote body positivity. It is also important to acknowledge that the benefits of using these social media platforms to challenge the status quo around beauty will inevitably result in a positive influence. The unrealistic beauty standards that are typically set by society have a higher chance of being deconstructed.

References

Alraddadi, A.S.: Mechanisms of technology affordance actualization critical realist case studies of information systems in Saudi Arabian SMEs (Issue March). Loughborough University (2020)

Audrezet, A., De Kerviler, G., Moulard, J.G.: Authenticity under threat: when social media influencers need to go beyond self-presentation. J. Bus. Res. **117**, 557–569 (2020)

Balcetis, E., Cole, S., Chelberg, M.B., Alicke, M.: Searching out the ideal: awareness of ideal body standards predicts lower global self-esteem in women. Self Identity **12**(1), 99–113 (2013)

Bhandari, A., Bimo, S.: TikTok and the "algorithmized self": A new model of online interaction. AoIR Selected Papers of Internet Research (2020)

Braun, V., Clarke, V.: Using thematic analysis in psychology. Qual. Res. Psychol. **3**(2) (2006)

Ceci, L.: TikTok- Statistics & facts, Statista. https://www.statista.com/topics/6077/tiktok/#dossierKeyfigures (2022)

Cohen, R., Irwin, L., Newton-John, T., Slater, A.: #bodypositivity: a content analysis of body positive accounts on Instagram. Body Image **29** (2019)

Farivar, S., Wang, F., Turel, O.: Followers' problematic engagement with influencers on social media: an attachment theory perspective. Comput. Hum. Behav. **133**, 107288 (2022)

Fioravanti, G., Bocci Benucci, S., Ceragioli, G., et al.: How the exposure to beauty Ideals on social networking sites influences body image: a systematic review of experimental studies. Adolescent Res. Rev. **7**, 419–458 (2022). https://doi.org/10.1007/s40894-022-00179-4

Haenlein, M., Anadol, E., Farnsworth, T., Hugo, H., Hunichen, J., Welte, D.: Navigating the new era of influencer marketing: how to be successful on Instagram, TikTok, & Co. California Manage. Rev. **63**(1) (2020)

Jiao, Z., Chen, J., Kim, E.: Modeling the use of online knowledge community: a perspective of needs-affordances-features. Comput. Intell. Neurosci. (2021)

Karahanna, E., Xu, S. X., Xu, Y., Zhang, N.: The needs-affordances-features perspective for the use of social media. MIS Quar. Manage. Inform. Syst. **42**(3) (2018)

Kim, D.H., Ellison, N.B.: From observation on social media to offline political participation: the social media affordances approach. New Media Soc. (2021)

Lazuka, R.F., Wick, M.R., Keel, P.K., Harriger, J.A.: Are we there yet? Progress in depicting diverse images of beauty in Instagram's body positivity movement. Body Image **34**, 85–93 (2020)

McComb, S.E., Mills, J.S.: The effect of physical appearance perfectionism and social comparison to thin-, slim-thick-, and fit-ideal Instagram imagery on young women's body image. Body Image **40**, 165–175 (2022)

Montle, M.E.: Debunking eurocentric ideals of beauty and stereotypes against African natural hair(styles): an Afrocentric Perspective. J. African Foreign Affairs **7**(1), 111–127 (2020)

Moore, C.D.: Impression Formation. In The Blackwell Encyclopedia of Sociology. G. Ritzer, Ed. Blackwell (2015)

Pozzi, G., Pigni, F., Vitari, C.: Affordance theory in the IS discipline: a review and synthesis of the literature. In: 20th Americas Conference on Information Systems (2014)

Ranzini, G., Lutz, C.: Love at first swipe? Explaining Tinder self-presentation and motives. Mobile Media Commun. **5**(1) (2017)

Ruiz-Gomez, A.: Digital fame and fortune in the age of social media: a classification of social media influencers. ADResearch: Int. J. Commun. Res. **19**(19), 08–29 (2019)

Saunders, M., Lewis, P., Thornhill, A.: Research Methods for Business Students. Pearson Education, vol. 5th (2009)

Schlosser, A.E.: Self-disclosure versus self-presentation on social media. Curr. Opin. Psychol. **31**, 1 (2020)

Scott, G.G.: More than friends: popularity on Facebook and its role in impression formation. J. Comput.-Mediat. Commun. **19**(3), 358–372 (2014)

Siddiqui, A.: Social media and its role in amplifying a certain idea of beauty. Infotheca **21**(1) (2021)

Strong, D., et al.: A Theory of organization-EHR affordance actualization. J Assoc. Inform. Syst. **15**(2), 53–85 (2014). https://doi.org/10.17705/1jais.00353

Sweet, K.S., LeBlanc, J.K., Stough, L.M., Sweany, N.W.: Community building and knowledge sharing by individuals with disabilities using social media. J. Comput. Assist. Learn. **36**(1), 1–11 (2020)

Thapa, D., Zheng, Y.: Capabilities and affordances in the ICT4D Context: similarities, differences, and complementarities. IFIP Adv. Inform. Commun. Technol. **552** (2019)

TikTok.: 5 tips for TikTok creators | TikTok Newsroom. https://newsroom.tiktok.com/en-us/5-tips-for-tiktok-creators (2020a)

TikTok.: How TikTok recommends videos #ForYou | TikTok Newsroom. https://newsroom.tiktok.com/en-us/how-tiktok-recommends-videos-for-you (2020b)

Tong, S.T., Corriero, E.F., Wibowo, K.A., Makki, T.W., Slatcher, R.B.: Self-presentation and impressions of personality through text-based online dating profiles: a lens model analysis. New Media Soc. **22**(5), 875–895 (2020)

Vaterlaus, J. M., Winter, M.: TikTok: an exploratory study of young adults' uses and gratifications. Soc. Sci. J. 1–20 (2021)

Vijay, D., Gekker, A.: Playing politics: how sabarimala played out on TikTok. Am. Behav. Sci. **65**(5) (2021)

Novel Blocking Techniques and Distance Metrics for Record Linkage

Nachiket Deo[1]([✉]), Joyanta Basak[1], Ahmed Soliman[1], Daniel Weinberg[2], Rebecca Steorts[2], and Sanguthevar Rajasekaran[1]

[1] University of Connecticut, Storrs, CT 06268, USA
nachiket.deo@uconn.edu
[2] US Census Bureau, 4600 Silver Hill Road, Hillcrest Heights, MD 20746, USA

Abstract. *Record Linkage* is the process of merging data from several sources and identifying records that are associated with the same entities, or individuals, where a unique identifier is not available. *Record Linkage* has applications in several domains such as master data management, law enforcement, health care, social networking, historical research, etc. A straight forward algorithm for record linkage would compare every pair of records and hence take at least quadratic time. In a typical application of interest, the number of records could be in the millions or more. Thus quadratic algorithms may not be feasible in practice. It is imperative to create novel record linkage algorithms that are very efficient. In this paper, we as address this crucial problem.

One of the popular techniques used to speedup record linkage algorithms is blocking. Blocking can be thought of as a step in which potentially unrelated record pairs are pruned from distance calculations. A large number of blocking techniques have been proposed in the literature. In this paper we offer novel blocking techniques that are based on mapping $k-$mers into a suitable range. In this paper, we also study the effect of distance metrics in the efficiency of record linkage algorithms. Specifically, we offer some novel variations of existing metrics that lead to improvements in the run times.

1 Introduction

The record linkage problem takes as input multiple data sets of records. The goal is to output clusters of records where each cluster has all the records of one entity only and it does not have any other records. An entity could be a person, organization, etc. Record linkage is also known as entity resolution in the literature.

Efficient and accurate record linkage and entity resolution are of vital importance in many applications spanning the government, health care, public safety, and national security. As an example, the public relies on statistics about the U.S. population and economy produced using entity resolution and record-linkage techniques for purposes such as distribution of public funds, entrepreneurs' decisions about where to locate their businesses, and monetary policy. Exact match

© The Author(s), under exclusive license to Springer Nature Switzerland AG 2023
P. Delir Haghighi et al. (Eds.): iiWAS 2023, LNCS 14416, pp. 431–446, 2023.
https://doi.org/10.1007/978-3-031-48316-5_40

data linking algorithms, such as JOIN, have been around for a long time and can be used effectively when no data errors exist [11]. In the 1970s, the US Census Bureau and the Social Security Administration carried out the 1973 CPS-SSA-IRS Exact Match study to improve policy models of the tax-transfer system, study the effects of alternative ways to price social security benefits, and summarize earning patterns of persons contributing to social security [7]. If all the records pertaining to the same individual are exactly correct with no errors in any of the (primary) attributes, the problem of record linkage will be straightforward to solve. The problem of record linkage is challenging for various reasons including: the absence of a global identifier (or key), many sources of error, and long run times. Several algorithms have been proposed in the literature for solving this problem. The algorithm of Fellegi and Sunter [9] assumes that the record pairs are independent and does not account for transitivity or other record linkage structure constraints. Sadinle and Fienberg [23] have extended the algorithm of [9] for multiple (i.e., more than 2) datasets. Unfortunately, the algorithm breaks down even for a moderately large number of or complex data sets. FEBRL [4] [5] is an open source system for record linkage that is very popular. It standardizes attributes of records such as names, addresses, and telephone numbers. As a result, it can link two datasets at a time. In this paper, we focus on algorithms that can link any number of data sets. Clustering-based approaches can integrate multiple datasets. Examples include Monge and Elkan [19], McVeigh, et al. [18], Tancredi and Liseo [27], and Steorts, et al. [25]. One drawback of these clustering approaches, however, is that they do not scale to large numbers of records and/or many component data tables. Some of the recent algorithms that employ clustering and which scale well can be found in [16]. In this paper, we provide novel blocking techniques that speedup existing algorithms. Our techniques are based on choosing an appropriate range for $k-$mers and using a cut-off threshold. A typical record has attributes such as last name, first name, address, etc. Many of the attributes are strings of characters from a finite alphabet Σ (with $|\Sigma| = s$). Consider any $k-$mer Q from one of the attributes. We can think of Q as an integer to the base s. In this case, any $k-$mer is mapped to an integer in the range $[0, s^k - 1]$. In this paper, we show that if we choose the mapping range appropriately, we can improve the performance of record linkage. We also study the effect of different distance metrics (used to compute the distance between two records) on linkage performance. We present some novel variants of existing metrics that enhance performance.

The rest of this paper is organized as follows: In Sect. 2 we provide a summary of some of the blocking techniques that have been proposed in the literature. In Sect. 3 we provide details on our novel blocking techniques. In Sect. 4 we review some of the popular metrics that are used to calculate the distance between any two records. Details on some novel distance metrics that we introduce are provided in Sect. 5. Section 6 is devoted to our experimental evaluations and results. In Sect. 7 we provide some concluding remarks.

2   A Summary of Blocking Techniques

A straight forward algorithm for record linkage will compute the distance between every pair of records resulting in a quadratic run time which can be improved in several ways. One such technique is called *blocking*. Blocking prunes potentially unrelated pairs from distance calculations. Blocking has been investigated extensively (see e.g., [21,26]). The idea of blocking is to partition the input records into groups such that records that belong to the same entity are likely to fall into the same block. Once the partitioning is done, pair-wise comparisons are done only within (and not across) the blocks. For example, if we partition n records into k equal sized (disjoint) blocks, then the number of distance calculations will reduce to $O\left(\frac{n^2}{k}\right)$. However, in some of the known blocking techniques, the partitioning may not be disjoint. The same record might fall into multiple blocks. In this case, there could be some redundant distance calculations. Even then, the overall run time could improve significantly. Blocking techniques are broadly classified into three types, local, global and hybrid methods [21].

2.1   Our Novel Blocking Techniques

In this paper we employ q-gram (also known as k-mer) based blocking. The basic idea can be explained as follows. Let R be any record. We can think of R as a string of characters from an alphabet Σ. Let $s = |\Sigma|$. A record might have multiple attributes (such as Lastname, Firstname, Gender, etc.). R could be thought of as a concatenation of (a subset of) the attribute strings. We choose an appropriate value for k. For instance, k could be 3 or 4. There will be a block corresponding to every possible k-mer. Specifically, there will be a total of s^k possible blocks. Many of these blocks could be empty. We consider every k-mer of R. For instance if $R = dabcaabde$ and $k = 3$, the k-mers of R will be $dab, abc, bca, caa, aab, abd$, and bde. The record R will be placed in the blocks corresponding to all the k-mers in it. For example, the record $R = dabcaabde$ will be placed in 7 blocks. After placing every input record into its blocks, pairwise comparisons are performed within the blocks to identify record pairs that are within a certain threshold τ. These record pairs form edges in a graph (where there is a node for every record and there will be an edge between two records if their distance is $\leq \tau$). If the distance between two records is $\leq \tau$, we assume that they belong to the same entity. The connected components of this graph are found and output as the final clusters.

In any k-mer based blocking scheme, we map a k-mer into an integer in the range $[0, s^k - 1]$ to get the ID of the corresponding block. The range of this mapping has a cardinality of s^k. In our prior work, we have realized that a value of $k = 3$ gives a better accuracy [16] but takes more time and a value of $k = 4$ takes less time but has a poorer accuracy. The optimal value for k can lie between 3 and 4! Unfortunately, k is an integer! Our innovation lies in the observation that we can look for optimality by changing the cardinality of the mapping we do on a k-mer to get its block ID. Also, after performing this mapping, we use a threshold T on the block IDs to prune blocks. In other words, we ignore blocks whose IDs exceed the threshold T. The rationale for this idea comes from our observation that if two records share a k-mer, then this k-mer (thought of as an integer) tends to be small (in real datasets).

For example, consider English alphabet with $s = 26$. Consider any k-mer $Q = c_1 c_2 \cdots c_k$, where each $c_i \in \Sigma$, $1 \leq i \leq k$. We can think of Q as an integer to the base $s = 26$. Specifically Q will correspond to the integer $c_k + c_{k-1} 26 + c_{k-2} 26^2 + \cdots + c_1 26^{k-1}$. (Here we use the same notation for a character and its integer mapping. For example, the character A can be mapped to 0, B can be mapped to 1, etc.) There are many ways in which we can change the cardinality of the range of the mapping. In general, we are interested in any mapping $f : \Sigma^k \to I$. In this paper we have studied the effect of three classes of such mappings and in each case we get better performances than employing the standard mapping. We summarize the mappings next.

1. Different Values for the Characters: In the standard mapping, we map the character A to 0, B to 1, C to 2, and so on. Our idea is to map the character A to an integer i, B to $i + 1$, etc. Here i is larger than 1 (100, for example).

2. Use of a Different Base: Our idea is to use a base b other than s. For instance when $s = 26$, we could use a base of $b = 50$. In this case, any k-mer $Q = c_1 c_2 \cdots c_k$ gets mapped to $c_k + c_{k-1} b + c_{k-2} b^2 + \cdots + c_1 b^{k-1}$.

3. Use of Hashing to Reduce Space: Clearly, we can employ the above ideas 1 and 2 together. When the values for the characters are large and/or the base value is large, we have to create a large number of blocks. We can reduce the space by applying a hash function on top of the above ideas. Specifically, we have to choose a hash function $h : I \to I$. For any k-mer Q, its block ID will then be computed as $h(f(Q))$. A simple choice for h could be: $h(x) = (ax + b) \bmod p$, where p is a randomly chosen prime, and a and b are $< p$. Universal hash families could also be employed.

We now prove a property of the above techniques.

Lemma 1. *When we use techniques 1 and 2, two records will fall into the same block if and only if they share at least one q-gram.*

Proof: If two records share a q-gram, $Q = c_1 c_2 \cdots c_k$, clearly, they will fall into a block whose label is $c_k + c_{k-1} b + c_{k-2} b^2 + \cdots + c_1 b^{k-1}$. Consider a block B that contains two records R_1 and R_2. Let $Q = c_1 c_2 \cdots c_k$ be the k-mer of R_1 that induced the inclusion of R_1 in B. Let $Q' = d_1 d_2 \cdots d_k$ be the k-mer of R_2 that induced the inclusion of R_2 in B. It follows that $c_k + c_{k-1} b + c_{k-2} b^2 + \cdots + c_1 b^{k-1} = d_k + d_{k-1} b + d_{k-2} b^2 + \cdots + d_1 b^{k-1}$. $c_k + c_{k-1} b + c_{k-2} b^2 + \cdots + c_1 b^{k-1}$ can be thought of as the integer $c_k c_{k-1} \cdots c_1$ and $d_k + d_{k-1} b + d_{k-2} b^2 + \cdots + d_1 b^{k-1}$ can be thought of as the integer $d_k d_{k-1} \cdots d_1$ both to the base b. These two integers will be equal only if they match in every 'digit', i.e., $c_i = d_i$, for $1 \leq i \leq k$.

3   Distance Metrics

For performing record linkage on any data set, we need the notion of a distance between two records and the distance between two sets of records. Rules for linking are typically specified using these distance metrics. For example, a linking rule might say that two records belong to the same entity if the distance between is $\leq \tau$, where τ is a user-specified threshold. Several distance metrics have been proposed in the literature. These metrics can be classified into three: Edit based, q-gram based, and heuristics based [28]. In this paper we study the effect of distance metrics on linkage performance (in terms of run times and accuracy). Note that similarity and distance are very closely related. For example, if the similarity between two records is high, then it means that the distance between them is low. In this paper we use these words interchangeably. Which of these is relevant will be clear from the context. In this section we define some of the well known distance metrics.

Definition 1 (Edit distance). *Edit distance, also known as Levenshtein distance, is a common measure for text similarity (see e.g., [6]). The edit distance between strings x and y is defined as the minimum number of edit operations (insertions, deletions, and substitutions) of single characters that are required to transform x to y.*

Lemma 2. *We can compute the edit distance between two strings x and y in $O(\ell m)$ time where $\ell = |x|$ and $m = |y|$.*

Definition 2 (q-gram). *A q-gram of a string Q is a substring of Q of length q. In this paper, we are exploring the application of q-gram based distance measure for the record linkage problem. We define the standard q-gram distance. We have created novel variations of this distance that increase the accuracy and reduce the run time (Sect. 5). Let Σ be a finite alphabet, and let Σ^* denote the set of all strings over Σ. Let $x = s_1 s_2 ... s_n$ be a string in Σ^*. The total number of q-mers in x is $n - q + 1$.*

Let x and y be strings in Σ^*, and let $q > 0$ be an integer.

Definition 3 (q-gram similarity). *The q-gram similarity $s_q(x,y)$ between the strings x and y is defined as the Jaccard similarity between strings x and y:*

$$s_q(x,y) = \frac{|\, qgrams(x) \cap qgrams(y)\,|}{|\, qgrams(x) \cup qgrams(y)\,|}$$

where $qgrams(x)$ and $qgrams(y)$ are the sets of q-grams in the strings x and y, respectively.

Lemma 3. *We can compute the q-gram similarity between two strings x and y in time $O((\ell + m)q)$, where $\ell = |x|$ and $m = |y|$.*

Proof: We can generate the q-gram of x and y in $O((\ell + m)q)$ time. Let the collection of q-grams in x be C_x and the collection of q-grams in y be C_y. Replace each q-gram u in C_x with a pair $(u, 1)$. Let the resultant collection be C'_x. Replace each q-gram v in C_y with a pair $(v.2)$. Let the resultant collection be C'_y. Put together C'_x and C'_y and sort them using integer sort. This can be done in $O((\ell + m)q)$ time (see e.g., [6]). Let the sorted sequence be C. We can scan through C to compute $C_x \cap C_y$ as well as $C_x \cup C_y$ in an additional $O((\ell + m)q)$ time. □

There are multiple attributes for each record in any data set and usually when linking the records we need more than one attribute.

Definition 4 ($q-gram$ similarity between a pair of records). *The q-gram similarity $S_q(x, y)$ between a pair of records x and y is*

$$S_q(x, y) = \frac{\sum_{i=1}^{k} s_q(x_i, y_i)}{k}$$

where k is number of attributes needed for calculating similarity between the pair of records. We assume that $\{x_1, x_2, \ldots, x_k\}$ is the set of attributes in x and $\{y_1, y_2, \ldots, y_k\}$ is the corresponding set of attributes in y.

Lemma 4. *If x and y are two records, we can compute the q-gram similarity between x and y in $O\left((\sum_{i=1}^{k}(|x_i| + |y_i|))q\right)$ time, where $\{x_1, x_2, \ldots, x_k\}$ is the set of attributes in x and $\{y_1, y_2, \ldots, y_k\}$ is the corresponding set of attributes in y.*

Proof: follows from the Proof of Lemma 2. □

Definition 5 (Hausdorff distance). *Given two finite sets X and Y of strings of the same length, the Hausdorff distance between them is defined as $max_{a \in X} \ min_{b \in Y} \ d(a, b)$ where $d(a, b)$ is the Hamming distance between the strings a and b.*

If S_1 and S_2 are two strings (not necessarily of the same length), we can define the Hausdorff distance between them with respect to the q-grams in them (for some suitable value of k). Specifically, let X be the set of q-gram in S_1 and let Y be the set of q-gram in S_2. The Hausdorff distance between S_1 and S_2 is the Hausdorff distance between X and Y.

Lemma 5. *If x and y are strings with lengths ℓ and m, respectively, we can compute the Hausdorff distance between x and y in $O(\ell m k)$ time (where the distance is computed with respect to k-mers).*

Proof: We can generate the q-grams of x and y in $O((\ell + m)k)$ time. Followed by this we compute the distance between each q-gram in x with each q-gram in y. This takes $O(\ell m k)$ time. □

Let Σ be a finite alphabet, and let Σ^* denote the set of all strings over Σ. Let x and y be strings in Σ^*.

Definition 6 (Jaro-Winkler similarity).
The Jaro *similarity between two records x and y is defined as follows*

$$s_j(x,y) = \frac{1}{3}\left(\frac{m}{|x|} + \frac{m}{|y|} + \frac{m-t}{m}\right)$$

where m is number of character matches and t is number of transpositions divided by 2. (A transposition refers to a pair of characters appearing in reverse order). The Jaro-Winkler similarity is defined as:

$$S_w(x,y) = \begin{cases} s_j(x,y), & \text{if } s_j(x,y) < \text{threshold} \\ s_j(x,y) + (l * p(1-d_j)), & \text{otherwise} \end{cases}$$

where l denotes the length of the longest common prefix between x and y with the maximum value of 4 and p is a scaling factor which is usually set to 0.1.

Lemma 6. *If x and y are strings with lengths ℓ and m, respectively, we can compute their Jaro-Winkler similarity in $O(\ell + m)$ time.*

Proof: Please see [1] for a proof. $\qquad\qquad\qquad\qquad\qquad\qquad\qquad\qquad\qquad\square$

4 Novel Distance Metrics

In this section we introduce some variants of known metrics. Our experimental results (Sect. 6) reveal that these variants result in better linkage performance.

To compute the distance between two records, we normally use multiple attributes (e.g., LastName, FirstName, and DateOfBirth). Given any two records R_1 and R_2, to compute their distance we compute the distance with respect to each attribute and calculate the total across all the attributes. In this process, if the partial distance computed exceeds the threshold τ, we skip the distance calculations with respect to the remaining attributes. Also, we use string lengths to avoid unnecessary distance computations. To be more specific, let the attributes of interest be $A_1, A_2, \ldots, A_k$. Each attribute is thought of as a string of characters. Let the lengths of these strings in R_1 and R_2 be $\ell_1^1, \ell_2^1, \ldots, \ell_k^1$, and $\ell_1^2, \ell_2^2, \ldots, \ell_k^2$, respectively. If $\sum_{i=1}^{k} |\ell_i^1 - \ell_i^2| > \tau$, then we skip the distance computation between R_1 and R_2. These pruning steps have a significant impact on run time of the linking process.

One of the distance metrics we have employed is the positional q-gram distance. The standard q-gram distance is a function of the number of common q-grams in the two records under concern. The positional q-gram distance not only cares about the common q-grams but also their relative positions in the two records. If there is a common q-gram between two records and if they occur in two entirely different positions, then this q-gram should not be taken as an evidence to the similarity between the two records.

We have also employed the Naive Hausdorff distance in our record linkage algorithms. We observed that Hausdorff distance leads to errors in linking when a string is substring of the other string. This leads to the minimum distance between them to be 0 (0 being perfect match). For example, if s_1 is 'Craft' and s_2 is 'Hopcraft' then the Hausdorff distance between them will be 0 and hence they will be output as belonging to the same entity. In order to overcome this issue, we have proposed a modification.

Definition 7 (Modified Hausdorff Distance). *The Modified Hausdorff distance $d_h(x, y)$ between a pair of records x and y is*

$$d_h(x, y) = \text{Hausdorff distance}(x, y) + |x| - |y|$$

Lemma 7 *If x and y are strings with lengths ℓ and m, respectively, we can compute the Modified Hausdorff distance between x and y in $O(\ell m k)$ time (where the distance is computed with respect to k-mers).*

Proof: follows from the proof of Lemma 6.   □

As we can see, Hausdorff distance is computationally intensive. In order to reduce the linking time, we have explored the idea of positional Modified Hausdorff distance (similar to positional q-gram distance).

Algorithm 1: Hybrid Hausdorff distance

Input: string s_1, string s_2, integer q
Output: Hybrid Hausdorff distance between s_1 and s_2
minDistance ← 0
hausdorffDistance ← 1
X ← generateQmersMap (s_1,q)
Y ← generateQmersMap (s_2,q)
minDistance ← 0
distance ← 0
for $i \leftarrow 0$ to X by 1 do
| distance ← calculateQgramDistance $(X_i, Y_i))$
| if distance < minDistance then
| | minDistance ← distance
| end
end
hausdorffDistance ← minDistance- α
return hausdorffDistance

Another modification that we explored is using q-gram distance instead of hamming distance in order to calculate string similarity between two q-gram. We have combined the ideas from Modified Hausdorff distance and q-gram distance in order to create this new distance metric. The Algorithm 1 describes to calculation of this similarity. An Interesting observation is that when we are performing the q-gram distance calculation between pair of q-grams, better performance was achieved in terms of linking time when we are using the value of q as 2 whereas the size of q-mers which are generated earlier in the algorithm is 3.

Please note that for Hausdorff distance we take the maximum of the minimum distances of pairs of q-gram, whereas in the Hybrid Hausdorff distance we take the minimum distance that was observed between all pairs of positional q-gram because for the q-gram distance the value closer to 1 is considered to be a better match than a value close to 0. Based on our experiments we have introduced hyper-parameter α.

5   Experimental Results

In this section, we present our experimental results on novel blocking and distance metrics. The basic algorithm used for record linkage is the one given in [16]. The performance of all the algorithms has been measured using the F1 score which is defined using precision and recall. **Precision:** Total number of records that are correctly clustered divided by the total number of records that are clustered together(including the ones that the algorithm miss classifies).
Recall: The total number of records that are correctly clustered together divided by the number of records that are correctly clustered plus the number of records that the algorithm was not able to correctly classify.
F1 Score: is defined as

$$\frac{2 * Precision * Recall}{Precision + Recall}.$$

5.1   Experimental Setup

All of our experiments shown in this section were carried out using 6 Intel(R) Core(TM) i5-8400 CPU @ 2.80GHz with 32GiB DDR4 2133MHz of main memory running on Ubuntu 22.04.1 LTS operating system.

5.2   Experimental Data

We have used two types of data sets in our experiments. Both data set types were curated from the *Social Security Death Master File* courtesy of SSDMF.INFO[1]. These data sets have FirstName, LastName, and Social Security Number (SSN) among other attributes. SSN is used for computing the linkage performance as it is treated as an error-free unique identifier in these data sets.

The first data set is publicly available for free on *figshare*[2]. This first data set, $dataset_1$, constitutes a total of $1,000,000$ unique records. Each experiment utilizing $dataset_1$ is configured to link four input data files where four copies of each entity are split across these input data files.

The second data set, $dataset_2$, is also publicly available on *figshare*[3] $dataset_2$ contains 10 sets of files of different sizes ranging from $100,000$ to $1,000,000$

---

[1] http://ssdmf.info/download.html.
[2] https://figshare.com/articles/dataset/**masked for double-anonymous review**.
[3] https://doi.org/**masked for double-anonymous review**.

records. Each set of files is prepared such that it contains exactly five records pertaining to each unique entity. These five records are divided into two groups. The first group consists of four exact copies of the original record. The second is a singleton group containing one corrupted record of the original. The corruption of the fifth record is done by introducing errors in the FirstName, LastName, or both fields.

5.3 Results for Distance Metrics

Please note that the algorithm of [16] uses the edit distance. Several experiments were conducted where we tried to improve the run time of the linking process using q-gram distance. One such experiment was to test several values of q and we observed that as we increase the value of q, the run time decreases but accuracy also decreases. A value of 3 for q yields the best run time and accuracy for $dataset_1$. The run time is better than that for edit distance. We also explored the idea of changing q dynamically as a function of the string lengths, but the results did not improve. Finally, when we implemented positional q-gram distance, we were able to observe better run times than for the edit distance. We were able to achieve the improvement in the run time with small reduction in the F1-score and very small difference in precision of the linking.

Hausdorff distance is computationally intensive and it took a large amount of time which is more than for edit or q-gram distance. We observed that a hybrid of positional Hausdorff distance with q-gram distance that we have proposed in this paper gave a better linking time than the edit distance. In our experiments, initially we generate q-gram of length 3 as we do for Hausdorff distance and while iterating over these q-grams, for each pair of q-grams we generate a q'-gram and perform the q-gram distance between them. Here, we experimented with different values for q'. We have observed that the performance is the best when q' is 2 for $dataset_1$ and $dataset_2$. For $dataset_2$, we have to use hyper-parameter α as 0.05 to get best results.

Table 1 presents accuracy results for six different distance metrics on $dataset_2$. As we can see all of the metrics perform well with F1-score higher than 95%. We could not generate F1-score for $dataset_1$ as it was corrupted in such a way that the ground truth is not reliable. Even then we observed that the percentage of clusters that contain all the records pertaining to single individuals and no other records of any other individuals is 99%.

Table 1. F1 score (%) for different distance metrics. Pos-Qgram stands for Positional Q-gram, and JW stands for Jaro-Winkler for *dataset₂*.

#Records	Pos-Qgram	Q-Gram	Hausdorff-Hybrid	Edit	JW
100000	99.1496	99.1008	99.2764	99.2826	99.1185
200000	99.0491	99.0534	98.8589	99.7311	98.9373
400000	98.9829	99.0157	98.7182	99.732	98.7936
600000	98.9024	98.9427	98.4077	99.7312	98.4601
800000	98.7415	98.8506	97.931	99.7227	98.1145
1000000	98.0843	98.1691	97.6193	99.7149	97.8969

Figure 1 shows the linkage times for applying different distance metrics on *dataset₁*.

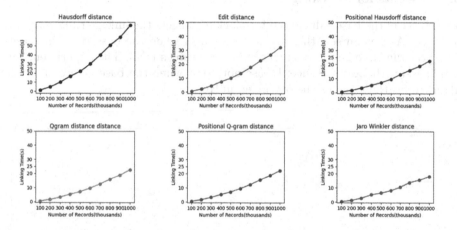

Fig. 1. Linkage Times for the different Distance Metrics for *dataset₁*

We have studied the impact of distance measures on linking *dataset₂* and the results are depicted in Fig. 3. We observe that the linking time for the Hybrid Hausdorff distance, that we have defined in this paper, performed slightly better than Edit distance in terms of linking time (Fig. 2).

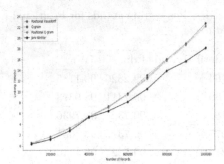
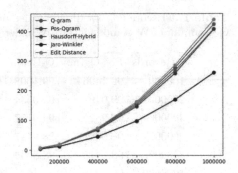

Fig. 2. Linkage Times for the 4 fastest distance metrics on $dataset_1$.

Fig. 3. Linkage Times for applying different distance metrics on $dataset_2$.

5.4 Results for Blocking

The choice of the base value, used for blocking, affects the linkage time, as shown in Fig. 4. As we can see, the run time decreases when the base value increases. The best run time is obtained when the base values is 45. The experiments are conducted with Edit distance. Please note that when the base values is 26, the algorithm is the same as the one given in [16].

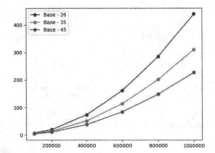
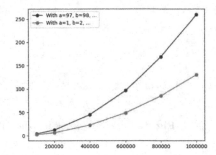

Fig. 4. Linkage Times with changes to Base for $dataset_2$

Fig. 5. Linkage Times with different values for the characters on $dataset_2$

Table 2 shows how F1-score changes with change in bases. F1-score definitely decreases with increase in the base but with 2 percent decrease in F1-score leads to reduction in run time by factor of 2.

Table 3 shows the accuracy obtained when we equated the character a with 97, b with 98, etc. Figure 5 shows the run times (orange) with $a = 1, b = 2, \ldots$ vs the run times (blue) with $a = 97, b = 98, \ldots$. For theses sets of experiments we have used Jaro-Winkler distance.

Table 2. F1- score with base change $dataset_2$

#Records	Base - 26	Base - 36	Base - 45
100000	99.2826	98.4164	96.5201
200000	99.7311	98.6905	97.4317
400000	99.732	98.6596	97.3716
600000	99.7312	98.6519	97.3526
800000	99.7227	98.671	97.3528
1000000	99.7149	98.6401	97.3266

Table 3. Different values for the characters for $dataset_2$

#Records	Linkage Time(s)	Precision
100000	2.25356	97.0832
200000	6.31206	96.8683
400000	22.716	96.7306
600000	48.8502	96.4281
800000	85.2045	96.1119
1000000	130.515	95.9135

Please note that if we use a standard blocking (with a base of 26), the run time for 1,000,000 records is around 250 s. On the other hand, if we use different values for the characters, the run time reduces to around 130 s, speeding up the process by approximately a factor of 2! Fig. 5 shows the run times for different values for characters. We also note that the F1-score drops from 97.89 to 95.91. Another point to note is that we have used total number of blocks as 75,000 instead of 26^3 which is 17576. This was done because our experiments shows that if we had used 17576 as the number of blocks, large number of blocks are empty and approximately clustering is affected negatively. This reduces the F1-score to 6%. Further increase in number of blocks would lead to similar run time and F1-score as standard blocking (with a base of 26).

The idea about hashing the blocking key was explored to understand its impact on accuracy and linkage time and it showed some promise. The $hashfunction_1$ is $((701*(blockingkey)+999983)\%99991)$ and the $hashfunction_2$ is $((6607 * x + 99991)\%58211)$. The linkage times for these two hash functions and their comparison without hashing are shown in Fig. 6 (Fig. 7).

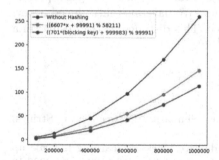

Fig. 6. Linkage Times with Hashing for $dataset_2$

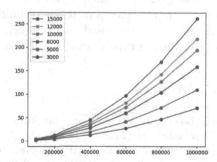

Fig. 7. Linkage Time with block reduction for $dataset_2$

We can see that $hashfunction_1$ reduces the linking time by factor of 1.5 and $hashfunction_2$ reduces the linking time by factor of 2.5. The F1-score for the linking decreases as specified in Table 4.

Table 4. Linking Accuracy(%) with Hashing on $dataset_2$

#Records	hf_1	hf_2
100000	88.2311	92.2436
200000	90.1346	94.1983
400000	90.1368	94.1157
600000	90.1807	94.1602
800000	90.1951	94.1778
1000000	90.1695	94.1353

Table 5. F1 score (%) for different block sizes for $dataset_2$.

#Records	15000	12000	10,000	8000	5000	3000
100000	99.1003	98.7846	98.5452	97.7146	94.7235	89.6927
200000	98.8919	98.6201	98.2922	97.3636	95.3752	91.9157
400000	98.7432	98.4699	98.1606	97.2322	95.1814	91.8065
600000	98.4165	98.1535	97.8574	96.9212	94.9675	91.6174
800000	98.0709	97.8209	97.5513	96.6044	94.7249	91.4155
1000000	97.848	97.5818	97.3206	96.4027	94.5761	91.289

Table 5 mentions the F1-score for different block sizes.

Record Linkage with Block reduction was explored. We reduced the number of blocks from 26^3 till 3000. We got similar results to what were achieved with other blocking techniques where the run time was reduced upon reduction in number of blocks with F1-Score getting reduced.

6   Conclusions

In this paper we have offered some novel blocking techniques that use an intrinsic property of real datasets in order to eliminate certain blocks. These algorithms achieve improved run times for record linkage with a small impact on accuracy. We have also presented variations of known distance metrics that yield performance improvements in terms of linking times. We have also introduced a new distance measure based on Hausdorff distance. This distance metric results in a better linking time than the edit distance.

References

1. Basak, J., et al.: On Computing the Jaro Similarity Between Two Strings, manuscript (2023)
2. Bilenko, M., Kamath, B., Mooney, R.J.: Adaptive blocking: learning to scale up record linkage. In: ICDM, pp. 87–96 (2006). https://doi.org/10.1109/icdm.2006.13
3. Christen, P.: A survey of indexing techniques for scalable record linkage and deduplication. IEEE Trans. Knowl. Data Eng. **24**(9), 1537–1555 (2012). https://doi.org/10.1109/TKDE.2011.127
4. Christen, P., Churches, T.: Febrl - freely extensible biomedical record linkage, Joint computer science technical report series (Online), TR-CS-02-05, [Canberra]: Australian national University, Dept. of Computer Science (2002)

5. Christen, P., Churches, T., Hegland, M.: Febrl – a parallel open source data linkage system. In: Dai, H., Srikant, R., Zhang, C. (eds.) PAKDD 2004. LNCS (LNAI), vol. 3056, pp. 638–647. Springer, Heidelberg (2004). https://doi.org/10.1007/978-3-540-24775-3_75
6. Cormen, T., Leiserson, C., Rivest, R., Stein, C.: Introduction to Algorithms, 4th edn. MIT Press, Cambridge (2022)
7. Curtis, K.: Pilots Arrested For Disability Payments. The Associated Press (2005)
8. Draisbach, U., Naumann, F.: A generalization of blocking and windowing algorithms for duplicate detection. In: ICDKE, pp. 18–24 (2011). https://doi.org/10.1109/icdke.2011.6053920
9. Fellegi, I.P., Sunter, A.B.: A theory for record linkage. J. Am. Stat. Assoc. 64(328), 1183–1210 (1969)
10. Hernández, M.A., Stolfo, S.J.: The merge/purge problem for large databases. In: SIGMOD, pp. 127–138 (1995). https://doi.org/10.1145/223784.223807
11. Herzog, T.N., Scheuren, F.J., Winkler, W.E.: Applications of record Linkage Techniques. www.soa.org/library/newsletters/the-actuary-magazine/2007/february/link2007feb/ (2007)
12. Jin, L., Li, C., Mehrotra, S.: Efficient record linkage in large data sets. In: DASFAA, pp. 137–146 (2003). https://doi.org/10.1109/dasfaa.2003.1192377
13. Karapiperis, D., Vatsalan, D., Verykios, V.S., Christen, P.: Efficient record linkage using a compact hamming space. In: EDBT, pp. 209–220 (2016). https://doi.org/10.5441/002/edbt.2016.21
14. Kim, H.-S., Lee, D.: HARRA: fast iterative hashed record linkage for large-scale data collections. In: EDBT, pp. 525–536 (2010). https://doi.org/10.1145/1739041.1739104
15. Kondrak, G.: N-gram similarity and distance. In: International Symposium on String Processing and Retrieval
16. Mamun, A.-A., Mi, T., Aseltine, R., Rajasekaran, S.: Efficient sequential and parallel algorithms for record linkage. J. Am. Med. Inform. Assoc. (2013). https://doi.org/10.1136/amiajnl-2013-002034
17. McCallum, A., Nigam, K., Ungar, H.: Efficient clustering of high-dimensional data sets with application to reference matching. In: Proceedings of the Sixth ACM SIGKDD International Conference on Knowledge Discovery and Data Mining, pp. 169–178. ACM (2000)
18. McVeigh, B.S., Spahn, B.T., Murray, J.S.: Scaling Bayesian probabilistic record linkage with post-hoc blocking: an application to the California great registers, arXiv e-prints. ArXiv:1905.05337 (2019)
19. Monge, A.E., Elkan, C.P.: An efficient domain-independent algorithm for detecting approximately duplicate database records. In: Proceedings of the SIGMOD 1997 Workshop on Research Issues on Data Mining and Knowledge Discovery, pp. 23–29 (1997)
20. Papadakis, G., Alexiou, G., Papastefanatos, G., Koutrika, G.: Schemaagnostic vs. schema-based configurations for blocking methods on homogeneous data. PVLDB 9(4), 312–323 (2015). https://doi.org/10.14778/2856318.2856326
21. Papadakis, G., Ioannou, E., Thanos, E., Palpanas, T.: The four generations of entity resolution. In: Jagadish, H.V., Özsu, M.T. (eds.) Synthesis Lectures on Data Management (2021)
22. Puhlmann, S., Weis, M., Naumann, F.: XML duplicate detection using sorted neighborhoods. In: Ioannidis, Y., et al. (eds.) EDBT 2006. LNCS, vol. 3896, pp. 773–791. Springer, Heidelberg (2006). https://doi.org/10.1007/11687238_46

23. Sadinle, M., Fienberg, S.E.: A generalized Fellegi-Sunter framework for multiple record linkage with application to homicide record systems. J. Am. Stat. Assoc. **108**(502), 385–397 (2013)
24. Shao, J., Wang, Q., Lin, Y.: Skyblocking: learning blocking schemes on the skyline. Inf. Syst. **85**(30–43), 21 (2018)
25. Steorts, R.C., Hall, R., Fienberg, S.E.: A Bayesian approach to graphical record linkage and de-duplication. J. Am. Stat. Assoc. (2015)
26. Steorts, R.C., Ventura, S.L., Sadinle, M., Fienberg, S.E.: A comparison of blocking methods for record linkage. In: Domingo-Ferrer, J. (ed.) PSD 2014. LNCS, vol. 8744, pp. 253–268. Springer, Cham (2014). https://doi.org/10.1007/978-3-319-11257-2_20
27. Tancredi, A., Liseo, B.: A hierarchical Bayesian approach to record linkage and size population problems. Ann. Appl. Stat. **5**(2B), 1553–1585 (2011)
28. van der Loo, M.P.J.: The stringdist package for approximate string matching. R J. **6/1** (2014)
29. Wang, Q., Cui, M., Liang, H.: Semantic-aware blocking for entity resolution. TKDE **28**(1), 166–180 (2016). https://doi.org/10.1109/tkde.2015.2468711
30. Zhao, Y., Karypis, G.: Evaluation of hierarchical clustering algorithms for document datasets. In: Proceedings of the Eleventh International Conference on Information and Knowledge Management, pp. 515–524. ACM (2002)

Efficiently Discovering Spatial Prevalent Co-location Patterns Without Distance Thresholds

Vanha Tran[✉][iD], Duyhai Tran, Anhthang Le, and Trongnguyen Ha

FPT University, Hanoi 155514, Vietnam
hatv14@fe.edu.vn,
{haitdhe153728,thanglahe153758,nguyenhthe153762}@fpt.edu.vn

Abstract. A spatial prevalent co-location pattern (SPCP) refers to a group of different features that their instances occur frequently within a spatial neighborhood. The neighbor of instances is typically evaluated based on the spatial separation between them. If the spatial separation is not greater than a threshold value set by users, they are considered to be neighboring each other. However, determining an appropriate distance threshold for each specific spatial dataset is challenging for users, as it requires careful analysis of the dataset. To address the issue, we propose an algorithm called Delaunay triangulation k-order clique (DTkC) to discover SPCPs without distance thresholds. This algorithm integrates three phases: creating the spatial neighbor hierarchy structure of instances based on Delaunay triangulation, employing k-order neighbors allows users to select an appropriate level from the neighbor structure, and designing a clique-based approach to quickly collect co-location instances of each candidate pattern and filter SPCPs. We conducted experimental analysis on both synthetic and real datasets, to demonstrate the effectiveness of DTkC in terms of generating the number of SPCPs, execution time, and memory consumption.

Keywords: Spatial prevalent co-location pattern · Delaunay triangulation · k-order neighbors · Clique

1 Introduction

Data analysis in the spatial domain is a crucial area in data mining where spatial prevalent co-location patterns (SPCPs) play a significant role as they exhibit clear associations of features among the studied objects in geographical space. Particularly, we not only investigate individual features of objects but also explore the relationships among multiple objects in space, their combinations and organization, which contain valuable hidden information that needs to be extracted to gain a deeper understanding of the overall spatial structure. Examining these associations can help us identify the general rules of these features, aiding in forecasting and making informed decisions while optimizing resource management and allocation. For example, when investigating the

© The Author(s), under exclusive license to Springer Nature Switzerland AG 2023
P. Delir Haghighi et al. (Eds.): iiWAS 2023, LNCS 14416, pp. 447–463, 2023.
https://doi.org/10.1007/978-3-031-48316-5_41

underlying causes of a specific issue, such as in the healthcare domain where the aim is to establish specialized healthcare facilities targeting specific diseases, an analysis of SPCPs becomes essential [18]. By studying SPCPs within residential areas, we can explore the associations between different diseases and the daily life habits of the population. These patterns provide valuable insights for decision-making regarding the development or enhancement of healthcare facilities in specific geographical locations while minimizing resource wastage. SPCPs are highly effective in various other domains such as criminology [3], public safety [4], business [10], disease control [5], transportation [14], and so on.

Most of the proposed SPCP mining algorithms use a distance threshold to identify neighbor relationships between spatial instances. Using a minimum distance threshold requires users to determine an appropriate threshold value. If this value is not carefully chosen, it can lead to overlooking important SPCPs or generating meaningless SPCPs. For example, important SPCPs are missed as a result of setting a small distance threshold, while a large value of that creates excessive computations, memory consumption, and too many redundant SPCPs.

Additionally, the minimum distance threshold can be influenced by data density. In high-density areas, a small value of the distance threshold can yield a large number of neighboring instances, while in low-density areas, it may lead to the omission of neighboring instances (even none neighbor relationship is formed). If the distance threshold is set to a large value, the neighbor relationship between instances are suitably constructed in the low-density areas. However, most of instances in the high-density areas form neighbor relationships. However, in which many inappropriate neighbor relationships are constructed. This issue makes the process of complex spatial datasets very challenging.

Moreover, the traditional SPCP mining algorithms, which follow a generation-test candidate framework [11,12,15,18,19] that is similar to the Apriori algorithm [6], are difficult to deal with when there are a large number of neighboring instances formed in the data set. Since these algorithms first need to generate a set of candidates, then they collect all co-location instances of each candidate by generating groups of instances and verifying the neighbor relationship of these instances in these groups. This step is quite time-consuming [10,18].

To overcome the above problems, the following work has been carried out:

(1) The neighbor relationship between instances is determined automatically by using Delaunay triangulation (DT).
(2) The concept of k-order neighbors in DT is used to allow users to adjust neighboring instances for their specific needs in exploring SPCPs.
(3) A modified clique-based SPCP mining algorithm is developed. First, all neighboring instances are enumerated by cliques. Next, these cliques are arranged into a special hash table structure. Then all co-location instances of any candidates can be conveniently queried from the structure. Finally, SPCPs can be filtered efficiently.

2   Related Work

SPCP is an important branch of data mining, so there are many algorithms have been proposed. Partial join [19] and join less [18] search for SPCPs by identifying co-location instances of candidates using separate cliques and star neighborhoods, respectively. However, both the two approaches face challenges in terms of computational complexity. To improve mining performance, co-location pattern instance-tree [11], improved co-location pattern instance-tree [12], CP-tree-based [17], clique-based instances driven schema (IDS) [2], and so on were developed to enhance the ability to search for SPCPs.

The above algorithms offer improving efficiency, but they may still face scalability challenges when dealing with large and dense datasets. The computational complexity can increase significantly as the dataset size grows, leading to longer processing times or even infeasibility. Thus, parallel SPCP mining algorithms have been proposed such as MapReduce [15], Hadoop [16], and GPU [1].

In the mentioned algorithms, a distance threshold is used as a parameter for the process of searching SPCPs. However, the inconvenience of using this parameter has been discussed above. Some studies have proposed to solve that problem, e.g., k nearest neighbor graph [7] and Delaunay triangulation (DT)-based [8,13]. A newly improved algorithm based on DT, that employs three filters (i.e., feature constraint, global edge constraint, and local constraint) to eliminate redundant edges on the original DT, has also been proposed [9]. Nevertheless, these algorithms suffer from challenges when dealing with large datasets or long patterns, as the number of neighboring instances expands exponentially, demanding significant storage space and posing difficulties in computational efficiency.

3   Method

3.1   Basic Concepts

Given a spatial dataset $S = \{S_1, ..., S_m\}$ where $S_i = \{f_{i_1}, ..., f_{i_m}\}$, $(1 \leq i \leq n)$ is a set of instances of a feature f_i and each instance f_{i_j} is in a three-element vector form $< f_i, ID, \text{location}(x, y) >$, we determine neighbor relationships R between instances and minimum prevalence threshold min_{prev} to compute SPCPs. The neighbor relationship R refers to the proximity or spatial closeness between instances in S. For example, Fig. 1 shows a point-of-interest dataset in which there are 12 instances (e.g., A.1, B.2, C.3) and these instances belong to 4 feature types, i.e., $F = \{A, B, C, D\}$. When the Euclidean distance metric is used to determine R, if the distance between two instances is smaller than a threshold d, the two instances are neighbors and they are connected by a solid line.

Definition 1 (Spatial co-location pattern). *A spatial co-location pattern c refers to a set of spatial features that is a subset of F, i.e., $c = \{f_1, ..., f_l\} \subseteq F$. The number of features in c is called the size of the pattern, c is a size l pattern.*

Definition 2 (Row instance). *A row instance of a pattern* $c = \{f_1, ..., f_l\}$ *is a set of instances that includes an instance of each feature type in c and each instance has the neighbor relationship with the remains. The set of all row instances of c is called the table instance,* $T(c)$. *The distinct instances of* f_i *in* $T(c)$ *is called the participating instances of* f_i *in c,* $Inst_{T(c)}(f_i)$.

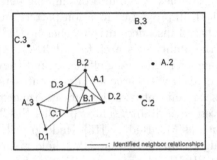

Fig. 1. A dataset with neighboring instances determined by a distance threshold.

Definition 3 (Participation ratio, PR). *The participation ratio of a feature* f_i *in a co-location pattern c represents the relative level of participation of the instances of* f_i *in c compared to the total instances of* f_i *in S and denoted as*

$$PR(c, f_i) = \frac{\text{Number of distinct instances of } f_i \text{ in } c}{\text{Number of instances of } f_i \text{ in } S} = \frac{|Inst_{T(c)}(f_i)|}{|Inst_S(f_i)|} \quad (1)$$

Definition 4 (Participation index, PI). *The participation index of a co-location pattern c is a measure that quantifies the level of involvement of the spatial features in c and is denoted as*

$$PI(c) = \min_{f_i \in c}\{PR(c, f_i)\} \quad (2)$$

Definition 5 (Prevalent spatial co-location pattern). *If the participation index of a co-location pattern c is not smaller than a minimum prevalence threshold* min_{prev} *given by users, c is a prevalent spatial co-location pattern, i.e.,* $PI(c) \geq min_{prev}$.

For example, we consider a co-location pattern $c = \{A, D\}$ in Fig. 1. Since A.1 and D.2 have a neighbor relationship, A.1, D.2 is a row instance of $\{A, D\}$. First, the table instance of $\{A, D\}$ is collected, i.e., $T(c) = \{\{A.1, D.2\}, \{A.1, D.3\}, \{A.3, D.1\}, \{A.3, D.3\}\}$. Thus, we have $Inst_{T(c)}(A) = \{A.1, A.3\}$ and $Inst_{T(c)}(D) = \{D.1, D.2, D.3\}$. Therefore, the PRs of A and D in c are computed, $PR(c, A) = \frac{|\{A.1, A.3\}|}{|\{A.1, A.2, A.3\}|} = \frac{2}{3}$ and $PR(c, D) = \frac{|\{D.1, D.2, D.3\}|}{|\{D.1, D.2, D.3\}|} = \frac{3}{3}$. After that, the PI of c is $PI(c) = min\{PR(c, A), PR(c, D)\} = min\{\frac{2}{3}, \frac{3}{3}\} = \frac{2}{3}$. Assuming a prevalent threshold of 0.5, $min_{prev} = 0.5$, is set by a user, since $PI(c) = \frac{2}{3} > min_{prev}$, $c = \{A, D\}$ is a SPCP.

3.2   Determining Neighboring Instances by Delaunay Triangulation

From Fig. 1 we can see, if the distance threshold d is set to a small value, all the instances in the upper right corner do not form the neighboring relationship. While a large value is set for d, all instances in the lower left corner are neighbors. The upper right corner and lower left corner correspond to sparse and dense areas, similar to the center and suburbs of a city. It is difficult to use a single distance threshold to determine whether all instances in the entire space have neighbor relationships.

Definition 6 Delaunay triangulation of S, $DT(S)$ [9]). *Delaunay triangulation of S is a geometric structure that consists of a set of non-overlapping triangles, forming a connected graph. DT is constructed in such a way that no point in S lies within the circumcircle of any triangle in the triangulation. This result is in a unique and explicit representation of the spatial data's topology.*

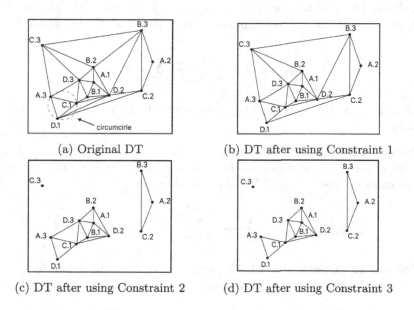

(a) Original DT   (b) DT after using Constraint 1

(c) DT after using Constraint 2   (d) DT after using Constraint 3

Fig. 2. Determining neighboring instances by Delaunay triangulation.

DT provides a comprehensive understanding of the relationships between instances, revealing the underlying connectivity and proximity within the dataset. For example, Fig. 2(a) shows the result of spatial data in Fig. 1 after executing DT. We consider two instances that are connected by an edge in DT having a neighbor relationship. However, some inappropriate edges are needed to remove, e.g., these edges connect two instances that belong to the same feature type, their length is too long, and so on. Therefore, three constraints were designed.

Definition 7 (Constraint 1). *The edges that connect two neighboring instances must belong to distinct feature types.*

Definition 8. *The global mean represents the overall average distance between connected instances in DT and is computed by*

$$\mu_{global} = \frac{1}{|E|} \sum_{e_t \in E} |e_t| \tag{3}$$

where E is a set of all edges in DT.

Definition 9. *The global standard deviation represents the variability or spread of edge lengths across all edges in DT and is computed by*

$$\sigma_{global} = (\frac{1}{|E| - 1} \sum_{e_t \in E} (|e_t| - \mu_{global})^2)^{\frac{1}{2}} \tag{4}$$

Definition 10. *The local mean of an instance f_{i_j} refers to the average length of all the edges that are directly connected to it in DT and is calculated by*

$$\mu_{local}(f_{i_j}) = \frac{1}{deg(f_{i_j})} \sum_{k=1}^{deg(f_{i_j})} |e_t| \tag{5}$$

where $deg(f_{i_j})$ is the number of edges connected to f_{i_j} and $|e_t|$ is the length of the edge.

Definition 11. *The local standard deviation of an instance f_{i_j} refers to the measure of variability or dispersion in the lengths of all the edges that are directly connected to the instance in DT and is calculated by*

$$\sigma_{local}(f_{i_j}) = (\frac{1}{deg(f_{i_j}) - 1} \sum_{t=1}^{deg(f_{i_j})} (|e_t| - \mu_{local}(f_{i_j}))^2)^{\frac{1}{2}} \tag{6}$$

Definition 12 (Constraint 2). *The length of an edge connecting to f_{i_j} is less than or equal to the specified global distance that is computed by*

$$const_{global}(f_{i_j}) = \mu_{global} + \sigma_{global} \frac{\mu_{global}}{\mu_{local}(f_{i_j})} \tag{7}$$

After running Constraints 1 and 2, we obtain distinct subgraphs $G_{sub}(V_{sub}, E_{sub})$ (e.g., as in Fig. 2(c)). But some long edges in each subgraph need to be removed.

Definition 13. *The mean local standard deviation of each subgraph $G_{sub}(V_{sub}, E_{sub})$ is computed by*

$$\mu_{\sigma_{local}}(G_{sub}) = \frac{\sum \sigma_{local}(f_{i_j})}{|E_{sub}|}, \forall f_{i_j} \in G_{sub} \tag{8}$$

Definition 14 (Constraint 3). *The length of an edge that is incident to f_{i_j} is not greater than the local distance constraint of f_{i_j} which is computed by*

$$const_{local}(f_{i_j}) = \mu_{local}^2(f_{i_j}) + \beta\mu_{\sigma_{local}}(G_{sub}) \qquad (9)$$

where $\mu_{local}^2(f_{i_j})$ represents the average length of the edges connecting the first-order and second-order neighbors of f_{i_j} and $\beta > 0$ is a factor to control the sensitiveness of the local distance constraint.

Definition 15 (k-order neighbor). *In DT, these instances that are connected directly to f_{i_j} is called the first-order of f_{i_j}. These points, that are directly connected to the first-order neighbors f_{i_j} and are not the first-order neighbors themselves, are called the second-order neighbors of f_{i_j}. The k-order neighbors of f_{i_j}, $N_k(f_{i_j})$, is conducted by continuing this process.*

For example, Fig. 2(d) shows the result after putting the three constraints on DT to construct neighbor relationships between instances automatically without setting distance thresholds. Table 1 shows the neighbors of each instance when applying Definition 15 with $k = 2$. The instances are sorted lexicographically.

Table 1. Neighboring instance sets with $k = 2$

f_{i_j}	$N_k(f_{i_j})$	f_{i_j}	$N_k(f_{i_j})$	f_{i_j}	$N_k(f_{i_j})$	f_{i_j}	$N_k(f_{i_j})$
A.1	B.1,B.2,C.1,D.2,D.3	B.2	C.1,D.2,D.3	C.1	D.1,D.2,D.3	D.1	–
A.2	B.3,C.2	B.3	C.2	C.2	-	D.2	–
A.3	B.1,C.1,D.1,D.2,D.3	B.1	C.1,D.1,D.2,D.3	C.3	–	D.3	–

4 DT k-Order Clique-Based Mining SPCP Algorithm

4.1 Overview of the Mining Algorithms

Figure 3 depicts the mining algorithm designed in this work. In Phase 1, users give a dataset and set a minimum prevalence threshold. Phase 2 constructs neighbor relationships between instances according to Definition 15. Next, all neighboring instances are preserved in a set of cliques in Phase 3. A hash table

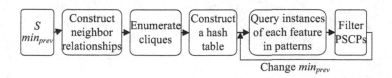

Fig. 3. DT k-order clique-based mining SPCP algorithm.

structure, that further compresses the neighbor relationships of instances, is designed. After that, the participation of the instances of each feature in any patterns can be queried from the hash structure. Finally, SPCPs are filtered.

Unlike the traditional generation-test candidate mining frameworks, our algorithm avoids the most time-consuming part of collecting all row instances for each pattern. In addition, although our algorithm adopts the same mining framework as IDS [2], there are two differences: first, the neighbor relationships of instances are automatically constructed without user-specified thresholds. Second, we designed depth-first search strategy to improve efficiency in enumerating cliques and reducing memory consumption.

4.2   Depth-First Search Clique Instance Drive Schema

Definition 16. *An instance clique tree, I-tree, is a hierarchical structure defined as follows: (1) It comprises a single root node labeled as root. (2) Each node contains an instance and a node link that points to the next sibling node that represents a larger instance. (3) An I-clique encompasses a collection of instances that is denoted by a leaf node and all its ancestor nodes. (4) Within an I-clique, every pair of instances satisfies the condition of being neighbors.*

The instance clique tree of instances with the neighbor relationships listed in Table 1 is shown in Fig. 4(a). However, if the data set is large and dense, the I-tree will become very large. If the entire I-tree is constructed before searching for cliques, it will waste execution time and consume storage space. Therefore, we designed a deep-first search strategy to build an I-tree, obtain cliques, and delete the nodes that have been traversed.

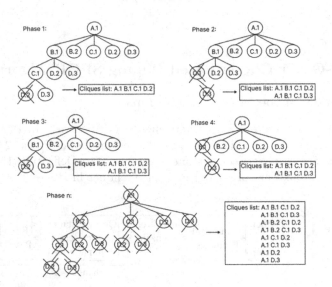

Fig. 4. An illustration of the deep-first search strategy for obtaining cliques.

Algorithm 1. Enumerating cliques by a deep-first search strategy

Input: S: dataset, N_k:is a set of all neighboring instances
Output: a set of cliques, $Clqs$

```
1:  iTree = Initialize_Itree()
2:  for f_{i_j} ∈ S do
3:      stack = Initialize_Stack()                          ▷ Depth-first manner
4:      headNode = iTree.AddHeadNode(f_{i_j})    ▷ Add headNode to the top of stack
5:      stack.push(N_k(f_{i_j}))
6:      oldInst = Initialize_Set();            ▷ Save all instances appeared in cliques
7:      while stack ≠ ∅ do
8:          curNode = stack.pop();                   ▷ Get a node from top of stack
9:          if oldInst.NotContain(curNode) then
10:             canCliq = True                      ▷ Mark as can generate new clique
11:             oldInst.Add(curNode)
12:         childNode = GetChildren(curNode)
13:         if childNode == ∅ then                       ▷ curNode is leaf node
14:             if canCliq == True then
15:                 canCliq = False
16:                 clique = GetClique(curNode)
17:                 Clqs.Add(clique)
18:             iTree.RemoveAncestors(curNode)
19:         else
20:             iTree.AddNode(curNode, childNode)
21:             stack.push(childNode.Reverse())
```

Algorithm 1 is explained by running an example on the cliques enumerated in Table 1. It takes A.1 as $headNode$ (Steps 2–4) and puts all neighbors of A.1 into a stack (Step 5), $stack = \{B.1,B.2,C.1,D.2, D.3\}$. $oldInst$ = records the instances that already visited (Step 6). While $stack$ is not empty, we pop one instance as $curNode = $ B.1 (Step 8). If this instance has not been visited yet, it is marked to use to generate new clique (Step 10) and added into $oldInst$. After that, the algorithm gets all children of $curNode$ by obtaining the intersection between the neighbors of it with its right siblings, $RSb(curNode)$ (Step 12), i.e., $childNode = N_k(B.1) \cap RSb(B.1) = \{B.2,C.1,D.2,D.3\} \cap \{C.1,D.1,D.2,D.3\} = \{C.1,D.2,D.3\}$. Sine $childNode \neq \emptyset$, all instances in $childNode$ are added as children of $curNode$, i.e., B.1 (Steps 20–21). The above process continues to be executed. When $curNode = $ D.2, since $childNode = N_k(D.2) \cap RSb(D.2) = $ (Step 13), $curNode$ is a leaf node, a clique is generated by combine it with all its ancestor nodes (Steps 15–17), i.e., $clique = \{A.1,B.1,C.1,D.2\}$. Then D.2 is removed form I-tree (Step 18). As shown in Fig. 4, Phases 2–4 describe processing other nodes and Phase n shows the enumerated cliques and the part of I-tree drawn by A.1 is deleted. As can be seen that a lot of storage space can be saved.

4.3 Compressed Clique Hash Table

Definition 17. *A compressed clique hash table, C-Hash, is a data structure consisting of key-value pairs: (1) The key represents a set of features, denoted as Fc. (2) The value is a collection of hash structures, each containing a key-value pair. Here, the key represents a specific feature f that belongs to Fc, and the value' represents a set of instances associated with feature f.*

For example, Fig. 5 shows the C-Hash that is build from the cliques listed by Algorithm 1 on the neighbors in Table 1.

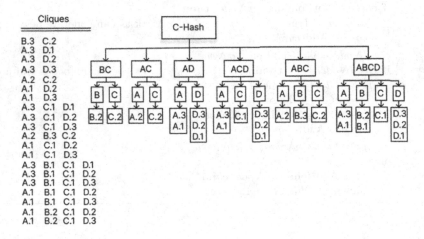

Fig. 5. The C-hash constructed based cliques enumerated from Algorithm 1.

4.4 The DTkC Algorithm

Algorithm 2 describes how to filter SPCPs from the compressed clique hash table structure. First, it iterates over the keys in CHash and adds them to the candidate set, *cands* (Steps 4–5). It then sorts the candidates in descending order of their size (Step 6). The algorithm enters a loop while where it retrieves the first candidate, *cand*, from the list and calculates its PI by iterating over the keys in CHash to get the values of keys that are supersets of *cand* (Steps 6–13). If the PI of the current candidate is not smaller than the minimum prevalence threshold, it is a SPCP and put into the result (Steps 14–15). After that, all direct subsets of *cand* are generated and added to *cands* as new candidates (Steps 16–17).

For example, we examine the prevalence of pattern $c=\{A, B\}$. The supersets of $\{A,B\}$ in CHash are ABCD and ABC. Thus, the instances of A and B in the pattern is the combination of the instances of A and B that are queried from the values of two keys ABCD and ABC, i.e., $Inst_{Tc} = \{\{A.3,A.1,A.2\}, \{B.2,B.1,B.3\}\}$. Therefore, the PI value of $\{A, B\}$ is $PI = min\{\frac{3}{3}, \frac{2}{3}\} = 1$.

Algorithm 2. The DTkC algorithm

Input: S: dataset, min_{prev}: minimum prevalence threshold
Output: a set of SPCPs, $SPCPs$

1: N_k=ConstructNeighborRelationship(S)   ▷ Based on Section 3.2
2: $Clqs$=EnumerateCliques(S, N_k)   ▷ Use Algorithm 1
3: $C - Hash$=ConstructCHash($Clqs$)
4: **for** $key \in C - Hash$ **do**
5:     $cands$.add(key)

6: $cands$.sort()
7: **while** $cands \neq \emptyset$ **do**
8:     $curCand= cands$.First
9:     $Inst_{Tc} = \emptyset$ ▷ Collect participating instances
10:     **for** $key \in C - Hash$ **do**
11:         **if** $cand \subseteq key$ **then**
12:             $Inst_{Tc}$.Add($value$)
13:     $PI = $ComputePI($Inst_{Tc}$)
14:     **if** $PI \geq min_{prev}$ **then**
15:         $SPCPs$.add($cand$)
16:     $subCands$=GenerateDirectSubsets($cand$)
17:     $cands$.add($subCands$)

5   Experimental Results and Analysis

5.1   Experiment Setting

In this section, a set of experiments are conducted to examine the performance of the DTkC algorithm. We choose joinless [18], CP-tree-based (named Condense) [17], and Delaunay triangulation-based co-location mining (DTC) [9] to compare. All programs in our experiments were coded using the Java programming language, available on GitHub[1], and were performed on a Laptop with Intel(R) Core (TM) i7-8550u CPU@1.8 - 4.0 GHz and 16 GB main memory.

Datasets: Four real datasets that are collected from points of interest in Beijing, China [2], Las Vegas, Toronto, USA[2], and United Kingdom (UK)[3], were used in our experiments. Moreover, two synthetic datasets, that were produced by a generator [18], were also used in our experiments. Table 1 lists some basic characteristics of the datasets used in this experiment (Table 2).

---

[1] https://shorturl.at/vyBJP.
[2] https://www.yelp.com/dataset.
[3] https://www.pocketgpsworld.com/.

Table 2. The datasets used in our experiments

Name	Area	# features	# instances	Distribution
Beijing	135 km × 224 km	17	90,257	Centralized + dense
Las Vegas	38 km × 63 km	19	31,592	Sparse + dense
Toronto	23 km × 56 km	19	20,309	Sparse + dense
UK	12,84 km × 13,867 km	26	143,621	Sparse + dense
Fig. 8(a), 9	5000 × 5000	15	*	Dense

5.2   Compare the Mining Performance

The first experiment compares the mining performance of the five algorithms including running time and memory consumption based on the variations of two parameters: the minimum distance threshold (only for Joinless and Condense) and the minimum prevalence threshold.

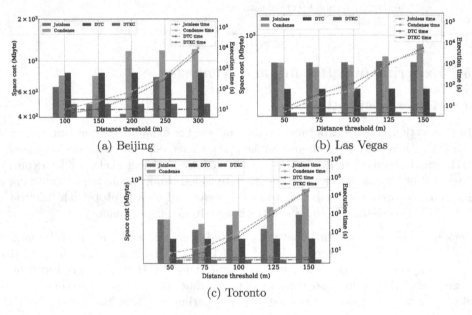

(a) Beijing   (b) Las Vegas

(c) Toronto

Fig. 6. The performance of compared algorithms on different distance thresholds ($min_{prev} = 0.2$ for all).

On Different Distance Thresholds: Figure 6 shows the result on both running time and memory consumption of the compared algorithms when modifying the minimum distance at values of 100 m, 150 m, 200 m, 250 m, and 300 m, and in our algorithm, DTkC sets $k = 2$, i.e., 2-order neighbors. We can observe that DTC and DTkC do not change their running time because they are not dependent on the minimum distance threshold parameter. Since the DTC algorithm only simply uses DT to obtain the neighbor relationship between instances, then it uses a merging strategy, that is, merging from triangles to quadrilaterals, merging from quadrilaterals to pentagons, etc., to find row instances of high size co-location patterns. However, the strategy generates only few high size patterns, so its execution time will be less than our algorithm. For Joinless and Condense, their running time will increase multiplicatively as distance thresholds increase. At lower values of distance thresholds, the running time of all algorithms is approximately equivalent. When increasing this parameter by a small amount, it leads to a significant increase in running time of Joinless and Condense, especially for dense data types like the ones we are using. Additionally, for Joinless and Condense, when the minimum distance threshold is increased, the number of neighboring instances also increases, leading to a higher number of candidate pattern evaluations and a larger volume of row instances. Consequently, a significant increase in memory consumption.

For DTC and DTkC algorithms, since they are not dependent on the minimum distance threshold, the memory consumption is always stable and lower compared to the aforementioned algorithms. However, DTkC exhibits significantly lower memory consumption than the DTC algorithm. This is attributed to the utilization of the depth-first clique search strategy instead of the merging operation used in DTC to generate row instances.

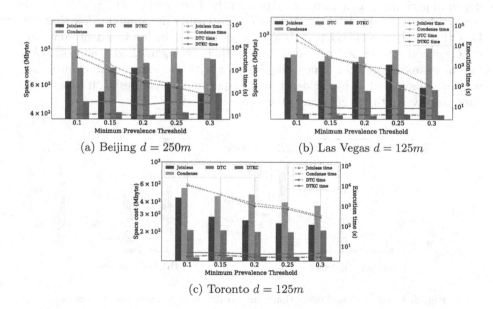

(a) Beijing $d = 250m$ (b) Las Vegas $d = 125m$

(c) Toronto $d = 125m$

Fig. 7. The performance of four algorithms on different prevalence thresholds.

On Different Prevalence Thresholds: Figure 7 describes the performance of the five algorithms on different prevalence thresholds. We observe that with a smaller prevalence threshold (e.g., 0.1), the computation times of Joinless and Condense are significantly large. Although the computation times decrease when the prevalence threshold is increased, they still remain considerably high compared to DTC and DTkC. The memory consumption of Joinless and Condense decreases to some extent when the prevalence threshold increases. This is because these algorithms start the computation from small candidate co-locations and gradually expand to larger ones. As a result, when the prevalence threshold increases, the number of high size patterns decreases, leading to a decrease in the number of candidate co-locations that need to be computed.

DTC and DTkC utilize obtaining table instances first and C-Hash structures for candidate co-locations, respectively. Therefore, changing the prevalence threshold does not significantly impact memory consumption during the computation of PIs for candidate co-locations and the filtering of prevalent patterns. However, DTkC still exhibits significantly lower memory consumption.

5.3   Evaluate the Scalability of DTkC

On Different Numbers of Instances: Figure 8 shows the computation time of the DTC and DTkC algorithms with an increasing number of instances ($min_{prev} = 0.2, k = 2$). We can see that in Fig. 8(a), the dataset is dense and the number of instances is large, the computation time for both the merging step and the depth-first clique search increases significantly. However, in Fig. 8(b), only the computation time for DTkC increases rapidly, while the computation time for DTC increases at a slower pace. This occurs because in the less dense dataset, DTC generates fewer new polygons through the merging method, whereas DTkC has an increasing number of new cliques along with the some of sub-cliques that were not eliminated all by the depth-first clique search. As a result, it takes more time to traverse the larger I-tree structure.

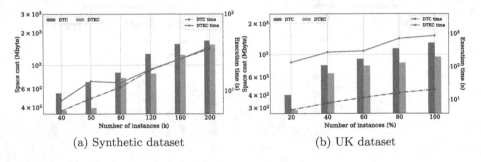

(a) Synthetic dataset   (b) UK dataset

Fig. 8. Space cost and execution time on different numbers of instances.

However, in both datasets in Fig. 8, the space cost of DTkC is always smaller than that of DTC. This is because the depth-first clique search generates fewer candidate co-locations compared to the merging method in DTC. In addition, another reason is that dataset in Fig. 8(b) has more features compared to Fig. 8(a), resulting in a larger average number of neighbors generated in DTkC compared to DTC. This also leads to a significantly larger number of cliques to traverse in the I-tree due to the higher average number of neighbors in DTkC, while the average number of neighbors in DTC is around 4–5.

Based on the above analysis, it can be seen that the DTkC algorithm is more suitable for dense datasets compared to DTC and datasets have fewer features. This is because it effectively reduces space cost while keeping the increase in execution time relatively low compared to the DTC algorithm (Fig. 9).

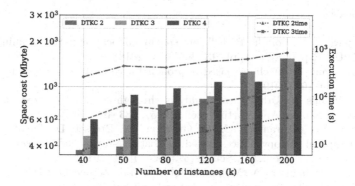

Fig. 9. Space cost and execution time on different k values ($min_{prev} = 0.2$).

On Different Values of k: Finally, we compare the scalability of DTkC based on the parameter k and the number of instances. It can be observed that both the execution time and space cost of DTkC show an increasing trend. However, the increase in space cost is not significant compared to the rate of increase in execution time. It is evident that the rapid increase in execution time of DTkC is an inherent characteristic of this dense dataset. However, it is uncommon to choose a large value for k, as the average number of neighbors can reach tens or more. The advantage lies in the fact that the space cost does not increase significantly, which is beneficial when dealing with dense data.

6   Conclusion

Mining SPCPs based on a distance threshold is challenging for users as it often leads to either missing or excessive patterns that may not align with their research objectives because it is difficult to find a suitable value of the threshold. This work proposes a combined algorithm called DTkC, which leverages a Delaunay triangulation-based approach to address the issue of determining neighbor relationships. The algorithm also incorporates the concept of k-order neighbors, allowing users to choose neighbor hierarchies based on their specific research needs rather than being limited to a fixed number of neighbors. Furthermore, DTkC uses a depth-first clique search strategy, resulting in enhanced computational efficiency and reduced memory consumption. The efficiency of DTkC is proved on both real and synthetic datasets and in multiple respects.

In the future, we aim to improve the performance of DTkC for datasets with moderate distribution density or datasets with a large number of features. As the parameter k increases by only one unit, the number of collected co-location patterns significantly increases. To address this issue and obtain a more accurate count of co-location patterns while avoiding data redundancy, we intend to explore and integrate suitable methods or techniques into the algorithm.

References

1. Andrzejewski, W., Boinski, P.: Efficient spatial co-location pattern mining on multiple GPUs. Expert Syst. Appl. **93**, 465–483 (2018)
2. Bao, X., Wang, L.: A clique-based approach for co-location pattern mining. Inf. Sci. **490**, 244–264 (2019)
3. Lee, I., Phillips, P.: Urban crime analysis through areal categorized multivariate associations mining. Appl. Artif. Intell. **22**(5), 483–499 (2008)
4. Leibovici, D.G., Claramunt, C., Le Guyader, D., Brosset, D.: Local and global spatio-temporal entropy indices based on distance-ratios and co-occurrences distributions. Int. J. Geogr. Inf. Sci. **28**(5), 1061–1084 (2014)
5. Li, J., Adilmagambetov, A., Mohomed Jabbar, M.S., Zaïane, O.R., Osornio-Vargas, A., Wine, O.: On discovering co-location patterns in datasets: a case study of pollutants and child cancers. GeoInformatica **20**(4), 651–692 (2016)
6. Luna, J.M., Fournier-Viger, P., Ventura, S.: Frequent itemset mining: a 25 years review. WIREs Data Min. Knowl. Discovery **9**(6), e1329 (2019)
7. Qian, F., Chiew, K., He, Q., Huang, H.: Mining regional co-location patterns with k NNG. J. Intell. Inf. Syst. **42**, 485–505 (2014)
8. Sundaram, V.M., Paneer, P., et al.: Discovering co-location patterns from spatial domain using a delaunay approach. Procedia Eng. **38**, 2832–2845 (2012)
9. Tran, V., Wang, L.: Delaunay triangulation-based spatial colocation pattern mining without distance thresholds. Stat. Anal. Data Min. **13**(3), 282–304 (2020)
10. Tran, V., Wang, L., Chen, H., Xiao, Q.: MCHT: a maximal clique and hash table-based maximal prevalent co-location pattern mining algorithm. Expert Syst. Appl. **175**, 114830 (2021)
11. Wang, L., Bao, Y., Lu, J., Yip, J.: A new join-less approach for co-location pattern mining. In: CIT, pp. 197–202. IEEE (2008)
12. Wang, L., Bao, Y., Lu, Z.: Efficient discovery of spatial co-location patterns using the iCPI-tree. Open Inf. Syst. J. **3**(1), 69–80 (2009)
13. Yang, X., Cui, W.: A novel spatial clustering algorithm based on delaunay triangulation. In: ICEODPA, vol. 7285, pp. 916–924. SPIE (2008)
14. Yao, X., Jiang, X., Wang, D., Yang, L., Peng, L., Chi, T.: Efficiently mining maximal co-locations in a spatial continuous field under directed road networks. Inf. Sci. **542**, 357–379 (2021)
15. Yoo, J.S., Boulware, D., Kimmey, D.: A parallel spatial co-location mining algorithm based on mapreduce. In: IEEE BigData, pp. 25–31. IEEE (2014)
16. Yoo, J.S., Boulware, D., Kimmey, D.: Parallel co-location mining with MapReduce and NoSQL systems. Knowl. Inf. Syst. **62**, 1433–1463 (2020)

17. Yoo, J.S., Bow, M.: A framework for generating condensed co-location sets from spatial databases. Intell. Data Anal. **23**(2), 333–355 (2019)
18. Yoo, J.S., Shekhar, S.: A joinless approach for mining spatial colocation patterns. IEEE T. Knowl. Data Eng. **18**(10), 1323–1337 (2006)
19. Yoo, J.S., Shekhar, S., Smith, J., Kumquat, J.P.: A partial join approach for mining co-location patterns. In: GIS, pp. 241–249 (2004)

Boosting Similar Compounds Searches via Correlated Subgraph Analysis

Yuma Naoi[1]($\boxtimes$) (ID) and Hiroaki Shiokawa[2] (ID)

[1] Department of Computer Science, University of Tsukuba, Tsukuba, Japan
naoi@kde.cs.tsukuba.ac.jp
[2] Center for Computational Sciences, University of Tsukuba, Tsukuba, Japan
shiokawa@cs.tsukuba.ac.jp

Abstract. Graph similarity search (GSS) models chemical compounds as a graph database. GSS is an essential tool for drug discovery because they can find similar graphs (compounds) for a query. Existing GSS methods have two critical limitations. First, handling large databases is time consuming. Second, finding compounds with the structure-activity relationship (SAR), which is vital in drug discovery, remains difficult. Herein a novel graph-based method for chemical compound searches is proposed to overcome these limitations. Since compounds with SAR share similar substructures, the proposed method extracts correlated subgraphs included in a query and explores similar compounds. In practical drug discovery task, our method achieves faster searches and improved accuracy compared to existing methods.

Keywords: Chemical compound database · Similarity search · Graph database

1 Introduction

Computer-aided drug design methods have contributed significantly to drug discovery processes. The demand for efficient algorithmic approaches to enhance drug discovery is increasing due to the exponential growth of chemical compound data. One example is ligand-based virtual screening (LBVS) [1,2]. LBVS is a common computational step to identify chemical compounds likely to bind to a drug target from a compound database. For effective screening, LBVS focuses on the so-called *structure-activity relationship (SAR)* because compounds with comparable chemical structures often exhibit similar chemical properties [10]. Thus, potential therapeutic targets for a specific disease may be effectively searched by finding structurally similar compounds in a database. Hence, similar compound searches are vital for LBVS.

Recently, graph-based similarity search (GSS) has drawn attention in LBVS since a labeled graph naturally represents a chemical compound [1,2,6,14,17]. Specifically, GSS models a chemical compound database as a graph database, which is a set of small graphs corresponding to compounds. Given a query graph (a chemical compound), GSS finds compounds most similar to the query in a database.

Several approaches can be used to measure the similarity between two graphs [2,6]. For instance, Cao et al. employed the *maximum common substructure* (MCS) [2] as a similarity measure in LBVS, where MCS measures the largest sized subgraphs shared between two graphs. Recently, Garcia et al. proposed the *graph edit distance* (GED)-based method [6]. Given two graphs G_i and G_j, the GED-based method evaluates the similarity by counting the number of node and edge insertions, deletions, and replacements necessary to transform G_i to G_j. Unlike MCS, the GED-based method can measure the similarity between graphs that do not share subgraphs. Hence, the GED-based method is now a de facto standard method in LBVS [4,25].

Although the GED-based method is effective in LBVS, it has two critical limitations. First, handling large-scale compound databases is expensive since a GED computation is an NP-hard problem [26]. Although A*-based approaches have been proposed to alleviate the high costs [5,19], they require $\mathcal{O}(\overline{n}^3)$ time, where $\overline{n}$ is the average size of graphs included in a graph database. Second, the GED-based method often fails to find similar compounds with SAR, significantly degrading the search accuracy in LBVS. This is because GED is not a scale-invariant measure. The GED-based method yields small similarities for two graphs if they have imbalanced graph sizes. Consequently, employing the GED-based method to perform LBVS on large-scale compound databases remains difficult.

1.1 Existing Approaches and Challenges

Recent studies have tried to address the aforementioned limitations [3]. Filter-and-verification methods [11,24,27,28] are the most common approaches to overcome the high complexity of GED-based methods. These methods exclude unpromising graphs from a database before running similarity searches. They initially construct offline indexes such as q-gram-based and subgraph-based ones over a graph database. Then for a given query graph and a given GED threshold, they filter out unpromising graphs from the database using offline indexes. Finally, they verify that the remaining graphs yield larger similarities than the given threshold. Since the indexes allow these methods to skip computing unpromising graphs, the number of computed graphs included in a graph database is reduced.

Although filter-and-verification methods decrease the running time of similarity searches, handling large-scale graph databases is burdensome because these methods still require expensive costs for each GED computation. For instance, the state-of-the-art method [28] repeatedly incurs $\mathcal{O}(\overline{n}^3)$ time in the worst case. Furthermore, as described above, GED-based methods often fail to find compounds with SAR since GED is not a scale-invariant measure. This limitation has yet to be resolved satisfactorily. Hence, efficiently finding similar compounds with SAR for LBVS remains a challenge.

1.2 Our Approach and Contributions

This paper aims to achieve efficient and accurate similar compound searches for LBVS. Specifically, we propose a novel graph-based algorithm to find compounds with SAR from a database. Existing approaches are not scale-invariant measures. Unlike existing approaches with a low search accuracy, the proposed method introduces correlated subgraph analysis to avoid scale-invariant similarity searches. Since compounds with SAR often share similar chemical structures, they should have a strong positive correlation in occurrences of their induced subgraphs. Consequently, our proposed algorithm finds similar compounds with SAR without a graph-size bias by measuring the occurrence correlation.

We devised our method using the following steps. First, for a given query, we theoretically derived the correlated subgraphs included in a graph database based on the state-of-the-art correlated subgraph analysis [9]. Second, we defined *correlation-aware graph vector* to characterize graphs in the database based on the correlated subgraphs. Finally, we provided a similar compound search algorithm using correlation-aware graph vectors. As a result, our proposed algorithm has the following attractive characteristics:

– **Efficient:** Our proposed method is faster than the state-of-the-art GED-based method (Sect. 4.2). On average, it is 228.5 times faster than the state-of-the-art method on practical datasets.
– **Effective:** Our correlation-aware approach effectively finds similar compounds with SAR in practical drug discovery scenarios (Sect. 4.1). We experimentally confirmed that our method has a higher search accuracy than the state-of-the-art method.
– **Scalable:** Our proposed method is more scalable than the state-of-the-art GED-based method (Sect. 4.2). Our method shows a nearly linear scalability against the average graph size of a database, whereas the GED-based method requires an exponential running time.

Our proposed algorithm is the first solution that focuses on the correlated subgraph structures included in compounds with SAR. We experimentally demonstrate that our algorithm outperforms the state-of-the-art GED-based method in terms of running time and search accuracy. For instance, our method finds SAR compounds from compounds targeting adenosine deaminase within 100 s, while the state-of-the-art GED-based method [3] did not finish the similarity search within 7,200 s. Although GSS now plays a crucial role in drug discovery, its applicability to larger databases is limited. However, our efficient approach should enhance the effectiveness of LBVS.

The rest of this paper is organized as follows. Section 2 describes the background. Section 3 introduces our proposed algorithm. Section 4 details our experimental results on real-world datasets. Finally, Sect. 5 concludes this paper.

2 Preliminary

Here, a chemical compound is modeled as a labeled undirected graph whose nodes and edges correspond to atoms and chemical bonds, respectively. Let $g =$

(V, E, L) be a labeled undirected graph, where V, E, and L are a set of nodes, a set of edges, and their labels, respectively. Hereafter, we denote $n = |V|$ and $m = |E|$ for simplicity.

A graph database $\mathcal{D}$ is a collection of N graphs, which are denoted by $\mathcal{D} = \{g_1, g_2, \ldots, g_N\}$. Given two graphs $g_i = (V_i, E_i, L_i)$ and $g_j = (V_j, E_j, L_j)$, $g_i \subseteq g_j$ if an injective function $f : V_i \rightarrow V_j$ exists. If $g_i \subseteq g_j$, then g_i is a *subgraph* of g_j (or g_j is a *supergraph* of g_i). Given graph database $\mathcal{D}$, we denote $\mathcal{D}_g = \{g' \mid g \subseteq g'\}$ as the set of all supergraphs of g included in $\mathcal{D}$.

Finally, we formulate the problem addressed in this paper. Let $sim(g_i, g_j)$ be a function to measure the similarity between two graphs, g_i and g_j. For a given query graph q, g_i is regarded as more similar to q than g_j if $sim(q, g_i) > sim(q, g_j)$ holds. Herein we focus on the top-k similar graph search problem, which is formalized as follows:

Problem 1. *Given query graph q, graph database $\mathcal{D}$, and similarity function $sim(g_i, g_j) : \mathcal{D} \times \mathcal{D} \rightarrow \mathbb{R}$, the top-$k$ similar graph search problem is a task to find k graphs in $\mathcal{D}$, $\mathcal{R}_k(q) = \{g_1, g_2, \ldots, g_N\}$ to maximize $\sum_{g_i \in \mathcal{R}_k(q)} sim(q, g_i)$.*

In Problem 1, existing GED-based methods employ the inverse of the graph edit distance as $sim(g_i, g_j)$. Not only are these approaches time-consuming since each GED computation incurs $\mathcal{O}(\overline{n}^3)$ time but their graph edit distance is not a scale-invariant measure. Thus, $\mathcal{R}_k(q)$ obtained by GED-based methods often excludes compounds with SAR.

3 Proposed Method: Correlation-Aware Approach

We present our correlation-aware approach to achieve efficient and accurate similar compound searches for LBVS.

3.1 Basic Ideas

Our proposed algorithm finds compounds with SAR within a short computation time. For Problem 1, existing GED-based methods measure the similarity between graphs using the whole of the graphs based on GED. Because GED is not scale-invariant, this approach degrades the search accuracy. In contrast, our algorithm selectively utilizes subgraphs in the graphs for a similarity computation. This avoids comparing the whole of the graphs. To this end, our proposed algorithm introduces the following approaches:

1. **Correlated Subgraph Extraction:** To select the subgraphs for the similarity computation, our algorithm invokes a *correlated subgraph extraction*. This extraction finds the most correlated subgraphs in $\mathcal{D}$ for a given query graph q. Since compounds with SAR should include many subgraphs correlated to the query, our algorithm generates a *correlation-aware graph vector* that is characterized by the presence of correlated subgraphs in each graph.

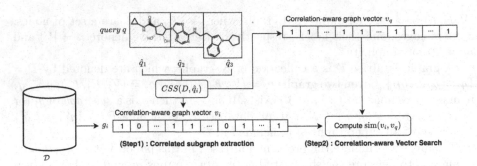

Fig. 1. Overview of the proposed method.

2. **Correlation-Aware Graph Search:** Given a set of graph vectors, our algorithm explores the top-k graphs that are the most similar to the query graph. As for the similarity function $sim(g_i, g_j)$ in Problem 1, our algorithm utilizes the correlation between the query and a graph in $\mathcal{D}$.

These simple approaches have two advantages. First, our algorithm can find compounds with SAR, even the graph sizes are imbalanced. Our algorithm measures the similarity between graphs based on the presence of subgraphs, which provides a scale-invariant comparison. Hence, our approach should outperform existing GED-based methods. Second, our algorithm can compute a graph similarity within a short computation time. Unlike GED-based methods, which require $\mathcal{O}(\overline{n}^3)$ time for each similarity computation, our correlation-aware graph search can compute similarity in a constant time. In Sect. 4, we experimentally discuss the effectiveness of our approach on practical compound databases.

3.2   Algorithm

Algorithm 1 shows the pseudocode of our proposed algorithm. Figure 1 overviews our algorithm. Given a graph database $\mathcal{D}$ and a query graph q, our algorithm returns the top-k graphs $\mathcal{R}_k(q)$, which are the most similar to q in $\mathcal{D}$. Algorithm 1 is roughly divided into two steps: (Step 1) correlated subgraph extraction and (Step 2) correlation-aware graph search.

(Step 1) Correlated Subgraph Extraction. The correlated subgraph extraction constructs the correlation-aware graph vector for each graph included in graph database $\mathcal{D}$. Graph vectors characterize graphs based on the presence of subgraphs correlated to the query graph. In this paper, we extend *Pearson's correlation* [18] to measure the correlation between two graphs. Formally, the correlation is defined as:

Algorithm 1. Proposed Method

Input: $\mathcal{D} = \{g_1, g_2, \ldots, g_N\}$, $q = (V_q. E_q, L_q)$, and $k, \in \mathbb{N}$;
Output: $\mathcal{R}_k(q)$;
1: $\mathcal{R}_k(q) \leftarrow \emptyset, \mathcal{C} \leftarrow \emptyset$;

▷ **(Step 1) Correlated subgraph extraction:**
2: $\mathcal{Q} = \{\hat{q_1}, \hat{q_2}, \ldots, \hat{q_p}\} \leftarrow \text{PARTITION}(q)$;
3: **for each** $\hat{q_i} \in \mathcal{Q}$ **do**
4:     $\mathcal{C}_t(\hat{q_i}) \leftarrow \text{CSS}(\mathcal{D}, \hat{q_i}, t)$;
5:     $\mathcal{C} \leftarrow \mathcal{C} \cup \{\mathcal{C}_k(\hat{q_i})\}$;

6: **for each** $g_i \in \mathcal{D}$ **do**
7:     Generate $\mathbf{v}_i \in \{0, 1\}^{(p \times t)}$ by Definition 4;

▷ **(Step 2) Correlation-aware graph search:**
8: **for each** $g_i \in \mathcal{D}$ **do**
9:     Obtain sim_k and g_k from $\mathcal{R}_k(q)$;
10:     **if** $sim(v_q, v_i) > sim_k$ **then**
11:         $\mathcal{R}_k(q) \leftarrow \{\mathcal{R}_k(q) \backslash \{g_k\}\} \cup \{g_i\}$;
12: **return** $\mathcal{R}_k(q)$;

Definition 1 (Correlation).   *Given two graphs g_i and g_j, a correlation between the graphs, denoted by $\phi(g_i, g_j)$, is defined as*

$$\phi(g_i, g_j) = \frac{sup(g_i, g_j) - sup(g_i)sup(g_j)}{\sqrt{sup(g_i)sup(g_j)(1 - sup(g_i))(1 - sup(g_j))}}, \qquad (1)$$

where $sup(g_i) = \frac{|\mathcal{D}_{g_i}|}{|\mathcal{D}|}$, and $sup(g_i, g_j) = \frac{|\mathcal{D}_{g_i} \cap \mathcal{D}_{g_j}|}{|\mathcal{D}|}$. Note that $\phi(g_i, g_j) = 0$ if $sup(g_i)sup(g_j)(1 - sup(g_i))(1 - sup(g_j)) = 0$.

$\phi(g_i, g_j)$ falls between -1 and 1. $\phi(g_i, g_j) = 0$ means that the occurrences of g_i and g_j in $\mathcal{D}$ are independent. If $\phi(g_i, g_j) > 0$, the occurrences of g_i and g_j are positively correlated in $\mathcal{D}$; otherwise, they are negatively correlated.

By Definition 1, we then define the correlated subgraphs to query graph g as follows:

Definition 2 (Correlated Subgraphs).   *Given graph database $\mathcal{D}$, graph g, and $t \in \mathbb{N}$, the correlated subgraphs of graphs in $\mathcal{D}$ is defined as $\mathcal{C}_t(g) = \{\hat{g_1}, \hat{g_2}, \ldots, \hat{g_t}\}$, where $\mathcal{C}_t(g)$ satisfies the following conditions:*

1. For each $\hat{g} \in \mathcal{C}_t(g)$, there exists $g' \in \mathcal{D}$ such that $\hat{g} \subseteq g'$.
2. $\mathcal{C}_t(g)$ maximizes $\sum_{\hat{g} \in \mathcal{C}_t(g)} \phi(g, \hat{g})$.

Definition 2 indicates that $\mathcal{C}_t(g)$ is the top-t correlated subgraph that yields the largest correlation with g such that $\forall \hat{g} \in \mathcal{C}_t(q), |\mathcal{D}_{\hat{g}}| \geq 1$. Here, we set $t = 30$ as the default setting.

To find $\mathcal{C}_t(g)$ from $\mathcal{D}$, several correlated subgraph search (CSS) methods have been proposed [7–9,17]. Our algorithm employs the state-of-the-art CSS method [9], which is denoted as CSS in Algorithm 1 (line 4), to find the top-t correlated subgraphs. Other CSS methods can also be applied in the same manner.

Finally, we define the correlation-aware graph vectors based on Definition 2. Prior to graph vector generation, our method partitions query graph q into subgraphs. Then it extracts top-t correlated subgraphs for each subgraph based on Definition 2. Specifically, as shown in Algorithm 1 (line 2), q is partitioned into p-disjoint subgraphs $\mathcal{Q} = \{\hat{q}_1, \hat{q}_2, \ldots, \hat{q}_p\}$ by graph partitioning methods [16,20–23]. After that, our method extracts the top-t correlated subgraphs $\mathcal{C} = \{\mathcal{C}_t(\hat{q}_1), \mathcal{C}_t(\hat{q}_2), \ldots, \mathcal{C}_t(\hat{q}_p)\}$ using the subgraphs in $\mathcal{Q}$.

For each correlated subgraph set in $\mathcal{C}$, we generate a local correlation-aware graph vector defined as follows:

Definition 3 (Local Correlation-Aware Graph Vector). *Given the top-t correlated subgraphs, $\mathcal{C}_t(\hat{q}_j) = \{\hat{g}_1, \hat{g}_2, \ldots, \hat{g}_t\}$, which are obtained by Definition 2, a local correlation-aware graph vector of $g_i \in \mathcal{D}$ is defined as $v_{i,j} \in \{0,1\}^t$, where its l-th element, $v_{i,j}^{(l)}$, is given by*

$$v_{i,j}^{(l)} = \begin{cases} 1 & (\hat{g}_l \subseteq g_i) \\ 0 & (\hat{g}_l \nsubseteq g_i) \end{cases}. \tag{2}$$

Based on Definition 3, the correlation-aware graph vector is defined as:

Definition 4 (Correlation-Aware Graph Vector). *For two vectors v_i and v_j, let $v_i \oplus v_j$ be a binary operation to concatenate v_i and v_j into the same vector.*

Given a set of query subgraphs $\mathcal{Q} = \{\hat{q}_1, \hat{q}_2, \ldots, \hat{q}_p\}$ and their corresponding correlated subgraphs $\mathcal{C} = \{\mathcal{C}_t(\hat{q}_1), \mathcal{C}_t(\hat{q}_2), \ldots, \mathcal{C}_t(\hat{q}_p)\}$, a correlation-aware graph vector of $g_i \in \mathcal{D}$, denoted by v_i, is defined as

$$v_i = v_{i,1} \oplus v_{i,2} \oplus \cdots \oplus v_{i,p}, \tag{3}$$

where $v_{i,j}$ is a local correlation-aware graph vector of $\mathcal{C}_t(\hat{q}_j)$ given by Definition 3.

Definition 4 indicates that $\mathbf{v}_i$ is a $(t \times p)$-dimensional vector of g_i, which represents the presence of correlated subgraphs included in $\mathcal{C}$.

(Step 2) Correlation-Aware Graph Search. In this step, our algorithm explores the top-k graphs that are the most similar to the query graph q. To find similar graphs based on correlations, our proposed method measures the similarity by utilizing the correlation-aware graph vectors obtained in Step 1. Specifically, for two given graph vectors, the similarity between two graphs is defined based on the Jaccard coefficient [12].

Definition 5 (Similarity). *Given two graphs g_i and g_j, the similarity between g_i and g_j, denoted by $sim(g_i, g_j)$, is defined as*

$$sim(g_i, g_j) = \frac{v_i \cdot v_j}{\|v_i\|_1 + \|v_j\|_1 - v_i \cdot v_j}, \tag{4}$$

Table 1. Statistics of datasets.

ID	Dataset	N	$\bar{n}$	# of actives	Drug target	Source
$\mathcal{D}_1$	ADA	5,554	23.3	104	Adenosine deaminase	[13]
$\mathcal{D}_2$	AKT2	7,137	29.1	237	Serine/threonine-protein kinase	[13]
$\mathcal{D}_3$	FABP4	2,797	26.8	47	Fatty acid binding protein adipocyte	[13]
$\mathcal{D}_4$	AA2AR	10,000	28.0	200	Adenosine A2A receptor	[13]
$\mathcal{D}_5$	ESR_ant	5,048	17.6	101	Estrogen receptor α	[15]
$\mathcal{D}_6$	TP53	4,245	17.5	78	Cellular tumor antigen p53	[15]
$\mathcal{D}_7$	ALDH1	10,000	23.8	250	Aldehyde dihydrogenase 1	[15]
$\mathcal{D}_8$	MAPK1	10,000	24.1	250	Mitogen-activated protein kinase 1	[15]

where v_i is the correlation-aware graph vector of g_i obtained by Definition 4, and $\|v_i\|_1$ is L^1-norm of v_i.

As shown in Definition 5, each similarity computation incurs $\mathcal{O}(t \cdot p)$ time since $\mathbf{v}_i$ and $\mathbf{v}_j$ are $(t \times p)$-dimensional vectors.

Based on Definition 5, our proposed method explores the top-k similar graphs from $\mathcal{D}$ for query graph q. As shown in Algorithm 1 (line 9), the k-th largest similarity value and its corresponding graph are maintained as sim_k and g_k in $\mathcal{R}_k(q)$ during the similarity searches. Finally, our algorithm outputs the top-k similarity search results $\mathcal{R}_k(q)$ after computing all similarities of graphs in $\mathcal{D}$.

4 Experimental Analysis

We experimentally evaluated the effectiveness of our proposed method by comparing it to the state-of-the-art GED-based method.

- **Proposed Method:** Our proposed algorithm is described in Sect. 3. We employed modularity-based partitioning [16] and TopCor [9] for the PARTITION and CSS invoked in Algorithm 1, respectively. Unless otherwise stated, we set $p = 4$.
- **GED-Based Method:** The state-of-the-art GED-based method [3] returns graphs that yield a smaller GED than a user-specified threshold τ. To solve Problem 1, τ was varied from 1 to $|V_q|$ until the top-k graphs were obtained.

Both methods were implemented using C++ and compiled by gcc 9.2.0 with the "-O3" option. All experiments were conducted on a Linux server with an Intel Xeon CPU 2.90 GHz and 1 TiB RAM. For reproducibility, we will make the codes available upon publication of this paper.

Datasets: We tested eight practical chemical compound databases published by DUD-E [13] and LIT-PCBA [15]. Table 1 shows their statistics, where $\bar{n}$ denotes the average number of nodes in each database. Each database contains two types of compounds: *active* and *inactive*. Active compounds can activate their corresponding drug target, while inactive ones cannot.

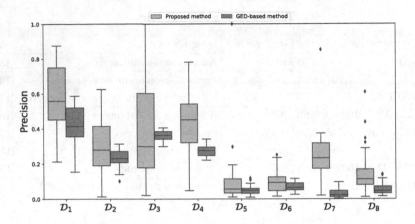

Fig. 2. Precision of the top-k search results.

Query: For the query graphs, active compounds were randomly selected from each database. Here, the results were averaged over the above ten queries. Unless otherwise stated, we set k to the same number of actives, excluding a query graph. For example, in the case of $\mathcal{D}_1$, k was set to 103.

4.1   Accuracy

Unlike the GED-based method, our proposed method provides a scale-invariant measure for finding the top-k similar graphs. Thus, we evaluated the top-k search accuracy against the ground-truth top-k search results to verify this advantage. We considered compounds categorized as active to be the ground-truth and used *precision* [12] to measure the accuracy compared with the ground-truth results.

Figure 2 compares the precision scores of our algorithm and the state-of-the-art GED-based method to the ground truth. Our algorithm yields higher precision scores than the GED-based method. Because our proposed algorithm evaluates the similarity between two graphs based on the presence of correlated subgraphs, it can fairly evaluate the similarity of graphs even if the node sizes are imbalanced. In contrast, a node size imbalance negatively affects the GED-based method since the graph edit distance is effective only if graphs have similar sizes. Therefore, our algorithm outperforms the GED-based method in terms of the top-k similarity search accuracy on chemical compound databases.

4.2   Efficiency

We experimentally investigated the efficiency of our proposed algorithm. Figure 3 shows the query processing time to find the top-k similar graphs on each database, where DNF indicates that the running time exceeded 7,200 s. Our algorithm achieves the highest overall performance. On average, it is 228.5 times faster than the state-of-the-art GED-based method. In some instances, our algorithm is up to 927.7 times faster than the GED-based method.

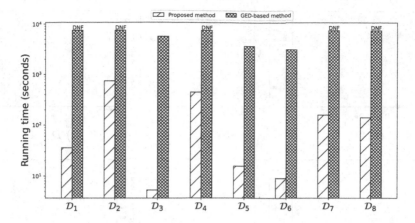

Fig. 3. Running time on real-world databases.

Additionally, our proposed method is more scalable than the GED-based method, even if a dataset has a large $\overline{n}$. As an example, consider the running times on $\mathcal{D}_1$ and $\mathcal{D}_5$ in Fig. 3. Although the two databases have roughly the same number of graphs, (*i.e.*, N is about 5,000), $\mathcal{D}_1$ has a larger $\overline{n}$ than $\mathcal{D}_5$.

The GED-based method has a much longer running time on $\mathcal{D}_1$ compared with that on $\mathcal{D}_5$ because it incurs $\mathcal{O}(\overline{n}^3)$ costs in the worst case. In contrast, our proposed algorithm introduces correlation-aware graph searches to mitigate the expensive similarity computation costs even as $\overline{n}$ increases. Consequently, our algorithm efficiently finds top-k similar graphs for large $\overline{n}$.

4.3   Impacts of Parameters

Finally, we experimentally assessed the impact of the inner parameter p included in our proposed method, where p is the number of query subgraphs partitioned from query graph q. To evaluate the impact of p, we investigated the running time and precision of our proposed method on real-world datasets by varying p as 2, 3, and 4.

Figure 4 and Fig. 5 show the running time and precision of our proposed method, respectively. Although the running time slightly improves for smaller p settings, increasing p has a minimal impact on the running time, except for $\mathcal{D}_2$. In contrast, smaller p settings yield a better precision than larger ones in the real-world databases, except for $\mathcal{D}_7$ and $\mathcal{D}_8$. Since every graph in the database can include small query subgraphs, it is difficult for a large p setting to characterize the graphs based on the correlation. Consequently, setting p to a smaller value for our proposed method is appropriate if the average graph size is small.

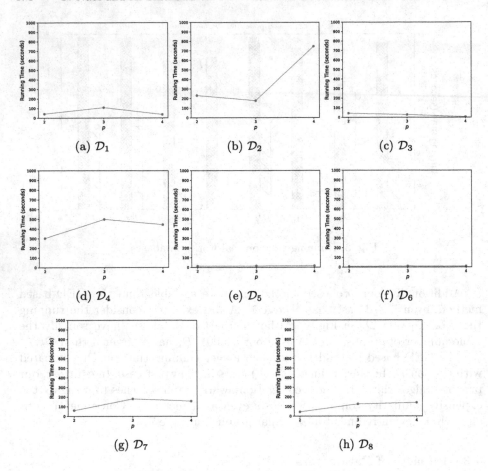

(a) $\mathcal{D}_1$ (b) $\mathcal{D}_2$ (c) $\mathcal{D}_3$

(d) $\mathcal{D}_4$ (e) $\mathcal{D}_5$ (f) $\mathcal{D}_6$

(g) $\mathcal{D}_7$ (h) $\mathcal{D}_8$

Fig. 4. Impact of p on the running time

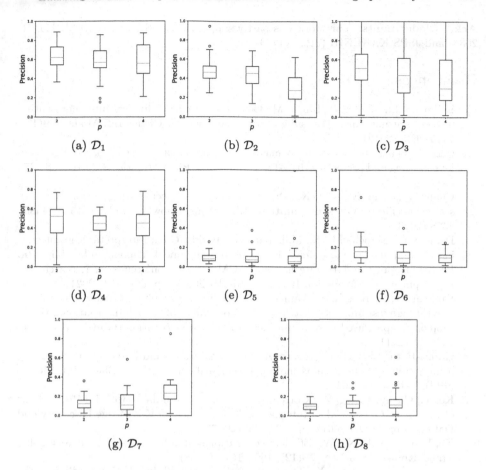

Fig. 5. Impact of p on the precision

5   Conclusion

Here, we address the problem of GSS for LBVS in drug discovery. Given a graph database composed of chemical compounds and a query compound, our proposed algorithm finds the top-k similar graphs for the query from the database. Our algorithm captures the correlated subgraph structures between the query and the database to realize a more accurate search compared to the existing GED-based method. Then by extracting the correlated subgraphs from the database, our proposed method generates correlation-aware graph vectors and performs vector-based similarity searches using scale-invariant similarity. Experiments demonstrate that the proposed method offers improved efficiency and top-k search accuracy on practical compound databases compared to the state-of-the-art GED-based method. Because GSS methods are essential in LBVS, employing our algorithm should advance the leading edge of drug discovery.

Acknowledgements. This work was partly supported by JST PRESTO (JPMJPR-2033) and JSPS KAKENHI (JP22K17894).

References

1. Bellmann, L., Penner, P., Rarey, M.: Connected subgraph fingerprints: representing molecules using exhaustive subgraph enumeration. J. Chem. Inf. Model. **59**(11), 4625–4635 (2019)
2. Cao, Y., Jiang, T., Girke, T.: A maximum common substructure-based algorithm for searching and predicting drug-like compounds. Bioinformatics **24**(13), i366–i374 (2008)
3. Chang, L., Feng, X., Yao, K., Qin, L., Zhang, W.: Accelerating graph similarity search via efficient GED computation. IEEE Trans. Knowl. Data Eng. **35**(5), 4485–4498 (2023)
4. Doan, K.D., Manchanda, S., Mahapatra, S., Reddy, C.K.: Interpretable graph similarity computation via differentiable optimal alignment of node embeddings. In: Proceedings of the 44th International ACM SIGIR Conference on Research and Development in Information Retrieval (SIGIR 2021), pp. 665–674 (2021)
5. Fankhauser, S., Riesen, K., Bunke, H.: Speeding up graph edit distance computation through fast bipartite matching. In: Proceedings of the 7th International Workshop on Graph-Based Representations in Pattern Recognition (GbRPR 2011), pp. 102–111 (2011)
6. Garcia-Hernandez, C., Fernández, A., Serratosa, F.: Ligand-based virtual screening using graph edit distance as molecular similarity measure. J. Chem. Inf. Model. **59**(4), 1410–1421 (2019)
7. Ke, Y., Cheng, J., Ng, W.: Correlation search in graph databases. In: Proceedings of the 13th ACM SIGKDD International Conference on Knowledge Discovery and Data Mining (KDD 2007), pp. 390–399 (2007)
8. Ke, Y., Cheng, J., Ng, W.: Efficient correlation search from graph databases. IEEE Trans. Knowl. Data Eng. **20**(12), 1601–1615 (2008)
9. Ke, Y., Cheng, J., Yu, J.X.: Top-k correlative graph mining. In: Proceedings of the 2009 SIAM International Conference on Data Mining (SDM 2009), pp. 1038–1049 (2009)
10. Lee, E.S.A., Fung, S., Sze-To, H.Y., Wong, A.K.C.: Discovering co-occurring patterns and their biological significance in protein families. BMC Bioinformatics **15**(S2), 13 (2014)
11. Liang, Y., Zhao, P.: Similarity search in graph databases: a multi-layered indexing approach. In: Proceedings of the 33rd IEEE International Conference on Data Engineering (ICDE 2017), pp. 783–794 (2017)
12. Manning, C.D., Raghavan, P., Schütze, H.: Introduction to Information Retrieval. Cambridge University Press, Cambridge (2008)
13. Mysinger, M.M., Carchia, M., Irwin, J.J., Shoichet, B.K.: Directory of useful decoys, enhanced (DUD-E): better ligands and decoys for better benchmarking. J. Med. Chem. **55**(14), 6582–6594 (2012)
14. Nguyen, D.D., Wei, G.W.: AGL-score: algebraic graph learning score for protein-ligand binding scoring, ranking, docking, and screening. J. Chem. Inf. Model. **59**(7), 3291–3304 (2019)
15. Nguyen, V.K.T., Jacquemard, C., Rognan, D.: LIT-PCBA: an unbiased data set for machine learning and virtual screening. J. Chem. Inf. Model. **60**(9), 4263–4273 (2020)

16. Onizuka, M., Fujimori, T., Shiokawa, H.: Graph partitioning for distributed graph processing. Data Sci. Eng. **2**(1), 94–105 (2017)
17. Prateek, A., Khan, A., Goyal, A., Ranu, S.: Mining top-k pairs of correlated subgraphs in a large network. Proc. VLDB Endowm. **13**(9), 1511–1524 (2020)
18. Reynolds, H.T.: The Analysis of Cross-classifications. The Free Press, New York (1977)
19. Riesen, K., Emmenegger, S., Bunke, H.: A novel software toolkit for graph edit distance computation. In: Proceedings of the 9th International Workshop on Graph-Based Representations in Pattern Recognition (GbRPR 2013), pp. 142–151 (2013)
20. Shiokawa, H., Amagasa, T., Kitagawa, H.: Scaling fine-grained modularity clustering for massive graphs. In: Proceedings of the 28th International Joint Conference on Artificial Intelligence (IJCAI 2019), pp. 4597–4604 (2019)
21. Shiokawa, H., Fujiwara, Y., Onizuka, M.: Fast algorithm for modularity-based graph clustering. In: Proceedings of the 27th AAAI Conference on Artificial Intelligence (AAAI 2013) (2013)
22. Shiokawa, H., Fujiwara, Y., Onizuka, M.: SCAN++: efficient algorithm for finding clusters, hubs and outliers on large-scale graphs. Proc. VLDB Endowm. **8**(11), 1178–1189 (2015)
23. Shiokawa, H., Takahashi, T.: DSCAN: distributed structural graph clustering for billion-edge graphs. In: Proceedings of the 31st International Conference on Database and Expert Systems Applications (DEXA 2020), pp. 38–54 (2020)
24. Wang, X., Ding, X., Tung, A.K., Ying, S., Jin, H.: An efficient graph indexing method. In: Proceedings of the 28th IEEE International Conference on Data Engineering (ICDE 2012), pp. 210–221 (2012)
25. Yagi, R., Shiokawa, H.: Fast top-k similar sequence search on DNA databases. In: Proceedings of the 24th International Conference on Information Integration and Web Intelligence (iiWAS 2022), pp. 145–150 (2022)
26. Zeng, Z., Tung, A.K.H., Wang, J., Feng, J., Zhou, L.: Comparing stars: on approximating graph edit distance. Proc. VLDB Endowm. **2**(1), 25–36 (2009)
27. Zhao, X., Xiao, C., Lin, X., Wang, W., Ishikawa, Y.: Efficient processing of graph similarity queries with edit distance constraints. VLDB J. **22**(6), 727–752 (2013)
28. Zhao, X., Xiao, C., Lin, X., Zhang, W., Wang, Y.: Efficient structure similarity searches: a partition-based approach. VLDB J. **27**(1), 53–78 (2018)

Efficient Similarity Searches for Multivariate Time Series: A Hash-Based Approach

Yuma Yasuda[1]([⊠]) and Hiroaki Shiokawa[2][ID]

[1] Department of Computer Science, University of Tsukuba, Tsukuba, Japan
yasuda@kde.cs.tsukuba.ac.jp
[2] Center for Computational Sciences, University of Tsukuba, Tsukuba, Japan
shiokawa@cs.tsukuba.ac.jp

Abstract. Various fields from biomedicine to sports science employ similarity searches in multivariate time series (MvTS) to identify patterns and trends. Given MvTS and a query time series, a similarity search extracts a set of subsequences in the MvTS that yield the most significant similarity to the query. Although this is a fundamental task, similarity searches become computationally expensive as the length of the MvTS increases. Herein an efficient method is proposed to accelerate the search process. Using hash-based indexes for MvTS, our proposed method effectively approximates the similarity of each subsequence pair, enhancing the computational efficiency. An experiment involving synthetic and real-world MvTS datasets demonstrates that our proposed method has a higher efficiency and search accuracy compared to existing approaches.

Keywords: Multivariate time series · Similarity search · Hash-based algorithm

1 Introduction

Diverse fields employ time series data because such data contain one-dimensional real numbers, which represent temporal changes in phenomena [25]. Due to advances in information sciences, multivariate time series (MvTS) has become prevalent in many applications. Previous studies on MvTS have focused on one-dimensional time series data processing [5, 7, 10–12, 14, 16, 23, 28]. Specifically, MvTS, which is comprised of sequences of multidimensional real numbers, plays a vital role in biomedical data analysis [22, 26], and behavior analysis in athletic sciences [8, 24]. For example, attaching motion capture devices to the arms and legs to record boxing movements generates four-dimensional MvTS [27].

A similar subsequence search is an essential building block because such applications often handle similar subsequences observed in MvTS. Given MvTS and an MvTS query, the problem is finding a set of subsequences most similar

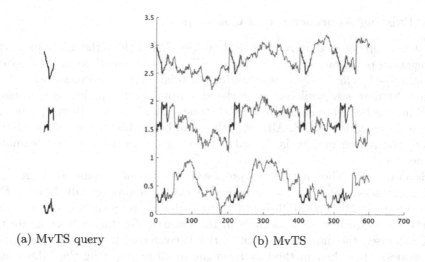

(a) MvTS query   (b) MvTS

Fig. 1. Example of a similar subsequence search on MvTS: Three-dimensional MvTS (right) is a toy dataset provided by [27]. Given a three-dimensional subsequence as a query (left), a similar subsequence search tries to find the subsequences highlighted in red from the MvTS.

to the query from MvTS. Because a similar subsequence search can identify subsequences with similar shapes of MvTS to the query, it is often used in MvTS-based analyses. Using the abovementioned boxing movements as an example, four-dimensional MvTS using a query representing the uppercut motion can identify an uppercut motion in the capture data.

Figure 1 shows an example of a similar subsequence search over MvTS for an MvTS query and an MvTS dataset. Once an MvTS query is inputted, the similar subsequence search outputs multivariate subsequences most similar to the query. The identified subsequences should represent the same motion, event, or phenomena as the query since they share very similar shapes.

Although a similar subsequence search is effective for MvTS-based analysis, it has a critical weakness. Large-scale MvTS datasets require expensive computational costs because all subsequences may be a candidate of the similar subsequences for a query. Consequently, the similarity between the query and each subsequence included in an MvTS dataset must be computed. Unlike traditional single-variate time series, MvTS includes multiple time series. Thus, a similar subsequence search requires a large query processing time if an MvTS dataset contains many long time series. This creates a critical problem in many practical applications since large-scale MvTS datasets are often utilized. For instance, Yamabe *et al.* reported that at least four-dimensional MvTS datasets must be computed to diagnose a sleep disorder, and each time series is composed of more than 15,552,000 real values (60 Hz × 72 h) [26]. Herein we propose an efficient search method for the similar subsequence search problem in MvTS.

1.1 Existing Approaches and Challenges

Classical approaches to overcome the above problem include the use of piecewise aggregate approximation (PAA) [7] and DFT [5]. These methods aim to reduce the data size by effectively approximating the original time series. Since they can reduce the data size while ensuring the similarity search quality, a reasonable speed up is achieved to handle large-scale time series. However, these approaches are not designed for MvTS. Although they can be applied to each dimension of MvTS, the search quality is degraded since each dimension is approximated independently.

Several approaches have been proposed to efficiently compute large-scale MvTS datasets. Tanaka *et al.* proposed a classic approach called the MDL-based method [23]. The MDL-based method detects frequently occurring multivariate subsequences as a motif from the dataset. To efficiently compute the MvTS dataset, the multivariate time series is converted into a one-dimensional time series. Then their method extracts the motif by applying the MDL-based approach to the one-dimensional time series. Recently, Yeh *et al.* reported a sophisticated approach, mSTAMP, which extracts motifs based on the Euclidean distance [27]. Before motif extraction, mSTAMP constructs the Matrix Profile [28],which stores the distance between a subsequence and its nearest neighbor for each time series in MvTS. By exploring various subsets of the multidimensional Matrix Profile, mSTAMP efficiently extracts semantically meaningful motifs from MvTS. The above approaches focus on extracting motifs. In contrast, our goal is to efficiently enumerate subsequences that are the most similar to a user-specified query MvTS. Since directly applying these approaches to query processing is difficult, achieving efficient similar subsequence searches on MvTS remains a challenge.

1.2 Our Approaches and Contributions

For a given MvTS query, we aim to find similar subsequences from an MvTS dataset efficiently. Our proposed search method outputs subsequences yielding a high Pearson coefficient [13] with the query. To improve the search efficiency, the proposed method pre-computes MvTS. In this pre-computation step, our method groups all subsequences in MvTS into clusters. Our method does not explore all subsequences in the MvTS since only clusters similar to the MvTS query are used.

The proposed method was developed in three steps. First, a locality-sensitive hash (LSH) function is defined for MvTS. Second, a subsequence clustering algorithm based on the LSH function is introduced by extending existing LSH-based approaches [1,6]. Using this clustering algorithm, our proposed method groups all subsequences into clusters. Finally, a similar subsequence search method over the clusters is realized. Our proposed method has the following attractive characteristics:

Table 1. Main symbols used in this paper.

Symbols	Definitions
$\mathbf{T}$	d-dimensional MvTS of length n (*i.e.*, $\mathbf{T} \in \mathbb{R}^{(d \times n)}$)
$T^{(i)}$	i-th one-dimensional time series in $\mathbf{T}$ (*i.e.*, $T^{(i)} \in \mathbf{R}^{(1 \times n)}$)
$t_j^{(i)}$	The j-th real value in $T^{(i)}$
d	Dimension of an MvTS $\mathbf{T}$
n	Length of an MvTS $\mathbf{T}$
$\mathbf{T}_{j,m}$	Subsequence of $\mathbf{T}$ that starts from its j-th element (*i.e.*, $\mathbf{T}_{j,m} \in \mathbb{R}^{(d \times m)}$)
$T_{j,m}^{(i)}$	Subsequence of $T^{(i)}$ that starts from its j-th element (*i.e.*, $T_{j,m}^{(i)} \in \mathbb{R}^{(1 \times m)}$)
$\mathbf{t}_{j,m}^k$	k-th column vector of $\mathbf{T}_{j,m}$ (*i.e.*, $\mathbf{t}_{j,m}^k \in \mathbb{R}^{(d \times 1)}$)
$\rho(\mathbf{T}_{i,m}, \mathbf{T}_{j,m})$	Peason correlation between $\mathbf{T}_{i,m}$ and $\mathbf{T}_{j,m}$ shown in Definition 1
$dist(\mathbf{T}_{i,m}, \mathbf{T}_{j,m})$	Distance between $\mathbf{T}_{i,m}$ and $\mathbf{T}_{j,m}$ shown in Definition 1
θ	User-specified threshold defined in Problem 1
$\mathcal{R}$	Set of similar subsequences to a query defined in Problem 1

- **Efficient:** Our method has a shorter query processing time (Sect. 4.1). Experiments demonstrate that the proposed method has a four times faster query processing time than existing alogrithms.
- **Scalable:** Our method is scalable (Sect. 4.2). It can perform searches efficiently regardless of the MvTS size.
- **Accurate:** Although our proposed method does not compute all subsequences, it has a higher accuracy than existing algorithms (Sect. 4.3). Experiments show that our method gives identical results to the ground truth.

Our proposed method has a higher efficiency and search accuracy compared to existing algorithms. Although a similar subsequence search is vital for biomedical and sports sciences, its applicability is limited for larger datasets. However, our hash-based approach should enhance the effectiveness of existing applications. The rest of this paper is organized as follows: Sect. 2 briefly describes the background of this paper. Section 3 introduces our proposed algorithm, while the experimental results on real-world datasets are provided in Sect. 4. Finally, Sect. 5 concludes this paper.

Organization: The rest of this paper is organized as follows: Sect. 2 briefly describes the backgrounds of this paper. Section 3 introduces our proposed algorithm, and we report experimental results on real-world datasets in Sect. 4. Finally, we conclude this paper in Sect. 5.

2 Preliminary

First, we introduce the basic notation. Table 1 summarizes the symbols and their corresponding definitions. MvTS, which is denoted by $\mathbf{T}$, is a set of z-normalized time series defined as $\mathbf{T} = \{T^{(1)}, T^{(2)}, \ldots, T^{(d)}\}$, where $T^{(i)}$ is a one-dimensional time series composed of n real values (*i.e.*, $T^{(j)} = \{t_1^{(i)}, t_2^{(i)}, \ldots, t_n^{(i)}\} \in \mathbb{R}^n$). That is, $\mathbf{T}$ is a d-dimensional time series whose length is equal to n (*i.e.*, $\mathbf{T} \in \mathbb{R}^{(d \times n)}$).

For a given one-dimensional time series $T^{(i)}$, its subsequence is defined as $T_{j,m}^{(i)} = \{t_j^{(i)}, t_{j+1}^{(i)}, \ldots, t_{j+m-1}^{(i)}\}$. The subsequence of length m starts from the j-th element of $T^{(j)}$. Additionally, we define a subsequence of MvTS $\mathbf{T}$ as $\mathbf{T}_{j,m} = \{T_{j,m}^{(1)}, T_{j,m}^{(2)}, \ldots, T_{j,m}^{(d)}\}$. That is, $\mathbf{T}_{j,m}$ can be regarded as a $(d \times m)$ matrix whose k-th column is defined as $\mathbf{t}_{j,m}^k = (t_{j+k-1}^{(1)}, t_{j+k-1}^{(2)}, \ldots, t_{j+k-1}^{(d)})^\top$ for $1 \leq k \leq m$. In this paper, we denote $\mathbf{T}_{j,m} \subseteq \mathbf{T}$ if $\mathbf{T}_{j,m}$ is a subsequence derived from $\mathbf{T}$.

We employ a similarity measure based on the Pearson coefficient [13], which is defined as follows:

Definition 1 (Pearson Coefficient).   *Given two subsequences of length m of MvTS, $\mathbf{T}_{i,m}$ and $\mathbf{T}_{j,m}$, the Pearson coefficient, which is denoted by $\rho(\mathbf{T}_{i,m}, \mathbf{T}_{j,m})$, is defined as*

$$\rho(\mathbf{T}_{i,m}, \mathbf{T}_{j,m}) = 1 - \frac{dist(\mathbf{T}_{i,m}, \mathbf{T}_{j,m})^2}{2m}, \tag{1}$$

where $dist(\mathbf{T}_{i,m}, \mathbf{T}_{j,m})$ is given by

$$dist(\mathbf{T}_{i,m}, \mathbf{T}_{j,m}) = \sqrt{\sum_{k=1}^{m} (t_{i,m}^k - t_{j,m}^k)^2}. \tag{2}$$

$\rho(\mathbf{T}_{i,m}, \mathbf{T}_{j,m})$ falls between -1 and 1. If $\mathbf{T}_{i,m}$ and $\mathbf{T}_{j,m}$ are similar subsequences, $\rho(\mathbf{T}_{i,m}, \mathbf{T}_{j,m})$ approaches 1.

Finally, based on the above definitions, we formalize the problem addressed in this paper.

Problem 1.   *Given MvTS $\mathbf{T} \in \mathbb{R}^{(d \times n)}$, MvTS query $\mathbf{T}_q \in \mathbb{R}^{(d \times m)}$, and threshold $\theta \in [0, 1]$, a similar subsequence search is a task to find a set of subsequences, which is denoted by $\mathcal{R}$, in $\mathbf{T}$ such that $\mathcal{R} = \{\mathbf{T}_{j,m} \subseteq \mathbf{T} \mid \rho(\mathbf{T}_q, \mathbf{T}_{j,m}) \geq \theta\}$.*

As shown in Problem 1, the similar subsequence search finds all subsequences in $\mathbf{T}$ that yield a Pearson coefficient greater than a user-specified threshold θ.

3   Proposed Method: A Hash-Based Approach

Our proposed algorithm achieves an efficient and accurate similarity search for an MvTS.

3.1   Basic Concept

For a given MvTS query, our proposed method aims to find a set of similar subsequences $\mathcal{R}$ from MvTS $\mathbf{T}$ within a short computation time. Our proposed method aims to reduce the number of computed subsequences during the query process. We employ an LSH-based approach. LSH attempts to project similar vectors into the same hash value using locality-sensitive hash functions [6]. Prior to query processing, our proposed method groups all subsequences based on LSH so that each group yields a significant Pearson coefficient. Then in the query processing step, our method initially identifies a set of groups most similar to the MvTS query. Hence, exploring all subsequences is avoided.

Our proposed method consists of three steps:

- **(Step 1) Projection:** First, each subsequence $T_{j,m} \subseteq T$ is projected into L-dimensional space using LSH functions, maintaining the Pearson coefficient between subsequences.
- **(Step 2) Grouping:** Then all subsequences are clustered into groups using the projected vectors derived in (Step 1) so that each group includes similar subsequences in terms of the Pearson coefficient.
- **(Step 3) Querying:** Finally, MvTS queries over the groups obtained in the previous step.

Sections 3.2, 3.3, and 3.4 explain the details of Steps 1, 2, and 3, respectively.

3.2   (Step 1) LSH-Based Subsequence Projection

In this step, our proposed method projects each subsequence $T_{j,m} \subseteq T$ into an L-dimensional subsequence vector based on the LSH function. First, we define the LSH function that maintains the Pearson coefficient between subsequences.

Definition 2 (LSH Function for MvTS). *Given a subsequence $T_{j,m} \subseteq T$, LSH function $h(T_{j,m})$ is defined as:*

$$h(T_{j,m}) = \frac{(T_{j,m}^\top v_a)^\top v_b + cw}{w}, \tag{3}$$

where $v_a \in \mathbb{R}^{(d \times 1)}$ and $v_b \in \mathbb{R}^{(m \times 1)}$ such that $v_a, v_b \sim \mathcal{N}(\mu, \sigma^2)$, $w \in \mathbb{R}$ is a constant value, and $c \in \mathbb{R}$ is a randomly selected constant value in $[0, w)$.

Note that Definition 2 outputs a single real value (*i.e.*, $h(T_{j,m}) \in \mathbb{R}$). Given a threshold $\theta \in [0, 1]$, we expected to hold $h(T_{i,m}) = h(T_{j,m})$ only if $\rho(T_{i,m}, T_{j,m}) \geq \theta$. By following [1,4], we set $w = \sqrt{2m(1 - \theta)}$.

Based on Definition 2, we define the L-dimensional subsequence vector as:

Definition 3 (L-Dimensional Subsequence Vector). *Let $h_1, h_2, \ldots, h_L$ be L LSH functions defined by Definition 2. For each subsequence $T_{j,m} \subseteq T$, the L-dimensional subsequence vector, which is denoted by $h_j \in \mathbb{R}^{(L \times 1)}$, is defined as $h_j = (h_1(T_{j,m}), h_2(T_{j,m}), \ldots, h_L(T_{j,m}))^\top$.*

Based on Definition 3, our proposed method generates the L-dimensional subsequence vector h_j for all subsequences $T_{j,m} \subseteq T$.

Algorithm 1. A Greedy Grouping Method

Input: $\mathcal{H} = \{\mathbf{h}_1, \mathbf{h}_2, \ldots, \mathbf{h}_{n-m+1}\}$, and $\theta \in [0,1]$;
Output: $\mathcal{G}$;
1: $\mathcal{G} \leftarrow \emptyset$;
2: **for each** $\mathbf{h}_i \in \mathcal{H}$ **do**
3:     $g_i \leftarrow \{i\}$;
4:     $\mathcal{G} \leftarrow \mathcal{G} \cup \{g_i\}$;
5: **for each** $g_i \in \mathcal{G}$ **do**
6:     **for each** $g_j \in \mathcal{G} \backslash \{g_i\}$ **do**
7:         $\langle \mathbf{h}_s, \mathbf{h}_t \rangle \leftarrow \arg \min_{s \in g_i, t \in g_j} \rho(\mathbf{h}_s, \mathbf{h}_t)$;
8:         **if** $\rho(\mathbf{h}_s, \mathbf{h}_t) \geq \theta$ **then**
9:             $g_i \leftarrow g_i \cup g_j$;
10:            $\mathcal{G} \leftarrow \mathcal{G} \backslash \{g_j\}$;
11: **return** $\mathcal{G}$;

3.3   (Step 2) Subsequence Grouping

In Step 2, our proposed algorithm clusters all subsequences in $\mathbf{T}$ by L-dimensional subsequence vectors, $\mathbf{h}_1, \mathbf{h}_2, \ldots, \mathbf{h}_{n-m+1}$, derived from $\mathbf{T}_{1,m}$, $\mathbf{T}_{2,m}$, $\ldots$, $\mathbf{T}_{n-m+1,m}$, respectively. For efficient query processing in the subsequent step, our algorithm clusters the subsequences into groups so that each group yields a Pearson coefficient greater than θ. Our proposed method employs a greedy subsequence grouping method, which uses the Pearson coefficient in Definition 1 as a similarity measure. Note that other clustering algorithms such as Lloyd's algorithms [17], graph-based algorithms [18,19], and density-based algorithms [20,21] are also applicable in this step.

Algorithm 1 shows a pseudocode of the greedy subsequence grouping method. The algorithm requires a set of L-dimensional subsequence vectors, $\mathcal{H}$, derived from Definition 3, and threshold θ. From $\mathcal{H}$ and θ, Algorithm 1 returns a set of groups of subsequences, $\mathcal{G}$. At the beginning of the algorithm, each subsequence is regarded as a singleton group (lines 2–3). Then the algorithm clusters the groups based on the Pearson coefficient (lines 5–10). Given two groups g_i and g_j, Algorithm 1 extracts a pair of subsequences vectors, say $\mathbf{h}_s$ and $\mathbf{h}_t$ such that $s \in g_i$ and $t \in g_j$, with the smallest Pearson coefficient among g_i and g_j (line 7). If $\rho(\mathbf{h}_s, \mathbf{h}_t) \geq \theta$, the algorithm merges g_i and g_j into the same group since any pairs of subsequences can yield a Pearson coefficient greater than θ (lines 8–10); otherwise, Algorithm 1 leaves g_i and g_j as different groups. In line 11, the algorithm returns $\mathcal{G}$.

3.4   (Step 3) LSH-Based Query Processing

In the final step, MvTS query $\mathbf{T}_q$ is performed using $\mathcal{G}$ obtained in Step 2. Algorithm 2 shows the pseudocode of this step. In line 2, our algorithm generates the L-dimensional subsequence vector $\mathbf{h}_q$ from query MvTS $\mathbf{T}_q$ based on Definitions 2 and 3. To compute LSH, Algorithm 2 needs to use the same

Algorithm 2. A MvTS Query Processing

Input: $\mathbf{T}_q$, $\mathbf{T}$, $\mathcal{G}$, $\mathcal{H} = \{\mathbf{h}_1, \mathbf{h}_2, \ldots, \mathbf{h}_{n-m+1}\}$, and $\theta \in [0,1]$;
Output: $\mathcal{R}$;
1: $\mathcal{R} \leftarrow \emptyset$;
2: $\mathbf{h}_q$ from $\mathbf{T}_q$ by Definitions 2 and 3;
3: **for each** $g \in \mathcal{G}$ **do**
4: $\quad \mathbf{c}_g \leftarrow \frac{1}{|g|}\sum_{i \in g}\mathbf{h}_i$;
5: $\quad$ **if** $\rho(\mathbf{h}_q, \mathbf{c}_g) \geq \theta$ **then**
6: $\quad\quad$ **for each** $i \in g$ **do**
7: $\quad\quad\quad$ **if** $\rho(\mathbf{T}_q, \mathbf{T}_{i,m}) \geq \theta$ **then**
8: $\quad\quad\quad\quad \mathcal{R} \leftarrow \mathcal{R} \cup \{\mathbf{T}_{i,m}\}$;
9: **return** $\mathcal{R}$;

Table 2. Statistics of datasets.

ID	Dataset	$|\mathbf{T}|$	d	m
$\mathcal{D}_1$	Matrix Profile dataset [27]	550	3	10
$\mathcal{D}_2$	Basketball dataset [15]	10,000	6	300
$\mathcal{D}_3$	Smartphone dataset [2]	152,888	9	800
$\mathcal{D}_4$	Mt. Tsukuba dataset [3]	158,422	11	1,000

LSH functions employed in Step 1. Then $\mathbf{h}_q$ and $\mathcal{G}$ are used to explore similar subsequences $\mathcal{R}$ (lines 3–8). To avoid computing all subsequences, Algorithm 2 filters out unpromising groups, which yield a smaller coefficient than θ (lines 3–5). Specifically, for each g, the algorithm generates an average vector $\mathbf{c}_g$ of the group (line 4) and it subsequently computes $\rho(\mathbf{h}_q, \mathbf{c}_g)$ (line 5). If $\rho(\mathbf{h}_q, \mathbf{c}_g) < \theta$, Algorithm 2 skips the computation for all subsequences included in group g. Otherwise, the algorithm proceeds to the validation phases (lines 6–8). Finally, Algorithm 2 outputs a set of subsequences $\mathcal{R}$ (line 9).

4 Experimental Analysis

We experimentally evaluated the effectiveness of our proposed method by comparing it tto several competitive methods.

- **Proposed Method:** Sect. 3 describes our proposed algorithm. In the experimental analysis, L, which represents the number of LSH functions is varied as 5, 10, and 25.
- **DFT Method:** A DFT-based algorithm approximates MvTS to reduce the size of each dimension by applying the existing DFT approach [5] for a one-dimensional time series. After reducing the size of each dimension, this method explores the subsequences like the MvTS query on the approximated MvTS.

- **Baseline Method:** This is a naïve implementation of a similar subsequence search. Given MvTS and an MvTS query, the Pearson coefficient is computed for all subsequences included in MvTS.

All algorithms were implemented by C++ and compiled by gcc with the "-O3" option. All experiments were conducted on a Linux server with an Intel CPU 2.90 GHz and 16 GiB RAM.

Datasets: We tested four real-world MvTS datasets published by [2,3,15,27]. Table 2 shows their statistics, where $\mathbf{T}$ is the length of MvTS, d is its dimension, and m is the length of each subsequence. We also tested synthetic MvTS datasets, which were randomly generated d-dimensional time series of length $|\mathbf{T}|$. To assess the scalability of our proposed method, we varied d and $|\mathbf{T}|$. Section 4.2 provides details of the synthetic datasets.

Query: For the MvTS query, we randomly selected 10 subsequences of length m shown in Table 2. Unless otherwise stated, we set $\theta = 0.70$. Here, we report the results averaged over the above 10 queries.

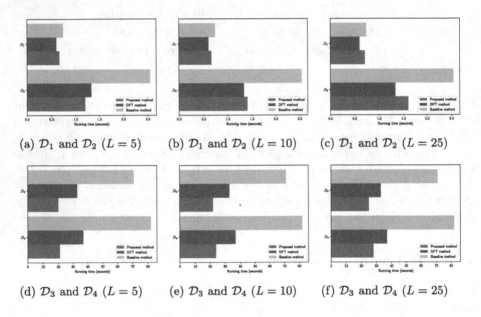

(a) $\mathcal{D}_1$ and $\mathcal{D}_2$ $(L = 5)$ (b) $\mathcal{D}_1$ and $\mathcal{D}_2$ $(L = 10)$ (c) $\mathcal{D}_1$ and $\mathcal{D}_2$ $(L = 25)$

(d) $\mathcal{D}_3$ and $\mathcal{D}_4$ $(L = 5)$ (e) $\mathcal{D}_3$ and $\mathcal{D}_4$ $(L = 10)$ (f) $\mathcal{D}_3$ and $\mathcal{D}_4$ $(L = 25)$

Fig. 2. Running time.

4.1   Efficiency

To demonstrate the efficiency of our proposed method, Table 2 compares the query processing time using real-world MvTS datasets. Figure 2 shows the query processing time to find all similar subsequences that yield a more significant Pearson coefficient than θ.

Our method is competitive with the others on low-dimensional datasets (*e.g.*, $\mathcal{D}_1$ and $\mathcal{D}_2$). However, our proposed algorithm outperforms the other methods in high-dimensional MvTS datasets (*e.g.*, $\mathcal{D}_3$ and $\mathcal{D}_4$). This is because our method is designed to mitigate the computational overhead incurred by MvTS with a large d. Unlike traditional methods such as the DFT method, which consecutively compute each time series in MvTS, our method simultaneously computes d-dimensional subsequences using Definition 2. Hence, our proposed method achieves a faster computation on high-dimensional large-scale MvTS datasets.

Furthermore, using the grouping algorithm, our proposed method effectively avoids computing all subsequences included in MvTS. Compared to the baseline method, our method has up to a four times faster query processing time.

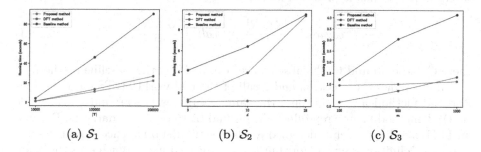

(a) $\mathcal{S}_1$ (b) $\mathcal{S}_2$ (c) $\mathcal{S}_3$

Fig. 3. Scalability test.

4.2 Scalability

To evaluate the scalability, we generated synthetic MvTS:

- $\mathcal{S}_1$: A synthetic MvTS to evaluate the impact of $|\mathbf{T}|$. We set $d = 3$ and $m = 1,000$, and varied $|\mathcal{T}|$ as 10,000, 100,000, and 200,000.
- $\mathcal{S}_2$: A synthetic MvTS to evaluate the impact of d. We fixed $|\mathbf{T}| = 10,000$ and $m = 1,000$, and varied d as 3, 10, and 25.
- $\mathcal{S}_3$: A synthetic MvTS to evaluate the impact of m. We set $|\mathbf{T}| = 10,000$ and $d = 3$, and varied m as 100, 500, and 1,0000.

Figure 3 shows the running time of each method under the above synthetic dataset settings. Our proposed method significantly outperforms the other methods if an MvTS dataset has a large d value. In the other settings, our method still shows competitive performances with the DFT method. In particular, as shown in Fig. 3(b), our method shows the best scalability for d. The running time of our method is almost constant for any d setting, while DFT exponentially increases its running time as d increases. As described earlier, recent applications must handle large-scale MvTS, including multiple time series. That is, our proposed method, which achieves a better scalability for the size of d, can improve the performance in MvTS applications.

Table 3. Accuracy.

	$\mathcal{D}_1$	$\mathcal{D}_2$	$\mathcal{D}_3$	$\mathcal{D}_4$
Precision@Proposed method	1.00	1.00	1.00	1.00
Recall@Proposed method	1.00	1.00	1.00	1.00
Precision@DFT method	1.00	0.97	0.91	0.92
Recall@DFT method	1.00	1.00	1.00	1.00

4.3 Accuracy

Finally, we assessed the similarity search accuracy using *precision* and *recall*. Based on [9], we define precision and recall as:

$$Precision = \frac{|\mathcal{G} \cap \mathcal{R}|}{|\mathcal{R}|}, \; Recall = \frac{|\mathcal{G} \cap \mathcal{R}|}{|\mathcal{G}|}, \tag{4}$$

where $\mathcal{G}$ is the ground truth subsequences obtained by the Baseline method.

Table 3 shows the precision and recall of the real-world MvTS datasets. Our proposed method always outputs the same results as the ground truth, while the DFT method fails to reproduce the ground truth on larger datasets. Because our LSH-based approach is designed to place similar subsequences into the same group by Definition 2 and Algorithm 1, our proposed method achieves the exact search even if the size of MvTS increases.

Our method offers an improved efficiency for high-dimensional large-scale MvTS datasets. Consequently, it outperforms existing methods in terms of efficiency and search accuracy.

5   Conclusion

A fast similar subsequence search method for MvTS is proposed to overcome the large computation time necessary for existing approaches, which must compute similarities for all subsequences included in MvTS. Our method employs a hash-based approach. By introducing LSH functions for MvTS, unpromising subsequences, which lack a large similarity with a user-specified query, are excluded. The proposed method outperforms existing algorithms with respect to efficiency and search accuracy in evaluations involving synthetic and real-world MvTS datasets.

Acknowledgements. This work was partly supported by JST PRESTO (JPMJPR-2033) and JSPS KAKENHI (JP22K17894). Part of this work used observational data from the Mt. Tsukuba Project in Center for Computational Sciences, University of Tsukuba.

References

1. Amagata, D., Hara, T.: Correlation set discovery on time-series data. In: Proceedings of the 30th International Conference on Database and Expert Systems Applications (DEXA 2019), pp. 275–290 (2019)
2. Barsocchi, P., Crivello, A., La Rosa, D., Palumbo, F.: A multisource and multivariate dataset for indoor localization methods based on WLAN and geo-magnetic field fingerprinting. In: Proceedings of the 2016 International Conference on Indoor Positioning and Indoor Navigation (IPIN 2016), pp. 1–8 (2016)
3. Center for Computational Sciences, U.o.T.: Mt. tsukuba project (2023). https://www.ccs.tsukuba.ac.jp/research_project/mt_tkb/. Accessed 25 July 2023
4. Datar, M., Immorlica, N., Indyk, P., Mirrokni, V.S.: Locality-sensitive hashing scheme based on p-stable distributions. In: Proceedings of the Twentieth Annual Symposium on Computational Geometry (SCG 2004), pp. 253–262 (2004)
5. Faloutsos, C., Ranganathan, M., Manolopoulos, Y.: Fast subsequence matching in time-series databases. ACM SIGMOD Record 23(2), 419–429 (1994)
6. Koga, H., Ishibashi, T., Watanabe, T.: Fast agglomerative hierarchical clustering algorithm using locality-sensitive hashing. Knowl. Inf. Syst. 12(1), 25–53 (2007)
7. Lin, J., Keogh, E., Lonardi, S., Chiu, B.: A symbolic representation of time series, with implications for streaming algorithms. In: Proceedings of the 8th ACM SIGMOD Workshop on Research Issues in Data Mining and Knowledge Discovery (DMKD 2003), pp. 2–11 (2003)
8. Maeda, T., Fujii, M., Hayashi, I.: Time series data analysis for sport skill. In: Proceedings of the 12th International Conference on Intelligent Systems Design and Applications (ISDA 2012), pp. 392–397 (2012)
9. Manning, C.D., Raghavan, P., Schütze, H.: Introduction to Information Retrieval. Cambridge University Press, Cambridge (2008)
10. Papapetrou, P., Athitsos, V., Potamias, M., Kollios, G., Gunopulos, D.: Embedding-based subsequence matching in time-series databases. ACM Trans. Datab. Syst. (ACM TODS) 36(3) (2011)
11. Rakthanmanon, T., et al.: Searching and mining trillions of time series subsequences under dynamic time warping. In: Proceedings of the 18th ACM SIGKDD International Conference on Knowledge Discovery and Data Mining (KDD 2012), pp. 262–270 (2012)
12. Ratanamahatana, C.A., Keogh, E.: Making time-series classification more accurate using learned constraints. In: Proceedings of the 2004 SIAM International Conference on Data Mining (SDM 2004), pp. 11–22 (2004)
13. Reynolds, H.T.: The Analysis of Cross-Classifications. The Free Press, New York (1977)
14. Sakurai, Y., Yoshikawa, M., Faloutsos, C.: FTW: fast similarity search under the time warping distance. In: Proceedings of the Twenty-Fourth ACM SIGMOD-SIGACT-SIGART Symposium on Principles of Database Systems (PODS 2005), pp. 326–337 (2005)
15. Salam, A., Hibaoui, A.E.: Comparison of machine learning algorithms for the power consumption prediction: case study of Tetouan city. In: Proceedings of the 6th International Renewable and Sustainable Energy Conference (IRSEC 2018), pp. 1–5 (2018)
16. Salvador, S., Chan, P.: Toward accurate dynamic time warping in linear time and space. Intell. Data Anal. 11(5), 561–580 (2007)

17. Shiokawa, H.: Scalable affinity propagation for massive datasets. Proc. AAAI Conf. Artif. Intell. **35**(11), 9639–9646 (2021)
18. Shiokawa, H., Amagasa, T., Kitagawa, H.: Scaling fine-grained modularity clustering for massive graphs. In: Proceedings of the 28th International Joint Conference on Artificial Intelligence (IJCAI 2019), pp. 4597–4604 (2019)
19. Shiokawa, H., Fujiwara, Y., Onizuka, M.: Fast algorithm for modularity-based graph clustering. In: Proceedings of the 27th AAAI Conference on Artificial Intelligence (AAAI 2013) (2013)
20. Shiokawa, H., Fujiwara, Y., Onizuka, M.: SCAN++: efficient algorithm for finding clusters, hubs and outliers on large-scale graphs. Proc. VLDB Endowm. **8**(11), 1178–1189 (2015)
21. Shiokawa, H., Takahashi, T.: DSCAN: distributed structural graph clustering for billion-edge graphs. In: Proceedings of the 31st International Conference on Database and Expert Systems Applications (DEXA 2020), pp. 38–54 (2020)
22. Suzuki, Y., Sato, M., Shiokawa, H., Yanagisawa, M., Kitagawa, H.: MASC: automatic sleep stage classification based on brain and myoelectric signals. In: Proceedings of the 33rd IEEE International Conference on Data Engineering (ICDE 2017), pp. 1489–1496 (2017)
23. Tanaka, Y., Iwamoto, K., Uehara, K.: Discovery of time-series Motif from multi-dimensional data based on MDL principle. Mach. Learn. **58**(2), 269–300 (2005)
24. Ten Holt, G.A., Reinders, M.J., Hendriks, E.A.: Multi-dimensional dynamic time warping for gesture recognition. In: Proceedings of 13th Annual Conference of the Advanced School for Computing and Imaging (ASCI 2007) (2007)
25. Yagi, R., Shiokawa, H.: Fast top-k similar sequence search on DNA databases. In: Proceedings of the 24th International Conference on Information Integration and Web Intelligence (iiWAS 2022), pp. 145–150 (2022)
26. Yamabe, M., Horie, K., Shiokawa, H., Funato, H., Yanagisawa, M., Kitagawa, H.: MC-SleepNet: large-scale sleep stage scoring in mice by deep neural networks. Sci. Rep. **9**(15793) (2019)
27. Yeh, C.C.M., Kavantzas, N., Keogh, E.: Matrix profile VI: meaningful multidimensional Motif discovery. In: Proceedings of 2017 IEEE International Conference on Data Mining (ICDM 2017), pp. 565–574 (2017)
28. Yeh, C.C.M., et al.: Matrix profile I: all pairs similarity joins for time series: a unifying view that includes Motifs, discords and shapelets. In: Proceedings of 2016 IEEE 16th International Conference on Data Mining (ICDM 2016), pp. 1317–1322 (2016)

Topic and Text Matching

A Machine Learning Approach to Enterprise Matchmaking Using Multilabel Text Classification Based on Semi-structured Website Content

Jan Vellmer[1]([✉]) [ID], Peter Mandl[1] [ID], Tobias Bellmann[2] [ID], Maximilian Balluff[1] [ID], Manuel Weber[1] [ID], Alexander Döschl[1] [ID], and Max-Emanuel Keller[1] [ID]

[1] HM Hochschule München University of Applied Sciences, Lothstraße 34, 80335 Munich, Germany
jan.vellmer@hm.edu

[2] SCIL Systems and Control Innovation Lab, Münchener Straße 20, 82234 Weßling, Germany

Abstract. Finding the right business partner to drive innovation or acquire technology transfer is a labor and time-intensive process. To simplify this process, there is a need for improved methods of automated matchmaking that can quickly identify the best potential collaboration partners. This paper presents a novel approach for semi-automated business matchmaking between companies and research institutes, that is applied to a first case study. For this purpose, we compare two transformer-based text classification models and evaluate how dataset quality affects few-shot learning performance. Flair's TARS classifier performed very well in our use case, requiring only 40 examples per class to achieve an F1 score of about 90%. This is already very close to the Hugging Face standard text classifier, which achieved an F1 score of 92% with much more annotation effort. The results show that few-shot learning models like TARS can achieve accurate results even with few training samples compared to regular transformer-based language models. Our novel approach allows the time-consuming and labor-intensive task of manual partner matchmaking to be significantly reduced.

Keywords: Research Partner · Open Innovation · Text Classification · Scoring · Transformer · Flair · Hugging Face · NLP · Matchmaking · TARS · Web Mining · BERT

1 Introduction

Keeping up with the increased demand for innovation is not only a labor-intensive and time-consuming but a highly cost-intensive challenge. Finding the right research partner to drive innovation with, is yet another time-consuming and complex business process, mostly still done manually today. Similarly time-consuming is the process of finding new customers through a variety of channels. Companies analyze indexes, relevant portals, purchase information from providers such as GENIOS[1] and search for potential customers via search engines for company websites.

---

[1] https://www.genios.de.

P. Delir Haghighi et al. (Eds.): iiWAS 2023, LNCS 14416, pp. 493–509, 2023.
https://doi.org/10.1007/978-3-031-48316-5_44

The better the pre-selection, the less effort the further acquisition process will take. According to [1] the effort involved in searching for technology partners is large, although an intensive search and evaluation process is more likely to lead to the identification of satisfactory partners. According to the authors, the decisive factor is not so much the breadth of the search, i.e., the number of partners identified, but rather the depth of the search, i.e., the quantity and quality of the information collected [1]. In technology transfer between universities, research institutes and companies, the acquisition of proper research partners goes through similar workflows.

One crucial channel is the official website of a potential innovation partner. The public website is so promising because it can easily be accessed to gather public information. For humans, it is comparatively easy to find out information about the industry a company is active in, about its products or about its capabilities, by just using the official website. However, this approach is very time-consuming and therefore cannot easily be done on a larger scale with thousands of websites. But finding and checking potential customers or partners automatically based on their websites is difficult because of the semi-structured nature of data, consisting of headings, text, images, and other type of resources.

Websites are usually structured quite differently, which makes broad crawls more difficult. The extraction of information is therefore time-consuming, and an automated evaluation of websites is not easily possible. Supportive tools that automate this process as much as possible and perform a semantic search could improve the partner search significantly.

Based on the shown problem space, this paper aims to provide a solution approach for semi-automated matchmaking. The goal of our project is to automate matchmaking between companies, research institutes or potential cooperation partners in general, quite similar to the search for partners in marriage or in multiplayer video games. In our project potential partners are to be found based on semi-structured website content by using the advantages of machine learning and text classification techniques. As a concrete case study, the search for partners for research cooperation is considered; a generalization of the matchmaking approach is the focus of further development. Based on the previous motivation, this paper makes the following contributions:

- A novel approach to business matchmaking via text classification based on websites content is presented. Our matchmaking uses text classification, which is about classifying a semi-structured or unstructured text assigned to predefined categories (target labels).
- Different classification algorithms based on several pre-trained BERT language models are compared. The performance of a few-shot learning approach is evaluated since less examples are needed to adapt the matchmaking concept to a new partner.
- To evaluate the new matchmaking approach, two datasets are created and tested on a TARS few-shot classifier and a standard text classifier. Here we also investigate how cleaning the dataset can improve the classification results. It can be shown that the dataset quality has a relevant impact on the model's precision performance.

The paper is organized as follows. In Sect. 2, we provide an overview of the state of the art in text classification as the basis of our matchmaking approach. Section 3 describes the new matchmaking approach with all the necessary steps. In Sect. 4, we address a use case that serves as the core for evaluating classification in the matchmaking approach. Section 5 describes and discusses the results of the experiments comparing the different classification algorithms.

2 State of the Art and Related Works

Automatic matchmaking has indeed been researched and used in many areas for quite some time. In recent years, more and more machine learning methods have been tested for this purpose, especially text classification. The search for suitable partners in the business environment is also referred to as "enterprise matchmaking", "B2B matchmaking", "company matchmaking" or "business matchmaking", although a uniform definition is lacking.

2.1 Enterprise Matchmaking

Matchmaking is intensively used, for example, in the search for suitable cloud services [2], but also to find the right influencers for brands in social networks [3], in online games to find players [4, 5] and when matching buyers and sellers on e-marketplaces [6]. Bringing companies together through automated matchmaking is still a relatively new approach, and to our knowledge there are currently few attempts based on machine learning. A literature search via Google Scholar, ACM Digital Library and Springerlink with the following search strings resulted in only a few papers dealing with AI-based enterprise matchmaking:

> ("Company Matchmaking" OR "Enterprise Matchmaking" OR "Business Match-making" OR "B2B Matchmaking") AND ("Artificial Intelligence" OR "Recommender" OR "AI" OR "Machine Learning").

Benramdane et al. [7] propose a recommender system with a hybrid matchmaking approach in two steps to match organizations of the same or even different market segments in digital platforms. In the first step, matchmaking was performed with static rules, and in the second step, the results of the first step were transformed into a ranking via machine learning. The recommender system uses Decision Tree Algorithm and Logistic Regression. The models were tested using a small dataset whose origin is not further specified. Non-existing attributes were automatically added in advance via the application of the MICE algorithm. The matchmaking results were published using confusion matrices. Neither with Decision Tree nor with Logistic Regression false positive or false negative predictions were made.

Li et al. [8] try to identify suitable products for customers with their matchmaking approach. They test TF-IDF- and transformer-based models such as RoBERTa, MiniLM and MPNet based on a dataset of IBM (IBM_CR) with more than 24,000 query documents about all IBM business units from 2010 to 2022 with longer texts. The texts are decomposed into chunks with a length of 256 tokens for the transformer models. The models were also tested in combination. Results were measured by precision, recall, and F-score at k (P@k, R@k, F@k), among others, where k refers to the top-k predictions. The best matching results were obtained with TD-IDF (R@10 was 30%, P@1 was

23%). Among the transformer-based models, MPNet performed best. The best model combination was obtained with TF-IDF and MPNet with a weighting of the models of 70 to 30.

Overall, however, it can be stated that Natural Language Processing, and specifically text classification [9, 10], is very well suited as a basis for a matchmaking method due to the abundance of company information available on the Internet. Our approach also uses this machine learning method. Therefore, we will briefly explain the basics that are important for our work in the following section.

2.2 Text Classification

Text classification is possible on document level, on paragraph level or on sentence level, whereas we will only consider the sentence level in the following. A distinction is made between multi-class and multi-label classification. In the former approach, each text is assigned to exactly one category out of at least two possible ones. Multi-label classification is particularly useful when the texts under consideration can be assigned to more than one category because there is overlap in content [11].

Data-driven methods based on Deep Learning have become popular for text classification [10]. Approaches such as transformer architectures and the attention mechanism [12] which was first implemented at Google [13] are currently dominating research. Meanwhile, there are many developments of Google BERT that have further improved the underlying model. RoBERTa [14] and XLNet [15] are prominent examples. Until recently, transformer models could only be trained and used for one task in computational linguistics. With Google's new T5 model [16] which is also based on the transformer architecture, a more advanced model has been developed that can now also be used for various tasks such as summarizing texts and for text classification. Recently, Google released the Pathways Language Model (PalM), with 540 billion model parameters, which can be used for many tasks [17]. Currently, the GPT models are in the headlines because they are the basis of OpenAI's ChatGPT chatbot (Chatbot Generative Pre-trained transformer) [18]. GPT-4 is called a multimodal model because it can process images as input in addition to text. GPT-3 and GPT-3.5 use a maximum of 175 billion parameters [19, 20], but the number of model parameters of GPT-4 has not been published yet.

Transformer models are very broad neural networks in which multi-dimensional language models are pre-trained with a large number of documents in a word embedding representation that also includes the context of words (contextual embedding). Google BERT currently uses 768 dimensions for word embedding in the default case [13]. A pre-trained model is usually fine-tuned for a specific task, requiring additional training examples for all categories (classes) to be recognized. The more training examples are available, the better the model training and thus the prediction. The conventional approach to text classification adds a linear classification layer (output layer) to the pre-trained neural network that computes a distribution over all categories of the prediction problem. The approach usually works well but requires an annotated training dataset as large as possible. However, often only a very small amount of manually generated training data is available.

Another approach worth mentioning, which originally comes from image processing, is zero-shot learning. This involves classifying objects in an image that have not previously appeared in the training data [21]. Applied to our problem, this means that a text is assigned a category that the model has not seen in training before. However, the category must be present in the list of predefined categories [22]. Unfortunately, in many cases zero-shot learning does not work very well, and the results are rather inaccurate, because the predictions are only determined from the pre-trained model, but the models have not been optimized for the actual application area [23]. In these situations, few-shot learning, i.e., training the model with only a few training data, can be used [19]. A promising implementation approach is the TARS model (Task-aware repre-sentation of sentences) [24]. In contrast to conventional text classification, TARS includes category labels in the model training in addition to the actual texts and the target label is either TRUE or FALSE, which reformulates the classification problem to a query. The following example shows which tuples TARS generates from our text samples:

   < *"Measuring instruments and measuring devices", "This began with the manufacture of variable area flowmeters."* > → *TRUE*

The sentence *"This began with the manufacture of variable area flowmeters"* is supplemented by the label *"Measuring instruments and measuring devices "*. A binary value, in this case "TRUE", is added as annotation.

This favors the zero- and few-shot features. Moreover, in the TARS model, extension of a trained classifier with additional categories is possible without loss of previous fine-tuning work, and the model is designed to support multiple text classification problems without loss of an already trained decoder layer. Few-shot learning is particularly suitable for our matchmaking problem, since only a small amount of training data is available in the general case, and category expansion should be possible without significant effort. This approach will therefore be considered in more detail.

3   Generic Matchmaking Approach

Our company matchmaking approach uses text classification methods to find suitable (partner) companies for a seeking instance. Therefore, we gather information from the semi-structured texts of company websites, as explained in Sect. 1. For a classification, the domain specific features that identify a company as a suitable candidate, have to be found in advance. We call these domain-specific features characteristics. These characteristics may be the products or services offered by a company. A thorough domain analysis is required to identify the domain-specific features. This process is not further discussed in this paper and should be performed by domain experts. The identified characteristics will be used to derive the actual classes to be used for the classification of a partner company. If, for example, companies dealing with control engineering are interesting as potential partners, the contents of the website are to be examined with regard to this characteristic. If several characteristics are relevant, the search should be broadened accordingly. A combination of the features under the most diverse aspects is also possible. The determination of characteristics is depending on the seeking instance and the characteristics analysis is individually performed for each use case. Nevertheless, this domain characteristic analysis should be generalized in the future.

The matchmaking approach matches companies to predefined categories based on their website content to derive a prediction about their suitability as partners. The input

498   J. Vellmer et al.

needed is on the one hand the URL of a company's website and on the other hand the list of categories necessary for an evaluation, which a company should fulfill or partially fulfill in order to be considered as a partner.

Our matchmaking approach uses a text classifier to classify a website into the given categories. For this purpose, the entire website content is segmented into individual texts. Each individual text is then classified. After classification, all outputs of the text classifier can serve as input for a rating of the respective company under consideration. In the rating, the specific rules for valuing a company are applied on the basis of the classification and, if necessary, using further information. The rating can also be performed using another proprietary machine learning method, provided that suitable input data is available.

As a supervised learning task, text classification normally requires as many data examples as possible. For a generic solution approach, however, it is desirable to use relatively few data examples for each category under consideration in order to avoid time consuming annotation for newly added categories. Thus, the aim is to find solutions that provide usable classification results with only a few training examples. Therefore, different classification algorithms are tested and compared in this paper.

Training language models from scratch is no longer practical today due to the immense effort involved. Instead, pre-trained models are used, which are based on algorithms such as Google BERT [9]. These models are trained with very rich data, incorporate the semantics of sentences by considering word context, and can be adapted to specific classification tasks in a fine-tuning step. For model fine-tuning, data examples are to be found and annotated in the target language and contain complete sentences or parts of sentences in which the categories resulting from the domain analysis are described. Each sentence is then categorized. How many samples are needed depends on the fine-tuning algorithm. Our solution approach for predicting a partner passes through a data processing pipeline consisting of the steps *extraction, preprocessing, classification, aggregation,* and *rating,* as shown in Fig. 1.

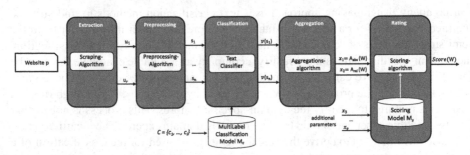

Fig. 1. Data processing pipeline for the matchmaking process

Extraction and Preprocessing. A website p usually consists of subpages u_1 to u_r and is structured as a tree of arbitrary depth. During extraction, all subpages are first identified and their contents are taken over as raw texts. Graphics and other non-textual content can be removed.

Since we use a sentence-wise classification strategy for the evaluation of a website p, the preprocessing step must segment all web pages of a website into individual sentences that can be classified separately. The web pages u_i are therefore cleaned of control characters and broken down into individual records for classification. Subpages that do not contain usable content are eliminated. All web pages u_i are thus segmented into a disjoint set W of individual texts or sentences s. Each sentence consists of a sequence of words that should not exceed a maximum length. This maximum length depends on the tokenization of the words, which may vary depending on the language model used. For Google BERT, for example the maximum is 512 tokens [25].

$$W = \{s_1, \ldots, s_n\} \tag{1}$$

The result of the extraction is the set W of independent individual text sentences or parts of sentences (referred to as sentence below), each with a maximum number of tokens. The order of the tokens in the sentence is relevant.

Classification. In the next step, a multilabel text classification is performed for each individual sentence $s \in W$ using a pre-trained and fine-tuned language model M_c. Each sentence is assigned to one or more categories by the text classifier T where a limited number of predefined categories $C = \{c_1, \ldots, c_l\}$ is supported. The inputs to the text classifier are individual sentences $s \in W$. The output of the text classifier is a vector v consisting of $|C|$ binary flags b_i indicating membership of the sentence s_i in category in c_i.

$$v_i(s_i) = (b_1, \ldots, b_l); b_i \in \{0, 1\}, 0 : s_i \text{ not in } c_i, 1 : s_i \text{ in } c_i \tag{2}$$

The individual values b_j indicate whether the considered sentence s_i fits into the respective category c_i of C. Each value is determined by the arrangement in the vector and assigned to a category.

Aggregation. The vectors $v_i(s_i)$ to all sentences from W represent the input for the next step, the aggregation. In this step, all vectors of the individual sentences are aggregated to an overall vector by interpreting the individual scores of each category, i.e. the binary values, as numerical values by summing them up. Thus, the result of the aggregation is again a vector $A_{abs}(W)$ which gives the absolute number of matching sentences s from W for each category c_i. Furthermore, the relative number of matching sentences related to the total number n of all sentences from W is determined and provided in a vector $A_{rel}(W)$:

$$A_{abs}(W) = (sum(c_1), \ldots, sum(c_l)), \text{ with } sum(c_j) = \sum\nolimits_{i=1}^{n} c_j \tag{3}$$

$$A_{rel}(W) = (rel(c_1), \ldots, rel(c_l)), \text{ with } rel(c_j) = \sum\nolimits_{i=1}^{n} \frac{sum(c_j)}{n} \tag{4}$$

Rating. This step uses the aggregated values, referred to as input values x_1 and x_2 in Fig. 1, to determine a rating for the company with website p. The scoring algorithm considers a weighting of individual categories and might respect threshold values for assignment to an individual category. In one use case, a category might play an important role and therefore be ranked with a high weight. In another use case, other categories could be more important. It is also possible that all categories are equally weighted in the ranking. Likewise, other input values $x_3, \ldots, x_p$ from other classification approaches or other information about the company can be taken into account. Output of the rating step is a score for the company, which indicates how well it matches the search criteria. An ordinal scale with values between 0 and 5 is suitable for the score, where 0 represents the worst rating (does not match at all) and 5 the best rating (matches ideally). In our case study, for example, the implementation of the scoring algorithm connects the categories via a set of rules that only selects research-intensive and cooperative companies that fulfill at least one other category. Threshold values for the individual categories are also included. Machine learning processes based on a Scoring Model M_s can be used to determine the threshold values if suitable training data with predefined company ratings are available.

In summary, for the explained approach, the input required is a website of a company that is addressed via a URL. Furthermore, an analysis must be performed to determine an arbitrary number of characteristics for a classification, which a potential partner should fulfill completely or partially. For each characteristic, a set of annotated sample data is required, which in the ideal case should be able to be as small as possible within a few-shot learning environment. As shown in Fig. 1, an individual scoring function uses the classification results and can include further features $x_3, \ldots, x_p$ for the rating.

Standard NLP procedures can be used to extract the data from the web pages. The aggregation is relatively trivial in our case. The main task to be solved is the classification of the text. The scoring-step is more of an individual step, depending on the preferred evaluation of the classification results.

In this paper, we pay more attention to the classification step inside the processing pipeline, shown in Fig. 1. Some classifier implementations base on pretrained models, which showed promising results in other tasks, were therefore selected and tested for matchmaking. These will be presented and compared in the following. All implementation approaches are based on a common data set, which is required for fine-tuning.

To apply our matchmaking process to a real-world example, we demonstrate this classification step on a case study.

4   Case Study

As a case study for an initial benchmark of the proposed matchmaking processes, we collaborated with a research laboratory, which specializes, among other things, in control engineering and simulation. The lab is looking for suitable research partners. Our goal was to understand how text classification can work in this context and how quality optimization of the dataset affects classification performance. In the case study we analyzed domain-specific characteristics for finding potential research partners and assigned them to categories for classification purposes.

Two different machine learning libraries were used to implement our classifiers:

- TARS few-shot classifier by Flair[2]
- Standard text classifier by Hugging Face[3]

We created a dataset, trained, and evaluated the two classifiers. Finally, we optimized our dataset for Few-Shot Learning and again trained and evaluated it.

In our case study, only German websites are considered. To make the findings more available for different readers, the German content was translated to English.

4.1 Defining Domain Characteristics

For our research laboratory, an extensive analysis was carried out by their domain experts to determine the key characteristics to seek for in the content of potential research partners' websites. As a result of the analysis, we found seven different areas which are of particular interest. These seven areas are *control engineering, sensor technology, measurement technology, virtualization/simulation, artificial intelligence, innovativeness, and willingness to cooperate.*

It's worth mentioning, that especially in the case of research cooperation, *innovativeness* and *willingness to cooperate* are important characteristics of a potential partner that we included in our characteristics. When our research lab is looking for a research partner, different characteristics play a role than when a software company is looking for suitable customers in the financial sector. Now these terms are used as keywords and searched for on the websites. From the absolute or relative occurrences of a keyword, it is possible to infer whether a company is a suitable candidate for cooperation. It makes even more sense to include the context of the sentences and to consider similar terms (synonyms). Both approaches have been tested, with the second being more promising. Hence, it is addressed in the following, using state of the art text classification. The seven dedicated characteristics from the domain analysis are used as classes for a text classifier on individual sentences. We conduct the classification as a multi-label classification problem.

4.2 Initial Dataset Creation

For the classification task, we created a dataset containing German examples for each of the seven domain-specific characteristics. Due to token limitation of the final model, single sentences were considered, not paragraphs or whole documents. The collection and annotation of our dataset was done semi-automatically. Subsequently, texts were selected from the Wikipedia categories *measuring device manufacturer, control engineering, sensor technology* and *artificial intelligence* using the Wikipedia API[4]. There were no corresponding Wikipedia categories for the categories *simulation and virtualization, innovativeness* and *willingness to cooperate.* Examples of these were added via a manual Google search and via a manual search of Wikipedia articles.

---

[2] https://github.com/flairNLP/flair.

[3] https://huggingface.co/.

[4] https://pypi.org/project/Wikipedia-API/.

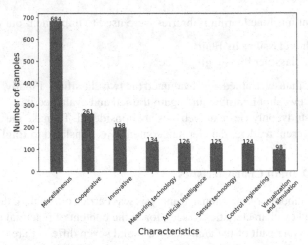

Fig. 2. Training sample distribution for initial raw dataset

We used the SBERT model [26] to determine the semantic similarity of the selected texts with given examples for each category. If the cosine-similarity exceeded 50%, a text was matched to the respective characteristic; if no similarity was found, a match was made to the *miscellaneous* category. This additional *miscellaneous* category was added to be able to also count the sentences that do not correspond to any of the seven characteristics searched for. Thus, an initial raw dataset with 1685 samples was created, which was distributed according to Fig. 2. The texts of a web page that are assigned to the *miscellaneous* category are not used in the ranking of companies.

4.3 Mapping Domain Characteristics to Categories

There is a distinguishment between characteristics and categories. When we speak of characteristics, we are referring to the domain-specific analysis. When we speak of categories, we are referring to the actual naming of the target values used for training. For each characteristic an own training category is defined, from which the following set C with altogether eight (including *miscellaneous*) categories can be derived:

$$C = \{C_1, C_2, \ldots, C_8\} \tag{5}$$

The following is an example text for the category *willingness to cooperate* from the corporate website of the Bosch company:

"At Bosch, we cooperate with various partners from science and industry. We focus on projects that have the potential to solve tomorrow's challenges today. This gives ideas the opportunity to quickly find their way into practice and survive there." [27].

Since we classified sentence by sentence, the text is first broken down into individual sentences in the extraction step. Each sentence is then matched to one or more categories by the classification process. In the example taken from [27], this could look like Table 1, where two of the records under consideration do not fall into any of the mentioned categories and are therefore matched to a residual category *miscellaneous*.

Table 1. Examples for sentences assigned to various categories C_m

Sentence	Category
At Bosch, we cooperate with various partners from science and industry	*willingness to cooperate*
We focus on projects that have the potential to solve tomorrow's challenges today	*miscellaneous*
This gives ideas the opportunity to quickly find their way into practice and survive there	*miscellaneous*

4.4 TARS Specific Data Set Optimization

To create a more optimized dataset, the raw dataset discussed in Sect. 4.2 was further optimized. In the follow-up cleansing, the following error classes were identified in the raw data set: Duplicates (ED), sentences with no semantic meaning (ES), sentences in which context was missing (EC), and incorrectly annotated labels (EL). The four specified error classes were removed from the raw dataset and an optimized training dataset with 1541 samples was created as a result.

For our multi-label classification problem, category class names must be determined. Remember, the domain characteristics are now transformed to actual category names for training. These category names tuned to TARS have no effect on Hugging Face standard text classification and thus could be used on the second model. In particular, special attention was paid when choosing the target labels, since the number of classes and their corresponding class names (target values) have an impact on the model performance of the few-shot TARS we used [24]. The number of selected characteristics does not necessarily have to be equal to the number of classes used for training. It may make sense to use more classes for training than the number of domain characteristics identified. To measure whether a more fine-grained distribution of the classes makes sense, the *coherence measure* according to Roeder [28] is a suitable metric. The coherence measure is a state-of-the-art metric to calculate topic coherence for topic models. It creates content vectors of words using their co-occurrences and, after that, calculates the score using normalized pointwise mutual information (NPMI) and the cosine similarity. The algorithm basically consists of the four-step pipeline segmentation, probability estimation, confirmation measure, and aggregation. To derive the target labels, we first used Latent Dirichlet Allocation to contrast different Topic Models with a variable number of topics. The combined Topic Models were thus used to find the N most frequent words for each category. Based on this, the coherence measure was determined for each class for the respective numbers of topics. If the coherence measure shows a high value for a low topic count (ideally for exactly one topic), it can be assumed that a further subdivision of the classes is not useful and that the example sentences have a high semantic similarity among each other. In our study, all determined coherence measures for a given class C_k were lower than 5. After creating the different topic models, representative category labels were determined by identified topic overlaps of the topic models and known domain-related synonyms.

These new, more fine-grained category labels C' (target labels) were then replaced with the original categories C to create the training dataset. Table 2 shows an example of the structure of the training data.

Table 2. Examples for training values transformed to new category label C'

Sentence	Category Label C	New Category Label C'
He laid the foundation for the later expansion of the company in the field of measurement technology	*Measuring technology*	*Measuring instruments and measuring devices*
We work with machine learning methods	*Artificial intelligence*	*Machine learning*
As a company, we are extremely proud of this innovative strength	*Cooperative*	*Collaboration and partnership*

In sum, the resulting dataset contains 1541 annotated examples, which are distributed according to Fig. 3. Here, it is particularly noticeable that for the category *miscellaneous* there are 596 examples in the dataset. All other categories have between 98 and 260 examples. This imbalance is mainly because it is easier to find texts or sentences that do not fit any of the seven categories and thus fall under *miscellaneous*.

When training the models, it was therefore necessary to observe whether overfitting of the *miscellaneous* class occurs through the imbalance of the data set. It was expected that there would be a large number of sentences on the websites of companies that should be matched to the category *miscellaneous*. Therefore, an overweight of this category in the training data is considered reasonable in order to stay as close to reality as possible. Since we translated the dataset labels to English for readability, reproducing our results with an English dataset may have an impact on the classification results.

4.5 Model Parametrization

First, we experimented with different models for both classifiers, e.g., *bert-base-german-cased*, *gbert-large*, *xlm-roberta-large-xnli-anli* and tried out different dataset sizes. Especially for TARS we tried out different amounts of given examples per class in the few-shot environment. In so doing we aimed at using as few examples as necessary and increased the amount successively. In our experiments, more than 40 training examples per class did not lead to a better performance. Different hyperparameters were tested and results are reported for the best.

We trained the TARS few shot classifier by Flair with an underlying German BERT Large[5] model with 40 training samples, 15 evaluation samples and 43 test samples per class, since the smallest class has 98 samples. The training was run for 40 epochs, with a learning rate of $5e^{-3}$.

---

[5] https://huggingface.co/deepset/gbert-large.

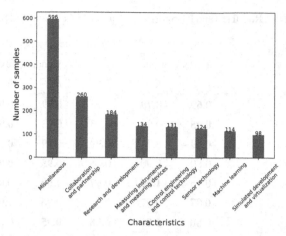

Fig. 3. Training sample distribution for optimized dataset with updated class labels

The standard text classifier by Hugging Face was trained on an underlying multi-lingual RoBERTa Large[6] model with a 70/15/15 train-eval-test split on the respective dataset with a learning rate of $4e^{-6}$ and 209 warmup steps. Here 20 epochs for training were sufficient, since more did not lead to better results.

5 Results

Table 3 and Table 4 summarize the classification results of both models on the raw dataset and the improved dataset. The columns show the accuracy, precision, recall, and F1-Score results. The left-hand side shows the affiliated results from TARS few-shot classifier in direct comparison to the standard text classifier by Hugging Face on the right-hand side. The micro, macro and weighted average metrics are also displayed for better comparison.

As shown in Table 3, both TARS and the standard text classifier show overall good results in precision, recall and F1-Score on the raw dataset. Top values for each column are highlighted in bold. The TARS model shows a higher recall value compared to precision. The F1-Score is equal to 0.89 on TARS and over 0.92 on the standard text classifier. The standard text classifier shows an overall higher score in precision and a significantly better score in detecting the *miscellaneous* class. For 6 out of 8 classes, the standard text classifier achieved an F1-Score over 0.9.

Table 4 shows that after dataset improvement, both TARS and the standard text classifier still show overall good results in precision, recall and F1-Score but not a significant F1-Score improvement compared to the raw dataset. Here both models show similar results in recall and precision. The F1-Score from the TARS model shows a subtle improvement by 0.1. However, we see a significant improvement in precision after dataset cleaning on the TARS classifier. For our use case, this improvement is favorable, since a higher precision means that we have a higher confidence that a predicted characteristic

---

[6] https://huggingface.co/xlm-roberta-large.

Table 3. Precision (*Pr*), Recall (*R*) and F1-Score (*F1*) for TARS Few Shot and Standard classifier on the raw dataset

Model	TARS Few Shot			Standard Text Classifier		
Class	*Pr*	*R*	*F1*	*Pr*	*R*	*F1*
Miscellaneous	0.69	0.79	0.73	**0.99**	**0.92**	**0.95**
Cooperative	**0.95**	0.91	0.93	0.93	**0.95**	**0.94**
Innovative	**0.89**	0.91	**0.90**	0.79	**0.95**	0.86
Measuring technology	0.80	0.90	0.85	**0.95**	**0.95**	**0.95**
Artificial Intelligence	0.95	**1.00**	0.97	**1.00**	0.94	0.97
Sensor technology	**0.87**	0.97	0.92	0.86	**1.00**	0.92
Control engineering	0.80	**1.00**	**0.88**	0.95	0.89	0.87
Virtualization and simulation	**0.93**	**1.00**	**0.96**	0.93	0.93	0.93
Micro average	0.85	**0.93**	0.89	**0.93**	**0.93**	**0.93**
Macro average	0.86	0.93	0.89	0.91	**0.94**	0.92
Weighted average	0.86	0.93	0.89	**0.94**	**0.94**	**0.94**

C on the partner website accurately represents reality. More generally speaking, we can say, that if we propose a partner to our seeking instance, we are more confident that our predictions about their characteristics are true. This is crucial in partner matchmaking and results in a more accurate selection of candidate partners, whereas a high recall increases the number of candidates, along with the need for manual reviewing.

Table 4. Precision (*Pr*), Recall (*R*) and F1-Score (*F1*) for TARS Few Shot and Standard classifier on the improved dataset

Model	TARS Few Shot			Standard Text Classifier		
Class	*Pr*	*R*	*F1*	*Pr*	*R*	*F1*
Miscellaneous	0.83	0.69	0.75	**0.97**	**0.89**	**0.93**
Collaboration and partnership	0.92	**0.96**	**0.94**	**0.97**	0.94	0.96
Research and development	0.81	**0.91**	0.86	**0.86**	0.90	**0.88**
Measuring instruments and measuring devices	0.84	0.88	0.86	**1.00**	**0.89**	**0.94**
Machine learning	**1.00**	0.97	**0.98**	0.82	**1.00**	0.90
Sensor technology	0.97	**1.00**	**0.98**	**1.00**	0.89	0.94
Control engineering and control technology	**0.92**	**0.90**	**0.91**	0.82	0.86	0.84

(continued)

Table 4. (*continued*)

Model	TARS Few Shot			Standard Text Classifier		
Class	*Pr*	*R*	*F1*	*Pr*	*R*	*F1*
Simulated development and virtualization	**0.91**	**0.97**	**0.94**	0.88	0.88	0.88
Micro average	0.90	**0.91**	0.90	**0.93**	**0.91**	**0.92**
Macro average	0.90	**0.91**	0.90	**0.91**	**0.91**	**0.91**
Weighted average	0.90	**0.91**	0.90	**0.93**	**0.91**	**0.92**

After all, the results show that Flair's TARS few-shot model is particularly suitable for training small data sets. TARS needed just 40 training samples per category to achieve remarkable results. With TARS we were able to derive a well performing multi-label classification model to achieve the goal of characteristic prediction for unknown partner websites. These predictions were then successfully used to propose partners for our seeking laboratory which was the goal of our case study.

6 Conclusion

The aim of this paper was to present a novel business matchmaking approach for semi-automated matchmaking between small and medium-sized enterprises. The matchmaking approach consists of the four steps data extraction, classification, aggregation, and scoring. This paper addressed the classification phase in particular. For this phase, two different text classifiers were demonstrated on a case study. Therefore, an initial raw dataset was created from publicly available websites data which was later fine-tuned. The goal of the text classification was to predict whether given categories of interest are found in the content of websites. From the classification results, it can be concluded that if there are 40 or more training examples per category, the use of pre-trained text classifiers and few-shot learning approaches are effective. It was shown that on a dataset with about 1500 examples and 8 different categories, the Hugging Face standard text classifier was able to achieve the highest F1-Score of 92%. But more mentionable are our results from Flair's TARS classifier. We found that Flair's TARS classifier is very suitable especially for few-shot learning, as it can achieve remarkable results even with only 40 examples per category. On both the raw and improved dataset the TARS classifier achieved an F1-Score about 90%, even with fewer training samples given. These results are also in consensus with the results originally obtained by the Flair developers [15].

Thus, we can conclude that in the scenario of partner matchmaking, where the creation of large training datasets is expensive and time consuming (expert-knowledge, manual sampling), Flair's TARS classifier is particularly suitable, since it can achieve sufficiently good classification results with only 40 examples per category in a few-shot learning environment. Despite the manual involvement in the training phase, after manually annotating training samples, the most time-consuming part is done. For us, the intense manual improvement of the raw dataset paid off due to higher precision results which eventually lead to a better matchmaking.

Once the classification model is calibrated to the seeking instance, the model can be applied in our matchmaking system. The matchmaking system is implemented in such a way that websites are automatically found, extracted, the characteristics classified (our described classification) and finally scored. During the scoring the explored company will be rated. In the future, our matchmaking prototype, which implements the data processing pipeline according to Fig. 1, could be further improved to a production-ready software solution and may be offered to interested industry partners. We also want to compare our previously implemented BERT-based classification approach with a GPT-based approach. Since the GPT model also supports few-shot learning, we hope to further reduce the required number of data examples per category with comparable classification performance by clever prompt engineering [29, 30]. In addition, we want to pre-train a larger set of standard categories.

Acknowledgments. Since this project was publicly founded, we would like to thank the German Federal Ministry of Education and Research, Funding reference number: 01IO1911.

References

1. Nijssen, E.J., et al.: Gathering and using information for the selection of technology partners. Technol. Forecast. Soc. Chang. **67**, 2–3 (2001)
2. Zilci, B.I., et al.: Cloud service matchmaking approaches: a systematic literature survey. In: 26th International Workshop on Database and Expert Systems Applications (DEXA) (2015)
3. Sweet, T., et al.: Machine learning techniques for brand-influencer matchmaking on the Instagram social network. http://arxiv.org/abs/1901.05949 (2019)
4. Christiansen, A.H., et al.: Multi-parameterised matchmaking: a framework. In: 2018 IEEE Conference on Computational Intelligence and Games (CIG). IEEE (2018)
5. Boroń, M., et al.: P2P matchmaking solution for online games. Peer Peer Netw. Appl. **13**, 137–150 (2020). https://doi.org/10.1007/s12083-019-00725-3
6. Joshi, M., et al.: A knowledge representation model for matchmaking systems in e-marketplaces. In: Proceedings of the 11th International Conference on Electronic Commerce. ACM, New York, NY, USA (2009)
7. Benramdane, M., et al.: Supervised machine learning for matchmaking in digital business ecosystems and platforms. Inf. Syst. Front. (2023). https://doi.org/10.1007/s10796-022-10357-3
8. Li, P., et al.: Long-form information retrieval for enterprise matchmaking. In: Proceedings of the 46th International ACM SIGIR Conference on Research and Development in Information Retrieval. ACM, New York, NY, USA (2023)
9. Gupta, S.: Text Classification: Applications and Use Cases. https://towardsdatascience.com/text-classification-applications-and-use-cases-beab4bfe2e62. Accessed 1 May 2021
10. Minaee, S., et al.: Deep learning based text classification: A comprehensive review. http://arxiv.org/abs/2004.03705 (2020)
11. Nooney, K.: Deep dive into multi-label classification..! https://towardsdatascience.com/journey-to-the-center-of-multi-labelclassification-384c40229bff. Accessed 1 May 2021
12. Vaswani, A., et al.: Attention is all you need. http://arxiv.org/abs/1706.03762 (2017)

13. Devlin, J., et al.: BERT: Pre-training of deep bidirectional Transformers for language understanding. http://arxiv.org/abs/1810.04805 (2018)
14. Liu, Y., et al.: RoBERTa: A robustly optimized BERT pretraining approach. http://arxiv.org/abs/1907.11692 (2019)
15. Yang, Z., et al: XLNet: Generalized Autoregressive Pretraining for Language Understanding. http://arxiv.org/abs/1906.08237 (2019)
16. Raffel, C., et al.: Exploring the limits of transfer learning with a unified text-to-text transformer. http://arxiv.org/abs/1910.10683 (2019)
17. Narang, S., Chowdhery, A.: Pathways Language Model (PaLM): Scaling to 540 Billion Parameters for Breakthrough Performance. https://ai.googleblog.com/2022/04/pathways-language-model-palm-scaling-to.html. Accessed 5 May 2022
18. OpenAI: GPT-4 Technical Report. https://doi.org/10.48550/arXiv.2303.08774 (2023)
19. Brown T., et al.: Language models are few-shot learners. Adv. Neural Inform. Process. Syst. **33**, 1877–1901 (2020)
20. Ye, J., et al.: A comprehensive capability analysis of GPT-3 and GPT-3.5 series models. http://arxiv.org/abs/2303.10420 (2023)
21. Xian, Y., et al.: Zero-Shot Learning - A Comprehensive Evaluation of the Good, the Bad and the Ugly. IEEE Transactions on Pattern Analysis and Machine Intelligence. http://arxiv.org/abs/1707.00600 (2017)
22. Munawwar, E.: Zero and Few Shot Learning. https://towardsdatascience.com/zero-and-few-shot-learning-c08e145dc4ed. Accessed 1 May 2022
23. Schopf, T., et al.: Evaluating Unsupervised Text Classification: Zero-shot and Similarity-based Approaches. https://arxiv.org/abs/2211.16285 (2022)
24. Halder, K., et al.: Task-aware representation of sentences for generic text classification. In: Proceedings of the 28th International Conference on Computational Linguistics. International Committee on Computational Linguistics, Stroudsburg, PA, USA (2020)
25. Sun, C., et al.: How to fine-tune BERT for text classification? In: Sun, M., Huang, X., Ji, H., Liu, Z., Liu, Y. (eds.) Chinese Computational Linguistics: 18th China National Conference, CCL 2019, Kunming, China, October 18–20, 2019, Proceedings, pp. 194–206. Springer International Publishing, Cham (2019). https://doi.org/10.1007/978-3-030-32381-3_16
26. Reimers N., Gurevych, I.: Sentence-BERT: Sentence embeddings using Siamese BERT-networks. https://arxiv.org/abs/1908.10084 (2019)
27. Robert Bosch GmbH Homepage. https://www.bosch.com/de/forschung/meet-bosch-research/kooperationen/. Accessed 16 June 2023
28. Roeder, M., et al.: Exploring the space of topic coherence measures. In: Proceedings of the Eighth ACM International Conference on Web Search and Data Mining - WSDM 2015. ACM Press, New York, New York, USA (2015)
29. White, J., et al.: A prompt pattern catalog to enhance prompt engineering with ChatGPT. http://arxiv.org/abs/2302.11382 (2023)
30. Liu, P., et al.: Pre-train, prompt, and predict: a systematic survey of prompting methods in natural language processing. ACM Comput. Surv. **55**(9), 1–35 (2023)

TraPM: A Framework for Online Pattern Matching Over Trajectory Streams

Rina Trisminingsih[1,3]([✉]), Salman Ahmed Shaikh[2], Toshiyuki Amagasa[1], Hiroyuki Kitagawa[1,2], and Akiyoshi Matono[2]

[1] University of Tsukuba, Tsukuba, Ibaraki, Japan
rinatrismi@kde.cs.tsukuba.ac.jp, {amagasa,kitagawa}@cs.tsukuba.ac.jp
[2] Artificial Intelligence Research Center, National Institute of Advanced Industrial Science and Technology, Tokyo, Japan
{shaikh.salman,a.matono}@aist.go.jp
[3] Department of Computer Science, IPB University, Bogor, Indonesia

Abstract. The proliferation of GPS-enabled devices has resulted in massive trajectory data streams. Moving objects' trajectories contain patterns which are useful for many applications, for instance, traffic monitoring, fleet management, etc. Pattern matching is a prerequisite of complex event processing, which is used to find complex patterns in data sequences. A number of distributed frameworks, like Apache Flink, Storm, etc., support pattern matching and complex event processing. However, they do not natively support pattern matching over trajectory streams. To address this problem, we propose a framework, TraPM, to support online pattern matching over trajectory streams. In addition, to accelerate spatial predicate evaluation, TraPM utilizes spatial indexing, i.e., Rtree and grid index. Moreover, it employs partition-based data distribution to distribute data across the cluster nodes. Extensive experiments on a real dataset demonstrate that our proposed framework can effectively detect patterns from trajectory streams and achieve higher throughput than the baseline approach.

Keywords: Pattern matching · Trajectory pattern matching · Online stream processing · Complex event processing · Spatial index

1 Introduction

With the extensive use of GPS-enabled devices, massive amount of moving objects' trajectory data is being generated. This data contain interesting patterns, which may be useful for a number of application domains [1]. A trajectory is a sequence of events and the identification of patterns in it can be useful for a variety of applications, for instance, ride-sharing applications, fleet management, route recommendation, etc. Given a trajectory stream and pattern query, pattern matching finds sequence of events which satisfy the given pattern over trajectory streams.

P. Delir Haghighi et al. (Eds.): iiWAS 2023, LNCS 14416, pp. 510–525, 2023.
https://doi.org/10.1007/978-3-031-48316-5_45

Example 1 (Real-time Driving Monitoring). Let us assume that a ride-sharing company wants to track the real-time driving behavior of its drivers. The company can easily obtain the real-time location of their vehicles via some vehicle tracking app; however, in addition, the company wants to get an alert if their drivers' driving is dangerous, violating speed limits or heading in the wrong direction. Such alerts are crucial to improve the quality of their service and to guarantee the safety of their passengers/deliveries. Such a monitoring system needs to process GPS points of thousands of vehicles in real time and to detect irregular driving, it must be capable of identifying complex patterns from thousands of trajectories, where each trajectory may consists of hundred of spatial points. Thus, we need a scalable system capable of handling spatial trajectories and detecting complex patterns in them in real time. This work proposes a real-time scalable system to detect complex patterns from spatial trajectory stream.

Many studies have proposed pattern-matching approaches using data stream mining [2–6]. These approaches mainly focus on discovering patterns that have occurred in the past instead of detecting complex patterns continuously from the trajectory data stream in real time as we do.

Complex Event Processing (CEP) is closely related to pattern matching. There are many CEP systems proposed in recent years [7]. Furthermore, state-of-the-art distributed stream processing systems like Apache Flink [8], Spark Streaming [9], and Storm [10] provide CEP capability, including pattern matching features. However, they do not natively support spatial trajectory pattern matching, i.e., they do not support spatial data types (points, lines, polygons, etc.), indexes, predicates and functions to enable pattern matching over trajectories. A few researchers have proposed CEP-based frameworks to detect complex patterns from trajectory data streams [11–14]. However, these frameworks suffer from at least one of the following issues: 1) lacking support of spatial predicates, 2) lacking query expressiveness, and 3) lacking scalability.

In this paper, we propose a framework TraPM (Trajectory Pattern Matching) to support online pattern matching over trajectory streams, which allows users to define patterns in expressive language. To enable scalable and distributed pattern matching, we make use of Apache Flink. The key contributions of this paper are summarized as follows.

(1) A novel framework for online pattern matching over trajectory streams. In addition to the trajectory points/events, the proposed framework considers nearby spatial objects (Point of Interests or Area of Interests) to detect complex patterns.
(2) An expressive spatial pattern matching operators which makes use of SQL:2021 to support spatial predicates and functions.
(3) Use of spatial indices to accelerate the performance of spatial pattern matching over trajectory streams.
(4) Extensive experiments to show the effectiveness and efficiency of the proposed framework using a real-life trajectory dataset from a ride-sharing company.

The rest of this paper is organized as follows. Section 2 presents the related works on general pattern matching, pattern matching over trajectories, and distributed stream processing. In Sect. 3, important preliminaries, definitions and problem formulation are presented. In Sect. 4, the proposed framework TraPM is presented, while Sect. 5 presents the experimental evaluation. Finally, in Sect. 6 conclusion and future direction are presented.

2   Related Work

In this section, we present the research work related to our research, particularly event pattern matching, pattern matching over trajectories, and distributed stream processing.

2.1   Event Pattern Matching

Our work is mainly related to complex event processing (CEP), a form of real-time stream processing that focuses on detecting patterns based on predicates from event stream. CEP systems generally provide pattern matching operators as their key feature. A number of CEP systems have been proposed in the literature during the last decade. Based on their pattern evaluation model, these approaches fall into three categories: 1) automata-based, 2) logic-based, and 3) tree-based [7].

Automata-based models, the most common category, translate patterns into nondeterministic automata as an evaluation model. For example, SASE and its derivatives [15,16], Cayuga [17], Siddhi [18], Esper [19], and FlinkCEP [20]. *Logic-based systems* rely on logic rules and inference to define patterns. Examples of such systems may be found in Event Calculus for Run-Time Reasoning (RTEC) [21] and Chronicle Recognition System (CRS) [22]. *Tree-based systems* such as [23] employs trees as a computational model. However, native support of spatial predicates for pattern matching on trajectory data has not been sufficiently addressed by these CEP systems.

2.2   Pattern Matching over Trajectories

Despite CEP systems' widespread usage, only a few attempts have addressed solutions which deal with spatial trajectory data. [11] proposed CEP-Traj, a CEP system that integrates trajectory streams and applies a series of pre-processing steps to ease pattern detection. [12] presented CEP systems based on RTEC, which detect patterns over trajectories in various application domains such as maritime monitoring and fleet management. For the RTEC systems, all patterns rely on rules that experts have designed. It makes these systems lack expressive querying in pattern matching. More recently, [13] presented a scalable CEP system on top of Wayeb CEP for processing big trajectory data streams. However, they did not consider the idea of spatial indexing in predicate evaluation to improve query performance. [14] proposed GeoT-Rex, a geospatial event processing for smart city applications. GeoT-Rex did not natively support trajectory pattern matching, but integrated geospatial operations and data models in CEP.

2.3 Distributed Stream Processing

To handle massive streaming trajectories, we need to enable CEP on distributed stream processing. Well-known distributed stream processing platforms, such as Apache Spark [9] and Storm [10], yet need to enable CEP independently. They have incorporated CEP engines, such as Siddhi [18] and Esper [19], as their embedded engines. On the other hand, Apache Flink [8] can incorporate CEP operators in the Flink program with the FlinkCEP built-in library in Data Stream API [20]. Flink also provides a pattern matching feature consolidating CEP and SQL API using the MATCH_RECOGNIZE clause [24]. This feature is based on a standard language for row pattern recognition in SQL:2021 [25]. However, Apache Flink, especially Flink SQL, does not provide native support for spatial data and operations required to process pattern matching over streaming trajectories. [27] utilized grid index to support processing of range, kNN, and join queries over trajectory streams, whereas [28,29] utilized it for spatial stream query processing. None of their solutions do not support CEP over trajectory streams. Thus, we extend Apache Flink, particularly Flink SQL, through spatial operators, predicates, and indices to support pattern matching queries over trajectory streams. To the best of our knowledge, this is the first work addressing real-time pattern matching over trajectory stream. Therefore, it is not possible to compare it with any other framework.

3 Preliminaries and Problem Definition

In this section, we present preliminaries and the problem definition.

3.1 Preliminaries

GPS-enabled moving objects, for instance, car, human, animal generate series of points, known as trajectory. We call each trajectory point an event. These events are generated continuously as an online data stream as the object move.

Definition 1 (Event). *An event e is a tuple consisting of location attribute given by latitude and longitude of a moving object at timestamp t.*

Definition 2 (Trajectory). *A trajectory T of a moving object is a sequence of discrete events $\{e_1, e_2, ..., e_n\}$ ordered by their timestamps $\{t_1, t_2, ..., t_n\}$, respectively, where $t_i < t_{(i+1)}$. Each trajectory is identified by trajectory identifier φ.*

Definition 3 (Trajectory Stream). *A trajectory stream S_Γ is an unbounded set of trajectories generated by multiple moving objects ordered by their timestamps.*

TraPM tries to find the query patterns in the trajectory stream. Since the stream is unbounded, window is used to bound the stream and the pattern is searched in the window-based sub-trajectory.

Definition 4 (Pattern). *A pattern or sequential pattern P is a sequence of predicates or conditions. The pattern is defined using regular expression and the trajectory stream events must fulfill the predicates in the pattern. The pattern is translated to Nondeterministic Finite Automata (NFA) as an evaluation model.*

Definition 5 (Predicate). *A predicate Pr is a condition that must be satisfied by S_Γ events. A predicate may consist of multiple conditions connected via Boolean operations.*

Example 2. [A query pattern to detect a specific driving pattern] A pattern to detect vehicles that passing certain point of interest (POI), later crossing an area of interest (AOI), and then taking a turn with bearing/angle more than 100°C. The pattern to detect such a driving can be formulated as a regular expression, **ABC**, consisting of three predicates, A, B, and C. Where, A: ST_IsNear_POI(ST_Point(A.lon, A.lat), 0.01); B: ST_Within_AOI(ST_Point (B.lon, B.lat)), and C: C.bearing > 100.

In pattern matching, a predicate can be categorized into constants, variables, simple mathematical operations, and user-defined. In this work we introduce several user-defined spatial predicates to support spatial pattern queries. Spatial predicates deal with topological relations between trajectories and nearby objects to identify complex patterns in a trajectory.

Definition 6 (Point of Interest (PoI)/Area of Interest (AoI)). *A static object, for instance, traffic signal, tree, shop, park, etc., whose location can be given by a spatial reference system (SRS) or coordinate reference system (CRS) on the surface of the Earth as coordinates. In particular, a PoI is a small object which can be represented by single coordinate, i.e., traffic signal, tree, etc.; whereas AoI is a larger object which can be represented by a polygon made up of multiple coordinates, i.e., park, school, etc.*

In our work, *PoIs* and *AoIs* are used in spatial predicates for trajectory pattern matching.

Definition 7 (Spatial Predicate). *A spatial predicate Pr_T is a predicate or condition that deals with spatial relation between trajectories and/or other spatial objects (PoI/AoI).*

Table 1 lists our proposed spatial functions that included spatial predicates. Since a trajectory stream is unbounded, we need a mechanism to bound the trajectories in trajectory stream so that pattern matching query may be executed on them. In stream processing, window is commonly used for this purpose.

Definition 8 (Window). *A window W is used to limit the number of trajectory events on which pattern matching query may be executed. Window could refer to specific time interval (time window) or to number of occurrences of events (count window).*

In this work, time-based window is used. However, it is straightforward to extend our work to count-based window.

Definition 9 (Pattern Matching Query). *A pattern matching query q over S_Γ detects patterns P, consisting of one or more predicates Pr, in S_Γ bounded by a sliding time window W. An output is generated if all the conditions in P are satisfied within W.*

Please refer Fig. 2b for a sample pattern matching query.

3.2   Problem Definition

This section formally defines the problem addressed in this work. In particular, we would like to detect complex patterns in trajectory stream continuously and in real time by utilizing the spatial predicates introduced in this work. Formally, the problem can be defined as follows:

Definition 10 (Online Trajectory Pattern Matching). *Given a pattern matching query q with ordinary (Pr) and spatial predicates (Pr_T), a real-time trajectory stream S_Γ, and a window W, continuously detect and output sequence of events bounded by W in S_Γ which satisfy q predicates.*

4   TraPM: A Framework for Online Pattern Matching over Trajectory Streams

In this section, we present TraPM's framework architecture, query language, pattern matching and distributed query processing.

4.1   Proposed Architecture

TraPM is implemented on top of Apache Flink to enable scalable stream processing, as depicted in Fig. 1. We use two APIs provided by Apache Flink, i.e., *Data Stream API* and *Table/SQL API* (FlinkSQL) for its development. The framework consumes moving objects' streaming trajectories via any pub/sub messaging system supported by Flink. The input stream is assumed to be totally ordered by timestamp. In the *Data Stream API layer*, Flink standard transformations are used to partition the input stream and translate the data stream into SQL API dynamic tables. In addition, this layer is responsible for generating PoIs and AoIs index.

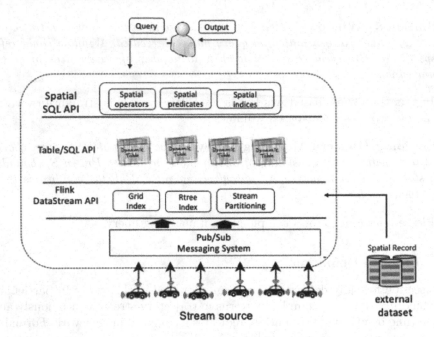

Fig. 1. TraPM Architecture

4.2 Query Language

For our proposed framework, we use the SQL query based on the standard language for pattern recognition (SQL:2021) [25]. It uses MATCH_RECOGNIZE clause for pattern matching. Flink SQL does not provide native support for spatial data and spatial operations; however, it supports SQL row pattern recognition for pattern matching via SQL API (SQL:2021). Thus, we extended Flink SQL with spatial functions, including spatial operators, predicates, and indices to support trajectory pattern matching. Users can register pattern matching queries to the TraPM framework through SQL API and its output is available via various sinks supported by Apache Flink, as illustrated in Fig. 1.

Figure 2a shows the basic syntax of the pattern matching query. In the query, SELECT and FROM clauses are used to specify the attributes to output, and the input stream, respectively. A MATCH_RECOGNIZE clause enables logical partitioning and ordering of the data that is used with the PARTITION BY and ORDER BY clauses. Furthermore, it enables defining patterns of rows to seek using the PATTERN clause. These patterns use a syntax similar to that of regular expressions. The logical components of the pattern variables are specified in the DEFINE clause. For the streaming use cases, it is often required that a pattern finishes within a given period of time. This allows for limiting the overall state size that Flink has to maintain internally. Therefore, Flink SQL supports the additional (non-standard SQL) WITHIN clause for defining time-based window for the pattern to occur completely. The clause can be defined after the PATTERN clause. If the time between the first and last event of a potential pattern match is longer than the given value, such a match will not be appended to the result. Figure 2b presents pattern matching query example using MATCH_RECOGNIZE clause for detecting a specific driving pattern as explained in Example 2.

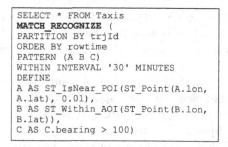

```
SELECT <selected attributes>
FROM <input stream>
MATCH_RECOGNIZE (
[PARTITION BY <attributes>]
[ORDER BY <time_attributes>]
PATTERN    <set   of   pattern
variables>
WITHIN <duration>
DEFINE <pattern definitions>)
```

```
SELECT * FROM Taxis
MATCH_RECOGNIZE (
PARTITION BY trjId
ORDER BY rowtime
PATTERN (A B C)
WITHIN INTERVAL '30' MINUTES
DEFINE
A AS ST_IsNear_POI(ST_Point(A.lon,
A.lat), 0.01),
B AS ST_Within_AOI(ST_Point(B.lon,
B.lat)),
C AS C.bearing > 100)
```

(a) Basic syntax   (b) Query to detect a driving pattern

Fig. 2. Pattern Matching Query

To enable pattern matching over spatial trajectory streams, we extended Flink SQL by adding a set of spatial functions. The spatial functions are implemented using Flink SQL User Defined Functions (UDFs). The implemented spatial functions include (1) Spatial constructors, to construct a geometry from the raw input stream; (2) Spatial operators, to execute a function on the given attribute; (3) Spatial predicates, to execute a logical judgement on the given

Table 1. TraPM Spatial Function

Category	Description	Implemented Functions for TraPM
Constructor	The functions which construct a geometry from raw input stream	ST_Point, ST_Polygon, ST_Line, ST_GeomFromText, ST_GeomFromWKB, ST_GeomFromWKT, etc
Operator	The functions which are executed directly on attribute values	ST_Distance, ST_Buffer, ST_Intersection, ST_Difference, etc
Predicate	The functions which execute a logical judgement on given attribute values and return Boolean	ST_Within, ST_Intersects, ST_Touches, ST_Equals, ST_IsNear_POI etc
Output	The functions that enable query to output in specified format	ST_AsBinary, ST_AsText

attributes and return boolean output; (4) Outputs, enable spatial pattern matching query output in specified format. Table 1 shows the list of spatial functions implemented for TraPM. Please refer Table 3 in the appendix section for the details of the functions.

4.3   Pattern Matching Evaluation

The evaluation model of Flink CEP module is based on NFA design of SASE++ [16]. This system translates patterns into non-deterministic automata equipped with predicates on their transitions. These transitions are triggered by the arrival of events.

Our spatial predicates require heavier processing than ordinary predicates as they need to check spatial trajectories' nearby objects. That is, the predicates may need to compute spatial distance between the trajectory and other spatial objects. The predicates in the baseline spatial trajectory pattern matching query follows brute-force approach, i.e., spatial distance is computed between all the events (points) of the trajectory and the objects in the database. However, such a approach is not useful for data streams due to the low-latency throughput requirement. Thus, to reduce the computation cost of spatial pattern matching, we propose index-based pruning. In particular, we made of use RTree and grid-based indices. The indices help to prune out the spatial objects which cannot help in the pattern matching and can be safely pruned.

Spatial index structures can be classified into two categories: 1) Tree-based, and 2) Grid-based. In this study, we use RTree and uniform grid index to accelerate the performance of pattern matching over trajectory streams. In TraPM query, RTree is constructed using PoIs and AoIs, whose distance need to be computed with trajectory stream during the pattern matching query execution. The RTree index is constructed once at the start of the query and then used continuously by trajectory stream for efficient query processing. On the other hand, grid index is constructed by partitioning the 2-dimensional space into cells of equal length. Just like RTree index, PoIs and AoIs are indexed, i.e., PoIs/AoIs are assigned grid cell IDs based on their spatial location, once at the start of the query. During the spatial trajectory pattern matching query execution, each incoming trajectory point is assigned a grid cell ID based on its spatial location. We then prune out the PoIs/AoIs which do not fall within the required distance of the trajectory events specified in the spatial predicate. For the grid-based pruning, we employ the idea of guaranteed and candidate neighbors proposed in in [27–29]. For the details on grid-based pruning, please refer [27–29].

4.4   Scalable Pattern Matching over Trajectory Streams

To enable distributed and scalable trajectory pattern matching query, we employ Flink native distributed approach, which divides the processing load into several distributed tasks. Particularly, We employ data partition based approach, where a trajectory stream is partitioned into smaller subsets based on trajectory IDs. This enables near uniform stream partitioning using the Flink's powerful data partitioning algorithm. In particular, we use Flink's *keyBy* operator, which logically partitions the input stream based on key or ID. Since in trajectory stream, the new trajectories arrive and old trajectories expire continuously, Flink *keyBy* operator dynamically assigns the new incoming stream to the Flink's task with the least amount of processing load, thus, keeping the data uniformly balanced during query execution. This approach also avoids data shuffling and broadcasting, resulting in higher throughput.

5   Experimental Evaluation

This section presents experimental evaluation of our proposed trajectory pattern matching framework.

5.1   Dataset

Datastream. We used Grab-Posisi [26], a real-world dataset collected by Grab company containing the GPS trajectories of drivers in Singapore and Jakarta. The dataset consist of 30 million tuples recorded from 2019-04-08 to 2019-04-21 in Singapore City. Each tuple consist of a trajectory ID, latitude, longitude, timestamp (UTC), data collection accuracy, bearing, and speed. We assume that the streaming tuples are in order with respect to time. The dataset is loaded into Apache Kafka messaging system and supplied as a distributed data stream to our framework.

PoIs. The dataset consists of 25,037 POIs of Singapore. Each tuple in the dataset consists of spatial location, name, and PoI category.

AoIs. The dataset of AoI is obtained from Singapore city and consist of 332 records.

5.2   Experimental Setting

All the experiments are performed on Apache Flink version 1.17.1 and all algorithms are implemented in Java, which is available as open source on Github[1]. All evaluations are performed on a machine running Ubuntu 20.04.5 LTS with 16 GB memory and Core i7 3.60 GHz x 8 CPU. In the experiments, we compared the following approaches:

- Baseline: Trajectory pattern matching query which does not utilize index.
- Grid index: Trajectory pattern matching query which uses grid index to index PoIs, AoIs and incoming trajectory stream points for efficient predicate evaluation.
- Rtree index: Trajectory pattern matching query which uses Rtree index to index PoIs and AoIs index for efficient predicate evaluation.

Table 2. Experimental parameters.

Parameter	Values
Grid cell width	10×10, $\mathbf{30 \times 30}$, 50×50, 100×100
# of PoI	1, 10, 100, **1000**, 10000, 20000, 25000
# of AoI	**1**, 10, 100, 200, 300
Parallelism	1, 5, **10**, 20
Window length	1, 5, **10**, 30 (minutes)

For the evaluation, we used the pattern matching query as shown in Fig. 3b and varied the parameters as summarized in Table 2, with the default values shown in bold. We report the performance of our framework in terms of throughput, which can be defined as the average number of tuples processed per second. It is obtained by dividing the total number of input stream tuples processed by the system with total processing time. Each experiment is performed three times and their average values are reported in the results.

We use Euclidean distance as the distance metric. As for the grid index, we construct a uniform grid index using a rectangular bounding box of Singapore region using the following top-right and bottom-left coordinates: bottom-left = 103.6, 1.21; top-right = 104.1, 1.47. To identify the most effective grid size, preliminary experiments are performed using the grid size shown in Table 2. In the preliminary experiments shown in Fig. 3a, we compare the throughput of the grid-based approach with the baseline by varying grid size. From the experiments we found that the grid size 30×30 produces the highest throughput. Thus, in the rest of the experiments, we use 30×30 as the default grid size parameter value.

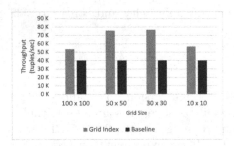

(a) Throughput evaluation by varying Grid-size

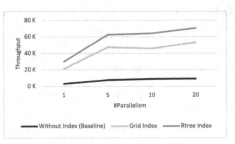

(b) Comparison of baseline approach with the index-based approaches

Fig. 3. Throughput evaluation

---

[1] https://github.com/rinatrismi/TraPM.

5.3 Experimental Result

Firstly, we compare the throughput of our proposed index-based (RTree and Grid) TraPR, with the baseline. We use the default parameter values for this experiment. Figure 3b shows that the throughput of proposed index-based approaches is better than the baseline. In particular, Grid index-based implementation can achieve over 4x and RTree based implementation can achieve over 6x higher throughput than the baseline. R-tree data retrieval efficiency is good with smaller number of objects. However, as the R-tree size increases, its retrieval efficiency degrades. Since in Fig. 3b, the number of PoI is only 1000, R-tree based query results in higher throughput.

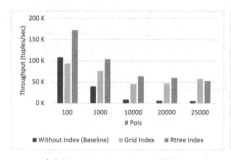

(a) Varying number of PoIs

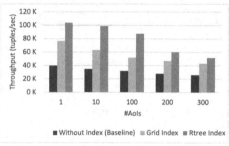

(b) Varying number of AoIs

Fig. 4. The throughput of query by varying number of PoIs and AoIs

Next, we examine the performance of our framework by varying the number of query objects. The experimental results of varying point of interest (PoI) are reported in Fig. 4a; while, Fig. 4b reports the performance results by of varying the number of Area of Interest (AoI). In both the figures, we see a decreasing throughput trend with the increase in PoIs or AoIs. In Fig. 4a, we see a sharp throughput decrease in the baseline and R-tree based implementations; whereas, the trend of grid-based implementation is not so steep and in fact flattens after 10,000 PoIs. This proves that R-tree based implementation is good when the number of PoIs are small, whereas, the grid-based implementation is good for very large number of PoIs. The reason in the sharp throughput decline in case of R-tree based implementation is the amount of overlapping among the tree index nodes and the number of candidates returned by the query. As the number of objects increase, the overlapping among the tree nodes increase, thus, each query to R-tree returns large number of candidates, thus requiring higher amount of processing. On the other hand, when using grid index, PoIs/AoIs are assigned grid cell IDs based on their location. The IDs are stored in a hash table. To identify neighboring PoIs/AoIs, each incoming streaming tuple is assigned grid cell ID and hashed. Unlike R-tree, grid index's hash table is not much affected by the number of PoIs/AoIs, thus the throughput decline in case of grid index is less steep than R-tree.

Finally, experiments are performed by varying the query parallelism to investigate the scalability of our pattern matching framework. The experimental results are shown in Fig. 5. From the figures, it is clear that our proposed framework is highly scalable. The scalability can be easily achieved by increasing the amount of query parallelism. Another thing to note in Fig. 5 is that for the small number of PoIs (i.e., 1000), R-tree based index gives the best throughput; whereas, for the larger number of PoIs, i.e., 10,000, 20,000 and 25,000, grid index based implementation gives the best result, for the reason discussed earlier.

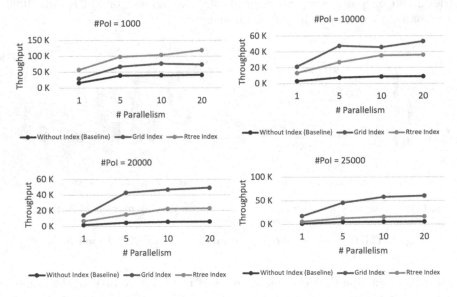

Fig. 5. Throughput evaluation by varying query parallelism.

6   Conclusion and Future Work

In this paper, we have proposed TraPM, a novel framework for scalable, online, and real-time pattern matching over spatial trajectory streams. TraPM utilizes spatial indexing, i.e., RTree and grid index, to accelerate spatial predicate evaluation. In addition, it employs a trajectory identifier based data distribution to distribute trajectory stream uniformly across the cluster nodes. The experimental study using a real dataset from a ride-sharing company demonstrated that our proposed framework can effectively perform pattern matching over trajectory stream and our proposed R-tree and grid-index based implementations can achieve higher throughput than the baseline approach. In the future, we plan to improve TraPM to tackle advanced patterns that consider road networks and enrich them with additional information, such as weather.

Acknowledgement. This paper is based on results obtained from "Research and Development Project of the Enhanced Infrastructures for Post-5G Information and Communication Systems" (JPNP20017) commissioned by NEDO, JPNP14004 commissioned by NEDO, JST CREST Grant Number JPMJCR22M2, AMED Grant Number JP21zf0127005, and JSPS KAKENHI Grant Numbers JP22H03694 and JP23H03399.

Appendix

Table 3. TraPM Functions for Spatial Pattern Matching

Function	Description
ST_Point(lon, lat)	Constructs a spatial Point from longitude and latitude
ST_Line(WKT)	Constructs Line from wkt text
ST_Polygon(WKT)	Constructs Polygon from wkt text
ST_GeomFromText(WKT)	Constructs Geometry from WKT
ST_GeomFromWKB(WKB)	Constructs Geometry from WKB
ST_AsText(A)	Returns WKT string representation of a geometry
ST_AsBinary(A)	Returns WKB representation of a geometry
ST_Distance(A, B)	Returns the Euclidean distance between A and B
ST_Buffer(A, r)	Returns a geometry whose distance from A $\leq$ radius r
ST_Intersection(A, B)	Returns the intersection of of A and B
ST_Difference(A, B)	Returns part of A that does not intersect B
ST_Within(A, B)	Returns true if A is fully contained by B
ST_Within_AOI(A)	Returns true if an AOI is fully contained by geometry g
ST_Intersects(A, B)	Returns true if A intersects B
ST_Touches(A, B)	Returns true if A touches B
ST_Equals(A, B)	Returns true if A equals B
ST_IsNear_POI(A, d)	Returns true if A is within distance d of given POI

A and B: Geometries, WKT: Well-known text, WKB: Well-Known Binary

References

1. Wang, S., Bao, Z., Shane Culpepper, J., Cong, G.: A survey on trajectory data management, analytics, and learning. ACM Comput. Surv. (CSUR) **54**(2), 1–36 (2021)
2. Masciari, E., Gao, S., Zaniolo, C.: Sequential pattern mining from trajectory data. In: 17th International Database Engineering & Applications (IDEAS'13), pp. 162–167 (2013)
3. Da Silva, T.C., Zeitouni, K., de Macedo, J., Casanova, M.: A framework for online mobility pattern discovery from trajectory data streams. In: 17th IEEE International Conference on Mobile Data Management (MDM), pp. 365–368 (2016)

4. Chen, L., Gao, Y., Fang, Z., Miao, X., Jensen, C.S., Guo, C.: Real-time distributed co-movement pattern detection on streaming trajectories. Proc. VLDB Endow. **12**(10), 1208–1220 (2019)
5. Fang, Z., Yunjun G.L., Chen, P.L., Miao, X., Jensen, C.S.: Coming: a real-time co-movement mining system for streaming trajectories. In: Proceedings of the 2020 ACM SIGMOD International Conference on Management of Data (SIGMOD'20), pp. 2777–2780 (2020)
6. Yadamjav, M., Bao, Z., Zheng, B., Choudhury, F., Samet, H.: Querying recurrent convoys over trajectory data. ACM Trans. Intell. Syst. Technol. **11**(5), 1–24 (2020)
7. Giatrakos, N., Alevizos, E., Artikis, A., Deligiannakis, A., Garofalakis, M.: Complex event recognition in the big data era: a survey. VLDB J. **29**, 313–352 (2020)
8. Apache Flink Project. https://flink.apache.org/. Accessed 15 July 2023
9. Spark Streaming. https://spark.apache.org/streaming/. Accessed 15 July 2023
10. Apache Storm. https://storm.apache.org/. Accessed 15 July 2023
11. Teroso-Saenz, F., Valdes-Vela, M., den Breejen, E., Hanckmann, P., Dekker, R., Skarmeta-Gomez, A.F.: CEP-traj: an event-based solution to process trajectory data. Inf. Syst. **52**, 34–54 (2015)
12. Patroumpas, K., Alevizos, E., Artikis, A., Vodas, M., Pelekis, N., Theodoridis, Y.: Online event recognition from moving vessel trajectories. GeoInformatica **21**(2), 389–427 (2017)
13. Ntoulias, E., Alevizos, E., Artikis, A., Akasiadis, C., Koumparos, A.: Online fleet monitoring with scalable event recognition and forecasting. GeoInformatica **26**, 613–644 (2022)
14. Khazael, B., Asl, M.V., Malazi, H.T.: Geospatial complex event processing in smart city applications. Simul. Model. Pract. Theory **122**, 102675 (2023)
15. Agrawal, J., Diao, Y., Gyllstrom, D., Immerman, N.: Efficient pattern matching over event streams. In: Proceedings of the 2008 ACM SIGMOD International Conference on Management of Data (SIGMOD '08), pp. 147–160 (2008)
16. Zhang, H., Diao, Y., Immerman, N.: On complexity and optimization of expensive queries in complex event processing. In: Proceedings of the 2014 ACM SIGMOD International Conference on Management of Data (SIGMOD'14), pp. 217–228 (2014)
17. Demers, A.J., Gehrke, J., Panda, B., Riedewald, M., Sharma, V., White, W.M.: Cayuga: a general-purpose event monitoring system. In: 3rd Biennial Conference on Innovative Data Systems Research (CIDR) (2007)
18. Siddhi CEP. https://github.com/wso2/siddhi. Accessed 18 July 2023
19. Esper. https://www.espertech.com/esper. Accessed 18 July 2023
20. FlinkCEP. https://nightlies.apache.org/flink/flink-docs-master/docs/libs/cep. Accessed 19 July 2023
21. Artikis, A., Sergot, M., Paliouras, G.: An event calculus for event recognition. IEEE Trans. Knowl. Data Eng. **27**(4), 895–908 (2014)
22. Dousson, C., Maigat, P.L.: Chronicle recognition improvement using temporal focusing and hierarchization. In: Proceedings of the 20th International Joint Conference on Artifical Intelligence (IJCAI'07), pp. 324–329 (2007)
23. Mei, Y., Madden, S.: ZStream: a cost-based query processor for adaptively detecting composite events. In: Proceedings of the 2009 ACM SIGMOD International Conference on Management of Data (SIGMOD), pp. 193–206 (2009)
24. Flink Pattern Recognition. https://nightlies.apache.org/flink/flink-docs-release-1.17/docs/dev/table/sql/queries/match_recognize/. Accessed 20 July 2023

25. ISO/IEC TR 19075–5:2021, Information technology - Guidance for the use of database language SQL. https://www.iso.org/standard/78936.html. Accessed 20 Jun 2023
26. Huang, X., et al.: Grab-Posisi: an extensive real-life GPS trajectory dataset in Southeast Asia. In: Proceedings of the 3rd ACM SIGSPATIAL International Workshop on Prediction of Human Mobility (PredictGIS'19), pp. 1–10 (2019)
27. Shaikh, S.A., Kitagawa, H., Matono, A., Kim, K.S.: TStream: a framework for real-time and scalable trajectory stream processing and analysis. In: Proceedings of the 30th International Conference on Advances in Geographic Information Systems (SIGSPATIAL'22), pp. 1–4 (2022)
28. Shaikh, S.A., Mariam, K., Kitagawa, H., Kim, K.S.: GeoFlink: a distributed and scalable framework for the real-time processing of spatial streams. In: Proceeding of the 29th ACM International Conference on Information and Knowledge Management (CIKM), pp. 3149–3156 (2020)
29. Shaikh, S.A., Kitagawa, H., Matono, A., Mariam, K., Kim, K.S.: GeoFlink: an efficient and scalable spatial data stream management system. IEEE Access **10**, 24909–24935 (2022)

Attention Based Stopword Generation for Neural Network Based Text Processing

Yuki Kuwabara[✉] and Yu Suzuki

Graduate School of Natural Science and Technology, Gifu University, 1–1 Yanagido, Gifu 5011193, Japan
kuwabara.yuki.e9@s.gifu-u.ac.jp, suzuki.yu.r4@f.gifu-u.ac.jp

Abstract. Stopwords are used to improve the accuracy of document classification and retrieval. We believe that setting appropriate stopwords improves classification accuracy. However, in our preliminary experiments, in document classification tasks using BERT, existing stopword lists are not effective for improving classification accuracy. In this method, words with high attention in misclassified input documents and low attention in correctly classified documents are treated as stopwords. We conduct experiments to confirm the effectiveness of our stopword generation methods. Our experimental results show that there are cases using stopwords generated by our methods that improve the classification accuracy. We find that the classification accuracy was higher when focusing on attention differences than when focusing only on attention in incorrect documents.

Keywords: Stopwords · Text classification · Attention · BERT · Machine learning · Natural language processing

1 Introduction

Stopwords are the words that are excluded from processing texts [1]. System developers use stopwords to improve the accuracies of document classification tasks and searching tasks. When we use inappropriate stopwords, the classification accuracies will decrease [2]. Existing stopword lists are not always effective in improving document classification accuracy using BERT [3]. Therefore, we need a method to generate stopwords to improve the classification accuracy.

This attention mechanism [4] used in BERT [5] is a mechanism that learns which parts of the input data to focus on for classifying documents. Using this *attention*, we can interpret the basis of the classifier's decision. We can find factors that would degrade classification performance from words the classifier uses as bases for its decisions. Therefore, we focus on attention when the classifier classifies documents using BERT.

When the classifier classifies text data, we define *correct documents* as text data that the classifier predicts the same label as the correct label. On the other hand, we define *incorrect documents* as text data that the classifier predicts a label different from the correct label. Words with high attention in incorrect documents are factors causing the classifier to make incorrect predictions. Therefore, it is good to generate stopwords by focusing on the attention in incorrect documents. However, if the system generates stopwords by focusing only on attention in incorrect documents, we expect that words with high attention in correct documents will also become stopwords. Words with high attention in correct documents help the classifier to make correct predictions. Generating stopwords by focusing only on attention in incorrect documents is not a good idea. Words with low attention in correct documents do not contribute to the classifier making correct predictions. It would be a good idea to use words with high attention in incorrect documents and low attention in correct documents as stopwords. We focus on the difference between attention in incorrect documents and attention in correct documents.

We propose two methods for generating a stopword list. We do not use these two methods at the same time. The first method is to generate a stopword list. In first method, we use the attention difference between incorrect and correct documents as the probability of words appearing in the stopword list. In this method, the system removes all words in the stopword list from input documents. The second is a method for generating stopword list with probability. We use the attention difference as the probability of word removal. The system probability decides whether or not to remove each word in input documents. In the second method, the system sometimes removes words from input documents and sometimes does not remove words from input documents, even if they are the same words.

We conduct experiments to confirm the effectiveness of our proposed stopword generation methods. We compare the accuracy of documents classification with and without stopwords removal. We show whether there is a significant difference in classification accuracy or not by statistical tests. Best stopwords will depend on datasets and the purpose of the classification. We perform classification with different purposes using the same dataset. We use three different datasets in our experiments. Experimental results show that there are cases using stopwords generated by our methods to improve classification accuracy. We find that the classification accuracy is higher when focusing on attention differences than when focusing only on attention in incorrect documents.

The contributions of our research is as follows:

- We generate stopwords that sometimes improve the classification accuracy in the document classification task using BERT.
- We find that the classification accuracy is higher when focusing on attention differences than when focusing on attention in incorrect documents.

2   Related Work

There are several studies on stopword generation. Kokubu et al. [6] generate stopwords that are effective in a keyword extraction task for guessing contents of texts. The keyword extraction method is to select words with a high frequency of occurrence base on certain criteria. Kokubu et al. use stopwords as a criterion for selecting words. There are three types of target words for stopwords: "Non-words," "Non-content words," and "Low-content words". "Non-words" are punctuation and symbols. "Non-content words" are words called function words. Function words are words that indicate grammatical relationships between words or sentences. Kokubu et al. remove non-content words based on part-of-speech information. "Low-content words" are words unlikely to help in guessing content. Kokubu et al. generate a list of "Low-content words". The stopword list is effective in the keyword extraction task.

Saiyed et al. [7] generate stopwords. There are two methods of creating stopwords. The first is to manually create a stopword list and compare all words to it. The second method is to create a stopword list automatically. The former is a static method. The latter is a dynamic method. The frequency of occurrence of the word follows Zipf's law. Saiyed et al. determine the words to be stopwords by setting a threshold at the top and bottom of the frequency of occurrence. The static method reduces document size by 44.53%. The dynamic method reduces document size by 52.53%. With dynamic methods, words that should not become stopwords may become stopwords.

Some studies apply the stopword concept to classification methods using neural networks. Kimura et al. [8] investigate the effect of stop phrases on document classification tasks. A phrase is a word sequence consisting of multiple words. Many of the most frequently occurring words are function words. Function words do not represent the content meaning of the document. There is an idea that frequently appearing words are stopwords [9]. Kimura et al. define stop phrases as frequently occurring phrases based on this concept of stopwords. Kimura et al. perform two experiments. The first is an experiment to add stop phrases to the tokenizer's vocabulary. The second is an experiment in multi-task learning of stop phrase extraction and document classification. Experimental results show that stop phrases are effective in improving classification accuracy.

Kokubu et al. consider low-content words with high frequency of occurrence as stopwords. Saiyed et al. determine the words to be stopwords by setting a threshold at the top and bottom of the frequency of occurrence. Kimura et al. consider frequently occurring phrases as stop phrases. In this study, we construct a system that generates stopwords by focusing on attention when the classifier classifies documents using BERT.

3   Proposed Method

First, we define *correct documents* as text data that the classifier predicts the same label as the correct label. On the other hand, we define *incorrect documents* as text data that the classifier predicts a label different from the correct label. We focus on the difference in attention below two cases: words appear in correct documents and words appear in incorrect documents. We use the difference in attention as the probability of word removal. We generate stopwords probabilistically. We show below the procedure for generating stopwords.

1. The system classifies text data without stopword removal.
2. The system calculates the average of attention of words in correct documents for each word. The system calculates the average of attention in incorrect documents for each word.
3. The system calculates the difference in the average attention for words in incorrect documents and words in correct documents.
4. We use the attention difference as a probability. We use the following two methods to remove stopwords.
   (a) Method 1 : Complete Removal
       i. The system decides with probability whether a word is a stopword or not.
       ii. The system adds a word to the stopword list if the system determines that the word is a stopword.
       iii. We remove from the input document all words that are in the stopword list that we have created.
   (b) Method 2 : Probabilistic Removal
       i. The system decides whether a word is a stopword based on the probability of word removal.
       ii. The system removes a word that is a stopword from the input document.
       iii. The system performs these steps i. and ii. for every word in input documents.

3.1   Attention

Attention mechanism is a mechanism that learns which parts of input data to focus on. BERT also uses the attention mechanism. We focus on the attention of the classifier when it makes a classification. We can interpret bases of the classifier's decision. We could find words that negatively affect classification performance based on the basis of the classification decision. Therefore, we focus on attention when the classifier classifies documents using BERT.

The system calculate the average attention for each word in input documents. We focus on the following two cases. When a word appears in the incorrect documents, and when the word appears in the correct documents. We define D as the document set of incorrect documents. We define N as the total number of documents in document set D. We define d_i as the ith document in document set D. The range of i values is 1 to N. We define n_i as the number of times the word w appears in document d_i. We define w_j as the jth appearing word w in document d_i. The range of j values is from 1 to n_i. We define $a(d_i, w_j)$ as the attention of a word w_j appearing in a document d_i. We define $a_m(w)$ as the average attention of the word w in the incorrect document. We show below the formula to calculate the average attention $a_m(w)$.

$$a_m(w) = \frac{1}{\sum_{i=1}^{N} n_i} \sum_{i=1}^{N} \sum_{j=1}^{n_i} a(d_i, w_j) \tag{1}$$

We define $a_c(w)$ as the average attention when the word w appears in the correct document. We calculate the average attention $a_c(w)$ using Eq. (1).

We can interpret the words with high attention in incorrect documents as the words the classifier focus on when it made the incorrect prediction. We consider that a word w with high attention in incorrect documents $a_m(w)$ should be a stopword. We believe that the removal of the misprediction factor would improve classification accuracy.

We consider a word w with high attention in correct documents $a_c(w)$. We can interpret these words as words that the classifier focuses on when it makes a correct prediction. We believe that words with high attention in the correct document $a_c(w)$ are useful words for classification. Therefore, it is not appropriate to remove those words from input documents. We consider that the method of generating stopwords by focusing only on attention in incorrect documents $a_m(w)$ is not a good idea. This method has the potential to remove factors that cause incorrect predictions while at the same time removing features that are important for correct predictions.

We consider words w with low attention in correct documents $a_c(w)$. These words do not contribute much to making correct predictions. It would be a good idea to use a word with high attention in incorrect documents $a_m(w)$ and low attention in correct documents $a_c(w)$ as a stopword. We focus on the difference between attention in the incorrect documents $a_m(w)$ and attention in correct documents $a_c(w)$. We show below the equation to calculate the difference of attention $a_d(w)$.

$$a_d(w) = a_m(w) - a_c(w) \qquad (2)$$

Words with a higher attention difference $a_d(w)$ have a negative impact on classification. Therefore, Words with higher attention difference $a_d(w)$ should be stopwords.

3.2   Probabilistic Stopword Removal

We generate stopwords by focusing on the attention difference $a_d(w)$. The following methods exist for determining stopwords: a method to determine the threshold value for the attention difference $a_d(w)$ and a method to determine the number of words that are stopwords. If researchers use the above methods, researchers must manually determine the threshold value and the number of stopwords. In this study, we automatically generate stopwords. We use the attention difference $a_d(w)$ as the probability that the word w is a stopword. Words with a higher attention difference $a_d(w)$ have a higher probability of being stopwords.

The range of the attention difference $a_d(w)$ depends on the data set used and the criteria used to perform the classification. We normalize the attention difference $a_d(w)$ so that the maximum is 1 and the minimum is 0. We define A as the whole set of attention differences $a_d(w)$. We define $\max A$ as the maximum attention difference $a_d(w)$. We define $\min A$ as the minimum attention difference $a_d(w)$. We show below the formula to calculate the normalized attention difference $a_n(w)$.

$$a_n(w) = \frac{a_d(w) - \min A}{\max A - \min A} \tag{3}$$

We use the normalized attention difference $a_n(w)$ as the probability that word w is a stopword. We show the probability $p(w)$ of a word w being a stopword in the following Eq. (4).

$$p(w) = a_n(w) \tag{4}$$

We use $p(w)$ to generate stopwords in two methods; complete removal or probabilistic removal.

Method 1: Complete Removal. The system generates a list of stopwords. In Method 1, the system removes the words in the stopword list from input documents.

System developers sometimes remove stopwords by deleting words in the stopword list from input documents. We find that existing stopword lists are ineffective in improving classification accuracy. Therefore, it is necessary to create a new stopword list that would be useful for improving classification accuracy.

We use $p(w)$ as the probability that the word w is a stopword. We show below the procedure for generating a stopword list.

1. The system determines whether word w is a stopword or not according to the probability $p(w)$.
2. The system adds the word w that the system determines to be a stopword to the stopword list.

If a word w_1 exists for which $p(w_1)$ is 0.9, the system adds the word w_1 to the stopword list with a probability of 90%. On the other hand, if a word w_2 exists for which $p(w_2)$ is 0.1, the system adds the word w_2 to the stopword list with a probability of 10%. The probability of adding a word with a higher $p(w)$ to the stopword list is high.

We show below the procedure for stopword removal.

1. The system checks whether a word in the input document exists in the stopword list.
2. If the word w exists in the stopword list, the system removes all words w in the input document.

Method 2: Probabilistic Removal. Method 2 is a method for probabilistically deciding whether or not to remove each word in input documents. In Method 1, the system removes all words in the stopword list from input documents. However, in Method 2, the system sometimes removes words from input documents and sometimes does not remove words from input documents, even if they are the same words. The two methods differ in the above points.

Words with high attention difference $a_d(w)$ have a negative effect on the classification accuracy. Words with high attention difference $a_d(w)$ do not necessarily have a negative effect on classification accuracy. Removing all words w

with high attention differences $a_d(w)$ from input documents would not be appropriate. We think about a method of not removing some of the words w in input documents. One problem with Method 1 is that words with high $p(w)$ are not present in the stopword list, and the system does not remove any words that negatively affect classification accuracy. The effectiveness of Method 1 depends on the successful generation of the stopword list. In Method 2, the system does not create a stopword list. The system removes stopwords automatically. The system decides whether or not to remove each word in input documents based on the probability of each word. The system removes more words with high $p(w)$ and fewer words with low $p(w)$.

The system removes stopwords without creating a stopword list. We use $p(w)$ as the probability that the word w is a stopword. We show below the procedure for stopword removal.

1. The system decides whether or not to remove each word in input documents based on the probability of each word.
2. The system removes words from input documents based on judgments of 1..

In Method 1, the system removes all words in the stopword list from input documents. However, in Method 2, the system sometimes removes words from input documents and sometimes does not remove words from input documents, even if they are the same words. The two methods differ in the above points. If there is a word w_1 with $p(w_1)$ equal to 0.9, the system removes word w_1 from the input document with a probability of 90%. We think of the case when there are a hundred words w_1 in input documents. We expect the system will remove about ninety words w_1. If there is a word w_2 with $p(w_2)$ equal to 0.1, the system removes the word w_2 from the input document with a probability of 10%. We think of the case when there are a hundred words w_2 in input documents. We expect the system will remove about ten words w_2. The system tends to remove more words w with higher $p(w)$.

4   Experiments

In this experiment, we confirm the effectiveness of the proposed method for stopword removal. We compare the accuracy of document classification with and without stopword removal. We show whether there is a significant difference in classification accuracy or not by statistical tests.

The best stopwords depend on datasets and the purpose of the classification. We perform four document classification tasks. For two of them, we use the Rakuten dataset. For one of them, we use the Twitter dataset. For the other classification, we use the livedoor news corpus.

4.1   Procedure

We show below the experimental procedure.

1. We collect data so that the number of data for each label is equal. The way to equalize the number of data differs for each dataset. For this reason, we describe them in the Sects. 4.2, 4.3, 4.4, and 4.5 sections.
2. We split the collected data so that the ratio of the number of data for training, validation, and testing is 8:1:1.
3. The system uses BERT to train on training data. We use a pre-trained model of BERT[1] published by Inui and Suzuki Lab at Tohoku University. We set the maximum number of epochs to 10,000. The system stops learning when it has not update the minimum value of loss in the validation data for 50 epochs. The system adopts the model when the loss in validation data is the smallest.
4. The system removes stopwords using the procedure shown in Sect. 3. We experiment with stopword removal using a complete removal and stopword removal using probabilistic removal. We do not use these two methods at the same time.
5. The system trains with BERT using training data with stopword removal. The learning conditions are the same as in 3. We create ten models for each stopword removal method.
6. The system classifies test data using the model created in 5. Each of the ten models classifies test data. We compare averages of accuracy.
7. We perform statistical tests. We test whether there is a significant difference in the averages of accuracies calculated by 6. The null hypothesis is "There is no difference in accuracy with and without stopword removal". The significance level is 5%. We perform an unpaired t-test. We reject the null hypothesis if the p-value is less than 0.05. We can say that there is a significant difference in accuracy.

Table 1. Results of Experiment 1 and 2: Classification accuracy and p-value

$p(w)$	method	Experiment 1		Experiment 2	
		accuracy	p-value	accuracy	p-value
No stopword		0.6828	-	0.5412	-
Attention in incorrect documents	Complete	0.6658	2.406×10^{-3}	0.5000	9.143×10^{-5}
	Probabilistic	0.6648	3.310×10^{-3}	0.4883	2.901×10^{-7}
Attention difference	Complete	**0.6858**	5.270×10^{-1}	**0.5413**	9.905×10^{-1}
	Probabilistic	**0.6838**	8.394×10^{-1}	**0.5475**	4.170×10^{-1}
Normalized attention difference	Complete	**0.6923**	1.157×10^{-1}	0.5395	7.686×10^{-1}
	Probabilistic	**0.6835**	8.959×10^{-1}	**0.5476**	2.946×10^{-1}

---

[1] https://huggingface.co/cl-tohoku/bert-base-japanese-whole-word-masking.

4.2   Experiment 1. Rakuten Dataset: Evaluation Point

Datasets. Rakuten Dataset[2] is a dataset published by the National Institute of Informatics. The Rakuten Ichiba data includes about 280 million product data, 70 million product review data, and 22.5 million store review data. We use the following two items from the Rakuten Ichiba product review data: review text and evaluation score. We assign labels to review texts based on evaluation points. We assign negative labels to texts with evaluation points of 1 and 2, neutral labels to texts with evaluation points of 3, and positive labels to texts with evaluation points of 4 and 5. We perform a 3-class classification: negative, neutral, and positive. We collect 2,000 data for each label.

Result and Discussion. We show the classification accuracy when classifying the test data and the p-value when performing the t-test in the column of Experiment 1 in Table 1. Column $p(w)$ in the table shows the value use as the probability of the word w is a stopword. "No stopword" indicates that the system classifies without stopword removal. The column of "method" shows the method of stopword removal proposed in Sect. 3.2. "Complete" indicates Method 1, which uses a stopword list. "Probabilistic" indicates Method 2, probabilistic removal. Bolded text indicates improvements in accuracy over the case without stopwords. We find the highest accuracy when we focus on the normalized attention difference and use the complete removal to remove stopwords.

We find that when we remove stopwords by focusing on the attention in incorrect documents, both methods are less accurate than when we do not remove stopwords. Therefore, it is better to generate stopwords by focusing on the attention difference or normalized attention difference rather than focusing on attention in incorrect documents.

The complete removal is more accurate than the probabilistic removal. For positive, negative, and neutral classification using the Rakuten dataset, it is better to use the complete removal to remove stopwords.

Figure 1 shows an example of a text that uses the complete removal based on normalized attention differences to remove stopwords. Words with much more attention are darker in color. We expect that darker-colored words are words the classifier focuses on when classifying. Without stopword removal, the classifier predicts a label different from the correct label. Without stopword removal, attention to the word "safely" is high. The system removes the word "safely" from the input document as a stopword by using the complete removal to remove stopwords. With stopword removal, the classifier predicts the same label as the correct label. We can say that we have successfully remove the words that cause incorrect predictions.

The average number of words in the stopword list is 142 when using the attention in incorrect documents, 38 when using the attention difference, and

---
[2] Rakuten Group, Inc. (2014) : Rakuten Dataset. Informatics Research Data Repository, National Institute of Informatics. (dataset). https://doi.org/10.32130/idr.2.0.

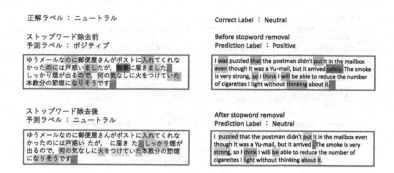

正解ラベル : ニュートラル   Correct Label : Neutral

ストップワード除去前   Before stopword removal
予測ラベル : ポジティブ   Prediction Label : Positive

ゆうメールなのに郵便屋さんがポストに入れてくれな   I was puzzled that the postman didn't put it in the mailbox
かったのには戸惑いましたが，無事に届きました。   even though it was a Yu-mail, but it arrived safely. The smoke
しっかり煙が出るので，何の気なしに火をつけていた   is very strong, so I think I will be able to reduce the number
本数分の節煙になりそうです。   of cigarettes I light without thinking about it.

ストップワード除去後   After stopword removal
予測ラベル : ニュートラル   Prediction Label : Neutral

ゆうメールなのに郵便屋さんがポストに入れてくれな   I puzzled that the postman didn't put it in the mailbox even
かったのには戸惑い たが， に届き た しっかり煙が   though it was a Yu-mail, but it arrived The smoke is very
出るので，何の気なしに火をつけていた本数分の節煙   strong, so I think I will be able to reduce the number of
になりそうです。   cigarettes I light without thinking about it.

Fig. 1. Comparison of attention before and after stopword removal in Experiment 1.

77 when using the normalized attention difference. The number of stopwords is large when focusing on the attention in incorrect documents. It seems likely that words that are useful for classification could be stopwords.

For positive, negative, and neutral classification using the Rakuten dataset, it is better to focus on the attention difference or normalized attention difference and to use the complete removal to remove stopwords.

4.3 Experiment 2. Rakuten Dataset: Usage

Datasets. We use the Rakuten dataset. We use the same dataset as in Experiment 1 presented in Sect. 4.2. We perform classification for different purposes on the same text data. In Experiment 2 we use a different item from Experiment 1. We use the following two items from the Rakuten Ichiba product review data: review text and usage. We use the "Usage" item in the dataset as a label. Six labels exist in the "Usage" items, such as "Practical and daily use", "Gifts," and so on. We use labels in the dataset to classify six classes.

Result and Discussion. We show the classification accuracy when classifying the test data and the p-value when performing the t-test in the column of Experiment 2 in Table 1. We find the highest accuracy when we focus on normalized attention differences and use probabilistic removal to remove stopwords.

When the system removes stopwords by focusing on incorrect documents, both methods result in less accurate text classification than when the system does not remove the stopwords.

attention difference, we find that the classification accuracy is higher with the probabilistic removal than with the complete removal. We can say that it is better to use probabilistic removal to remove stopwords when classifying the usage of products using the Rakuten dataset.

The accuracy of classification with probabilistic removal does not change much before and after normalizing for differences in attention. Attention differences have a minimum value of 0 and a maximum value of 0.92. Normalizing the range of values from 0 to 1 do not change values much. Therefore, the removal

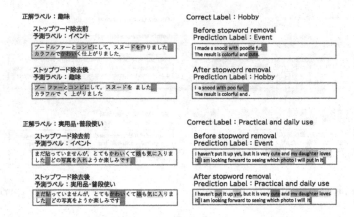

Fig. 2. Comparison of attention before and after stopword removal in Experiment 2.

probability of each word does not change much, and the accuracy does not differ much.

Figure 2 shows two examples. These two examples are cases of stopword removal by probabilistic removal focusing on the normalized attention difference. In the above example, "cute" has high attention before stopword removal. Therefore, "cute" is likely to be a factor causing incorrect prediction. The system remove "cute" from the input document by probabilistic removal. The classifier can predict correctly by removing words causing incorrect predictions. The below example shows that the system does not remove "cute". Figure 2 shows that attention to the word "cute" is higher after the stopword removal than before the stopword removal. The classifier can predict correctly by focusing on "cute". There are documents that the classifier could classify correctly by removing "cute". There are documents that the classifier could classify correctly without removing "cute". Even words with high attention when the classifier makes incorrect predictions do not necessarily have a negative effect on classification accuracy. Therefore, it is not appropriate to remove all those words.

For classification by usage of products using the Rakuten dataset, it is better to use probabilistic removal to remove stopwords by focusing on the normalized attention difference.

4.4   Experiment 3. Twitter Dataset

Datasets. Twitter Japanese Reputation Analysis Dataset [10]³ is a dataset published by Suzuki Laboratory, Gifu University. The dataset contains tweet IDs for tweets circa 2015-2016, IDs for genres such as cell phones, status IDs to get the tweet text, and three types of labels: positive, negative, and neutral. In our experiment, we use tweet texts and three types of labels: positive, negative, and neutral. In the dataset, there are texts with multiple labels. We use texts

---

³ https://www.db.info.gifu-u.ac.jp/sentiment_analysis/.

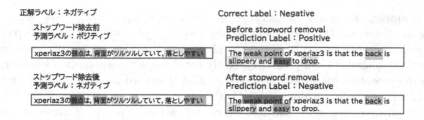

Fig. 3. Comparison of attention before and after stopword removal in Experiment 3.

with one label: positive, negative, or neutral. We perform a 3-class classification: positive, negative, and neutral. We collect 1,400 data for each label.

Result and Discussion. We show the classification accuracy when classifying the test data and the p-value when performing the t-test in the column of Experiment 3 in Table 2. We find the highest accuracy when we focus on the attention difference and use the complete removal to remove stopwords.

We find that when we remove stopwords by focusing on the attention in incorrect documents, both methods are less accurate in text classification than when we do not remove stopwords. Therefore, it is better to generate stopwords by focusing on the attention difference or normalized attention difference rather than focusing on attention in incorrect documents.

We find that the classification accuracy is higher with the complete removal than with tha probabilistic removal. For positive, negative, and neutral classification using the Twitter dataset, it is better to use the complete removal to remove stopwords.

Figure 3 shows a text that the classifier can predict the correct label by stopword removal. The above example shows a visualization of attention when the system classifies without stopword removal. The below example shows a visualization of attention when the system classifies with stopword removal. We focus on the attention difference and remove stopwords using a stopword list. Figure 3 shows no change in the input document before and after stopword removal. For

Table 2. Results of Experiment 3 and 4: Classification accuracy and p-value

$p(w)$	method	Experiment 3		Experiment 4	
		accuracy	p-value	accuracy	p-value
No stopword		0.7297	-	0.8971	-
Attention in incorrect documents	Complete	0.6738	7.929×10^{-6}	0.8971	9.999×10^{-1}
	Probabilistic	0.6983	3.372×10^{-3}	0.8911	7.238×10^{-2}
Attention difference	Complete	**0.7364**	4.587×10^{-1}	0.8969	9.468×10^{-1}
	Probabilistic	**0.7307**	9.126×10^{-1}	**0.9013**	2.343×10^{-1}
Normalized attention difference	Complete	**0.7360**	5.356×10^{-1}	**0.9016**	2.583×10^{-1}
	Probabilistic	**0.7326**	7.646×10^{-1}	**0.8984**	7.471×10^{-1}

this example, the system does not remove words likely to cause incorrect predictions. However, the prediction label change before and after the stopword removal. It seems that attention has change to be able to classify correctly. Sometimes classifiers can predict correctly by changing the attention when train with documents with stopword removal. The stopword removal also affect the classification results for documents that do not contain stopwords.

For positive, negative, and neutral classification using the Twitter dataset, it is better to focus on the attention difference and to use the complete removal to remove stopwords.

4.5   Experiment 4. Livedoor News Corpus

Datasets. Livedoor news corpus[4] is a dataset published by RONDHUIT. This corpus is a collection of data from livedoor news website operated by NHN JAPAN Corp. The dataset contains 7,376 news articles, including URL, date, title, and body text. There are nine categories of news articles. Each category contains between 512 and 901 news articles. We perform a 9-class classification that predicts categories from the body text of news articles. There is a bias in the number of data across categories. Therefore, we set each category to have the same number of data as the category with the least number of data. We collect 500 data for each label.

Result and Discussion. We show the classification accuracy when classifying the test data and the p-value when performing the t-test in the column of Experiment 4 in Table 2. We find the highest accuracy when we focus on the normalized attention difference and use the complete removal to remove stopwords.

We discuss the case of using stopwords focusing on the attention in incorrect documents. There is no change in accuracy when we use the complete removal. Accuracy decrease when we use the probabilistic removal. Stopwords focusing on attention in incorrect documents are not effective in improving accuracy. It is better to generate stopwords by focusing on the attention difference or normalized attention difference.

We focus on accuracy when we use the stopword list. Accuracy is high when we focus on normalized attention differences. By normalized attention differences, The system has set stopwords well. Using the attention difference is less accurate in text classification than without stopwords. The system does not remove enough words causing incorrect predictions. When the number of removed words is small, there is a possibility that the classification accuracy will decrease.

For classification by news categories using the livedoor news corpus, it is better to focus on the normalized attention difference and to use the complete removal to remove stopwords.

---

[4] http://www.rondhuit.com/download.html#ldcc

5   Conclusions

In this paper, we propose methods to generate stopword list to improve the accuracy of a document classification task for classifiers using BERT. We construct a system that generates stopwords using the attention of words that appear in incorrectly classified documents but not in correctly classified documents.

The words with high attention in incorrect documents are the factors causing the classifier to make incorrect predictions. Therefore, we generate stopwords by focusing on the attention in incorrect documents. Words with high attention in correct documents help the classifier to make correct predictions. We consider generating stopwords by focusing only on attention in incorrect documents is not a good idea. It would be a good idea to use words with high attention in incorrect documents and low attention in correct documents as stopwords. We focus on the difference between attention in incorrect documents and in correct documents.

We propose two methods for generating stopwords. The first method is to generate a stopword list. The system removes the words in the stopword list from input documents. The second is a method that the system probability decides whether or not to remove each word in input documents.

We conduct experiments to confirm the effectiveness of stopword generation using our methods. Experimental results show that there are cases using stopwords generated by our method that improve the classification accuracy. We can see texts for which the classifier predicts the correct label by removing words with a large attention difference. Words with high attention in incorrect documents are factors causing the classifier to make incorrect predictions. Removing these words from input documents improves classification accuracy. Sometimes classifiers can predict correctly by changing the attention when train with documents with stopword removal. We found that when we remove stopwords by focusing on the attention in incorrect documents, both methods are less accurate in text classification than when we do not remove stopwords. Stopword generation focusing only on attention in incorrect documents was not a good idea. This method has the potential to remove words that are important for correct predictions. We cannot say that words with high attention in incorrect documents are necessary factors that lead to incorrect predictions. It is better to generate stopwords by focusing on the difference in attention rather than focusing on attention in incorrect documents.

In some cases, stopwords generated by our methods improve classification accuracy. Generating stopwords by focusing on attention may improve classification accuracy. There is a significant difference of 88%, but it is not significant enough. Therefore, we aim to generate stopwords that can improve classification accuracy significantly enough. In our proposed methods, after the system builds the model, the system classifies the test data and sets the probability of word removal. After that, the system builds a classification model by learning the text data with stopwords removal. Our method requires the construction of two classification models. We aim to improve classification accuracy by setting an appropriate probability of word removal for each word in only one model. We think of a method to determine the probability of word removal for each word in input documents during model training. In addition, we have only experimented on Japanese datasets. In the future, we would like to test our method on texts in other languages to see if it is effective.

Acknowledgements. This paper is partly supported by JSPS KAKENHI 19H04218, 23H03694.

References

1. Anand, R., David, U.J.: Mining of massive datasets. Cambridge University Press (2011)
2. Saif, H., Fernández, M., He, Y., Alani, H.: On stopwords, filtering and data sparsity for sentiment analysis of twitter. In: Proceedings of the Ninth International Conference on Language Resources and Evaluation (LREC2014), pp. 810–817 (2014)
3. Kuwabara, Y., Suzuki, Yu.: An analysis of stopwords in document classification tasks with BERT. Inf. Fundamentals Access Technol. (IFAT) **2022**(41), 1–6 (2022). (in Japanese)
4. Vaswani, A., et al.: Attention is all you need. In: Advances in Neural Information Processing Systems 30 (2017)
5. Devlin, J., Chang, M.-W., Lee, K., Toutanova, K.: BERT: pre-training of deep bidirectional transformers for language understanding. In: Proceedings of the 2019 Conference of the North American Chapter of the Association for Computational Linguistics: Human Language Technologies, Volume 1 (Long and Short Papers), pp. 4171–4186, Minneapolis, Minnesota (2019). Association for Computational Linguistics
6. Kokubu, H., Yamazaki, H., Nosaka, M.: Japanese stopword list making for keyword extraction suitable for semantic interpretation. Trans. Japan Soc. Kansei Eng. **12**(4), 511–518 (2013). (in Japanese)
7. Saiyed, S., Sajja, P.: Empirical analysis of static and dynamic stopword generation approaches. In: Tuba, M., Akashe, S., Joshi, A. (eds.) ICT Systems and Sustainability. LNNS, vol. 321, pp. 149–156. Springer, Singapore (2022). https://doi.org/10.1007/978-981-16-5987-4_16
8. Kimura, Y., Komamizu, T., Hatano, K.: Document classification with stop-phrase extraction. In: 14th Forum on Data Engineering and Information Management (DEIM2022), pp. A23–A24 (2022). (in Japanese)
9. Fox, C.: A stop list for general text. ACM SIGIR Forum **24**, 19–21 (1989)
10. Suzuki, Yu.: Filtering method for twitter streaming data using human-in-the-loop machine learning. J. Inf. Process. **27**, 404–410 (2019)

Digital Index Card Creation and Management for Memorizing What You See on the Web

Yuna Saka[1], Yoshiyuki Shoji[1,2]($\boxtimes$) (iD), Hiroaki Ohshima[3] (iD), and Kouzou Ohara[1] (iD)

[1] Aoyama Gakuin University, Sagamihara, Kanagawa 252–5258, Japan
`yuna@sw.it.aoyama.ac.jp`, `ohara@it.aoyama.ac.jp`
[2] Shizuoka University, Hamamatsu, Shizuoka 432–8011, Japan
`shojiy@inf.shizuoka.ac.jp`
[3] University of Hyogo, Kobe, Hyogo 651–2197, Japan
`ohshima@ai.u-hyogo.ac.jp`

Abstract. This paper proposes a method of enabling users to memorize important information obtained from daily Web browsing by letting them manage their browsing history as cards. People always encounter a lot of information on websites, but most of it is forgotten even if needed later. Therefore, we implemented a memory retention support system based on card creation and management. This system allows users to make cards semi-manually using their website browsing history. The system displays the cards in an easy-to-view manner and provides management functions. By creating and organizing the cards that summarize their daily browsing activities and reviewing the cards they collected, users can realize what they value and recall necessary information more easily. The results of the user study in which the participants used the system for a Web search task demonstrated that the proposed semi-manual card creation has positive effects on memory retention after four days.

Keywords: Information Access · Memory · Browsing History · Index Card

1 Introduction

Historically, people have used cards to summarize unorganized information and make it stick in their memory. Such cards used to manage and learn from information are generally called "Index Cards," and many applications and styles are being introduced. Organizing and remembering information through card management is common and leads to the proposal of various applications.

Here, let us consider a method to apply such card-based memory retention techniques to Web browsing. Organizing miscellaneous information on the Web as cards will likely make it stay in one's memory. In addition, looking back at

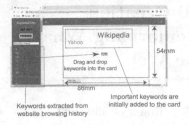

Fig. 1. A screenshot of the proposed semi-manual card creation.

Fig. 2. A screenshot of the proposed card list for review.

the created cards and comparing them with the previously accumulated cards will make the user aware of their interest and aid in decision-making.

To this end, this paper proposes a system that takes a day's website browsing history as an input and allows users to summarize it as cards semi-manually. Figure 1 shows an overview of the system. With the support of this system, users can summarize information gained from the websites visited on that day into a card about the size of a business card.

The system also allows users to collect and manage the cards they created, as shown in Fig. 2. Before proceeding to the card-making process, the system shows the list of cards the user has previously created. As a result, users can create, collect, and manage cards daily, allowing them to organize and make use of important or interesting information from the Web.

For evaluation, we implemented a Google Chrome browser extension prototype to prove that such a system is helpful. We conducted a subject experiment that lets participants use our prototype system for an information retrieval task, and checked the degree of memory retention after four days.

2   Related Work

This section introduces some related studies on website browser history analysis, card-making in the field of education, and lifelog analysis and visualization.

2.1   Web Browsing History Analysis

The analysis of Web browsing history that aims at making browsing experiences more comfortable and meaningful has been researched frequently. As an example, Wexelblat *et al.* [7] propose a method to visualize the users' paths during website browsing as a graph. There are several studies that visualize website browsing history and encourage knowledge retention. For instance, Xu *et al.* [8] express website browsing history as an undirected semantic graph based on a spring model. Our research focuses on encouraging users to look back at websites and also keep important information in memory. Also, our approach expects positive effects from creating cards semi-manually. This relates to the effect in which people feel attached to things they make on their own, known as the "Ikea Effect [3]."

2.2 Card Making in Education

Since information cards written in the past are considered precious information resources, there are some studies attempting to digitize such cards [2]. "Hyper-Card", one of the most famous Wiki-like electronic card management systems, is proven to be effective for education [1]. Hidayat *et al.* [4] propose a method to associate paper information cards and electronic devices with an education support system for smartphones using AR (Augmented Reality) technology. Our study aims to apply such phenomenon that these cards are effective for memory retention and organization to Web browsing.

As a method to create paper cards from operation history, Shoji *et al.* [6] propose an application to automatically presume the interests of the visitors from their museum guide device and create a postcard as a souvenir.

2.3 Lifelog Analysis

Website browsing history is related to lifelog analysis, which analyzes photographs and activity data for visualizing and recording what users saw. As an example, Pirsiavash *et al.* [5] propose a method to analyze photographs as lifelogs and determine what events occurred at certain times.

In contrast to such lifelogging strategies, webpage information is more complex since it contains more detailed information and involves doing several tasks simultaneously using multiple tabs. Therefore, we propose a method to manage information semi-manually instead of classifying and choosing a representative out of it automatically.

3   Method

This section will cover our methods using the actual implementations for Google Chrome as an example. Our system consists of a Google Chrome extension API module for loading website browsing history, a front-end module for card making, and a server-side module for storing and organizing cards.

3.1   Extraction of Phrase Candidates from Website Browsing History

First, the system reads the webpage contents from the website browsing history using the Google Chrome API and infers important keywords. Next, morphological analysis is applied to the webpage titles in the loaded website browsing history. After extracting all words with the analyzer, words analyzed as nouns are selected as candidates for the important keywords. The keywords' importance is chosen from three ranks according to the number of times they appeared in the titles of the accessed webpages.

3.2   Memory Retention Support with Semi-Manual Card Making

When the user calls the system, it will call the API, extract words from the day's browsing history, and calculate the importance of each word. Words with relatively high importance ranks are added to the cards automatically. In the initial state, the font size of the keywords is proportional to the three ranks of importance, and the font colors are set based on this ranking as well.

Users can edit the keywords on this card by adding keywords from the given list or the keyword input textbox and removing keywords from the card. The rotation angle, size, and color of the keywords on the card and the card's background color can be modified. In addition, users can add tags to the cards for grouping.

3.3   Reflection Support with Card Management Interface

Immediately after activating the system, the screen shows a random list of the cards the user created. The cards on the list can be rearranged in the order of their creation date, or they can be grouped based on their keywords or tags. Additionally, the view of the list can be changed to only show certain cards by indicating keywords or tags the cards contain in common. Each card on the list can be enlarged, and users can revisit the links they have visited from the URLs associated with each keyword on the card.

The system tries to increase the frequency with which users look back at cards created in the past. Therefore, the card-making button does not appear on the initial screen, and the user has to scroll through the card list screen to find the button at the end.

4   Evaluation

We empirically evaluated the memory-retention-support effect of the proposed method through short-term website search tasks.

4.1   Comparison Methods

In the experiment, the effects of making cards semi-manually and reviewing cards are evaluated by comparing the following five methods:

- **Semi-manual creation + Review**: participants can create cards semi-manually and review them by managing the cards;
- **Semi-manual creation + No Review**: participants can create cards semi-manually, but they cannot review the cards;
- **Automatic creation + Review**: participants only get to review the cards created automatically;
- **Automatic creation + No Review**: participants only get to see the cards immediately after they are automatically generated;
- **No assistance**: participants are not involved in card-making or reviewing.

Digital Index Card Creation and Management   545

Table 1. The average ratio and number of items remembered immediately after the task and four days later (two subjects for each task, maximum of seven items).

	Immediately after	4 days later
Semi-manual Creation + Review	1.00 (7.0 / 7.0)	0.93 (6.5 / 7.0)
Semi-manual Creation + No Review	1.00 (7.0 / 7.0)	**1.00 (7.0 / 7.0)**
Automatic Creation + Review	0.93 (6.5 / 7.0)	0.57 (4.0 / 7.0)
Automatic Creation + No Review	1.00 (7.0 / 7.0)	0.86 (6.0 / 7.0)
No Assistance	1.00 (7.0 / 7.0)	0.79 (5.5 / 7.0)

4.2 Experimental Tasks

In the short-term evaluation experiment, the participants were provided with one of these two tasks:

- Make a travel plan to Hamamatsu City (a local area in Japan);
- Think of a menu for a casual wedding party.

Participants were assigned to each of the ten patterns that can be formed from the combination of the two tasks and the five methods (see Sect. 4.1). Each participant was assigned seven items consisting of a decision target and several requirements to investigate for the given task.

The participants were given 20 min to search the Web for information to help them decide about the items in the task. After searching, the participants either started making cards, reviewed the cards they created, or simply did nothing, according to the assigned card-making method. When the participants finished these, they were orally asked about their decisions for each item in the topic. Four days later, the participants were asked what they remembered about their final decisions for the items again.

4.3 Experimental Results

Table 1 shows the average number and ratio of the items the participants could recall on the day of the short-term experiment task and four days after that day. In evaluating the memory consistency of the items immediately after the task and several days later, cases in which participants forgot the main contents were judged as "inconsistent memory."

The results show that the memory consistency rates of the participant groups that made cards semi-manually were relatively high on the day of task execution and several days later. However, regardless of card making, the participant groups that reviewed the cards had lower memory consistency rates.

5 Discussion

This section discusses the effectiveness of creating cards semi-manually and reviewing them based on the results of the evaluation experiments.

The participants who edited the cards tended to have a high memory consistency rate several days later. From this result, it can be inferred that editing cards manually has a specific effect on memory retention. On the other hand, participants involved in card management had comparatively lower memory consistency rates than those who were not involved. Therefore, we could not seek a positive effect from organizing cards.

6   Conclusion

In this paper, we proposed a system that allows users to retain the information they gained from the internet on a particular day by summarizing and organizing their website browsing history with cards. From the results of the short-term evaluation experiment, it can be concluded that the proposed semi-manual card-making has some effect on memory retention.

We plan to conduct a long-term experiment to verify the effects of card editing and organizing in the future. Furthermore, we would like to upgrade the system's functions to improve its usability and increase the memory retention support effect.

Acknowledgements. This work was supported by JSPS KAKENHI Grants Number 21H03775, 21H03774, and 22H03905. The research was also supported by ROIS NII Open Collaborative Research 2023 (Grant Number 22S1001).

References

1. Bowers, D., Tsai, C.: Hypercard in educational research: an introduction and case study. Educ. Technol. **30**(2), 19–24 (1990)
2. Downton, A., et al.: Constructing web-based legacy index card archives-architectural design issues and initial data acquisition. In: ICDAR 2001, pp. 854–858 (2001)
3. Norton, M.I., Mochon, D., Ariely, D.: The IKEA effect: when labor leads to love. J. Consum. Psychol. **22**(3), 453–460 (2012)
4. Nur Hidayat, W., Akhsan Hakiki, M., Fajar Nashrullah, M., Elmunsyah, H., Atmadji Sutikno, T.: Development of mobile learning application based on augmented reality with index card match method. In: ICOVET 2020, pp. 304–309 (2020)
5. Pirsiavash, H., Ramanan, D.: Detecting activities of daily living in first-person camera views. In: CVPR 2012, pp. 2847–2854 (2012)
6. Shoji, Y., et al.: Museum experience into a souvenir: generating memorable postcards from guide device behavior log. In: JCDL 2021, pp. 120–129 (2021)
7. Wexelblat, A., Maes, P.: Footprints: history-rich web browsing. In: RIAO 1997, pp. 75–84 (1997)
8. Xu, L., Fernando, Z.T., Zhou, X., Nejdl, W.: LogCanvas: visualizing search history using knowledge graphs. In: SIGIR 2018, pp. 1289–1292 (2018)

Multitask, Cross-Lingual Recipe Classification Using Joint Fine-Tuning Mechanisms

Vlad-Andrei Negru$^{(\boxtimes)}$, Camelia Lemnaru[ID], and Rodica Potolea[ID]

Technical University of Cluj-Napoca, Cluj-Napoca, Romania
negru.li.vlad@student.utcluj.ro

Abstract. We explore solutions for text classification applied to online cooking recipes, in a multitask, multilingual approach. The main objective is designing a solution that ensures high accuracy on the prediction tasks from, but not constrained to, 6 European Languages, considering also the cross-lingual transferability. The challenges of the problem are structured on two main dimensions: (1) data driven - such as imbalance and noise in the training data, and (2) solution driven - such as multilingualism, or the need to easily extend the model to new languages. We propose a solution focused on the XLM-R architecture, fine-tuned jointly on all tasks. We apply self-supervised domain adaptation via additional pre-training and analyze the enhancements produced by performing a 0-shot evaluation for under-represented languages. Compared to basic language modeling solutions, we obtained an increase of 1.32% and 2.42%, respectively for the two most difficult classification tasks. In the 0-shot context, the absolute improvements are of 16.71% and 7.83% respectively, on underrepresented languages.

Keywords: Language Models · Multitask · Multilingual · Text Classification · Domain Adaptation · Cross-lingual transfer · Knowledge transfer

1 Introduction

With the advent of large language models and their increased semantic compositionality abilities, learning to perform multiple tasks, in multiple languages, at the same time, has become more or less common practice. In this paper we explore such a setup, in which we solve three recipe classification problems in a parallel manner, using a pre-trained large language model as backbone, on which we perform additional in-domain pre-training and joint fine-tuning. We perform preliminary experiments on three encoder-based models, and find that XLM-RoBERTa (XLM-R) [1] obtains the best overall results. We further investigate the multilingual and cross-lingual capabilities of the best fine-tuned model, and find that the language imbalance has a significant effect on classification performance, for all three problems. The contributions of the current paper are:

- to propose a joint, multi-lingual recipe classification model which solves three related text classification tasks

© The Author(s), under exclusive license to Springer Nature Switzerland AG 2023
P. Delir Haghighi et al. (Eds.): iiWAS 2023, LNCS 14416, pp. 547–552, 2023.
https://doi.org/10.1007/978-3-031-48316-5_48

- to perform an ablation study on which parts of the recipe are the most informative
- perform in-domain pre-training to boost performance in under-represented and low resource languages
- perform an analysis on the 0-shot capabilities of the model (language-wise)

2   Proposed Solution

The data contains three separate classification tasks, related to various technical aspects of a cooking recipe. This information is not specifically present in the text of the recipes and must be inferred by having a solid understanding of the recipe as a whole. The first classification task, *protein*, refers to the presence or absence of meat in the dish. *Way of browning* describes the type of browning and caramelization of the final product (also a binary classification problem). This is known to be affected by the ingredients of the dish, the method of cooking and the thickness of the dish. *Way of drying* is the hardest task, as it is multilabel and heavily imbalanced. It is also a multiclass problem, influenced by many factors from the recipe, such as the cooking technique, ingredients, the thickness of the food, the category of the recipe and so on.

2.1   Data Description

The dataset consists of 53.000 oven recipes, inequally distributed across 6 European languages. For each recipe in the dataset, we have the url, the language and a set of annotations performed by domain experts, including the labels for the three target tasks. We use the *recipe_scrapers* library[1] to extract various information from the raw *html*, such as: recipe title and cooking instructions, ingredients, etc. The data poses two important challenges: multilingualism, and imbalance in all three classification problems.

2.2   Joint Classification Model

The proposed solution relies on fine-tuning a pre-trained, multi-lingual, large language model belonging to the MLM family [1,2]. We use a single linear layer on top of the [CLS] token produced by the language model, to which we apply dropout regularization and Softmax to produce the output. All the layers of the model are affected by backpropagation during fine-tuning.

Since we have to solve three classification tasks, which might share a certain amount of information between them, we should use three different models. However, we choose to train a single, multitask model for all three. Figure 1 illustrates this process. By training for the three tasks in such a joint manner, we aim to exploit their relations and similarities and also decrease training, inference, deployment and maintenance costs. As Fig. 1 shows, the new global loss function is a linear combination of the individual losses of the required classification tasks [3]. We used uniform weighing in the loss combination strategy.

---

[1] Available at: https://github.com/hhursev/recipe-scrapers.

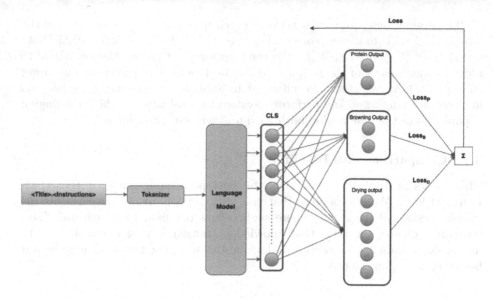

Fig. 1. Joint classification model architecture

In-Domain Pre-training. Because of the language imbalance challenge posed by the data, we need to consider a strategy for enhancing the model for the underrepresented languages, since we assume that fine-tuning on the available data will not be sufficient to reach an acceptable performance in all languages. Consequently, we apply unsupervised, in-domain pre-training using Masked Language Modeling on a set of 490.000 unlabeled recipes in the six languages, especially targeting the underrepresented ones. Apart from potentially increasing the value of the context semantics extracted by the model, this technique should also enhance the cross-lingual transfer ability of the model. As a result, we expect the model not only to have a better performance on the richly represented languages in the labeled dataset, but also to better transfer the knowledge gained via fine-tuning to other languages that were not seen at this step (like Spanish or Portuguese). This method also provides an efficient mechanism of extending the supported languages of the model, without the need of labeling new recipes.

3   Experiments

We have used stratified sampling to split the available data into: a training dataset, comprising 80% of the total recipes, a validation dataset, 10% of the data, and a test dataset containing the remaining 10%. The solutions that used transformer-based language models were fine-tuned for a maximum of 6 epochs. As training parameters, we used batches of size 32, a learning rate of 5e-5 and AdamW as optimizer. During the fine-tuning process we also clipped the gradients to 1 in order to limit overfitting.

The evaluations addressed several research questions: first, we compared the joint model with baselines, considering several backbone models: mBERT [4], Longformer [5] and XLM-R [1]. We then perform a feature ablation study, to identify which parts of the recipe hold the best predictive power on the target concepts. Third, we study the effect of in-domain pre-training, especially on low resource languages, and perform a systematic evaluation of the cross-lingual capabilities of the best model, both with and without pre-training.

3.1 Comparison with Baselines

The results in Table 1 indicate that the best performing model is the XLM-R model joint. We also observe that the joint version always outperforms the simple versions of the model, where we fine-tune one model for each task. This strongly indicates the value that knowledge transfer has for our tasks, as the model learns valuable knowledge and semantics from one task that may help it better inferring on the other.

Table 1. Accuracy of baseline models

Model	Protein	Way of Browning	Way of Drying
Bag Of Words + Logistic Regression	95.47%	82.58%	77.82%
TF-IDF + Logistic Regression	95.22%	84.69%	80.86%
Longformer	96%	87.10%	82.61%
Longformer Joint	96.60%	89.20%	82.50%
mBERT Joint	96.40%	88.60%	82.50%
XLM-RoBERTa	**97.15%**	88.40%	82.61%
XLM-RoBERTa Joint	96.69%	**89.36%**	**82.89%**

3.2 Feature Ablation Study

We consider various types of data included in the recipe, exploring multiple forms of the information: text features, numerical features or encoded features. The information blocks we experimented with are the title, instructions, oven settings and the ingredients of the recipe. Based on experimental results, we conclude that the use of the title and recipe instructions in textual form is sufficient for our tasks, as it has good performance and low degree of added complexity to the language model architecture.

3.3 Effect of In-Domain Pre-training

As explained in Sect. 2.2, we also perform in-domain model adaptation, using two different approaches, both based on Masked Language Modeling. First one treats each individual recipe as a different entry (Individual). The second merges all the recipes and considers blocks of 512 tokens for the MLM Process (Block).

Table 2 presents the comparison between the default XLM-R model and the pre-trained versions in a joint training context. We can see that both pre-trained solutions are outperforming the default model, especially for Way of Drying task. Thus, the domain adaptation proves to bring enhancements in the overall performance, especially for the individual method.

Table 2. Accuracy of domain adapted models

Model	Protein	Way of Browning	Way of Drying
XLM-R Joint (No Pre-train)	96.69%	89.36%	82.89%
XLM-R Joint (Individual)	**96.94%**	**89.72%**	**85.03%**
XLM-R Joint (Block)	96.67%	89.77%	84.72%

Another aspect that must be considered is the enhancements brought for each language. We are expecting to enhance the performance of underrepresented languages using the domain adaptation, as we want to increase the cross-lingual transferability of the model for the cooking domain. We can see in Table 3 the comparisons of accuracy per language for the classification problems. The greatest enhancements are for the underreprèsented languages, especially for the Way of Browning and Way of Drying tasks, for French, Swedish and Italian.

Table 3. Pre-training enhancements across languages - Accuracy

Model	German	English	French	Italian	Dutch	Swedish
No Pre-train - Protein	97.34%	**96.99%**	97.23%	95.22%	**93.55%**	**96.47%**
Individual- Protein	**97.64%**	96.94%	**97.52%**	**97.56%**	**93.55%**	95.06%
No Pre-train - Browning	90.55%	**89.09%**	87.89%	88.04%	86.95%	80.00%
Individual - Browning	**90.82%**	88.26%	**93.26%**	**89.27%**	**87.10%**	**81.48%**
No Pre-train - Drying	84.73%	83.79%	76.47%	78.47%	78.46%	74.12%
Individual - Drying	**87.12%**	**85.29%**	**78.72%**	**81.95%**	**79.19%**	**82.72%**

3.4   Cross-Lingual Capabilities

In order to assess and quantify the cross-lingual capabilities of the model we perform a 0-shot evaluation. We want to evaluate the behaviour of the model on the classification tasks for languages that were not seen at fine-tuning. Thus we can measure how well the model transfers the knowledge obtained in the fine-tuning step to other languages. We fine-tune the model on the well represented languages from our labeled dataset. This represents 76% of recipes, in English and German. Then we measure the performance on the rest of the languages, comparing the pre-trained model with the default XLM-R language model.

The results in Table 4 show a great improvement brought by the pre-training on the cross-lingual transferability. We can see that – for every language – the overall accuracy improved, heavily enhancing the performance for the *Way of Browning* task, where the final scores are comparable to the scores of the model fine-tuned on all the languages. The cross-lingual transfer of the model is minimal for the most difficult task, *Way of Drying*, proving that for harder tasks, a mere pre-training does not reach similar scores as fine-tuning the model in the desired language.

Table 4. 0-shot analysis - Accuracy

Model	Language	Protein	Way of Browning	Way of Drying
XLM-R Pre-trained	nl	**92.02%**	**82.35%**	**72.97%**
XLM-R	nl	90.97%	68.26%	64.18%
XLM-R Pre-trained	fr	**94.58%**	**82.58%**	**69.33%**
XLM-R	fr	94.47%	50.09%	52.93%
XLM-R Pre-trained	it	**96.06%**	**84.62%**	**60.71%**
XLM-R	it	95.36%	68.50%	51.52%
XLM-R Pre-trained	sv	94.53%	**70.89%**	54.87%
XLM-R	sv	**94.93%**	66.76%	**57.94%**

4   Conclusions

In this paper we propose performing fine-tuning on a pre-trained language model in a joint manner, to exploit hidden interactions between three text classification tasks related to the cooking domain. Preliminary experiments indicate that XLM-R obtains the best overall performance. We additionally apply in-domain pre-training to improve its behavior on underrepresented languages. Also, we investigate its multilingual and cross-lingual capabilities and find that the language imbalance has a significant effect on classification performance, for all three tasks, but in-domain pre-training significantly alleviates this issue.

References

1. Conneau, A., et al.: Unsupervised Cross-lingual Representation Learning at Scale (2020)
2. Vaswani, A., et al.: Attention Is All You Need. arXiv: 1706.03762 (2017)
3. Chen, S., Zhang, Y., Yang, Q.: 2021 Multi-Task Learning in Natural Language Processing: An Overview. arXiv:2109.09138 (2021)
4. Devlin, J., Chang, M.W., Lee, K., Toutanova, K.: BERT: Pre-training of Deep Bidirectional Transformers for Language Understanding (2019)
5. Beltagy, I., Peters, M.E., Cohan, A.: Longformer: The Long-Document Transformer, arXiv: 2004.05150 (2020)

Correction to: Integration of Knowledge Bases and External Information Sources via Magic Properties and Query-Driven Entity Linking

Yuuki Ohmori (ID), Hiroyuki Kitagawa (ID), Toshiyuki Amagasa (ID),
and Akiyoshi Matono (ID)

Correction to:
Chapter 30 in: P. Delir Haghighi et al. (Eds.):
Information Integration and Web Intelligence, **LNCS 14416,**
https://doi.org/10.1007/978-3-031-48316-5_30

The book was inadvertently published with a typo in the first author's family name in chapter 30. The current family name "Ohmroi" is incorrect. Correctly it should read "Ohmori". This has been corrected in the corresponding chapter accordingly.

The updated version of this chapter can be found at
https://doi.org/10.1007/978-3-031-48316-5_30

© The Author(s), under exclusive license to Springer Nature Switzerland AG 2024
P. Delir Haghighi et al. (Eds.): iiWAS 2023, LNCS 14416, p. C1, 2024.
https://doi.org/10.1007/978-3-031-48316-5_49

Author Index

P. Delir Haghighi et al. (Eds.): iiWAS 2023, LNCS 14416, pp. 553–555, 2023.
https://doi.org/10.1007/978-3-031-48316-5

Printed in the United States
by Baker & Taylor Publisher Services

Printed in the United States
by Baker & Taylor Publisher Services